Contents

II   Driving abroad – a cautionary tale
IV   Driving regulations
VII Ski resorts

1   Route planning maps

1   Key to route planning map pages

24   Road maps

24   Key to road map pages · Distance table

201   City plans and approach maps

Alicante C	201	Luxembourg C	215
Amsterdam C U	202	Lyon C U	215
Antwerpen C	201	Madrid U C	215
Athina U C	202	Málaga C	216
Barcelona C U	203	Marseille C	216
Basel C	203	Milano C U	217
Beograd C	205	Moskva C U	218
Berlin C U	204	München C U	218
Bordeaux C U	205	Nápoli C U	219
Bruxelles U C	205	Oslo U C	219
Budapest C U	206	Paris C U	220
Dublin C U	207	Praha C U	222
Düsseldorf C U	207	Roma C U	223
Edinburgh C	207	Rotterdam C	222
Firenze Florence C	209	Sankt Peterburg U	222
Frankfurt C	209	Sevilla C	224
Genève Geneva C	209	Stockholm C U	225
Génova Genoa C	209	Strasbourg C U	224
Göteborg C	210	Stuttgart C	224
Granada C	210	Torino U C	226
Hamburg C U	210	Venézia C	226
Helsinki C U	211	Warszawa C U	227
İstanbul U	211	Wien U C	227
København C U	212	Zagreb C	228
Köln Cologne C	212	Zürich C	228
Lisboa C U	213	C City street plan	
London C U	213	U Urban area map	

229   Index to road maps

www.philips-maps.co.uk

First published in 1998 by Philip's,
a division of Octopus Publishing Group Ltd
www.octopusbooks.co.uk
Carmelite House, 50 Victoria Embankment
London EC4Y 0DZ
An Hachette UK Company · www.hachette.co.uk

Twenty-fifth edition 2017, first impression 2017

 This product includes mapping data licensed from Ordnance Survey®, with the permission of the Controller of Her Majesty's Stationery Office © Crown copyright 2017.
All rights reserved. Licence number 100011710

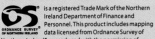 is a registered Trade Mark of the Northern Ireland Department of Finance and Personnel. This product includes mapping data licensed from Ordnance Survey of Northern Ireland®, reproduced with the permission of Land and Property Services under delegated authority from the Controller of Her Majesty's Stationery Office, © Crown Copyright 2017.

The information in this atlas is provided without any representation or warranty, express or implied and the Publisher cannot be held liable for any loss or damage due to any use or reliance on the information in this atlas, nor for any errors, omissions or subsequent changes in such information.

The representation in this atlas of any road, drive or track is not evidence of the existence of a right of way.

The maps of Ireland on pages 26 to 30 and the urban area map and town plan of Dublin are based upon the Crown Copyright and are reproduced with the permission of Land & Property Services under delegated authority from the Controller of Her Majesty's Stationery Office, © Crown Copyright and database right 2017, PMLPA No 100503, and on Ordnance Survey Ireland by permission of the Government © Ordnance Survey Ireland / Government of Ireland Permit number 9075.

Cartography by Philip's, Copyright © Philip's 2017

*Nielsen BookScan Travel Publishing Year Book 2015 data
**Independent research survey, from research carried out by Outlook Research Limited, 2005/06

Photographic acknowledgements:
Pages II and III: all photographs by Stephen Mesquita

Legend to route planning maps

 CW00496250

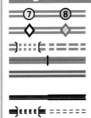

Motorway, tunnel	
Toll motorway	
Main road	
European	
National road number	
Distances – in kilometres	
International boundary, national boundary	
Car ferry and destination	
Mountain pass, international airport, height (metres)	

Town – population

MOSKVA	5 million +
BERLIN	2–5 million
MINSK	1–2 million
Oslo	500000–1 million
Århus	200000–500000
Turku	100000–200000

Gävle	50000–100000
Nybro	20000–50000
Ikast	10000–20000
Skjern	5000–10000
Lillesand	0–5000

The green version of the symbol indicates towns with Low Emission Zones

Scale · pages 2–23

1:3 200 000
1 in = 50.51 miles
1 cm = 32km

| 0 | 10 | 20 | 30 | 40 | 50 | 60 | 70 | 80 | 90 | 100 | 110 miles |
| 0 | 20 | 40 | 60 | 80 | 100 | 120 | 140 | 160 | 180 km |

Legend to road maps pages 26–200

Motorway with junctions – full, restricted access	
services, rest area	
tunnel, under construction	
Toll Motorway – with toll barrier	
Pre-pay motorway – (A) (CH) (CZ) (H) (SK) 'Vignette' must be purchased before travel	
Principal trunk highway – single / dual carriageway	
tunnel, under construction	
Other main highway – single / dual carriageway	
Other important road, other road	
E25 A49 European road number, motorway number	
135 National road number	
Col Bayard 1248 Mountain pass	
Scenic route, gradient – arrow points uphill	
Distances – in kilometres major 143	
minor 28	
Principal railway with tunnel	
Ferry route	
Short ferry route	
International boundary, national boundary	
National park, natural park	

✈ Airport		⛷ Ski resort	
Ancient monument		Theme park	
⚵ Beach		◉ World Heritage site	
Castle or house		1754▲ Spot height	
⌂ Cave		Sevilla World Heritage town	
✦ Other place of interest		Verona Town of tourist interest	
Park or garden		■ ● City or town with Low Emission Zone	
✝ Religious building			

Scale · pages 26–181

1:753 800
1 inch = 12 miles
1 cm = 7.5km

| 0 | 2 | 4 | 6 | 8 | 10 | 12 | 14 | 16 | 18 | 20 | 22 | 24 | 26 miles |
| 0 | 4 | 8 | 12 | 16 | 20 | 24 | 28 | 32 | 36 | 40km |

Scale · pages 182–200

1:1 507 600
1 inch = 24 miles
1 cm = 15km

| 0 | 4 | 8 | 12 | 16 | 20 | 24 | 28 | 32 | 36 | 40 | 44 | 48 | 52 miles |
| 0 | 8 | 16 | 24 | 32 | 40 | 48 | 56 | 64 | 72 | 80km |

Driving abroad –
a cautionary tale

by Stephen Mesquita,
Philip's On the Road Correspondent

15/06/2016 07:10:39 LS300W   *******

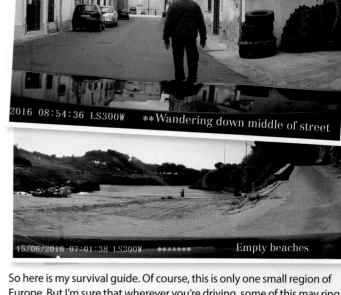

5/06/2016 07:05:10 LS300W   ****** Timeless pastoral scenes

2016 08:54:36 LS300W   ** Wandering down middle of street

15/06/2016 07:01:38 LS300W   ******   Empty beaches

At last, you're on holiday. You can relax, leave your troubles behind you and soak in the sun, the food and the way of life. That's all true, of course – if you don't have to drive.

When you're driving in a strange country, relaxing is the last thing you should be doing. In fact, when you're driving on roads you don't know – and on the 'wrong' side of the road – you need to pay attention at all times and be ultra defensive.

Take one of my favourite places to visit – the very end of the heel of Italy. If you're only used to the UK's roads, driving there is a whole different kettle of fish. Or '*un altro paio di maniche*' (another pair of sleeves), as it should be.

These are the idyllic images you might have :

- Empty roads with great views.
- Timeless pastoral scenes.
- Village locals wandering down the middle of the street.
- Driving down to empty beaches for a swim before breakfast (only if you're really keen).

But the reality's a lot different. It's not that the Southern Italians are any better or worse drivers than we are. But there are different laws, different conventions, different road conditions and different driving styles.

So here is my survival guide. Of course, this is only one small region of Europe. But I'm sure that wherever you're driving, some of this may ring bells – and perhaps even be useful.

Here are my Top 10 Tips from last year's holiday, illustrated with real-time dashcam video...

1 Being overtaken

Overtaking is more of a national sport on the continent than it is in the UK. What's disconcerting is the way that the overtaking car pulls in so sharply after overtaking. It takes a bit of getting used to but it's generally not (quite) as dangerous as it looks.

13/06/2016 08:43:35 LS300W   *******

2 Tailgating

It's probably no worse than in the UK; but tailgating can still be intimidating and distracting. If you feel threatened, try to pull off the road if it's safe to do it. Or try my favourite ploy – go round a roundabout twice to escape your tailgater.

3 Motorway Slip Roads

Beware short slip roads on to motorways. They give merging motorists little chance to join the traffic at anything other than a snail's pace, leading them into narrow lanes of fast traffic. Not for the faint-hearted. Check your mirror as often as you can.

4 Oncoming traffic driving on your side of the road

On narrow country roads, this is a hazard everywhere. It's probably worse in the UK than it is in Southern Italy. But, as the picture shows, it can produce some heart-stopping moments.

5 Pulling out of side roads and hoping

Pulling out of side roads and hoping. A lot of this goes on at crossroads in small towns and villages. Given the configuration of the roads, there's not much you can do about it – except be very cautious, even when it's your right of way or, as here, the traffic lights only work at certain times of day

6 Petrol stations

Many country petrol stations are unmanned. Those that are manned sometimes charge you more for the privilege of having someone serve you. It may be worth it: the unmanned ones are not easy to operate. In a richly comic episode, I had to seek assistance to discover that I had paid for €40 of petrol at a pump some distance from the one at which my car was parked.

7 Parking Meters

In this region, almost every town has the blue road markings which indicate that, if you want to park here, you'll need to buy a ticket. You'll need coins – many don't accept notes or credit cards. No change is given. If you're lucky, as you put the coins in, the expiry time is shown. If you're unlucky, this panel will be dirty or scratched so that you can't read it. The times you need to pay for vary from town to town, depending on the time of year (always in the tourist season) and the time of day (siesta time is sometimes not charged). A crash course in the language is recommended. In 11 days, I spent over €65 on meters.

8 Sat Nav – beware of speed limits

Even though I'm an atlas publisher, I would strongly recommend you take a sat nav – as well as this atlas, of course. It really reduces the stress of navigating on unfamiliar roads (it's not so good for route planning). But beware if your sat nav tells you the speed limit – those on the screen seem to bear little resemblance to the signs at the side of the road.

9 Speed limits Part 2

Even relying on the roadside signs, it can be hard to work out the speed limits. Can you work out what's happening here (answer at the foot of the page)?

10 Cameras

These pictures cost me €200. They show me at the wheel of my stylish Fiat 500 (that's what the website said anyway) being distracted by two cyclists as they went through a red light. The red light is hidden in the hedge. This deserted spot in the middle of the countryside boasts the only traffic camera ever seen in the region. I stupidly had my eye on the cyclists, not the light. First I received a bill from Hertz for €47.90 – which I innocently thought was for the 'offence'. But no, it was for supplying my name and address (with almost every word misspelt) to the local authority. A year later, a bill arrived from said local authority, for €145 if paid within 5 days (or €220 if not).

And I haven't even got to that most thrilling part of your holiday 'At the Car Hire Desk' (damage waiver rip-off's, not getting the car you ordered, should you photograph the car, and is it worth having another driver), documentation (the code you have to get now from the DVLA if you're hiring a car) and taking a spare pair of glasses. And do watch how much you drink. See the next section for all the rules and regulations for each country, including the alcohol limits. If in doubt, don't drink and drive. Now turn over and read the driving laws of the country you're going to. Buon Viaggio.

Answer to point 9: the speed limit is normally 90kph but it's 50kph when it's foggy or visibility is less than 100m.

Driving regulations

Vehicle A national vehicle identification plate is always required when taking a vehicle abroad.

Fitting headlamp converters or beam deflectors when taking a right-hand drive car to a country where driving is on the right (every country in Europe except the UK and Ireland) is compulsory.

Within the EU, if not driving a locally hired car, it is compulsory to have either Europlates or a country of origin (e.g. GB) sticker. Outside the EU (and in Andorra) a sticker is compulsory, even with Europlates.

Documentation All countries require that you carry a valid passport, vehicle registration document, hire certificate or letter of authority for the use of someone else's vehicle, full driving licence/International Driving Permit and insurance documentation (and/or green card outside the EU). Some non-EU countries also require a visa. Minimum driving ages are often higher for people holding foreign licences. New exit checks at the Eurotunnel and ferry terminals mean that drivers taking vehicles from the UK should allow extra time. Drivers of vehicles over three years old should ensure that the MOT is up to date.

EHIC cards are free and give you entitlement to healthcare in other EU countries and Switzerland. *www.gov/european-health-insurance-card*

Licence A photo licence is preferred; with an old-style paper licence, an International Driving Permit (IDP) should also be carried. In some countries, an IDP is compulsory, whatever form of licence is held. Non-EU drivers should always have both a licence and IDP. UK (except NI) drivers should check in advance whether a hire company will wish to check for endorsements and vehicle categories. If so, visit *www.gov.uk/view-driving-licence* to create a digital code (valid for 72 hours) that allows their details to be shared. For more information, contact the DVLA (0300790 6802, *www.dft.gov.uk/dvla*).

Insurance Third-party cover is compulsory across Europe. Most insurance policies give only basic cover when driving abroad, so you should check that your policy provides at least third-party cover for the countries in which you will be driving and upgrade it to the level that you require. You may have to take out extra cover at the frontier if you cannot produce acceptable proof of adequate insurance. Even in countries in which a green card is not required, carrying one is recommended for extra proof of insurance.

Motorcycles It is compulsory for all motorcyclists and passengers to wear crash helmets.

Other In countries in which visibility vests are compulsory, one for each person should be carried in the passenger compartment, or panniers on a motorbike, where they can be reached easily.

Warning triangles should also be carried in the passenger compartment.

The penalties for infringements of regulations vary considerably from one country to another. In many countries the police may impose on-the-spot fines (ask for a receipt). Penalties can be severe for serious infringements, particularly for exceeding the blood-alcohol limit; in some countries this can result in immediate imprisonment.

In some countries, vignettes for toll roads are being replaced by electronic tags.

Please note that driving regulations may change, and that it has not been possible to cover all the information for every type of vehicle. The figures given for capitals' populations are for the whole metropolitan area.

The symbols used are:

- Motorway
- Dual carriageway
- Single carriageway
- Surfaced road
- Unsurfaced or gravel road
- Urban area
- Speed limit in kilometres per hour (kph). These are the maximum speeds for the types of roads listed. In some places and under certain conditions they may be considerably lower. Always obey local signs.
- Seat belts
- Children
- Blood alcohol level
- Warning triangle
- First aid kit
- Spare bulb kit
- Fire extinguisher
- Minimum driving age
- Additional documents required
- Mobile phones
- Dipped headlights
- Winter driving
- LEZ Low Emission Zone
- Other information

The publishers have made every effort to ensure that the information given here was correct at the time of going to press. No responsibility can be accepted for any errors or their consequences.

Andorra Principat d'Andorra (AND)

Area 468 km² (181 mi²) **Population** 85,500 **Capital** Andorra la Vella (44,000) **Languages** Catalan (official), French, Castilian and Portuguese **Currency** Euro = 100 cents **Website** http://visitandorra.com

	Motorway	Dual carriageway	Single carriageway	Urban area
Speed limit	n/a	90	60/90	50

- Seat belts: Compulsory
- Children: Under 10 and below 150 cm must travel in an EU-approved restraint system adapted to their size in the rear. Airbag must be deactivated if a child is in the front passenger seat.
- Blood alcohol: 0.05% • Warning triangle: Compulsory • First aid kit: Recommended
- Spare bulb kit: Compulsory • Fire extinguisher: Recommended • Minimum driving age: 18
- Mobile phones: Not permitted whilst driving
- Dipped headlights: Compulsory for motorcycles during day and for other vehicles during poor daytime visibility.
- Winter driving: Winter tyres or snow chains compulsory in poor conditions or when indicated by signs
- ★ On-the-spot fines imposed
- ★ Visibility vests compulsory

Austria Österreich (A)

Area 83,859 km² (32,377 mi²) **Population** 8,663,000 **Capital** Vienna / Wien (2,600,000) **Languages** German (official) **Currency** Euro = 100 cents **Website** www.austria.gv.at

	Motorway	Dual carriageway	Single carriageway	Urban area
Speed limit	130	100	100	50
If towing trailer under 750kg / over 750 kg	100	100	100/80	50

- Seat belts: Compulsory
- Children: Under 14 and under 150cm cannot travel as a front or rear passenger unless they use a suitable child restraint; under 14 over 150cm must wear adult seat belt
- Blood alcohol: 0.049% • 0.01% if licence held less than 2 years
- Warning triangle: Compulsory • First aid kit: Compulsory
- Spare bulb kit: Recommended • Fire extinguisher: Recommended
- Minimum driving age: 18 (16 for motorbikes under 50 cc, 20 over 50 cc)
- Mobile phones: Only allowed with hands-free kit
- LEZ: LEZ On A12 motorway non-compliant vehicles banned and certain substances banned, night-time speed restrictions; Steermark province has LEZs affecting lorries
- Dipped headlights: Must be used during the day by all road users. Headlamp converters compulsory
- Winter driving: Winter tyres compulsory 1 Nov–15 Apr
- ★ On-the-spot fines imposed
- ★ Radar detectors and dashcams prohibited
- ★ To drive on motorways or expressways, a motorway sticker must be purchased at the border or main petrol station. These are available for 10 days, 2 months or 1 year. Vehicles 3.5 tonnes or over must display an electronic tag.
- ★ Visibility vests compulsory

Belarus (BY)

Area 207,600 km² (80,154 mi²) **Population** 9,499,000 **Capital** Minsk (2,101,000) **Languages** Belarusian, Russian (both official) **Currency** Belarusian ruble = 100 kopek **Website** www.belarus.by/en/government

	Motorway	Dual carriageway	Single carriageway	Urban area
Speed limit	110	90	90	60*
If towing trailer under 750kg	90	70	70	

*In residential areas limit is 20 km/h • Vehicle towing another vehicle 50 kph limit • If full driving licence held for less than two years, must not exceed 70 kph

- Seat belts: Compulsory in front seats, and rear seats if fitted
- Children: Under 12 not allowed in front seat and must use appropriate child restraint
- Blood alcohol: 0.00% • Warning triangle: Compulsory • First aid kit: Compulsory
- Spare bulb kit: Recommended • Fire extinguisher: Compulsory • Minimum driving age: 18
- Additional documents: Visa, vehicle technical check stamp, international driving permit, green card, health insurance. Even with a green card, local third-party insurance may be imposed at the border
- Mobile phones: Use prohibited
- Dipped headlights: Compulsory during the day Nov–Mar and at all other times in conditions of poor visibility or when towing or being towed.
- Winter driving: Winter tyres compulsory; snow chains recommended
- ★ A temporary vehicle import certificate must be purchased on entry and driver must be registered
- ★ Fees payable for driving on highways
- ★ It is illegal for vehicles to be dirty
- ★ On-the-spot fines imposed
- ★ Radar-detectors prohibited
- ★ Vehicles registered outside Eurasion Economic Union or over 3.5 tons are required to use BelToll device for automatic payment of motorway tolls. See www.beltoll.by/index.php/en

Belgium Belgique (B)

Area 30,528 km² (11,786 mi²) **Population** 11,260,000 **Capital** Brussels/Bruxelles (1,666,000) **Languages** Dutch, French, German (all official) **Currency** Euro = 100 cents **Website** www.belgium.be/en

	Motorway	Dual carriageway	Single carriageway	Urban area
Speed limit	120*	120*	90	50**
If towing trailer	90	90	60	50
Over 3.5 tonnes	90	90	60	50

*Minimum speed of 70kph may be applied in certain conditions on motorways and some dual carriageways **Near schools, hospitals and churches the limit may be 30kph

- Seat belts: Compulsory
- Children: All under 19s under 135 cm must wear an appropriate child restraint. Airbags must be deactivated if a rear-facing child seat is used in the front
- Blood alcohol: 0.049% • Warning triangle: Compulsory • First aid kit: Recommended
- Spare bulb kit: Recommended • Fire extinguisher: Compulsory • Minimum driving age: 18
- Mobile phones: Only allowed with a hands-free kit
- Dipped headlights: Mandatory at all times for motorcycles and advised during the day in poor conditions for other vehicles
- ★ Cruise control must be deactivated on motorways where indicated
- ★ On-the-spot fines imposed
- ★ Radar detectors prohibited
- ★ Sticker indicating maximum recommended speed for winter tyres must be displayed on dashboard if using them
- ★ Visibility vest compulsory

Bosnia Herzegovina Bosna i Hercegovina (BIH)

Area 51,197 km² (19,767 mi²) **Population** 3,872,000 **Capital** Sarajevo (688,000) **Languages** Bosnian/Croatian/Serbian **Currency** Convertible Marka = 100 convertible pfenniga **Website** www.fbihvlada.gov.ba/english/index.php

	Motorway	Dual carriageway	Single carriageway	Urban area
Speed limit	130	100	80	50

- Seat belts: Compulsory if fitted
- Children: Under 12s must sit in rear using an appropriate child restraint. Under-2s may travel in a rear-facing child seat in the front only if the airbags have been deactivated.
- Blood alcohol: 0.03% • Warning triangle: Compulsory • First aid kit: Compulsory
- Spare bulb kit: Compulsory • Minimum driving age: 18
- Fire extinguisher: Compulsory for LPG vehicles
- Additional documents: Visa, International Driving Permit, green card
- Mobile phones: Prohibited
- Dipped headlights: Compulsory for all vehicles at all times
- Winter driving: Winter tyres compulsory 15 Nov–15 Apr; snow chains recommended
- ★ GPS must have fixed speed camera function deactivated; radar detectors prohibited.
- ★ On-the-spot fines imposed
- ★ Visibility vest, tow rope or tow bar compulsory
- ★ Spare wheel compulsory, except for two-wheeled vehicles

Bulgaria Bulgariya (BG)

Area 110,912 km² (42,822 mi²) **Population** 7,202,000 **Capital** Sofia (1,543,000) **Languages** Bulgarian (official), Turkish **Currency** Lev = 100 stotinki **Website** www.government.bg

	Motorway	Dual carriageway	Single carriageway	Urban area
Speed limit	130	90	90	50
If towing trailer	100	70	70	50

- Seat belts: Compulsory in front and rear seats
- Children: Under 3s not permitted in vehicles with no child restraints; 3–10 year olds must sit in rear
- Blood alcohol: 0.05% • Warning triangle: Compulsory • First aid kit: Compulsory
- Spare bulb kit: Recommended • Fire extinguisher: Compulsory • Minimum driving age: 18
- Additional documents: Photo driving licence preferred; a paper licence must be accompanied by an International Driving Permit. Green card or insurance specific to Bulgaria.
- Mobile phones: Only allowed with a hands-free kit
- Dipped headlights: Compulsory
- Winter driving: Snow chains should be carried from 1 Nov–1 Mar
- ★ Fee at border
- ★ GPS must have fixed speed camera function deactivated; radar detectors prohibited
- ★ On-the-spot fines imposed
- ★ Road tax stickers (annual, monthly or weekly) must be purchased at the border and displayed prominently with the vehicle registration number written on them.
- ★ Visibility vest compulsory

Croatia Hrvatska (HR)

Area 56,538 km² (21,829 mi²) **Population** 4,825,000 **Capital** Zagreb (1,113,000) **Languages** Croatian **Currency** Kuna = 100 lipa **Website** https://vlada.gov.hr/en

	Motorway	Dual carriageway	Single carriageway	Urban area
Speed limit	130	110	90	50
Under 24	120	100	80	50
If towing	110	80	80	50

- Seat belts: Compulsory if fitted
- Children: Children under 12 not permitted in front seat and must use appropriate child seat or restraint in rear.
- Blood alcohol: 0.05% • 0.00 % for drivers under 24
- Warning triangle: Compulsory • First aid kit: Compulsory
- Spare bulb kit: Compulsory • Fire extinguisher: Recommended • Minimum driving age: 18
- Additional documents: Green card recommended
- Mobile phones: Only allowed with hands-free kit
- Dipped headlights: Compulsory
- Winter driving: Winter tyres, snow chains and shovel compulsory in winter
- ★ On-the-spot fines imposed
- ★ Radar detectors prohibited
- ★ Tow bar and rope compulsory
- ★ Visibility vest compulsory

Czechia Česko (CZ)

Area 78,864 km² (30,449 mi²) **Population** 10,553,000 **Capital** Prague/Praha (2,156,000) **Languages** Czech (official), Moravian **Currency** Czech Koruna = 100 haler **Website** www.vlada.cz/en/

	Motorway	Dual carriageway	Single carriageway	Urban area
Speed limit	130	90	90	50
If towing	80	80	80	50

- Seat belts: Compulsory in front seats and, if fitted, in rear
- Children: Children under 36 kg and 150 cm must use appropriate child restraint. Only front-facing child retraints are permitted in the front in vehicles with airbags fitted. Airbags must be deactivated if a rear-facing child seat is used in the front.
- Blood alcohol: 0.00% • Warning triangle: Compulsory • First aid kit: Compulsory
- Spare bulb kit: Compulsory • Fire extinguisher: Compulsory
- Minimum driving age: 18 (17 for motorcycles under 125 cc)
- Mobile phones: Only allowed with a hands-free kit
- LEZ: Two-stage LEZ in Prague for vehicles over 3.5 and 6 tonnes. Permit system.
- Dipped headlights: Compulsory at all times
- Winter driving: Winter tyres compulsory November-March, roads are icy/snow-covered or snow is expected
- ★ GPS must have fixed speed camera function deactivated; radar detectors prohibited
- ★ On-the-spot fines imposed
- ★ Replacement fuses must be carried
- ★ Spectacles or contact lens wearers must carry a spare pair in their vehicle at all times
- ★ Vignette needed for motorway driving, available for 1 year, 60 days, 15 days. Toll specific to lorries introduced 2006, those over 12 tonnes must buy an electronic tag
- ★ Visibility vest compulsory

Denmark Danmark (DK)

Area 43,094 km² (16,638 mi²) **Population** 5,707,000 **Capital** Copenhagen / København (2,016,000) **Languages** Danish (official) **Currency** Krone = 100 øre **Website** www.denmark.dk/en

	Motorway	Dual carriageway	Single carriageway	Urban area
Speed limit	110-130	80-90	80	50*
If towing	80	70	70	50*

*Central Copenhagen 40 kph

- Seat belts: Compulsory front and rear
- Children: Under 135cm must use appropriate child restraint; in front permitted only in an appropriate rear-facing seat with any airbags disabled.
- Blood alcohol: 0.05% • Warning triangle: Compulsory • First aid kit: Recommended
- Spare bulb kit: Recommended • Fire extinguisher: Recommended • Minimum driving age: 18
- Mobile phones: Only allowed with a hands-free kit
- LEZ: Aalborg, Arhus, Copenhagen, Frederiksberg and Odense. Proofs of emissions compliance or compliant filter needed to obtain sticker. Non-compliant vehicles banned.
- Dipped headlights: Must be used at all times
- ★ On-the-spot fines imposed
- ★ Radar detectors prohibited
- ★ Tolls apply on the Storebaeltsbroen and Oresundsbron bridges.
- ★ Visibility vest recommended

Estonia Eesti (EST)

Area 45,100 km² (17,413 mi²)
Population 1,316,000 **Capital** Tallinn (543,000)
Languages Estonian (official), Russian
Currency Euro = 100 cents **Website** valitsus.ee/en

⏱	🚗	⚠	🏭
n/a	90*	90	50

If full driving licence held for less than two years

⏱			
90	90	90	50

*In summer, the speed limit on some dual carriageways may be raised to 100/110 kph

- Compulsory if fitted
- Children too small for adult seatbelts must wear a seat restraint appropriate to their size. Rear-facing safety seats must not be used in the front if an air bag is fitted, unless this has been deactivated.
- 0.00% △ Compulsory 🔺 Compulsory
- Recommended 🔦 Compulsory ⊖ 18
- Only allowed with a hands-free kit
- Compulsory at all times
- Winter tyres are compulsory from Dec–Mar. Studded winter tyres are allowed from 15 Oct–31 Mar, but this can be extended to start 1 October and/or end 30 April
- ★ A toll system is in operation in Tallinn
- ★ On-the-spot fines imposed

Finland Suomi (FIN)

Area 338,145 km² (130,557 mi²)
Population 5,489,000 **Capital** Helsinki (1,442,000)
Languages Finnish, Swedish (both official)
Currency Euro = 100 cents
Website http://valtioneuvosto.fi/en/frontpage

⏱	🚗	⚠	🏭
120	100	80-100	20/50

Vans, lorries and if towing

⏱			
80	80	60	20/50

*100 in summer • If towing a vehicle by rope, cable or rod, max speed limit 60 kph • Maximum of 80 kph for vans and lorries • Speed limits are often lowered in winter

- Compulsory in front and rear
- Below 135 cm must use a child restraint or seat
- 0.05% △ Compulsory 🔺 Recommended
- Recommended 🔦 Recommended
- ⊖ 18 (motorbikes below 125cc 16)
- Only allowed with a hands-free kit
- Must be used at all times
- Winter tyres compulsory Dec–Feb
- ★ On-the-spot fines imposed ★ Radar-detectors are prohibited ★ Visibility vest compulsory

France (F)

Area 551,500 km² (212,934 mi²)
Population 64,570,000 **Capital** Paris (12,405,000)
Languages French (official), Breton, Occitan
Currency Euro = 100 cents
Website www.diplomatie.gouv.fr/en/

⏱	🚗	⚠	🏭
130	110	90	50

On wet roads or if full driving licence held for less than 2 years

⏱			
110	100	80	50

If towing below / above 3.5 tonnes gross

⏱			
110/90	100/90	90/80	50

50kph on all roads if fog reduces visibility to less than 50m • Licence will be lost and driver fined for exceeding speed limit by over 50kph

- Compulsory in front seats and, if fitted, in rear
- In rear, 4 or under must have a child safety seat (rear facing if up to 9 months); if 5–10 must use an appropriate restraint system. Under 10 permitted in the front only if rear seats are fully occupied by other under 10s or there are no rear safety belts. In front, if child is in rear-facing child seat, any airbag must be deactivated.
- 0.05% • If towing or with less than 2 years with full driving licence, 0.00% • All drivers/motorcyclists must carry an unused breathalyser to French certification standards, showing an NF number.
- △ Compulsory 🔺 Recommended
- Recommended ⊖ 18
- Use not permitted whilst driving
- LEZ An LEZ operates in the Mont Blanc tunnel. Cars and vans registered before 1997 and motorcycles before 1999 are banned from anywhere inside the Paris Boulevard Périphérique between 8 am and 8 pm on weekdays. Classic cars more than 30 years old are exempt.
- Compulsory in poor daytime visibility and at all times for motorcycles
- Winter tyres recommended. Carrying snow chains recommended in winter as these may have to be fitted if driving on snow-covered roads, in accordance with signage.
- GPS must have fixed speed camera function deactivated; radar-detection equipment is prohibited ★ It is compulsory to carry a French-authority-recognised (NF) breathalyser. ★ On-the-spot fines imposed ★ Tolls on motorways. Electronic tag needed if using automatic tolls.
- ★ Visibility vests, to be worn on the roadside in case of emergency or breakdown, must be carried for all vehicle occupants. ★ Motorcyclists and passengers must have four reflective stickers on their helmets (front, back and both sides) and carry visibility vests to be worn on the roadside in case of emergency or breakdown.

Germany Deutschland (D)

Area 357,022 km² (137,846 mi²)
Population 81,459,000 **Capital** Berlin (5,871,000)
Languages German (official) **Currency** Euro = 100 cents **Website** www.bundesregierung.de

⏱	🚗	⚠	🏭
*	*	100	50

If towing

⏱			
80	80	80	50

*no limit, 130 kph recommended

- Compulsory
- Aged 3-12 and under 150cm must use an appropriate child seat or restraint and sit in the rear. In the front, if child under 3 is in a rear-facing child seat, airbags must be deactivated
- 0.05% • 0.0% for drivers 21 or under or with less than two years full licence
- △ Compulsory 🔺 Compulsory
- Recommended 🔦 Recommended
- ⊖ 18 (motorbikes: 16 if under 50cc)
- Use permitted only with hands-free kit – also applies to drivers of motorbikes and bicycles
- LEZ More than 60 cities have or are planning LEZs. Proof of compliance needed to acquire sticker. Non-compliant vehicles banned.
- Compulsory during poor daytime visibility and in tunnels; recommended at other times. Compulsory at all times for motorcyclists.
- Winter tyres compulsory in all winter weather conditions; snow chains recommended
- ★ GPS must have fixed speed camera function deactivated; radar detectors prohibited
- ★ On-the-spot fines imposed ★ Visibility vest compulsory ★ Tolls on autobahns for lorries

Greece Ellas (GR)

Area 131,957 km² (50,948 mi²)
Population 10,955,000 **Capital** Athens / Athina (3,754,000) **Languages** Greek (official)
Currency Euro = 100 cents
Website www.primeminister.gr/english

⏱	🚗	⚠	🏭
130	110	90	50

Motorbikes, and if towing

⏱			
90	70	70	40

- Compulsory in front seats and, if fitted, in rear
- Under 12 or below 135cm must use appropriate child restraint. In front if child is in rear-facing child seat, any airbags must be deactivated
- 0.05% • 0.00% for drivers with less than 2 years' full licence and motorcyclists
- △ Compulsory 🔺 Compulsory
- Recommended 🔦 Compulsory
- ⊖ 18 🚬 Not permitted.
- Compulsory during poor daytime visibility and at all times for motorcycles
- Snow chains permitted on ice- or snow-covered roads
- ★ Radar-detection equipment is prohibited
- ★ Tolls on several newer motorways.

Hungary Magyarország (H)

Area 93,032 km² (35,919 mi²)
Population 9,856,000 **Capital** Budapest (3,304,000)
Languages Hungarian (official)
Currency Forint = 100 filler
Website www.kormany.hu/en

⏱	🚗	⚠	🏭
130	110	90	50

If towing

⏱			
80	70	70	50

- Compulsory
- Under 135cm and over 3 must be seated in rear and use appropriate child restraint. Under 3 allowed in front only in rear-facing child seat with any airbags deactivated.
- 0.00% △ Compulsory 🔺 Compulsory
- Compulsory 🔦 Recommended ⊖ 17
- Only allowed with a hands-free kit
- LEZ Budapest has vehicle restrictions on days with heavy dust and is planning an LEZ.
- Compulsory during the day outside built-up areas; compulsory at all times for motorcycles
- Snow chains compulsory where conditions dictate
- ★ Many motorways are toll and operate electronic vignette system with automatic number plate recognition, tickets are available for 4 days, 7 days, 1 month, 1 year ★ On-the-spot fines issued ★ Radar detectors prohibited ★ Tow rope recommended ★ Visibility vest compulsory

Iceland Ísland (IS)

Area 103,000 km² (39,768 mi²)
Population 333,000 **Capital** Reykjavik (210,000)
Languages Icelandic **Currency** Krona = 100 aurar
Website www.government.is/

⏱	🚗	🚙	🏭
n/a	90	80	50

- Compulsory in front and rear seats
- Under 12 or below 150cm not allowed in front seat and must use appropriate child restraint.
- 0.05% △ Compulsory 🔺 Compulsory
- Compulsory 🔦 Compulsory
- ⊖ 18; 21 to drive a hire car; 25 to hire a jeep
- Only allowed with a hands-free kit
- Compulsory at all times
- Winter tyres compulsory c.1 Nov–14 Apr (variable)
- ★ Driving off marked roads is forbidden
- ★ Highland roads are not suitable for ordinary cars
- ★ On-the-spot fines imposed

Ireland Eire (IRL)

Area 70,273 km² (27,132 mi²)
Population 4,635,000 **Capital** Dublin (1,801,000)
Languages Irish, English (both official)
Currency Euro = 100 cents **Website** www.gov.ie/en/

⏱	🚗	⚠	🏭
120	100	80	50

If towing

⏱			
80	80	80	50

- Compulsory where fitted. Driver responsible for ensuring passengers under 17 comply
- Children 3 and under must be in a suitable child restraint system. Airbags must be deactivated if a rear-facing child seat is used in the front. Those under 150cm and 36 kg must use appropriate child restraint.
- 0.05% • 0.02% for novice and professional drivers
- △ Compulsory 🔺 Recommended
- Recommended 🔦 Recommended
- ⊖ 17 (16 for motorbikes up to 125cc; 18 for over 125cc; 18 for lorries; 21 bus/minibus)
- Only allowed with a hands-free kit
- Compulsory for motorbikes at all times and in poor visibility for other vehicles
- ★ Driving is on the left ★ GPS must have fixed speed camera function deactivated; radar detectors prohibited ★ On-the-spot fines imposed ★ Tolls are being introduced on some motorways; the M50 Dublin has barrier-free tolling with number-plate recognition.

Italy Italia (I)

Area 301,318 km² (116,338 mi²)
Population 60,671,000 **Capital** Rome / Roma (4,321,000) **Languages** Italian (official)
Currency Euro = 100 cents **Website** www.italia.it

⏱	🚗	⚠	🏭
130	110	90	50

If towing

⏱			
80	70	70	50

Less than three years with full licence

⏱			
100	90	90	50

When wet

⏱			
100	90	90	50

Some motorways with emergency lanes have speed limit of 150 kph

- Compulsory in front seats and, if fitted, in rear
- Under 12 not allowed in front seats except in child safety seat; children under 3 must have special seat in the back. For foreign-registered cars, the country of origin's legislation applies.
- 0.05% • 0.00% for professional drivers or with less than 3 years full licence
- △ Compulsory 🔺 Recommended
- Compulsory 🔦 Recommended
- ⊖ 18 • 14 for mopeds, 16 up to 125cc, 20 up to 350cc
- Only allowed with a hands-free kit
- LEZ Most northern and several southern regions operate seasonal LEZs and many towns and cities have various schemes that restrict access. There is an LEZ in the Mont Blanc tunnel
- Compulsory outside built-up areas, in tunnels, on motorways and dual carriageways and in poor visibility; compulsory at all times for motorcycles
- Snow chains compulsory where signs indicate 15 Oct–15 Apr
- ★ On-the-spot fines imposed ★ Radar-detection equipment is prohibited ★ Tolls on motorways. Blue lanes accept credit cards; yellow lanes restricted to holders of Telepass pay-toll device.
- ★ Visibility vest compulsory

Kosovo Republika e Kosoves / Republika Kosovo (RKS)

Area 10,887 km² (4203 mi²) **Population** 1,859,000
Capital Pristina (504,000) **Languages** Albanian, Serbian (both official), Bosnian, Turkish, Roma
Currency Euro (Serbian dinar in Serb enclaves)
Website www.kryeministri-ks.net/?page=2,1

⏱	🚗	⚠	🏭
130	80	80	50

- Compulsory
- Under 12 must sit in rear seats
- 0.03% • 0.00% for professional, business and commercial drivers
- △ Compulsory 🔺 Compulsory
- Compulsory 🔦 Compulsory
- ⊖ 18 (16 for motorbikes less than 125 cc, 14 for mopeds)
- International driving permit, locally purchased third-party insurance (green card is not recognised), documents with proof of ability to cover costs and valid reason for visiting. Visitors from many non-EU countries require a visa.
- Only allowed with a hands-free kit
- Compulsory at all times
- Winter tyres or snow chains compulsory in poor winter weather conditions

Latvia Latvija (LV)

Area 64,589 km² (24,942 mi²) **Population** 1,974,000
Capital Riga (1,018,000) **Languages** Latvian (official), Russian **Currency** Euro = 100 cents
Website www.mk.gov.lv/en

⏱	🚗	⚠	🏭
n/a	100	90	50

If towing

⏱			
n/a	80	80	50

In residential areas limit is 20kph • If full driving licence held for less than two years, must not exceed 80 kph

- Compulsory in front seats and if fitted in rear
- If under 12 years and 150cm must use child restraint in front and rear seats
- 0.05% • 0.02% with less than 2 years experience
- △ Compulsory 🔺 Compulsory
- Recommended 🔦 Compulsory ⊖ 18
- Only allowed with hands-free kit
- Must be used at all times all year round
- Winter tyres compulsory for vehicles up to 3.5 tonnes Dec–Feb, but illegal May–Sept
- ★ On-the-spot fines imposed ★ Pedestrians have priority ★ Radar-detection equipment prohibited ★ Visibility vests compulsory

Lithuania Lietuva (LT)

Area 65,200 km² (25,173 mi²)
Population 2,876,000 **Capital** Vilnius (543,000)
Languages Lithuanian (official), Russian, Polish
Currency Euro = 100 cents **Website** http://lrv.lt/en

⏱	🚗	⚠	🏭
130	110	90	50

If towing

⏱			
n/a	70	70	50

If licence held for less than two years

⏱			
130	90	70	50

In winter speed limits are reduced by 10–20 km/h

- Compulsory
- Under 12 or below 135 cm not allowed in front seats unless in a child safety seat; under 3 must use appropriate child seat and sit in rear
- 0.04% • 0.02% if full licence held less than 2 years
- △ Compulsory 🔺 Compulsory
- Recommended 🔦 Compulsory ⊖ 18
- Licences without a photograph must be accompanied by photographic proof of identity, e.g. a passport
- Only allowed with a hands-free kit
- Must be used at all times
- Winter tyres compulsory 10 Nov–1 Apr
- ★ On-the-spot fines imposed
- ★ Visibility vest compulsory

Luxembourg (L)

Area 2,586 km² (998 mi²) **Population** 563,000
Capital Luxembourg (107,000)
Languages Luxembourgian / Letzeburgish (official), French, German **Currency** Euro = 100 cents
Website www.luxembourg.public.lu/en/

⏱	🚗	⚠	🏭
130/110	90	90	50

If towing

⏱			
90	75	75	50

If full driving licence held for less than two years, must not exceed 75 kph • In 20 km/h zones, pedestrians have right of way.

Compulsory

Children under 3 must use an appropriate restraint system. Airbags must be disabled if a rear-facing child seat is used in the front. Children 3–18 and/or under 150 cm must use a restraint system appropriate to their size. If over 36kg a seatbelt may be used in the back only

0.05% • 0.02 for young drivers, drivers with less than 2 years experience and drivers of taxis and commercial vehicles

Compulsory Compulsory (buses)

Compulsory 18

Compulsory (buses, transport of dangerous goods)

Use permitted only with hands-free kit

Compulsory for motorcyclists and in poor visibility for other vehicles

Winter tyres compulsory in winter weather

★ On-the-spot fines imposed ★Visibility vest compulsory

Macedonia Makedonija (MK)

Area 25,713 km² (9,927 mi²) **Population** 2,069,000 **Capital** Skopje (507,000) **Languages** Macedonian (official), Albanian **Currency** Denar = 100 deni **Website** www.vlada.mk/?language=en-gb

120	100	80	50
Newly qualified drivers or if towing			
100	80	60	50

Compulsory

Under 12 not allowed in front seats

0.05% • 0.00% for business, commercial and professional drivers and with less than 2 years experience

Compulsory Compulsory

Compulsory 18 (mopeds 16)

Recommended; compulsory for LPG vehicles

International driving permit; visa

Use not permitted whilst driving

Compulsory at all times

Winter tyres or snow chains compulsory 15 Nov–15 Mar

★ GPS must have fixed speed camera function deactivated; radar detectors prohibited ★Novice drivers may only drive between 11pm and 5am if there is someone over 25 with a valid licence in the vehicle. ★ On-the-spot fines imposed ★ Visibility vest must be kept in the passenger compartment and worn to leave the vehicle in the dark outside built-up areas ★Tolls apply on many roads ★Tow rope compulsory

Moldova (MD)

Area 33,851 km² (13,069 mi²) **Population** 3,418,000 **Capital** Chisinau (736,000) **Languages** Moldovan / Romanian (official) **Currency** Leu = 100 bani **Website** www.moldova.md

90	90	90	60
If towing or if licence held under 1 year			
70	70	70	60

Compulsory in front seats and, if fitted in rear seats

Under 12 not allowed in front seats

0.00% Compulsory Compulsory

Recommended Compulsory

18 (mopeds and motorbikes, 16; vehicles with more than eight passenger places, taxis or towing heavy vehicles, 21)

International Driving Permit (preferred), visa

Only allowed with hands-free kit

Must use dipped headlights at all times

Winter tyres recommended Nov–Feb

Montenegro Crna Gora (MNE)

Area 14,026 km², (5,415 mi²) **Population** 677,000 **Capital** Podgorica (187,000) **Languages** Serbian (of the Ijekavian dialect) **Currency** Euro = 100 cents **Website** www.gov.me/en/homepage

n/a	100	80	50

80kph speed limit if towing a caravan

Compulsory in front and rear seats

Under 12 not allowed in front seats. Under-5s must use an appropriate child seat.

0.03 % Compulsory Compulsory

Compulsory Compulsory

18 (16 motorbikes under 125cc; 14 mopeds)

Prohibited Must be used at all times

From mid-Nov to March, driving wheels must be fitted with winter tyres

★ An 'eco' tax vignette must be obtained when crossing the border and displayed in the upper right-hand corner of the windscreen ★ On-the-spot fines imposed ★ Tolls on some primary roads and in the Sozina tunnel between Lake Skadar and the sea ★Visibility vest compulsory

Netherlands Nederland (NL)

Area 41,526 km² (16,033 mi²) **Population** 17,000,000 **Capital** Amsterdam 2,431,000 • administrative capital 's-Gravenhage (The Hague) 1,051,000 **Languages** Dutch (official), Frisian **Currency** Euro = 100 cents **Website** www.government.nl

130	80/100	80/100	50

Compulsory

Under 3 must travel in the back, using an appropriate child restraint; 3–18 and under 135cm must use an appropriate child restraint. A rear-facing child seat may be used in front only if airbags are deactivated.

0.05% • 0.02% with less than 5 years experience or moped riders under 24

Compulsory Recommended

Recommended Recommended 18

Only allowed with a hands-free kit

LEZ About 20 cities operate or are planning LEZs. A national scheme is planned.

Recommended in poor visibility and on open roads. Compulsory for motorcycles.

★ On-the-spot fines imposed

★ Radar-detection equipment is prohibited

Norway Norge (N)

Area 323,877 km² (125,049 mi²) **Population** 5,215,000 **Capital** Oslo (1,718,000) **Languages** Norwegian (official), Lappish, Finnish **Currency** Krone = 100 øre **Website** www.norway.org.uk

90/100	80	80	30/50
If towing trailer with brakes			
80	80	80	50
If towing trailer without brakes			
60	60	60	50

Compulsory in front seats and, if fitted, in rear

Children less than 150cm tall must use appropriate child restraint. Children under 4 must use child safety seat or safety restraint (cot). A rear-facing child seat may be used in front only if airbags are deactivated.

0.01% Compulsory Recommended

Recommended Recommended

18 (heavy vehicles 18/21)

Only allowed with a hands-free kit

LEZ Oslo (administered through national road-toll scheme), with plans for other cities

Must be used at all times

Winter tyres or summer tyres with snow chains compulsory for snow- or ice-covered roads

★ On-the-spot fines imposed ★Radar-detectors prohibited ★ Tolls apply on some bridges, tunnels and access roads into Bergen, Oslo, Trondheim & Stavangar. Several use electronic fee collection only. ★ Visibility vest compulsory

Poland Polska (PL)

Area 323,250 km² (124,807 mi²) **Population** 38,484,000 **Capital** Warsaw / Warszawa (3,106,000) **Currency** Zloty = 100 groszy **Website** www.premier.gov.pl/en.html

Motor-vehicle only roads[1], under/over 3.5 tonnes			
130[2]/80[2]	110/80	100/80	n/a
Motor-vehicle only roads[1] if towing			
n/a	80	80	n/a
Other roads, under 3.5 tonnes			
n/a	100	90	50/60[3]
Other roads, 3.5 tonnes or over			
n/a	80	70	50/60[3]
Other roads, if towing			
n/a	60	60	30

[1]Indicated by signs with white car on blue • [2]Minimum speed 40 kph • [3]50 kph 05.00–23.00; 60 kph 23.00–05.00; 20 kph in marked residential areas

Compulsory in front seats and, if fitted, in rear

Under 12 and below 150 cm must use an appropriate child restraint. Rear-facing child seats not permitted in vehicles with airbags.

0.02% Compulsory Recommended

Recommended Compulsory

18 (mopeds and motorbikes under 125cc – 16)

Only allowed with a hands-free kit

Compulsory for all vehicles

Snow chains permitted only on roads completely covered in snow

★ On-the-spot fines imposed ★ Radar-detection equipment is prohibited ★ Vehicles over 3.5 tonnes (including cars towing caravans) must have a VIAbox for the electronic toll system ★Visibility vests compulsory for drivers of Polish-registered vehicles

Portugal (P)

Area 88,797 km² (34,284 mi²) **Population** 10,427,000 **Capital** Lisbon / Lisboa (2,822,000) **Languages** Portuguese (official) **Currency** Euro = 100 cents **Website** www.portugal.gov.pt/en.aspx

120*	90/100	90	50/20
If towing			
100*	90	80	50

*50kph minimum; 90kph maximum if licence held under 1 year

Compulsory in front seats and, if fitted, in rear

Under 12 and below 135cm must travel in the rear in an appropriate child restraint; rear-facing child seats permitted in front only if airbags deactivated

0.05% • 0.02% for drivers with less than 3 years with a full licence

Compulsory Recommended

Recommended Recommended

18 (motorcycles under 50cc 17)

MOT certificate for vehicles over 3 years old, photographic proof of identity (e.g. driving licence or passport) must be carried at all times.

Only allowed with hands-free kit

LEZ An LEZ prohibits vehicles without catalytic converters from certain parts of Lisbon. There are plans to extend the scheme city-wide

Compulsory for motorcycles, compulsory for other vehicles in poor visibility and tunnels

Visibility vest compulsory

★ On-the-spot fines imposed ★ Radar-detectors prohibited ★Tolls on motorways; do not use green lanes, these are reserved for auto-payment users. Some motorways require an automatic toll device. ★ Wearers of spectacles or contact lenses should carry a spare pair

Romania (RO)

Area 238,391 km² (92,042 mi²) **Population** 19,511,000 **Capital** Bucharest / Bucuresti (2,272,000) **Languages** Romanian (official), Hungarian **Currency** Romanian leu = 100 bani **Website** www.gov.ro

Cars and motorcycles			
120/130	100	90	50
Vans			
110	90	80	40
Motorcycles			
100	80	80	50

For motor vehicles with trailers or if full driving licence has been held for less than one year, speed limits are 20kph lower than those listed above • Jeep-like vehicles: 70kph outside built-up areas but 60kph in all areas if diesel. For mopeds, the speed limit is 45 kph.

Compulsory

Under 12s not allowed in front and must use an appropriate restraint in the rear

0.00% Compulsory Compulsory

Compulsory Compulsory 18

Only allowed with hands-free kit

Compulsory outside built-up areas, compulsory everywhere for motorcycles

Winter tyres compulsory Nov–Mar if roads are snow- or ice-covered, especially in mountainous areas

★ Electronic road tax system; price depends on emissions category and length of stay

★ Compulsory road tax can be paid for at the border, post offices and some petrol stations

★ It is illegal for vehicles to be dirty ★On-the-spot fines imposed ★ Tolls on motorways

★ Visibility vest compulsory

Russia Rossiya (RUS)

Area 17,075,000 km² (6,592,800 mi²) **Population** 144,192,000 **Capital** Moscow / Moskva (11,504,000) **Languages** Russian (official), and many others **Currency** Russian ruble = 100 kopeks **Website** government.ru/en/

110	90	90	60/20
If licence held for under 2 years			
70	70	70	60/20

Compulsory if fitted

Under 12s permitted only in an appropriate child restraint

0.03 % Compulsory Compulsory

Compulsory Compulsory 18

International Driving Permit with Russian translation, visa, green card endorsed for Russia, International Certificate for Motor Vehicles

Only allowed with a hands-free kit

Compulsory during the day

Winter tyres compulsory December-February

★ On-the-spot fines imposed ★Picking up hitch-hikers is prohibited ★ Radar detectors/blockers prohibited ★Road tax payable at the border

Serbia Srbija (SRB)

Area 77,474 km² (29,913 mi²) **Population** 7,042,000 **Capital** Belgrade / Beograd (1,167,000) **Languages** Serbian **Currency** Dinar = 100 paras **Website** www.srbija.gov.rs

120	100	80	60

Novice drivers limited to 90% of speed limit and not permitted to drive 11pm–5 a.m.

Compulsory in front and rear seats

Age 3–12 must be in rear seats and wear seat belt or appropriate child restraint; under 3 in rear-facing child seat permitted in front only if airbag deactivated

0.03% • 0.0% for commercial drivers, motor-cyclists, or if full licence held less than 1 year

Compulsory Compulsory

Compulsory Compulsory 18 (16 for motorbikes less than 125cc; 14 for mopeds)

International Driving Permit, green card or locally bought third-party insurance

Compulsory

Winter tyres compulsory Nov–Apr for vehicles up to 3.5 tonnes. Carrying snow chains recommended in winter as these may have to be fitted if driving on snow-covered roads, in accordance with signage.

★ 3-metre tow bar or rope ★ 80km/h speed limit if towing a caravan ★ Spare wheel compulsory ★ On-the-spot fines imposed ★Radar detectors prohibited ★Tolls on motorways and some primary roads ★Visibility vest compulsory

Slovakia Slovenska Republika (SK)

Area 49,012 km² (18,923 mi²) **Population** 5,416,000 **Capital** Bratislava (660,000) **Languages** Slovak (official), Hungarian **Currency** Euro = 100 cents **Website** www.government.gov.sk

130/90	90	90	50

Compulsory

Under 12 or below 150cm must be in rear in appropriate child restraint

0.0% Compulsory Compulsory

Compulsory Recommended

18 (15 for mopeds)

International driving permit, proof of health insurance

Only allowed with a hands-free kit

Compulsory at all times

Winter tyres compulsory

★ On-the-spot fines imposed ★Radar-detection equipment is prohibited ★ Tow rope recommended ★Vignette required for motorways, car valid for 1 year, 30 days, 7 days; lorry vignettes carry a higher charge. ★Visibility vests compulsory

Slovenia Slovenija (SLO)

Area 20,256 km² (7,820 mi²) **Population** 2,063,000 **Capital** Ljubljana (279,000) **Languages** Slovene **Currency** Euro = 100 cents **Website** www.gov.si

130	90*	90*	50
If towing			
80	80*	80*	50

*70kph in urban areas

Compulsory

Below 150cm must use appropriate child restraint. A rear-facing baby seat may be used in front only if airbags are deactivated.

0.05% • 0.0% for commercial drivers, under 21s or with less than one year with a full licence

Compulsory Compulsory

Compulsory Recommended

18 (motorbikes up to 125cc 16; up to 350cc 18)

Licences without photographs must be accompanied by an International Driving Permit

Only allowed with hands-free kit

Must be used at all times

Snow chains or winter tyres compulsory mid-Nov to mid-March, and in wintery conditions at other times

★ On-the-spot fines imposed

★ Vignettes valid for variety of periods compulsory for vehicles below 3.5 tonnes for toll roads. Write your vehicle registration number on the vignette before displaying it. For heavier vehicles electronic tolling system applies; several routes are cargo-traffic free during high tourist season.

★ Visibility vest compulsory

Spain España (E)

Area 497,548 km² (192,103 mi²)
Population 46,423,000 **Capital** Madrid (6,489,000)
Languages Castilian Spanish (official), Catalan, Galician, Basque **Currency** Euro = 100 cents
Website www.lamoncloa.gob.es/lang/en/Paginas/index.aspx

	120*	100*	90	50
If towing				
	80	80	70	50

*Urban motorways and dual carriageways 80 kph

- Compulsory
- Under 135cm and below 12 must use appropriate child restraint
- 0.05% • 0.03% if less than 2 years full licence or if vehicle is over 3.5 tonnes or carries more than 9 passengers
- Two compulsory (one for in front, one for behind)
- Recommended   Compulsory
- Recommended
- 18 (21 for heavy vehicles; 16 for motorbikes up to 125cc)
- Compulsory for motorcycles and in poor daytime visibility for other vehicles.
- Snow chains recommended for mountainous areas in winter
- ★ Drivers who wear spectacles or contact lenses must carry a spare pair. ★ Radar-detection equipment is prohibited ★ Spare wheel compulsory ★ Tolls on motorways ★ Visibility vest compulsory

Sweden Sverige (S)

Area 449,964 km² (173,731 mi²)
Population 9,875,000 **Capital** Stockholm (2,192,000)
Languages Swedish (official), Finnish
Currency Swedish krona = 100 ore
Website www.sweden.gov.se

	90–120	80	70–100	30–60
If towing trailer with brakes				
	80	80	70	50

- Compulsory in front and rear seats
- Under 15 or below 135cm must use an appropriate child restraint and may sit in the front only if airbag is deactivated; rear-facing baby seat permitted in front only if airbag deactivated.
- 0.02%   Compulsory   Recommended
- Recommended   Recommended   18
- Licences without a photograph must be accompanied by photographic proof of identity, e.g. a passport
- LEZ Gothenberg, Helsingborg, Lund, Malmo, Mölndal and Stockholm have LEZs, progressively prohibiting vehicles 6 or more years old.
- Must be used at all times
- 1 Dec–31 Mar winter tyres, anti-freeze and shovel compulsory
- ★ On-the-spot fines imposed
- ★ Radar-detection equipment is prohibited

Switzerland Schweiz (CH)

Area 41,284 km² (15,939 mi²)
Population 8,212,000 **Capital** Bern (407,000) **Languages** French, German, Italian, Romansch (all official) **Currency** Swiss Franc = 100 centimes / rappen **Website** www.admin.ch

	120	80	80	50/30
If towing up to 1 tonne / over 1 tonne				
	80	80	60/80	30/50

- Compulsory
- Up to 12 years or below 150 cm must use an appropriate child restraint. Children 6 and under must sit in the rear.
- 0.05%, but 0.0% for commercial drivers or with less than three years with a full licence
- Compulsory   Recommended
- Recommended   Recommended
- 18 (mopeds up to 50cc – 16)
- Only allowed with a hands-free kit
- Compulsory
- Winter tyres recommended Nov–Mar; snow chains compulsory in designated areas in poor winter weather
- ★ GPS must have fixed speed camera function deactivated; radar detectors prohibited
- ★ Motorways are all toll and for vehicles below 3.5 tonnes a vignette must be purchased at the border. The vignette is valid for one calendar year. Vehicles over 3.5 tonnes must have an electronic tag for travel on any road.
- ★ On-the-spot fines imposed ★ Pedestrians have right of way ★ Picking up hitchhikers is prohibited on motorways and main roads ★ Spectacles or contact lens wearers must carry a spare pair in their vehicle at all times

Turkey Türkiye (TR)

Area 774,815 km² (299,156 mi²)
Population 79,464,000 **Capital** Ankara (5,150,000)
Languages Turkish (official), Kurdish
Currency New Turkish lira = 100 kurus
Website www.mfa.gov.tr/default.en.mfa

	120	90	90	50
If towing				
	80	80	80	40

- Compulsory if fitted
- Under 150 cm and below 36kg must use suitable child restraint. If above 136 cm may sit in the back without child restraint. Under 3s can only travel in the front in a rear facing seat if the airbag is deactivated. Children 3–12 may not travel in the front seat.
- 0.00%
- Two compulsory (one in front, one behind)
- Compulsory   Compulsory
- Compulsory   18
- International driving permit advised, and required for use with licences without photographs; note that Turkey is in both Europe and Asia, green card/UK insurance that covers whole of Turkey or locally bought insurance, e-visa obtained in advance.
- Prohibited
- Compulsory in daylight hours
- ★ Spare wheel compulsory ★ On-the-spot fines imposed ★ Several motorways, and the Bosphorus bridges are toll roads ★ Tow rope and tool kit must be carried

Ukraine Ukraina (UA)

Area 603,700 km² (233,088 mi²)
Population 44,429,000 **Capital** Kiev / Kyyiv (3,375,000) **Languages** Ukrainian (official), Russian
Currency Hryvnia = 100 kopiykas
Website www.kmu.gov.ua/control/en

	130	110	90	60
If towing				
	80	80	80	60

Speed limit in pedestrian zone 20 kph

- Compulsory in front and rear seats
- Under 12 and below 145cm must use an appropriate child restraint and sit in rear
- 0.02% – if use of medication can be proved. Otherwise 0.00%
- Compulsory   Compulsory
- Optional   Compulsory   18
- International Driving Permit, visa, International Certificate for Motor Vehicles, green card
- No legislation
- Compulsory in poor daytime and from Oct–Apr
- Winter tyres compulsory Nov–Apr in snowy conditions
- ★ A road tax is payable on entry to the country.
- ★ On-the-spot fines imposed
- ★ Tow rope and tool kit recommended

United Kingdom (GB)

Area 241,857 km² (93,381 mi²)
Population 65,716,000 **Capital** London (13,880,000)
Languages English (official), Welsh (also official in Wales), Gaelic **Website** www.direct.gov.uk
Currency Sterling (pound) = 100 pence

	112	112	96	48
If towing				
	96	96	80	48

- Compulsory in front seats and if fitted in rear seats
- Under 3 not allowed in front seats except with appropriate restraint, and in rear must use child restraint if available; in front 3–12 or under 135cm must use appropriate child restraint, in rear must use appropriate child restraint (or seat belt if no child restraint is available, e.g. because two occupied restraints prevent fitting of a third).
- 0.08% (England, Northern Ireland, Wales) • 0.05% (Scotland)
- Recommended   Recommended
- Recommended   Recommended
- 17 (16 for mopeds)
- Only allowed with hands-free kit
- LEZ London's LEZ operates by number-plate recognition; non-compliant vehicles face hefty daily charges. Foreign-registered vehicles must register.
- ★ Driving is on the left
- ★ On-the-spot fines imposed
- ★ Smoking is banned in all commercial vehicles
- ★ Some toll motorways and bridges

Ski resorts

The resorts listed are popular ski centres, therefore road access to most is normally good and supported by road clearing during snow falls. However, mountain driving is never predictable and drivers should make sure they take suitable snow chains as well as emergency provisions and clothing. Listed for each resort are: the atlas page and grid square; the resort/minimum piste altitude (where only one figure is shown, they are at the same height) and maximum altitude of its own lifts; the number of lifts and gondolas (the total for lift-linked resorts); the season start and end dates (snow cover allowing); whether snow is augmented by cannon; the nearest town (with its distance in km) and, where available, the website and/or telephone number of the local tourist information centre or ski centre ('00' prefix required for calls from the UK).

The ❄ symbol indicates resorts with snow cannon

Andorra

Pyrenees

Pas de la Casa / Grau Roig 146 B2 ❄ 2050–2640m • 31 lifts • Dec–Apr • Andorra La Vella (30km) www.pasdelacasa.com • *Access via Envalira Pass (2407m), highest in Pyrenees, snow chains essential.*

Austria

Alps

Bad Gastein 109 B4 ❄ 1050/1100–2700m • 50 lifts • Dec–Mar • St Johann im Pongau (45km) +43 6432 3393 0 www.gastein.com

Bad Hofgastein 109 B4 ❄ 860–2295m • 50 lifts • Dec–Mar • St Johann im Pongau (40km) +43 6432 3393 0 www.gastein.com/en/region-villages/bad-hofgastein

Bad Kleinkirchheim 109 C4 ❄ 1070–2310m • 27 lifts • Dec–Mar • Villach (35km) +43 4240 8212 www.badkleinkirchheim.at

Ehrwald 108 B1 ❄ 1000–2965m • 24 lifts • Dec–Apr • Imst (30km) +43 5673 2395 www.wetterstein-bahnen.at/en

Innsbruck 108 B2 ❄ 574/850–3200m • 59 lifts • Dec–Apr • Innsbruck +43 512 56 2000 www.innsbruck.info/en/ • *Motorway normally clear. The motorway through to Italy and through the Arlberg Tunnel are both toll roads.*

Ischgl 107 B5 ❄ 1340/1380–2900m • 101 lifts • Dec–May • Landeck (25km) +43 50990 100 www.ischgl.com • *Car entry to resort prohibited between 2200hrs and 0600hrs.*

Kaprun 109 B3 ❄ 885/770–3030m, • 25 lifts • Nov–Apr • Zell am See (10km) +43 6542 770 www.zellamsee-kaprun.com

Kirchberg in Tirol 109 B3 ❄ 860–2000m • 197 lifts • Nov–Apr • Kitzbühel (6km) +43 57507 2100 www.kitzbueheler-alpen.com • *Easily reached from Munich International Airport (120 km)*

Kitzbühel (Brixen im Thale) 109 B3 ❄ 800/1210–2000m • 197 lifts • Dec–Apr • Wörgl (40km) www.kitzbueheler-alpen.com/en +43 57057 2200

Lech/Oberlech 107 B5 ❄ 1450–2810m • 66 lifts • Dec–Apr • Bludenz (50km) +43 5583 2161 0 www.lechzuers.com • *Roads normally cleared but keep chains accessible because of altitude.*

Mayrhofen 108 B2 ❄ 630–2500m • 57 lifts • Dec–Apr • Jenbach (35km) +43 5285 6760 www.mayrhofen.at • *Chains rarely required.*

Obertauern 109 B4 ❄ 1740/1640–2350m • 26 lifts • Dec–Apr • Radstadt (20km) +43 6456 7252 www.obertauern.com • *Roads normally cleared but chain accessibility recommended. Camper vans and caravans not allowed; park these in Radstadt*

Saalbach Hinterglemm 109 B3 ❄ 1030/1100–2100m • 70 lifts • Nov–Apr • Zell am See (19km) +43 6541 6800-68 www.saalbach.com • *Both village centres are pedestrianised and there is a good ski bus service during the daytime*

St Anton am Arlberg 107 B5 ❄ 1300–2810m • 41 lifts • Dec–Apr • Innsbruck (104km) +43 5446 22690 www.stantonamarlberg.com

Schladming 109 B4 ❄ 745–1900m • 85 lifts • Dec–Mar • Schladming +43 36 87 233 10 www.schladming-dachstein.at

Serfaus 108 B1 ❄ 1427/1200–2820m • 67 lifts • Dec–Apr • Landeck (30km) +43 5476 6239 www.serfaus-fiss-ladis.at • *Private vehicles banned from village. Use Dorfbahn Serfaus, an underground funicular which runs on an air cushion.*

Sölden 108 C2 ❄ 1380–3250m, • 33 lifts • Sep-Apr (glacier); Nov-Apr (main area) • Imst (50km) +43 57200 200 www.soelden.com • *Roads normally cleared but snow chains recommended because of altitude. The route from Italy and the south over the Timmelsjoch via Obergurgl is closed Oct–May and anyone arriving from the south should use the Brenner Pass motorway.*

Zell am See 109 B3 ❄ 750–1950m • 53 lifts • Dec–Mar • Zell am See +43 6542 770 www.zellamsee-kaprun.com • *Low altitude, so good access and no mountain passes to cross.*

Zell im Zillertal (Zell am Ziller) 109 B3 ❄ 580/930–2410m • 22 lifts • Dec–Apr • Jenbach (25km) +43 5282 7165–226 www.zillertalarena.com

Zürs 107 B5 ❄ 1720/1700–2450m • 97 lifts • Dec–Apr • Bludenz (30km) +43 5583 2245 www.lech-zuers.at • *Roads normally cleared but keep chains accessible because of altitude. Village has garage with 24-hour self-service gas/petrol, breakdown service and wheel chains supply.*

France

Alps

Alpe d'Huez 118 B3 ❄ 1860–3330m • 85 lifts • Dec–Apr • Grenoble (63km) www.alpedhuez.com • *Snow chains may be required on access road to resort.*

Avoriaz 118 A3 ❄ 1800/1100–2280m • 35 lifts • Dec–May • Morzine (14km) +33 4 50 74 72 72 www.morzine-avoriaz.com • *Chains may be required for access road from Morzine. Car-free resort, park on edge of village. Horse-drawn sleigh service available.*

Chamonix-Mont-Blanc 119 B3 ❄ 1035–3840m • 49 lifts • Dec–Apr • Martigny (38km) +33 4 50 53 99 98 www.chamonix.com

Chamrousse 118 B2 ❄ 1700–2250m • 26 lifts • Dec–Apr • Grenoble (30km) www.chamrousse.com • *Roads normally cleared, keep chains accessible because of altitude.*

Châtel 119 A3 ❄ 1200/1110–2200m • 41 lifts • Dec–Apr • Thonon-Les-Bains (35km) http://info.chatel.com/english-version.html +33 4 50 73 22 44

Courchevel 118 B3 ❄ 1750/1300–2470m • 67 lifts • Dec–Apr • Moûtiers (23km) www.courchevel.com • *Roads normally cleared but keep chains accessible. Traffic 'discouraged' within the four resort bases.*

Flaine 118 A3 ❄ 1600–2500m • 26 lifts • Dec–Apr • Cluses (25km) +33 4 50 90 80 01 www.flaine.com • *Keep chains accessible for D6 from Cluses to Flaine. Car access for depositing luggage and passengers only. 1500-space car park outside resort. Near Sixt-Fer-á-Cheval.*

La Clusaz 118 B3 ❄ 1100–2600m • 55 lifts • Dec–Apr • Annecy (32km) www.laclusaz.com • *Roads normally clear but keep chains accessible for final road from Annecy.*

La Plagne 118 B3 ❄ 2500/1250–3250m • 109 lifts • Dec–Apr Moûtiers (32km) www.la-plagne.com • *Ten different centres up to 2100m altitude. Road access via Bozel, Landry or Aime normally cleared. Linked to Les Arcs by cablecar*

Les Arcs 119 B3 ❄ 1600/1200–3230m • 77 lifts • Dec–May • Bourg-St-Maurice (15km) +33 4 79 07 12 57 www.lesarcs.com • *Four base areas up to 2000 metres; keep chains accessible. Pay parking at edge of each base resort. Linked to La Plagne by cablecar*

Les Carroz d'Araches 118 A3 ❄ 1140–2500m • 80 lifts • Dec–Apr • Cluses (13km) www.lescarroz.com

Les Deux-Alpes 118 C3 ❄ 1650/1300–3600m • 55 lifts • Dec–Apr • Grenoble (75km) +33 4 76 79 22 00 www.les2alpes.com/en • *Roads normally cleared, however snow chains recommended for D213 up from valley road (D1091).*

Les Gets 118 A3 ❄ 1170/1000–2000m • 52 lifts • Dec–Apr • Cluses (18km) +33 4 50 75 80 80 www.lesgets.com

Les Ménuires 118 B3 ❄ 1815/1850–3200m • 40 lifts www.lesmenuires.com • Dec–Apr • Moûtiers (27km) • *Keep chains accessible for D117 from Moûtiers.*

Les Sept Laux Prapoutel 118 B3 ❄ 1350–2400m • 24 lifts • Dec–Apr • Grenoble (38km) www.les7laux.com (in French only) • *Roads normally cleared, however keep chains accessible for mountain road up from the A41 motorway. Near St Sorlin d'Arves.*

Megève 118 B3 1100/1050–2350m • 79 lifts • Dec–Apr • Sallanches (12km) www.megeve.com • *Horse-drawn sleigh rides available.*

Méribel 118 B3 1400/1100–2950m • 61 lifts • Dec–May • Moûtiers (18km) +33 4 79 08 60 01 www.meribel.net • *Keep chains accessible for 18km to resort on D90 from Moûtiers.*

Morzine 118 A3 1000–2460m • 67 lifts, • Dec–Apr • Thonon-Les-Bains (30km) +33 4 50 74 72 72 www.morzine-avoriaz.com

Pra Loup 132 A2 1600/1500–2500m • 53 lifts • Dec–Apr • Barcelonnette (10km) +33 4 92 84 10 04 www.praloup.com • *Roads normally cleared but chains accessibility recommended.*

Risoul 118 C3 1850/1650–2750m • 59 lifts • Dec–Apr • Briançon (40km) +33 4 92 46 02 60 www.risoul.com • *Keep chains accessible. Near Guillestre. Linked with Vars Les Claux*

St-Gervais Mont-Blanc 118 B3 850/1150–2350m • 27 lifts • Dec–Apr • Sallanches (10km) +33 4 50 47 76 08 www.saintgervais.com/en

Serre Chevalier 118 C3 1350/1200–2800m • 77 lifts • Dec–Apr • Briançon (10km) + 33 4 92 24 98 98 www.serre-chevalier.com • *Made up of 13 small villages along the valley road, which is normally cleared.*

Tignes 119 B3 2100/1550–3450m • 87 lifts • Jan–Dec • Bourg St Maurice (26km) +33 4 79 40 04 40 www.tignes.net • *Keep chains accessible because of altitude.*

Val d'Isère 119 B3 1850/1550–3450m • 87 lifts • Dec–Apr • Bourg-St-Maurice (30km) +33 4 79 06 06 60 www.valdisere.com • *Roads normally cleared but keep chains accessible.*

Val Thorens 118 B3 2300/1850–3200m • 29 lifts • Dec–Apr • Moûtiers (37km) +33 4 79 00 08 08 www.valthorens.com • *Chains essential – highest ski resort in Europe. Obligatory paid parking on edge of resort.*

Valloire 118 B3 1430–2600m • 34 lifts • Dec–Apr • Modane (20km) +33 4 79 59 03 96 www.valloire.net • *Road normally clear up to the Col du Galbier, to the south of the resort, which is closed from 1st November to 1st June. Linked to Valmeinier.*

Valmeinier 118 B3 1500–2600m • 34 lifts • Dec–Apr • St Michel de Maurienne (47km) +33 4 79 59 53 69 www.valmeinier.com • *Access from north on D1006/D902. Col du Galbier, to the south of the resort closed from 1st November to 1st June. Linked to Valloire.*

Valmorel 118 B3 1400–2550m • 90 lifts • Dec–Apr • Moûtiers (15km) +33 4 79 09 85 55 www.valmorel.com • *Near St Jean-de-Belleville. Linked with ski areas of Doucy-Combelouvière and St François-Longchamp.*

Vars Les Claux 118 C3 1850/1650–2750m • 59 lifts • Dec–Apr • Briançon (40km) +33 4 92 46 51 31 www.vars.com/en/winter • *Four base resorts up to 1850 metres. Keep chains accessible. Linked with Risoul.*

Villard de Lans 118 B2 1050/1160–2170m • 28 lifts • Dec–Apr • Grenoble (32km) +33 4 76 95 10 38 www.villarddelans.com

Pyrenees

Font-Romeu 146 B3 1800/1600–2200m • 25 lifts • Nov–Apr • Perpignan (87km) +33 4 68 30 68 30 www.font-romeu.fr • *Roads normally cleared but keep chains accessible.*

Saint-Lary Soulan 145 B4 31 lifts • Dec–Mar • 830/1650/1700–2515m • Tarbes (75km) +33 5 62 39 50 81 www.saintlary.com • *Access roads constantly cleared of snow.*

Vosges

La Bresse-Hohneck 106 A1 500/900–1350m • 33 lifts • Dec–Mar • Cornimont (6km) +33 3 29 25 41 29 www.labresse.net

Germany

Alps

Garmisch-Partenkirchen 108 B2 700–2830m • 38 lifts • Dec–Apr • Munich (95km) +49 8821 180 700 www.gapa.de • *Roads usually clear, chains rarely needed.*

Oberaudorf 108 B3 480–1850m • 30 lifts • Dec–Apr • Kufstein (15km) www.oberaudorf.de • *Motorway normally kept clear. Near Bayrischzell.*

Oberstdorf 107 B5 815m • 26 lifts • Dec–Apr • Sonthofen (15km) +49 8322 7000 www.oberstdorf.de/en

Rothaargebirge

Winterberg 81 A4 700/620–830m • 19 lifts • Dec–Mar • Brilon (30km) +49 2981 925 00 www.winterberg.de (German and Dutch only) • *Roads usually cleared, chains rarely required.*

Greece

Central Greece

Mount Parnassos: Kelaria-Fterolakka 182 E4 1640–2260m • 16 lifts • Dec–Apr • Amfiklia +30 22340 22694-5 www.parnassos-ski.gr

Mount Parnassos: Gerondovrahos 182 E4 1800–1900m • 3 lifts • Dec–Apr • Amfiklia +30 29444 70371

Peloponnisos

Mount Helmos: Kalavrita Ski Centre 184 A3 1650–2100m • 7 lifts • Dec–Mar • Kalavrita +30 276920 24451-2 www.kalavrita-ski.gr

Mount Menalo: Ostrakina 184 B3 1500–1600m • 4 lifts • Dec–Mar • Tripoli +30 27960 22227

Macedonia

Mount Falakro: Agio Pnevma 183 B6 • 9 lifts • 1720/1620–2230m • Dec–Apr • Drama + 30 25210 23691

Mount Vasilitsa: Vasilitsa 182 C3 • Dec–Mar • 1750/1800–2113m • 8 lifts • Konitsa +30 24620 84850 www.vasilitsa.com (Greek only)

Mount Vermio: Seli 182 C4 1500–1900m • 11 lifts • Dec–Mar • Kozani +30 23310 26237 www.seli-ski.gr (in Greek)

Mount Vermio: Tria-Pente Pigadia 182 C3 1420–2005m • 7 lifts • Dec–Mar • Ptolemaida www.3-5pigadia.gr (Greek only) +30 23320 44464

Mount Verno: Vigla 182 C3 1650–1900m • 5 lifts • Dec–Mar • Florina +30 23850 22354 www.vigla-ski.gr (in Greek)

Mount Vrondous: Lailias 183 B5 1600–1850m • 4 lifts • Dec–Mar • Serres +30 23210 53790

Thessalia

Mount Pilio: Agriolefkes 183 D5 1300–1500m • 4 lifts • Dec–Mar • Volos +30 24280 73719

Italy

Alps

Bardonecchia 118 B3 1312–2750m • 21 lifts • Dec–Apr • Bardonecchia + 39 122 99032 www.bardonecchiaski.com • *Resort reached through the 11km Frejus tunnel from France, roads normally cleared.*

Bórmio 107 C5 1200/1230–3020m • 24 lifts • Dec–Apr • Tirano (40km) www.bormio.com • *Tolls payable in Ponte del Gallo Tunnel, open 0800hrs–2000hrs.*

Breuil-Cervinia 119 B4 2050–3500m • 21 lifts • Jan–Dec • Aosta (54km) +39 166 944311 www.cervinia.it • *Snow chains strongly recommended. Bus from Milan airport.*

Courmayeur 119 B3 1200–2760m • 21 lifts • Dec–Apr • Aosta (40km) +39 165 841612 www.courmayeurmontblanc.it • *Access via Mont Blanc tunnel from France. Roads constantly cleared.*

Limone Piemonte 133 A3 1000/1050–2050m • 29 lifts • Dec–Apr • Cuneo (27km) www.limonepiemonte.it • *Roads normally cleared, chains rarely required.*

Livigno 107 C5 1800–3000m • 31 lifts • Nov–May • Zernez (CH) (27km) +39 342 052200 www.livigno.com • *Keep chains accessible. The traffic direction through Munt la Schera Tunnel to/from Zernez is regulated on Saturdays. Check in advance.*

Sestrière 119 C3 2035/1840–2840m • 92 lifts • Dec–Apr • Oulx (22km) +39 122 755444 www.sestriere-online.com • *One of Europe's highest resorts; although roads are normally cleared keep chains accessible.*

Appennines

Roccaraso – Aremogna 169 B4 1285/1240–2140m • 24 lifts • Dec–Apr • Castel di Sangro (7km) +39 864 62210 www.roccaraso.net (in Italian)

Dolomites

Andalo – Fai della Paganella 121 A3 1042/1050/2125m • 19 lifts • Dec–Apr • Trento (40km) www.visitdolomitipaganella.it +39 461 585836

Arabba 108 C2 1600/1450–2950m • 29 lifts • Dec–Mar • Brunico (45km) +39 436 780019 www.arabba.it • *Roads normally cleared but keep chains accessible.*

Cortina d'Ampezzo 108 C3 1224/1050–2930m • 37 lifts • Dec–Apr • Belluno (72km) www.cortina.dolomiti.org • *Access from north on route 51 over the Cimabanche Pass may require chains.*

Corvara (Alta Badia) 108 C2 1568–2500m • 56 lifts • Dec–Apr • Brunico (38km) www.altabadia.it • *Roads normally clear but keep chains accessible.*

Madonna di Campiglio 121 A3 72 lifts • Dec–Apr • 1550/1500–2600m • Trento (60km) +39 465 447501 www.campigliodolomiti.it/homepage • *Roads normally cleared but keep chains accessible. Linked to Folgarida and Marilleva.*

Moena di Fassa (Sorte/Ronchi) 108 C2 1184/1450–2520m • 8 lifts • Dec–Apr • Bolzano (40km) +39 462 609770 www.fassa.com

Selva di Val Gardena/Wolkenstein Groden 108 C2 1563/1570–2450m • 81 lifts • Dec–Apr • Bolzano (40km) +39 471 777777 www.valgardena.it • *Roads normally cleared but keep chains accessible.*

Norway

Hemsedal 47 B5 700/640–1450m • 24 lifts • Nov–May • Honefoss (150km) +47 32 055030 www.hemsedal.com • *Be prepared for extreme weather conditions.*

Slovakia

Chopok (Jasna-Chopok) 99 C3 900/950–1840m • 17 lifts • Dec–Apr • Jasna +421 907 886644 www.jasna.sk

Donovaly 99 C3 913–1360m • 17 lifts • Nov–Apr • Ruzomberok +421 48 4199900 www.parksnow.sk/zima

Martinské Hole 98 B2 1250/1150–1456m • 8 lifts • Nov–May • Zilina +421 43 430 6000 www.martinky.com (in Slovak only)

Plejsy 99 C4 470–912m • 9 lifts • Dec–Mar • Krompachy +421 53 429 8015 www.plejsy.sk

Strbske Pleso 99 B4 1380–1825m • 7 lifts • Dec–Mar • Poprad +421 917 682 260 www.vt.sk

Slovenia

Julijske Alpe

Kanin (Bovec) 122 A2 460/1600–2389m • 5 lifts • Dec–Apr • Bovec +386 5 384 1919 www.boveckanin.si

Kranjska Gora 122 A2 800–1210m • 19 lifts • Dec–Mar • Kranjska Gora +386 4 5809 440 www.kranjska-gora.si

Vogel 122 A2 570–1800m • 11 lifts • Dec–Apr • Bohinjska Bistrica +386 4 5729 712 www.vogel.si

Kawiniške Savinjske Alpe

Krvavec 122 A3 1450–1970m • 10 lifts • Dec–Apr • Kranj 386 4 25 25 911 www.rtc-krvavec.si

Pohorje

Rogla 123 A4 1517/1050–1500m • 13 lifts • Dec–Apr • Slovenska Bistrica +386 3 75 77 100 www.rogla.eu

Spain

Pyrenees

Baqueira-Beret/Bonaigua 145 B4 1500–2500m • 33 lifts • Dec–Apr • Vielha (15km) +34 902 415 415 www.baqueira.es • *Roads normally clear but keep chains accessible. Near Salardú.*

Sistema Penibetico

Sierra Nevada 163 A4 2100–3300m • 24 lifts • Dec–May • Granada (32km) +34 902 70 80 90 http://sierranevada.es • *Access road designed to be avalanche safe and is snow cleared.*

Sweden

Idre Fjäll 199 D9 590–890m • 33 lifts • Nov–Apr • Mora (140km) +46 253 41000 www.idrefjall.se • *Be prepared for extreme weather conditions.*

Sälen 49 A5 360m • 100 lifts • Nov–Apr • Malung (70km) +46 771 84 00 00 www.skistar.com/salen • *Be prepared for extreme weather conditions.*

Switzerland

Alps

Adelboden 106 C2 1353m • 94 lifts • Dec–Apr • Frutigen (15km) www.adelboden.ch • *Linked with Lenk.*

Arosa 107 C4 1800m • 16 lifts • Dec–Apr • Chur (30km) +41 81 378 70 20 www.arosa.ch • *Roads cleared but keep chains accessible due to high altitude.*

Crans Montana 119 A4 1500–3000m • 34 lifts • Dec–Apr, Jul–Oct • Sierre (15km) • *Roads normally cleared but keep chains accessible for ascent from Sierre.*

Davos 107 C4 1560/1100–2840m • 55 lifts • Nov–Apr • Davos. +41 81 415 21 21 www.davos.ch • *Linked with Klosters*

Engelberg 106 C3 1000/1050–3020m • 26 lifts • Nov–May • Luzern (39km) +41 41 639 77 77 www.engelberg.ch • *Straight access road normally cleared.*

Flums (Flumserberg) 107 B4 1400/1000–2220m • 17 lifts • Dec–Apr • Buchs (25km) +41 81 720 18 18 www.flumserberg.ch • *Roads normally cleared, but 1000-metre vertical ascent; keep chains accessible.*

Grindelwald 106 C3 1050–2950m • 20 lifts • Dec–Apr • Interlaken (20km) +41 33 854 12 12 www.jungfrauregion.ch

Gstaad – Saanenland 106 C2 1050/950–3000m • 74 lifts • Dec–Apr • Gstaad +41 33 748 81 81 www.gstaad.ch • *Linked to Anzère.*

Klosters 107 C4 1191/1110–2840m • 55 lifts • Dec–Apr • Davos (10km). +41 81 410 20 20 www.davos.ch/klosters • *Linked with Davos. Roads normally clear but keep chains accessible.*

Leysin 119 A4 2263/1260–2330m • 16 lifts • Dec–Apr • Aigle (6km) +41 24 493 33 00 www.leysin.ch

Mürren 106 C2 1650–2970m • 12 lifts • Dec–Apr • Interlaken (18km) +41 33 856 86 86 www.mymuerren.ch • *No road access. Park in Strechelberg (1500 free places) and take the two-stage cable car.*

Nendaz 119 A4 1365/1400–3300m • 20 lifts • Nov–Apr • Sion (16km) +41 27 289 55 89 www.nendaz.ch • *Roads normally cleared, however keep chains accessible for ascent from Sion. Near Vex.*

Saas-Fee 119 A4 1800–3500m • 23 lifts • Jan–Dec • Brig (35km) +41 27 958 18 58 www.saas-fee.ch/en/ • *Roads normally cleared but keep chains accessible because of altitude.*

St Moritz 107 C4 1856/1730–3300m • 24 lifts • Nov–May • Chur (89km) +41 81 837 33 33 www.stmoritz.ch • *Roads normally cleared but keep chains accessible.*

Samnaun 107 C5 1846/1400–2900m • 40 lifts • Dec–May • Scuol (30km) +41 81 861 88 30 www.engadin.com • *Roads normally cleared but keep chains accessible.*

Verbier 119 A4 1500–3330m • 17 lifts • Nov–Apr • Martigny (27km) +41 27 775 38 38 www.verbier.ch • *Roads normally cleared.*

Villars-Gryon 119 A4 1253/1200–2100m • 16 lifts • Dec–Apr, Jun–Jul • Montreux (35km) +41 24 495 32 32 www.villars.ch • *Roads normally cleared but keep chains accessible for ascent from N9. Near Bex.*

Wengen 106 C2 1270–2320m • 19 lifts • Dec–Apr • Interlaken (12km) +41 33 856 85 85 http://wengen.ch • *No road access. Park at Lauterbrunnen and take mountain railway.*

Zermatt 119 A4 1620–3900m • 40 lifts, • all year • Brig (42km) +41 27 966 81 00 www.zermatt.ch • *Cars not permitted in resort, park in Täsch (3km) and take shuttle train.*

Turkey

North Anatolian Mountains

Uludag 186 B4 1770–2320m • 15 lifts • Dec–Mar • Bursa (36km) +90 224 285 21 11 http://skiingturkey.com/resorts/uludag.html

To the best of the Publisher's knowledge the information in this table was correct at the time of going to press. No responsibility can be accepted for any errors or their consequences.

Skiing near Valmorel, France
Jacques Pierre / hemis.fr / Alamy

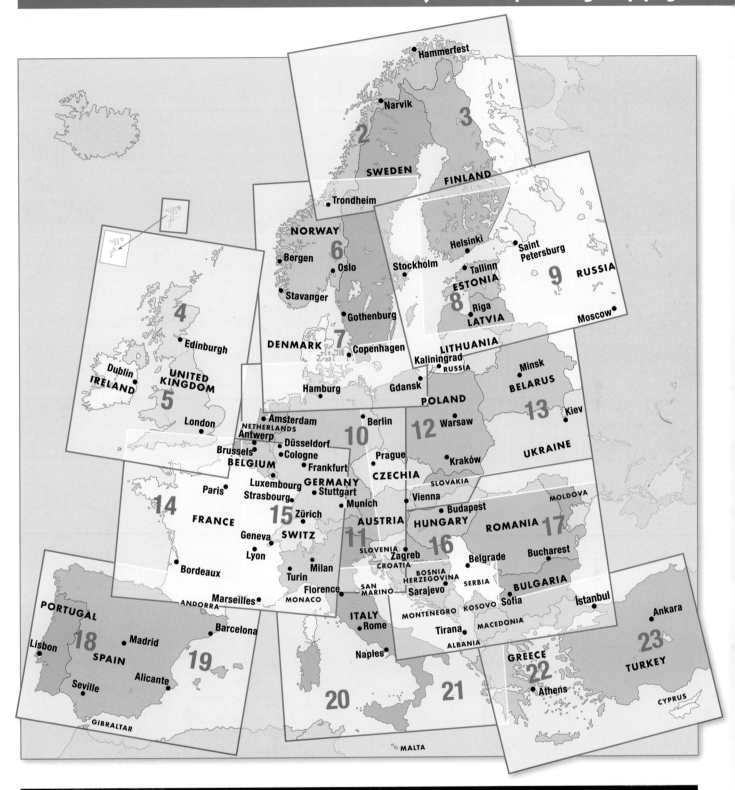

Motorway vignettes

Some countries require you to purchase (and in some cases display) a vignette before using motorways.

In Austria you will need to purchase and display a vignette on the inside of your windscreen. Vignettes are available for purchase at border crossings and petrol stations. More details from www.asfinag.at/toll/toll-sticker

In Belarus all vehicles over 3.5 tonnes and cars and vans under 3.5 tonnes registered outside the Eurasion Economic Union are required to have a *BelToll* unit installed. This device exchanges data with roadside gantries, enabling motorway tolls to be automatically deducted from the driver's account. http://www.beltoll.by/index.php/en/beltoll-system/five-steps#

In Czechia, you can buy a vignette at the border and also at petrol stations. Make sure you write your vehicle registration number on the vignette before displaying it. The roads without toll are indicated by a traffic sign saying "Bez poplatku". More details from www.motorway.cz

In Hungary a new e-vignette system was introduced in 2008. It is therefore no longer necessary to display the vignette, though you should make doubly sure the information you give on your vehicle is accurate. Vignettes are sold at petrol stations throughout the country. Buy online at http://toll-charge.hu/

In Slovakia, an electronic vignette must purchased before using the motorways. Vignettes may be purchased online, via a mobile app or at Slovak border crossings and petrol stations displaying the 'eznamka' logo. More details from https://eznamka.sk/selfcare/home/

In Switzerland, you will need to purchase and display a vignette before you drive on the motorway. Bear in mind you will need a separate vignette if you are towing a caravan. www.ezv.admin.ch/zollinfo_privat/04338/04340/04916/index.html?lang=en

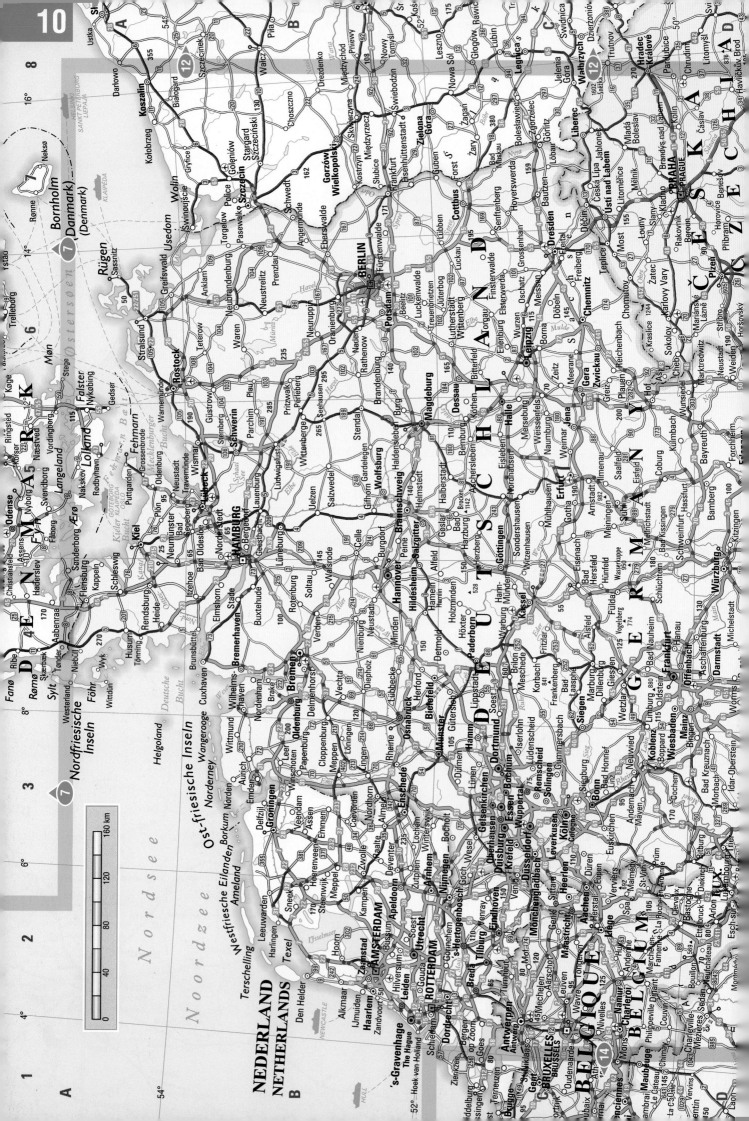

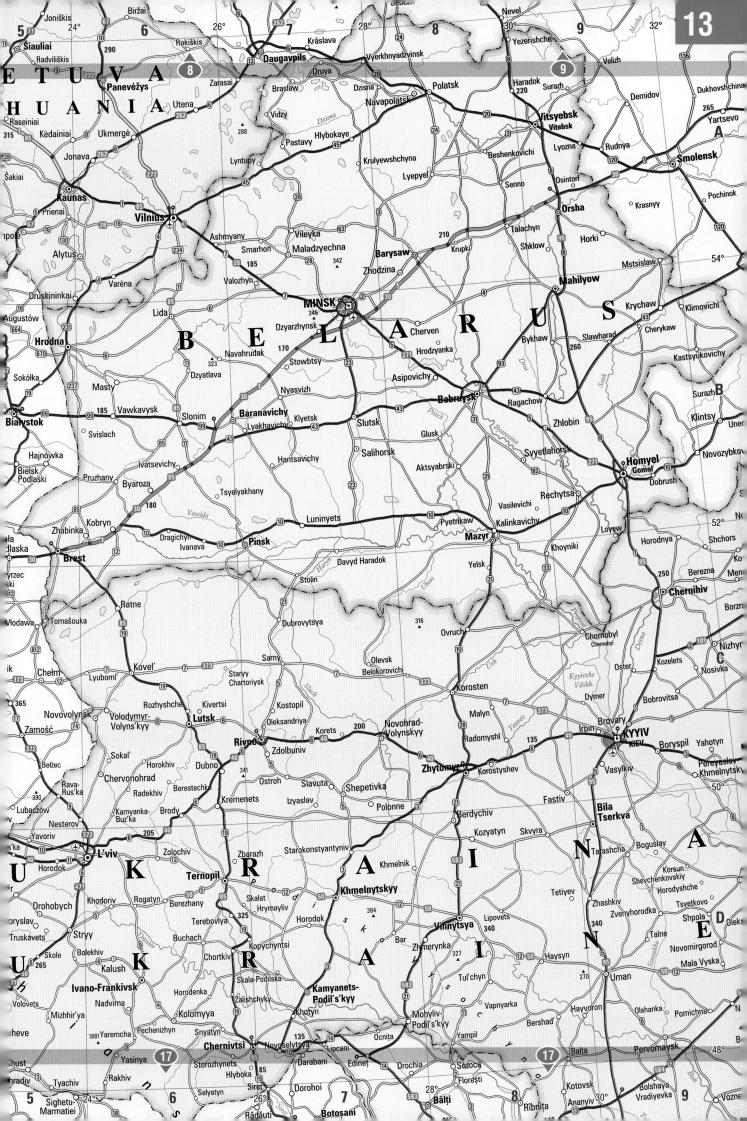

Key to road map pages

Distance table

Amsterdam
2945 **Athina**
1505 3192 **Barcelona**
1484 3742 2803 **Bergen**
650 2412 1863 1309 **Berlin**
197 2895 1308 1586 764 **Bruxelles**
2245 1219 2644 3037 1707 2181 **Bucuresti**
1420 1530 1999 2212 882 1358 852 **Budapest**
367 3100 1269 1783 956 215 2398 1573 **Calais**
533 3630 1817 270 1504 763 3021 2196 548 **Dublin**
1093 3826 1995 176 1696 941 3124 2299 726 346 **Edinburgh**
441 2499 1313 1508 550 383 1804 979 575 1123 1301 **Frankfurt**
1029 3080 2362 819 668 1145 1734 1550 1342 477 176 1067 **Göteborg**
447 2719 1780 1023 286 563 2014 1189 760 477 1486 485 582 **Hamburg**
1560 2539 2338 1063 475 1239 1834 1009 1431 1318 1236 1598 505 1113 **Helsinki**
2756 1145 2990 3653 2223 2706 690 1341 2911 3537 3657 2314 2891 2530 2350 **İstanbul**
965 2782 2090 1103 370 1081 2077 1252 1278 752 479 795 284 518 803 2593 **København**
256 2684 1376 1427 566 198 1983 1158 390 938 1116 180 986 404 1517 2499 714 **Köln**
2331 4460 1268 3723 2869 3141 3917 3222 2069 2617 2795 2400 3282 2700 3817 4342 3014 2339 **Lisboa**
480 3200 1387 458 1074 333 2591 1766 118 430 608 693 122 878 1991 3107 1188 508 2187 **London**
406 2661 1190 1613 749 209 2052 1227 424 972 1150 240 1172 590 1703 2472 900 186 2160 542 **Luxembourg**
1790 3809 617 3183 2364 1600 3262 2622 1528 1634 2254 1930 2742 2160 3276 3589 2473 1798 651 1646 1628 **Madrid**
1210 2683 509 2435 1541 1030 2154 1505 1063 1588 1789 1023 1994 1412 2525 2479 1722 1006 1777 1182 822 1126 **Marseille**
1085 2182 1038 2141 1060 890 1668 992 1072 1620 1798 683 1700 1118 1535 1993 1428 868 2315 1190 679 1655 538 **Milano**
2457 2930 3655 2223 1821 2585 1761 2099 2800 3348 3526 2312 1665 2115 1160 2605 2325 2387 4875 2918 2852 4224 3270 3027 **Moskva**
839 2106 1340 1788 594 789 1497 672 994 1524 1720 398 1347 765 1069 1907 969 580 2545 1094 555 2010 1011 473 2305 **München**
1347 3372 2680 503 960 1463 2667 1842 1660 773 729 1385 316 900 697 3089 590 1304 3604 1778 1490 3063 2312 2018 1823 1559 **Oslo**
510 2917 988 1922 1051 320 2307 1482 281 829 1007 591 1481 899 2012 2727 1209 495 1821 399 351 1280 782 857 2903 810 1799 **Paris**
950 2067 1750 1675 345 888 1362 537 1097 1635 1816 512 1013 652 770 1878 715 690 2870 1205 753 2329 1399 853 1853 388 1305 1061 **Praha**
1691 1140 1385 2706 1502 1520 1904 1263 1678 2226 2404 1289 2265 1683 1977 2237 1993 1474 2653 1796 1285 2002 876 606 3362 918 2583 1389 1309 **Roma**
2347 4223 1031 3736 2894 2150 3709 3010 2078 2626 2804 2344 3295 2713 3826 4034 3023 2318 401 2196 2178 550 1540 2078 4774 2371 3613 1830 2781 2446 **Sevilla**
2206 828 2453 3103 1673 2156 391 790 2361 2891 3087 1764 2341 1980 1800 550 2043 1949 3706 2461 1922 3037 1929 1443 2252 1367 2632 2177 1328 1687 3484 **Sofiya**
1393 3418 2726 1063 1006 1509 2713 1888 1673 2254 1069 1431 505 946 167 3185 590 1350 3650 1824 1536 3109 2358 2064 1228 1600 530 1845 1351 2629 3659 2679 **Stockholm**
1256 2128 2366 1909 606 1350 1473 648 1542 2110 2268 1136 1274 886 361 1989 956 1152 3480 1680 1345 2960 2015 1469 1245 996 1506 1677 616 1853 3397 1439 1612 **Warszawa**
1168 1772 1856 1970 640 1114 1067 242 1308 1954 2034 731 1308 947 1088 1583 1010 916 3100 1524 993 2473 1353 818 2137 430 1600 1240 295 1126 2876 1033 1646 727 **Wien**
816 2426 1030 1938 863 619 1810 985 804 1352 1530 464 1497 915 2164 2323 1433 589 2296 922 410 1647 699 292 2552 303 1815 592 691 898 2061 1173 1861 1307 743 **Zürich**

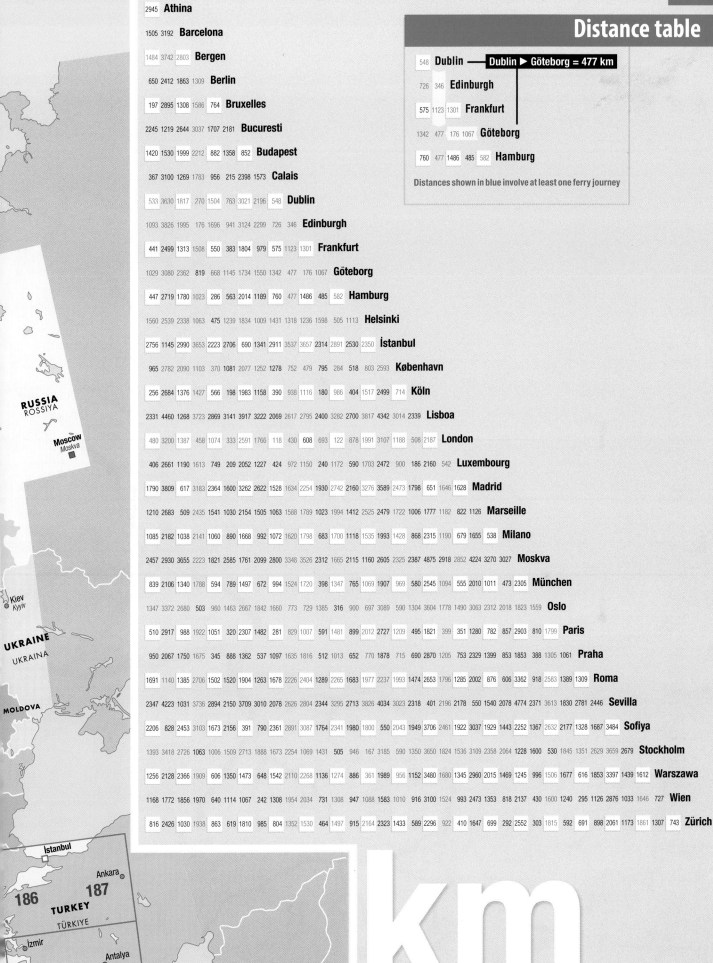

548 **Dublin** — Dublin ▶ Göteborg = 477 km
726 346 **Edinburgh**
575 1123 1301 **Frankfurt**
1342 477 176 1067 **Göteborg**
760 477 1486 485 582 **Hamburg**

Distances shown in blue involve at least one ferry journey

km

186 187
TURKEY
TÜRKIYE
188 189
CYPRUS
KYPROS

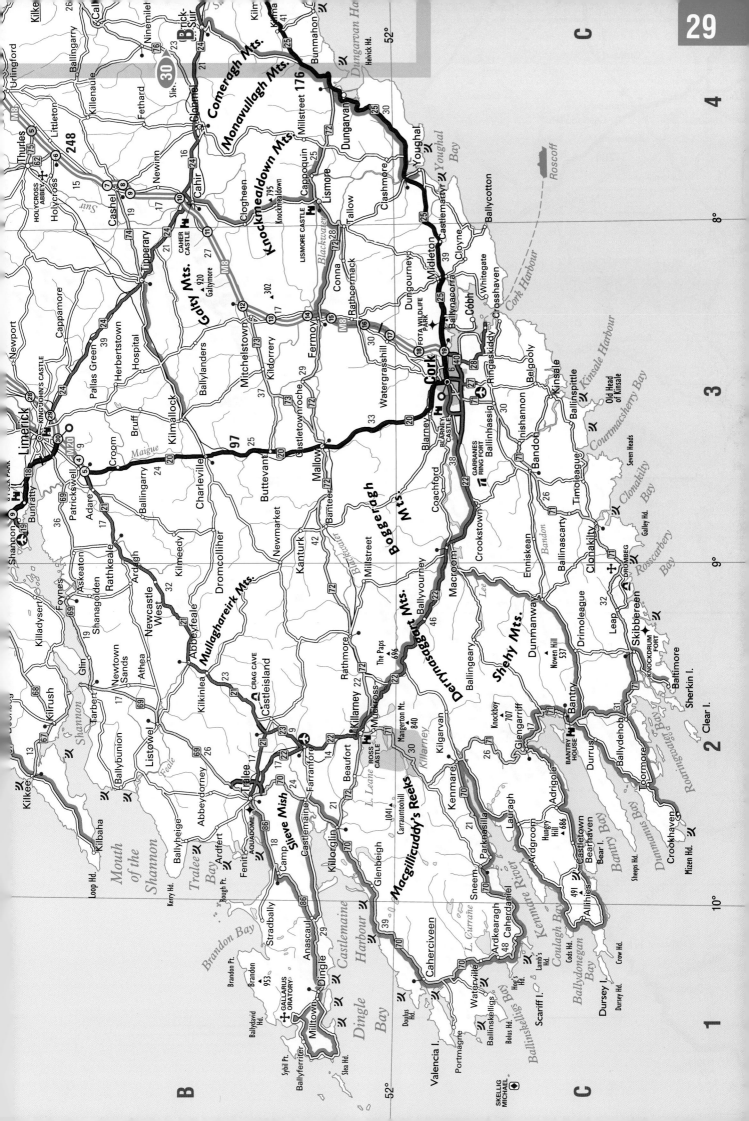

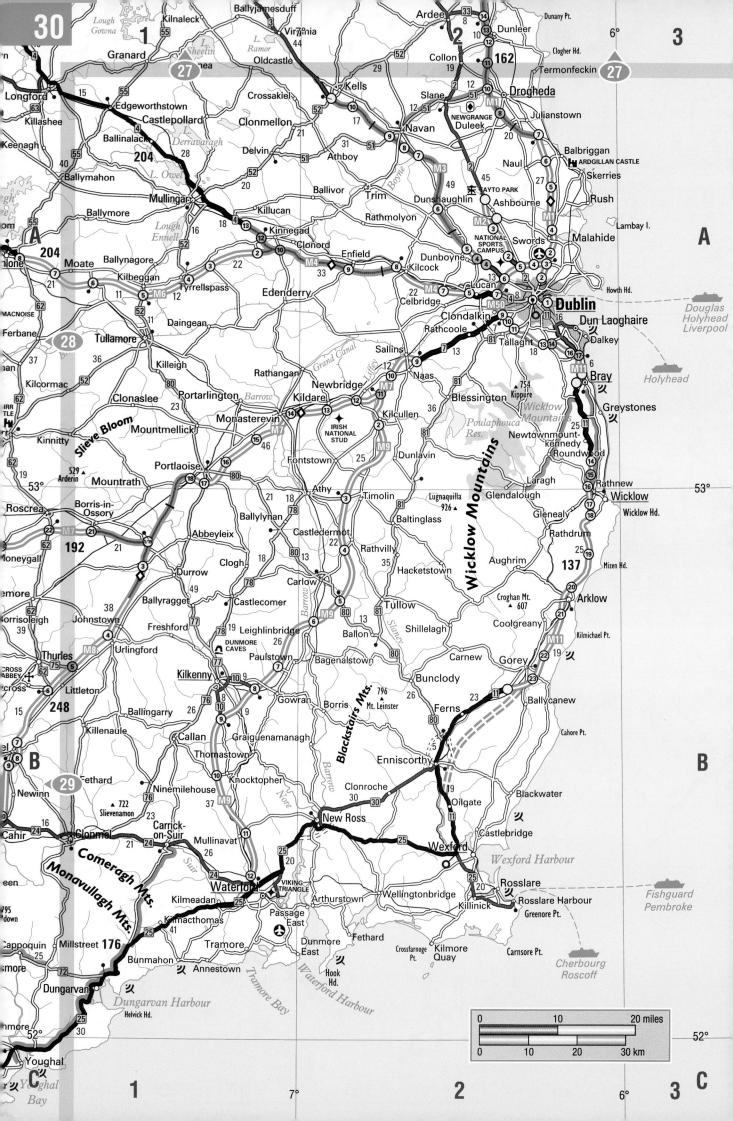

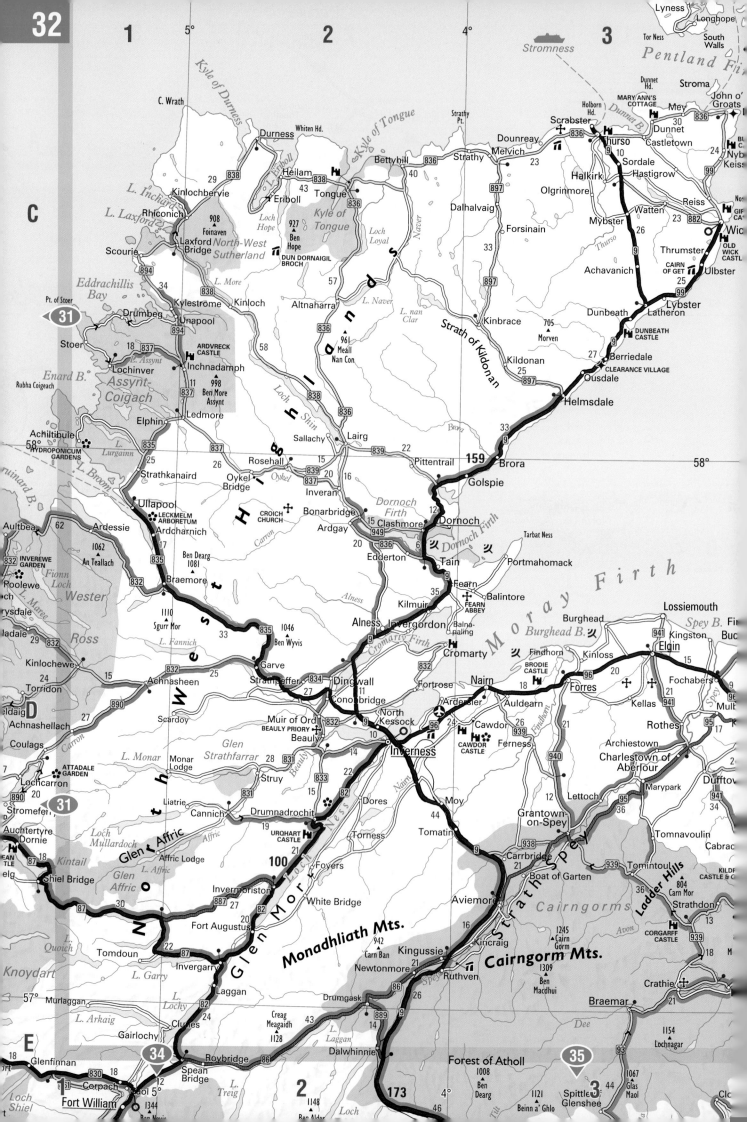

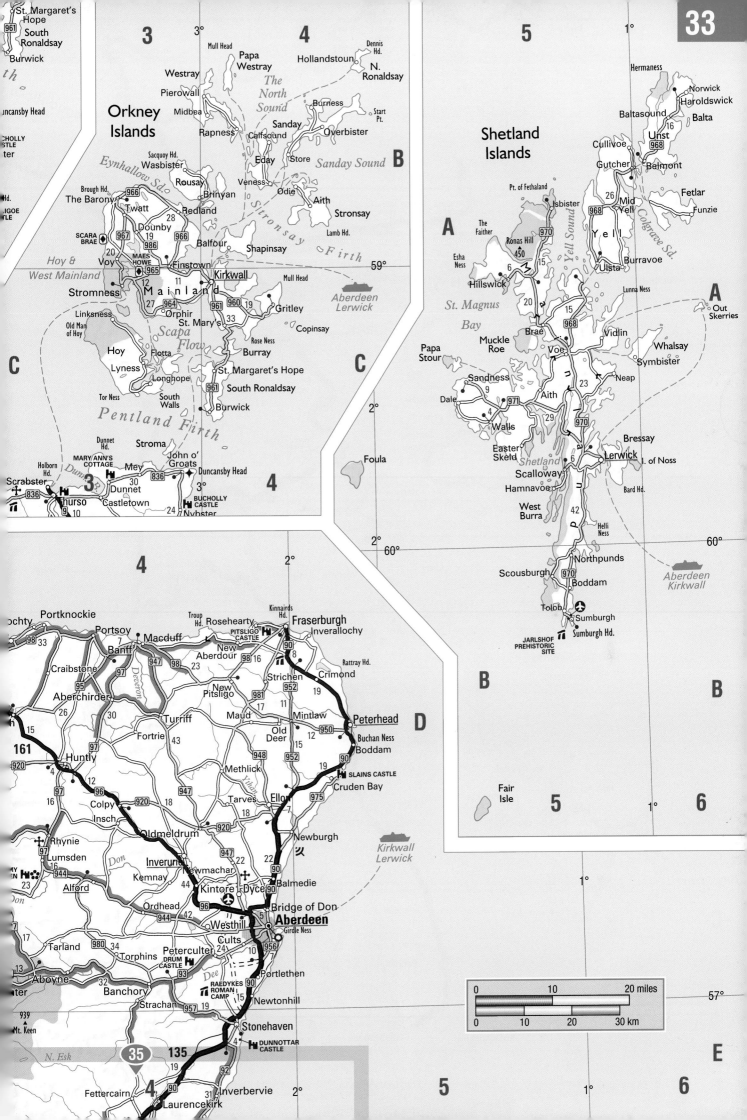

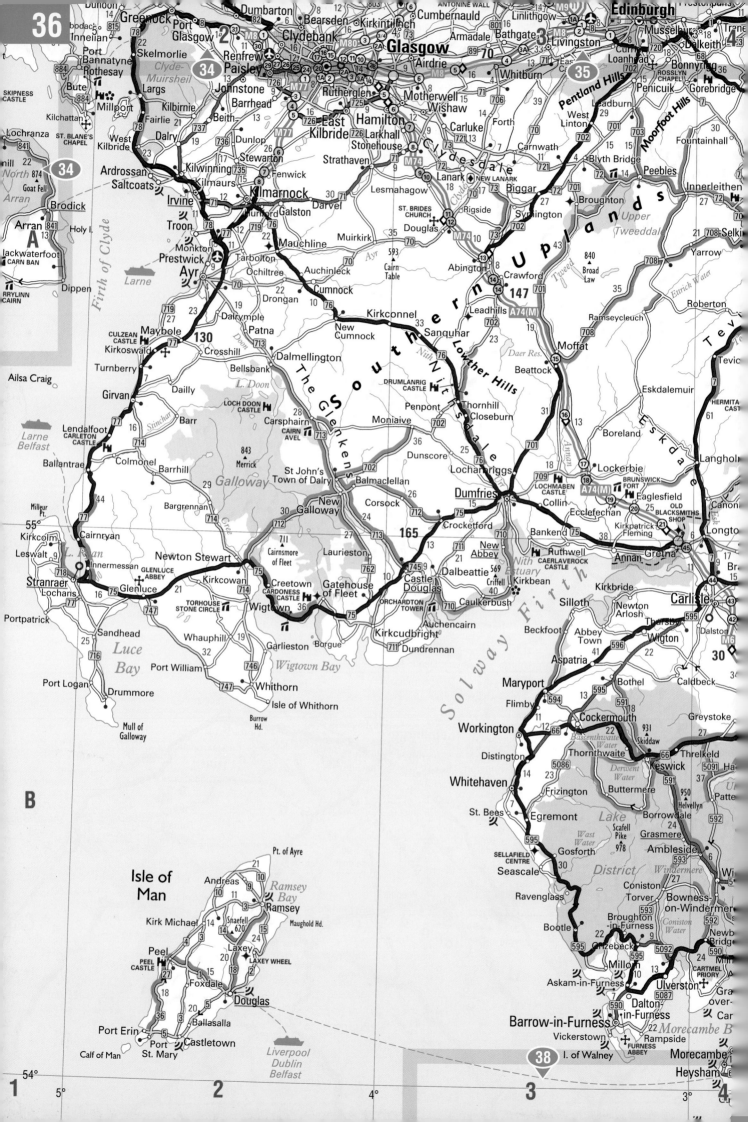

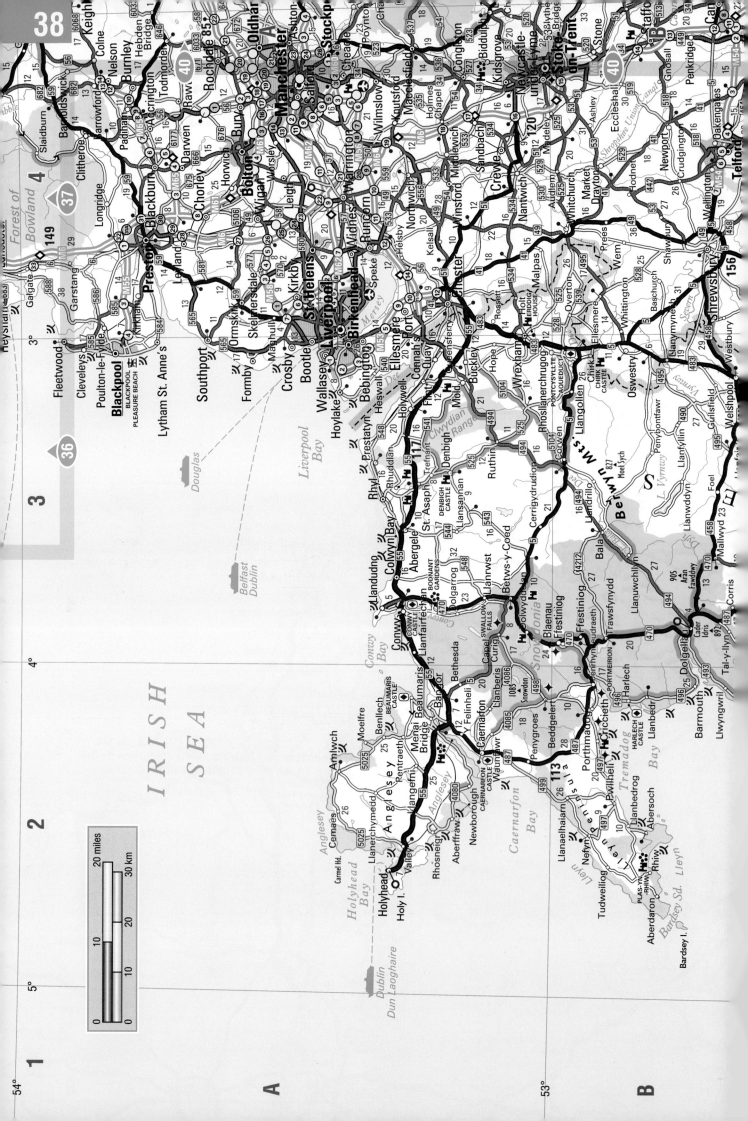

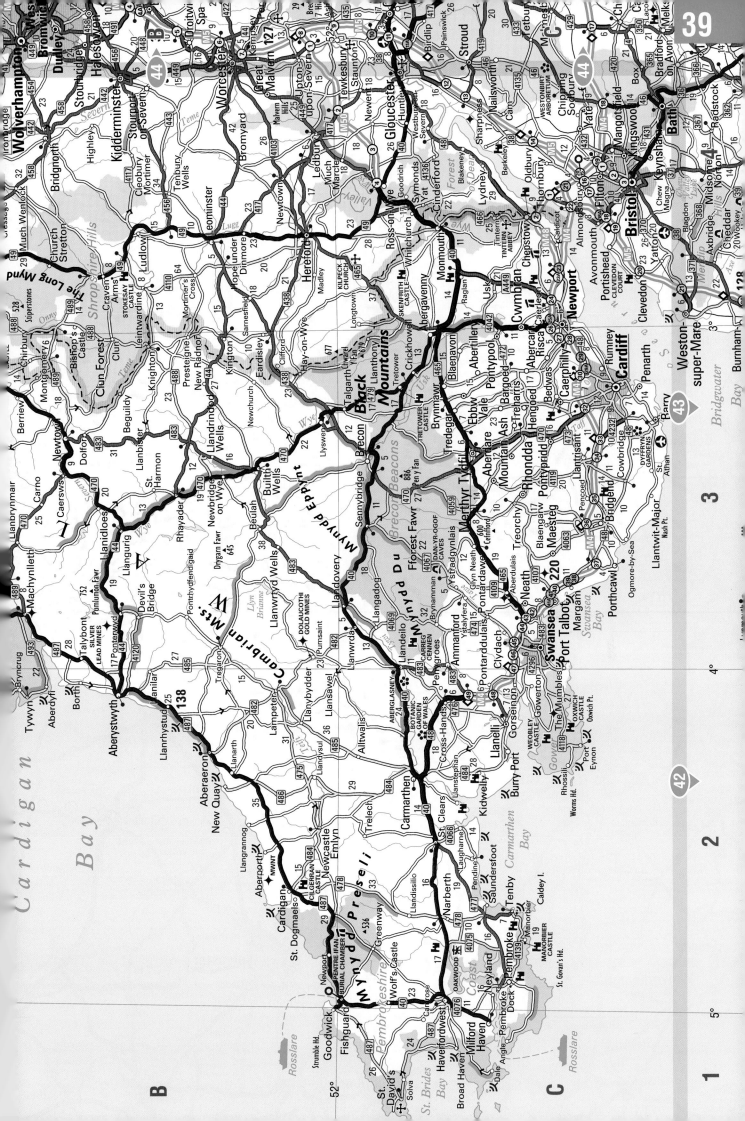

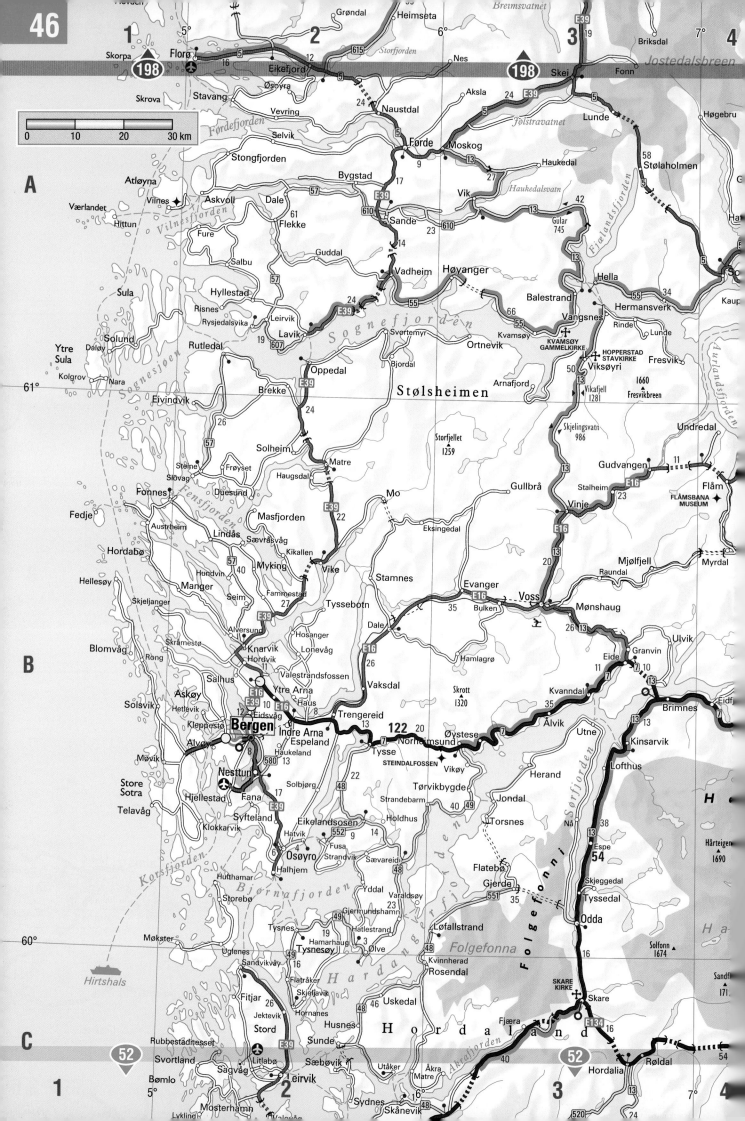

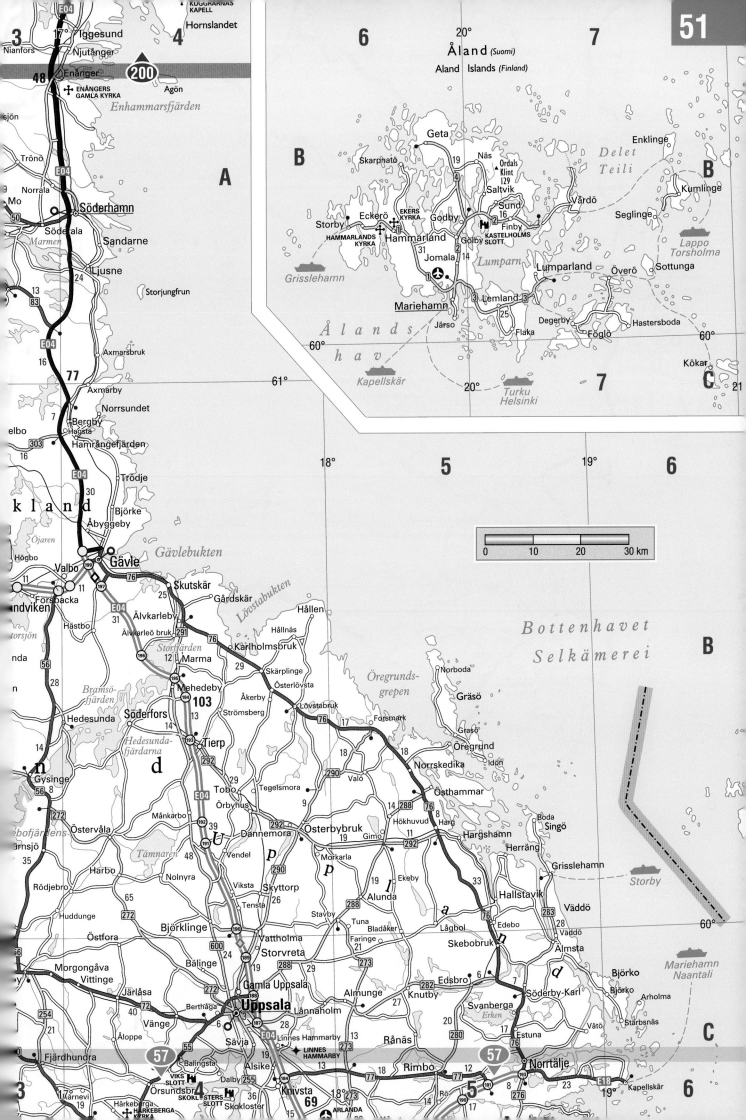

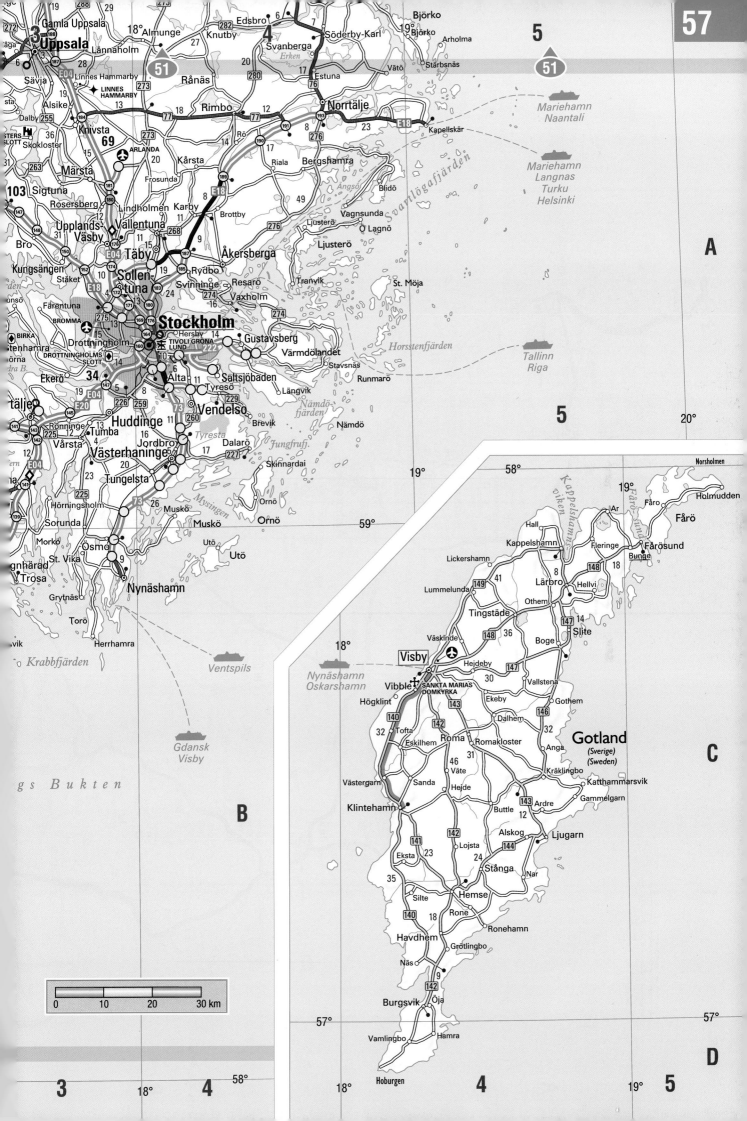

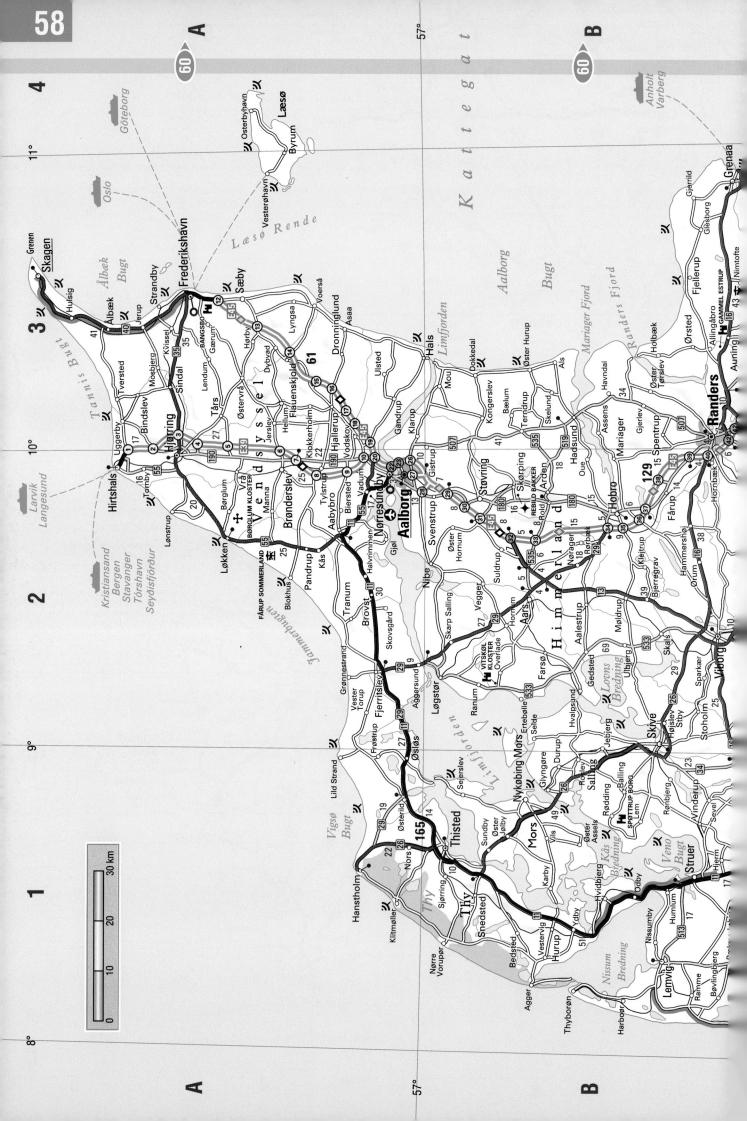

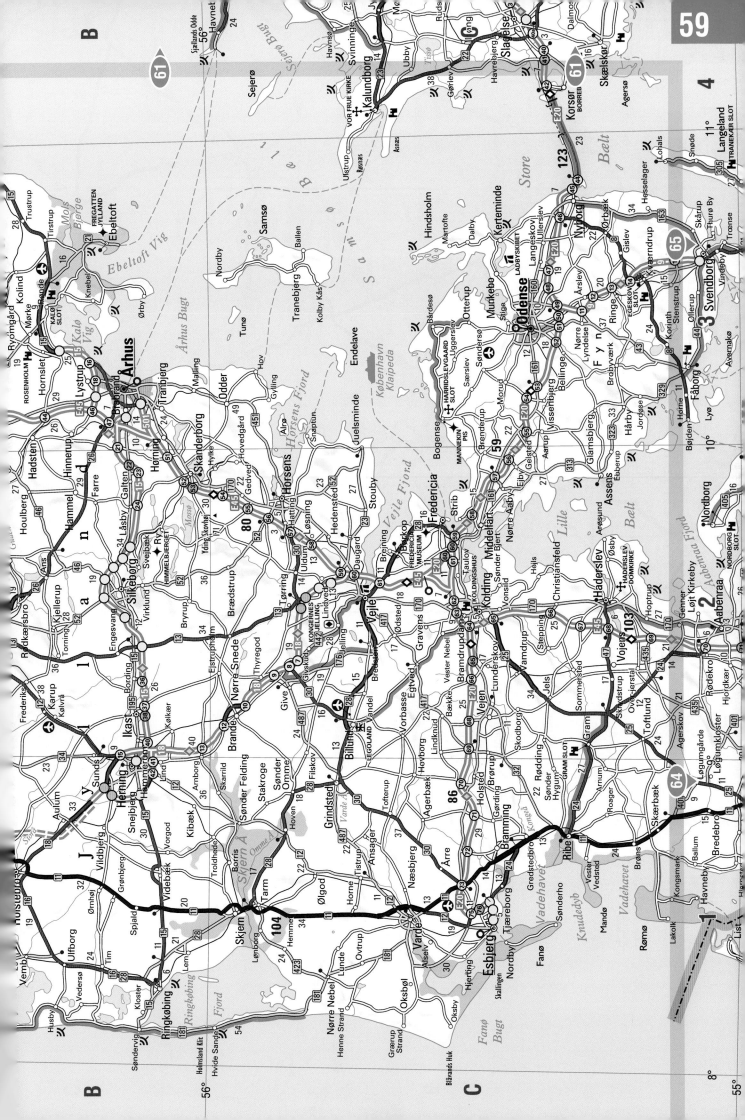

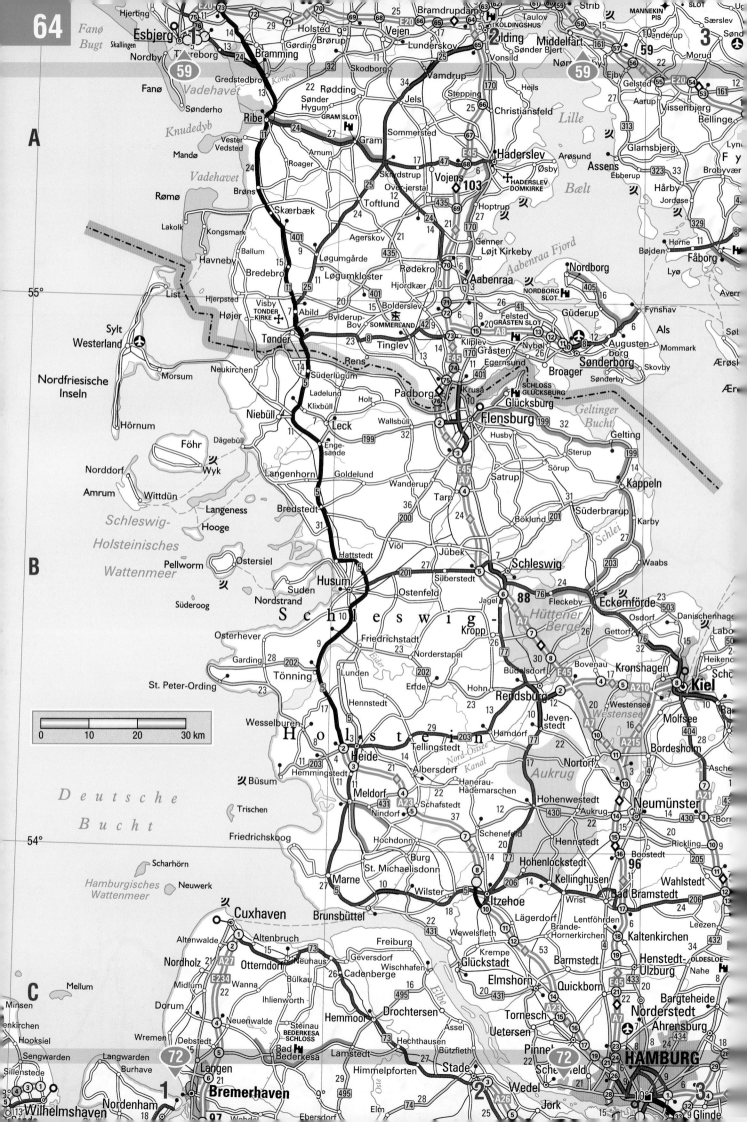

KØBENHAVN
COPENHAGEN

Malmö
13°

Bjärred
Lomma
Staffanstorp
Dalby
Veberöd
Sjöbo

Södra
Sandby
Harlösa
ÖVEDSKLOSTER
Lövestad

Vollsjö

Brösarp
Kiv

14°

Skåne-
Tranås

Sankt
Olof

Taastrup
Grevestrand
Amager
Dragør

Oxie
Vellinge
Höllviksnäs
Skanör med
Falsterbo
FALSTERBO
SLOT
Trelleborg

Klågerup
Blentarp
TORUP SLOT
Svedala
Anderslöv
Skurup
Rydsgärd
Klagstorp
Skivarp
Beddingestrand
Smygehamn
Abbekås

SÖVDEBORG
SLOT
Sövestad
St. Herrestad
Ystad

Tomelilla
Hammenhög
Köpingebro
Borrby

Gärsn

GL

Kåseberga
Sandhamn

Osted
Havdrup
Borup
Køge
Herfølge
VALLØ
SLOT
Hårlev
Karise
Store
Heddinge
Stevns Klint

Haslev
GISSELFELD
SLOT
Dalby
Rønnede
Fakse
FAKSE SLOT
Rødvig
Fakse
Ladeplads

Fakse
Bugt

Klaipeda
Ystad

Travemünde

Rønne

Rostock
Travemünde

København

Swinoujście

Bor

Præstø
Mern
Ørslev
Kalvehave
Borre
Stege
Møns Klint
Nyby
Møn
St. Damme
Stubbekøbing
Horbelev

Eskilstrup
Nykøbing
Falster
Væggerløse
Bøte By
Gedser

Trelleborg
Helsinki

Wittow
Dranske
Kloster
Hiddensee
Neuendorf
Trent
Prerow
Zingst
Ahrenshoop
Wustrow
Barth
Bodstedt
Dierhagen
Graal-Müritz
Ribnitz-
Damgarten
Gresenhorst
Marlow
Bad Sülze
Tribsees
Rövershagen
Bentwisch
Sanitz
Tessin
Rostock
Ziesendorf
Schwaan
Selow
Bützow
Laage
Weitendorf
Lüssow
Güstrow
Thürkow
Prüzen
Teterow
Malchin
Wokern
Ziddorf
Gielow

Kap Arkona
Altenkirchen
Wiek
Rügen
Sagard
Jasmund
Sassnitz
Gingst
Bergen
Binz
Sellin
Putbus
Garz
Göhren
Thiessow

Darsser Ort

Vorpommersche
Boddenlandschaft

Saaler Bodden

Löbnitz
Veglast
Richtenberg
Franzburg
Grimmen
Rakow

Hohendorf
Samtens
Stralsund
Brandshagen
Zudar

Reinberg
Miltzow
Poggendorf
Görmin
Loitz
Dargun
Jördenstorf
Neukalen
Verchen
Demmin
Tutow
Jarmen
Gützkow

Rügen

Greifswalder
Bodden

Greifswald
Züssow

Peenemünde
Kröslin
Lubmin
Kemnitz
Lassan
Murchin
Anklam

Zinnowitz
Koserow
Wolgast
Zemitz

Usedom

Bansin
Ahl
Usedom
Swi

Stettin

Kummerower
See

Tollense

Peene

Abbaue
Burow
Spantekow
Sarnow
Albinshof
Ducherow
Rathebur
Leopoldshagen
Mönkebude
Ueckermünde
Altentrep
Eggesin

Mecklenburg

12°
13°
14°

Stenshuvud 3 15° 4 16° 5

Vik

Simrishamn

MINGEHUS

Skillinge

A

holmsgattet

Ertholmene

Hammeren

HAMMARSHUS Sandvig-Allinge

Tejn

Bornholm Rø Gudhjem

(Danmark)

(Denmark) Hasle Klemensker

Nyker Svaneke

Øster-
marie

Køge Nylars Åkirkeby

Rønne 38 28 Neksø

Pedersker Snogebaek

55°

Jaroslawiec

J. Kopań B

J.

203 64 *Wieprza*

Darłowo Stary
Jaroslaw

MUZEUM
Dąbki DARŁOWO Sławno

J. Bukowo 68

Łazy E28 32 Ostrowiec

203 6

Mielno *J. Jamno* Jamno Lejkowo

Ystad Sarbinowo Sianów

Ustronie 42 **Koszalin** 206 35 Nacław

Morskie 11 Bonin

Kołobrzeg 11 Dobrzyca ZAMEK W.
KOSZALINIE

Mrzeżyno 5 Wrzosowo 26 Biesiekierz Manowo

Dygowo 163

Niechorze 27 Rosnowo Mostowo

102 162 Niedalino *Rade...*

Rewal 21 Trzebiatów Karlino 166

Pobierowo 102 31 Goścíno 19 31 167 37 11

Dziwnów 103 Białogard Dargiń

Międzywodzie Cerkwica 18 Gorawino E28 16 19 25 Bobolice

8 Kamień 109 6 163 12 169 C

Wolinski Pomorski 23 Sławoborze Tychowo 171

102 32 Kolczewo Swierzno 17 Rymań 167 Tychówka

Międzyzdroje 105 Rzeszníkowo 33 Rabino 17 Białowąs 29 Grzmiąca

11 Mechowo Gryfice 6 23 23 30

3 21 15 13 Ząbrowo 162 Połczyn- 172

Lubin 107 18 Zdrój Barwice

Wolin Gołczewo 20 Płoty Resko Rusinowo Sława 21 ZAMEK W. 163 24 172

Haff E65 75 E28 152 Świdwin 75 POLCZYNIE Ostropole

Zalew 106 16°

Szczeciński 108 Starogard 4 Bierzwina

Jowe Warpno 3 Przybiernów 15° Żabowo 18 151

Radowo Brzeżno *Drawski* 27

0 10 20 30 km

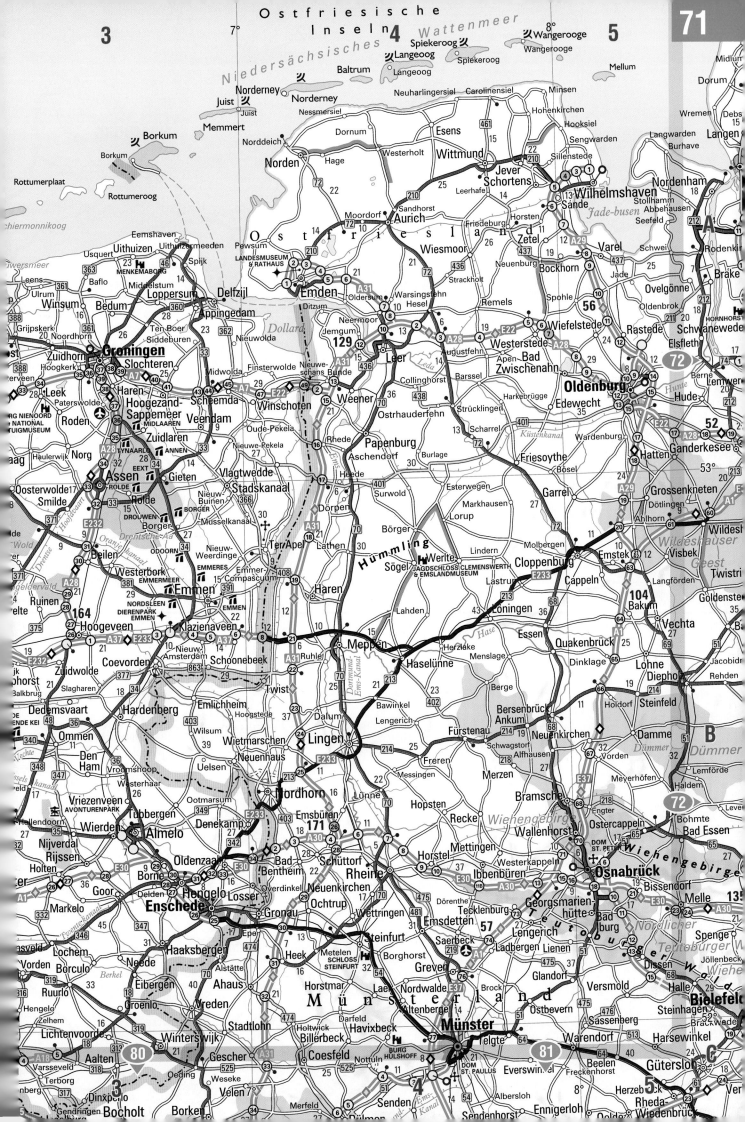

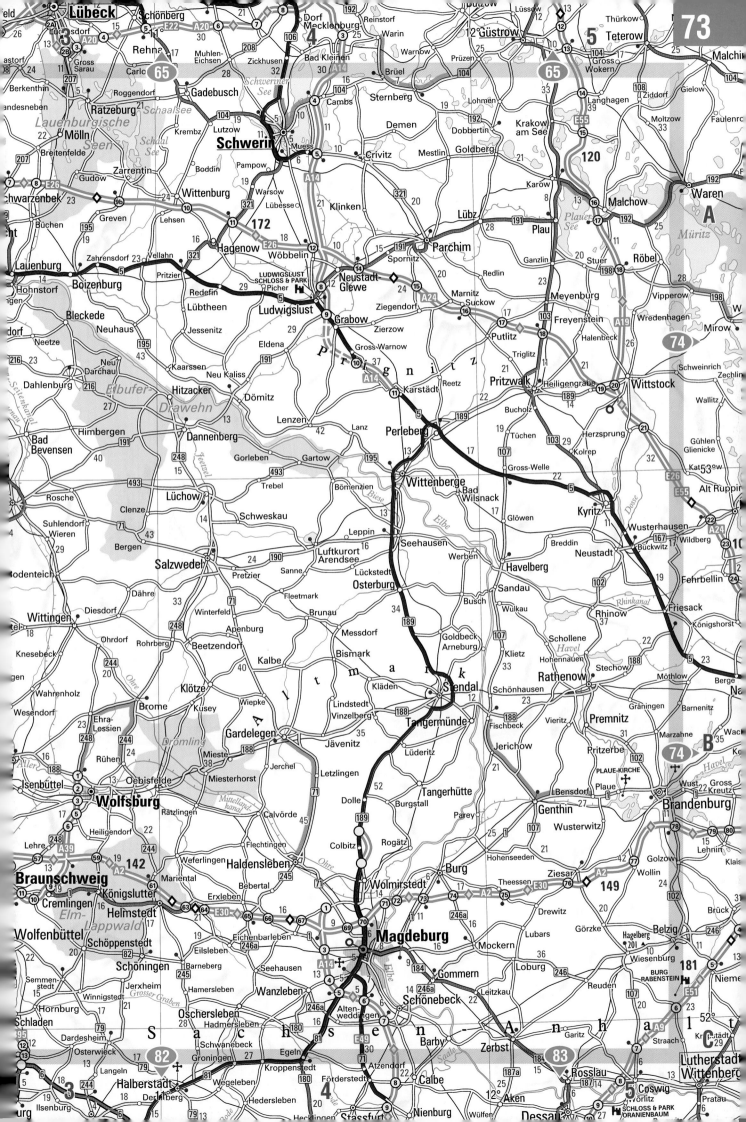

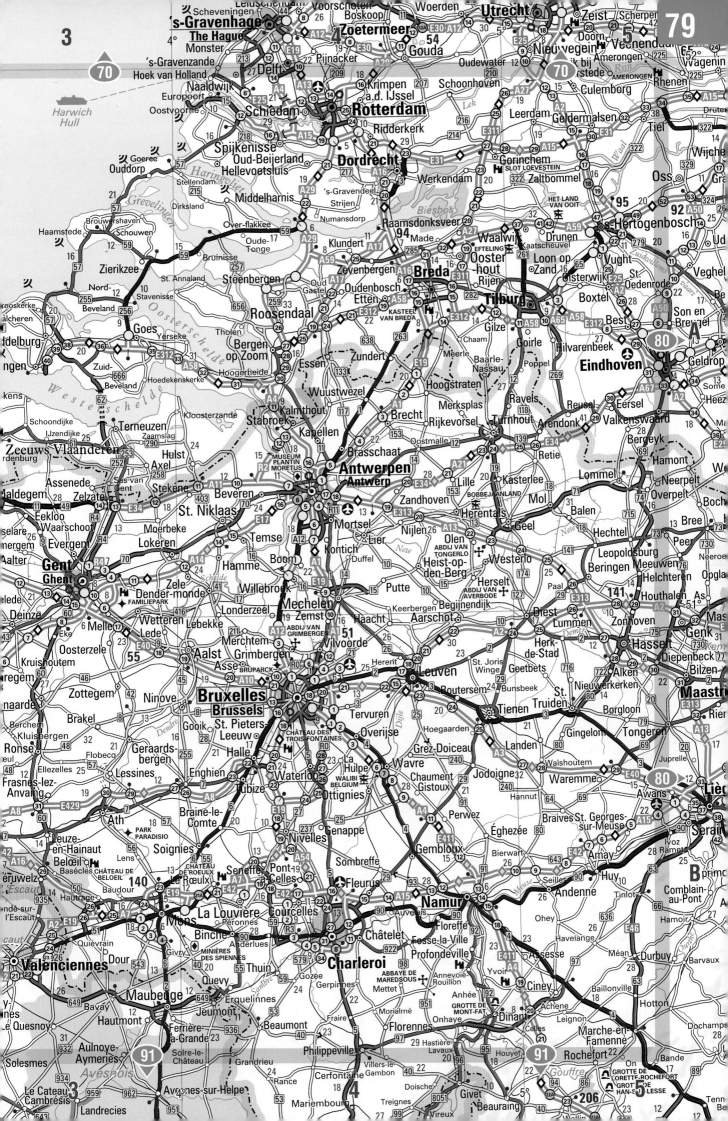

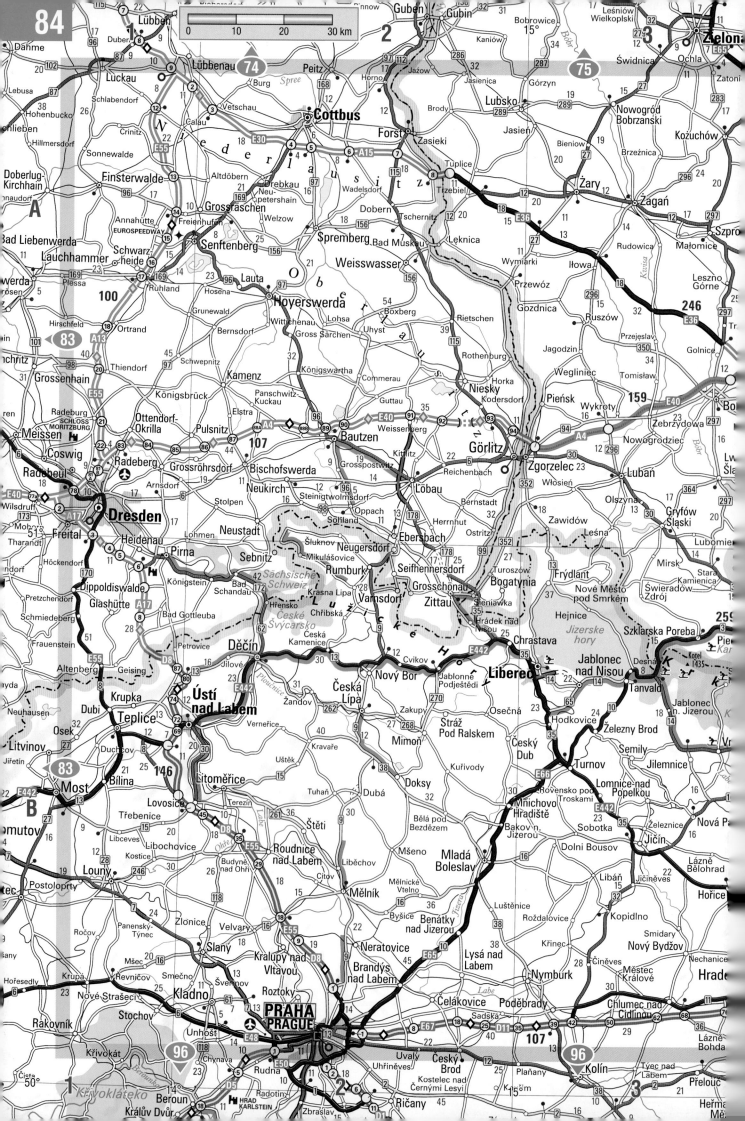

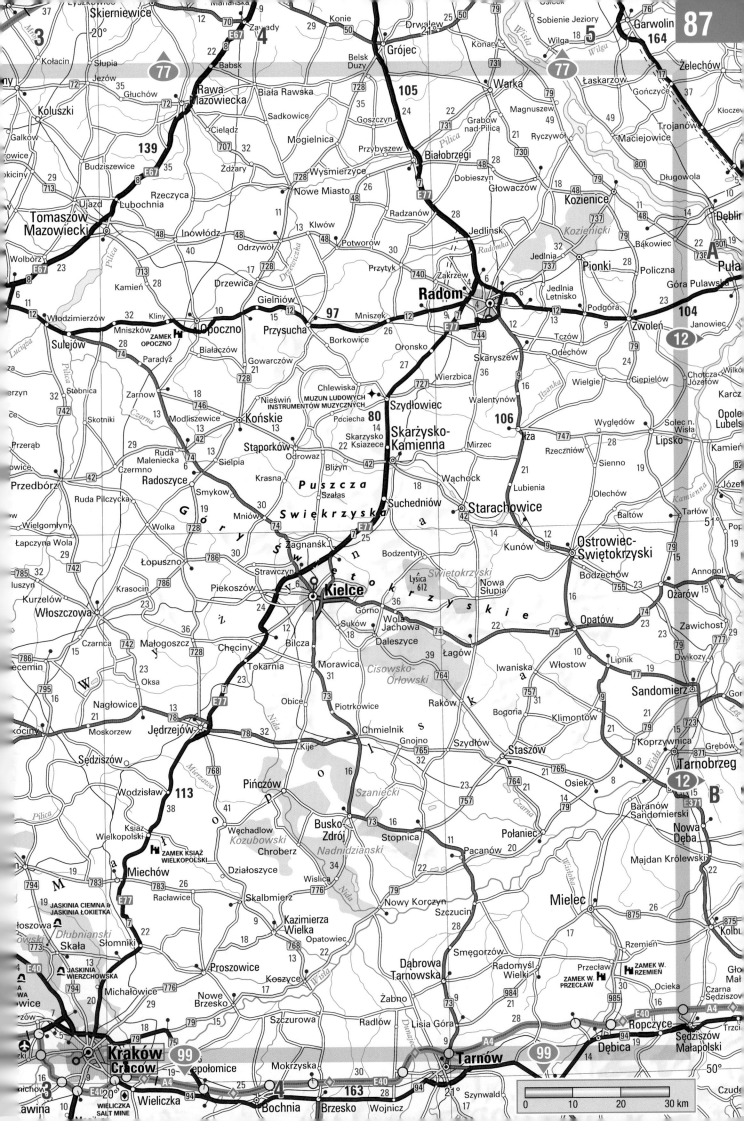

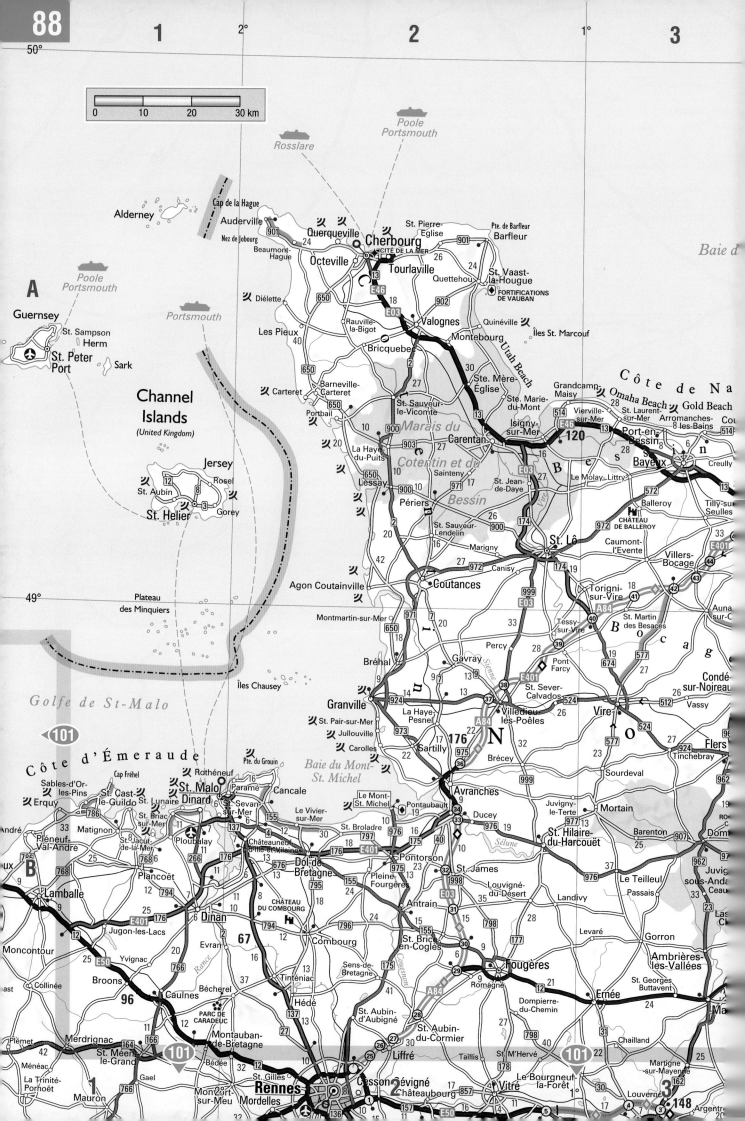

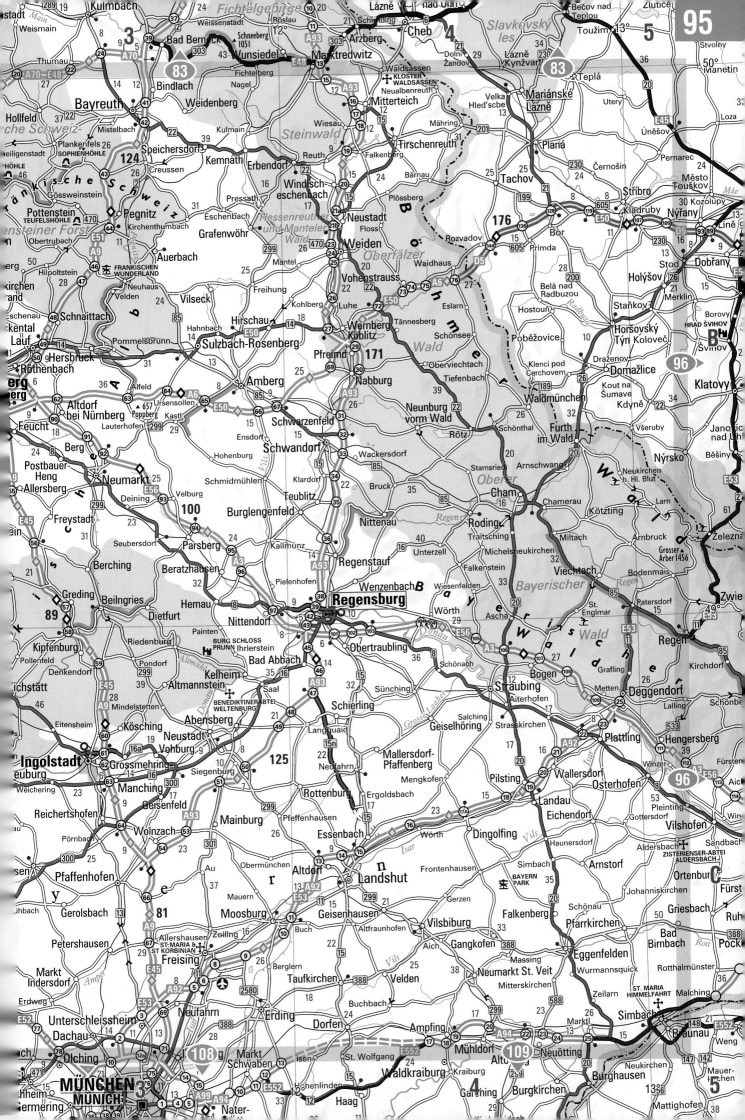

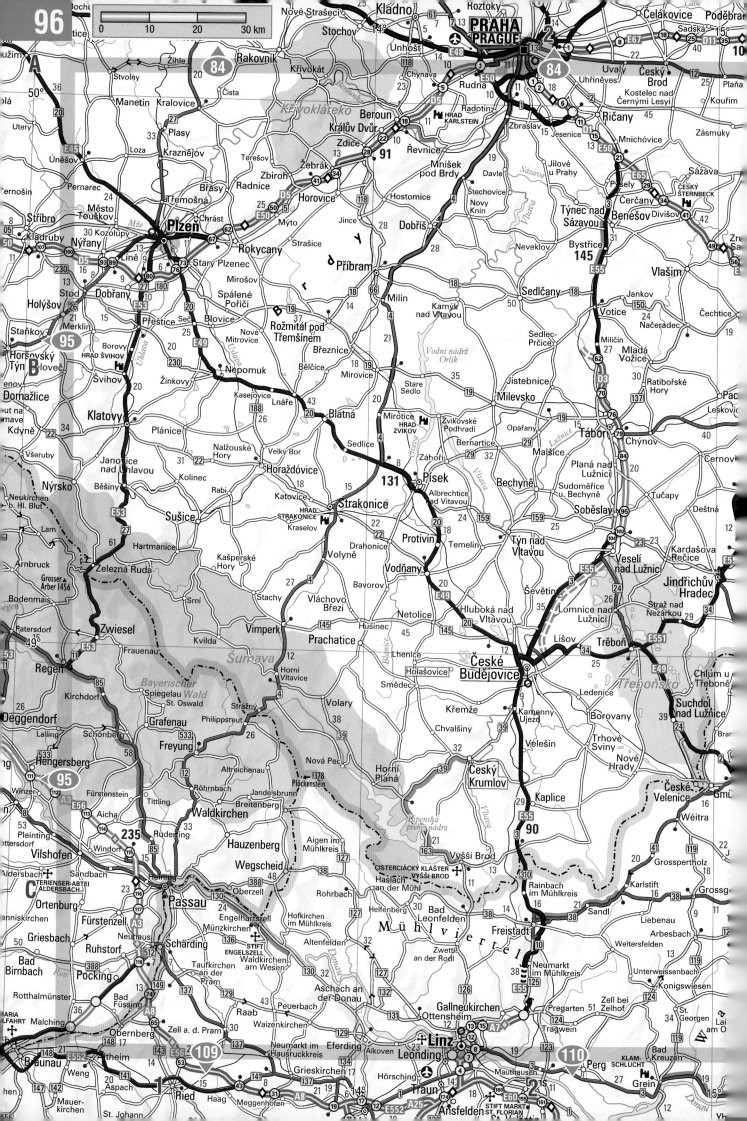

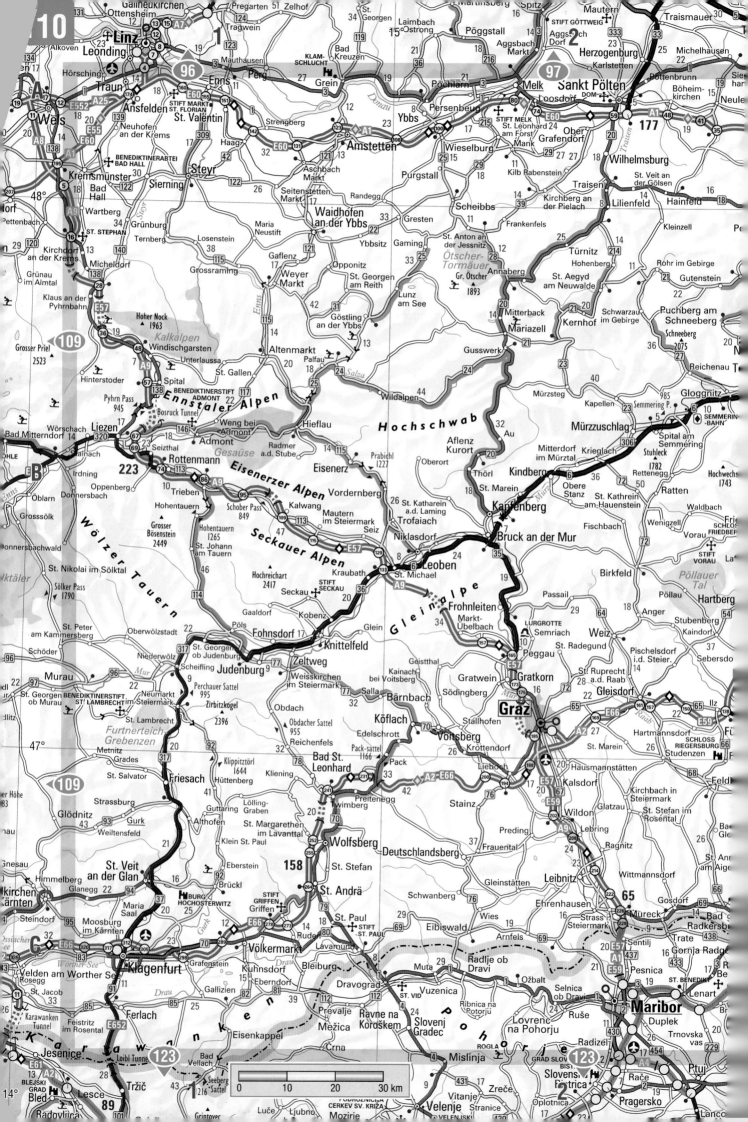

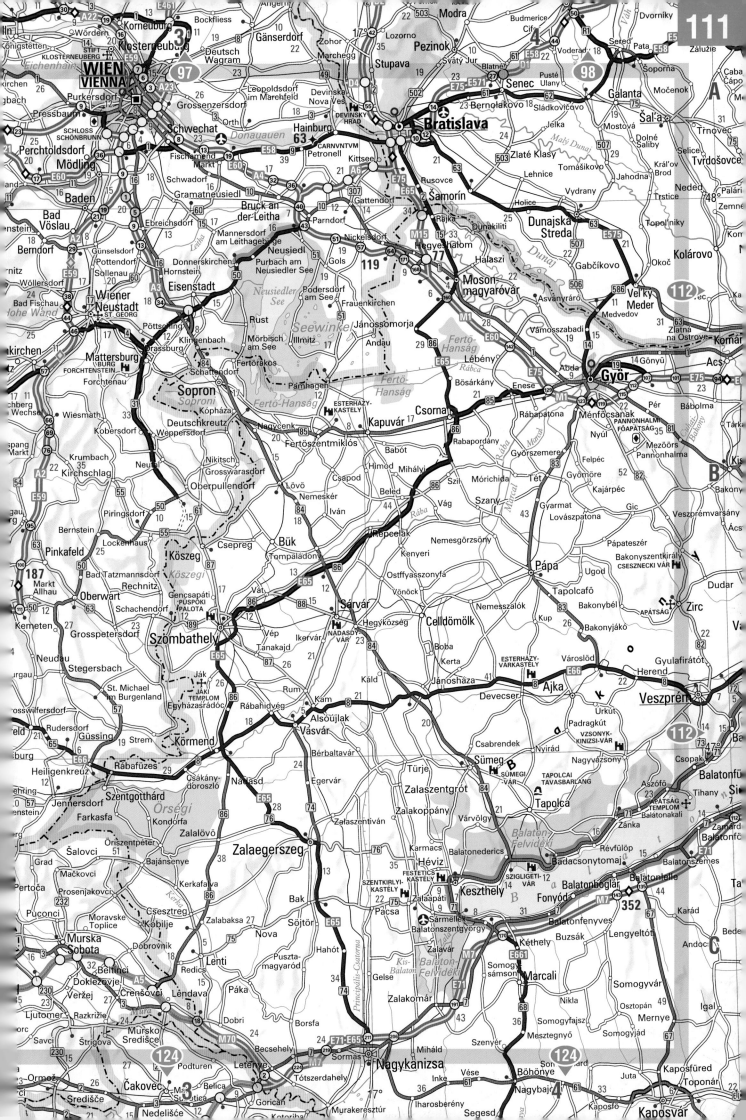

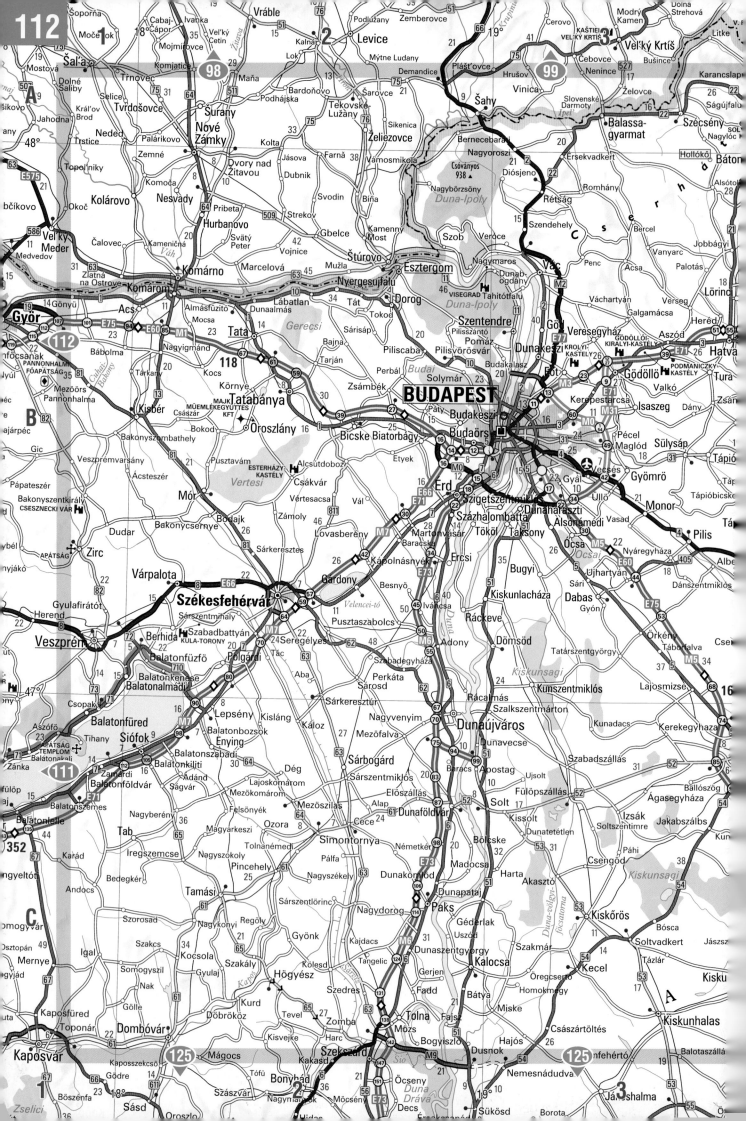

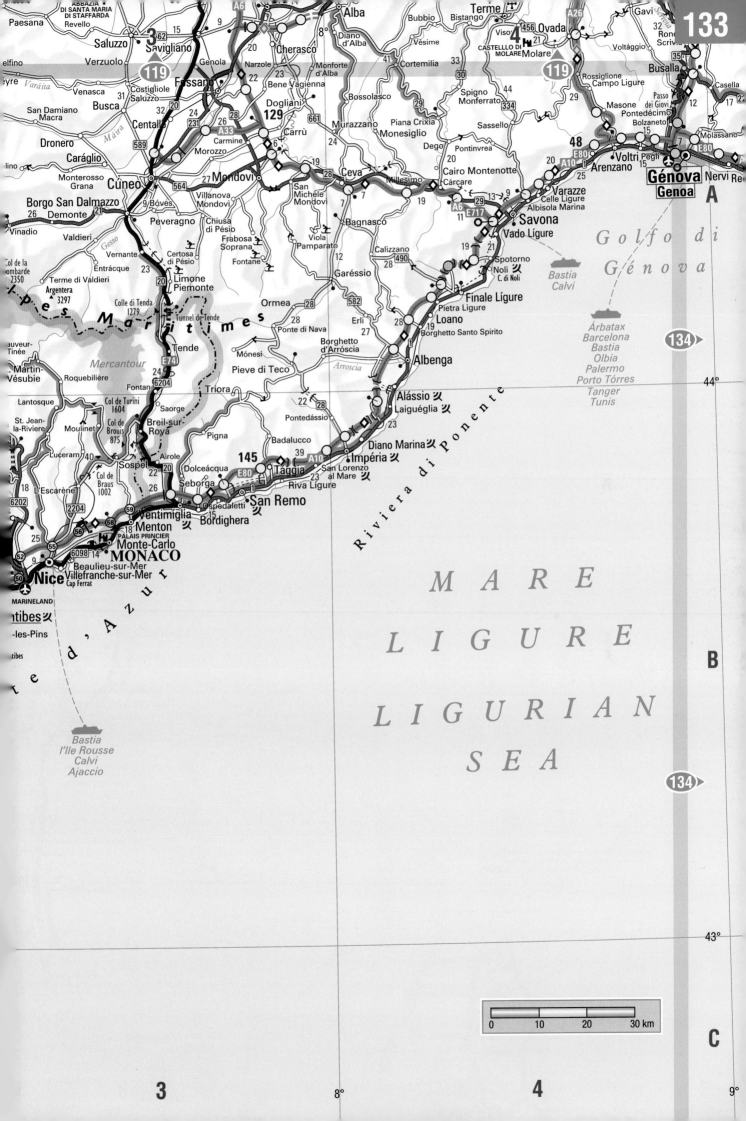

Unije
Nerezine
Čunski
Pula
3

Susak
Mali Lošinj
Veli Lošinj
123

Silba
Olib
Premuda
Ist
Virsko more
Molat

Prizna
15°
Stara Novalja
Novalja
Cesarica
Karlobag
E65
928
25
Metajna
Pag
Pag
AENONA
Gorica
Lukovo Šugorje
29

Vir
Vir
Povljana
Barič Draga
Tribanj
Kruščica
Starigrad-Paklenica

Privlaka
Vrsi
Nin
Ražanac
Poličnik
12 E65
Posedarje
8

AENONA
Nin
17
8
Novigrad
10

Sestrunj
Petrčane
Murvica
Zemunik Donji
56
21

Božava
Zadar
18
424
Bibinje
Sukošan
17
Benkovac
ASSERIA
A1

Ugljan
Preko
TVRĐAVA SV. MIHOVILA
Kali
26
Miranje
A1
21

Brbinj
Kuklijca
Turanj
27
56

Dugi Otok
Pašman
Pašman
Biograd na Moru
Stankovci
49

Zaglav
Sali
Tkon
Pakoštane
Vransko Jezero
39
E65

Telašćica
Žut
8
Pirovac
27
16

Kornati
Kornat
Tisno
Murter
Vodice
8

Žirje
KATEDRALA SV JAKOVA
Zablaće
149
Krapanj

A D R I A T I C   S E A

Zadar

Split
Starigrad
Durrës
Trieste

Ancona

Jabucka

Svetac

Primošten

Rogoznica
B

43°

15°
4

0   10   20   30 km

C

gli Abruzzi
3
15°
4

Klanac
Lički Osik
odlapača
Jošan
Donj
4

Gospić
389
Vrebac
Udbina
123
218

Brušane
29
Bilaj
Gornja Ploča
17
1
Kremen
1591
Mazin
A

Medak
Vaganski vrh
1757
Raduč
7
Sveti Rok
Bruvno
21
33

Paklenica
28
A1
50
21
26
Gračac
16

Velebit
27
20
Dori

Jasenice
54
27
Zrmanja
Kaštel Zegarski
26

12
Obrovac
16
Ervenik
Mokro Polj

27
Medvide
Kista
Krka

BURNUM
44
59
Đevrske
33

MANASTIR KRKA
22
Skradin
33

Šibenik

29

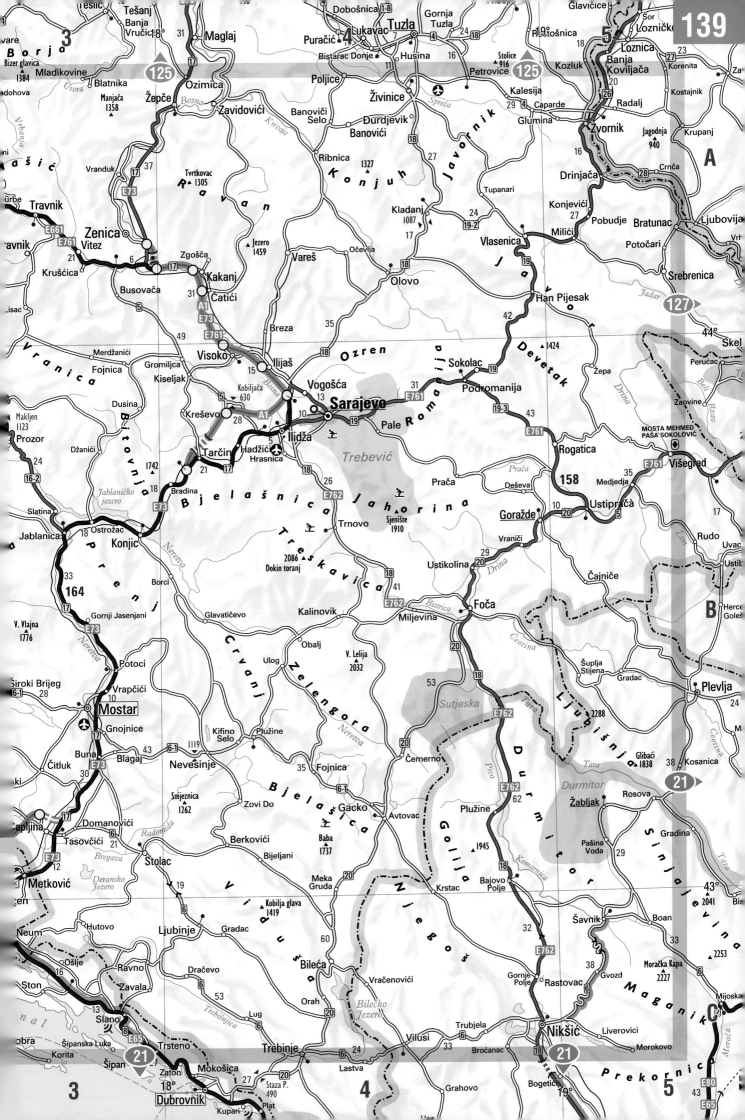

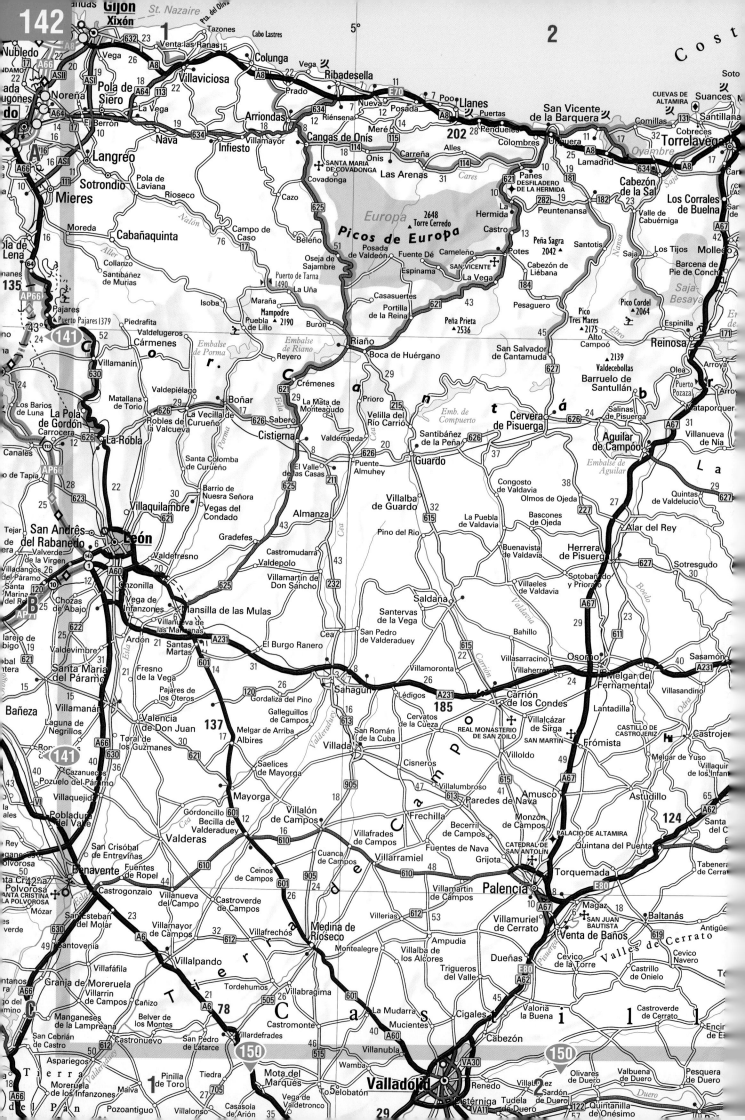

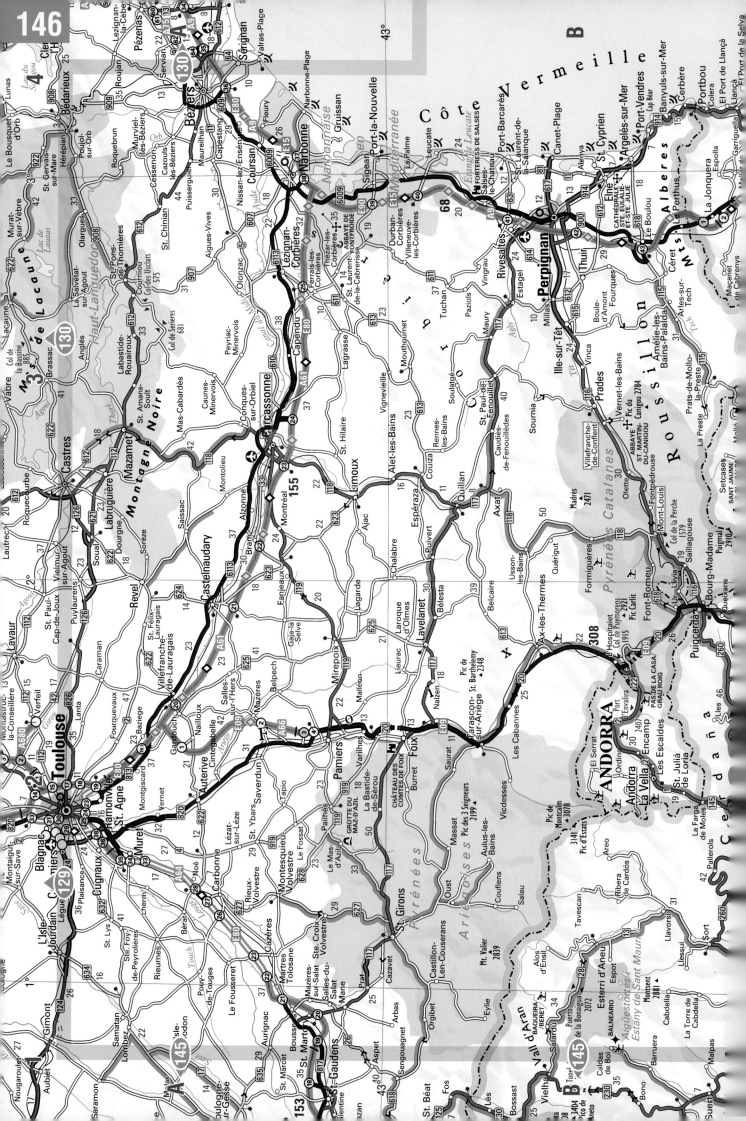

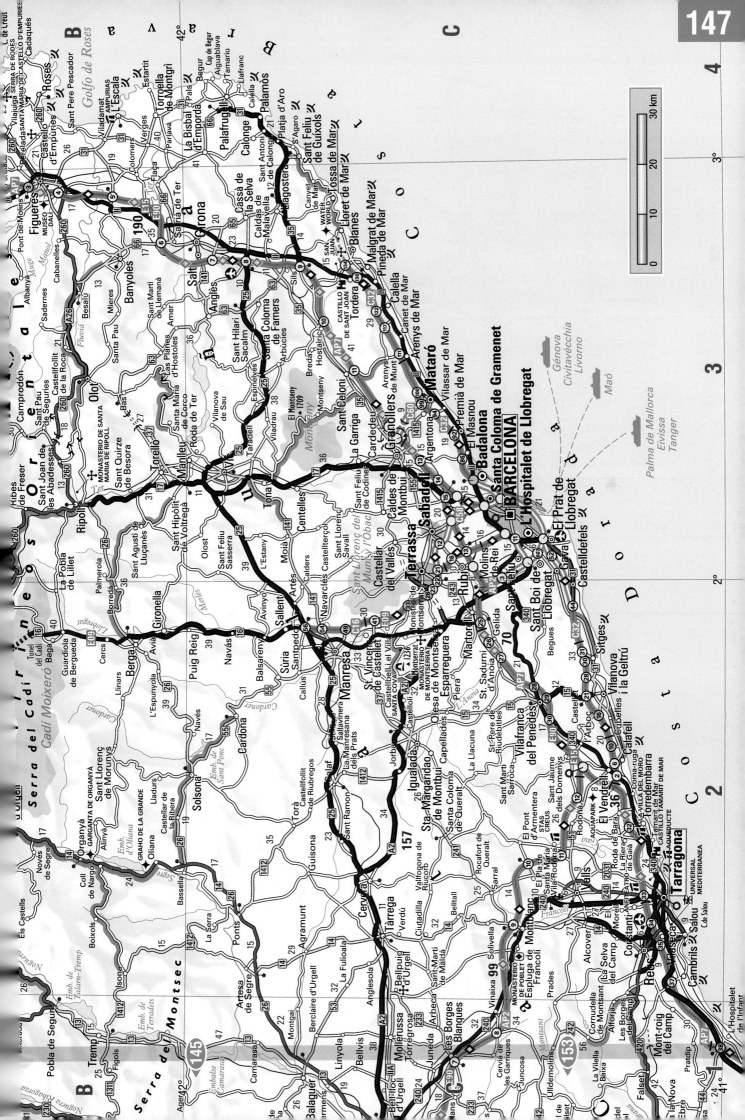

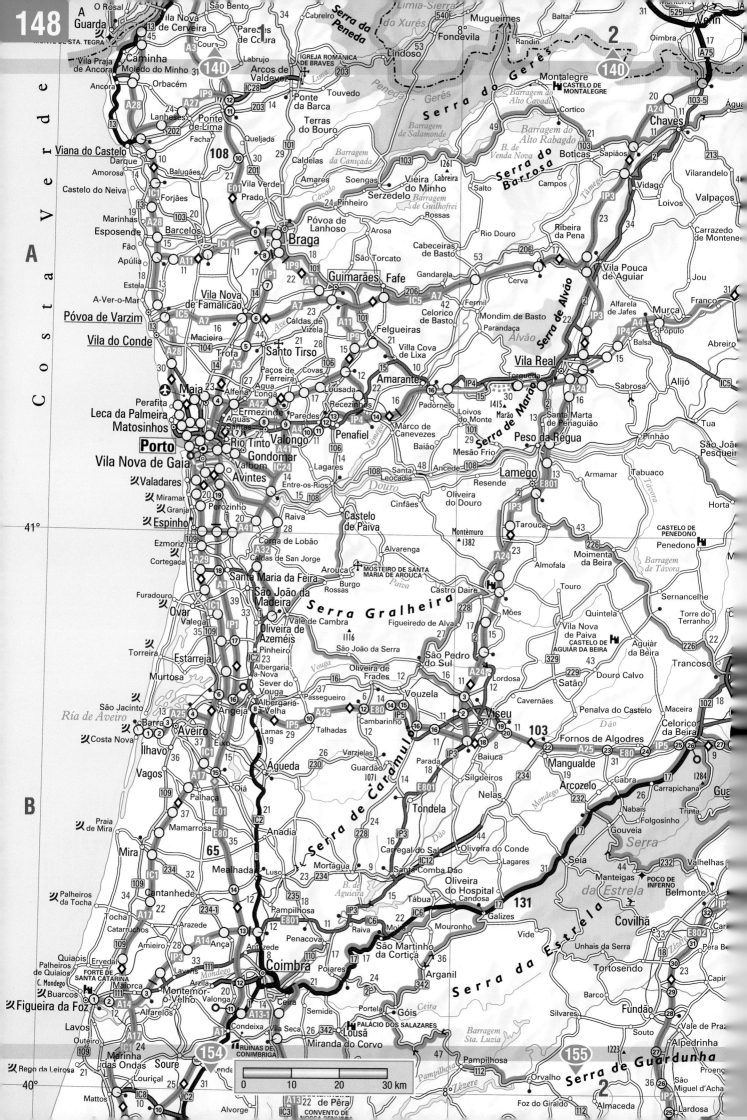

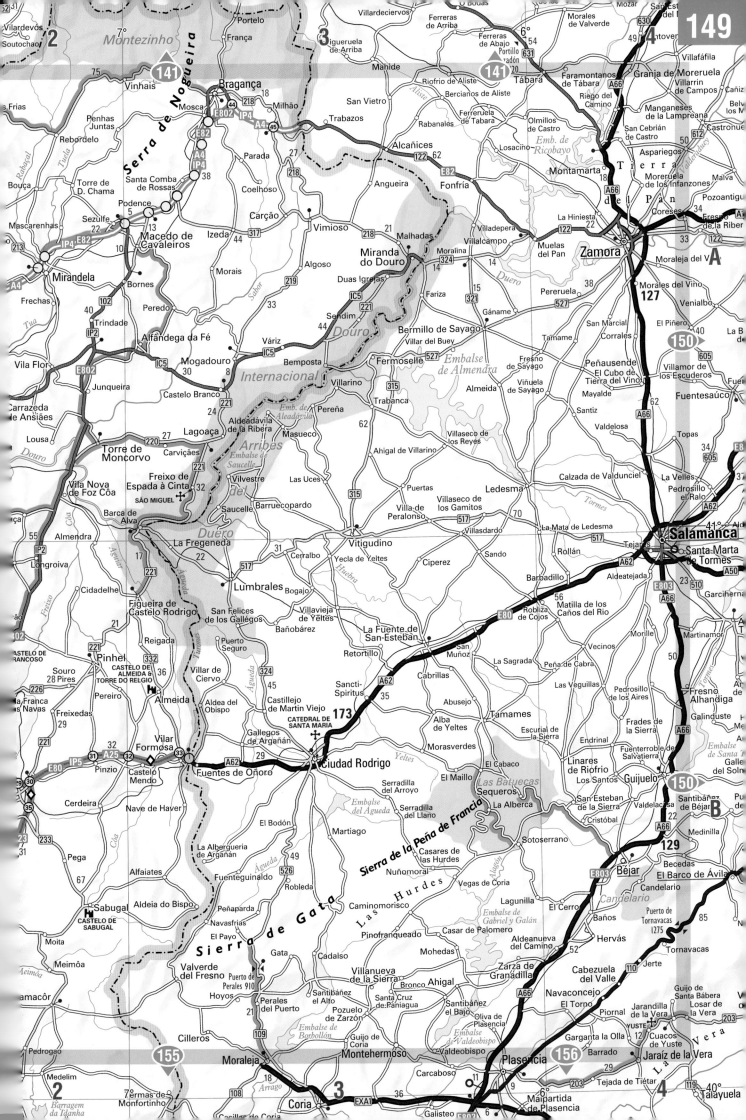

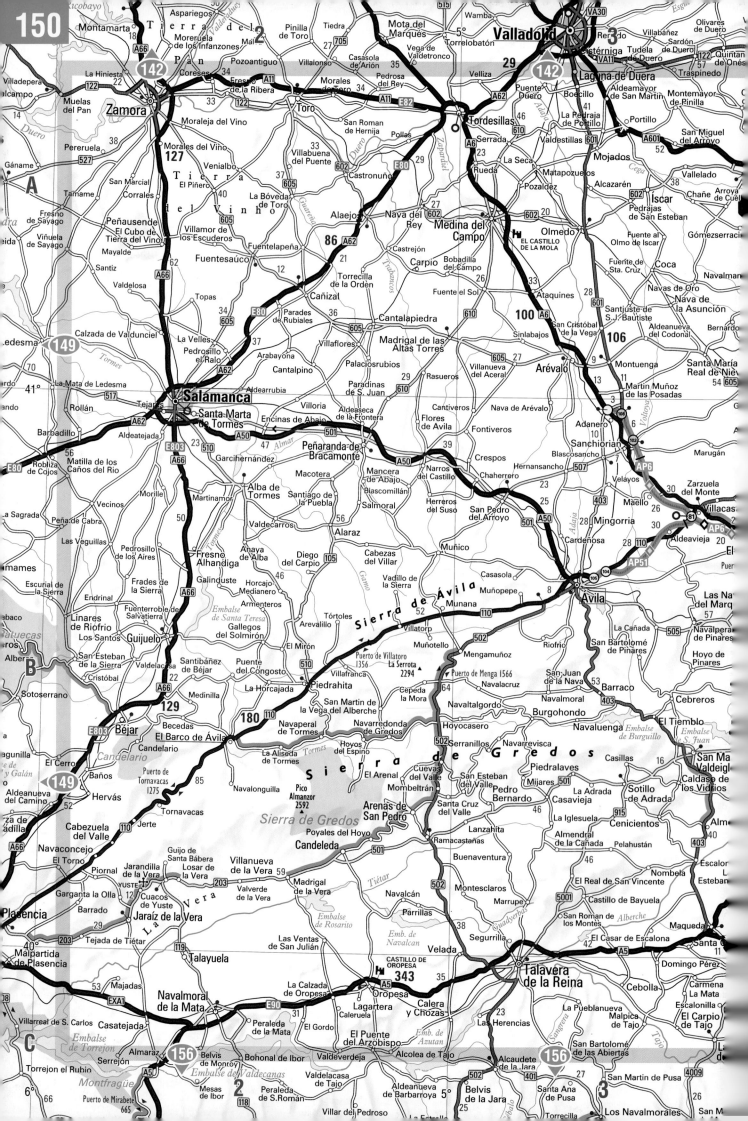

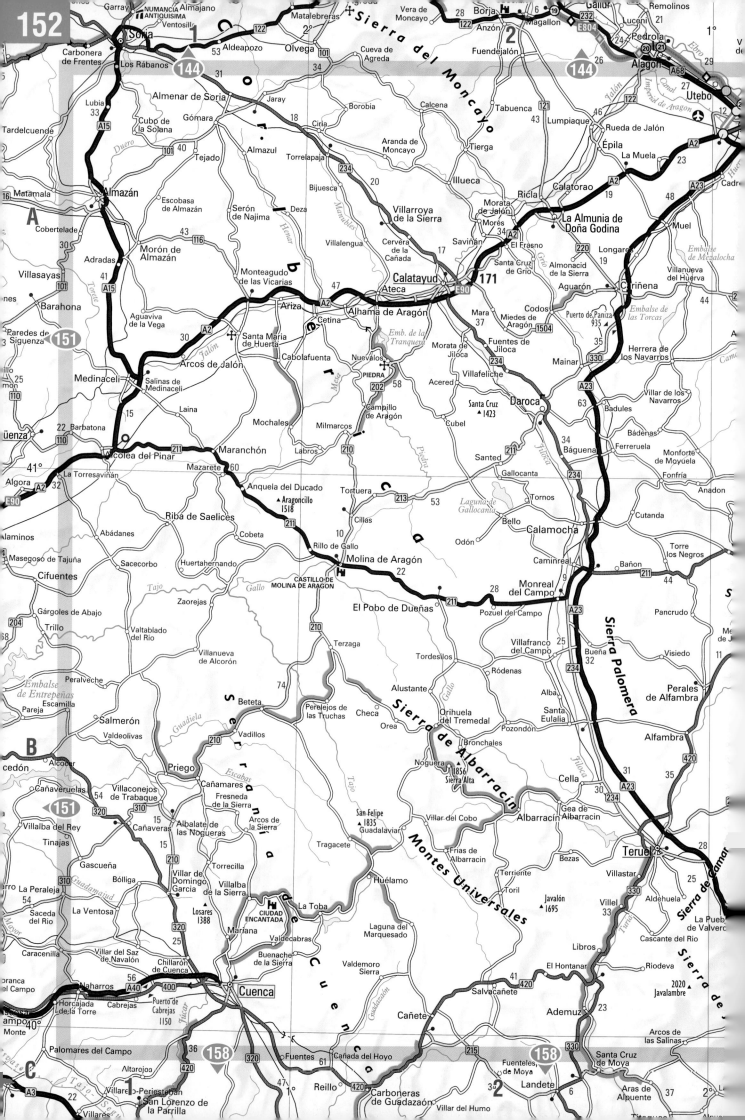

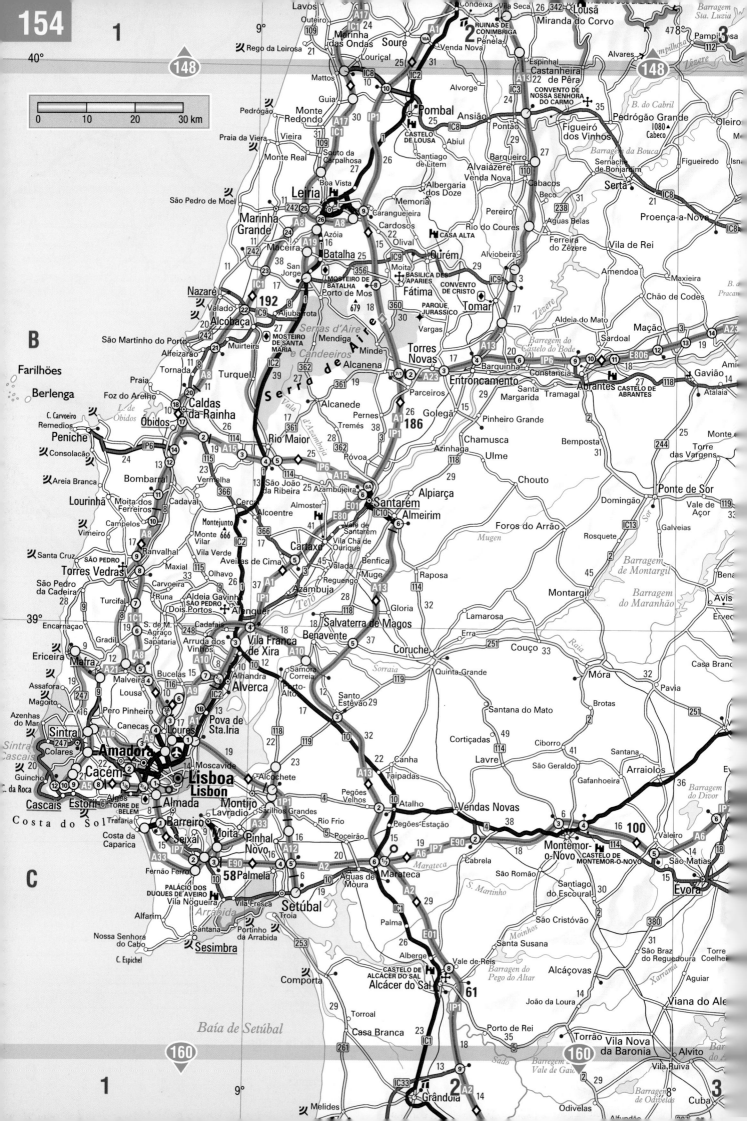

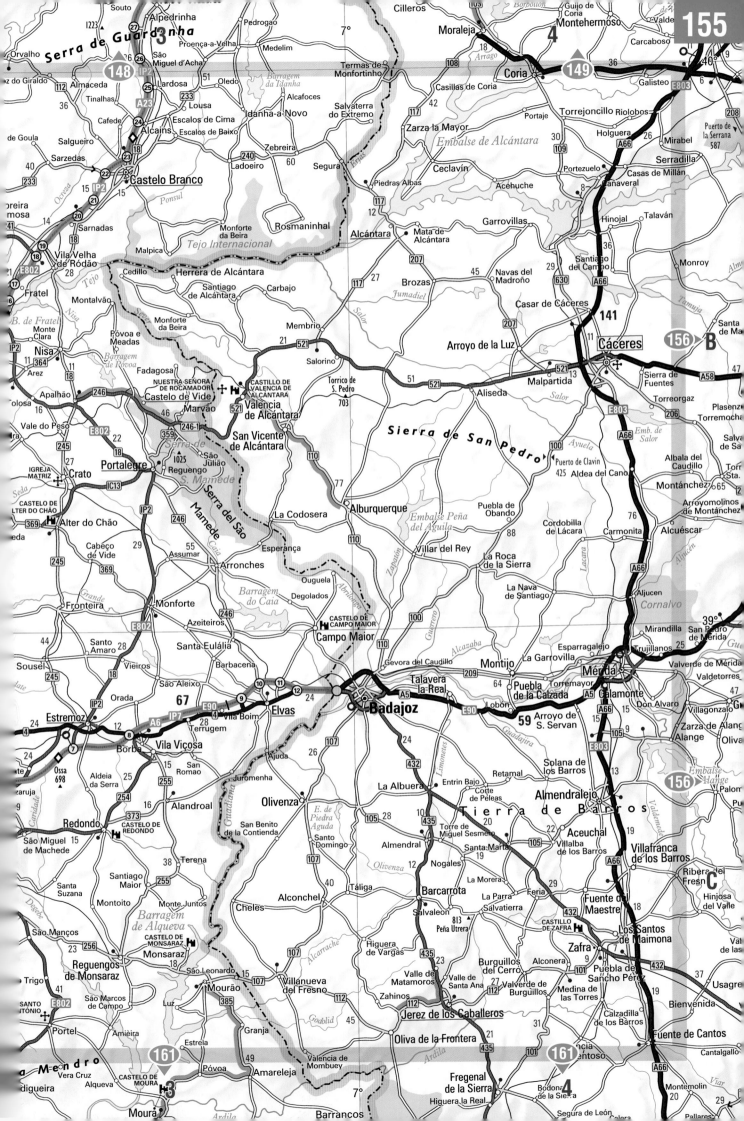

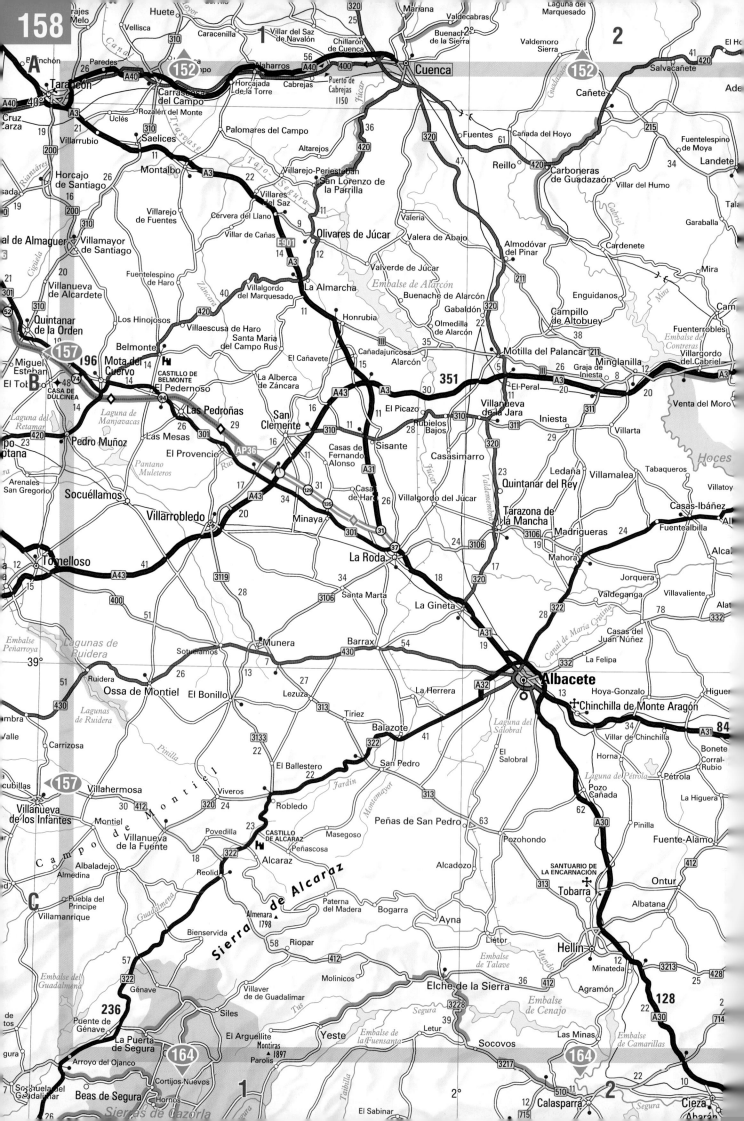

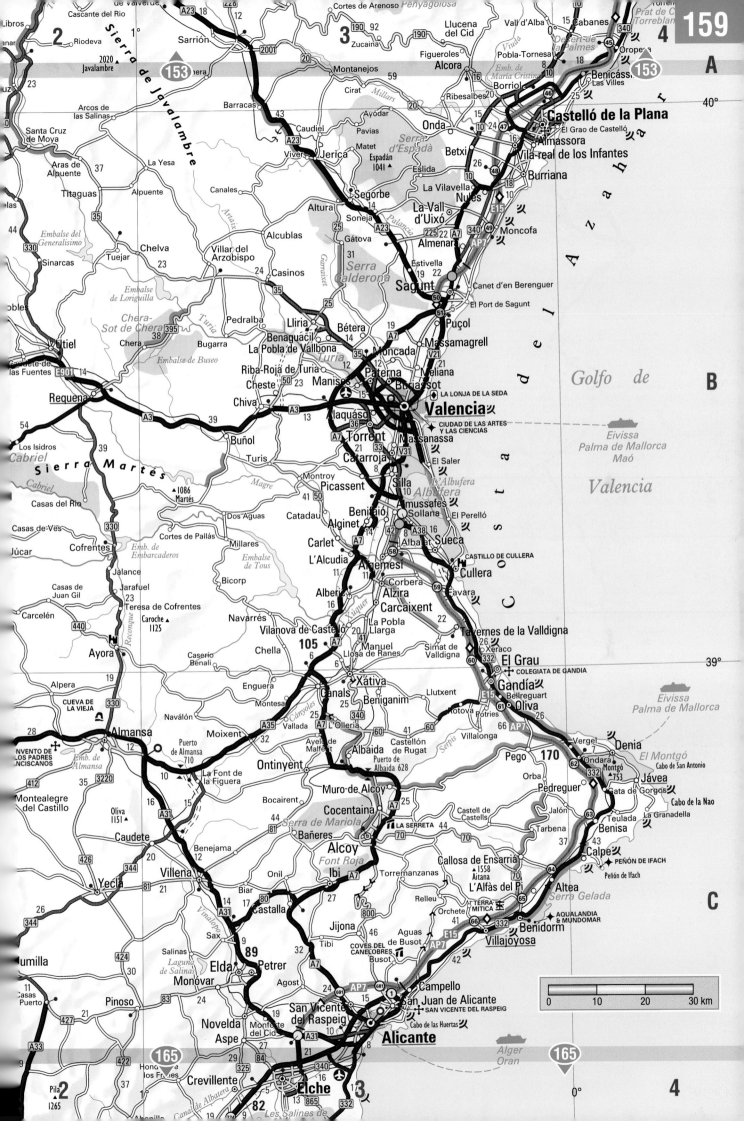

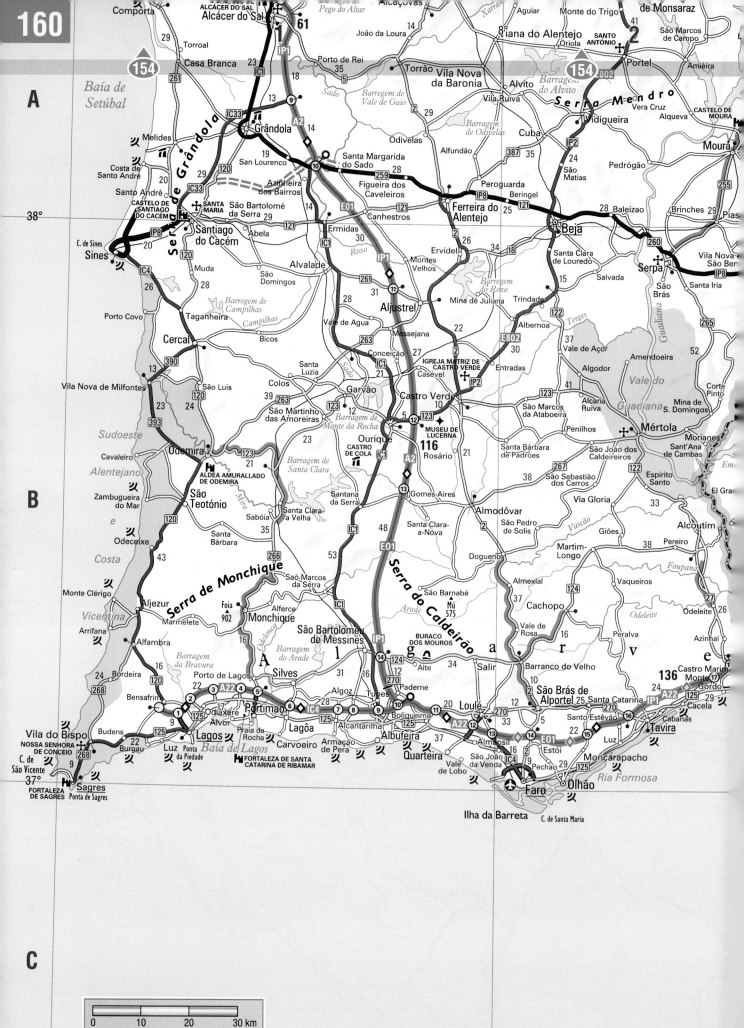

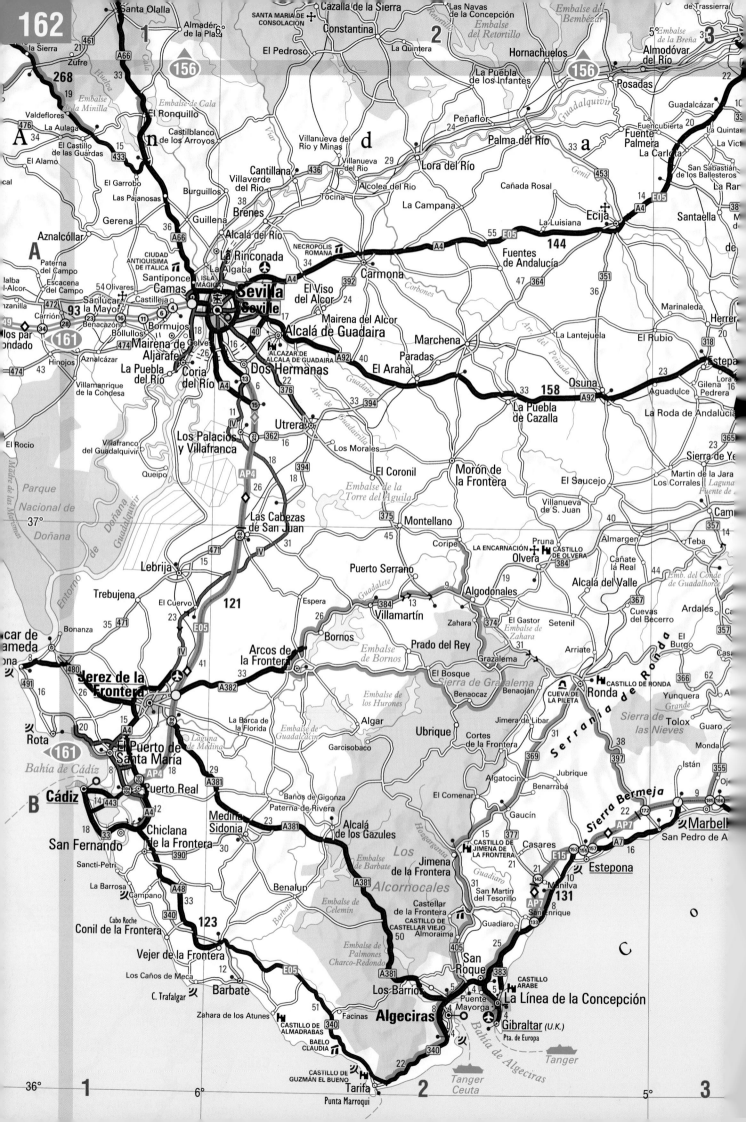

A

B

C

3

4

A

1   2°   2

40°

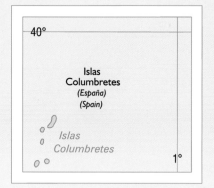

Islas
Columbretes
(España)
(Spain)

40°

*Islas
Columbretes*

1°

ISLAS
BALEARES

BALEARIC
ISLANDS

Port de Sóller

Sóll

Deia   Tune
Sóllé

Valldemossa   Al

Banyalbufar   Bunya

Estellencs   39   Esporles   11
Puigpunyent   Marrat

Sa Dragonera   10   **Palma de**
Mallorca   4   8

Andratx   15   25
Port d'Andratx   Calvià   13   12
Barcelona   Peguera   17 14   MA1   6   10
Santa Ponça   Palma
Nova   Can
Pastilla
Magaluf   S'Arenal
Cap Enderrocat

Valencia   Cap de Cala Figuera   *Bahía
de Palma*

Maó

*Eivissa
Denia*   **Mallorca**
Majorca

B

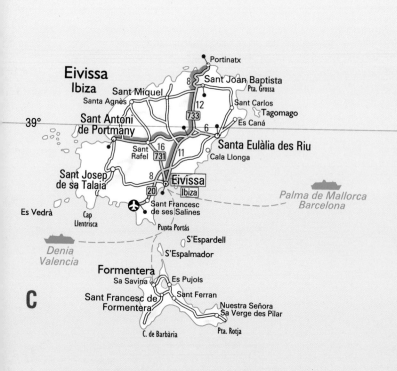

39°

Eivissa
Ibiza

Portinatx

Sant Miquel   Sant Joan Baptista
Santa Agnès   Pta. Grossa
8   Sant Carlos
Sant Antoni   12   Sant Carlos
de Portmany   733   Tagomago
6   Es Caná

Sant   16   Santa Eulàlia des Riu
Rafel   731   11   Cala Llonga

Sant Josep   8
de sa Talaia   20   Eivissa
Ibiza

Es Vedrà   Sant Francesc
Cap   de ses Salines
Llentrisca   Punta Portás

*Denia
Valencia*   S'Espardell
S'Espalmador

Formentera
Sa Savina   Es Pujols
Sant Francesc de   Sant Ferran
Formentera   Nuestra Señora
Sa Verge des Pilar
C. de Barbària   Pta. Rotja

*Palma de Mallorca
Barcelona*

C

1   2°   2

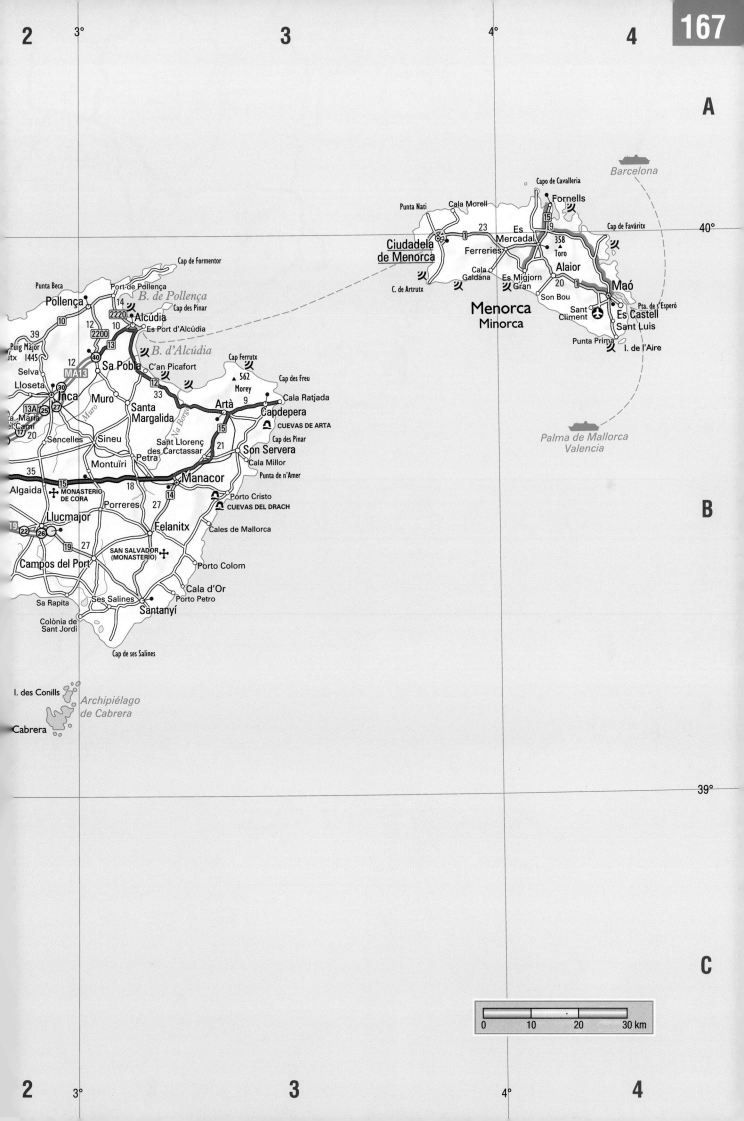

2 3° 3 4° 4

A

40°

B

39°

C

Barcelona

Capo de Cavalleria
Punta Nati Cala Morell Fornells
15
9
23 Es
Cap de Favàritx
Ciudadela Mercadal 358
de Menorca Ferreries Toro
Cala Alaior
Galdana Es Migjorn 20 1 Maó
Menorca Gran Son Bou PTA. de s'Esperó
Minorca Sant Es Castell
Climent Sant Luis
Punta Prima I. de l'Aire

Palma de Mallorca
Valencia

Cap de Formentor
Punta Beca Port de Pollença
Pollença 14 B. de Pollença
10 2220 Alcúdia Cap des Pinar
12 10 Es Port d'Alcúdia
39 2200 13 B. d'Alcúdia
Puig Major 40 Cap Ferrutx
itx 1445 12 Sa Pobla C'an Picafort
Selva MA13 12 ▲ 562 Cap des Freu
Lloseta 33 Morey
30 Inca Muro Artà 9 Cala Ratjada
a Maria 13A 25 27 Santa 15 Capdepera
el Camí 17 20 Margalida CUEVAS DE ARTA
Sencelles Sineu Petra Cap des Pinar
Montuïri Sant Llorenç 21 Son Servera
35 des Carctassar Cala Millor
Algaida 15 18 Manacor Punta de n'Amer
MONASTERIO 14 Porto Cristo
DE CORA Porreres CUEVAS DEL DRACH
19 Llucmajor 27
22 26 Felanitx Cales de Mallorca
19 27 SAN SALVADOR Porto Colom
Campos del Port (MONASTERIO)
Cala d'Or
Sa Rapita Ses Salines Porto Petro
Santanyí
Colònia de
Sant Jordi
Cap de ses Salines

I. des Conills
Archipiélago
de Cabrera
Cabrera

Puig Major
Na Borja
Muro
C. de Artrutx

0 10 20 30 km

2 3° 3 4° 4

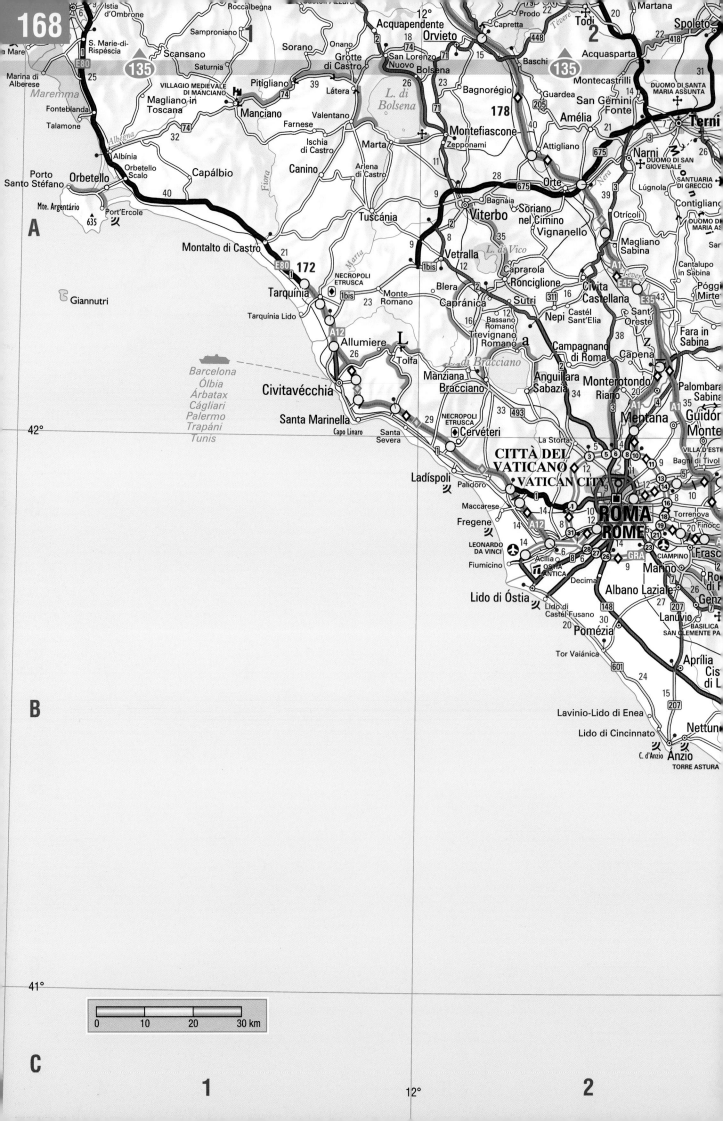

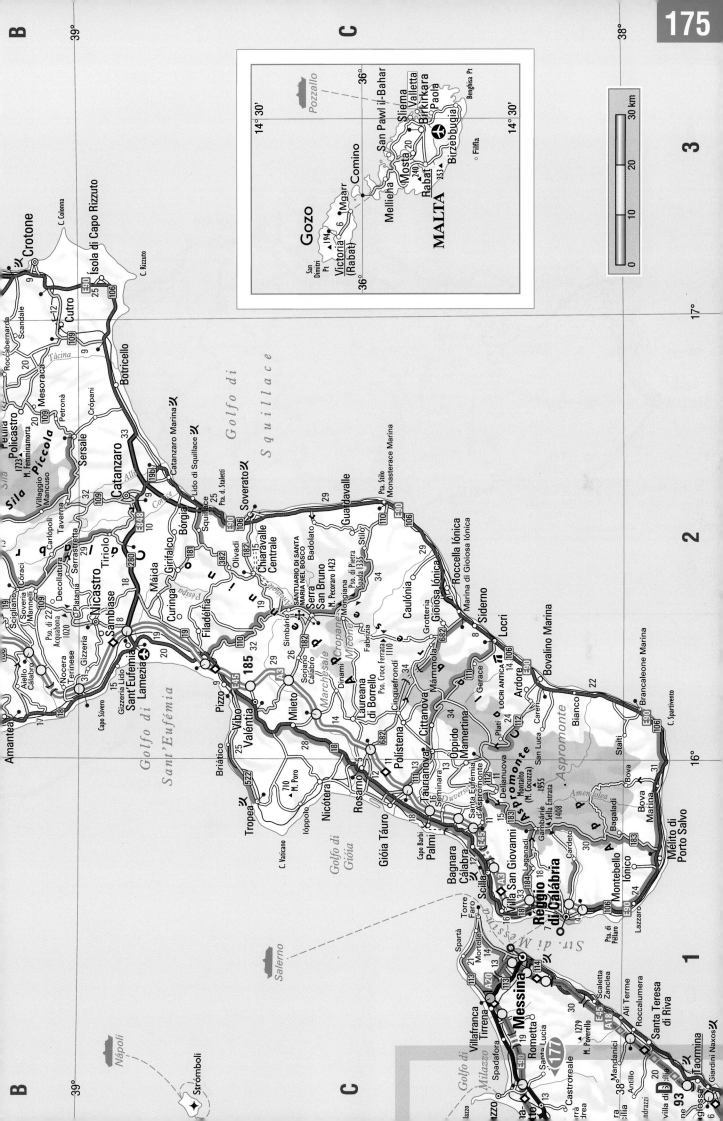

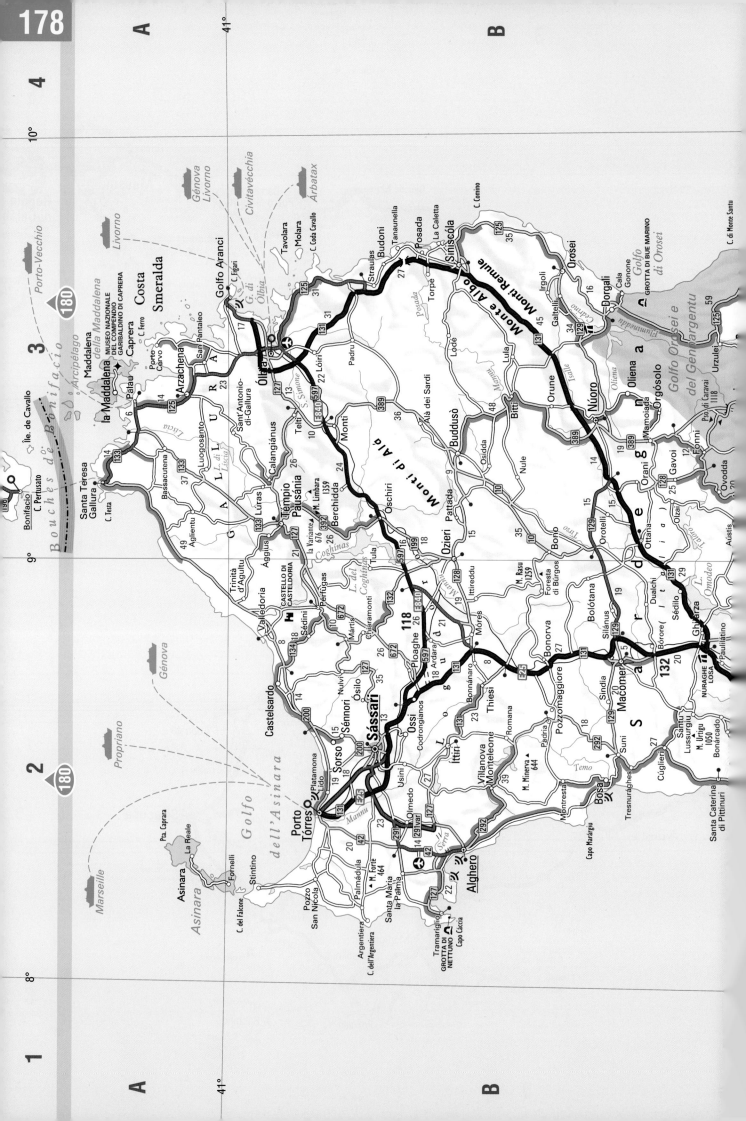

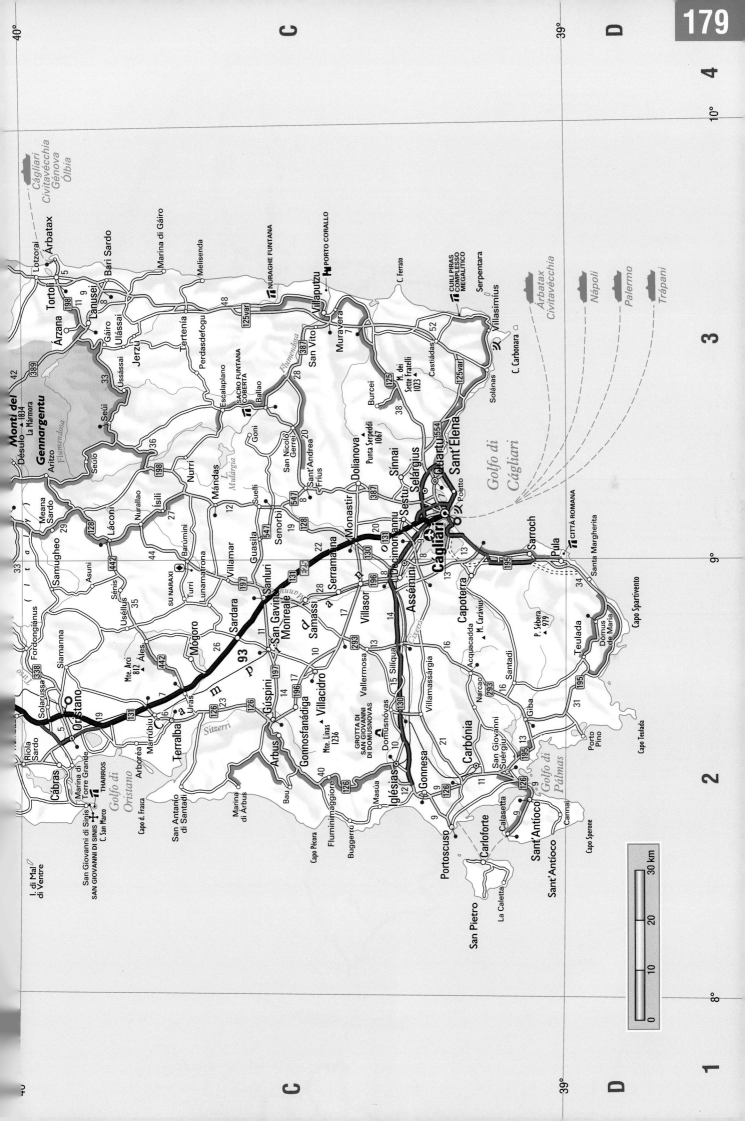

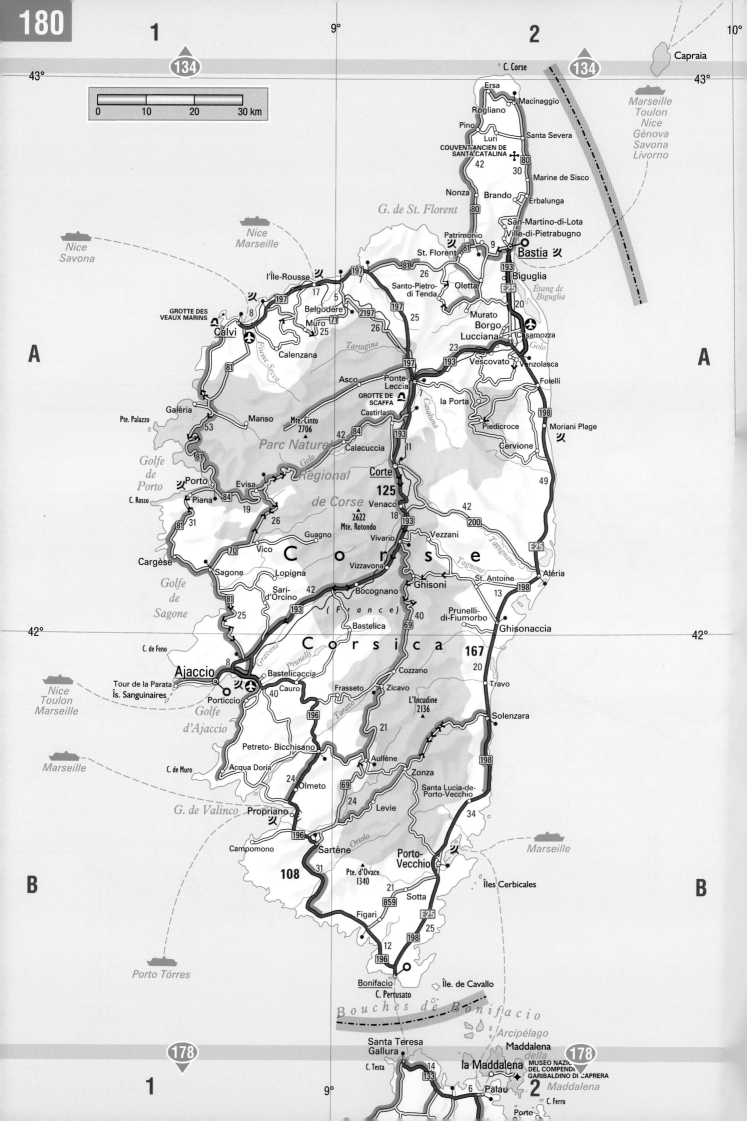

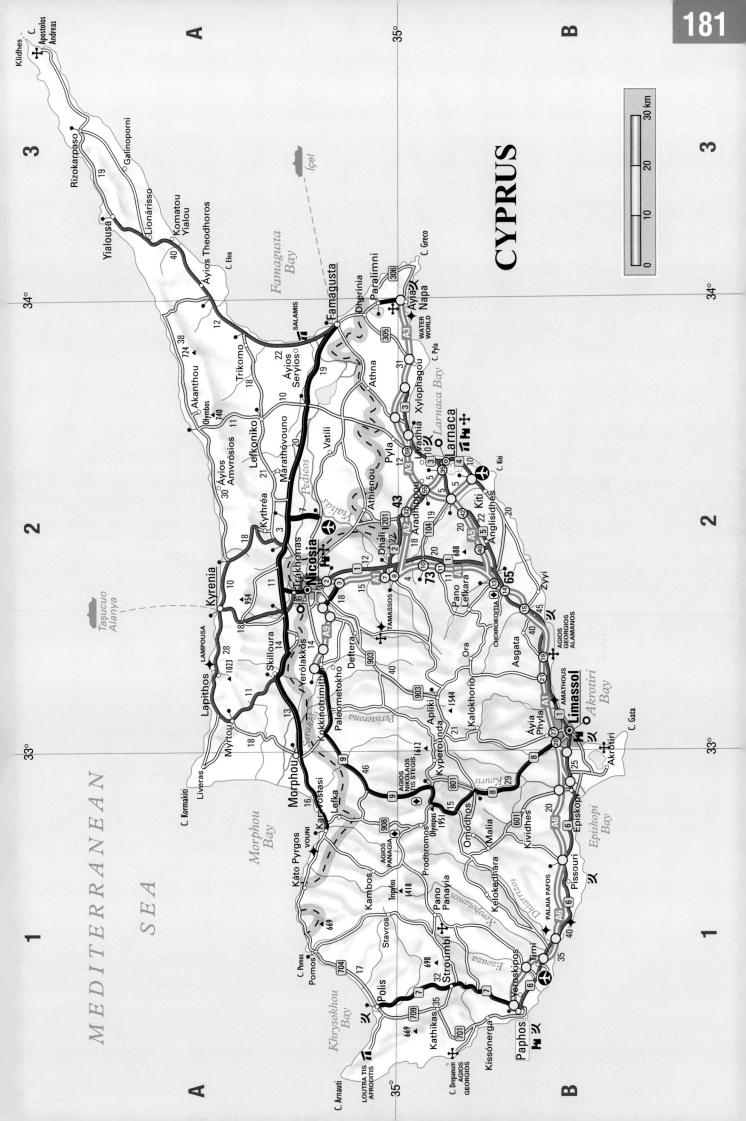

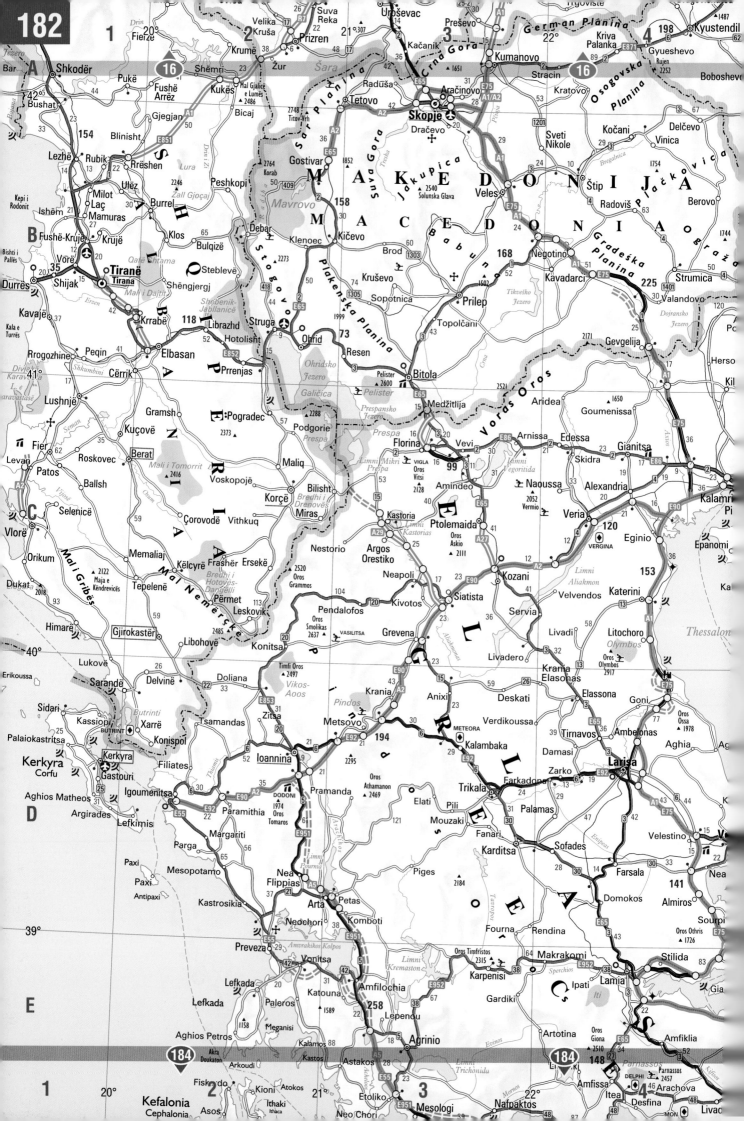

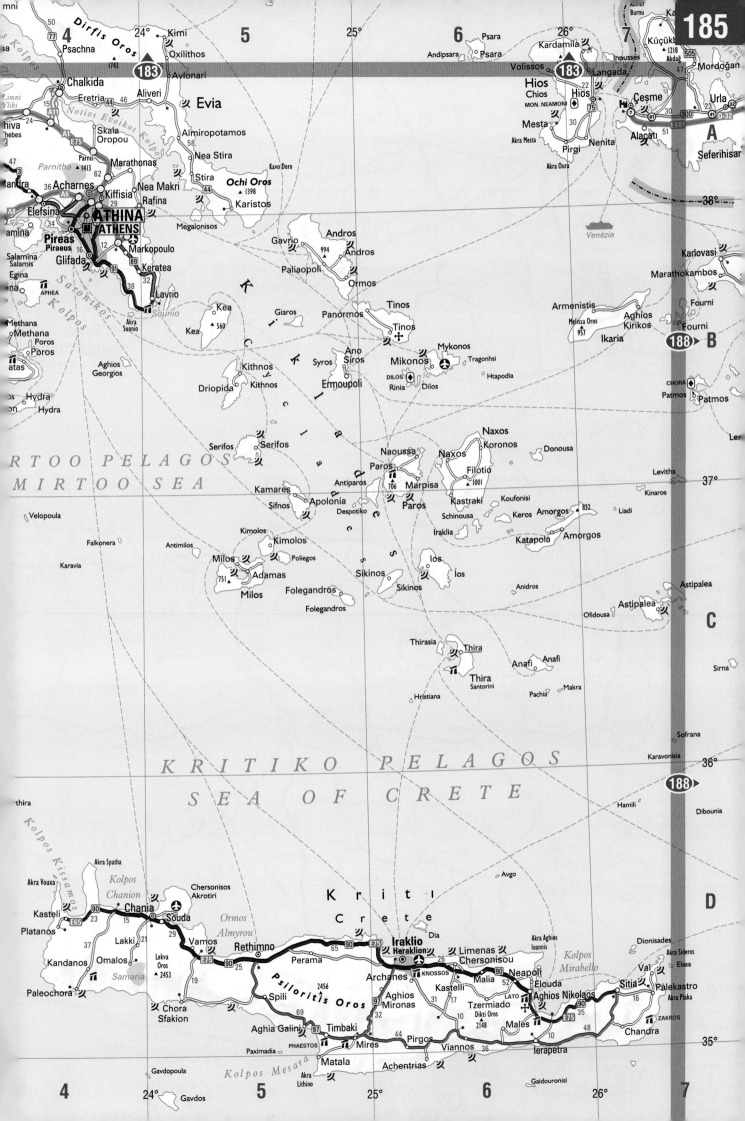

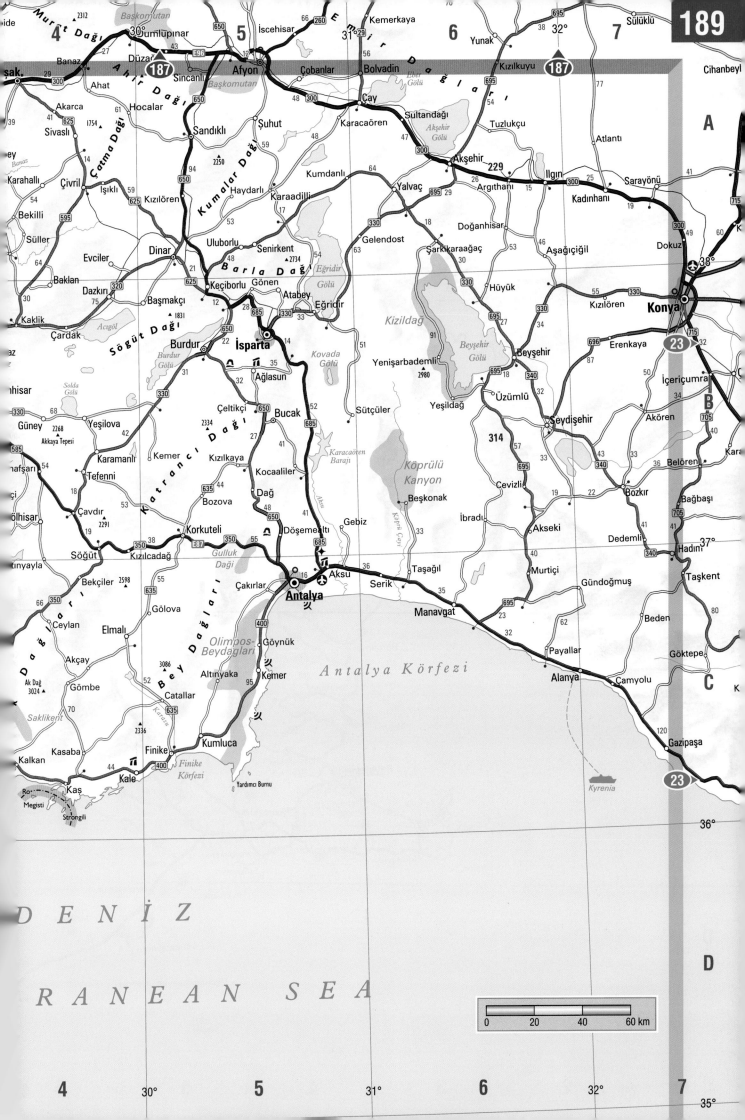

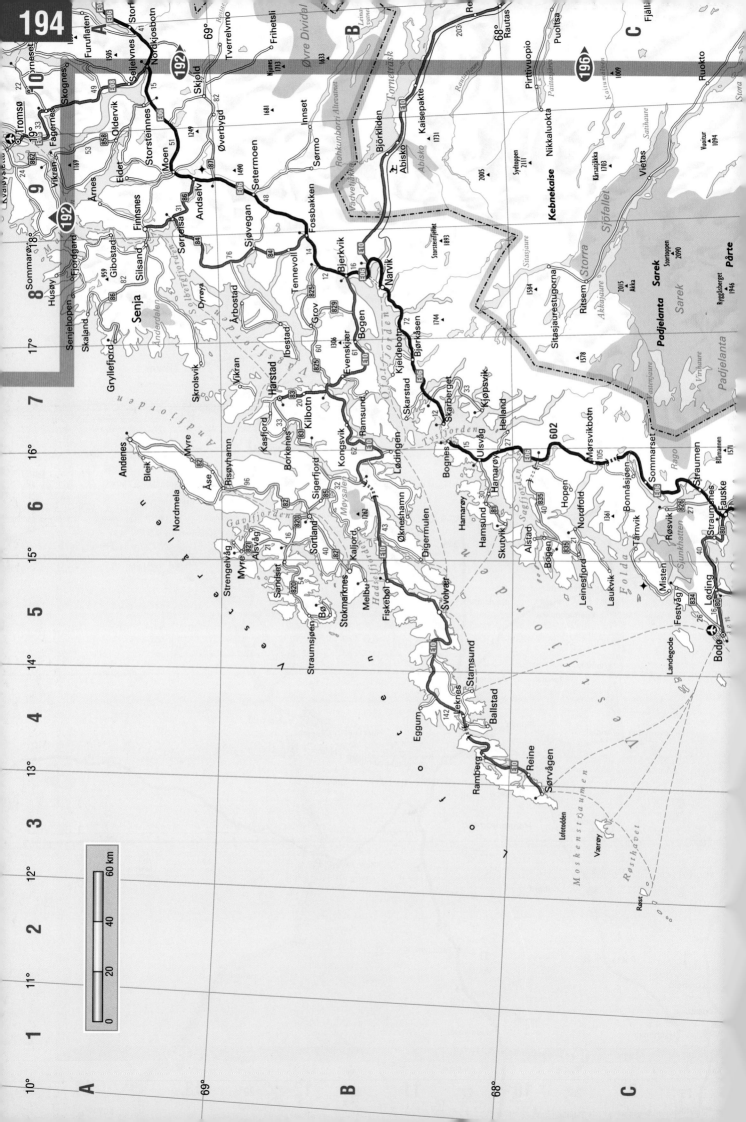

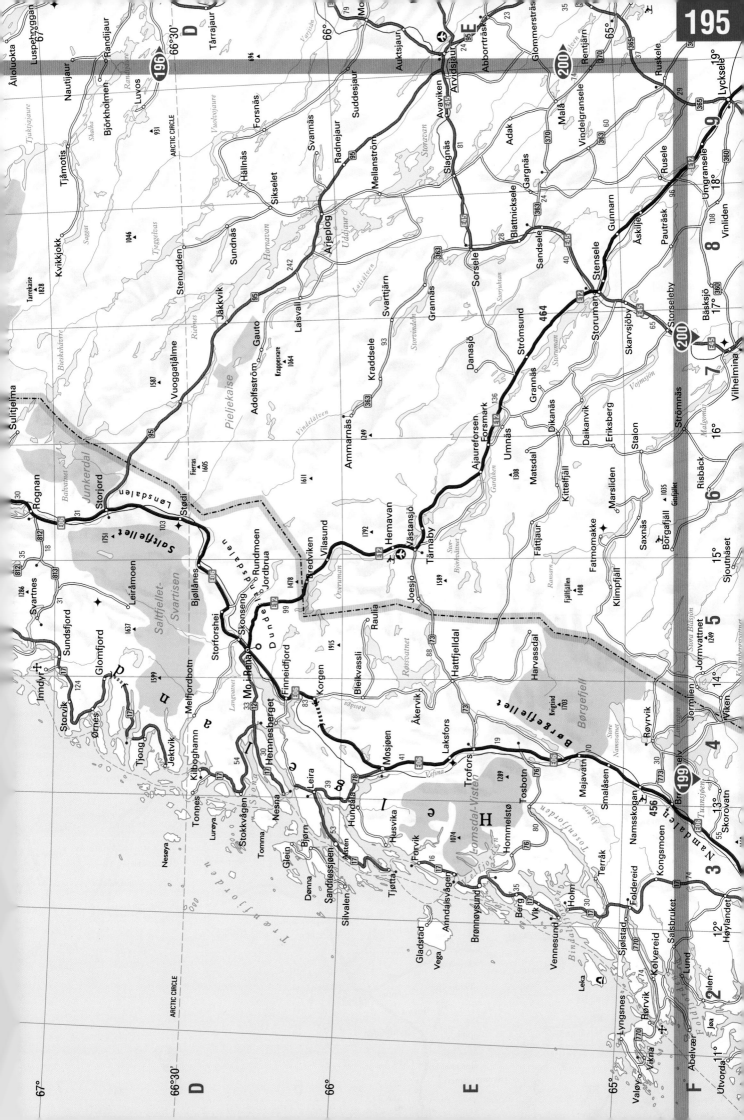

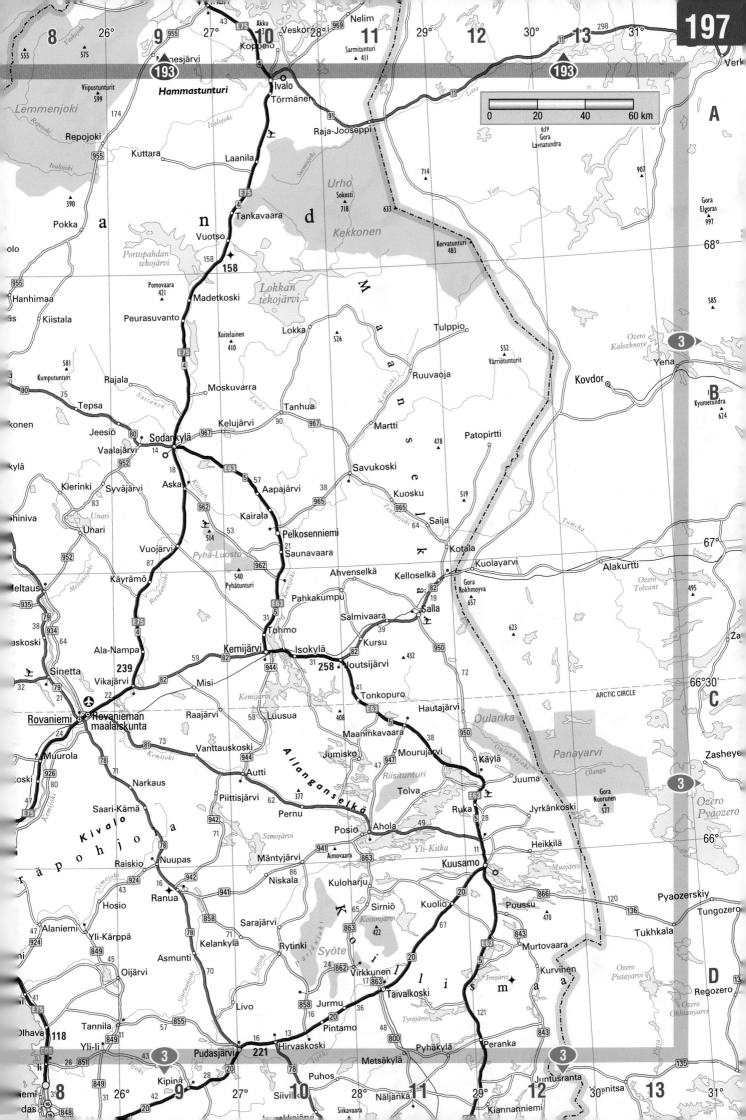

NORSKEHAVET

NORWEGIAN SEA

Frohavet

Harsv
Ratvi
Lysøysund
Nes   Bo
Uthaug   Brekst
Frøya   Sistranda
Titran   Agdenes   Å
Hitra   Fillan
Veidholmen   Hitra
                    Sandstad
Dyrnes   Forsnes   Lensvik
        Smøla   Heim   Snillfjord
    Edøy
                    Aure   Kyrksæterøra
    Gullstein
        Tustna   Aresvika   Vinje   80
                    E39   65   10
Kristiansund
Bremsnes   Halsa   Hennset   Storås   Løkk
    64   19   70   85   25   Åsskard   Mo   Meld
Hustad   13   Tingvoll   63   65   Rindal   49
Bud   69   Averøya   70   16   Surnadalsøra   700
Eide   E39   Kvenna   Rennebu
Elnesvågen   30   Batnfjordsøra   40   Todal   Troll-
Gossa   62   70   Eidsvåg   1667   heimen
    12   Hjelset   62   Storli   18
Molde   16   Sunndalsøra
Otterøya   Åfarnes   Eresfjord   Driva   70   Lønset   65   70   Oppd
Vestnes   Isfjorden   18   1880   Gjøra
Brattvåg   30   64   Andalsnes
Søvik   Tomra   45   Voll   850   155   Eikesdal   Dovrefjell-   46   Drivst
Ålesund   14   E39   Sjøholt   17   63   Verma   100   Sunndalsfjella   E06
Spjelkavik   26   Tresfjord   55   2286   Dovrefjell
Hareid   Sykkylven   Stordal   63   Lesjaskog   1026   Hjerkinn
Ulsteinvik   Festøy   60   Stranda   26   Sylte   Pyttegga   Lora   28   29
    E39   42   26   1999   624   E136   Fokstua   Dovre   Fo
Larsnes   Eidsdal   60   56   Tafjord   Nyseter   Dombås
Leikanger   Volda   34   Hellesylt   63   Reinheimen   Dovre   E06
Selje   37   Åheim   651   Storfjorden   40   60   Djupvasshytta   258   1139   Grotli   15   Pollfoss   73   Bismo   Vågåmo   37   155   Otta   Ro
Raudeberg   61   Totland   Hornindal   46   Videseter   Breheimen   Lom   22   Lalm   16
Måløy   15   Stårheim   34   Stryn   15   Sotaseter   2068   Randsverk   29   Sjoa
Isane   12   Nordfjordeid   Innvik   Lodalskåpa   Bøverdal   Glittertind   17   Kva
Kalvåg   614   Sandane   Byrkjelo   50   Olden   2083   Jostedalsbreen   2470   47   51   E06
Florø   16   Eikefjord   615   59   Hyen   16   46   Nørdstedalsseter   1140   2469   Skåbu
Stavang   12   Skei   19   Jostedal   119   Leirvassbu   99
Stongfjorden   E39   Naustd   Moskog   33   Skjolden   Jotunheimen   55   Giendesheim   Dalsete

City plans • Plans de villes
Stadtpläne • Piante di città

Motorway	Autoroute	Autobahn	Autostrada
Major through route	Route principale majeur	Hauptstrecke	Strada di grande communicazione
Through route	Route principale	Schnellstrasse	Strada d'importanza regionale
Secondary road	Route secondaire	Nebenstrasse	Strada d'interesse locale
Dual carriageway	Chaussées séparées	Zweispurig Schnellstrasse	Strada a carreggiate doppie
Other road	Autre route		
Tunnel	Tunnel	Nebenstrecke	Altra strada
Limited access / pedestrian road	Rue réglementée / rue piétonne	Tunnel	Galleria stradale
One-way street	Sens unique	Beschränkter Zugang/ Fussgängerzone	Strada pedonale / a accesso limitato
Parking	Parc de stationnement	Einbahnstrasse	Senso unico
Motorway number	Numéro d'autoroute	Parkplatz	Parcheggio
National road number	Numéro de route nationale	Autobahnnummer	Numero di autostrada
European road number	Numéro de route européenne	Nationalstrassen-nummer	Numero di strada nazionale
Destination	Destination	Europäische Strassennummer	Numero di strada europea
Car ferry	Bac passant les autos	Ziel	Destinazione
Railway	Chemin de fer	Autofähre	Traghetto automobili
Rail/bus station	Gare / gare routière	Eisenbahn	Ferrovia
Underground, metro station	Station de métro	Bahnhof / Busstation	Stazione ferrovia / pullman
Cable car	Téléférique	U-Bahnstation	Metropolitano
Abbey, cathedral	Abbaye, cathédrale	Drahtseilbahn	Funivia
Church of interest	Église intéressante	Abtei, Kloster, Kathedrale	Abbazia, duomo
Synagogue	Synagogue	Interessante Kirche	Chiesa da vedere
Hospital	Hôpital	Synagoge	Sinagoga
Police station	Police	Krankenhaus	Ospedale
Post office	Bureau de poste	Polizeiwache	Polizia
Tourist information	Office de tourisme	Postamt	Ufficio postale
Place of interest	Autre curiosité	Informationsbüro	Ufficio informazioni turistiche
		Sonstige Sehenswürdigkeit	Luogo da vedere

Approach maps • Agglomérations
Carte régionale • Regionalkarte

Toll motorway – with motorway number	Autoroute à péage – avec numéro d'autoroute	Gebührenpflichtige Autobahn – mit Autobahnnummer	Autostrada a pedaggio – con numero
Toll-free motorway – with European road number	Autoroute – avec numéro de route européenne	Gebührenfreie Autobahn – Europäische Strassennummer	Autostrada – con numero di strada europea
Pre-pay motorway – vignette required	Autoroute – 'vignette'	Autobahn – 'vignette'	Autostrada – 'vignette'
Motorway services	Aire de service	Autobahnservice	Area di servizio autostradale
Motorway junction full access, restricted access	Échangeur d'autoroute – accès libre, accès réglementé	Autobahnkreuz – voller/begrenzter Zugang	Raccordi autostradali – completo/parziali
Under construction	En construction	Im Bau	In construzione
Tunnel	Tunnel	Tunnel	Galleria stradale
Major route dual carriageway single carriageway	Route principale chaussées séparées chausée sans séparation	Hauptstrecke – zweispurige Schnellstrasse	Strada di grande communicazione carreggiata doppia carreggiata unica
Secondary route dual carriageway single carriageway	Route secondaire chaussées séparées chausée sans séparation	Nebenstrasse – zweispurige Schnellstrasse	Strada d'interesse locale carreggiata doppia carreggiata unica
Other road	Autre route	Nebenstrecke	Altra strada
Car ferry	Bac passant les autos	Autofähre	Traghetto automobili
Destination	Destination	Ziel	Destinazione
Railway	Chemin de fer	Eisenbahn	Ferrovia
Railway station	Gare	Hauptbahnhof	Stazione ferrovia
Height – in metres	Altitude – en mètres	Höhe – über dem Meeresspiegel	Altezza in metri
Airport	Aéroport principal	Flughafen	Aeroporto
Airfield	Autre aéroport	Flugplatz	Aerodromo/ campo d'aviazione
City plan coverage area	Région de plan de ville	Vom Stadtplan abgedecktes Gebiet	Area della pianta della città

Alicante

0 km 0.5

Antwerpen Antwerp

0 km 1

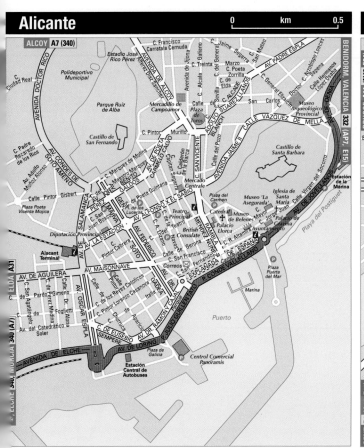

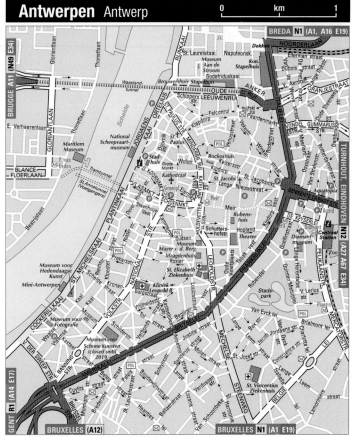

Amsterdam

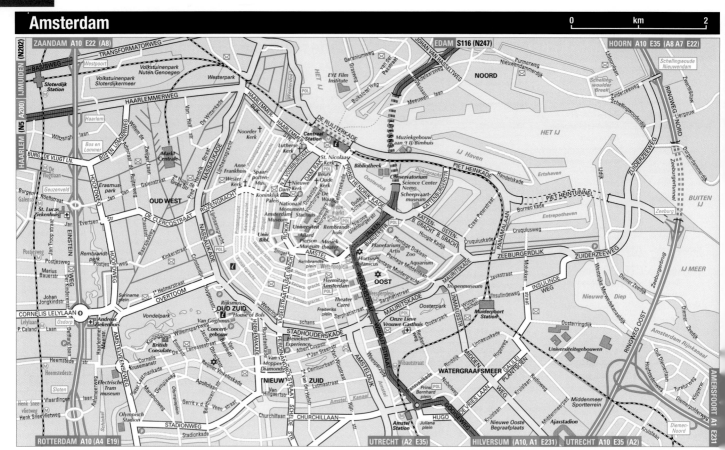

Amsterdam

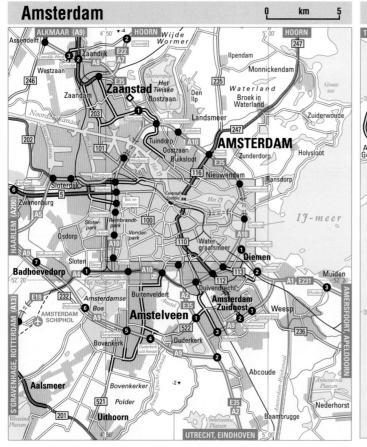

Athina Athens

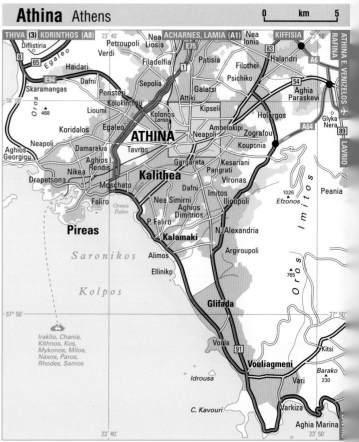

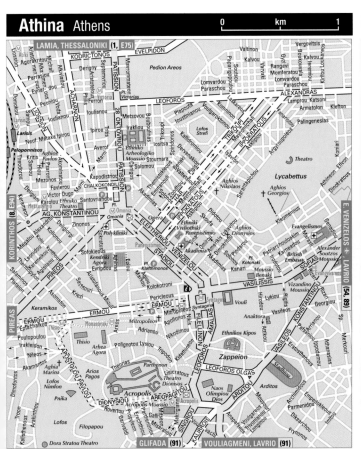

Athina Athens

0 km 1

Basel

0 km 0.5

Barcelona

0 km 5

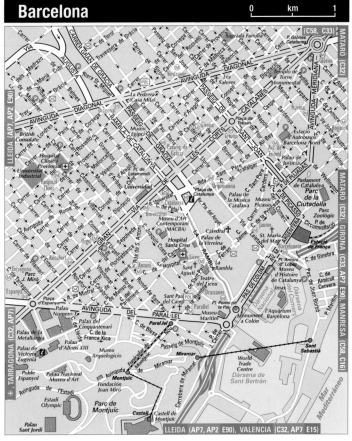

Barcelona

0 km 1

Berlin

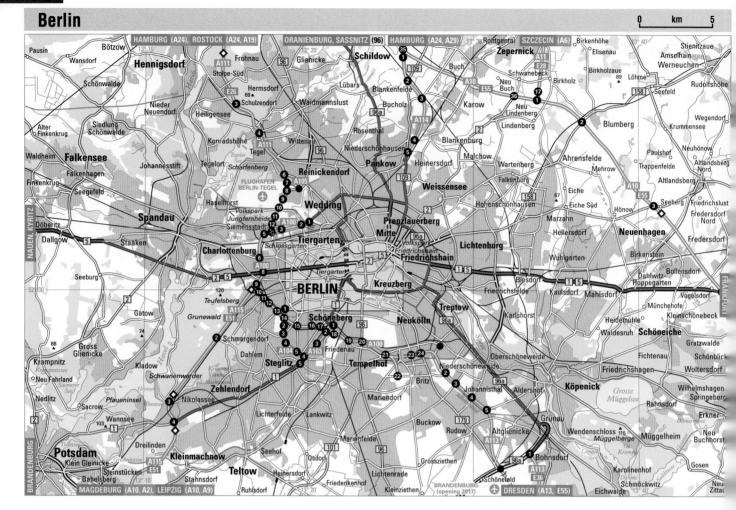

Berlin

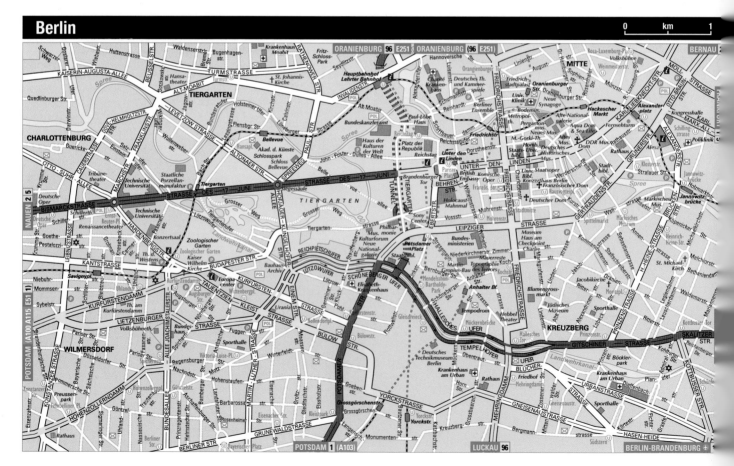

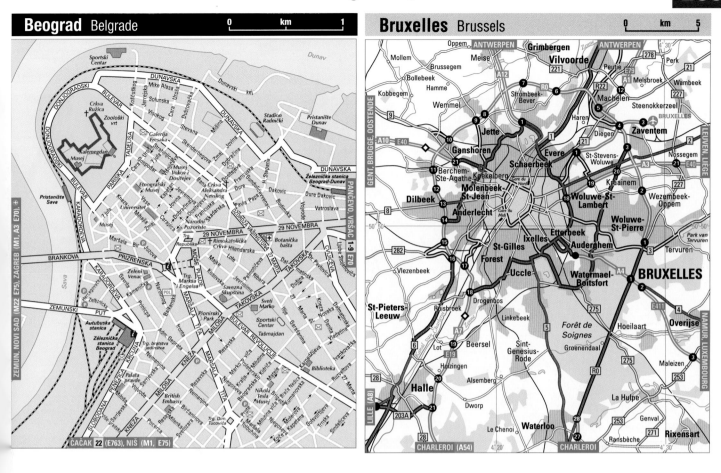

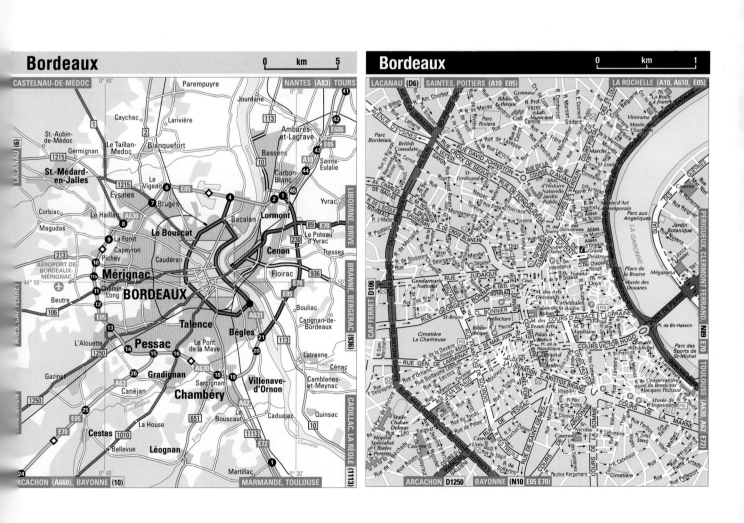

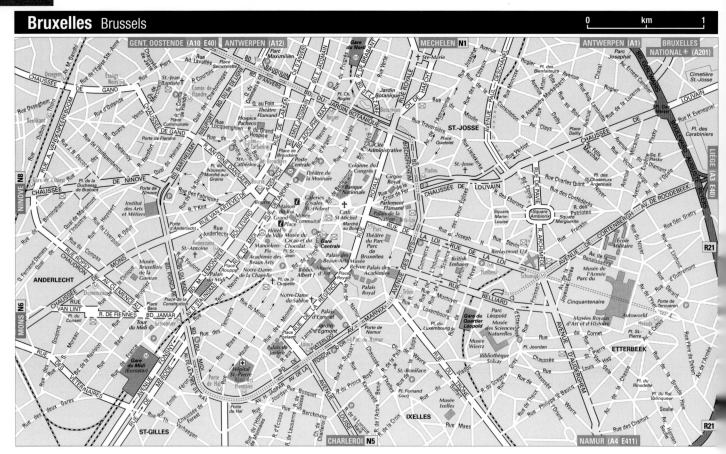

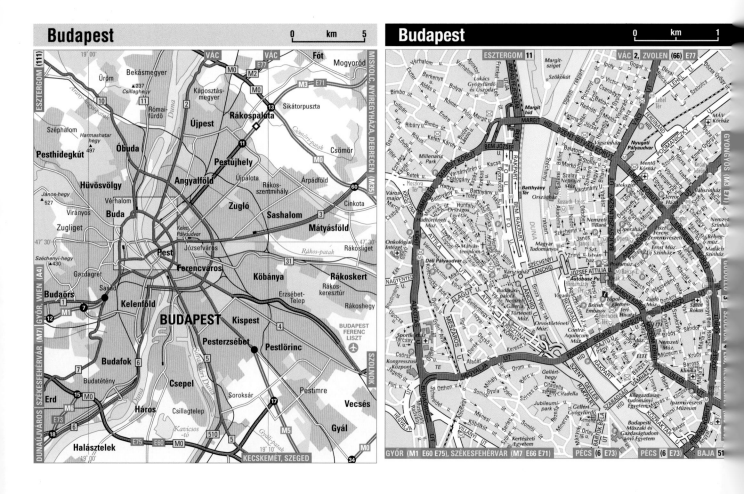

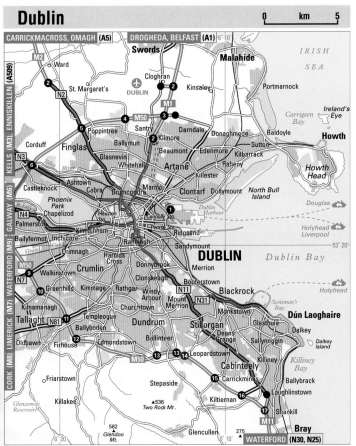

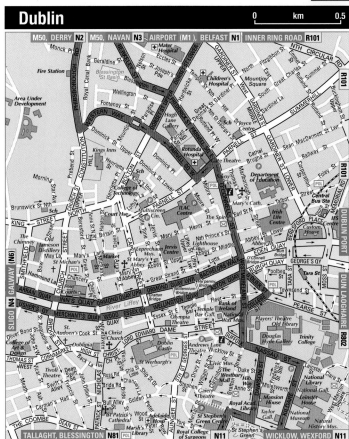

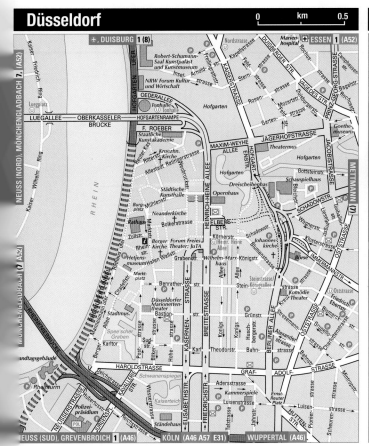

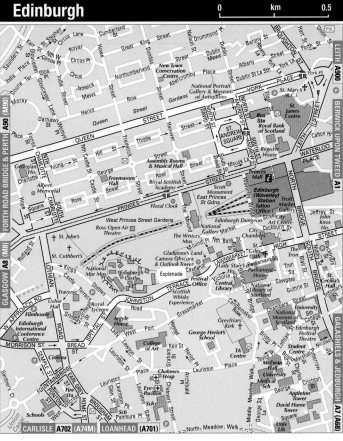

For **Cologne** see page 212

For **Copenhagen** see page 212

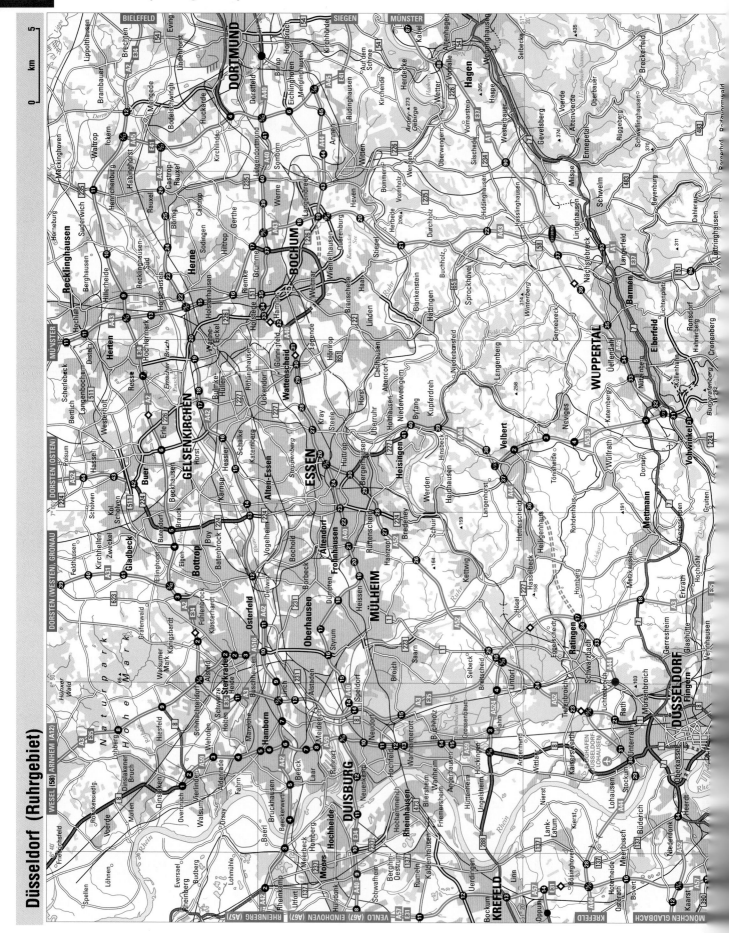

Firenze Florence

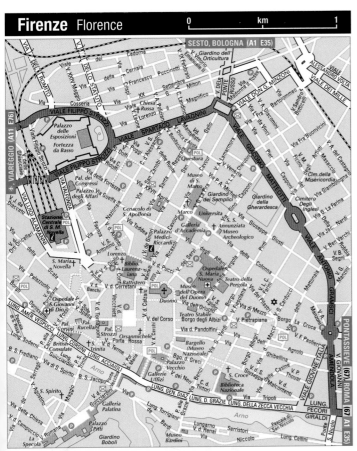

Frankfurt

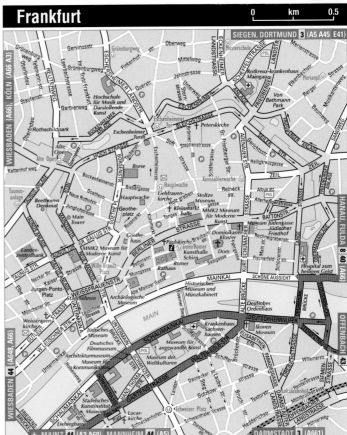

Genève Geneva

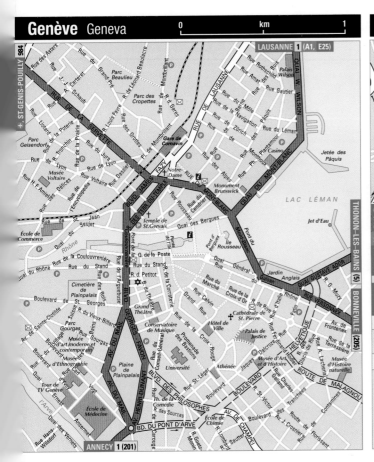

Génova Genoa

Granada

Göteborg Gothenburg

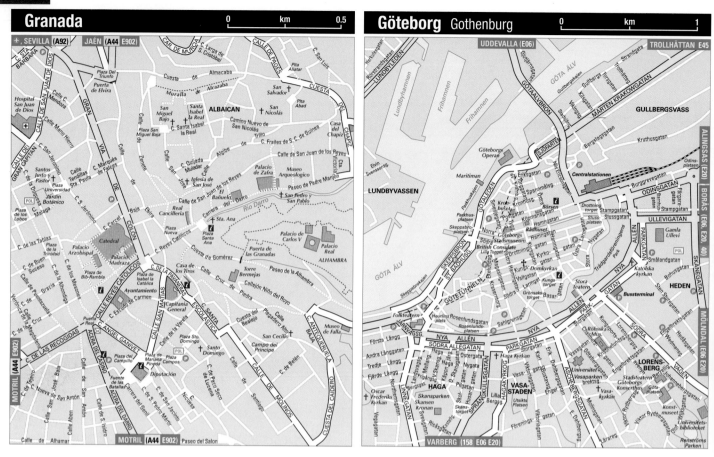

Hamburg

Hamburg

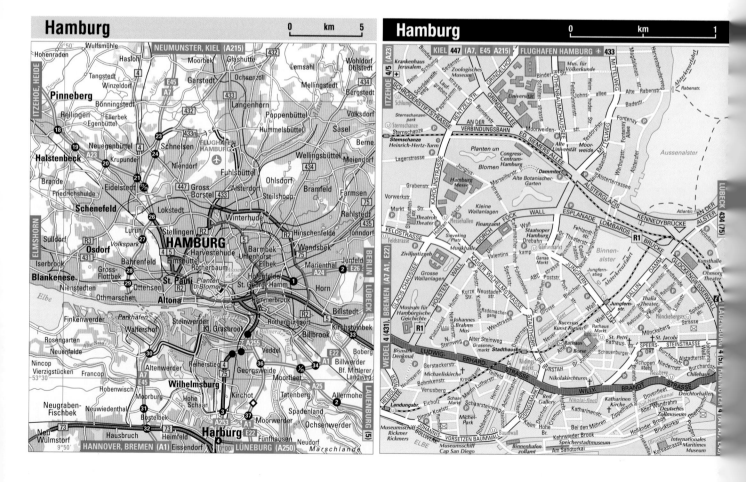

Helsinki

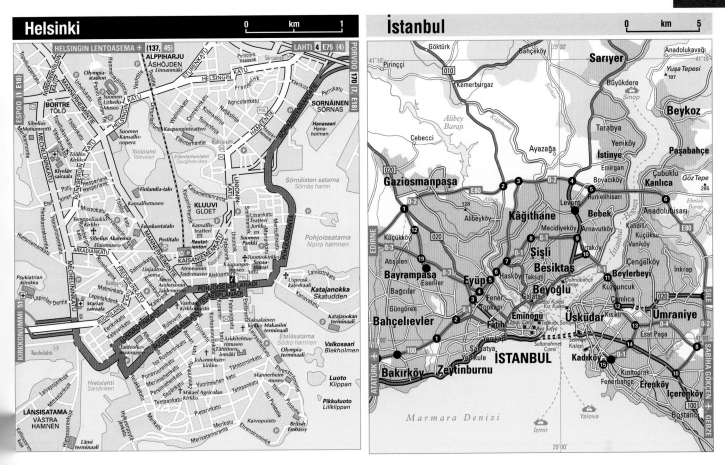

İstanbul

Helsinki

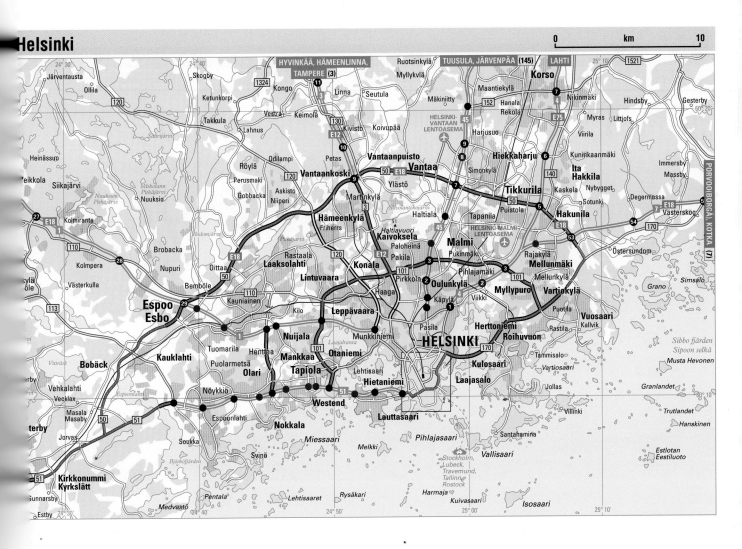

København Copenhagen

Köln Cologne

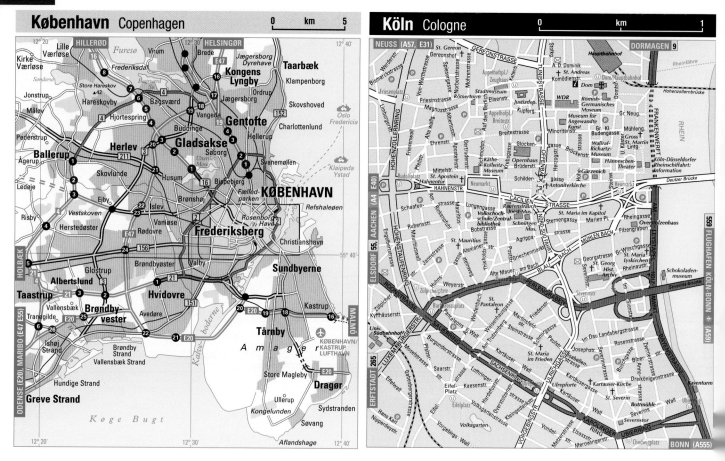

København Copenhagen

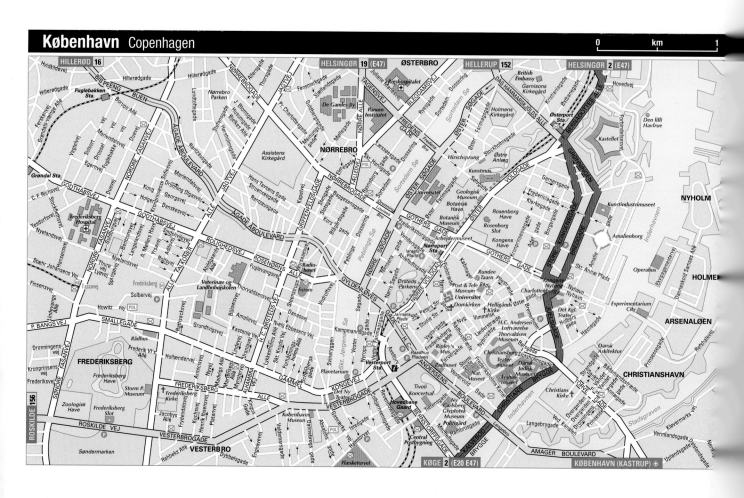

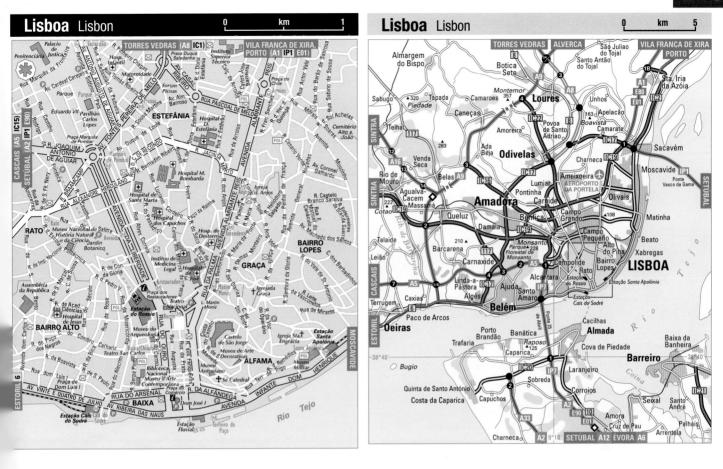

Lisboa Lisbon

London

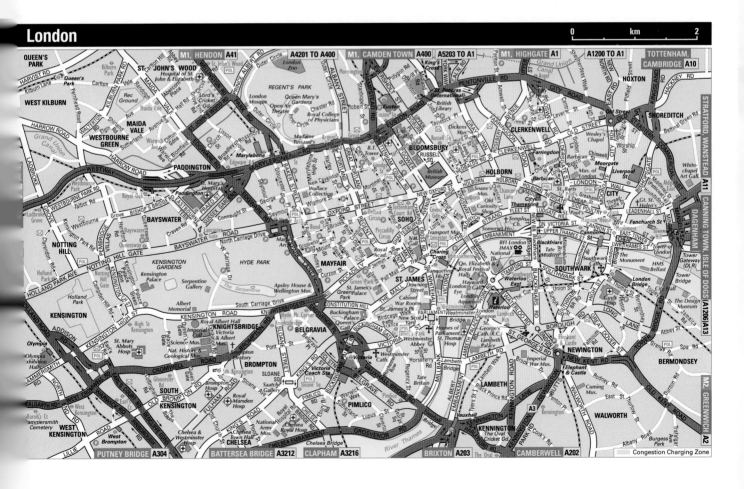

0   km   10

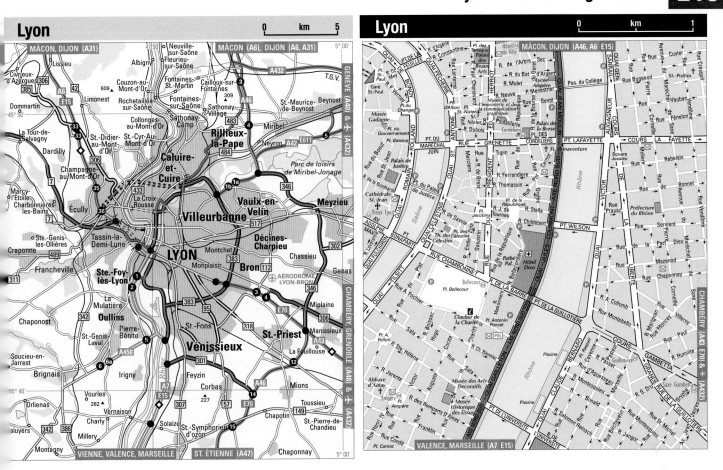

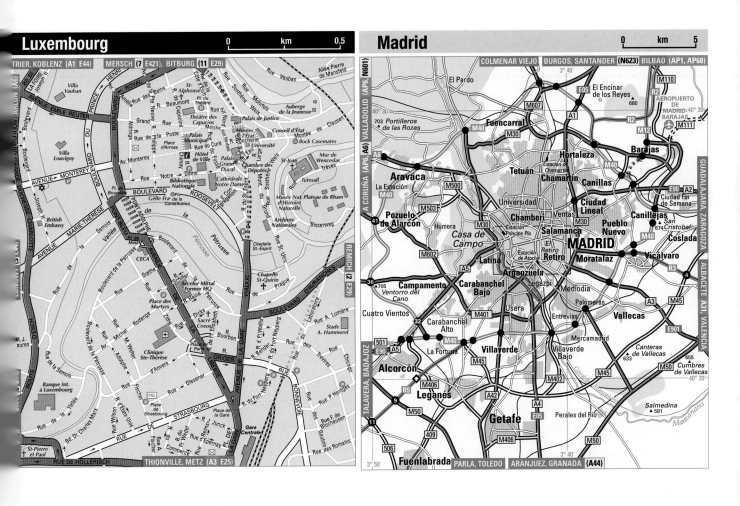

Madrid

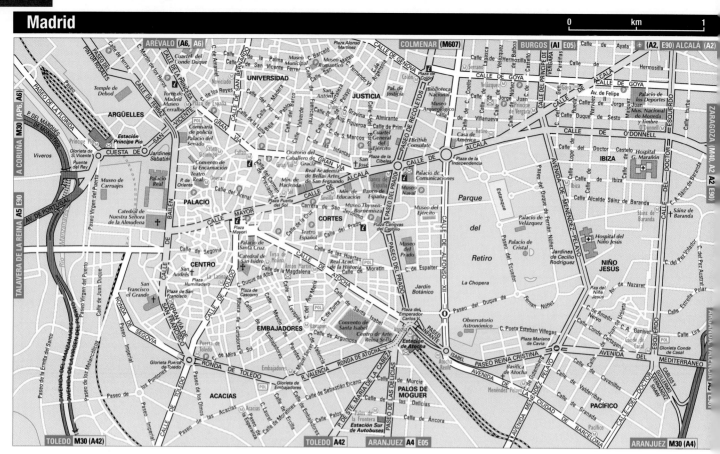

Málaga

Marseille / Marseilles

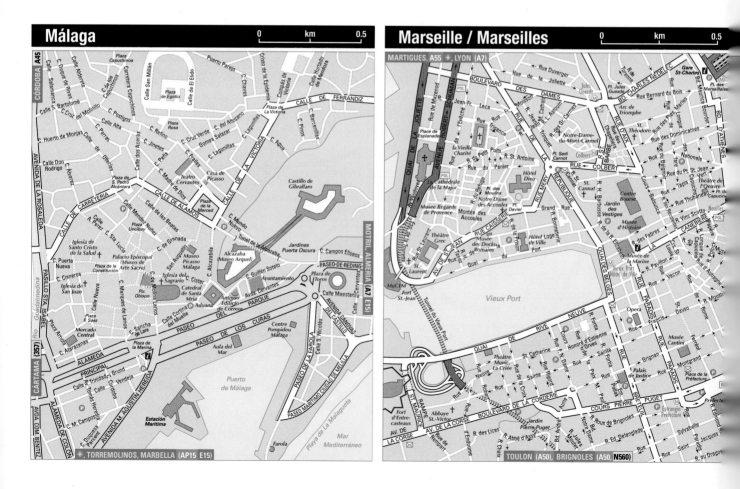

Milano Milan

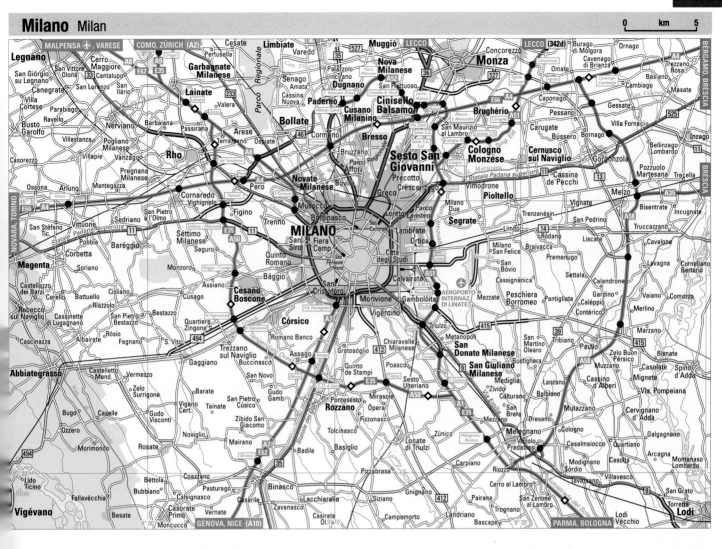

Milano Milan

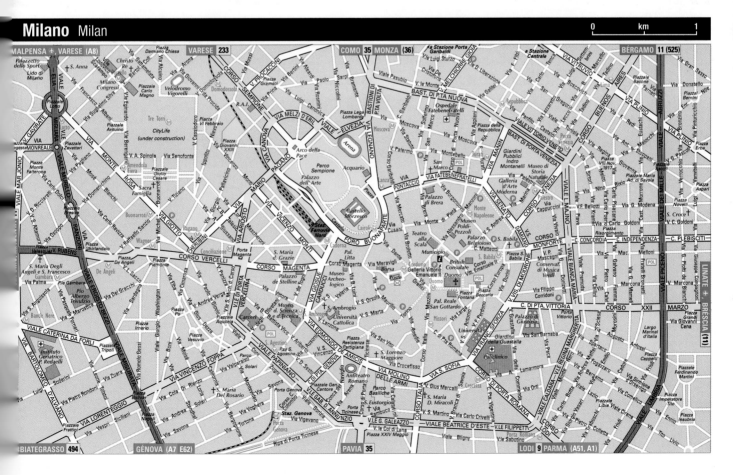

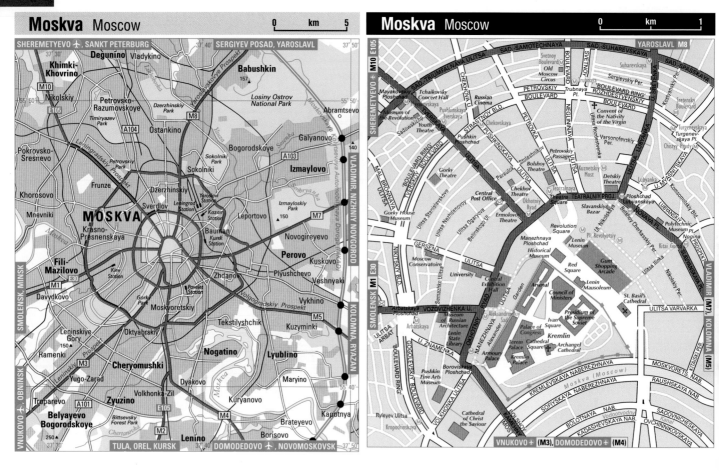

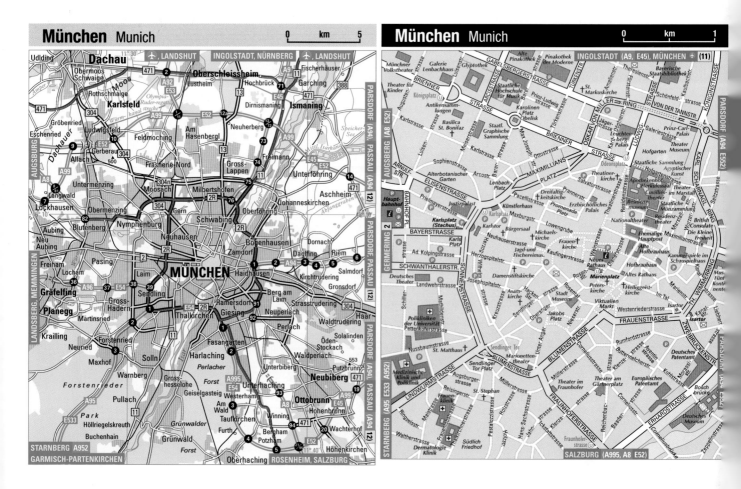

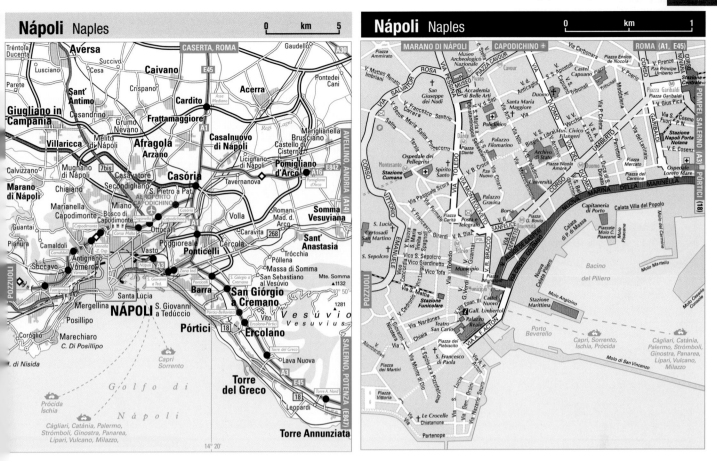

Nápoli Naples

BERGEN · CASERTA, ROMA · AVELLINO, ANDRIA (A14) · SALERNO POTENZA (E847)

Trentola Ducenta, Aversa, Lusciano, Succivo, Caivano, Gaudello, Parete, Cesa, Crispano, Acerra, Sant' Antimo, Cardito, Frattamaggiore, Casandrino, Frattaminore, Casalnuovo di Nápoli, Giugliano in Campania, Grumo Nevano, Afragola, Arzano, Licignano di Nápoli, Pomigliano d'Arco, Villaricca, Melito di Nápoli, Casoria, Tavernanova, Calvizzano, Mughano di Nápoli, Casavatore, Casandrino, S. Pietro a Pat., Marano di Nápoli, Chiaiano, Secondigliano, Miano, Volla, Romani Mad. d. Arco, Somma Vesuviana, Marianella, Capodimonte, Bosco di Capodimonte, Ottocalli, Cércola, Caravita, Sant' Anastasia, Guantai, Pianura, Camaldoli, Antignano, Vomero, Vasto, Poggioreale, Ponticelli, Trócchia, Póllena, Massa di Somma, San Sebastiano al Vesúvio, Soccavo, Fuorigrotta, Barra, San Giórgio a Cremano, Mte. Somma 1132, Mergellina, Santa Lucia, NÁPOLI, S. Giovanni a Tedúccio, Pórtici, Ercolano, Vesúvio Vesuvius 1281, Posillipo, Marechiaro, C. Di Posillipo, Coróglio, M. di Nísida, Capri Sorrento, Torre del Greco, Lava Nuova, Prócida Ischia, Golfo di Nápoli, Cágliari, Catánia, Palermo, Strómboli, Ginostra, Panarea, Lípari, Vulcano, Milazzo, Torre del Greco, Leopárdi, Torre Annunziata

Nápoli Naples

MARANO DI NÁPOLI · CAPODICHINO · ROMA (A1, E45) · POMPEI SALERNO (A3) · PÓRTICI (18)

Museo Archeologico Nazionale, Piazza Ammirato, Piazza Cavour, Piazza Enrico de Nicola, Piazza Principe Umberto, Stazione Centrale, Accademia di Belle Arti, San Giuseppe dei Nudi, Santa Maria Maggiore, Castel Capuano, Tribunali, Piazza Garibaldi, DUOMO, Policlinico, Palazzo Dante, Palazzo Filomarino, Mus. Civico Filangeri, Archivio di Stato, Piazza Mercato, Ospedale dei Pellegrini, Spirito Santo, V. B. Croce, Universitá, Piazza d. Carmine, Ospedale Loreto Mare, Stazione Cumana, Palazzo Gravina, Borsa, Piazza G. Bovio, Capitaneria di Porto, Calata Villa del Popolo, Municipio, Calata di P. di Massa, Piazzale Molo C. Pisacane, Certosa di San Martino, S. Lucia, Piazza Municipio, Nuova Calata Piliero, Castel Nuovo, Molo Martello, Gall. Umberto I, Stazione Funicolare, Teatro San Carlo, Palazzo Reale, Stazione Marittima, Molo Angioino, Bacino del Piliero, Chiaia, Piazza del Plebiscito, Porto Beverello, Piazza dei Martiri, S. Francesco di Paola, Molo di San Vincenzo, Molo Cesaro Console, Piazza Vittoria, Le Crocelle, Chiatamone, Partenope, Piazza Amedeo, Cágliari, Catánia, Palermo, Strómboli, Ginostra, Panarea, Lípari, Vulcano, Milazzo, Capri, Sorrento, Ischia, Prócida

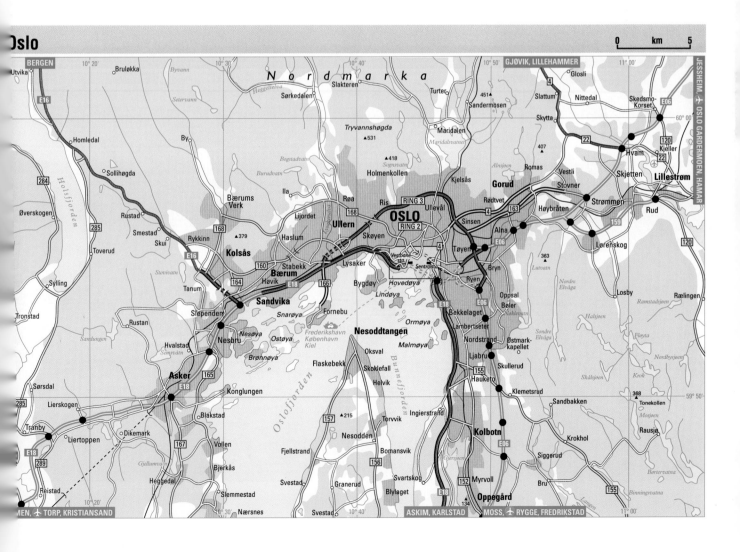

Oslo

BERGEN · GJØVIK, LILLEHAMMER · JESSHEIM, OSLO GARDERMOEN, HAMAR

Utvika, Bruløkka, Byvann, Nordmarka, Slakteren, Glosli, Homledal, Sørkedalen, Sandermosen, Nittedal, Slattum, Skedsmo-Korset, By, Maridalen, Turter, Skytta, Hvam, Kjeller, Sollihøgda, Tryvannshøgda, Holmenkollen, Skjetten, Lillestrøm, Øverskogen, Rustad, Bærums Verk, Ila, Røa, Ris, Kjelsås, Rødtvet, Gorud, Vestli, Stovner, Strømmen, Rud, Smestad, Lijordet, Ullevål, RING 3, Sinsen, Høybråten, Lørénskog, Toverud, Skui, Rykkinn, Haslum, Ullern, Skøyen, OSLO, RING 2, Alna, Losby, Sylling, Kolsås, Stabekk, Lysaker, Vestbane sta., Tøyen, Bryn, Ryen, Oppsal, Rælingen, Tanum, Høvik, Bærum, Bygdøy, Hovedøya, Sentralst., Bøler, Østmark-kapellet, Sandvika, Slependen, Fornebu, Lindøya, Bekkelaget, Lambertseter, Nesøya, Snarøya, Frederikshavn København Kiel, Ormøya, Nesoddtangen, Nordstrand, Nesbru, Ostøya, Brønnøya, Flaskebekk, Malmøya, Ljabru, Skullerud, Hvalstad, Konglungen, Oksval, Skoklefall, Helvik, Hauketo, Klemetsrud, Sandbakken, Asker, Blåkstad, Torvvik, Ingierstrand, Sørsdal, Lierskogen, Nesodden, Bomansvik, Kolbotn, Tránby, Liertoppen, Vollen, Fjellstrand, Svartskog, Krokhol, Siggerud, Reistad, Heggedal, Bjerkås, Slemmestad, Granerud, Blylaget, Myrvoll, Bru, Dikemark, Oppegård, Svelvik, Nærnes, Svestad, TORP, KRISTIANSAND, ASKIM, KARLSTAD, MOSS, RYGGE, FREDRIKSTAD

Oslo

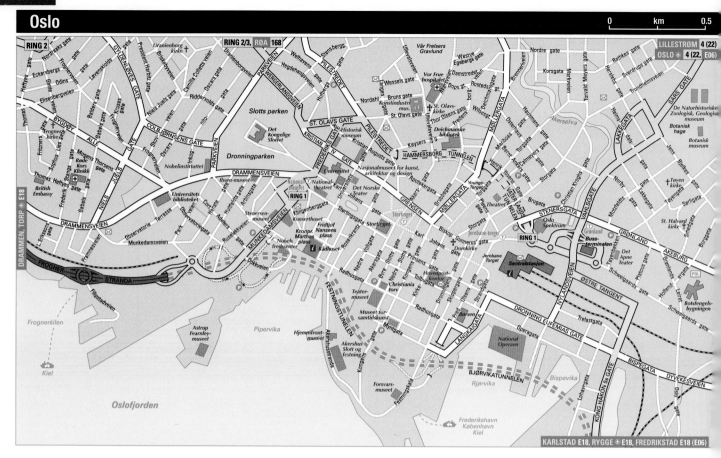

Paris

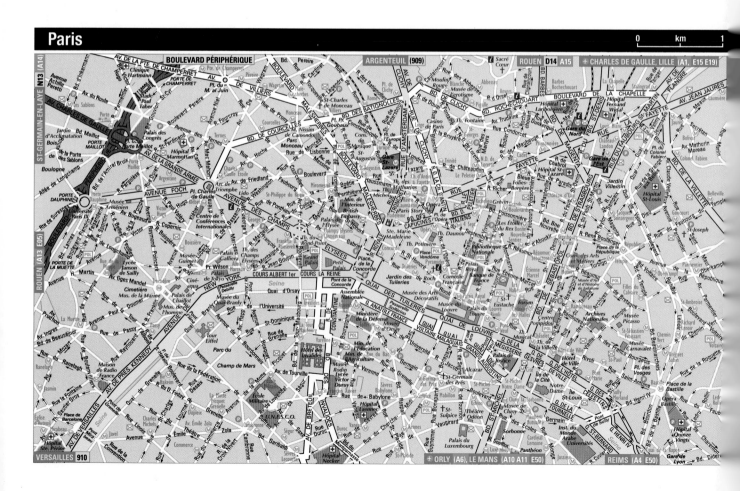

Praha Prague

0 km 5

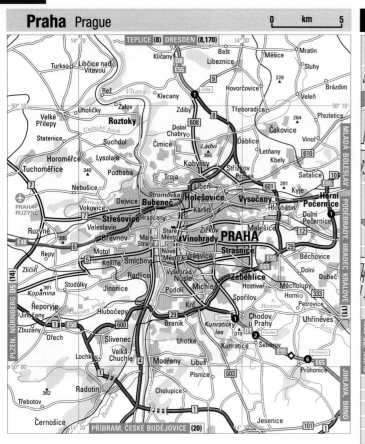

Praha Prague

0 km 1

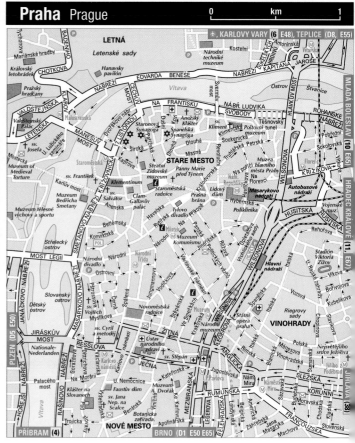

Rotterdam

0 km 1

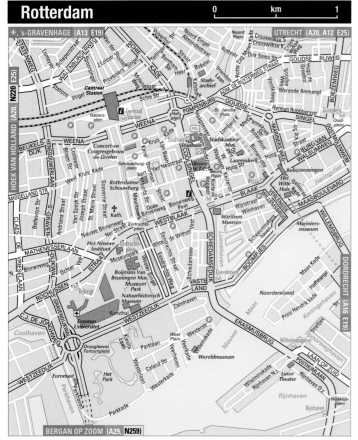

Sankt-Peterburg St. Petersburg

0 km 5

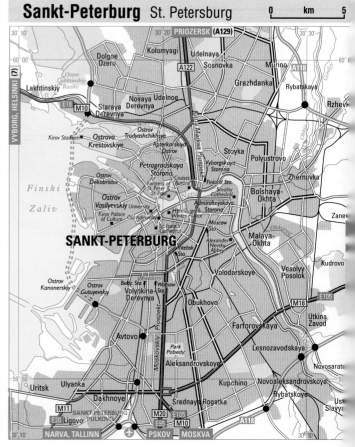

Roma Rome

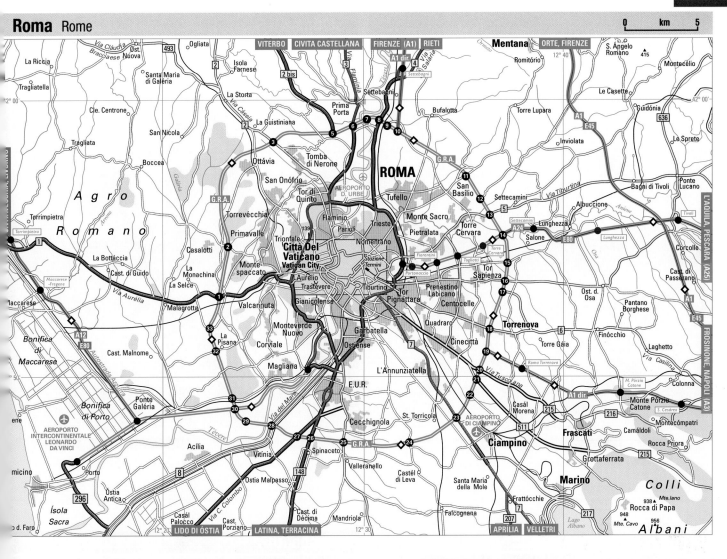

Roma Rome

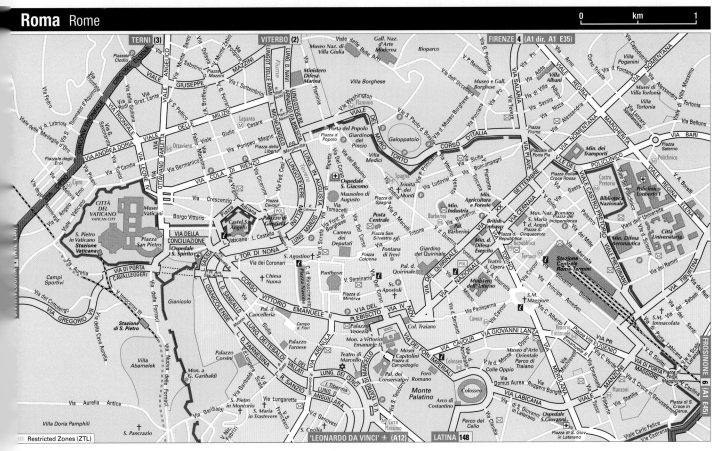

Sevilla Seville

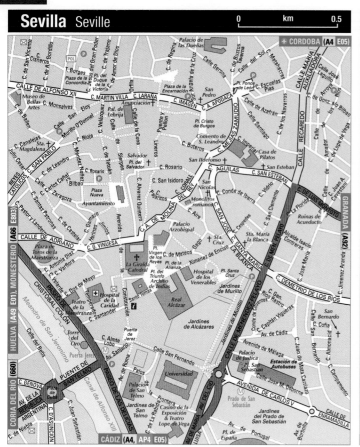

Stuttgart

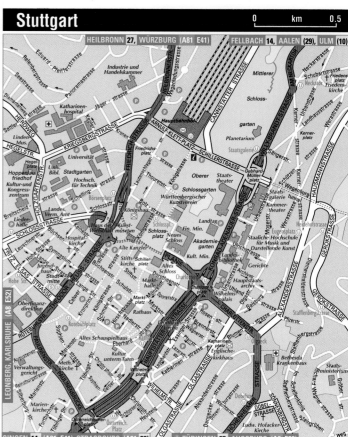

Strasbourg

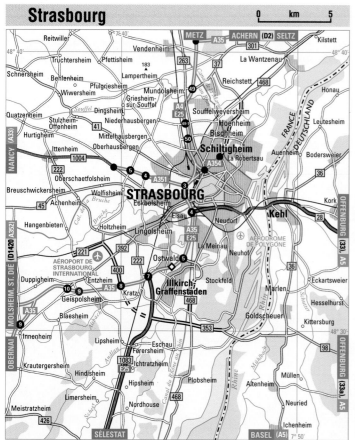

Strasbourg

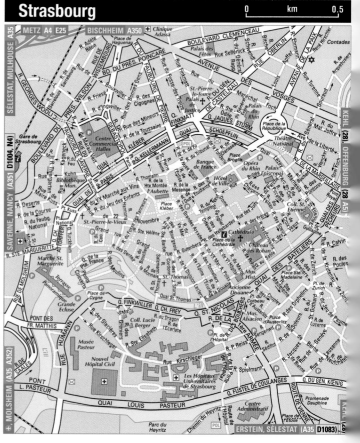

Stockholm

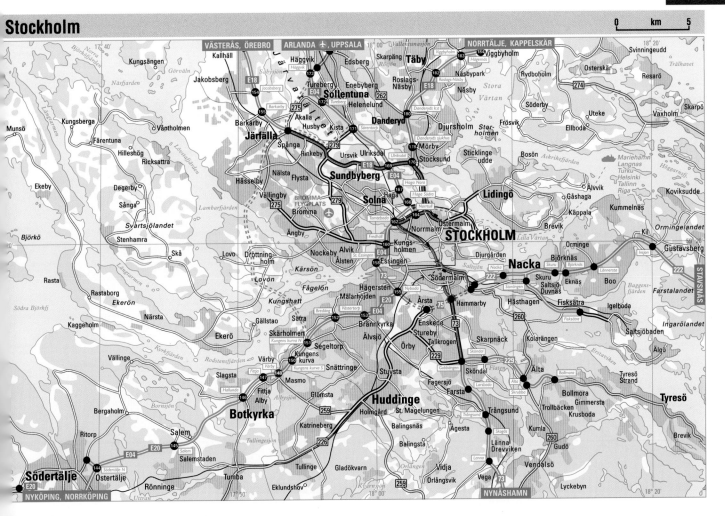

Stockholm

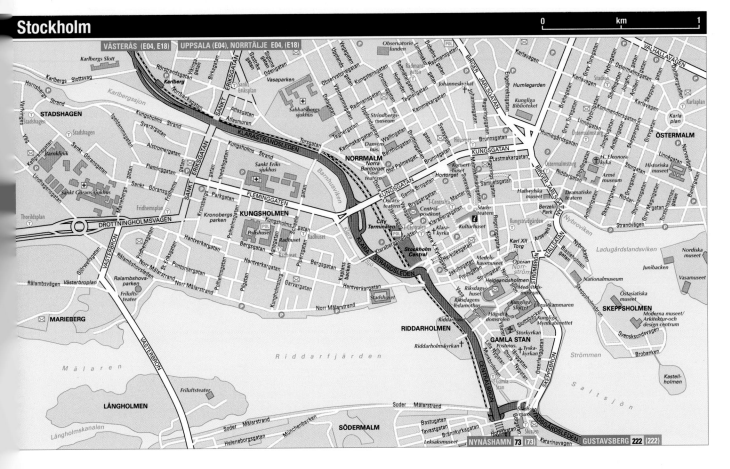

Torino Turin

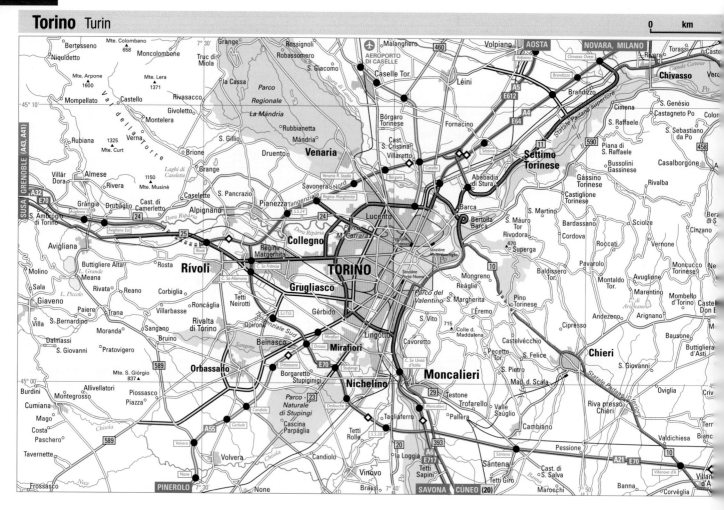

Venézia Venice

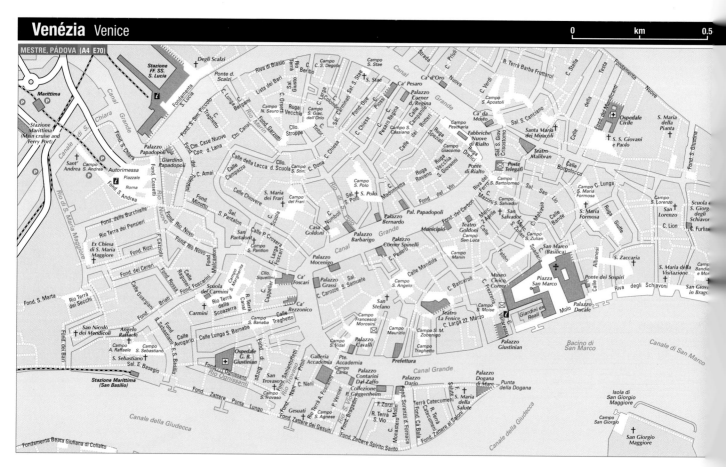

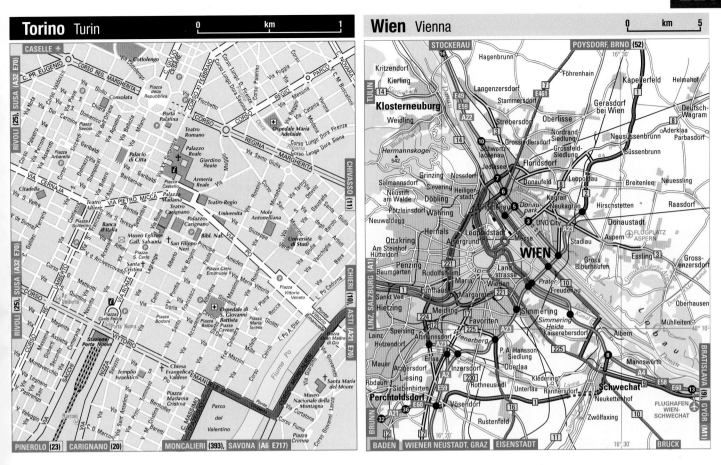

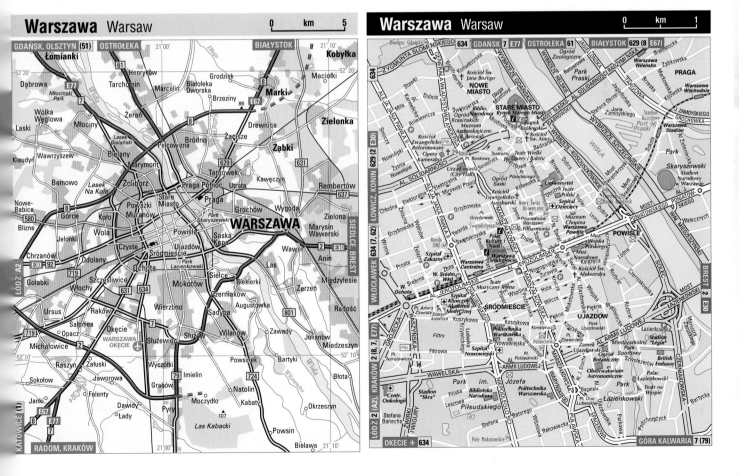

Wien Vienna

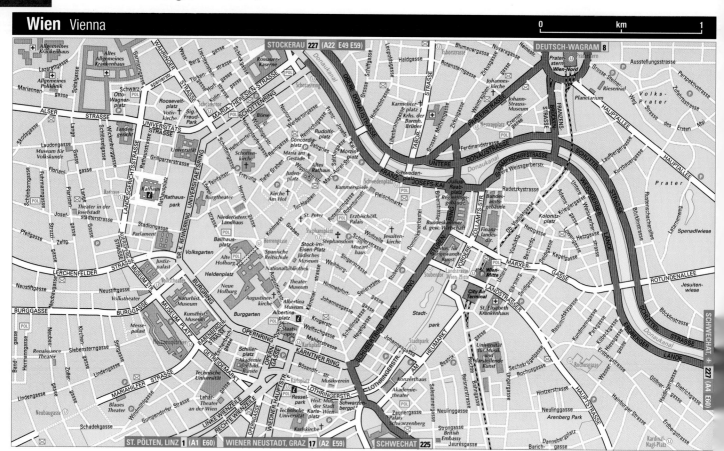

Zagreb

Zürich

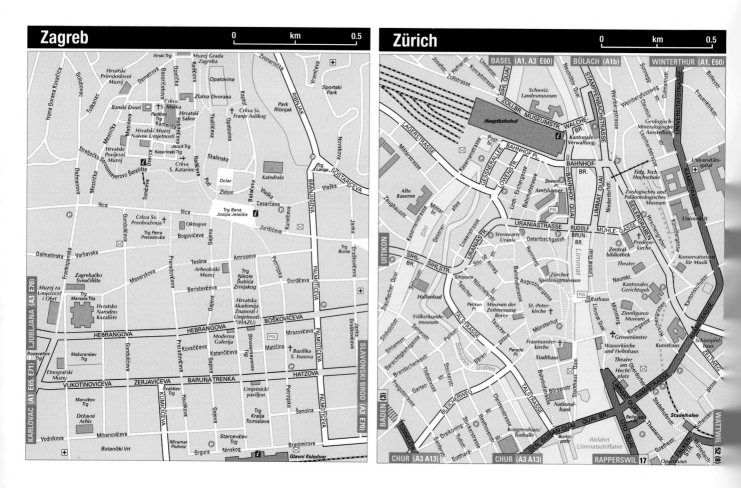

Index

Code	English	Français	Deutsch	Italiano
A	Austria	Autriche	Österreich	Austria
AL	Albania	Albanie	Albanien	Albania
AND	Andorra	Andorre	Andorra	Andorra
B	Belgium	Belgique	Belgien	Belgio
BG	Bulgaria	Bulgarie	Bulgarien	Bulgaria
BIH	Bosnia-Herzegovin	Bosnie-Herzegovine	Bosnien-Herzegowina	Bosnia-Herzogovina
BY	Belarus	Belarus	Weissrussland	Bielorussia
CH	Switzerland	Suisse	Schweiz	Svizzera
CY	Cyprus	Chypre	Zypern	Cipro
CZ	Czechia	République Tchèque	Tschechische Republik	Repubblica Ceca
D	Germany	Allemagne	Deutschland	Germania
DK	Denmark	Danemark	Dänemark	Danimarca
E	Spain	Espagne	Spanien	Spagna
EST	Estonia	Estonie	Estland	Estonia
F	France	France	Frankreich	Francia
FIN	Finland	Finlande	Finnland	Finlandia
FL	Liechtenstein	Liechtenstein	Liechtenstein	Liechtenstein
FO	Faeroe Islands	Îles Féroé	Färöer-Inseln	Isole Faroe
GB	United Kingdom	Royaume Uni	Grossbritannien und Nordirland	Regno Unito
GBZ	Gibraltar	Gibraltar	Gibraltar	Gibilterra
GR	Greece	Grèce	Greichenland	Grecia
H	Hungary	Hongrie	Ungarn	Ungheria
HR	Croatia	Croatie	Kroatien	Croazia
I	Italy	Italie	Italien	Italia
IRL	Ireland	Irlande	Irland	Irlanda
IS	Iceland	Islande	Island	Islanda
KOS	Kosovo	Kosovo	Kosovo	Kosovo
L	Luxembourg	Luxembourg	Luxemburg	Lussemburgo
LT	Lithuania	Lituanie	Litauen	Lituania
LV	Latvia	Lettonie	Lettland	Lettonia
M	Malta	Malte	Malta	Malta
MC	Monaco	Monaco	Monaco	Monaco
MD	Moldova	Moldavie	Moldawien	Moldavia
MK	Macedonia	Macédoine	Makedonien	Macedonia
MNE	Montenegro	Monténégro	Montenegro	Montenegro
N	Norway	Norvège	Norwegen	Norvegia
NL	Netherlands	Pays-Bas	Niederlande	Paesi Bassi
P	Portugal	Portugal	Portugal	Portogallo
PL	Poland	Pologne	Polen	Polonia
RO	Romania	Roumanie	Rumanien	Romania
RSM	San Marino	Saint-Marin	San Marino	San Marino
RUS	Russia	Russie	Russland	Russia
S	Sweden	Suède	Schweden	Svezia
SK	Slovakia	République Slovaque	Slowak Republik	Repubblica Slovacca
SLO	Slovenia	Slovénie	Slowenien	Slovenia
SRB	Serbia	Serbie	Serbien	Serbia
TR	Turkey	Turquie	Türkei	Turchia
UA	Ukraine	Ukraine	Ukraine	Ucraina

A

Aabenraa DK 64 A2
Aabybro DK 58 A2
Aach D 107 B4
Aachen D 80 B2
Aalborg DK 58 A2
Aalen D 94 C2
Aalestrup DK 58 B2
Aalsmeer NL 70 B1
Aalst B 79 B4
Aalten NL 71 C3
Aalter B 79 A3
Äänekoski FIN 8 A4
Aapajärvi FIN . . .197 B10
Ağapınar TR 187 C5
Aarau CH 106 B3
Aarberg CH 106 B2
Aarburg CH 106 B2
Aardenburg NL 79 A3
Aars DK 58 B2
Aarschot B 79 B4
Aarup DK 59 C3
Aba H 112 B2
Abádanes E 152 B1
Abades E 151 B3
Abadin E 141 A3
Abádszalók H 113 B4
Abaliget H 125 A4
Abana TR 23 A8
A Baña E 140 B2
Abanilla E 165 A3
Abano Terme I 121 B4
Abarán E 165 A3
Abasár H 113 B4
Abbadia San Salvatore
I 135 C4
Abbaue D 74 A2
Abbehausen D 72 A1
Abbekäs S 66 A2
Abbeville F 90 A1
Abbey IRL 28 A3
Abbeydorney IRL . . .29 B2
Abbeyfeale IRL 29 B2
Abbeyleix IRL 30 B1
Abbey Town GB 36 B3
Abbiategrasso I . . .120 B1
Abborrträsk S 196 D2
Abbots Bromley
GB 40 C2
Abbotsbury GB 43 B4
Abda H 111 B4
Abejar E 143 C4
Abela P 160 B1
Abelvær N 199 A8
Abenberg D 94 B2
Abenójar E 157 B3
Abensberg D 95 C3
Aberaeron GB 39 B2
Abercarn GB 39 C3
Aberchirder GB 33 D4
Aberdare GB 39 C3
Aberdaron GB 38 B2
Aberdeen GB 33 D4
Aberdulais GB 39 C3
Aberdyfi GB 39 B2
Aberfeldy GB 35 B4
Aberffraw GB 38 A2
Aberfoyle GB 34 B3
Abergavenny GB . . .39 C3
Abergele GB 38 A3
Abergynolwyn GB . . .38 B3
Aberporth GB 39 B2
Abersoch GB 38 B2
Abertillery GB 39 C3
Abertura E 156 A2
Aberystwyth GB 39 B2
Abetone I 135 A3
Abfaltersbach A . . .109 C3
Abide
Çanakkale TR . . .186 B1
Kütahya TR 187 D4
Abiego E 145 B3
Abild DK 64 B1
Abingdon-on-Thames
GB 44 B2
Abington GB 36 A3
Abisko S 194 B9
Abiul P 154 B2

Abla E 164 B2
Ablis F 90 C1
A Bola E 140 B3
Abondance F 118 A3
Abony H 113 B4
Aboyne GB 33 D4
Abrantes P 154 B2
Abreiro P 148 A2
Abreschviller F 92 C3
Abrest F 117 A3
Abriès F 119 C3
Abrud RO 17 B5
Absdorf A 97 C3
Abtenau A 109 B4
Abtsgmünd D 94 C1
Abusejo E 149 B3
Åby
Kronoberg S 62 A2
Östergötland S . . .56 B2
Åbyggeby S 51 B4
Åbytorp S 55 A6
A Cañiza E 140 B2
A Capela E 140 A2
Acate I 177 B3
Accadía I 171 B3
Accéglio I 132 A2
Accettura I 172 B2
Acciaroli I 170 C3
Accous F 145 A3
Accrington GB 40 B1
Accúmoli I 169 A3
Acedera E 156 A2
Acered E 152 A2
Acerenza I 172 B1
Acerno I 170 C3
Acerra I 170 C2
Aceuchal E 155 C4
Acharacle GB 34 B2
Acharnes GR 185 A4
Achavanich GB 32 C3
Achene B 79 B5
Achenkirch A 108 B2
Achensee A 108 B2
Achenthal A 108 B2
Achentrias GR 185 E6
Achern D 93 C4
Acheux-en-Amienois
F 90 A2
Achiltibuie GB 32 C1
Achim D 72 A2
Achladokambos
GR 184 B3
Achnasheen GB . . .32 D1
Achnashellach GB . .32 D1
Achosnich GB 34 B1
Aci Castello I 177 B4
Aci Catena I 177 B4
Acilia I 168 B2
Acıpayam TR 189 B4
Acireale I 177 B4
Acle GB 41 C5
A Coruña E 140 A2
Acquacadda I 179 C2
Acqua Doria F 180 B1
Acquanegra sul Chiese
I 121 B3
Acquapendente I . . .168 A1
Acquasanta Terme
I 136 C2
Acquasparta I 168 A2
Acquaviva I 135 B4
Acquaviva delle Fonti
I 171 C4
Acquaviva Picena
I 136 C2
Acquigny F 89 A5
Acqui Terme I 119 C5
Acri I 174 B2
Acs H 112 B2
Acsa H 112 B3
Ácsteszér H 112 B1
Acy-en-Multien F . . .90 B2
Ada SRB 126 B2
Adak S 195 E9
Ådalsbruk N 48 B3
Adamas GR 185 C5
Adamsfjord N 193 B10
Adamuz E 157 B3
Adana TR 23 C8

Ádánd H 112 C2
Adanero E 150 B3
Adare IRL 29 B3
Adaševci SRB 125 B5
Adeanueva de Ebro
E 144 B2
Adelboden CH 106 C2
Adelebsen D 82 A1
Adélfia I 173 A2
Adelmannsfelden
D 94 C2
Adelsheim D 94 B1
Adelsö S 57 A3
Ademuz E 152 B2
Adenau D 80 B2
Adendorf D 72 A3
Adinkerke B 78 A2
Adjud RO 17 B7
Adliswil CH 107 B3
Admont A 110 B1
Ádneram N 52 A2
Adolfström S 195 D7
Adony H 112 B2
Adorf
Hessen D 81 A4
Sachsen D 83 B4
Adra E 164 C1
Adradas E 152 A1
Adrall E 147 B2
Adrano I 177 B3
Ádria I 121 B5
Adrigole IRL 29 C2
Adwick le Street
GB 40 B2
Adzaneta E 153 B3
Aesch CH 106 B2
A Estrada E 140 B2
Afandou GR 188 C3
Åfarnes N 198 C4
Affing D 94 C2
Affoltern CH 106 B3
Affric Lodge GB 32 D1
Afjord N 199 B7
Aflenz Kurort A . . .110 B2
A Fonsagrada E . . .141 A3
Afragóla I 170 C2
Afritz A 109 C4
Áfyon TR 187 D5
Ágasegyháza H . . .112 C3
Agay F 132 B2
Agazzano I 120 C2
Agde F 130 B2
Agdenes N 198 B6
Ager E 145 C4
Agerbæk DK 59 C1
Agersø DK 65 A4
Agerskov DK 64 A2
Agger DK 58 B1
Aggersund DK 58 A2
Aggius I 178 B3
Aggsbach Dorf A . . .97 C3
Aggsbach Markt A . .97 C3
Aggtelek H 99 C4
Aghalee GB 27 B4
Aghia I 182 D4
Aghia Anna GR . . .183 E5
Aghia Galini GR . . .185 D5
Aghia Marina GR . .101 D1
Aghia Paraskevi
GR 186 C1
Aghia Pelagia GR . .184 C3
Aghia Triada GR . . .184 B2
Aghiokambos GR . .182 D4
Aghios Efstratios
GR 183 D6
Aghios Kirikos
GR 185 B7
Aghios Matheos
GR 182 D1
Aghios Mironas
GR 185 D6
Aghios Nikolaos
GR 185 D6
Aghio Theodori
GR 184 B4
Agiči BIH 124 C2
Agira I 177 B3
Aglientu I 178 A3
Agnières F 118 C2

Agno CH 120 B1
Agnone I 170 B2
Agolada E 140 B2
Agon Coutainville
F 88 A2
Ágordo I 121 A5
Agost E 165 A4
Agramón E 158 C2
Agramunt E 147 C2
Agreda E 144 C2
Agria GR 183 D5
Agrigento I 176 B2
Agrinio GR 182 E3
Agrón E 163 A4
Agrópoli I 170 C2
Aguadulce
Almería E 164 C2
Sevilla E 162 A3
Agualada E 140 A2
Agua Longa P 148 A1
A Guarda E 140 C2
Aguarón E 152 A2
Aguas E 145 B3
Aguas Belas P 154 B2
Aguas de Busot I . .159 C3
Aguas de Moura
P 154 C2
Águas Frias P 148 A2
Águas Santas P . . .148 A1
Aguaviva E 153 B3
Aguaviva de la Vega
E 152 A1
A Gudiña E 141 B3
Agudo E 156 B3
Águeda P 148 B1
Aguessac F 130 A2
Aguglianó I 136 B2
Agugliano I 136 B2
Aguiar P 154 C2
Aguiar da Beira P . .148 B2
Aguilafuente E 151 A3
Aguilar de Campóo
E 142 B2
Aguilar de la Frontera
E 163 A3
Aguilas E 164 B3
Ahat TR 187 D4
Ahaus D 71 B3
Åheim N 198 C2
Ahigal E 149 B3
Ahigal de Villarino
E 149 A3
Ahillones E 156 B2
Ahlbeck
Mecklenburg-
Vorpommern D . .66 C3
Mecklenburg-
Vorpommern D . .74 A3
Ahlen D 81 A3
Ahlhorn D 71 B5
Ahmetbey TR 186 A2
Ahmetler TR 188 A4
Ahmetli TR 188 A2
Ahoghill GB 27 B4
Ahola FIN 197 C11
Ahrensbök D 65 B3
Ahrensburg D 72 A3
Ahrenshoop D 66 B1
Ahun F 116 A2
Åhus S 63 C2
Ahvenselkä FIN . .197 C11
Aibar E 144 B2
Aich D 95 C4
Aicha D 96 C1
Aichach D 94 C3
Aidone I 177 B3
Aiello Cálabro I . . .175 B2
Aigen im Mühlkreis
A 96 C1
Aigle CH 119 A3
Aignan F 128 C3
Aignay-le-Duc F . . .104 B3
Aigre F 115 C4
Aigrefeuille-d'Aunis
F 114 B3
Aigrefeuille-sur-Maine
F 101 B4
Aiguablava E 147 C4
Aiguebelette-le-Lac
F 118 B2
Aiguebelle F 118 B3
Aigueperse F 116 A3

Aigues-Mortes F . .131 B3
Aigues-Vives F . . .130 B1
Aiguilles F 119 C3
Aiguillon F 129 B3
Aigurande F 103 C3
Ailefroide F 118 C3
Aillant-sur-Tholon
F 104 B2
Ailly-sur-Noye F . . .90 B2
Ailly-sur-Somme F . .90 B2
Aimargues F 131 B3
Aime F 118 B3
Ainaži LV 8 D4
Ainet A 109 C3
Ainsa E 145 B4
Airaines F 90 B1
Aird GB 34 B2
Aird Asaig Tairbeart
GB 31 B2
Airdrie GB 35 C4
Aire-sur-l'Adour F .128 C2
Aire-sur-la-Lys F . . .78 B2
Airole I 133 B3
Airolo CH 107 C3
Airvault F 102 C1
Aisey-sur-Seine F . .104 B3
Aïssey F 105 B5
Aisy-sur-Armançon
F 104 B3
Aith
Orkney GB 33 B4
Shetland GB 33 A5
Aitona E 153 A4
Aitrach D 107 B5
Aiud RO 17 B5
Aix-en-Othe F 104 A2
Aix-en-Provence
F 131 B4
Aixe-sur-Vienne F .115 C5
Aix-les-Bains F . . .118 B2
Aizenay F 114 B2
Aizkraukle LV 8 D4
Aizpute LV 8 D2
Ajac F 146 A3
Ajaccio F 180 B1
Ajain F 116 A1
Ajaureforsen S . . .195 E6
Ajdovščina SLO . . .122 B2
Ajka H 111 B4
Ajo E 143 A3
Ajofrin E 157 A4
Ajos FIN 196 D7
Ajuda P 155 C3
Akanthou CY 181 A2
Akarca TR 189 A4
Akasztó H 112 C3
Akçakoca TR 187 A6
Akçaova TR 187 A6
Akçay TR 189 C4
Aken D 83 A4
Åkerby S 51 B4
Åkernes N 52 B3
Åkersberga S 57 A4
Åkers styckebruk
S 56 A3
Åkervik N 195 E4
Akhisar TR 186 D2
Akırkeby DK 67 A3
Akkrum NL 70 A2
Akören TR 189 B7
Åkra N 46 B2
Akranes IS 190 C4
Åkrehamn N 52 A1
Akrotiri CY 181 B1
Aksaray TR 23 B8
Akşehir TR 189 A6
Akseki TR 189 B6
Aksla N 46 A3
Aksu TR 189 C5
Aktsyabrski BY 13 B8
Akureyri IS 191 B7
Åkvåg N 53 B5
Akyazı TR 187 B5
Ål N 47 B5
Ala I 121 B4
Alaca TR 23 A8

Alaçam TR 23 A8
Alaçatı TR 188 A1
Alàdei Sardi I 178 B3
Ala di Stura I 119 B4
Alagna Valsésia I . .119 B4
Alagón E 144 C2
Alaior E 167 B4
Alájar E 161 B3
Alakurtti RUS 197 C13
Alakylä FIN 196 B7
Alameda E 163 A3
Alameda de la Sagra
E 151 B4
Alamedilla E 163 A4
Alamillo E 156 B3
Alaminos E 151 B5
Ala-Nampa FIN . . .197 C9
Alanäs S 199 A12
Alandroal P 155 C3
Alange E 156 B1
Alaniemi FIN 197 D8
Alanís E 161 B3
Alanno I 169 A3
Ålansbro S 200 D3
Alanya TR 189 C7
Alap H 112 C2
Alaquáso E 159 B3
Alaraz E 150 B2
Alarcón E 158 B1
Alar del Rey E 142 B2
Alaró E 167 B2
Alaşehir TR 188 A3
Alássio I 133 A4
Alastaro FIN 8 A3
Alata F 180 B1
Alatoz E 158 B2
Alatri I 169 B3
Alavus FIN 8 A3
Alba
E 152 B2
I 119 C5
Alba Adriática I . . .136 C2
Albacete E 158 C2
Alba de Tormes E .150 B2
Alba de Yeltes E . .149 B3
Albaida E 159 C3
Alba-Iulia RO 17 B5
Ålbæk DK 58 A3
Albaladejo E 158 C1
Albala del Caudillo
E 156 A1
Albalat E 159 B3
Albalate de Cinca
E 145 C4
Albalate del Arzobispo
E 153 A3
Albalate de las
Nogueras E 152 B1
Albalate de Zorita
E 151 B5
Alban F 130 B1
Albánchez E 164 B2
Albanchez de Ubeda
E 163 A4
Albano Laziale I . . .168 B2
Albanyà E 147 B3
Albaredo d'Adige
I 121 B4
Albares E 151 B4
Albarracín E 152 B2
Albatana E 158 C2
Albatarrec E 153 A4
Albatera E 165 A4
Albbruck D 106 B3
Albedin E 163 A3
Albelda de Iregua
E 143 B4
Albenga I 133 A4
Álberga
Södermanland S . .56 A2
Södermanland S . .56 B2
Albergaria-a-Nova
P 148 B1
Albergaria-a-Velha
P 148 B1
Albergaria dos Doze
P 154 B2
Alberge P 154 C2
Alberic E 159 B3

Aab–Alc

Albernoa P 160 B2
Alberobello I 173 B3
Alberoni I 122 B1
Albersdorf D 64 B2
Albersloh D 81 A3
Albert F 90 A2
Albertirsa H 112 B3
Albertville F 118 B3
Alberuela de Tubo
E 145 C3
Albi F 130 B1
Albidona I 174 B2
Albínia I 168 A1
Albino I 120 B2
Albires E 142 B1
Albisola Marina I . .133 A4
Albocácer E 153 B4
Albolote E 163 A4
Albondón E 164 C1
Alborea E 158 B2
Albox E 164 B2
Albrechtice nad
Vitavou CZ 96 B2
Albstadt D 107 A4
Albufeira P 160 B1
Albuñol E 164 C1
Albuñuelas E 163 B4
Alburquerque E . . .155 B3
Alby
Öland S 63 B4
Västernorrland S 200 D1
Alcácer do Sal P . .154 C2
Alcáçovas P 154 C2
Alcadozo E 158 C2
Alcafoces P 155 B3
Alcains P 155 B3
Alcalá de Guadaira
E 162 A2
Alcalá de Gurrea
E 144 B3
Alcalá de Henares
E 151 B4
Alcalá de la Selva
E 153 B3
Alcalá del Júcar E .158 B2
Alcalá de los Gazules
E 162 B2
Alcalá del Río E . . .162 A2
Alcalá del Valle E . .162 B2
Alcalá del Xivert E .153 B4
Alcalá la Real E . . .163 A4
Álcamo I 176 B1
Alcampell E 145 C4
Alcanadre E 144 B1
Alcanar E 153 B4
Alcanena P 154 B2
Alcañices E 149 A3
Alcántara E 155 B4
Alcantarilha P 160 B1
Alcantarilla E 165 B3
Alcañz E 153 A3
Alcara il Fusi I 177 A3
Alcaraz E 158 C1
Alcaria Ruiva P . . .160 B2
Alcarraz E 153 A4
Alcaudete E 163 A3
Alcaudete de la Jara
E 150 C3
Alcázar de San Juan
E 157 A4
Alcazarén E 150 A3
Alcester GB 44 A2
Alcoba E 157 A3
Alcobaça P 154 B1
Alcobendas E 151 B4
Alcocer E 151 B5
Alcochete P 154 C2
Alcoentre P 154 B2
Alcolea
Almería E 164 C2
Córdoba E 156 C3
Alcolea de Calatrava
E 157 B3

Alcolea de Cinca
E 145 C4
Alcolea del Pinar
E 152 A1
Alcolea del Río E .162 A4
Alcolea de Tajo E .150 C2
Alcollarín E 156 A2
Alconchel E. 155 C3
Alconera E. 155 C4
Alcontar E 164 B2
Alcora E. 153 B3
Alcorcón E. 151 B4
Alcorisa E 153 B3
Alcossebre E 153 B4
Alcoutim P. 160 B2
Alcover E 147 C2
Alcoy E 159 C3
Alcsútdoboz H . . .112 B2
Alcubierre E 145 C4
Alcubilla de Avellaneda
E 143 C4
Alcubilla de Nogales
E 141 B5
Alcubillas E. 157 B4
Alcublas E. 159 B3
Alcúdia E 167 B3
Alcudia de Guadix
E 164 B1
Alcuéscar E 155 B4
Aldbrough GB. 41 B3
Aldeacentenera E 156 A2
Aldeadávila de la
Ribera E 149 A3
Aldea del Cano E .155 B4
Aldea del Fresno
E 151 B3
Aldea del Obispo
E 149 B3
Aldea del Rey E . .157 B4
Aldea de Trujillo
E 156 A2
Aldealcorvo E 151 A4
Aldealuenga de Santa
Maria E 151 A4
Aldeamayor de San
Martín E. 150 A3
Aldeanueva de
Barbarroya E . .150 C2
Aldeanueva del Camino
E 149 B4
Aldeanueva del
Codonal E. 150 A2
Aldeanueva de San
Bartolomé E . . .156 A2
Aldeapozo E 144 C1
Aldeaquemada E. .157 B4
Aldea Real E 151 A3
Aldearrubia E 150 A2
Aldeaseca de la
Frontera E. 150 B2
Aldeasoña E 151 A3
Aldeatejada E 150 B2
Aldeavieja E 150 B3
Aldeburgh GB. 45 A5
Aldehuela E 152 B2
Aldehuela de
Calatañazor E . .143 C4
Aldeia da Serra P .155 C3
Aldeia do Bispo P 149 B3
Aldeia do Mato P. .154 B2
Aldeia Gavinha P .154 B1
Aldeire E 164 B1
Aldenhoven D 80 B2
Aldersbach D 95 C5
Aldershot GB. 44 B3
Aldudes F 144 A2
Åled S 60 C2
Aledo E. 165 B3
Alegria E 143 B4
Aleksandrovac
SRB. 127 C3
Aleksandrów Kujawski
PL. 76 B3
Aleksandrów Łódźki
PL. 86 A3
Aleksa Šantić
SRB 126 B1
Ålem S 62 B4
Alençon F 89 B4
Alenquer P. 154 B1
Alenya F. 146 B3
Aléria F 180 A2
Alès F 131 A3
Áles I 179 C2
Alessándria I 120 C1
Alessándria della
Rocca I 176 B2
Alessano I 173 C4
Ålesund N 198 C3
Alet-les-Bains F . .146 B3
Alexandria
GB 34 C3
GR 182 C4
RO 17 D6
Alexandroupoli
GR. 183 C7
Aleyrac F 131 A3
Alézio I 173 B4
Alfacar F 163 A4
Alfaiates P 149 B3
Alfajarin E 153 A3
Alfambra
E 152 B2
P. 160 B1
Alfândega da Fé
P 149 A3
Alfarela de Jafes
P 148 A2
Alfarelos P. 148 B1
Alfarim P 154 C1
Alfarnate E. 163 B3
Alfaro E 144 B2
Alfarrás E. 145 C4
Alfaz del Pi E 159 C3
Alfedena I 169 B4
Alfeizarão P. 154 B1

Alfeld
Bayern D 95 B3
Niedersachsen D. 72 C2
Alfena P. 148 A1
Alferce P 160 B1
Alfhausen D. 71 B4
Alfonsine I 135 A5
Alford
Aberdeenshire
GB. 33 D4
Lincolnshire GB . .41 B4
Alforja E. 147 C1
Alfoz E 141 A3
Alfreton GB 40 B2
Alfta S 50 A3
Alfundão P. 160 A1
Algaida E 167 B2
Algar E. 162 B2
Ålgarås S. 55 B5
Algarinejo E. 163 A3
Algarrobo E 163 B3
Algatocin E 162 B2
Algeciras E 162 B2
Algemesí E 159 B3
Algés P. 154 C1
Algete E. 151 B4
Alghero I 178 B2
Älghult S 62 A3
Alginet E 159 B3
Algodonales E . . .162 B2
Algodor
E 151 C4
P. 160 B2
Algora E 151 B5
Algoso P 149 A3
Algoz P 160 B1
Älgsjö S 200 B3
Alguaire E 145 C4
Alguazas E 165 A3
Algutsrum S 63 B4
Algyö H 126 A2
Alhama de Almería
E 164 C2
Alhama de Aragón
E 152 A2
Alhama de Granada
E 163 B4
Alhama de Murcia
E 165 B3
Alhambra E 157 B4
Alhandra P. 154 C1
Alhaurin de la Torre
E 163 B3
Alhaurin el Grande
E 163 B3
Alhendin E 163 A4
Alhóndiga E 151 B5
Alia E 156 A2
Ália I 176 B2
Aliağa TR 186 D1
Aliaga E 153 B3
Alibunar SRB. . . .127 B2
Alicante E 165 A4
Alicún de Ortega
E 164 B1
Alife I 170 B2
Alija del Infantado
E 141 B5
Alijó P. 148 A2
Alimena I 177 B3
Alingsås S 60 B2
Alinyà E 147 B2
Aliseda E 155 B4
Ali Terme I 177 A4
Aliveri GR 185 A5
Alixan F 117 C5
Aljaraque E 161 B2
Aljezur P 160 B1
Aljorra E. 165 B3
Aljubarrota P 154 B2
Aljucen E 155 B4
Aljustrel P 160 B1
Alken B 79 B5
Alkmaar NL 70 B1
Alkoven A 96 C2
Allaines F. 103 A3
Allaire F 101 B3
Allanche F 116 B2
Alland A 111 A3
Allariz E 140 B3
Allassac F 129 A4
Allauch F 131 B4
Alleen N. 52 B3
Allègre F 117 B3
Allemont F 118 B3
Allendale Town GB 37 B4
Allendorf D 81 B4
Allelev DK. 59 C1
Alsfeld D 81 B5
Allensteig A 97 C3
Allepuz E 153 B3
Allersberg D 95 B3
Allershausen D . . .95 C3
Alles E 142 A2
Allevard F 118 B3
Allgunnen S. 62 A3
Allihies IRL 29 C1
Allingåbro DK. 58 B3
Allmannsdorf D. . .107 B4
Allo E 144 B1
Alloa GB. 35 B4
Allogny F 103 B4
Ålloluokta S. 196 B2
Allones
Eure et Loire F. .90 C1
Maine-et-Loire F 102 B2
Allonnes F 102 B2
Allons F 128 B2
Allos F 132 A2
Allstedt D. 82 A3
Alltwalis GB. 39 C2
Allumiere I 168 A1
Almaceda P. 155 B3
Almacelles E 145 C4
Almachar E 163 B3
Almada P. 154 C1
Almadén de la Plata
E 161 B3
Almadenejos E . . .156 B3
Almadrones E 151 B5

Almagro E 157 B4
Almajano E 144 C1
Almansa E 159 C2
Almansil P 160 B1
Almanza E 142 B1
Almaraz E 150 C2
Almargen E 162 B2
Almarza E 143 C4
Almásfüzitö H 112 B2
Almassora E 159 B3
Almazán E. 152 A1
Almazul E 152 A1
Alme D. 81 A4
Almedina E 158 C1
Almedinilla E 163 A3
Almeida
E 149 A3
P. 149 B3
Almeirim P. 154 B2
Almelo NL 71 B3
Almenar E 145 C4
Almenara E 159 B3
Almenar de Soria
E 152 A1
Almendra P. 149 B2
Almendral E 155 C4
Almendral de la
Cañada E 150 B3
Almendralejo E . . .155 C4
Almenno San
Bartolomeo I . . .120 B2
Almere NL 70 B2
Almería E 164 C2
Almerimar E 164 C2
Almese I 119 B4
Almexial P. 160 B2
Ålmhult S. 63 B2
Almiropotamos
GR. 185 A5
Almiros GR 182 D4
Almodôvar P 160 B1
Almodóvar del Campo
E 157 B3
Almodóvar del Pinar
E 158 B2
Almodóvar del Río
E 162 A2
Almofala P. 148 B2
Almogia E 163 B3
Almoharin E 156 A1
Almonacid de la Sierra
E 152 A2
Almonacid de Toledo
E 157 A4
Almonaster la Real
E 161 B3
Almondsbury GB . .43 A4
Almonte E 161 B3
Almoradí E. 165 A4
Almoraima E 162 B2
Almorox E 150 B3
Almoster P 154 B2
Almsele S 200 B3
Älmsta S 51 C5
Almudena E 164 A3
Almudévar E 145 B3
Almuñécar E 163 B4
Almunge S. 51 C5
Almuradiel E 157 B4
Almussafes E 159 B3
Almvik S. 62 A4
Alness GB. 32 D2
Alnmouth GB. 37 A5
Alnwick GB. 37 A5
Åloppe S 51 C4
Álora E. 163 B3
Alos d'Ensil E . . .146 B2
Alosno E 161 B2
Alozaina E 162 B3
Alpbach A 108 B2
Alpedrete de la Sierra
E 151 B4
Alpedrinha P 148 B2
Alpen D 80 A2
Alpera E 159 C2
Alphen aan de Rijn
NL 70 B1
Alpiarça P 154 B2
Alpignano I 119 B4
Alpirsbach D 93 C4
Alpu TR 187 C5
Alpuente E 159 B2
Alqueva P 160 A2
Alquézar E 145 B4
Als DK 58 B3
Alsasua E 144 B1
Alsdorf D 80 B2
Alselv DK. 59 C1
Alsfeld D 81 B5
Alsike S. 57 A3
Alskog S 57 C4
Alsleben D. 83 A4
Alsónémedi H 112 B3
Alsótold H 112 B3
Alsóújlak H 111 B3
Alstad N. 194 C6
Alstätte D. 71 B3
Alsterbro S 62 B3
Alstermo S. 62 B3
Alston GB 37 B4
Alsvåg N 194 B6
Alsvik N 194 C5
Alta N 192 C7
Ålta S 57 A4
Altamura I 172 B2
Altarejos E. 158 B1
Altaussee A 109 B4
Altavilla Irpina I . .170 B2
Altavilla Silentina
I 170 C3
Altdöbern D 84 A2
Altdorf
CH 107 C3
D. 95 C4
Altdorf bei Nürnberg
D 95 B3
Alte P 160 B1
Altea E 159 C3
Altedo I 121 C4
Altena D 81 A3

Altenau D. 82 A2
Altenberg D 84 B1
Altenberge D 71 B4
Altenbruch D. 64 C1
Altenburg D 83 B4
Altenfelden A. 96 C1
Altengronau D 82 B1
Altenheim D. 93 C3
Altenhundem D. . . .81 A4
Altenkirchen
Mecklenburg-
Vorpommern D . .66 B2
Radom D. 81 B3
Altenkunstadt D . .82 B3
Altenmarkt
A. 110 B1
Altenmarkt im Pongall
A. 109 B4
Altensteig D. 93 C4
Altentreptow D . . .74 A2
Altenwalde D. 64 C1
Alten-weddingen D 73 B4
Alter do Chão P. . .155 B3
Altfraunhofen D . . .95 C4
Altheim
A. 109 A4
D. 94 B1
Althofen A 110 C1
Altınoluk TR. 186 C1
Altınova TR 186 C1
Altıntaş TR. 187 C5
Altınyaka TR 189 C5
Altınyayla TR. . . .189 B4
Altkirch F. 106 B2
Altlandsberg D. . . .74 B2
Altlewin D 74 B3
Altmannstein D. . . .95 C3
Altmorschen D 82 A1
Altmunster A 109 B4
Altnaharra GB. . . .32 C2
Alto Campoó E . . .142 A2
Altofonte I 176 A2
Altomonte I 174 B2
Alton
Hampshire GB. . .44 B3
Staffordshire GB . 40 C2
Altopáscio I 135 B3
Altötting D 109 A3
Altreichenau D 96 C1
Alt Ruppin D 74 B1
Altshausen D. 107 B4
Altstätten CH. 107 B4
Altura E 159 B3
Altusried D 107 B5
Alūksne LV. 8 D5
Alunda S 51 B5
Alustante E 152 B2
Alva GB. 35 B4
Alvaiázere P. 154 B2
Alvalade P. 160 B1
Älvängen S 60 B2
Alvarenga P. 148 B1
Alvares P 154 A2
Alvdal N 199 C7
Älvdalen S 49 A6
Alverca P 154 C1
Alversund N 46 B2
Alvesta S 62 B2
Alvignac F 129 B4
Alvignano I 170 B2
Ålvik N 46 B3
Alvik S. 50 B1
Alvimare F 89 A4
Alviobeira P. 154 B2
Alvito P 160 A2
Älvkarleby S 51 B4
Älvkarleö̈bruk S . .51 B4
Alvor P. 160 B1
Alvorge P. 154 B2
Alvøy N 46 B2
Ålvros S. 199 C11
Älvsbacka S 55 A4
Älvsbyn S 196 D4
Älvsered S. 60 B2
Alwernia PL. 86 B3
Alwinton GB 37 A4
Alyth GB 35 B4
Alytus LT. 13 A6
Alzénau D 93 A5
Alzey D. 93 B4
Alzira E 159 B3
Alzonne F 146 A3
Amadora P. 154 C1
Åmål S 55 A3
Amalfi I 170 C2
Amaliada GR 184 B2
Amance F 105 B5
Amancey F 105 B5
Amándola I 136 C2
Amantea I 175 B2
Amarante P. 148 A1
Amareleja P. 161 A2
Amares P. 148 A1
Amaseno I 169 B3
Amasra TR 187 A7
Amatrice I 169 A3
Amay B 79 B5
Ambarnyy RUS. . . .3 D13
Ambazac F. 115 C5
Ambelonas GR . . .182 D4
Amberg D 95 B3
Ambérieu-en-Bugey
F. 118 B2
Ambérieux-en-Dombes
F. 117 A4
Ambés F 128 A2
Ambjörby S 49 B5
Ambjörnarp S 60 B3
Amble GB. 37 A5
Ambleside GB 36 B4
Ambleteuse F 78 B1
Amboise F 102 B2
Ambrières-les-Vallées
F. 88 B3
Amden CH 107 B4
Amel B. 80 B2
Amélia I 168 A2

Amélie-les-Bains-
Palalda F. 146 B3
Amelinghausen D . .72 A3
Amendoa P 154 B2
Amendoeira P . . .160 B2
Améndola I 171 B3
Amendolara I 174 B2
A Merca E 140 B3
Amerongen NL 70 B2
Amersfoort NL. 70 B2
Amersham GB. 44 B3
Amesbury GB 44 B2
Amfiklia GR. 182 E4
Amfilochia GR. . . .182 E3
Amfipoli GR. 183 C5
Amfissa GR 184 A3
Amièira P. 155 C3
Amieira P. 154 B3
Amieiro P. 148 B1
Amiens F 90 B2
Amindeo GR 182 C3
Åminne S. 60 B3
Åmli N 53 B4
Ammanford GB. . . .39 C3
Ammarnäs S 195 E7
Åmmeberg S 55 B5
Amorbach D 94 B1
Amorebieta E 143 A4
Amorgos GR. 185 C6
Amorosa P. 148 A1
Amorosi I 170 B2
Åmot
Buskerud N 48 C1
Telemark N 53 A3
S. 50 B3
Åmotfors S 54 A3
Åmotsdal N 53 A4
Amou F 128 C2
Ampezzo I 122 A1
Ampfing D. 95 C4
Ampflwang A. 109 A4
Amplepuis F 117 B4
Amposta E 153 B4
Ampthill GB. 44 A3
Ampudia E 142 C2
Ampuero E 143 A3
Amriswil CH 107 B4
Åmsele S 200 B5
Amstelveen NL. . . .70 B1
Amsterdam NL 70 B1
Amstetten A. 110 A1
Amtzell D. 107 B4
Amulree GB. 35 B4
Amurrio E 143 A4
Amusco E 142 B2
Anacapri I 170 C2
Anadia P. 148 B1
Anadon E. 152 B2
Anafi GR 185 C6
Anagni I. 169 B3
Anamur TR 23 C7
Ananyiv UA 17 B8
Anascaul IRL 29 B1
Ånaset S 2 D7
Anatoliko GR 182 C3
Anaya de Alba E . .150 B2
Ança P. 148 B1
Ancaster GB 40 C3
Ancede P. 148 A1
Ancenis F 101 B4
Ancerville F. 91 C5
Anchuras E 156 A3
Ancona I 136 B2
Ancora P. 148 A1
Ancrum GB. 35 C5
Ancy-le-Franc F . .104 B3
Andalo I 121 A3
Åndalsnes N 198 C4
Andance F 117 B4
Andau A. 111 B4
Andeer D. 53 A6
Andelfingen CH. . .107 C4
Andelot-Blancheville
F. 105 A4
Andelot-en-Montagne
F. 105 C4
Andenes N. 194 A7
Andenne B. 79 B5
Anderlues B. 79 B4
Andermatt CH 107 C3
Andernach D. 80 B3
Andernos-les-Bains
F. 128 B1
Anderslöv S. 66 A2
Anderstorp S. 60 B3
Andijk NL. 70 B2
Andoain E 144 A1
Andocs H. 112 C1
Andolsheim F. . . .106 A2
Andorra E 153 B3
Andorra La Vella
AND. 146 B2
Andosilla E 144 B2
Andover GB. 44 B2
Andratx E 166 B2
Andreapol RUS. . . .9 D8
Andreas GB. 36 B2
Andréspol PL. 86 A3
Andrest F 145 A4
Andretta I 172 B1
Andrezieux-Boutheon
F. 117 B4
Andria I 171 B4
Andrijevica MNE . .16 D3
Andritsena GR . . .184 B2
Andros GR. 185 B5
Andrychów PL. 99 B3
Andselv N 194 A9
Andújar E. 157 B3
Anduze F 131 A2
Åneby N 48 B2
Aneby S 62 A2
Añes E 143 A3
Anet F 90 C1
Anfo I 121 B3
Ang S 62 A2

Anga S 57 C4
Angaïs F 145 A3
Ånge S 199 B11
Änge S 200 D1
Ångeja P 148 B1
Ängelholm S 61 C2
Ängelsberg S 50 C3
Anger A 110 B2
Angera I 120 B1
Angermünde D 74 A3
Angern A 97 C4
Angers F 102 B1
Angerville F. 90 C2
Anghiari I. 135 B5
Angle GB. 39 C1
Anglés E 147 C3
Anglés F 130 B1
Angles F 114 B2
Anglesola E. 147 C2
Angles sur l'Anglin
F. 115 B4
Anglet F 128 C1
Anglisidhes CY . .181 B2
Anglure F 91 C3
Angoulême F. . . .115 C4
Angoulins F. 114 B2
Angsö S 56 A2
Angueira P 149 A3
Angües E 145 B3
Anguiano E 143 B4
Anguillara Sabazia
I 168 A2
Anguillara Véneta
I 121 B4
Anhée B 79 B4
Anholt DK 60 C1
Aniane F 130 B2
Aniche F 78 B3
Ånimskog S 54 B3
Anina RO 16 C4
Anixi GR 182 D3
Anizy-le-Château F 91 B3
Anjalankoski FIN. . .8 B5
Anjan S 199 B9
Ankara TR 187 C7
Ankaran SLO. . . .122 B2
Ankarsrum S. 62 A4
Ankerlia N 192 C4
Anklam D. 66 C2
Ankum D 71 B4
Anlauftal A. 109 B4
Anlezy F. 104 C2
Ånn S 199 B9
Annaberg A 110 B2
Annaberg-Buchholz
D 83 B5
Annaberg im
Lammertal A . . .109 B4
Annaburg D 83 A5
Annahütte D 84 A1
Annalong GB. 27 B5
Annan GB 36 B3
Anndalsvågen N . .195 E3
Anneberg
Halland S. 60 B2
Jönköping S. 62 A2
Annecy F 118 B3
Annelund S 60 B3
Annemasse F 118 A3
Annenskiy Most
RUS. 9 B10
Annerstad S 60 C3
Annestown IRL . . .30 B1
Annevoie-Rouillon
B 79 B4
Annonay F 117 B4
Annot F 132 B2
Annweiler D. 93 B3
Ano Poroia GR . . .183 B5
Añora E 156 B3
Ano Siros GR 185 B5
Anould F 106 A1
Anquela del Ducado
E 152 B1
Anröchte D 81 A4
Ans DK. 59 B2
Ansager DK. 59 C1
Ansbach D. 94 B2
Anse F 117 B4
Anseroeul B. 79 B3
Ansfelden A. 110 A1
Ansião P 154 B2
Ansó E 144 B3
Ansoain E 144 B2
Anstruther GB. . . .35 B5
Antalya TR. 189 C5
Antas E 164 B3
Antegnate I. 120 B2
Antequera E 163 B3
Anterselva di Mezzo
I 108 C3
Antibes F. 132 B3
Antigüedad E 142 C2
Antillo I 177 B4
Antirio GR. 184 A2
Antnäs S 196 D5
Antoing B. 79 B3
Antonin PL. 86 A1
Antrain F. 88 B2
Antrim GB. 27 B4
Antrodoco I 169 A3
Antronapiana I . . .119 A5
Anttis S 196 B5
Antuzede P 148 B1
Antwerp = Antwerpen
B 79 A4
Antwerpen = Antwerp
B 79 A4
Anversa d'Abruzzi
I 169 B3
Anvin F 78 B2
Anzat-le-Luguet F 116 B3
Anzi I 172 B1
Anzio I 168 B2
Anzola d'Emilia I .135 A4
Anzón E 144 C2
Aoiz E 144 B2
Aosta I 119 B4

Apalhão P 155 B3
Apátfalva H 126 A2
Apatin SRB 125 B5
Apatity RUS. 3 C13
Apc H 112 B3
Apécchio I 136 B1
Apeldoorn NL 70 B2
Apen D. 71 A4
Apenburg D. 73 B4
Apensen D. 72 A2
A Peroxa E 140 B3
Apiro I 136 B2
Apliki CY 181 B2
Apolda D 82 A3
Apolonia GR 185 C5
A Pontenova E. . .141 A3
Apostag H 112 C2
Appelbo S 49 B6
Appennino I 136 C2
Appenzell CH 107 B4
Appiano I 108 C2
Appingedam NL . . .71 A3
Appleby-in-
Westmorland GB .37 B4
Applecross GB . . .31 B3
Appledore GB 42 A2
Appoigny F 104 B2
Apremont-la-Forêt
F. 92 C1
Aprica I 120 A3
Apricena I 171 B3
Aprigliano I 174 B2
Aprília I 168 B2
Apt F 131 B4
Apúlia P. 148 A1
Aquiléia I 122 B2
Aquilónia I 172 B1
Aquino I 169 B3
Ar S 57 C4
Arabayona E 150 A2
Arabba I 108 C2
Araç TR 23 A7
Aracena E 161 B3
Arachova GR. . . .184 A3
Aračinovo MK . . .182 A3
Arad RO. 126 A3
Aradac SRB. 126 B2
Aradhippou CY . . .181 B2
Aragnouet F 145 B4
Aragona I. 176 B2
Aramits F. 144 A3
Aramon F 131 B3
Aranda de Duero
E 143 C3
Aranda de Moncayo
E 152 A2
Arandjelovac SRB 127 C2
Aranjuez E. 151 B4
Arantzazu E 143 B4
Aranzueque E . . .151 B4
Aras de Alpuente
E 159 B2
Arauzo de Miel E .143 C3
Arazede P 148 B1
Arbas F 145 B4
Árbatax I 179 C3
Arbeca E 147 C1
Arberg D 94 B2
Arbesbach A 96 C2
Arboga S. 56 A1
Arbois F 105 C4
Arbon CH. 107 B4
Arboréa I 179 C2
Arbório I 119 B5
Årbostad N 194 B8
Arbrå S. 50 A3
Arbroath GB. 35 B5
Arbúcies E. 147 C3
Arbuniel E 163 A4
Arbus I 179 C2
Arcachon F 128 B1
Arce I 169 B3
Arcen NL. 80 A2
Arc-en-Barrois F .105 B3
Arces-Dilo F 104 A2
Arc-et-Senans F . .105 B4
Arcévia I 136 B1
Arcey F. 106 B1
Archanes GR. . . .185 D6
Archangelos GR .188 C3
Archena E 165 A3
Archez E 163 B4
Archiac F 115 C3
Archidona E 163 A3
Archiestown GB . .32 D3
Archivel E 164 A3
Arcidosso I 135 C4
Arcille I 135 C4
Arcis-sur-Aube F .91 C4
Arc-lès-Gray F . .105 B4
Arco I 121 B3
Arcones E 151 A4
Arcos E 143 B3
Arcos de Jalón E .152 A1
Arcos de la Frontera
E 162 B2
Arcos de la Sierra
E 152 B1
Arcos de las Salinas
E 159 B2
Arcos de Valdevez
P 148 A1
Arcozelo P. 148 B2
Arc-sur-Tille F . . .105 B4
Arcy-sur-Cure F . .104 B2
Ardagh IRL. 29 B2
Årdal N. 52 A2
Ardala S 55 B4
Ardales E. 162 B3
Årdalstangen N . . .47 A4
Ardara
I 178 B2
IRL 26 B2
Ardarroch GB 31 B3
Ardbeg GB. 34 C1
Ardcharnich GB . .32 D1
Ardchyle GB 34 B3
Ardee IRL. 27 C4
Arden DK. 58 B2

Ardentes F 103 C3
Ardenza I 134 B3
Ardersier GB 32 D2
Ardes F 116 B3
Ardessie GB 32 D1
Ardez CH 107 C5
Ardfert IRL 29 B2
Ardgay GB 32 D2
Ardglass GB 27 B5
Ardgroom IRL 29 C2
Ardhasig GB 31 B2
Ardino BG 183 B7
Ardisa E 144 B3
Ardkearagh IRL 29 C1
Ardlui GB 34 B3
Ardlussa GB 34 B2
Ardón E 142 B1
Ardooie B 78 B3
Ardore I 175 C2
Ardre S 57 C4
Ardres F 78 B1
Ardrishaig GB 34 B2
Ardrossan GB 34 C3
Are N 52 A1
Åre S 199 B10
Areia Branca P 154 B1
Aremark N 54 A2
Arenales de San
Gregorio E 157 A4
Arenas E 163 B3
Arenas de Iguña
E 142 A2
Arenas del Rey E 163 B4
Arenas de San Juan
E 157 A4
Arenas de San Pedro
E 150 B2
Arendal N 53 B4
Arendonk B 79 A5
Arengosse F 128 B2
Arentorp S 55 B3
Arenys de Mar E 147 C3
Arenys de Munt E 147 C3
Arenzano I 133 A4
Areo E 146 B2
Areopoli GR 184 C3
Ares E 140 A2
Arès F 128 B1
Ares del Maestrat
E 153 B3
Aresvika N 198 B5
Arette F 144 A3
Aretxabaleta E 143 A4
Arevalillo E 150 B2
Arévalo E 150 A3
Arez P 155 B3
Arezzo I 135 B4
Arfeuilles F 117 A3
Argalasti GR 183 D5
Argallón E 156 B2
Argamasilla de Alba
E 157 A4
Argamasilla de
Calatrava E 157 B3
Arganda E 151 B4
Arganil P 148 B1
Argasion GR 184 B1
Argegno I 120 B2
Argelès-Gazost F 145 A3
Argelès-sur-Mer F 146 B4
Argenta I 121 C4
Argentan F 89 B3
Argentat F 116 B1
Argentera I 132 A2
Argenteuil F 90 C2
Argenthal D 93 B3
Argentiera I 178 B2
Argentona E 147 C3
Argenton-Château
F 102 C1
Argenton-sur-Creuse
F 103 C3
Argentré F 102 A1
Argentré-du-Plessis
F 101 A4
Argent-sur-Sauldre
F 103 B4
Argirades GR 182 D1
Argithani TR 189 A6
Argos GR 184 B3
Argos Orestiko
GR 182 C3
Argostoli GR 184 A1
Argote E 143 B4
Arguedas E 144 B2
Argueil F 90 B1
Arholma S 51 C6
Århus DK 59 B3
Ariano Irpino I 170 B3
Ariano nel Polésine
I 121 C5
Aribe E 144 B2
Aridea GR 182 C4
Arienzo I 170 B2
Arild S 61 C2
Arileod GB 34 B1
Arinagour GB 34 B1
Ariño E 153 A3
Arinthod F 118 A2
Arisaig GB 34 B2
Arisgotas E 157 A4
Aritzo I 179 C3
Ariza E 152 A1
Årjäng S 54 A3
Arjeplog S 195 D8
Arjona E 157 C3
Arjonilla E 157 C3
Arkasa GR 188 D2
Arkelstorp S 63 B2
Arkösund S 56 B2
Arklow IRL 30 B2
Arla S 56 A2
Arlanc F 117 B3
Arlanzón E 143 B3
Arlebosc F 117 B4
Arlena di Castro I 168 A1
Arles F 131 B3
Arles-sur-Tech F 146 B3
Arló H 113 A4
Arlon B 92 B1
Armação de Pera
P 160 B1
Armadale
Highland GB 31 B3
West Lothian GB 35 C4
Armagh GB 27 B4
Armamar P 148 A2
Armenistis GR 185 B7
Armeno I 119 B5
Armenteros E 150 B2
Armentières F 78 B2
Armilla E 163 A4
Armiñón E 143 B4
Armoy GB 27 A4
Armuña de Tajuña
E 151 B4
Armutlu
Bursa TR 186 B3
İzmir TR 188 A2
Arnac-Pompadour
F 115 C5
Arnafjord N 46 A3
Arnage F 102 B2
Arnas F 117 A4
Årnäs S 55 B4
Arnay-le-Duc F 104 B3
Arnborg DK 59 B2
Arnbruck D 95 B4
Arnea GR 183 C5
Arneberg
Hedmark N 48 A2
Hedmark N 49 B4
Arneburg D 73 B5
Arnedillo E 144 B1
Arnedo E 144 B1
Arneguy F 144 A2
Arnés E 153 B4
Árnes IS 190 A4
Årnes
Akershus N 48 B3
Troms N 194 A9
Arnfels A 110 C2
Arnhem NL 70 C2
Arnissa GR 182 C3
Arno S 56 B3
Arnold GB 40 B2
Arnoldstein A 109 C4
Arnsberg D 81 A4
Arnschwang D 95 B4
Arnsdorf D 84 A1
Årnset N 198 B6
Arnside GB 37 B4
Arnstadt D 82 B2
Arnstein D 94 B1
Arnstorf D 95 C4
Arnum DK 59 C1
Aroche E 161 B3
Ároktő H 113 B4
Arolla CH 119 A4
Arolsen D 81 A5
Arona I 119 B5
Äros N 54 A1
Arosa
CH 107 C4
P 148 A1
Ærøskøbing DK 65 B3
Arøsund DK 59 C2
Arouca P 148 B1
Årøysund N 54 A1
Arpajon F 90 C2
Arpajon-sur-Cère
F 116 C2
Arpela FIN 196 C7
Arpino I 169 B3
Arquata del Tronto
I 136 C2
Arques F 78 B2
Arques-la-Bataille
F 89 A5
Arquillos E 157 B4
Arraia-Maeztu E 143 B4
Arraiolos P 154 C2
Arrancourt F 92 C2
Arras F 78 B2
Arrasate E 143 A4
Årre DK 59 C1
Arreau F 145 B4
Arredondo E 143 A3
Arrens-Marsous F 145 B3
Arriate E 162 B2
Arrifana P 160 B1
Arrigorriaga E 143 A4
Arriondas E 142 A1
Arroba de los Montes
E 157 A3
Arrochar GB 34 B3
Arromanches-les-Bains
F 88 A3
Arronches P 155 B3
Arroniz E 144 B1
Arrou F 103 A3
Arroya E 142 B2
Arroya de Cuéllar
E 150 A3
Arroyal E 142 B2
Arroyo de la Luz
E 155 B4
Arroyo del Ojanco
E 164 A2
Arroyo de San Servan
E 155 C4
Arroyomolinos de
León E 161 A3
Arroyomolinos de
Montánchez E 156 A1
Arruda dos Vinhos
P 154 C1
Arsac F 128 B2
Ars-en-Ré F 114 B2
Arsiè I 121 B4
Arsiero I 121 B4
Årslev DK 59 C3
Ársoli I 169 A3
Ars-sur-Moselle F 92 B2
Årsunda S 50 B3
Artà E 167 B3
Arta GR 182 D3
Artajona E 144 B2
Artegna I 122 A2
Arteixo E 140 A2
Artemare F 118 B2
Arten I 121 A4
Artena I 169 B2
Artenay F 103 A3
Artern D 82 A3
Artés E 147 C2
Artesa de Segre E 147 C2
Arth CH 107 B3
Arthez-de-Béarn
F 145 A3
Arthon-en-Retz F 101 B4
Arthurstown IRL 30 B2
Artieda E 144 B3
Artix F 145 A3
Artotina GR 182 E4
Artsyz UA 17 B8
Artziniega E 143 A3
A Rúa E 141 B3
Arudy F 145 A3
Arundel GB 44 C3
Arveyres F 128 B2
Arvidsjaur S 196 D2
Arvieux F 118 C3
Arvika S 54 A3
Åryd
Blekinge S 63 B3
Kronoberg S 62 B2
Arzachena I 178 A3
Arzacq-Arraziguet
F 128 C2
Árzana I 179 C3
Arzano F 100 B2
Aržano HR 138 B2
Arzberg D 95 A4
Arzignano I 121 B4
Arzila P 148 B1
Arzl im Pitztal A 108 B1
Arzúa E 140 B2
As B 80 A1
Aš CZ 83 B4
Ås N 54 A1
Åsa S 60 B2
Asaa DK 58 A3
Aşağıçiğil TR 189 A6
Ašanja SRB 127 C2
Åsarna S 199 C11
Åsarøy N 52 A2
Åsarp S 55 B4
Asasp F 145 A3
Åsbro S 55 A6
Åsby S 60 B2
Åsby S 62 A3
Asbygri IS 191 A9
Ascain F 144 A2
Ascea I 172 B1
Ascha D 95 B4
Aschach an der Donau
A 96 C2
Aschaffenburg D 93 B5
Aschbach Markt A 110 A1
Ascheberg
Nordrhein-Westfalen
D 81 A3
Schleswig-Holstein
D 65 B3
Aschendorf D 71 A4
Aschersleben D 82 A3
Asciano I 135 B4
Ascó E 153 A4
Asco F 180 A2
Áscoli Piceno I 136 C2
Áscoli Satriano I 171 B3
Ascona CH 120 A1
Ascot GB 44 B3
Ascoux F 103 A4
Åse N 194 A6
Åseda S 62 A3
Åsele S 200 B3
Åsen
N 199 B8
S 49 A5
Asendorf D 72 B2
Asenovgrad BG 183 A6
Åsensbruk S 54 B3
Åseral N 52 B3
Asfeld F 91 B4
Åsgårdstrand N 54 A1
Ásgarður IS 190 B1
Asgate CY 181 B2
Ash
Kent GB 45 B5
Surrey GB 44 B3
Åshammar S 50 B3
Ashbourne
GB 40 B2
IRL 30 A2
Ashburton GB 43 B3
Ashby-de-la-Zouch
GB 40 C2
Ashchurch GB 44 B1
Åsheim N 199 D8
Ashford GB 45 B4
Ashington GB 37 A5
Ashley GB 38 B4
Ashmyany BY 13 A6
Ashton Under Lyne
GB 40 B1
Ashwell GB 44 A3
Asiago I 121 B4
Asipovichy BY 13 B8
Aska FIN 197 B9
Askam-in-Furness
GB 36 B3
Askeaton IRL 29 B3
Asker N 48 C2
Askersund S 55 B5
Åskilje S 200 B3
Askim N 54 A2
Askland N 53 B4
Äsköping S 56 A2
Askvoll N 46 A2
Asljunga S 61 C3
Asmunti FIN 197 D9
Asnæs DK 61 D1
As Neves E 140 B2
As Nogaís E 141 B3
Ásola I 120 B3
Asolo I 121 B4
Asos GR 184 A1
Asotthalom H 126 A1
Aspach A 109 A4
Aspang Markt A 111 B3
Aspariegos E 149 A4
Asparn an der Zaya
A 97 C4
Aspatria GB 36 B3
Aspberg S 55 A4
Aspe E 165 A4
Aspet F 145 A4
Äspö S 63 B3
As Pontes de García
Rodríguez E 140 A3
Aspres-sur-Buëch
F 132 A1
Aspsele S 200 C4
Assafora P 154 C1
Asse B 79 B4
Assebakte N 193 C9
Assel D 72 A2
Asselborn L 92 A1
Assémini I 179 C2
Assen NL 71 B3
Assenede B 79 A3
Assens
Aarhus Amt. DK 58 B3
Fyns Amt. DK 59 C2
Assesse B 79 B5
Assisi I 136 B1
Åsskard N 198 B5
Assling D 108 B3
Asso I 120 B2
Asson F 145 A3
Ássoro I 177 B3
Assumar P 155 B3
Åsta N 48 A3
Astaffort F 129 B3
Astakos GR 184 A2
Asten NL 80 A1
Asti I 119 C5
Astipalea GR 188 C1
Astorga E 141 B4
Åstorp S 61 C2
Åsträsk S 200 B5
Astudillo E 142 B2
Asuni I 179 C2
Asványráró H 111 B4
Aszód H 112 B3
Aszófő H 111 C4
Atabey TR 189 B5
Atalaia P 154 B3
Atalandi GR 182 E4
Atalho P 154 C2
Átány H 113 B4
Atanzón E 151 B4
Ataquines E 150 A3
Atarfe E 163 A4
Atça TR 188 B3
Ateca E 152 A2
A Teixeira E 141 B3
Atella I 172 B1
Atessa I 169 A4
Ath B 79 B3
Athboy IRL 30 A2
Athea IRL 29 B2
Athenry IRL 28 A3
Athens = Athina
GR 185 B4
Atherstone GB 40 C2
Athienou CY 181 A2
Athies F 90 B2
Athies-sous-Laon
F 91 B3
Athina = Athens
GR 185 B4
Athleague IRL 28 A3
Athlone IRL 28 A4
Athna CY 181 A2
Athy IRL 30 B2
Atienza E 151 A5
Atina I 169 B3
Atkár H 113 B3
Atlantı TR 189 A7
Atna N 199 D7
Åtorp S 55 A5
Atrå N 47 C5
Ätran S 60 B2
Atri I 169 A3
Atripalda I 170 C2
Atsiki GR 183 D7
Attendorn D 81 A3
Attichy F 90 B3
Attigliano I 168 A2
Attigny F 91 B4
Attleborough GB 41 C5
Åtvidaberg S 56 B1
Atzendorf D 73 C4
Au
Steiermark A 110 B2
Vorarlberg A 107 B4
Bayern D 95 C3
Bayern D 108 B2
Aub D 94 B2
Aubagne F 132 B1
Aubange B 92 B1
Aubel B 80 B1
Aubenas F 117 C4
Aubenton F 91 B4
Auberive F 105 B4
Aubeterre-sur-Dronne
F 128 A3
Aubiet F 129 C3
Aubigné F 115 B3
Aubigny F 114 B2
Aubigny-au-Bac F 78 B3
Aubigny-en-Artois
F 78 B2
Aubigny-sur-Nère
F 103 B4
Aubin F 130 A1
Aubonne CH 105 C5
Aubrac F 116 C2
Aubusson F 116 B2
Auch F 129 C3
Auchencairn GB 36 B3
Auchinleck GB 36 A2
Auchterarder GB 35 B4
Auchtermuchty GB 35 B4
Auchtertyre GB 31 B3
Auchy-au-Bois F 78 B2
Audenge F 128 B1
Auderville F 88 A2
Audierne F 100 A1
Audincourt F 106 B1
Audlem GB 38 B4
Audruicq F 78 B2
Audun-le-Roman F 92 B1
Audun-le-Tiche F 92 B1
Aue
Nordrhein-Westfalen
D 81 A4
Sachsen D 83 B4
Auerbach
Bayern D 95 B3
Sachsen D 83 B4
Auffach A 108 B3
Augher GB 27 B3
Aughnacloy GB 27 B4
Aughrim IRL 30 B2
Augignac F 115 C4
Augsburg D 94 C2
Augusta I 177 B4
Augusten-borg DK 64 B2
Augustfehn D 71 A4
Augustów PL 12 B5
Aukrug D 64 B2
Auktsjaur S 196 D2
Auldearn GB 32 D3
Aulendorf D 107 B4
Auletta I 172 B1
Aulla I 134 A2
Aullène F 180 B2
Aulnay F 115 B3
Aulnoye-Aymeries
F 79 B3
Ault F 90 A1
Aultbea GB 31 B3
Aulum DK 59 B1
Aulus-les-Bains F 146 B2
Auma D 83 B3
Aumale F 90 B1
Aumetz F 92 B1
Aumont-Aubrac F 116 C3
Aunay-en-Bazois
F 104 B2
Aunay-sur-Odon F 88 A3
Aune N 199 A10
Auneau F 90 C1
Auneuil F 90 B1
Auning DK 58 B3
Aunsetra N 199 A9
Aups F 132 B2
Aura D 82 B1
Auray F 100 B3
Aurdal N 47 B6
Aure N 198 B5
Aurich D 71 A4
Aurignac F 145 A4
Aurillac F 116 C2
Auriol F 132 B1
Auritz-Burguette
E 144 B2
Aurlandsvangen N 47 B4
Auronzo di Cadore
I 109 C3
Auros F 128 B2
Auroux F 117 C3
Aurskog N 48 C3
Aursmoen N 48 C3
Ausónia I 169 B3
Ausservillgraton
A 109 C3
Austad N 52 B3
Austbygda N 47 B5
Aústis I 178 B3
Austmarka N 49 B4
Austre Moland N 53 B4
Austre Vikebygd N 52 A1
Austrheim N 46 B2
Auterive F 146 A2
Autheuil-Authouillet
F 89 A5
Authon F 132 A2
Authon-du-Perche
F 102 A2
Autol E 144 B2
Autreville F 92 C1
Autrey-lès-Gray F 105 B4
Autti FIN 197 C10
Autun F 104 C3
Auty-le-Châtel F 103 B4
Auvelais B 79 B4
Auvillar F 129 B3
Auxerre F 104 B2
Auxi-le-Château F 78 B2
Auxon F 104 A2
Auxonne F 105 B4
Auxy F 104 C3
Auzances F 116 A2
Auzon F 117 B3
Ağva TR 187 A4
Availles-Limouzine
F 115 B4
Avaldsnes N 52 A1
Avallon F 104 B2
Avantas GR 183 C7
Avaviken S 195 E9
Avebury GB 44 B2
A Veiga E 141 B3
Aveiras de Cima
P 154 B2
Aveiro P 148 B1
Avelgem B 79 B3
Avellino I 170 C2
Avenches CH 106 C2
A-Ver-o-Mar P 148 A1
Aversa I 170 C2
Avesnes-le-Comte
F 78 B2
Avesnes-sur-Helpe
F 91 A3
Avesta S 50 B3
Avetrana I 173 B3
Avezzano I 169 A3
Avià E 147 B2
Aviano I 122 A1
Aviemore GB 32 D3
Avigliana I 119 B4
Avigliano I 172 B1
Avignon F 131 B3
Ávila E 150 B3
Avilés E 141 A5
Avilley F 105 B5
Avintes P 148 A1
Avinyo E 147 C2
Àvio I 121 B3
Avioth F 92 B1
Avis P 154 B3
Avize F 91 C4
Avlonari GR 185 A5
Ávola I 177 C4
Avon F 90 C2
Avonmouth GB 43 A4
Avord F 103 B4
Avranches F 88 B2
Avril F 92 B1
Avrillé F 102 B1
Avtovac BIH 139 B4
Awans B 79 B5
Axams A 108 B2
Axat F 146 B3
Axbridge GB 43 A4
Axel NL 79 A3
Ax-les-Thermes F 146 B2
Axmarby S 51 B4
Axmarsbruk S 51 A4
Axminster GB 43 B3
Axvall S 55 B4
Ay F 91 B4
Aya E 144 A1
Ayamonte E 161 B2
Ayancık TR 23 A8
Ayaş TR 187 B7
Aydın TR 188 B2
Ayelo de Malferit
E 159 C3
Ayer CH 119 A4
Ayerbe E 144 B3
Ayette F 78 B2
Ayia Napa CY 181 B2
Áyia Phyla CY 181 B2
Áyios Amvrósios
CY 181 A2
Áyios Seryios CY 181 A2
Áyios Theodhoros
CY 181 A3
Aykirikçi TR 187 C5
Aylesbury GB 44 B3
Ayllón E 151 A4
Aylsham GB 41 C5
Ayna E 158 C1
Ayódar E 159 B3
Ayora E 159 B2
Ayr GB 36 A2
Ayrancı TR 23 C7
Ayrancılar TR 188 A2
Ayron F 115 B4
Aysgarth GB 37 B4
Ayton GB 35 C5
Aytos BG 17 D7
Ayvacık TR 186 C1
Ayvalık TR 186 C1
Aywaille B 80 B1
Azaila E 153 A3
Azambuja P 154 B2
Azambujeira P 154 B2
Azanja SRB 127 C2
Azannes-et-
Soumazannes F 92 B1
Azanúy-Alins E 145 C4
Azaruja P 155 C3
Azay-le-Ferron F 115 B5
Azay-le-Rideau F 102 B2
Azcoitia E 143 A4
Azé F 117 A4
Azeiteiros P 155 B3
Azenhas do Mar P 154 C1
Azinhaga P 154 B2
Azinhal P 160 B2
Azinheira dos Bairros
P 160 A1
Aznalcázar E 161 B3
Aznalcóllar E 161 B3
Azóia P 154 B2
Azpeitia E 144 A1
Azuaga E 156 B2
Azuara E 153 A3
Azuqueca de Henares
E 151 B4
Azur F 128 C1
Azzano Décimo I 122 B1

B

Baad A 107 B5
Baamonde E 140 A3
Baar CH 107 B3
Bağarasi TR 188 B2
Baarle-Nassau B 79 A4
Baarn NL 70 B2
Babadağ TR 188 B3
Babadag RO 17 C8
Babaeski TR 186 A2
Babayevo RUS 9 C9
Babenhausen
Bayern D 107 A5
Hessen D 93 B4
Babiak PL 76 B3
Babice PL 86 B3
Babigoszcz PL 75 A3
Babimost PL 75 B4
Babina Greda HR 125 B4
Babócsa H 124 A3
Bábolma H 112 B1
Baborów PL 86 B1
Baboszewo PL 77 B5
Babót H 111 B4
Babruysk BY 13 B8
Babsk PL 87 A4
Bac GB 31 A2
Bač SRB 125 B5
Bacares E 164 B2
Bacău RO 17 B7
Baccarat F 92 C2
Bacharach D 93 A3
Backa S 50 B2
Bačka Palanka
SRB 126 B1
Backaryd S 63 B3
Bačka Topola
SRB 126 B1
Backe S 200 C2
Bäckebo S 62 B4
Bäckefors S 54 B3
Bäckhammar S 55 A5
Bački Breg SRB 125 B4
Bački-Brestovac
SRB 126 B1
Bački Monoštor
SRB 125 B4
Bački Petrovac
SRB 126 B1
Bački Sokolac
SRB 126 B1
Backnang D 94 C1
Bačko Gradište
SRB 126 B2
Bačko Novo Selo
SRB 125 B5
Bačko Petrovo Selo
SRB 126 B2
Bácoli I 170 C2
Bacqueville-en-Caux
F 89 A5
Bácsalmás H 126 A1
Bácsbokod H 125 A5
Bad Abbach D 95 C4
Badacsonytomaj
H 111 C4
Bad Aibling D 108 B3
Badajoz E 155 C4
Badalona E 147 C3
Badalucco I 133 B3
Bad Aussee A 109 B4
Bad Bederkesa D 72 A1
Bad Bentheim D 71 B4
Bad Bergzabern D 93 B3
Bad Berka D 82 B3
Bad Berleburg D 81 A4
Bad Berneck D 95 A3
Bad Bevensen D 73 A3
Bad Bibra D 82 A3
Bad Birnbach D 95 C5
Bad Blankenburg
D 82 B3
Bad Bleiberg A 109 C4
Bad Brambach D 83 B4
Bad Bramstedt D 64 C2
Bad Breisig D 80 B3
Bad Brückenau D 82 B1
Bad Buchau D 107 A4
Bad Camberg D 81 B4
Badderen N 192 C6
Bad Doberan D 65 B4
Bad Driburg D 81 A5
Bad Düben D 83 A4
Bad Dürkheim D 93 B4
Bad Dürrenberg D 83 A4
Bad Dürrheim D 107 A3
Bad Elster D 83 B4
Bad Ems D 81 B3
Baden
A 111 A3
CH 106 B3
Bádenas E 152 A2
Baden-Baden D 93 C4
Bad Endorf D 109 B3
Badenweiler D 106 B2
Baderna HR 122 B2
Bad Essen D 71 B5
Bad Fischau A 111 B3
Bad Frankenhausen
D 82 A3
Bad Freienwalde D 74 B3
Bad Friedrichshall
D 93 B5
Bad Füssing D 96 C1
Bad Gandersheim
D 82 A2
Bad Gastein A 109 B4
Bad Gleichenberg
A 110 C2
Bad Goisern A 109 B4
Bad Gottleuba D 84 B1
Bad Grund D 82 A2
Bad Hall A 110 A1
Bad Harzburg D 82 A2
Bad Herrenalb D 93 C4
Bad Hersfeld D 82 B1
Bad Hofgastein A 109 B4
Bad Homburg D 81 B4
Bad Honnef D 80 B3
Bad Hönningen D 80 B3
Badia Calavena I 121 B4
Badia Polésine I 121 B4
Badia Pratáglia I 135 B4
Badia Tedalda I 135 B5
Bad Iburg D 71 B5
Bad Innerlaterns
A 107 B4
Bad Ischl A 109 B4
Bad Karlshafen D 81 A5
Bad Kemmeriboden
CH 106 C2
Bądki PL 69 B3
Bad Kissingen D 82 B2
Bad Kleinen D 65 C4
Bad Kohlgrub D 108 B2
Bad König D 93 B5
Bad Königshofen
D 82 B2
Bad Köstritz D 83 B4
Badkowo PL 76 B3
Bad Kreuzen A 110 A1
Bad Kreuznach D 93 B3
Bad Krozingen D 106 B2
Bad Laasphe D 81 B4
Bad Langensalza D 82 A2
Bad Lauchstädt D 83 A3
Bad Lausick D 83 A4
Bad Lauterberg D 82 A2
Bad Leonfelden A 96 C2
Bad Liebenwerda
D 83 A5
Bad Liebenzell D 93 C4
Bad Lippspringe D 81 A4

Badljevina HR 124 B3
Bad Meinberg D 81 A4
Bad Mergentheim D 94 B1
Bad Mitterndorf A 109 B4
Bad Münder D 72 B2
Bad Münstereifel D 80 B2
Bad Muskau D 84 A2
Bad Nauheim D 81 B4
Bad Nenndorf D 72 B2
Bad Neuenahr-Ahrweiler D 80 B3
Bad Neustadt D 82 B2
Bad Oeynhausen D 72 B1
Badolato I 175 C2
Badolatosa E 163 A3
Bad Oldesloe D 65 C3
Badonviller F 92 C2
Bad Orb D 81 B5
Badovinci SRB 127 C1
Bad Peterstal D 93 C4
Bad Pyrmont D 72 C2
Bad Radkersburg A 110 C2
Bad Ragaz CH 107 C4
Bad Rappenau D 93 B5
Bad Reichenhall D 109 B3
Bad Saarow-Pieskow D 74 B3
Bad Sachsa D 82 A2
Bad Säckingen D 106 B2
Bad Salzdetfurth D 72 B3
Bad Salzig D 81 B3
Bad Salzuflen D 72 B1
Bad Salzungen D 82 B2
Bad Sankt Leonhard A 110 C1
Bad Sassendorf D 81 A4
Bad Schandau D 84 B2
Bad Schmiedeberg D 83 A4
Bad Schönborn D 93 B4
Bad Schussenried D 107 A4
Bad Schwalbach D 81 B4
Bad Schwartau D 65 C3
Bad Segeberg D 64 C3
Bad Soden D 81 B4
Bad Soden-Salmünster D 81 B5
Bad Sooden-Allendorf D 82 A1
Bad Sulza D 83 A3
Bad Sülze D 66 B1
Bad Tatzmannsdorf A 111 B3
Bad Tennstedt D 82 A2
Bad Tölz D 108 B2
Badules E 152 A2
Bad Urach D 94 C1
Bad Vellach A 110 C1
Bad Vilbel D 81 B4
Bad Vöslau A 111 B3
Bad Waldsee D 107 B4
Bad Wiessee D 108 B2
Bad Wildungen D 81 A5
Bad Wilsnack D 73 B4
Bad Windsheim D 94 B2
Bad Wörishafen D 108 A1
Bad Wurzach D 107 B4
Bad Zwesten D 81 A5
Bad Zwischenahn D 71 A5
Baells E 145 C4
Baena E 163 A3
Baesweiler D 80 B2
Baeza E 157 C4
Baflo NL 71 A3
Baga E 147 B2
Bagaladi I 175 C1
Bagenkop DK 65 B3
Baggetorp S 56 A2
Bagh a Chaisteil GB 31 C1
Bagheria I 176 A2
Bagn N 47 B6
Bagnacavallo I 135 A4
Bagnáia I 168 A2
Bagnara Cálabra I 175 C1
Bagnasco I 133 A4
Bagnères-de-Bigorre F 145 A4
Bagnères-de-Luchon F 145 B4
Bagni del Másino I 120 A2
Bagni di Lucca I 134 A3
Bagni di Rabbi I 121 A3
Bagni di Tivoli I 168 B2
Bagno di Romagna I 135 B4
Bagnoles-de-l'Orne F 89 B3
Bagnoli dei Trigno I 170 B2
Bagnoli di Sopra I 121 B4
Bagnoli Irpino I 170 C3
Bagnolo Mella I 120 B3
Bagnols-en-Forêt F 132 B2
Bagnols-sur-Cèze F 131 A3
Bagnorégio I 168 A2
Bagolino I 121 B3
Bagrationovsk RUS 12 A4
Bagrdan SRB 127 C3
Báguena E 152 A2
Bahabón de Esgueva E 143 C3
Bahillo E 142 B2
Báia delle Zágare I 171 B4
Báia Domizia I 169 B3
Baia Mare RO 17 B5
Baiano I 170 C2
Baião P 148 A1
Baiersbronn D 93 C4
Baiersdorf D 94 B3
Baignes-Ste Radegonde F 115 C3
Baigneux-les-Juifs F 104 B3
Baildon GB 40 B2
Bailén E 157 B4
Băileşti RO 17 C5
Baileux B 91 A4
Bailieborough IRL 27 C4
Bailleul F 78 B2
Baillonville B 79 B5
Bailó E 144 B3
Bain-de-Bretagne F 101 B4
Bains F 117 B3
Bains-les-Bains F 105 A5
Bainton GB 40 B3
Baio E 140 A2
Baiona E 140 B2
Bais F 89 B3
Baiso I 134 A3
Baiuca P 148 B2
Baja H 125 A4
Bajánsenye H 111 C3
Bajina Bašta SRB 127 D1
Bajmok SRB 126 B1
Bajna H 112 B2
Bajovo Polje MNE 139 B4
Bajša SRB 126 B1
Bak H 111 C3
Bakar HR 123 B3
Bakewell GB 40 B2
Bakio E 143 A4
Bakka N 47 C6
Bakkafjörður IS 191 A11
Bakkagerði IS 191 B12
Bække DK 59 C2
Bakken N 48 B3
Baklan TR 189 B4
Bækmarksbro DK 58 B1
Bakonybél H 111 B4
Bakonycsernye H 112 B2
Bakonyjákó H 111 B4
Bakonyszentkirály H 111 B4
Bakonyszombathely H 112 B1
Bakov nad Jizerou CZ 84 B2
Bąkowiec PL 87 A5
Baks H 113 C4
Baksa H 125 B4
Bakum D 71 B5
Bala GB 38 B3
Bâlâ TR 23 B7
Balaguer E 145 C4
Balassagyarmat H 112 A3
Balástya H 113 C4
Balatonakali H 111 C4
Balatonalmádi H 112 B2
Balatonboglár H 111 C4
Balatonbozsok H 112 C2
Balatonederics H 111 C4
Balatonfenyves H 111 C4
Balatonföldvár H 112 C1
Balatonfüred H 112 C1
Balatonfűzfő H 112 B2
Balatonkenese H 112 B2
Balatonkiliti H 112 C2
Balatonlelle H 111 C4
Balatonszabadi H 112 C2
Balatonszemes H 111 C4
Balatonszentgyörgy H 111 C4
Balazote E 158 C1
Balbeggie GB 35 B4
Balbigny F 117 B4
Balboa E 141 B4
Balbriggan IRL 30 A2
Balchik BG 17 D8
Balçova TR 188 A2
Baldock GB 44 B3
Bale HR 122 B2
Baleira E 141 A3
Baleizao P 160 A2
Balen B 79 A5
Balerma E 164 C2
Balestrand N 46 A3
Balestrate I 176 A2
Balfour GB 33 B4
Bälganet S 63 B3
Balıkesir TR 186 C2
Balıklıçeşme TR 186 B2
Bälinge S 51 C4
Balingen D 107 A3
Balingsta S 56 A3
Balintore GB 32 D3
Balizac F 128 B2
Balk NL 70 B2
Balkbrug NL 71 B3
Balla IRL 28 A2
Ballachulish GB 34 B2
Ballaghaderreen IRL 26 C2
Ballancourt-sur-Essonne F 90 C2
Ballantrae GB 36 A2
Ballao I 179 C3
Ballasalla GB 36 B2
Ballater GB 32 D3
Ballen DK 59 C3
Ballenstedt D 82 A3
Ballerias E 145 C3
Balleroy F 88 A3
Ballerup DK 61 D2
Ballesteros de Calatrava E 157 B4
Ballı TR 186 B2
Ballina IRL 26 B1
Ballinalack IRL 30 A1
Ballinamore IRL 26 B3
Ballinascarty IRL 29 C3
Ballinasloe IRL 28 A3
Ballindine IRL 28 A3
Balling DK 58 B1
Ballingarry
 Limerick IRL 29 B3
 Tipperary IRL 30 B1
Ballingeary IRL 29 C2
Ballinhassig IRL 29 C3
Ballinluig GB 35 B4
Ballino I 121 B3
Ballinrobe IRL 28 A2
Ballinskelligs IRL 29 C1
Ballinspittle IRL 29 C3
Ballintra IRL 26 B2
Ballivor IRL 30 A2
Ballobar E 153 A4
Ballon
 F 102 A2
 IRL 30 B2
Ballószög H 112 C3
Ballsh AL 182 C1
Ballstad N 194 B4
Ballum DK 64 A1
Ballybay IRL 27 B4
Ballybofey IRL 26 B3
Ballybunion IRL 29 B2
Ballycanew IRL 30 B2
Ballycarry GB 27 B5
Ballycastle
 GB 27 A4
 IRL 26 B1
Ballyclare GB 27 B5
Ballyconneely IRL 28 A1
Ballycotton IRL 29 C3
Ballycroy IRL 26 B1
Ballydehob IRL 29 C2
Ballyferriter IRL 29 B1
Ballygawley GB 27 B3
Ballygowan GB 27 B5
Ballyhaunis IRL 28 A3
Ballyheige IRL 29 B2
Ballyjamesduff IRL 27 C3
Ballylanders IRL 29 B3
Ballylynan IRL 30 B1
Ballymahon IRL 28 A4
Ballymena GB 27 B4
Ballymoe IRL 28 A3
Ballymoney GB 27 A4
Ballymore IRL 28 A4
Ballymote IRL 26 B2
Ballynacorra IRL 29 C3
Ballynagore IRL 30 A1
Ballynahinch GB 27 B5
Ballynure GB 27 B5
Ballyragget IRL 30 B1
Ballysadare IRL 26 B2
Ballyshannon IRL 26 B2
Ballyvaughan IRL 28 A2
Ballyvourney IRL 29 C2
Ballywalter GB 27 B5
Balmaclellan GB 36 A2
Balmaseda E 143 A3
Balmazújváros H 113 B5
Balme I 119 B4
Balmedie GB 33 D4
Balmuccia I 119 B5
Balna-paling GB 32 D2
Balneario de Panticosa E 145 B3
Balotaszállás H 126 A1
Balsa P 148 A2
Balsareny E 147 C2
Balsorano-Nuovo I 169 B3
Bålsta S 57 A3
Balsthal CH 106 B2
Balta UA 17 A8
Baltanás E 142 C2
Baltar E 140 C3
Baltasound GB 33 A6
Bălţi MD 17 B7
Baltimore IRL 29 C2
Baltinglass IRL 30 B2
Baltiysk RUS 69 A4
Baltów PL 87 A5
Balugães P 148 A1
Bælum DK 58 B3
Balve D 81 A3
Balvi LV 8 D5
Balvicar GB 34 B2
Balya TR 186 C2
Balzo I 136 C2
Bamberg D 94 B2
Bamburgh GB 37 A5
Banatska Palanka SRB 127 C3
Banatski Brestovac SRB 127 C2
Banatski Despotovac SRB 126 B2
Banatski Dvor SRB 126 B2
Banatski-Karlovac SRB 127 B3
Banatsko Arandjelovo SRB 126 A2
Banatsko-Novo Selo SRB 127 C2
Banaz TR 187 D4
Banbridge GB 27 B4
Banbury GB 44 A2
Banchory GB 33 D4
Bande
 B 79 B5
 E 140 B3
Bandholm DK 65 B4
Bandırma TR 186 B2
Bandol F 132 B1
Bandon IRL 29 C3
Bañeres E 159 C3
Banff GB 33 D4
Bangor
 F 100 B2
 Down GB 27 B5
 Gwynedd GB 38 A2
 IRL 26 B1
Bangsund N 199 A8
Banie PL 74 A3
Banja Koviljača SRB 127 C1
Banjaloka SLO 123 B3
Banja Luka BIH 124 C3
Banjani SRB 127 C1
Banja Vručica BIH 125 C3
Banka SK 98 C1
Bankekind S 56 B1
Bankend GB 36 A3
Bankeryd S 62 A2
Bankfoot GB 35 B4
Banloc RO 126 B3
Bannalec F 100 B2
Bannes F 91 C3
Bannockburn GB 35 B4
Bañobárez E 149 B3
Bañon E 152 B2
Banon F 132 A1
Baños E 149 B4
Baños de Gigonza E 162 B2
Baños de la Encina E 157 B4
Baños de Molgas E 140 B3
Baños de Rio Tobia E 143 B4
Baños de Valdearados E 143 C3
Bánov CZ 98 C1
Banova Jaruga HR 124 B2
Bánovce nad Bebravou SK 98 C2
Banovići BIH 139 A4
Banoviči Selo BIH 139 A4
Bánréve H 99 C4
Bansin D 66 C3
Banská Belá SK 98 C2
Banská Bystrica SK 99 C3
Banská Štiavnica SK 98 C2
Bansko BG 183 B5
Banstead GB 44 B3
Banteer IRL 29 B3
Bantheville F 91 B5
Bantry IRL 29 C2
Bantzenheim F 106 B2
Banyalbufar E 166 B2
Banyoles E 147 B3
Banyuls-sur-Mer F 146 B4
Bapaume F 90 A2
Bar
 MNE 16 D3
 UA 13 D7
Barabhas GB 31 A2
Barači BIH 138 A2
Baracs H 112 C2
Baracska H 112 B2
Barahona E 151 A5
Barajes de Melo E 151 B5
Barakaldo E 143 A4
Baralla E 141 B3
Barañain E 144 B2
Baranavichy BY 13 B7
Báránd H 113 B5
Baranda SRB 127 B2
Baranello I 170 B2
Baranów Sandomierski PL 87 B5
Baraqueville F 130 A1
Barasoain E 144 B2
Barbacena P 155 C3
Barbadás E 140 B3
Barbadillo E 149 B4
Barbadillo de Herreros E 143 B3
Barbadillo del Mercado E 143 B3
Barbadillo del Pez E 143 B3
Barban HR 123 B3
Barbarano Vicento I 121 B4
Barbariga HR 122 C2
Barbaros TR 186 B2
Barbastro E 145 B4
Barbate E 162 B2
Barbatona E 152 A1
Barbâtre F 114 B1
Barbazan F 145 A4
Barbeitos E 141 A3
Barbentane F 131 B3
Barberino di Mugello I 135 A4
Barbezieux-St Hilaire F 115 C3
Barbonne-Fayel F 91 C3
Barbotan-les-Thermes F 128 C2
Barby D 73 C4
Bárcabo E 145 B4
Barca de Alva P 149 A3
Barcarrota E 155 C4
Barcellona-Pozzo di Gotto I 177 A4
Barcelona E 147 C3
Barcelonette F 132 A2
Barcelos P 148 A1
Bárcena del Monasterio E 141 A4
Barcena de Pie de Concha E 142 A2
Barchfeld D 82 B2
Barcin PL 76 B2
Barcino PL 68 A1
Bárcis I 122 A1
Barco P 148 B2
Barcones E 151 A5
Barcs H 124 B3
Barcus F 144 A3
Bardejov SK 12 D4
Bårdesø DK 59 C3
Bardi I 120 C2
Bardney GB 40 B3
Bardo PL 85 B4
Bardolino I 121 B3
Bardonécchia I 118 B3
Bardoñovo SK 112 A2
Barèges F 145 B4
Barenstein D 83 B5
Barentin F 89 A4
Barenton F 88 B3
Barevo BIH 138 A3
Barfleur F 88 A2
Barga I 134 A3
Bargas E 151 C3
Barge I 119 C4
Bargemon F 132 B2
Barghe I 120 B3
Bargoed GB 39 C3
Bargrennan GB 36 A2
Bargteheide D 64 C3
Barham GB 45 B5
Bari I 173 A2
Barič Draga HR 137 A4
Barilović HR 123 B4
Bari Sardo I 179 C3
Barisciano I 169 A3
Barjac F 131 A3
Barjols F 132 B1
Barjon F 105 B3
Bårkåker N 54 A1
Barkald N 199 D7
Barkowo
 Dolnośląskie PL 85 A4
 Pomorskie PL 68 B2
Bârlad RO 17 B7
Bar-le-Duc F 91 C5
Barles F 132 A2
Barletta I 171 B4
Barlinek PL 75 B4
Barmouth GB 38 B2
Barmstedt D 64 C2
Barnard Castle GB 37 B5
Barnarp S 62 A2
Bärnau D 95 B4
Bärnbach A 110 B2
Barneberg D 73 B4
Barnenitz D 74 B1
Barnet GB 44 B3
Barnetby le Wold GB 40 B3
Barneveld NL 70 B2
Barneville-Carteret F 88 A2
Barnoldswick GB 40 B1
Barnowko PL 75 B3
Barnsley GB 40 B2
Barnstädt D 83 A3
Barnstaple GB 42 A2
Barnstorf D 72 B1
Barntrup D 72 C2
Baron F 90 B2
Baronissi I 170 C2
Barqueiro P 154 B2
Barquinha P 154 B2
Barr
 F 93 C3
 GB 36 A2
Barra P 148 B1
Barracas E 159 A3
Barraco E 150 B3
Barrado E 150 B2
Barrafranca I 177 B3
Barranco do Velho P 160 B2
Barrancos P 161 A3
Barrax E 158 B1
Barrbaar D 94 C2
Barre-des-Cevennes F 130 A2
Barreiro P 154 C1
Barreiros E 141 A3
Barrême F 132 B2
Barret-le-Bas F 132 A1
Barrhead GB 34 C3
Barrhill GB 36 A2
Barrio de Nuesra Señora E 142 B1
Barrowford GB 40 B1
Barrow-in-Furness GB 36 B3
Barrow upon Humber GB 40 B3
Barruecopardo E 149 A3
Barruelo de Santullán E 142 B2
Barruera E 145 B4
Barry GB 39 C3
Bårse DK 65 A4
Barsinghausen D 72 B2
Barssel D 71 A4
Bar-sur-Aube F 104 A3
Bar-sur-Seine F 104 A3
Barth D 66 B1
Bartholomä D 94 C1
Bartin TR 187 A7
Barton upon Humber GB 40 B3
Barúmini I 179 C2
Baruth D 74 B2
Barvaux B 80 B1
Barver D 72 B1
Barwatd PL 99 B3
Barwice PL 68 B1
Barysaw BY 13 A8
Barzana E 141 A5
Bârzava RO 16 B4
Bárzio I 120 B2
Bas E 147 B3
Bašaid SRB 126 B2
Basaluzzo I 120 C1
Basarabeasca MD 17 B8
Basauri E 143 A4
Baschi I 168 A2
Baschurch GB 38 B4
Basconcillos del Tozo E 143 B3
Bascones de Ojeda E 142 B2
Basécles B 79 B3
Basel CH 106 B2
Basélice I 170 B2
Basildon GB 45 B4
Basingstoke GB 44 B2
Baška
 CZ 98 B2
 HR 123 C3
Baška Voda HR 138 B2
Bäsksjö S 200 B3
Baslow GB 40 B2
Başmakçı TR 189 B5
Basovizza I 122 B2
Bassacutena I 178 A3
Bassano del Grappa I 121 B4
Bassano Romano I 168 A2
Bassecourt CH 106 B2
Bassella E 147 B2
Bassevuovdde N 193 D9
Bassou F 104 B2
Bassoues F 128 C3
Bassum D 72 B1
Båstad S 61 C2
Bastardo I 136 C1
Bastelica F 180 A2
Bastelicaccia F 180 B1
Bastia
 F 180 A2
 I 136 B1
Bastogne B 92 A1
Baston GB 40 C3
Bastuträsk S 200 B6
Bata H 125 A4
Batajnica SRB 127 C2
Batak BG 183 B6
Batalha P 154 B2
Bátaszék H 125 A4
Batea E 153 A4
Batelov CZ 97 B3
Bath GB 43 A4
Bathgate GB 35 C4
Batida H 126 A2
Batignano I 135 C4
Batina HR 125 B4
Bátka SK 99 C4
Batković BIH 125 C5
Batley GB 40 B2
Batnfjordsøra N 198 C4
Batočina SRB 127 C3
Bátonyterenye H 113 B3
Batrina HR 125 B3
Båtsfjord N 193 B13
Båtskärsnäs S 196 D6
Battaglia Terme I 121 B4
Bätterkinden CH 106 B2
Battice B 80 B1
Battipáglia I 170 C2
Battle GB 45 C4
Battonya H 126 A3
Batuša SRB 127 C3
Bátya H 112 C2
Bau I 179 C2
Baud F 100 B2
Baudour B 79 B3
Baugé F 102 B1
Baugy F 103 B4
Bauma CH 107 B3
Baume-les-Dames F 105 B5
Baumholder D 93 B3
Baunatal D 81 A5
Baunei I 178 B3
Bauska LV 8 D4
Bautzen D 84 A2
Bavanište SRB 127 C2
Bavay F 79 B3
Bavilliers F 106 B1
Bavorov CZ 96 B2
Bawdsey GB 45 A5
Bawinkel D 71 B4
Bawtry GB 40 B2
Bayat TR 187 D5
Bayel F 105 A3
Bayeux F 88 A3
Bayındır TR 188 A2
Bayon F 92 C2
Bayonne F 128 C1
Bayons F 132 A2
Bayramiç TR 186 C1
Bayreuth D 95 B3
Bayrischzell D 108 B3
Baza E 164 B2
Bazas F 128 B2
Baziege F 146 A2
Bazoches-les-Gallerandes F 103 A4
Bazoches-sur-Hoëne F 89 B4
Bazzano I 135 A4
Beaconsfield GB 44 B3
Beade E 140 B2
Beadnell GB 37 A5
Beaminster GB 43 B4
Bearsden GB 34 C3
Beas E 161 B3
Beasain E 144 A1
Beas de Segura E 164 A2
Beattock GB 36 A3
Beaubery F 117 A4
Beaucaire F 131 B3
Beaufort
 F 118 B3
 IRL 29 B2
Beaufort-en Vallée F 102 B1
Beaugency F 103 B3
Beaujeu
 Alpes-de-Haute-Provence F 132 A2
 Rhône F 117 A4
Beaulac F 128 B2
Beaulieu
 F 103 B4
 GB 44 C2
Beaulieu-sous-la-Roche F 114 B2
Beaulieu-sur-Dordogne F 129 B4
Beaulieu-sur-Mer F 133 B3
Beaulon F 104 C2
Beauly GB 32 D2
Beaumaris GB 38 A2
Beaumesnil F 89 A4
Beaumetz-lès-Loges F 78 B2
Beaumont
 B 79 B4
 F 129 B3
Beaumont-de-Lomagne F 129 C3
Beaumont-du-Gâtinais F 103 A4
Beaumont-en-Argonne F 91 B5
Beaumont-Hague F 88 A2
Beaumont-la-Ronce F 102 B2
Beaumont-le-Roger F 89 A4
Beaumont-sur-Oise F 90 B2
Beaumont-sur-Sarthe F 102 A2
Beaune F 105 B3
Beaune-la-Rolande F 103 A4
Beaupréau F 101 B5
Beauraing B 91 A4
Beaurepaire F 117 B5
Beaurepaire-en-Bresse F 105 C4
Beaurières F 132 A1
Beauvais F 90 B2
Beauval F 90 A2
Beauville F 129 B3
Beauvoir-sur-Mer F 114 B1
Beauvoir-sur-Niort F 114 B3
Beba Veche RO 126 A2
Bebertal D 73 B4
Bebington GB 38 A3
Bebra D 82 B1
Bebrina HR 125 B3
Beccles GB 45 A5
Becedas E 150 B2
Beceite E 153 B4
Bečej SRB 126 B2
Becerreá E 141 B3
Becerril de Campos E 142 B2
Bécherel F 101 A4
Bechhofen D 94 B2
Bechyně CZ 96 B2
Becilla de Valderaduey E 142 B1
Beckfoot GB 36 B3
Beckingham GB 40 B3
Beckum D 81 A4
Beco P 154 B2
Bécon-les-Granits F 102 B1
Bečov nad Teplou CZ 83 B4
Becsehely H 111 C3
Bedale GB 37 B5
Bedames E 143 A3
Bédar E 164 B3
Bédarieux F 130 B2
Bédarrides F 131 A3
Bedburg D 80 B2
Beddgelert GB 38 A2
Beddingestrand S 66 A2
Bédée F 101 A4
Bedegkér H 112 C2
Beden TR 189 C7
Bedford GB 44 A3
Będków PL 87 A3
Bedlington GB 37 A5
Bedlno PL 77 B4
Bedmar E 163 A4
Bédoin F 131 A4
Bedónia I 134 A2
Bedretto CH 107 C3
Bedsted DK 58 B1
Bedum NL 71 A3
Bedwas GB 39 C3
Bedworth GB 40 C2
Będzin PL 86 B3
Beekbergen NL 70 B2
Beek en Donk NL 80 A1
Beelen D 71 C5
Beelitz D 74 B1
Beer GB 43 B3
Beerfelde D 74 B3
Beerfelden D 93 B4
Beernem B 78 A3
Beeskow D 74 B3
Beetsterzwaag NL 70 A3
Beetzendorf D 73 B4
Beflelay CH 106 B2
Begaljica SRB 127 C2
Bégard F 100 A2
Begejci SRB 126 B2
Begijar E 157 C4
Begijnendijk B 79 A4
Begndal N 48 B1
Begues E 147 C2
Beguildy GB 39 B3
Begur E 147 C4
Beho B 80 B1
Behringen D 82 A2
Beilen NL 71 B3
Beilngries D 95 B3
Beine-Nauroy F 91 B4
Beinwil CH 106 B3
Beiseförth D 82 A1
Beith GB 34 C3
Beitostølen N 47 A5
Beiuş RO 16 B5
Beja P 160 A2
Béjar E 149 B
Bekçiler TR 189 C
Békés H 113 C
Békéscsaba H 113 C
Bekilli TR 189 A
Bekkarfjord N 193 B1
Bela SK 98 B
Bélâbre F 115 B
Bela Crkva SRB 127 C
Belalcázar E 156 B
Belánad Radbuzou CZ 95 B
Belanovica SRB 127 C
Bélapátfalva H 113 A
Bělápod Bezdězem CZ 84 B
Belcaire F 146 B

Bełchatów PL 86 A3
Belchite E 153 A3
Bělčice CZ 96 B1
Belcoo GB 26 B3
Belecke D 81 A4
Beled H 111 B4
Belej HR 123 C3
Beleño E 142 A1
Bélesta F 146 B2
Belevi TR 188 A2
Belfast GB 27 B5
Belford GB 37 A5
Belfort F 106 B1
Belgentier F 132 B1
Belgern D 83 A5
Belgioioso I 120 B2
Belgodère F 180 A2
Belgooly IRL 29 C3
Belgrade = Beograd SRB 127 C2
Belhade F 128 B2
Belica HR 124 A2
Beli Manastir HR 125 B4
Belin-Bèliet F 128 B2
Belinchón E 151 B4
Belišće HR 125 B4
Bělkovice-Lašťany CZ 98 B1
Bella I 172 B1
Bellac F 115 B5
Bellágio I 120 B2
Bellananagh IRL 27 C3
Bellano I 120 A2
Bellária I 136 A1
Bellavary IRL 26 C1
Belleau F 90 B3
Belleek GB 26 B2
Bellegarde
Gard F 131 B3
Loiret F 103 B4
Bellegarde-en-Diois F 132 A1
Bellegarde-en-Marche F 116 B2
Bellegarde-sur-Valserine F 118 A2
Belle-Isle-en-Terre F 100 A2
Bellême F 89 B4
Bellenaves F 116 A3
Bellentre F 118 B3
Bellevaux F 118 A3
Bellevesvre F 105 C4
Belleville F 117 A4
Belleville-sur-Vie F 114 B2
Bellevue-la-Montagne F 117 B3
Belley F 118 B2
Bellheim D 93 B4
Bellinge DK 59 C3
Bellingham GB 37 A4
Bellinzago Novarese I 120 B1
Bellinzona CH 120 A2
Bell-lloc d'Urgell E 153 A4
Bello E 152 B2
Bellpuig d'Urgell E 147 C2
Bellreguart E 159 C3
Bellsbank GB 36 A2
Belltall E 147 C2
Belluno I 121 A5
Bellver de Cerdanya E 146 B2
Bellvis E 147 C1
Bélmez E 156 B2
Belmez de la Moraleda E 163 A4
Belmont GB 33 A6
Belmont-de-la-Loire F 117 A4
Belmonte
Asturias E 141 A4
Cuenca E 158 B1
P 148 B2
Belmonte de San José E 153 B3
Belmonte de Tajo E 151 B4
Belmont-sur-Rance F 130 B1
Belmullet IRL 26 B1
Belobreşca RO 127 C3
Beloeil B 79 B3
Belogradchik BG 16 D5
Belokorovichi UA 13 C8
Belorado E 143 B3
Belotič SRB 127 C1
Bělotin CZ 98 B1
Belovo BG 183 A6
Belozersk RUS 9 C10
Belp CH 106 C2
Belpasso I 177 B3
Belpech F 146 A2
Belper GB 40 B2
Belsay GB 37 A5
Belsk Duzy PL 87 A4
Beltinci SLO 111 C3
Beltra IRL 26 C1
Belturbet IRL 27 B3
Beluša SK 98 B2
Belvedere Marittimo I 174 B1
Belver de Cinca E 153 A4
Belver de los Montes E 142 C1
Belvès F 129 B3
Belvezet F 130 A2
Belvis de la Jara E 150 C3
Belvis de Monroy E 150 C2
Belyy RUS 9 E8
Belz F 100 B2
Bełżec PL 13 C5
Belzig D 73 B5
Bembibre E 141 B4
Bembridge GB 44 C2
Bemmel NL 80 A1
Bemposta
Bragança P 149 A3
Santarém P 154 B2
Benabarre E 145 B4
Benacazón E 161 B3
Benaguacil E 159 B3
Benahadux E 164 C2
Benalmádena E 163 B3
Benalúa de Guadix E 164 B1
Benalúa de las Villas E 163 A4
Benalup E 162 B2
Benamargosa E 163 B3
Benamaurel E 164 B2
Benameji E 163 A3
Benamocarra E 163 B3
Benaocaz E 162 B2
Benaoján E 162 B2
Benarrabá E 162 B2
Benasque E 145 B4
Benátky nad Jizerou CZ 84 B2
Benavente
E 142 B1
P 154 C2
Benavides de Órbigo E 141 B5
Benavila P 154 B3
Bendorf D 81 B3
Benedikt SLO 110 C2
Benejama E 159 C3
Benejúzar E 165 A4
Benešov CZ 96 B2
Bénestroff F 92 C2
Benet F 114 B3
Bene Vagienna I 133 A3
Bénévent-l'Abbaye F 116 A1
Benevento I 170 B2
Benfeld F 93 C3
Benfica P 154 B2
Bengtsfors S 54 A3
Bengtsheden S 50 B2
Beničanci HR 125 B4
Benicarló E 153 B4
Benicássim E 153 B4
Benidorm E 159 C3
Benifaió E 159 B3
Beniganim E 159 C3
Benington GB 41 B4
Benisa E 159 C4
Benkovac HR 137 A4
Benllech GB 38 A2
Benneckenstein D 82 A2
Bénodet F 100 B1
Benquerencia de la Serena E 156 B2
Bensafrim P 160 B1
Bensbyn S 196 D5
Bensdorf D 73 B5
Benshausen D 82 B2
Bensheim D 93 B4
Bentley GB 44 B3
Bentwisch D 65 B5
Beočin SRB 126 B1
Beograd = Belgrade SRB 127 C2
Beragh GB 27 B3
Beranga E 143 A3
Berat AL 182 C1
Bérat F 146 A2
Beratzhausen D 95 B3
Bérbaltavár H 111 B3
Berbegal E 145 C3
Berbenno di Valtellina I 120 A2
Berberana E 143 B3
Bercedo E 143 A3
Bercel H 112 B3
Bercenay-le-Hayer F 91 C3
Berceto I 134 A2
Berchem B 79 B3
Berchidda I 178 B3
Berching D 95 B3
Berchtesgaden D 109 B4
Bérchules E 163 B4
Bercianos de Aliste E 149 A3
Berck F 78 B1
Berclaire d'Urgell E 147 C1
Berdoias E 140 A1
Berducedo E 141 A4
Berdún E 144 B3
Berdychiv UA 13 D8
Bere Alston GB 42 B2
Bereguardo I 120 B2
Berehommen N 53 A3
Berehove UA 16 A5
Berek BIH 124 B3
Beremend H 125 B4
Bere Regis GB 43 B4
Berestechko UA 13 C6
Berettyóújfalu H 113 B5
Berezhany UA 13 D6
Berezivka UA 17 B9
Berezna UA 13 C9
Berg
D 95 B3
N 195 E3
S 56 B2
Berga
Sachsen-Anhalt D 82 A3
Thüringen D 83 B4
E 147 B2
S 62 A4
Bergama TR 186 C2
Bérgamo I 120 B2
Bergara E 143 A4
Bergby S 51 B4
Berge
Brandenburg D 74 B1
Niedersachsen D 71 B4
Telemark N 53 A4
Telemark N 53 A4
Bergeforsen S 200 D3
Bergen
Mecklenburg-Vorpommern D 66 B2
Niedersachsen D 72 B2
Niedersachsen D 73 B3
N 46 B2
NL 70 B1
Bergen op Zoom NL 79 A4
Bergerac F 129 B3
Bergères-lés-Vertus F 91 C4
Bergeyk NL 79 A5
Berghausen D 93 C4
Bergheim D 80 B2
Berghem S 60 B2
Berg im Gau D 95 C3
Bergisch Gladbach D 80 B3
Bergkamen D 81 A3
Bergkvara S 63 B4
Berglern D 95 C3
Bergnäset S 196 D5
Bergneustadt D 81 A3
Bergsäng S 49 B5
Bergshamra S 57 A4
Bergsjö S 200 E3
Bergs slussar S 56 B1
Bergsviken S 196 D4
Bergtheim D 94 B2
Bergues F 78 B2
Bergum NL 70 A2
Bergün Bravuogn CH 107 C4
Bergwitz D 83 A4
Berhida H 112 B2
Beringel P 160 A2
Beringen B 79 A5
Berja E 164 C2
Berkåk N 199 C7
Berkeley GB 43 A4
Berkenthin D 65 C3
Berkhamsted GB 44 B3
Berkheim D 107 A5
Berkhof D 72 B2
Berkovići BIH 139 B4
Berkovitsa BG 17 D5
Berlanga E 156 B2
Berlanga de Duero E 151 A5
Berlevåg N 193 B13
Berlikum NL 70 A2
Berlin D 74 B2
Berlstedt D 82 A3
Bermeo E 143 A4
Bermillo de Sayago E 149 A3
Bern CH 106 C2
Bernalda I 174 A2
Bernardos E 150 A3
Bernartice
Jihočeský CZ 96 B2
Vychodočeský CZ 85 B3
Bernau
Baden-Württemberg D 106 B3
Bayern D 109 B3
Brandenburg D 74 B2
Bernaville F 90 A2
Bernay F 89 A4
Bernburg D 83 A3
Berndorf A 111 B3
Berne D 72 A1
Bernecebarati H 112 A2
Bernhardsthal A 97 C4
Bernkastel-Kues D 92 B3
Bernolakovo SK 111 A4
Bernsdorf D 84 A2
Bernstadt D 84 A2
Bernstein A 111 B3
Bernués E 145 B3
Beromünster CH 106 B3
Beroun CZ 96 B2
Berovo MK 182 B4
Berre-l'Etang F 131 B4
Berriedale GB 32 C3
Berriew GB 39 B3
Berrocal E 161 B3
Bersenbrück D 71 B4
Bershad' UA 13 D8
Bertamiráns E 140 B2
Berthåga S 51 C4
Berthelming F 92 C2
Bertincourt F 90 A2
Bertinoro I 135 A5
Bertogne B 92 A1
Bertrix B 91 B5
Berufjörður IS 191 C11
Berville-sur-Mer F 89 A4
Berwick-upon-Tweed GB 37 A4
Berzasca RO 16 C4
Berzence H 124 A3
Berzocana E 156 A2
Besalú E 147 B3
Besançon F 105 B5
Besenfeld D 93 C4
Besenyötelek H 113 B4
Besenyszög H 113 B4
Beshenkovichi BY 13 A8
Besigheim D 93 C5
Běšiny CZ 96 B1
Beška SRB 126 B2
Beşkonak TR 189 B6
Besle F 101 B4
Besnyö H 112 B2
Bessais-le-Fromental F 103 C4
Bessan F 130 B2
Besse-en-Chandesse F 116 B2
Bessèges F 131 A3
Bessé-sur-Braye F 102 B2
Bessines-sur-Gartempe F 115 B5
Best NL 79 A5
Bestorp S 56 B1
Betanzos E 140 A2
Betelu E 144 A2
Bétera E 159 B3
Beteta E 152 B1
Béthenville F 91 B4
Bethesda GB 38 A2
Béthune F 78 B2
Beton-Bazoches F 90 C3
Bettembourg L 92 B2
Betterdorf L 92 B2
Bettna S 56 B2
Béttola I 120 C2
Bettona I 136 B1
Bettyhill GB 32 C2
Betws-y-Coed GB 38 A3
Betxi E 159 B3
Betz F 90 B2
Betzdorf D 81 B3
Beuil F 132 A2
Beulah GB 39 B3
Beuzeville F 89 A4
Bevagna I 136 C1
Bevens-bruk S 56 A1
Beveren B 79 A4
Beverley GB 40 B3
Bevern D 81 A5
Beverstedt D 72 A1
Beverungen D 81 A5
Beverwijk NL 70 B1
Bex CH 119 A4
Bexhill GB 45 C4
Beyazköy TR 186 A2
Beychevelle F 128 A2
Beydağ TR 188 A3
Beyeğaç TR 188 B3
Beykoz TR 186 A4
Beynat F 129 A4
Beyoğlu TR 186 A4
Beypazarı TR 187 B6
Beyşehir TR 189 B6
Bezas E 152 B2
Bezau A 107 B4
Bezdan SRB 125 B4
Bèze F 105 B4
Bezenet F 116 A2
Bezhetsk RUS 9 D10
Béziers F 130 B2
Bezzecca I 121 B3
Biadki PL 85 A5
Biała
Łódzkie PL 77 C4
Opolskie PL 85 B5
Białaczów PL 87 A4
Biała Podlaska PL 13 B5
Biała Rawska PL 87 A4
Biale Błota PL 76 A2
Białobloty PL 76 B2
Białobrzegi PL 87 A4
Białogard PL 67 C4
Białośliwie PL 76 A2
Białowąs PL 68 B1
Biały Bór PL 68 B1
Białystok PL 13 B5
Biancavilla I 177 B3
Bianco I 175 C2
Biandrate I 119 B5
Biar E 159 C3
Biarritz F 144 A2
Bias F 128 B1
Biasca CH 120 A1
Biatorbágy H 112 B2
Bibbiena I 135 B4
Bibbona I 134 B3
Biberach
Baden-Württemberg D 93 C4
Baden-Württemberg D 107 A4
Bibinje HR 137 A4
Bibione I 122 B2
Biblis D 93 B4
Bibury GB 44 B2
Bicaj AL 182 B2
Biccari I 171 B3
Bicester GB 44 B2
Bichl D 108 B2
Bichlbach A 108 B1
Bicorp E 159 B3
Bicos P 160 B1
Bicske H 112 B2
Bidache F 128 C1
Bidart F 144 A2
Biddinghuizen NL 70 B2
Biddulph GB 40 B1
Bideford GB 42 A2
Bidford-on-Avon GB 44 A2
Bidjovagge N 192 C6
Bie S 56 A2
Bieber D 81 B5
Biebersdorf D 74 C2
Biedenkopf D 81 B4
Biel E 144 B3
Bielany Wroclawskie PL 85 A4
Bielawa PL 85 B4
Bielawy PL 77 B4
Biel/Bienne CH 106 B2
Bielefeld D 72 B1
Biella I 119 B5
Bielsa E 145 B4
Bielsk PL 77 B4
Bielsko-Biała PL 99 B3
Bielsk Podlaski PL 13 B5
Bienenbuttel D 72 A3
Bieniow PL 84 A3
Bienservida E 158 C1
Bienvenida E 156 B1
Bierdzany PL 86 B2
Bierné F 102 B1
Biersted DK 58 A2
Bierun PL 86 B3
Bierutów PL 85 A5
Bierwart B 79 B5
Bierzwina PL 75 A4
Bierzwnik PL 75 A4
Biescas E 145 B3
Biesenthal D 74 B2
Biesiekierz PL 67 B5
Bietigheim-Bissingen D 93 C5
Bièvre B 91 B5
Bieżuń PL 77 B4
Biga TR 186 B2
Bigadiç TR 186 C3
Biganos F 128 B2
Bigas P 148 B2
Bigastro E 165 A4
Bigbury GB 42 B3
Biggar GB 36 A3
Biggin Hill GB 45 B4
Biggleswade GB 44 A3
Bignasco CH 119 A5
Biguglia F 180 A2
Bihać BIH 124 C1
Biharnagybajom H 113 B5
Bijeljani BIH 139 B4
Bijeljina BIH 125 C5
Bijuesca E 152 A2
Bilaj HR 137 A4
Bila Tserkva UA 13 D9
Bilbao E 143 A4
Bilcza PL 87 B4
Bildudalur IS 190 B2
Bileća BIH 139 C4
Bilecik TR 187 B4
Biled RO 126 B2
Biłgoraj PL 12 C5
Bilhorod-Dnistrovskyy UA 17 B9
Bílina CZ 84 B1
Bilisht AL 182 C2
Bilje HR 125 B4
Billdal S 60 B1
Billerbeck D 71 C4
Billericay GB 45 B4
Billesholm S 61 C2
Billingborough GB 40 C3
Billinge S 61 D3
Billingham GB 37 B5
Billinghay GB 41 B3
Billingsfors S 54 B3
Billingshurst GB 44 B3
Billom F 116 B3
Billsta S 200 C4
Billund DK 59 C2
Bílovec CZ 98 B2
Bilstein D 81 A4
Bilthoven NL 70 B2
Bilto N 192 C5
Bilzen B 80 B1
Bíňa SK 112 B2
Binaced E 145 C4
Binasco I 120 B2
Binbrook GB 41 B3
Binche B 79 B4
Bindlach D 95 B3
Bindslev DK 58 A3
Binefar E 145 C4
Bingen D 93 B3
Bingham GB 40 C3
Bingley GB 40 B2
Bingsjö S 50 A2
Binic F 100 A3
Binz D 66 B2
Biograd na Moru HR 137 B4
Bionaz I 119 B4
Bioska SRB 127 D1
Birda RO 126 B3
Birdlip GB 44 B1
Biri N 48 B2
Birkeland N 53 B4
Birkenfeld
Baden-Württemberg D 93 C4
Rheinland-Pfalz D 92 B3
Birkenhead GB 38 A3
Birkerød DK 61 D2
Birkfeld A 110 B2
Birkirkara M 175 C3
Birmingham GB 40 C2
Birr IRL 28 A4
Birresborn D 80 B2
Birstein D 81 B5
Biržai LT 8 D4
Birzebbugia M 175 C3
Bisáccia I 172 A1
Bisacquino I 176 B2
Bisbal de Falset E 153 A4
Biscarosse F 128 B1
Biscarosse Plage F 128 B1
Biscarrués E 144 B3
Biscéglie I 171 B4
Bischheim F 93 C3
Bischofsheim D 82 B1
Bischofshofen A 109 B4
Bischofswerda D 84 A2
Bischofswiesen D 109 B3
Bischofszell CH 107 B4
Bischwiller F 93 C3
Bisenti I 169 A3
Bishop Auckland GB 37 B5
Bishop's Castle GB 39 B4
Bishops Lydeard GB 43 A3
Bishop's Stortford GB 45 B4
Bishop's Waltham GB 44 C2
Bisignano I 174 B2
Bisingen D 93 C4
Biskupice-Oławskie PL 85 A5
Biskupiec PL 69 B4
Bismark D 73 B4
Bismo N 198 D5
Bispgården S 200 C2
Bispingen D 72 A2
Bissen L 92 B2
Bissendorf D 71 B5
Bisserup DK 65 A4
Bistango I 119 C5
Bistarac Donje BIH 139 A4
Bistrica BIH 124 C3
Bistrica ob Sotli SLO 123 A4
Bistriţa RO 17 B6
Bitburg D 92 B2
Bitche F 93 B3
Bitetto I 171 B4
Bitola MK 182 B3
Bitonto I 171 B4
Bitschwiller F 106 B2
Bitterfeld D 83 A4
Bitti I 178 B3
Biville-sur-Mer F 89 A5
Bivona I 176 B2
Biwer L 92 B2
Bizeljsko SLO 123 A4
Bizovac HR 125 B4
Bjåen N 52 A3
Bjärnum S 61 C3
Bjärred S 61 D3
Bjästa S 200 C4
Bjelland
Vest-Agder N 52 B2
Vest-Agder N 52 B3
Bjelovar HR 124 B2
Bjerkreim N 52 B2
Bjerkvik N 194 B8
Bjerreby DK 65 B3
Bjerregrav DK 58 B2
Bjerringbro DK 59 B2
Bjøberg N 47 B5
Bjøllånes N 195 D5
Björbo S 50 B1
Bjordal N 46 A2
Björg IS 191 B8
Bjørkåsen N 194 B7
Björke
Gävleborg S 51 B4
Östergötland S 56 B1
Bjørkelangen N 48 C3
Björketorp S 60 B2
Björkholmen S 196 C2
Björkliden S 194 B9
Björklinge S 51 B4
Björko S 51 C6
Björkö S 60 B1
Björköby S 62 A2
Björkvik S 56 B2
Bjørn N 195 D3
Björna S 200 C4
Björneborg S 55 A5
Björnerod S 54 A2
Bjørnevatn N 193 C13
Björnlunda S 56 A3
Bjørnstad N 193 C14
Björsäter S 56 B2
Bjurberget S 49 B4
Bjurholm S 200 C5
Bjursås S 50 B2
Bjurtjärn S 55 A5
Bjuv S 61 C2
Blachownia PL 86 B2
Blackburn GB 38 A4
Blackpool GB 38 A3
Blackstad S 62 A4
Blackwater IRL 30 B2
Blackwaterfoot GB 34 C2
Blacy F 91 C4
Bladåker S 51 B5
Blaenau Ffestiniog GB 38 B3
Blaenavon GB 39 C3
Blaengarw GB 39 C3
Blagaj
BIH 124 B2
BIH 139 B3
Blagdon GB 43 A4
Blagnac F 129 C4
Blagoevgrad BG 183 A5
Blaichach D 107 B5
Blain F 101 B4
Blainville-sur-l'Eau F 92 C2
Blair Atholl GB 35 B4
Blairgowrie GB 35 B4
Blajan F 145 A4
Blakeney GB 39 C4
Blakstad N 53 B4
Blâmont F 92 C2
Blanca E 165 A3
Blancos E 140 C3
Blandford Forum GB 43 B4
Blanes E 147 C3
Blangy-sur-Bresle F 90 B1
Blankaholm S 62 A4
Blankenberge B 78 A3
Blankenburg D 82 A2
Blankenfelde D 74 B2
Blankenhain D 82 B3
Blankenheim D 80 B2
Blanquefort F 128 B2
Blansko CZ 97 B4
Blanzac F 115 C4
Blanzy F 104 C3
Blaricum NL 70 B2
Blarney IRL 29 C3
Blascomillán E 150 B2
Blascosancho E 150 B3
Błaszki PL 86 A2
Blatná CZ 96 B1
Blatné SK 111 A4
Blatnice CZ 98 C1
Blatnika BIH 139 A3
Blato HR 138 C2
Blato na Cetini HR 138 B2
Blatten CH 119 A4
Blattnicksele S 195 E8
Blatzheim D 80 B2
Blaubeuren D 94 C1
Blaufelden D 94 B1
Blaustein D 94 C1
Blaydon GB 37 B5
Blaye F 128 A2
Blaye-les-Mines F 130 A1
Blázquez E 156 B2
Bleckede D 73 A3
Blecua E 145 B3
Bled SLO 123 A3
Bleiburg A 110 C1
Bleichenbach D 81 B5
Bleicherode D 82 A2
Bleik N 194 A6
Bleikvassli N 195 E4
Bléneau F 104 B1
Blentarp S 61 D3
Blera I 168 A2
Blérancourt F 90 B3
Bléré F 102 B2
Blesle F 116 B3
Blessington IRL 30 A2
Blet F 103 C4
Bletchley GB 44 B3
Bletterans F 105 C4
Blidö S 57 A4
Blidsberg S 60 B3
Blieskastel D 92 B3
Bligny-sur-Ouche F 104 B3
Blikstorp S 55 B5
Blinisht AL 182 B1
Blinja HR 124 B2
Blizanówek PL 76 C3
Bliżyn PL 87 A4
Blois F 103 B3
Blokhus DK 58 A2
Blokzijl NL 70 B2
Blombacka S 55 A4
Blomberg D 72 C2
Blomskog S 54 A3
Blomstermåla S 62 B4
Blomvåg N 46 B1
Blönduós IS 190 B5
Błonie PL 77 B5
Blonville-sur-Mer F 89 A4
Blötberget S 50 B2
Blovice CZ 96 B1
Bloxham GB 44 A2
Blšany CZ 83 B5
Bludenz A 107 B4
Bludov CZ 97 B4
Blumberg D 107 B3
Blyberg S 49 A6
Blyth
Northumberland GB 37 A5
Nottinghamshire GB 40 B2
Blyth Bridge GB 35 C4
Blythburgh GB 45 A5
Blythe Bridge GB 40 C1
Bø
Nordland N 194 B5
Telemark N 53 A5
Boal E 141 A4
Boan MNE 139 C5
Boario Terme I 120 B3
Boat of Garten GB 32 D3
Boa Vista P 154 B2
Boğazkale TR 23 A8
Boğazlıyan TR 23 B8
Boba H 111 B4
Bobadilla
Logroño E 143 B4
Málaga E 163 A3
Bobadilla del Campo E 150 A2
Bobadilla del Monte E 151 B4
Bóbbio I 120 C2
Bóbbio Pellice I 119 C4
Bobigny F 90 C2
Bobingen D 94 C2
Böblingen D 93 C5
Bobolice PL 68 B1
Boboras E 140 B2
Boboshevo BG 182 A4
Bobowa PL 99 B4
Bobrová CZ 97 B4
Bobrovitsa UA 13 C9
Bobrowice PL 75 C4
Bobrówko PL 75 B4
Boca de Huérgano E 142 B2
Bocairent E 159 C3
Bočar SRB 126 B2
Bocchigliero I 174 B2
Boceguillas E 151 A4
Bochnia PL 99 B4
Bocholt
B 80 A1
D 80 A2
Bochov CZ 83 B5
Bochum D 80 A3
Bockara S 62 A4
Bockenem D 72 B3
Bockfliess A 97 C4
Bockhorn D 71 A5
Bočna SLO 123 A3
Bocognano F 180 A2
Boconád H 113 B4
Bőcs H 113 A4
Boczów PL 75 B3
Boda S 50 B2
Böda S 62 A5
Boda
Stockholm S 51 B5
Värmland S 55 A4
Västernorrland S 200 D2
Bodafors S 62 A2
Boda Glasbruk S 63 B3
Bodajk H 112 B2
Boddam
Aberdeenshire GB 33 D5
Shetland GB 33 B5
Boddin D 73 A4
Bödefeld-Freiheit D 81 A4
Boden S 196 D4
Bodenmais D 95 B5
Bodenteich D 73 B3
Bodenwerder D 72 C2
Bodiam GB 45 B4
Bodinnick GB 42 B2
Bodio CH 120 A1
Bodjani SRB 125 B5
Bodmin GB 42 B2
Bodø N 194 C5

Bodonal de la Sierra
E 161 A3
Bodrum TR 188 B2
Bodstedt D 66 B1
Bodträskfors S 196 C3
Bodzanów PL 77 B5
Bodzanowice PL 86 B2
Bodzechów PL 87 B5
Bodzentyn PL 87 B4
Boecillo E 150 A3
Boëge F 118 A3
Boën F 117 B3
Bogács H 113 B4
Bogadmindszent
H 125 B4
Bogajo E 149 B3
Bogarra E 158 C1
Bogarre E 163 A4
Bogatić SRB 127 C1
Bogatynia PL 84 B2
Bogda RO 126 B3
Bogdaniec PL 75 B4
Boge S 57 C4
Bogen
D 95 C4
Nordland N 194 B7
Nordland N 194 C6
S 49 B4
Bogense DK 59 C3
Bognanco Fonti I .119 A5
Bognelv N 192 B6
Bognes N 194 B7
Bogno CH 120 A2
Bognor Regis GB . .44 C3
Bogoria PL 87 B5
Bograngen S 49 B4
Boguchwały PL 69 B5
Bogumiłowice PL . . .86 A3
Boguslav UA 13 D9
Boguszów-Gorce
PL 85 B4
Bogyiszló H 112 C2
Bohain-en-Vermandois
F 91 B3
Böheimkirchen A . .110 A2
Bohinjska Bistrica
SLO 122 A2
Böhlen D 83 A4
Böhmenkirch D 94 C1
Bohmte D 71 B5
Bohonal de Ibor E .150 C2
Böhönye H 124 A3
Bohumin CZ 98 B2
Boiro E 140 B2
Bois-d'Amont F 105 C5
Boisseron F 131 B3
Boitzenburg D 74 A2
Boixols E 147 B2
Boizenburg D 73 A3
Bojadła PL 75 C4
Bojano I 170 B2
Bojanowo PL 85 A4
Bøjden DK 64 A3
Bojkovice CZ 98 B1
Bojná SK 98 C2
Bojnice SK 98 C2
Boka SRB 126 B2
Bököln D 64 B2
Bökshölm S 62 A2
Boksitogorsk RUS . . .9 C8
Bol HR 138 B2
Bolaños de Calatrava
E 157 B4
Bolayır TR 186 B1
Bolbec F 89 A4
Bölcske H 112 C2
Bolderslev DK 64 B2
Boldog H 112 B3
Boldva H 113 A4
Böle S 196 D4
Bolea E 145 B3
Bolekhiv UA 13 D5
Bolesławiec PL 84 A3
Boleszkowice PL 74 B3
Bolewice PL 75 B5
Bólgheri I 134 B3
Bolhrad UA 17 C8
Boliden S 200 B6
Bolimów PL 77 B5
Boliqueime P 160 B1
Boljevci SRB 127 C2
Boljkovci SRB 127 C2
Bolków PL 85 B4
Bollebygd S 60 B2
Bollène F 131 A3
Bólliga E 152 B1
Bollnäs S 50 A3
Bollstabruk S 200 D3
Bollullos E 161 B3
Bollullos par del
Condado E 161 B3
Bologna I 135 A4
Bologne F 105 A4
Bolognetta I 176 B2
Bolognola I 136 C2
Bologoye RUS 9 D9
Bolótana I 178 B2
Bolsena I 168 A1
Bolshaya Vradiyevka
UA 17 B9
Bolsover GB 40 B2
Bolstad S 54 B3
Bolsward NL 70 A2
Boltaña E 145 B4
Boltenhagen D 65 C4
Boltigen CH 106 C2
Bolton GB 38 A4
Bolu TR 187 B6
Bolungarvík IS 190 A2
Bolvadin TR 187 D6
Bóly H 125 B4
Bolzano I 133 A4
Bolzano I 108 C2
Bomba I 169 A4
Bombarral P 154 B1
Bömenzien D 73 B4

Bomlitz D 72 B2
Bømlo N 52 A1
Bøn N 48 B3
Bona F 104 B2
Bonaduz CH 107 C4
Bonanza E 161 C3
Boñar E 142 B1
Bonarbridge GB 32 C2
Bonárcado I 178 B2
Bonares E 161 B3
Bonäs S 50 A1
Bonassola I 134 A2
Bonawe GB 34 B2
Bondal N 53 A4
Bondeno I 121 C4
Bondorf D 93 C4
Bondstorp S 60 B3
Bon-Encontre F 129 B3
Bonete E 158 C2
Bonifacio F 180 B2
Bonigen CH 106 C2
Bonin PL 67 B5
Bonn D 80 B3
Bonnánaro I 178 B2
Bonnåsjøen N 194 C6
Bonnat F 116 A1
Bonndorf D 106 B3
Bonnétable F 102 A2
Bonneuil-les-Eaux
F 90 B2
Bonneuil-Matours
F 115 B4
Bonneval F 103 A3
Bonneval-sur-Arc
F 119 B4
Bonneville F 118 A3
Bonnières-sur-Seine
F 90 B1
Bonnieux F 131 B4
Bönnigheim D 93 B5
Bonnyrigg GB 35 C4
Bonny-sur-Loire F . .103 B4
Bono
E 145 B4
S 54 A1
Bonorva I 178 B2
Bønsnes N 48 B2
Bonyhád H 125 A4
Boom B 79 A4
Boos F 89 A5
Boostedt D 64 B3
Bootle
Cumbria GB 36 B3
Merseyside GB 38 A3
Bopfingen D 94 C2
Boppard D 81 B3
Boqueixón E 140 B2
Bor
CZ 95 B4
S 62 A2
SRB 16 C5
TR 23 C8
Boran-sur-Oise F . . .90 B2
Borås S 60 B2
Borba P 155 C3
Borbona I 169 A3
Borča SRB 127 C2
Borci BIH 139 B4
Borculo NL 71 B3
Bordány H 126 A1
Bordeaux F 128 B2
Bordeira P 160 B1
Bordesholm D 64 B3
Borðeyri IS 190 B4
Bordighera I 133 B3
Bording DK 59 B2
Bordón E 153 B3
Bore I 120 C2
Borehamwood GB . .44 B3
Borek Strzeliński
PL 85 B5
Borek Wielkopolski
PL 76 C2
Boreland GB 36 A3
Borello I 135 A5
Borensberg S 56 B1
Borgafjäll S 199 A12
Borgarnes IS 190 C4
Borgentreich D 81 A5
Börger D 71 B4
Borger NL 71 B3
Borggård S 56 B1
Borghamn S 55 B5
Borghetto di Vara
I 134 A2
Borghetto d'Arróscia
I 133 A3
Borghetto Santo Spirito
I 133 A4
Borgholm S 62 B4
Borghorst D 71 B4
Bórgia I 175 C2
Borgloon B 79 B5
Børglum DK 58 A2
Borgo F 180 A2
Borgo alla Collina
I 135 B4
Borgo a Mozzano
I 134 B3
Borgoforte I 121 B3
Borgofranco d'Ivrea
I 119 B4
Borgomanero I 119 B5
Borgomasino I 119 B4
Borgonovo Val Tidone
I 120 B2
Borgo Pace I 135 B5
Borgorose I 169 A3
Borgo San Dalmazzo
I 133 A3
Borgo San Lorenzo
I 135 B4
Borgosésia I 119 B5
Borgo Val di Taro
I 134 A2
Borgo Valsugana
I 121 A4
Borgo Vercelli I 119 B5

Borgstena S 60 B3
Borgue GB 36 B2
Borgund N 47 A4
Borgvik S 55 A3
Borja E 144 C2
Bork D 80 A3
Borken D 80 A2
Borkenes N 194 B7
Borkheide D 74 B1
Borkowo PL 77 B5
Borkum D 71 A3
Borlänge S 50 B2
Borlu TR 186 D3
Bormes-les-Mimosas
F 132 B2
Bórmio I 107 C5
Bormujos E 161 B3
Borna D 83 A4
Borne NL 71 B3
Bornes P 149 A2
Borne Sulinowo PL .68 B1
Bornheim D 80 B2
Bornhöved D 64 B3
Börnicke D 74 B1
Bornos E 162 B2
Borobia E 152 A2
Borodino RUS 9 E10
Borohrádek CZ 85 B4
Boronów PL 86 B2
Bórore I 178 B2
Boroszów PL 86 B2
Borota H 126 A1
Borovany CZ 96 C2
Borovichi RUS 9 C8
Borovnica SLO 123 B3
Borovo HR 125 B4
Borox E 151 B4
Borrby S 66 A3
Borre
DK 65 B5
N 54 A1
Borredà E 147 B2
Borrenes E 141 B4
Borriol E 159 A3
Borris
DK 59 C1
IRL 30 B2
Borris-in-Ossory
IRL 28 B4
Borrisokane IRL 28 B3
Borrisoleigh IRL 28 B4
Borrowdale GB 36 B3
Børrud N 49 C4
Borsa RO 17 B6
Borsdorf D 83 A4
Børselv N 193 B9
Borsfa H 111 C3
Borský Mikuláš
SK 98 C1
Borsodivánka H . . .113 B4
Borsodnádasd H . .113 A4
Börte N 53 A3
Borth GB 39 B2
Bort-les-Orgues F .116 B2
Börtnan S 199 C10
Børtnes N 47 B6
Borup DK 61 D1
Boryslav UA 13 D5
Boryspil UA 13 C9
Boryszyn PL 75 B4
Borzęciczki PL 85 A5
Borzęcin PL 77 B5
Borzonasca I 134 A2
Borzyszkowy PL 68 A2
Borzytuchom PL 68 A2
Bosa I 178 B2
Bošáca SK 98 C1
Bosanci HR 123 B4
Bosanska Dubica
BIH 124 B2
Bosanska Gradiška
BIH 124 B3
Bosanska Kostajnica
BIH 124 B2
Bosanska Krupa
BIH 124 C2
Bosanski Brod
BIH 125 B3
Bosanski Novi
BIH 124 B2
Bosanski Petrovac
BIH 124 C2
Bosanski Šamac
BIH 125 B4
Bosansko Grahovo
BIH 138 A2
Bošany SK 98 C2
Bösárkány H 111 B4
Bosau D 65 B3
Bósca H 112 C3
Boscastle GB 42 B2
Bosco I 120 C1
Bosco Chiesanuova
I 121 B4
Bösdorf D 65 B3
Bösel D 71 A4
Bosham GB 44 C3
Bösingfeld D 72 B2
Bosjön S 49 C5
Boskoop NL 70 B1
Boskovice CZ 97 B4
Bošnjaci HR 125 B4
Bošnjane SRB 127 D3
Bossast E 145 B4
Bossolasco I 133 A4
Boštanj SLO 123 A4
Boston GB 41 C3
Bostrak N 53 A4
Böszénfa H 125 A3
Bot E 153 A4
Botajica BIH 125 C4
Bøte By DK 65 B4
Bothel GB 36 B3
Boticas P 148 A2
Botngård N 198 B6

Botoš SRB 126 B2
Botoşani RO 17 B7
Botricello I 175 C2
Botsmark S 200 B6
Bottendorf D 81 A4
Bottesford GB 40 C3
Bottnaryd S 60 B3
Botunje SRB 127 C3
Bötzingen D 106 A2
Bouaye F 101 B4
Bouça P 149 A2
Boucau F 128 C1
Bouchain F 78 B3
Bouchoir F 90 B2
Boudreville F 105 B3
Boudry CH 106 C1
Bouesse F 103 C3
Bouguenais F 101 B4
Bouhy F 104 B2
Bouillargues F 131 B3
Bouillon B 91 B5
Bouilly F 104 A2
Bouin F 114 B2
Boulay-Moselle F . . .92 B2
Boulazac F 129 A3
Boule-d'Amont F . . .146 B3
Bouligny F 92 B1
Boulogne-sur-Gesse
F 145 A4
Boulogne-sur-Mer
F 78 B1
Bouloire F 102 B2
Bouquemaison F . . .78 B2
Bourbon-Lancy F . .104 C2
Bourbon-l'Archambault
F 104 C2
Bourbonne-les-Bains
F 105 B4
Bourbourg F 78 B2
Bourbriac F 100 A2
Bourcefranc-le-Chapus
F 114 C2
Bourdeaux F 131 A4
Bouresse F 115 B4
Bourg F 128 A2
Bourg-Achard F 89 A4
Bourganeuf F 116 B1
Bourg-Argental F . .117 B4
Bourg-de-Péage
F 117 B5
Bourg-de-Thizy F . .117 A4
Bourg-de-Visa F . . .129 B3
Bourg-en-Bresse
F 118 A2
Bourges F 103 B4
Bourg-et-Comin F . .91 B3
Bourg-Lastic F 116 B2
Bourg-Madame F . .146 B2
Bourgneuf-en-Retz
F 114 A2
Bourgogne F 91 B4
Bourgoin-Jallieu
F 118 B2
Bourg-St Andéol
F 131 A3
Bourg-St Maurice
F 119 B3
Bourgtheroulde F . .89 A4
Bourgueil F 102 B2
Bourmont F 105 A4
Bournemouth GB . . .43 B5
Bourneville F 89 A4
Bournezeau F 114 B2
Bourran F 129 B3
Bourret F 129 C4
Bourron-Marlotte F .90 C2
Bourton-on-The-Water
GB 44 B2
Boussac F 116 A2
Boussens F 145 A4
Boutersem B 79 B4
Bouttencourt F 90 B1
Bouvières F 131 A4
Bouvron F 101 B4
Bouxwiller F 93 C3
Bouzas F 140 B2
Bouzonville F 92 B2
Bova I 175 D1
Bovalino Marina I . .175 C2
Bovallstrand S 54 B2
Bova Marina I 175 D1
Bovec SLO 122 A2
Bóveda E 141 B3
Bóvegno I 120 B3
Bovenau D 64 B2
Bovenden D 82 A1
Bøverdal N 198 D5
Boves F 90 B2
Bóves I 133 A3
Bovey Tracey GB . . .43 B3
Bovino I 171 B3
Bøvlingbjerg DK 58 B1
Bovolenta I 121 B4
Bovolone I 121 B4
Bowes GB 37 B5
Bowmore GB 34 C1
Bowness-on-
Windermere GB . .36 B4
Box GB 43 A4
Boxberg
Baden-Württemberg
D 94 B1
Sachsen D 84 A2
Boxholm S 55 B6
Boxmeer NL 80 A1
Boxtel NL 79 A5
Boyabat TR 23 A8
Boyalica TR 187 B4
Boyalık TR 186 B3
Bozan TR 187 C6
Božava HR 137 A3
Bozburun TR 188 C3
Bozcaada TR 186 C1
Bozdoğan TR 188 B3
Bozec By DK 65 B4
Bozepole Wielkie
PL 68 A2
Boticas P 148 A2
Boževac SRB 127 C3

Božice CZ 97 C4
Boži Dar CZ 83 B4
Bozkir TR 189 B7
Bozouls F 130 A1
Bozova TR 189 B9
Bozüyük TR 187 C5
Bózzolo I 121 B3
Bra I 119 C4
Braås S 62 A3
Brabrand DK 59 B3
Bracadale GB 31 B2
Bracciano I 168 A2
Bracieux F 103 B3
Bräcke S 199 C12
Brackenheim D 93 B5
Brackley GB 44 A2
Bracklin IRL 27 C4
Bracknell GB 44 B3
Brackwede D 72 C1
Braco GB 35 B4
Brad RO 16 B5
Bradford GB 40 B2
Bradford on Avon
GB 43 A4
Bradina BIH 139 B4
Brådland N 52 B2
Brae GB 33 A5
Braemar GB 32 D3
Braemore GB 32 D1
Braga P 148 A1
Bragança P 149 A3
Bräila RO 17 C7
Braine F 91 B3
Braine-le-Comte B . .79 B4
Braintree GB 45 B4
Braives B 79 B5
Brake D 72 A1
Brakel
D 81 A5
B 79 B3
Bräkne-Hoby S 63 B3
Brålanda S 54 B3
Bralin PL 86 A1
Brallo di Pregola I . .120 C2
Bram F 146 A3
Bramafan F 132 B2
Bramberg am
Wildkogel A 109 B3
Bramdrupdam DK . .59 C2
Bramming DK 59 C1
Brampton GB 37 B4
Bramsche D 71 B4
Branca I 136 B1
Brancaleone Marina
I 175 D2
Brancaster GB 41 C4
Brand
Nieder Österreich
A 96 C3
Vorarlberg A 107 B4
Brandbu N 48 B2
Brande DK 59 C2
Brande-Hornerkirchen
D 64 C2
Brandenberg A 108 B2
Brandenburg D 73 B5
Brand-Erbisdorf D . .83 B5
Brandis D 83 A4
Brando F 180 A2
Brandomil E 140 A2
Brandon GB 45 A4
Brandshagen D 66 B2
Brandval N 49 B4
Brandýs nad Labem
CZ 84 B2
Branice PL 98 A1
Braničevo SRB 127 C3
Braniewo PL 69 A4
Branik SLO 122 B2
Brankovina SRB . . .127 C1
Branky CZ 98 B1
Branne F 128 B2
Brannenburg-
Degerndorf D 108 B3
Brantôme F 115 C4
Branzi I 120 A2
Bras d'Asse F 132 B2
Braskereidfoss N . . .48 B3
Braslaw BY 13 A7
Brasparts F 100 A2
Brassac F 130 B1
Brassac-les-Mines
F 116 B3
Brasschaat B 79 A4
Brastad S 54 B2
Břasy CZ 96 B1
Brąszewice PL 86 A2
Bratislava SK 111 A4
Brattfors S 55 A5
Brattvåg N 198 C3
Bratunac BIH 127 C1
Braubach D 81 B3
Braunau A 95 C5
Braunfels D 81 B4
Braunlage D 82 A2
Braunsbedra D 83 A3
Braunschweig D 73 B3
Bray IRL 30 A2
Bray Dunes F 78 A2
Bray-sur-Seine F . . .90 C3
Bray-sur-Somme F . .90 B2
Brazatortas E 157 B3
Brazey-en-Plaine
F 105 B4
Brbinj HR 137 A4
Brčko BIH 125 C4
Brdani SRB 127 D2
Brdów PL 76 B3
Brea de Tajo E 151 B4
Brécey F 88 B2
Brechen D 81 B4
Brechin GB 35 B5
Brecht B 79 A4
Breckerfeld D 80 A3
Břeclav CZ 97 C4
Brecon GB 39 C3
Brécy F 103 B4

Breda
E 147 C3
NL 79 A4
Bredaryd S 60 B3
Bredbyn S 200 C4
Breddin D 73 B5
Bredebro DK 64 A1
Bredelar D 81 A4
Bredenfelde D 74 A2
Bredsjö S 50 C1
Bredstedt D 64 B1
Bredsten DK 59 C2
Bredträsk S 200 C4
Bredviken S 195 D5
Bree B 80 A1
Bregana HR 123 B4
Breganze I 121 B4
Bregenz A 107 B4
Bréhal F 88 B2
Brehna D 83 A4
Breiðdalsvík IS 191 C11
Breidenbach D 93 B3
Breil-sur-Roya F . . .133 B3
Breisach D 106 A2
Breitenbach
CH 106 B2
D 81 B5
Breitenberg D 96 C1
Breitenfelde D 73 A3
Breitengussbach D .94 B2
Breivikbotn N 192 B6
Brejning DK 59 C2
Brekke N 46 A2
Brekken N 199 C8
Brekkestø N 53 B4
Brekkvasselv N 199 A10
Brekstad N 198 B6
Breland N 53 B3
Bremanger N 198 D1
Bremen D 72 A1
Bremerhaven D 72 A1
Bremervörde D 72 A2
Bremgarten CH 106 B3
Bremsnes N 198 B4
Brem-sur-Mer F 114 B2
Brenderup DK 59 C2
Brenes E 162 A2
Brengova SLO 110 C2
Brenna PL 98 B2
Breno I 120 B3
Brénod F 118 A2
Brensbach D 93 B4
Brentwood GB 45 B4
Brescello I 121 C3
Bréscia I 120 B3
Breskens NL 79 A3
Bresles F 90 B2
Bresnica SRB 127 D2
Bressana I 120 B2
Bressanone I 108 C2
Bressuire F 102 C1
Brest
BY 13 B5
F 100 A1
HR 122 B2
Brestač SRB 127 C1
Brestanica SLO 123 A4
Brestova HR 123 B3
Brestovac HR 125 B3
Bretenoux F 129 B4
Breteuil
Eure F 89 B4
Oise F 90 B2
Brétigny-sur-Orge
F 90 C2
Bretten D 93 B4
Bretteville-sur-Laize
F 89 A3
Brettheim D 94 B2
Breuil-Cervínia I . . .119 B4
Breukelen NL 70 B2
Brevik
N 53 A5
Stockholm S 57 A4
Västra Götaland
S 55 B5
Breza BIH 139 A4
Brežice SLO 123 B4
Bréziers F 132 A2
Breznica HR 124 A2
Breznica Našička
HR 125 B4
Brezno SK 99 C3
Brezolles F 89 B5
Březovánad Svitavou
CZ 97 B4
Brezovápod Bradlom
SK 98 C1
Brezovica
SK 99 B4
SLO 123 A3
Brezovo Polje Selo
BIH 125 C4
Briançon F 118 C3
Brianconnet F 132 B2
Briare F 103 B4
Briatexte F 129 C4
Briático I 175 C2
Briaucourt F 105 A4
Bribir HR 123 B3
Bricquebec F 88 A2
Bridgend
Argyll & Bute GB . .34 C1
Bridgend GB 39 C3
Bridge of Cally GB . .35 B4
Bridge of Don GB . . .33 D4
Bridge of Earn GB . .35 B4
Bridge of Orchy
GB 34 B3
Bridgnorth GB 39 B4
Bridgwater GB 43 A4
Břidličná CZ 98 B1
Bridlington GB 41 A3
Bridport GB 43 B4
Brie-Comte-Robert
F 90 C2
Briec F 100 A1
Brie-Comte-Robert
F 90 C2

Brienon-sur-Armançon
F 104 B2
Brienz CH 106 C3
Brienza I 172 B1
Briesen D 74 B3
Brieskow Finkenheerd
D 74 B3
Brietlingen D 72 A3
Brieva de Cameros
E 143 B4
Briey F 92 B1
Brig CH 119 A5
Brigg GB 40 B3
Brighouse GB 40 B2
Brightlingsea GB . . .45 B5
Brighton GB 44 C3
Brignogan-Plage
F 100 A1
Brignoles F 132 B2
Brigstock GB 40 C3
Brihuega E 151 B5
Brijuni HR 122 C2
Brillon-en-Barrois
F 91 C5
Brilon D 81 A4
Brimnes N 46 B3
Brinches P 160 A2
Brindisi I 173 B3
Brinje HR 123 B4
Brinon-sur-Beuvron
F 104 B2
Brinon-sur-Sauldre
F 103 B4
Brinyan GB 33 B3
Brión E 140 B2
Briones E 143 B4
Brionne F 89 A4
Brioude F 117 B3
Brioux-sur-Boutonne
F 115 B3
Briouze F 89 B3
Briscous F 144 A2
Brisighella I 135 A4
Brissac-Quincé F . .102 B1
Brissago CH 120 A1
Bristol GB 43 A4
Brive-la-Gaillarde
F 129 A4
Briviesca E 143 B3
Brixham GB 43 B3
Brixlegg A 108 B2
Brjánslækur IS 190 B2
Brka BIH 125 C4
Brnaze HR 138 B2
Brněnec CZ 97 B4
Brno CZ 97 B4
Bro S 57 A3
Broadclyst GB 43 B3
Broadford
GB 31 B3
IRL 28 B3
Broad Haven GB 26 B1
Broadstairs GB 45 B5
Broadstone GB 43 B4
Broadway GB 44 A2
Broager DK 64 B2
Broaryd S 60 B3
Broby S 61 C4
Brobyværk DK 59 C3
Bročanac BIH 138 B3
Brocas F 128 B2
Brock D 71 B4
Brockel D 72 A2
Brockenhurst GB . . .44 C2
Broczyno PL 75 A5
Brod MK 182 B3
Brodalen S 54 B2
Broddbo S 50 C3
Brodek u Přerova
CZ 98 B1
Broden-bach D 80 B3
Brodick GB 34 C2
Brod na Kupi HR . . .123 B3
Brodnica PL 69 B4
Brodnica Graniczna
PL 68 A3
Brodowe Łąki PL . . .77 A6
Brody
Lubuskie PL 75 B4
Lubuskie PL 84 A2
Mazowieckie PL . . .77 B5
UA 13 C6
Broglie F 89 B4
Brójce PL 75 B4
Brokind S 56 B1
Brolo I 177 A3
Brome D 73 B3
Bromley GB 45 B4
Bromölla S 63 B2
Bromont-Lamothe
F 116 B2
Brömsebro S 63 B3
Bromsgrove GB 44 A1
Bromyard GB 39 B4
Bronchales E 152 B2
Bronco E 149 B3
Brønderslev DK 58 A2
Broni I 120 B2
Brønnøysund N 195 E3
Brøns DK 59 C1
Bronte I 177 B3
Bronzani Mejdan
BIH 124 C2
Bronzolo I 121 A4
Broons F 101 A3
Broquies F 130 A1
Brora GB 32 C3
Brørup DK 59 C2
Brösarp S 63 C2
Brossac F 115 C3
Brostrud N 47 B5
Brotas P 154 C2
Brötjärna S 50 B2
Broto E 145 B3
Brottby S 57 A4
Brøttum N 48 A2
Brou F 103 A3
Brouage F 114 C2
Brough GB 37 B4
Broughshane GB . . .27 B4

Broughton GB.....35 C4
Broughton-in-Furness
  GB.........36 B3
Broumov CZ.....85 B4
Broût-Vernet F..116 A3
Brouvelieures F..106 A1
Brouwershaven NL 79 A3
Brovary UA......13 C9
Brovst DK......58 A2
Brownhills GB....40 C2
Brozas E......155 B4
Brozzo I......120 B3
Brtnice CZ......97 B3
Brtonigla HR..122 B2
Bruay-la-Buissière
  F.........78 B2
Bruchhausen-Vilsen
  D.........72 B2
Bruchsal D......93 B4
Bruck D......95 B4
Brück D......74 B1
Bruck an der
  Grossglocknerstrasse
  A.........109 B3
Bruck an der Leitha
  A.........111 A3
Bruck an der Mur
  A.........110 B2
Brückl A......110 C1
Bruckmühl D....108 B2
Brue-Auriac F ..132 B1
Brüel D......65 C4
Bruen CH......107 C3
Bruère-Allichamps
  F.........103 C4
Bruff IRL......29 B3
Bruflat N......47 B6
Brugg CH......106 B3
Brugge B......78 A3
Brüggen D......80 A2
Brühl D......80 B2
Bruinisse NL....79 A4
Brûlon F......102 B1
Brumano I......120 B2
Brumath F......93 C3
Brummen NL....70 B3
Brumov-Bylnice
  CZ.........98 B2
Brumunddal N...48 B2
Brunau D......73 B4
Brunehamel F...91 B4
Brünen D......80 A2
Brunete E......151 B3
Brunflo S......199 B11
Brunico I......108 C2
Brunkeberg N...53 A4
Brunn D......74 A2
Brunnen CH....107 C3
Brunsbüttel D....64 C2
Brunssum NL....80 B1
Bruntál CZ......98 B1
Brušane HR....137 A4
Brusasco I......119 B5
Brusio CH......120 A3
Brusno SK......99 C3
Brusque F......130 B1
Brussels = Bruxelles
  B.........79 B4
Brusson I......119 B4
Brüssow D......74 A3
Brusy PL......68 B2
Bruton GB......43 A4
Bruvno HR......138 A1
Bruvoll N......48 B3
Bruxelles = Brussels
  B.........79 B4
Bruyères F......106 A1
Bruz F......101 A4
Bruzaholm S....62 A3
Brwinów PL......77 B5
Brynamman GB...39 C3
Bryncrug GB......39 B2
Bryne N......52 B1
Brynmawr GB....39 C3
Bryrup DK......59 B2
Brzeg PL......85 B5
Brzeg Dolny PL....85 A4
Brześć Kujawski
  PL.........76 B3
Brzesko PL......99 B4
Brzeszcze PL....99 B3
Brzezie PL......68 B2
Brzeziny
  Łódzkie PL....87 A3
  Wielkopolskie PL..86 A2
Brzeźnica PL....84 A3
Brzeźnica Nowa PL 86 A3
Brzeźno PL......75 A4
Brzotin SK......99 C4
Brzozie Lubawskie
  PL.........69 B4
Bua S......60 B2
Buarcos P......148 B1
Buaveg N......52 A1
Bubbio I......119 C5
Bubry F......100 B2
Buca TR......188 A2
Bucak TR......189 B5
Bučany SK......98 C1
Buccheri I......177 B3
Buccino I......172 B1
Bucelas P......154 C1
Buch
  Bayern D....94 C2
  Bayern D....95 C4
Buchach UA......13 D6
Bucharest = Bucureşti
  RO.........17 C7
Buchbach D......95 C4
Buchboden A....107 B4
Buchen D......94 B1
Büchen D......73 A3
Buchenberg D....107 B5
Buchères F......104 A3
Buchholz D......72 A2
Buchloe D......108 A1
Buchlovice CZ....98 B1
Buchlyvie GB....34 B3
Buchs CH......107 B4

Buchy F......89 A5
Bückeburg D....72 B2
Buckfastleigh GB..42 B3
Buckhaven GB....35 B4
Buckie GB......33 D4
Buckingham GB...44 A3
Buckley GB......38 A3
Bückwitz D......73 B5
Bučovice CZ......97 B5
Bucsa H......113 B5
Bucureşti = Bucharest
  RO.........17 C7
Bucy-lès-Pierrepont
  F.........91 B3
Buczek PL......86 A3
Bud N......198 C3
Budakalasz H....112 B3
Budakeszi H....112 B2
Budal N......199 C7
Budaörs H......112 B2
Budapest H......112 B3
Buðardalur IS...190 B4
Budča SK......99 C3
Buddusò I......178 B3
Bude GB......42 B2
Budeč CZ......97 B3
Büdelsdorf D....64 B2
Budens P......160 B1
Budia E......151 B5
Budimlić-Japra
  BIH.........124 C2
Büdingen D......81 B5
Budinšćina HR..124 A2
Budišov CZ......98 B1
Budleigh Salterton
  GB.........43 B3
Budmerice SK....98 C1
Budoni I......178 B3
Búdrio I......135 A4
Budva MNE......16 D3
Budyněnad Ohří
  CZ.........84 B2
Budziszewice PL..87 A3
Budzyń PL......76 B1
Bue N......52 B1
Bueña E......152 B2
Buenache de Alarcón
  E.........158 B1
Buenache de la Sierra
  E.........152 B2
Buenaventura E ..150 B3
Buenavista de Valdavia
  E.........142 B2
Buendia E......151 B5
Bueu E......140 B2
Buezo E......143 B3
Bugac H......112 C3
Bugarra E......159 B3
Bugeat F......116 B1
Bugenhagen N...179 C2
Bugojno BIH....138 A3
Bugøyfjord N...193 C13
Bugøynes N...193 C13
Bugyi H......112 B3
Buharkent TR..188 B3
Bühl
  Baden-Württemberg
  D.........93 C4
  Bayern D....107 B5
Bühlertal D......93 C4
Bühlertann D....94 B1
Buia I......122 A2
Buin N......47 B6
Buis-les-Baronnies
  F.........131 A4
Buitenpost NL...70 A3
Buitrago del Lozoya
  E.........151 B4
Bujalance E......157 C3
Bujaraloz E......153 A3
Buje HR......122 B2
Bujedo E......143 B3
Bük H......111 B3
Bükkösd H......125 A3
Bükkzsérc H....113 B4
Bukovci SLO....124 A1
Bukowiec PL....75 B5
Bukowina Tatrzańska
  PL.........99 B4
Bukownica PL...86 A2
Bukowno PL....86 B3
Bülach CH......107 B3
Búland IS......191 D7
Buldan TR......188 A3
Bulgari BG......17 D7
Bulgnéville F...105 A4
Bulgurca TR......188 A2
Bülkau D......64 C1
Bulken N......46 B3
Bulkowo PL......77 B5
Bullas E......164 A3
Bulle CH......106 C2
Büllingen B......80 B2
Bullmark S......200 B6
Bulqizë AL......182 B2
Buna BIH......139 B3
Bunahowen IRL...26 B1
Bunbeg IRL......26 A2
Bunclody IRL....30 B2
Buncrana IRL....27 A3
Bunde
  Niedersachsen D...71 A4
  Nordrhein-Westfalen
  D.........72 B1
Bünde D......72 B1
Bundoran IRL....26 B2
Bunessan GB....34 B1
Bungay GB......45 A5
Bunge S......57 C5
Bunić HR......123 C4
Bunmahon IRL...30 B1
Bunnyconnellan
  IRL.........26 B1
Buño E......140 A2
Buñol E......159 B3
Buñuel E......144 C2
Bunyola E......166 B2
Buonabitácolo I..172 B1
Buonalbergo I...170 B2

Buonconvento I ..135 B4
Buonvicino I....174 B1
Burano I......122 B1
Burbach D......81 B4
Burcei I......179 C3
Burdons-sur-Rognon
  F.........105 A4
Büren D......81 A4
Büren an der Aare
  CH.........106 B2
Burford GB......44 B2
Burg
  Cottbus D......84 A1
  Magdeburg D...73 B4
  Schleswig-Holstein
  D.........64 C2
Burgas BG......17 D7
Burgau
  A.........111 B3
  D.........94 C2
  P.........160 B1
Burg auf Fehmarn
  D.........65 B4
Burgbernheim D..94 B2
Burgdorf
  CH.........106 B2
  D.........72 B3
Burgebrach D....94 B2
Bürgel D......83 B3
Burgess Hill GB..44 C3
Burghaslach D...94 B2
Burghausen D...109 A3
Burghead GB....32 D3
Burgheim D......94 C3
Burg le Marsh GB 41 B4
Búrgio I......176 B2
Burgkirchen D...109 A3
Burgkunstadt D..82 B3
Burglengenfeld D ..95 B4
Burgo P......148 B1
Burgoberbach D..94 B2
Burgohondo E...150 B3
Burgos E......143 B3
Burgsinn D......82 B1
Burgstädt D......83 B4
Burgstall D......73 B4
Burg Stargard D ..74 A2
Burgsvik S......57 C4
Burgui E......144 B3
Burguillos E......162 A2
Burguillos del Cerro
  E.........155 C4
Burguillos de Toledo
  E.........151 C4
Burhaniye TR..186 C1
Burhave D......71 A5
Burie F......114 C3
Burjassot E......159 B3
Burk D......94 B2
Burkhardtsdorf D ..83 B4
Burlada E......144 B2
Burladingen D...107 A4
Burlage D......71 A4
Burnes GB......33 B4
Burnham GB....44 B3
Burnham Market
  GB.........41 C4
Burnham-on-Crouch
  GB.........45 B4
Burnham-on-Sea
  GB.........43 A4
Burniston GB....40 A3
Burnley GB......40 B1
Burntisland GB...35 B4
Burón E......142 A1
Buronzo I......119 B5
Burovac SRB...127 C3
Burow D......74 A2
Burravoe GB....33 A5
Burrel AL......182 B2
Burret F......146 B2
Burriana E......159 B3
Burry Port GB....39 C2
Bürs A......107 B4
Bursa TR......186 B4
Burseryd S......60 B3
Bürstadt D......93 B4
Burton GB......37 B4
Burton Agnes GB..41 A3
Burton Bradstock
  GB.........43 B4
Burton Latimer GB 44 A3
Burton upon Stather
  GB.........40 B3
Burton upon Trent
  GB.........40 C2
Burträsk S......200 B6
Burujón E......151 C3
Burwell GB......45 A4
Burwick GB......33 C4
Bury GB......40 B1
Bury St Edmunds
  GB.........45 A4
Burzenin PL......86 A2
Busachi I......179 B2
Busalla I......134 A1
Busana I......134 A3
Busano I......119 B4
Busca I......133 A3
Busch D......73 B4
Buševec HR....124 B2
Bushat AL......182 B1
Bushey GB......44 B3
Bushmills GB....27 A4
Bušince SK......112 A3
Buskhyttan S....56 B2
Busko-Zdrój PL...87 B4
Busot E......159 C3
Busovača BIH...139 A3
Busquístar E....163 B4
Bussang F......106 B1
Busseto I......120 C3
Bussière-Badil F ..115 C4
Bussière-Poitevine
  F.........115 B4
Bussolengo I...121 B3
Bussoleno I......119 B4

Bussum NL......70 B2
Busto Arsízio I...120 B1
Büsum D......64 B1
Butera I......177 B3
Butgenbach B....80 B2
Butler's Bridge IRL 27 B3
Butryny PL......77 A5
Bütschwil CH...107 B4
Buttermere GB...36 B3
Buttevant IRL....29 B3
Buttle S......57 C4
Buttstädt D......82 A3
Butzbach D......81 B4
Butzfleth D......72 A2
Bützow D......65 C4
Buxières-les-Mines
  F.........104 C1
Buxtehude D....72 A2
Buxton GB......40 B2
Buxy F......104 C3
Büyükçekmece
  TR.........186 A3
Büyükkarıştıran
  TR.........186 A2
Büyükorhan TR..186 C3
Buzançais F....103 C3
Buzancy F......91 B4
Buzău RO......17 C7
Buzet HR......122 B2
Buziaş RO......126 B3
Buzsák H......111 C4
Buzy F......145 A3
By S......50 B3
Byala BG......17 D6
Byaroza BY......13 B6
Byczyna PL......86 A2
Bydalen S......199 B10
Bydgoszcz PL....76 A3
Bydgin N......47 A5
Bygdisiljum S...200 B6
Bygland N......53 B3
Byglandsfjord N..53 B3
Bygstad N......46 A2
Bykhaw BY......13 B9
Bykle N......52 A3
Bylderup-Bov DK..64 B2
Byrkjedal N......52 B2
Byrkjelo N......198 D3
Byrum DK......58 A3
Byšice CZ......84 B2
Býškovice CZ....98 B1
Bysław PL......76 A2
Bystré CZ......97 B4
Bystřice CZ......96 B2
Bystřice CZ......98 B2
Bystřice nad
  Pernštejnem CZ ..97 B4
Bystřice pod
  Hostýnem CZ....98 B1
Bystrzyca Kłodzka
  PL.........85 B4
Bytča SK......98 B2
Bytnica PL......75 B4
Bytom PL......86 B2
Bytom Odrzański
  PL.........85 A3
Bytów PL......68 A2
Byxelkrok S......62 A5
Bzenec CZ......98 C1
Bzince SK......98 C1

C

Çağa TR......187 B7
Cabacos P......154 B2
Cabaj-Čápor SK ..98 C2
Cabana E......140 A2
Cabanac-et-Villagrains
  F.........128 B2
Cabañaquinta E..142 A1
Cabanas P......160 B2
Cabañas del Castillo
  E.........156 A2
Cabañas de Yepes
  E.........151 C4
Cabanelles E....147 B3
Cabanes E......153 B4
Cabanillas E....144 B2
Čabar HR......123 B3
Cabasse F......132 B2
Cabdella E......146 B2
Cabeceiras de Basto
  P.........148 A1
Cabeço de Vide P ..155 B3
Cabella Ligure I..120 C2
Cabeza del Buey
  E.........156 B2
Cabeza la Vaca E..161 A3
Cabezamesada E .151 C4
Cabezarados E..157 B3
Cabezarrubias del
  Puerto E......157 B3
Cabezas del Villar
  E.........150 B2
Cabezas Rubias E 161 B2
Cabezón E......142 C2
Cabezón de la Sal
  E.........142 A2
Cabezón de Liébana
  E.........142 A2
Cabezuela E....151 A4
Cabezuela del Valle
  E.........149 B4
Cabo de Gata E..164 C2
Cabo de Palos E..165 B4
Cabolafuente E..152 A1
Cabourg F......89 A3
Cabra
  E.........163 A3
  P.........148 B2
Cabra del Santo Cristo
  E.........163 A4
Cábras I......179 C2
Cabreiro P......140 C2
Cabreiros E......140 A3
Cabrejas E......152 B1
Cabrela P......154 C2

Cabrillas E......149 B3
Cabuna HR......125 B3
Cacabelos E....141 B4
Čačak SRB......127 D2
Cáccamo I......176 B2
Caccuri I......174 B2
Cacela P......160 B2
Cacém P......154 C1
Cáceres E......155 B4
Cachafeiro E....140 B2
Cachopo P......160 B2
Čachtice SK......98 C1
Cacin E......163 A4
Cadafais P......154 C1
Cadalen F......129 C5
Cadalso E......149 B3
Cadaqués E....147 B4
Cadaval P......154 B1
Cadavedo E......141 A4
Čadavica BIH...138 A2
Cadéac F......145 B4
Cadelbosco di Sopra
  I.........121 C3
Cadenazzo CH...120 A1
Cadenberge D....64 C2
Cadenet F......131 B4
Cadeuil F......114 C3
Cádiar E......164 C1
Cadillac F......128 B2
Cádiz E......162 B1
Čadjavica HR...125 B3
Cadouin F......129 B3
Cadours F......129 C4
Cadrete E......152 A3
Caen F......89 A3
Caerleon GB....39 C4
Caernarfon GB...38 A2
Caerphilly GB...39 C3
Caersws GB......39 B3
Cafede P......155 B3
Caggiano I......172 B1
Cagli I......136 B1
Cágliari I......179 C3
Čaglin HR......125 B3
Cagnano Varano I 171 B3
Cagnes-sur-Mer F 132 B3
Caher IRL......29 B4
Caherciveen IRL..29 C1
Caherdaniel IRL...29 C1
Cahors F......129 B4
Cahul MD......17 C8
Caiazzo I......170 B2
Caion E......140 A2
Cairndow GB....34 B3
Cairnryan GB....36 B1
Cairo Montenotte
  I.........133 A4
Caister-on-Sea GB .41 C5
Caistor GB......41 B3
Caivano I......170 C2
Cajarc F......129 B4
Çakırlar TR......189 C5
Çakmak TR......187 C6
Çal TR......189 A4
Cala E......161 B3
Calabritto I......172 B1
Calaceite E......153 B4
Calacuccia F....180 A2
Cala d'Or E......167 B3
Calaf E......147 C2
Calafat RO......17 C5
Calafell E......147 C2
Cala Galdana E..167 B3
Cala Gonone I...178 B3
Calahonda
  Granada E....163 B4
  Málaga E......163 B3
Calahorra E......144 B2
Calais F......78 B1
Cala Llonga E...166 C1
Calalzo di Cadore
  I.........109 C3
Cala Millor E....167 B3
Calamocha E....152 B2
Calamonte E....155 C4
Cala Morell E...167 A3
Calanais GB......31 A2
Calañas E......161 B3
Calanda E......153 B3
Calangiánus I...178 B3
Călăraşi RO......17 C7
Cala Ratjada E...167 B3
Calascibetta I...177 B3
Calasetta I......179 C2
Calasparra E....164 A3
Calatafimi I......176 B1
Calatayud E......152 A2
Calatorao E......152 A2
Calau D......84 A1
Calbe D......73 B4
Calcena E......152 A2
Calcinelli I......136 B1
Calco I......120 B2
Caldaro sulla strada del
  Vino I......121 A4
Caldarola I......136 B2
Caldas da Rainha
  P.........154 B1
Caldas de Bo i E ..145 B4
Caldas de Malavella
  E.........147 C3
Caldas de Reis E..140 B2
Caldas de San Jorge
  P.........148 B1
Caldas de Vizela
  P.........148 A1
Caldaso de los Vidrios
  E.........150 B3
Caldbeck GB....36 B3
Caldearenas E...145 B3
Caldelas P......148 A1
Calders E......147 C2
Caldes de Montbui
  E.........147 C3
Caldicot GB......39 C4
Caldirola I......120 C2

Caledon GB......27 B4
Calella
  Barcelona E....147 C3
  Girona E......147 C4
Calenzana F....180 A1
Calera de León E..161 A3
Calera y Chozas
  E.........150 C3
Caleruega E....143 C3
Caleruela E......150 C2
Cales de Mallorca
  E.........167 B3
Calestano I......134 A3
Calfsound GB....33 B4
Calgary GB......34 B1
Calimera I......173 B4
Calitri I......172 B1
Calizzano I......133 A4
Callac F......100 A2
Callan IRL......30 B1
Callander GB....35 B3
Callas F......132 B2
Calliano
  Piemonte I....119 B5
  Trentino Alto Adige
  I.........121 B4
Callington GB...42 B2
Callosa de Ensarriá
  E.........159 C3
Callosa de Segura
  E.........165 A4
Callús E......147 C2
Čalma SRB......127 B1
Calmbach D......93 C4
Calne GB......43 A5
Calolziocorte I..120 B2
Calonge E......147 C4
Calonne F......155 B3
Calpe E......159 C4
Caltabellotta I...176 B2
Caltagirone I....177 B3
Caltanissetta I...177 B3
Caltavuturo I....176 B2
Çaltılıbük TR...186 C3
Caltojar E......151 A5
Caluire-et-Cuire F 117 B4
Caluso I......119 B4
Calvello I......172 B1
Calvi F......180 A1
Calviá E......166 B2
Calvinet F......116 C2
Calvisson F......131 B3
Calvörde D......73 B4
Calw D......93 C4
Calzada de Calatrava
  E.........157 B4
Calzada de Valdunciel
  E.........150 A2
Calzadilla de los Barros
  E.........155 C4
Cam GB......43 A4
Camaiore I......134 B3
Camarasa E....145 C4
Camarena E....151 B3
Camarès F......130 B1
Camaret-sur-Aigues
  F.........131 A3
Camaret-sur-Mer
  F.........100 A1
Camarillas E....153 B3
Camariñas E....140 A1
Camarma E......151 B4
Camarzana de Tera
  E.........141 B4
Camas E......162 A1
Camastra I......176 B2
Cambados E....140 B2
Cambarinho P...148 B1
Camberley GB...44 B3
Cambil E......163 A4
Cambligeu F......78 B2
Cambo-les-Bains
  F.........144 A2
Camborne GB...42 B1
Cambrai F......78 B3
Cambre E......140 A2
Cambridge GB...45 A4
Cambrils E......147 C2
Cambs D......65 C4
Camburg D......83 A3
Camden GB......44 B3
Cameleño E......161 B3
Camelford GB...42 B2
Camerano I......136 B2
Camerino I......136 B2
Camerota I......172 B1
Camigliatello Silano
  I.........174 B2
Caminha P......148 A1
Caminomorisco E 149 B3
Caminreal E....152 B2
Camisano Vicentino
  I.........121 B4
Camlidere TR...187 B7
Cammarata I....176 B2
Camogli I......134 A2
Camors F......100 B3
Camp IRL......29 B2
Campagna I......172 B1
Campagnano di Roma
  I.........168 A2
Campagnático I..135 C4
Campan F......145 A4
Campana I......174 B2
Campanario E...156 B2
Campanillas E...163 B3
Campano E......162 B1
Campaspero E..151 A3
Campbeltown GB .34 C2
Campello E......165 A4
Campelos P......154 B1
Campi Bisénzio I 135 B4
Campico López E 165 B3
Campíglia Maríttima
  I.........134 B3
Campillo de Altobuey
  E.........158 B2

Campillo de Aragón
  E.........152 A2
Campillo de Arenas
  E.........163 A4
Campillo de Llerena
  E.........156 B2
Campillos E......162 A3
Câmpina RO......17 C6
Campi Salentina I 173 B4
Campli I......136 C2
Campo E......145 B4
Campobasso I...170 B2
Campobello di Licata
  I.........176 B2
Campobello di Mazara
  I.........176 B1
Campo da Feira E 140 A3
Campodársego I 121 B4
Campo de Bacerros
  E.........141 B3
Campo de Caso E 142 A1
Campo de Criptana
  E.........157 A4
Campodolcino I..120 A2
Campofelice di
  Roccella I......176 B2
Campofiorito I...176 B2
Campofórmido I 122 A2
Campofranco I...176 B2
Campofrío E......161 B3
Campogalliano I 121 C3
Campo Ligure I..133 A4
Campolongo I...109 C3
Campo Lugar E..156 A2
Campo Maior P..155 B3
Campomanes E..141 A5
Campomarino I..170 B3
Campo Molino I..133 A3
Campomono F...180 B1
Campo Real E...151 B4
Camporeale I....176 B2
Camporeggiano I 136 B1
Camporrells E...145 C4
Camporrobles E..158 B2
Campos P......148 A2
Camposa P......148 A2
Camposampiero I 121 B4
Camposanto I...121 C4
Campos del Port
  E.........167 B3
Camposines E...153 A4
Campotéjar E...163 A4
Campotosto I....169 A3
Campo Túres I...108 C2
Camprodón E...147 B3
Campsegret F...129 B3
Camrose GB......39 C1
Camuñas E......157 A4
Çamyolu TR......189 C7
Çan TR......186 B2
Cana I......135 C4
Cañada del Hoyo
  E.........158 B2
Cañadajuncosa E 158 B1
Cañada Rosal E..162 A2
Çanak HR......123 C4
Çanakkale TR...186 B1
Canale I......119 C4
Canales
  Asturias E....141 B5
  Castellón de la Plana
  E.........159 B3
Canals E......159 C3
Canal San Bovo I 121 A4
Cañamares E....152 B1
Cañamero E......156 A2
Cañar E......163 B4
Cañate la Real E..162 B2
Cañaveral E......155 B4
Cañaveral de León
  E.........161 A3
Cañaveras E....152 B1
Cañaveruelas E..151 B5
Canazei I......108 C2
Cancale F......88 B2
Cancellara I......172 B1
Cancello ed Arnone
  I.........170 B2
Cancon F......129 B3
Canda E......141 B4
Candamil E......140 A3
Candanchu E...145 B3
Candas E......141 A5
Candasnos E....153 A4
Candé F......101 B4
Candela I......172 A1
Candelario E....150 B2
Candeleda E......150 B2
Cándia Lomellina
  I.........120 B1
Candide
  Casamazzago I 109 C3
Candin E......141 B4
Candosa P......148 B2
Canecas P......154 C1
Canelli I......119 C5
Canena E......157 B4
Canencia E......151 B4
Canero E......141 A4
Canet F......130 B2
Canet de Mar E..147 C3
Canet d'en Berenguer
  E.........159 B3
Cañete E......158 A2
Cañete de las Torres
  E.........163 A3
Canet-Plage F...146 B4
Canfranc E......145 B3
Cangas
  Lugo E......141 A4
  Pontevedra E..140 B2
Cangas de Narcea
  E.........141 A4
Cangas de Onis E 142 A1
Canha P......154 C2
Canhestros P....160 A1

Canicatt i I	176	B2
Canicattini Bagni		
I	177	B4
Canicosa de la Sierra		
E	143	C3
Caniles E	164	B2
Canillas de Aceituno		
E	163	B3
Canino I	168	A1
Canisy F	88	A2
Cañizal E	150	A2
Cañizo E	142	C1
Canjáyar E	164	C2
Çankırı TR	23	A7
Cannai I	179	C2
Cannara I	136	B1
Cánnero Riviera I	120	A1
Cannes F	132	B3
Canneto		
Sicilia I	177	A3
Toscana I	135	B3
Canneto sull'Oglio		
I	120	B3
Cannich GB	32	D2
Cannóbio I	120	A1
Cannock GB	40	C1
Canonbie GB	36	A4
Canosa di Púglia		
I	171	B4
Can Pastilla I	166	B2
C'an Picafort I	167	B3
Cantalapiedra E	150	A2
Cantalejo E	151	A4
Cantalgallo E	161	A3
Cantalice I	169	A2
Cantalpino E	150	A2
Cantalupo in Sabina		
I	168	A2
Cantanhede P	148	B1
Cantavieja E	153	B3
Čantavir SRB	126	B1
Canterbury GB	45	B5
Cantiano I	136	B1
Cantillana E	162	A2
Cantiveros E	150	B3
Cantoria E	164	B2
Cantù I	120	B2
Canvey GB	45	B4
Cany-Barville F	89	A4
Canyet de Mar E	147	C3
Caol GB	34	B2
Cáorle I	122	B1
Caorso I	120	B2
Capáccio I	172	B1
Capaci I	176	A2
Capálbio I	168	A1
Capánnori I	134	B3
Caparde BIH	139	A4
Caparroso E	144	B2
Capbreton F	128	C1
Capdenac-Gare F	116	C2
Capdepera I	167	B3
Cap-de-Pin F	128	B2
Capel Curig GB	38	A3
Capellades E	147	C2
Capena I	168	A2
Capendu F	146	A3
Capestang F	130	B2
Capestrano I	169	A3
Cap Ferret F	128	B1
Capileira E	163	B4
Capinha P	148	B2
Ca'Pisani I	122	C1
Capistrello I	169	B3
Capizzi I	177	B3
Čaplje BIH	124	C2
Čapljina BIH	139	B3
Capo di Ponte I	120	A3
Caposile I	122	B1
Capoterra I	179	C2
Cappamore IRL	29	B3
Cappeln D	71	B5
Cappoquin IRL	29	B4
Capracotta I	169	B4
Capránica I	168	A2
Caprarola I	168	A2
Capretta I	135	C5
Capri I	170	C2
Capriati a Volturno		
I	170	B2
Caprino Veronese		
I	121	B3
Captieux F	128	B2
Cápua I	170	B2
Capurso I	173	A2
Capvern F	145	A4
Carabaña E	151	B4
Carabias E	151	A4
Caracal RO	17	C6
Caracenilla E	152	B1
Carágio I	133	A3
Caraman F	146	A2
Caramánico Terme		
I	169	A4
Caranga E	141	A4
Caranguejeira P	154	B2
Caransebeş RO	16	C5
Carantec F	100	A2
Carapelle I	171	B3
Carasco I	134	A2
Carate Brianza I	120	B2
Caravaca de la Cruz		
E	164	A3
Caravággio I	120	B2
Carbajal E	163	B3
Carbajo E	155	B3
Carballeda E	140	B3
Carballeda de Avia		
E	140	B2
Carballo E	140	A2
Carbis Bay GB	42	B1
Carbon-Blanc F	128	B2
Carbonera de Frentes		
E	143	C4
Carboneras E	164	C3
Carboneras de		
Guadazaón E	158	B2
Carbonero el Mayor		
E	151	A3
Carboneros E	157	B4
Carbónia I	179	C2
Carbost		
Highland GB	31	B2
Highland GB	31	B2
Carcaboso E	149	B3
Carcabuey E	163	A3
Carcaixent E	159	B3
Carcans F	128	A1
Carcans-Plage F	128	A1
Carção P	149	A3
Carcar E	144	B2
Cárcare I	133	A4
Carcassonne F	146	A3
Carcastillo E	144	B2
Carcedo de Burgos		
E	143	B3
Carcelén E	159	B2
Carcès F	132	B2
Carchelejo E	163	A4
Çardak		
Çanakkale TR	186	B1
Denizli TR	189	B4
Cardedeu E	147	C3
Cardeña E	157	B3
Cardenete E	158	B2
Cardeñosa E	150	B3
Cardeto I	175	C1
Cardiff GB	39	C3
Cardigan GB	39	B2
Cardona E	147	C2
Cardosos P	154	B2
Carei RO	16	B5
Carentan F	88	A2
Carentoir F	101	B3
Careri I	175	C2
Carevdar HR	124	A2
Cargèse F	180	A1
Carhaix-Plouguer		
F	100	A2
Caria P	148	B2
Cariati I	174	B2
Carignan F	91	B5
Carignano I	119	C4
Cariñena E	152	A2
Carini I	176	A2
Carinola I	170	B1
Carisbrooke GB	44	C2
Carlabhagh GB	31	A2
Carlepont F	90	B3
Carlet E	159	B3
Carlingford IRL	27	B4
Carlisle GB	36	B4
Carloforte I	179	C2
Carlópoli I	175	B2
Carlow		
D	65	C3
IRL	30	B2
Carlton GB	40	C2
Carluke GB	35	C4
Carmagnola I	119	C4
Carmarthen GB	39	C2
Carmaux F	130	A1
Carmena E	150	C3
Cármenes E	142	B1
Carmine I	133	A3
Carmona E	162	A2
Carmonita E	155	B4
Carmyllie GB	35	B5
Carnac F	100	B2
Carndonagh IRL	27	A3
Carnew IRL	30	B2
Carnforth GB	37	B4
Cárnia I	122	A2
Carnlough GB	27	B5
Carno GB	39	B3
Carnon Plage F	131	B2
Carnota E	140	B1
Carnoustie GB	35	B5
Carnwath GB	35	C4
Carolei I	174	B2
Carolinensiel D	71	A4
Carolles F	88	B2
Caronia I	120	A2
Caronía I	177	A3
Carovigno I	173	B3
Carovilli I	170	B2
Carpaneto Piacentino		
I	120	C2
Carpegna I	135	B5
Carpenédolo I	121	B3
Carpentras F	131	A4
Carpi I	121	C3
Carpignano Sésia		
I	119	B5
Carpineti I	134	A3
Carpineto Romano		
I	169	B3
Cárpino I	171	B3
Carpinone I	170	B2
Carpio E	150	A2
Carquefou F	101	B4
Carqueiranne F	132	B2
Carral E	140	A2
Carranque E	151	B4
Carrapichana P	148	B2
Carrara I	134	A3
Carraroe IRL	28	A2
Carrascalejo E	156	A2
Carrascosa del Campo		
E	151	B5
Carratraca E	162	B3
Carrazeda de Ansiães		
P	148	A2
Carrazedo de		
Montenegro P	148	A2
Carrbridge GB	32	D3
Carregal do Sal P	148	B1
Carreña E	142	A2
Carrick IRL	26	B2
Carrickart IRL	26	A3
Carrickfergus GB	27	B5
Carrickmacross		
IRL	27	C4
Carrick-on-Shannon		
IRL	26	C2
Carrick-on-Suir IRL	30	B1
Carrigallen IRL	27	C3
Carrión E	161	B3
Carrión de Calatrava		
E	157	A4
Carrión de los Condes		
E	142	B2
Carrizo de la Ribera		
E	141	B5
Carrizosa E	157	B5
Carro F	131	B4
Carrocera E	142	B1
Carros F	133	B3
Carrouge CH	106	C1
Carrouges F	89	B3
Carrù I	133	A3
Carryduff GB	27	B5
Carry-le-Rouet F	131	B4
Carsóli I	169	A3
Carsphairn GB	36	A2
Cartagena E	165	B4
Cártama E	163	B3
Cartaxo P	154	B2
Cartaya E	161	B2
Carteret F	88	A2
Cartes E	142	A2
Carúnchio I	170	B2
Carviçães P	149	A3
Carvin F	78	B2
Carvoeira P	154	B1
Carvoeiro P	160	B1
Casabermeja E	163	B3
Casa Branca		
Portalegre P	154	C3
Setúbal P	154	C2
Casacalenda I	170	B2
Casa Castalda I	136	B1
Casaio E	141	B4
Casal di Principe		
I	170	B2
Casalécchio di Reno		
I	135	A4
Casale Monferrato		
I	119	B5
Casalina I	136	C1
Casalmaggiore I	121	C3
Casalnuovo		
Monterotaro I	170	B3
Casaloldo I	121	B3
Casalpusterlengo		
I	120	B2
Casamássima I	173	B2
Casamicciola Terme		
I	170	C1
Casamozza F	180	A2
Casarabonela E	162	B3
Casarano I	173	B4
Casar de Cáceres		
E	155	B4
Casar de Palomero		
E	149	B3
Casarejos E	143	C3
Casares E	162	B2
Casares de las Hurdes		
E	149	B3
Casariche E	163	A3
Casarrubios del Monte		
E	151	B3
Casas de Don Pedro		
E	156	A2
Casas de Fernando		
Alonso E	158	B1
Casas de Haro E	158	B1
Casas de Juan Gil		
E	159	B2
Casas del Juan Núñez		
E	158	B2
Casas del Puerto		
E	159	C2
Casas del Río E	159	B2
Casas de Millán E	155	B4
Casas de Reina E	156	B2
Casas-…Ves E	159	B2
Casas-…nez E	158	B1
Casasimarro E	158	B1
Casas Nuevas E	164	B3
Casasola E	150	B3
Casasola de Arión		
E	150	A2
Casasuertes E	142	A2
Casatejada E	150	C2
Casavieja E	150	B3
Casazza I	120	B2
Cascais P	154	C1
Cascante E	144	C2
Cascante del Rio		
E	152	B2
Cáscia I	169	A3
Casciana Terme I	134	B3
Cáscina I	134	B3
Cáseda E	144	B2
Casekow D	74	A3
Casella I	134	A2
Caselle Torinese I	119	B4
Casemurate I	135	A5
Casenove I	136	C1
Caseres E	153	A4
Caserío Benalí E	159	B3
Caserta I	170	B2
Casével P	160	B1
Cashel IRL	29	B4
Casillas E	150	B3
Casillas de Coria		
E	155	B4
Casina I	134	A3
Casinos E	159	B3
Čáslav CZ	97	B3
Cásola Valsénio I	135	A4
Cásole d'Elsa I	135	B4
Cásoli I	169	A4
Casória I	170	C2
Caspe E	153	A3
Cassàde la Selva		
I	147	C3
Cassagnas F	130	A2
Cassagnes-Bégonhès		
F	130	A1
Cassano allo Iónio		
I	174	B2
Cassano d'Adda I	120	B2
Cassano delle Murge		
I	171	C4
Cassano Magnago		
I	120	B1
Cassano Spinola I	120	C1
Cassel F	78	B2
Cassibile I	177	C4
Cassine I	119	C5
Cassino I	169	B3
Cassis F	132	B1
Cassolnovo I	120	B1
Cassuéjouls F	116	C2
Častá SK	98	C1
Castagnaro I	121	B4
Castagneto Carducci		
I	134	B3
Castagnola CH	120	A1
Castalla E	159	C3
Castañar de Ibor		
E	156	A2
Castanheira de Pêra		
P	154	A2
Cástano Primo I	120	B1
Castasegna CH	120	A2
Castéggio I	120	B2
Casteição P	148	B2
Castejón E	144	B2
Castejón de Monegros		
E	153	A3
Castejón de Sos		
E	145	B4
Castejón de Valdejasa		
E	144	C3
Castèl Baronia I	172	A1
Castel Bolognese		
I	135	A4
Castelbuono I	177	B3
Casteldáccia I	176	A2
Castel d'Aiano I	135	A3
Castel d'Ario I	121	B3
Castel de Cabra E	153	B3
Casteldelfino I	132	A3
Castél del Monte I	169	A4
Castel del Piano I	135	C4
Castèl di Iúdica I	177	B3
Castèl di Rio I	135	A4
Castèl di Sangro I	169	B4
Castèl di Tora I	169	A2
Castelfidardo I	136	B2
Castelfiorentino I	135	B3
Castelforte I	169	B3
Castelfranco Emilia		
I	121	C4
Castelfranco in		
Miscano I	170	B3
Castelfranco Véneto		
I	121	B4
Castél Frentano I	169	A4
Casteljaloux F	128	B3
Castellabate I	170	C2
Castellammare del		
Golfo I	176	A1
Castellammare di		
Stábia I	170	C2
Castellamonte I	119	B4
Castellana Grotte		
I	173	B3
Castellane F	132	B2
Castellaneta I	173	B2
Castellaneta Marina		
I	173	B2
Castellar E	157	B4
Castellarano I	135	A3
Castellar de la Frontera		
E	162	B2
Castellar de la Ribera		
E	147	B2
Castellar del Vallés		
E	147	C3
Castellar de Santiago		
E	157	B4
Castell Arquato I	120	C2
Castell'Azzara I	135	C4
Castellbell i Villar		
E	147	C2
Castelldans E	153	A4
Castell de Cabres		
E	153	B4
Castelldefels E	147	C2
Castell de Ferro E	163	B4
Castelleone I	120	B2
Castellet E	147	C2
Castelletto di Brenzone		
I	121	B3
Castellfollit de la Roca		
E	147	B3
Castellfollit de		
Riubregos E	147	C2
Castellfort E	153	B3
Castellina in Chianti		
I	135	B4
Castellina Marittima		
I	134	B3
Castellóde Farfaña		
E	145	C4
Castellóde la Plana		
E	159	B3
Castello d'Empúries		
E	147	B4
Castello di Fiemme		
I	121	A4
Castelloli E	147	C2
Castellón de Rugat		
E	159	C3
Castellote E	153	B3
Castello Tesino I	121	A4
Castellterçol E	147	C3
Castellúccio de'Sáuri		
I	171	B3
Castelluccio Inferiore		
I	174	B1
Castelmassa I	121	B4
Castelmáuro I	170	B2
Castelmoron-sur-Lot		
F	129	B3
Castelnaudary F	146	A2
Castelnau-de-Médoc		
F	128	A2
Castelnau-de-		
Montmirail F	129	C4
Castelnau-Magnoac		
F	145	A4
Castelnau-Montratier		
F	129	B4
Castelnou E	153	A3
Castelnovo ne'Monti		
I	134	A3
Castelnuovo		
Berardenga I	135	B4
Castelnuovo della		
Dáunia I	170	B3
Castelnuovo di		
Garfagnana I	134	A3
Castelnuovo di Val di		
Cécina I	135	B3
Castelnuovo Don		
Bosco I	119	B4
Castelnuovo Scrivia		
I	120	C1
Castelo Branco		
Bragança P	149	A3
Castelo Branco P	155	B3
Castelo de Paiva		
P	148	A1
Castelo de Vide P	155	B3
Castelo do Neiva		
P	148	A1
Castelo Mendo P	149	B3
Castelraimondo I	136	B2
Castel San Gimignano		
I	135	B4
Castèl San Giovanni		
I	120	B2
Castèl San Pietro		
Terme I	135	A4
Castelsantángelo		
I	136	C2
Castèl Sant'Elia I	168	A2
Castelsaraceno I	174	B1
Castelsardo I	178	B2
Castelserás E	153	A3
Casteltérmini I	176	B2
Castelvecchio		
Subéquo I	169	A3
Castelvetrano I	176	B1
Castél Volturno I	170	B1
Castenédolo I	120	B3
Castets F	128	C1
Castiádas I	179	C3
Castiglioncello I	134	B3
Castiglione I	169	A3
Castiglione Chiavarese		
I	134	A2
Castiglione d'Adda		
I	120	B2
Castiglione dei Pepoli		
I	135	A4
Castiglione del Lago		
I	135	B5
Castiglione della		
Pescáia I	135	C3
Castiglione delle		
Stiviere I	121	B3
Castiglione di Sicilia		
I	177	B4
Castiglione d'Órcia		
I	135	B4
Castiglione Messer		
Marino I	170	B2
Castiglione Messer		
Raimondo I	169	A3
Castiglion Fibocchi		
I	135	B4
Castiglion Fiorentino		
I	135	B4
Castilblanco E	156	A2
Castilblanco de los		
Arroyos E	161	B3
Castil de Peones		
E	143	B3
Castilfrío de la Sierra		
E	144	C1
Castilgaleu E	145	B4
Castilisar E	144	B2
Castilleja E	161	B3
Castillejar E	164	B2
Castillejo de Martin		
Viejo E	149	B3
Castillejo de Mesleón		
E	151	A4
Castillejo de Robledo		
E	151	A4
Castillo de Bayuela		
E	150	B3
Castillo de Locubín		
E	163	A3
Castillonès F	129	B3
Castillon-la-Bataille		
F	128	B2
Castillon-Len-		
Couserans F	146	B2
Castillonroy E	145	C4
Castilruiz E	144	C1
Castione CH	120	A2
Castions di Strada		
I	122	B2
Castirla F	180	A2
Castlebar IRL	28	A2
Castlebellingham		
IRL	27	C4
Castleblaney IRL	27	B4
Castlebridge IRL	30	B2
Castle Cary GB	43	A4
Castlecomer IRL	30	B1
Castlederg GB	27	B3
Castledermot IRL	30	B2
Castle Douglas GB	36	B3
Castleford GB	40	B2
Castleisland IRL	29	B2
Castlemaine IRL	29	B2
Castlemartyr IRL	29	C3
Castlepollard IRL	30	A1
Castlerea IRL	28	A3
Castleton GB	40	B2
Castletown		
Highland GB	32	C3
Isle of Man GB	36	B2
Castletown Bearhaven		
IRL	29	C2
Castletownroche		
IRL	29	B3
Castlewellan GB	27	B5
Casto I	120	B3
Castrejón E	150	A2
Castrelo del Valle		
E	141	B3
Castres F	130	B1
Castricum NL	70	B1
Castries F	131	B2
Castrignano del Capo		
I	173	C4
Castril E	164	B2
Castrillo de Duero		
E	151	A4
Castrillo de la Vega		
E	143	C3
Castrillo de Onielo		
E	142	C2
Castro		
E	142	A2
I	173	B4
Castrocabón E	141	B5
Castro-Caldelas E	141	B3
Castrocaro Terme		
I	135	A4
Castrocontrigo E	141	B4
Castro Daire P	148	B2
Castro dei Volsci I	169	B3
Castro del Río E	163	A3
Castro de Rey E	141	A3
Castrofilippo I	176	B2
Castrogonzalo E	142	B1
Castrojeriz E	142	B2
Castro Laboreiro		
P	140	B2
Castro Marim P	160	B2
Castromonte E	142	C1
Castromudarra E	142	B1
Castronuevo E	142	C1
Castronuño E	150	A2
Castropol E	141	A3
Castroreale I	177	A4
Castroserracin E	151	A4
Castro-Urdiales E	143	A3
Castroverde E	141	A3
Castro Verde P	160	B1
Castroverde de		
Campos E	142	C1
Castroverde de Cerrato		
E	142	C2
Castuera E	156	B2
Cataéggio I	120	A2
Catalca TR	186	A3
Catallar TR	189	C5
Çatalzeytin TR	23	A8
Catánia I	177	B4
Catanzaro I	175	C2
Catanzaro Marina		
I	175	C2
Catarroja E	159	B3
Catarruchos P	148	B1
Catcleugh GB	37	A4
Catenanuova I	177	B3
Caterham GB	44	B3
Cati E	153	B4
Čatići BIH	139	A4
Catignano I	169	A3
Catillon F	91	A3
Catoira E	140	B2
Caton GB	37	B4
Catral E	165	A4
Catterick GB	37	B5
Cáttólica I	136	B1
Cattólica Eraclea		
I	176	B2
Catton GB	37	B4
Caudebec-en-Caux		
F	89	A4
Caudete E	159	C3
Caudete de las Fuentes		
E	159	B2
Caudiel E	159	B3
Caudiès-de-		
Fenouillèdes F	146	B3
Caudry F	91	A3
Caulkerbush GB	36	B3
Caulnes F	101	A3
Caulónia I	175	C2
Caumont-l'Evente		
F	88	A3
Caunes-Minervois		
F	146	A3
Cauro F	180	B1
Caussade F	129	B4
Causse-de-la-Selle		
F	130	B2
Cauterets F	145	B3
Cava de Tirreni I	170	C2
Cavaglia I	119	B5
Cavaillon F	131	B4
Cavalaire-sur-Mer		
F	132	B2
Cavaleiro P	160	B1
Cavalese I	121	A4
Cavallermaggiore		
I	119	C4
Cavallino I	122	B1
Cavárzere I	121	B5
Cavdarhisar TR	187	C4
Çavdır TR	189	B4
Cavernães P	148	B2
Cavezzo I	121	C4
Cavignac F	128	A2
Čavle HR	123	B3
Cavo I	134	C3
Cavour I	119	C4
Cawdor GB	32	D3
Çay TR	187	D6
Çaycuma TR	187	A7
Cayeux-sur-Mer F	78	B1
Cayiralan TR	23	B8
Çayırhan TR	187	B6
Caylus F	129	B4
Cayres F	117	C3
Cazalilla E	157	C4
Cazalla de la Sierra		
E	156	C2
Cazals F	129	B4
Cazanuecos E	142	B1
Cazaubon F	128	C2
Cazaux F	128	B1
Cazavet F	146	A2
Cazères F	146	A2
Cazin BIH	124	C1
Cazis CH	107	C4
Čazma HR	124	B2
Cazo E	142	A1
Cazorla E	164	B2
Cazouls-lès-Béziers		
F	130	B2
Cea		
León E	142	B1
Orense E	140	B3
Ceánuri E	143	A4
Ceauce F	88	B3
Cebolla E	150	C3
Čebovce SK	112	A3
Cebreros E	150	B3
Čečava BIH	125	C3
Ceccano I	169	B3
Cece H	112	C2
Cecenowo PL	68	A2
Čechtice CZ	96	B3
Čechtín CZ	97	B3
Cécina I	134	B3
Ceclavin E	155	B4
Cedégolo I	120	A3
Cedeira E	140	A2
Cedillo E	155	B3
Cedillo del Condado		
E	151	B4
Cedrillas E	153	B3
Cedynia PL	74	B3
Cée E	140	B1
Cefalù I	177	A3
Céggia I	122	B1
Cegléd H	113	B3
Céglédbercel H	112	B3
Céglie Messápica		
I	173	B3
Cehegín E	164	A3
Ceilhes-et-Rocozels		
F	130	B2
Ceinos de Campos		
E	142	B1
Ceira P	148	B1
Čejč CZ	97	C4
Cekcyn PL	76	A3
Cela BIH	124	C2
Čelákovice CZ	84	B2
Celano I	169	A3
Celanova E	140	B3
Celbridge IRL	30	A2
Čelebič BIH	138	B2
Celenza Valfortore		
I	170	B2
Čelić BIH	125	C4
Čelinac BIH	124	C3
Celje SLO	123	A4
Cella E	152	B2
Celldömölk H	111	B4
Celle D	72	B3
Celle Ligure I	133	A4
Celles B	79	B4
Celles-sur-Belle F	115	B3
Cellino San Marco		
I	173	B3
Celorico da Beira		
P	148	B2
Celorico de Basto		
P	148	A1
Çeltik TR	187	C6
Çeltikçi TR	189	B5
Cemaes GB	38	A2
Cembra I	121	A4
Cemerno BIH	139	B4
Cenad RO	126	A2
Cencenighe Agordino		
I	121	A4
Cenei RO	126	B2
Ceneselli I	121	B4
Cenicero E	143	B4
Cenicientos E	150	B3
Censeau F	105	C5
Čenta SRB	126	B2
Centallo I	133	A3
Centelles E	147	C3
Cento I	121	C4
Centúripe I	177	B3
Cepeda la Mora E	150	B2
Cépet F	129	C4
Čepin HR	125	B4
Čepinski Martinci		
HR	125	B4
Cepovan SLO	122	A2
Čeprano I	169	B3
Čeralije HR	125	B3
Cerami I	177	B3
Cerano I	120	B1
Cérans Foulletourte		
F	102	A2
Ceraso I	172	B1
Cerbaia I	135	B4
Cerbère F	146	B4
Cercadillo E	151	A5
Cercal		
Lisboa P	154	B1
Setúbal P	160	B1
Čerčany CZ	96	B2
Cerceda E	151	B4
Cercedilla E	151	B3
Cercemaggiore I	170	B2
Cercs E	147	B2

Cercy-la-Tour F . . .104 C2
Cerda I 176 B2
Cerdedo E 140 B2
Cerdeira P 149 B2
Cerdon F 103 B4
Cerea I 121 B4
Ceres
GB 35 B5
I 119 B4
Cerese I 121 B3
Ceresole-Reale I . .119 B4
Cereste F 132 B1
Céret F 146 B3
Cerezo de Abajo
E 151 A4
Cerezo de Riotírón
E 143 B3
Cerfontaine B 79 B4
Cergy F 90 B2
Cerignola I 171 B3
Cerilly F 103 C4
Cerisiers F 104 A2
Cerizay F 114 B3
Çerkeş TR 23 A7
Çerkezköy TR 186 A3
Cerkije SLO 123 A3
Cerknica SLO 123 B3
Cerkno SLO 122 A2
Cerkwica PL 67 C4
Cerna RO 125 B4
Černá Hora CZ 97 B4
Cernavodă RO. . . .17 C8
Cernay F 106 B2
Cerne Abbas GB . .43 B4
Cernégula E. 143 B3
Cernik HR 124 B3
Černóbbio I 120 B2
Cernik F 95 B4
Černošin CZ 95 B4
Černovice CZ 96 B2
Cérons F 128 B2
Cerovlje HR 123 B3
Cerovo SK 99 C3
Cerqueto I 135 C5
Cerralbo E 149 B3
Cerreto d'Esi I 136 B1
Cerreto Sannita I . .170 B2
Cerrigydrudion GB .38 A3
Cërrik AL 182 B1
Cerro Muriano E . .156 B3
Certaldo I 135 B4
Certosa di Pésio I .133 A3
Cerva P 148 A2
Cervaro I 169 B3
Cervatos de la Cueza
E 142 B2
Červená Řečice CZ 97 B3
Červená-Skala SK . .99 C4
Cervená Voda CZ .97 A4
Cerveny Kostelec
CZ 85 B4
Cervera E 147 C2
Cervera de la Cañada
E 152 A2
Cervera del Llano
E 158 B1
Cervera del Río Alhama
E 144 B2
Cervera de Pisuerga
E 142 B2
Cervéteri I 168 B2
Cérvia I 135 A5
Cerviáde les Garriques
E 147 C1
Cervignano del Friuli
I 122 B2
Cervinara I 170 B2
Cervione F 180 A2
Cervo E 141 A3
Cervon F 104 B2
Cesana Torinese I .119 C3
Cesarica HR 137 A4
Cesarò I 177 B3
Cesena I 135 A5
Cesenático I 135 A5
Cēsis LV 8 D4
Česká Bělá CZ. . . .97 B3
Česká Kamenice
CZ 84 B2
Česká Lípa CZ. . . .84 B2
Česká Skalice CZ. .85 B4
Česká Třebová CZ .97 B4
České Budějovice
CZ 96 C2
České Velenice CZ .96 C2
Český Brod CZ. . . .96 A2
Český Dub CZ. . . .84 B2
Český Krumlov CZ .96 C2
Český Těšín CZ. . .98 B2
Češljeva Bara
SRB 127 C3
Çeşme TR 188 A1
Cessenon F 130 B2
Cesson-Sévigné
F. 101 A4
Cestas F. 128 B2
Čestobrodica SRB 127 C2
Cesuras E 140 A2
Cetina E 152 A2
Cetin Grad HR 123 B4
Cetinje MNE 16 D3
Cetraro I 174 B1
Ceuti E 165 A3
Ceva I 133 A4
Cevico de la Torre
E 142 C2
Cevico Navero E . .142 C2
Cevins F 118 B3
Cévio CH 119 A5
Cevizli TR 189 B6
Cewice PL 68 A2
Ceylan TR 189 C4
Ceyrat F 116 B3
Ceyzériat F 118 A2
Chaam NL 79 A4
Chabanais F 115 C4
Chabeuil F 117 C5
Chabielice PL 86 A3
Chablis F 104 B2
Chabons F 118 B2
Chabówka PL 99 B3

Chabreloche F. . . .117 B3
Chabris F. 103 B3
Chagford GB 42 B3
Chagny F 105 C3
Chagoda RUS. 9 C9
Chaherrero E. 150 B3
Chailland F 88 B3
Chaillé-les-Marais
F. 114 B2
Chailles F. 103 B3
Chailley F 104 A2
Chalabre F. 146 B3
Chalamont F 118 B2
Châlette-sur-Loing
F. 103 A4
Chalindrey F 105 B4
Chalkida GR 185 A4
Challacombe GB. . .42 A3
Challans F 114 B2
Challes-les-Eaux
F. 118 B2
Chalmazel F 117 B3
Chalmoux F 104 C2
Chalonnes-sur-Loire
F. 102 B1
Châlons-en-
Champagne F. . .91 C4
Chalon-sur-Saône
F. 105 C3
Chalupy PL 69 A3
Châlus F 115 C4
Cham
CH 106 B3
D. 95 B4
Chamberet F 116 B1
Chambéry F 118 B2
Chambilly F 117 A4
Chambley F 92 B1
Chambly F 90 B2
Chambois F 89 B4
Chambon-sur-Lac
F. 116 B2
Chambon-sur-Voueize
F. 116 A2
Chambord F 103 B3
Chamborigaud F . .131 A2
Chamboulive F 116 B1
Chamonix-Mont Blanc
F. 119 B3
Chamoux-sur-Gelon
F. 118 B3
Champagnac-le-Vieux
F. 117 B3
Champagney F 106 B1
Champagnole F . . .105 C4
Champagny-Mouton
F. 115 B4
Champaubert F 91 C3
Champdeniers-St Denis
F. 114 B3
Champdieu F 117 B4
Champdôtre F 105 B4
Champeix F 116 B3
Champéry CH 119 A3
Champigne F 102 B1
Champignelles F . .104 B2
Champigny-sur-Veude
F. 102 B2
Champlitte-et-le-Prelot
F. 105 B4
Champoluc I 119 B4
Champoly F 117 B3
Champorcher I 119 B4
Champrond-en-Gâtine
F. 89 B5
Champs-sur-Tarentaine
F. 116 B2
Champs-sur-Yonne
F. 104 B2
Champtoceaux F. .101 B4
Chamrousse F 118 B2
Chamusca F 154 B2
Chanac F 130 A2
Chanaleilles F 117 C3
Chandler's Ford
GB 44 C2
Chandra GR. 185 D7
Chandrexa de Queixa
E 141 B3
Chañe E 150 A3
Changy F 117 A3
Chania GR. 185 D5
Channes F 104 B3
Chantada E 140 B3
Chantelle F 116 A3
Chantenay-St Imbert
F. 104 C2
Chanteuges F 117 B3
Chantilly F 90 B2
Chantonnay F 114 B2
Chão de Codes P .154 B2
Chaource F 104 A3
Chapa E 140 B2
Chapareillan F 118 B2
Chapel en le Frith
GB 40 B2
Chapelle Royale F 103 A3
Chapelle-St Laurent
F. 102 C1
Charbonnat F 104 C3
Chard GB. 43 B4
Charenton-du-Cher
F. 103 C4
Charlbury GB 44 B2
Charleroi B 79 B4
Charlestown
GB 42 B2
IRL 26 C2
Charlestown of
Aberlour GB. . . .32 D3
Charleville IRL 29 B3
Charleville-Mézières
F. 91 B4
Charlieu F 117 A4
Charlottenberg S . .49 C4
Charlton Kings GB .44 B1
Charly F 90 C3
Charmes F 92 C2

Charmes-sur-Rhône
F. 117 C4
Charmey CH 106 C2
Charminster F 43 B4
Charmont-en-Beauce
F. 103 A4
Charny F 104 B2
Charolles F 117 A4
Chârost F 103 C4
Charquemont F . . .106 B1
Charrin F 104 C2
Charroux F 115 B4
Chartres F 90 C1
Charzykow PL 68 B2
Chassenoeuil-sur-
Bonnieure F . . .115 C4
Chassigny F 105 B4
Château-Arnoux
F. 132 A2
Châteaubernard
F. 115 C3
Châteaubourg F . .101 A4
Châteaubriant F . .101 B4
Château-Chinon
F. 104 B2
Château-d'Oex
CH 106 C2
Château-d'Olonne
F. 114 B2
Château-du-Loir
F. 102 B2
Châteaudun F 103 A3
Châteaugiron F . . .101 A4
Château-Gontier
F. 102 B1
Château-Landon
F. 103 A4
Château-la-Vallière
F. 102 B2
Château-l'Evêque
F. 129 A3
Châteaulin F 100 A1
Châteaumeillant
F. 103 C4
Châteauneuf
Nièvre F 104 B2
Saône-et-Loire F .117 A4
Châteauneuf-de-
Randon F 117 C3
Châteauneuf-d'Ille-et-
Vilaine F 88 B2
Châteauneuf-du-Faou
F. 100 A2
Châteauneuf-du-Pape
F. 131 A3
Châteauneuf-en-
Thymerais F 89 B5
Châteauneuf la-Forêt
F. 116 B1
Châteauneuf-le-Rouge
F. 132 B1
Châteauneuf-sur-
Charente F 115 C3
Châteauneuf-sur-Cher
F. 103 C4
Châteauneuf-sur-Loire
F. 103 B4
Châteauneuf-sur-
Sarthe F 102 B1
Châteauponsac F .115 B5
Château-Porcien F .91 B4
Châteauredon F . .132 A2
Châteaurenard
Bouches du Rhône
F. 131 B3
Loiret F 104 B1
Château-Renault
F. 102 B2
Châteauroux F 103 C3
Châteauroux-les-Alpes
F. 118 C3
Château-Salins F . .92 C2
Château-Thierry F. .91 B3
Châteauvillain F . .105 A3
Châtel F 119 A3
Châtelaillon-Plage
F. 114 B2
Châteaudren F . . .100 A3
Châtel-Censoir F . .104 B2
Châtel-de-Neuvre
F. 116 A3
Châtelet B 79 B4
Châtelguyon F 116 B3
Châtellerault F 115 B4
Châtel-Montagne
F. 117 A3
Châtel-St Denis
CH 106 C1
Châtel-sur-Moselle
F. 92 C2
Châtelus-Malvaleix
F. 116 A2
Châtenois F 105 A4
Châtenois-les-Forges
F. 106 B1
Chatham GB 45 B4
Châtillon I 119 B4
Châtillon-Coligny
F. 103 B4
Châtillon-en-Bazois
F. 104 B2
Châtillon-en-Diois
F. 118 C2
Châtillon-sur
Chalaronne F . . .117 A4
Châtillon-sur-Indre
F. 103 C3
Châtillon-sur-Loire
F. 103 B4
Châtillon-sur-Marne
F. 91 B3
Châtillon-sur-Seine
F. 104 B3
Châtres F 91 C3
Chatteris GB 45 A4
Chatton GB 37 A4
Chauchina E 163 A4
Chaudes-Aigues
F. 116 C3
Chaudrey F 91 C4

Chauffailles F 117 A4
Chaulnes F 90 B2
Chaument Gistoux
B 79 B4
Chaumergy F 105 C4
Chaumont F 105 A4
Chaumont-en-Vexin
F. 90 B1
Chaumont-Porcien
F. 91 B4
Chaumont-sur-Aire
F. 91 C5
Chaumont-sur-Loire
F. 103 B3
Chaunay F 115 B4
Chauny F 90 B3
Chaussin F 105 C4
Chauvigny F 115 B4
Chavagnes-en-Paillers
F. 114 B2
Chavanges F 91 C4
Chaves P 148 A2
Chavignon F 91 B3
Chazelles-sur-Lyon
F. 117 B4
Chazey-Bons F . . .118 B2
Cheadle
Greater Manchester
GB. 40 B1
Staffordshire GB . 40 C2
Cheb CZ. 83 B4
Chebsara RUS. 9 C11
Checa E. 152 B2
Chęciny PL 87 B4
Cheddar GB. 43 A4
Cheddleton GB. . . .40 B1
Chef-Boutonne F .115 B3
Cheles E 155 C3
Chella E 159 B3
Chelles F 90 C2
Chełm PL 13 C5
Chełmno
Kujawsko-Pomorskie
PL 76 A3
Wielkopolskie PL .76 B3
Chelmsford GB. . . .45 B4
Chelmuzhi RUS. . . .9 A9
Chełmża PL 76 A3
Cheltenham GB. . . .44 B1
Chelva E 159 B2
Chémery F 103 B3
Chemery-sur-Bar F 91 B4
Chemillé F 102 B1
Chemin F 105 C4
Chemnitz D 83 B4
Chénerailles F 116 A2
Cheniménil F 105 A5
Chenonceaux F . . .103 B3
Chenôve F 105 B3
Chepelare BG 183 B6
Chepstow GB 39 C4
Chera E 159 B3
Cherasco I 119 C4
Cherbonnières F . .115 C3
Cherbourg F 88 A2
Cherchiara di Calábria
I 174 B2
Cherepovets RUS .9 C10
Cherni Vit UA. 13 C9
Chernivtsi UA 17 A6
Chernobyl = Chornobyl
UA 13 C9
Chernyakhovsk
RUS. 12 A4
Chéroy F 104 A1
Cherven BY 13 B8
Chervonohrad UA. .13 C6
Cherykaw BY. 13 B9
Chesham GB. 44 B3
Cheshunt GB. 44 B3
Chessy-lès-Pres
F. 104 A2
Cheste E 159 B3
Chester GB 38 A4
Chesterfield GB. . . .40 B2
Chester-le-Street
GB 37 B5
Chevagnes F 104 C2
Chevanceaux F . . .115 C3
Chevillon F 91 C5
Chevilly F 103 A3
Chew Magna GB . .43 A4
Chézery-Forens F .118 A2
Chialamberto I 119 B4
Chiampo I 121 B4
Chianale I 119 C4
Chianciano Terme
I. 135 B4
Chiaramonte Gulfi
I. 177 B3
Chiaramonti I. 178 B2
Chiaravalle I 136 B2
Chiaravalle Centrale
I. 175 C2
Chiaréggio I 120 A2
Chiari I. 120 B2
Chiaromonte I 174 A2
Chiasso CH 120 B2
Chiávari I. 134 A2
Chiavenna I 120 A2
Chiché F 102 C1
Chichester GB. 44 C3
Chiclana de la Frontera
E 162 B1
Chiclana de Segura
E 164 A1
Chiddingfold GB . . .44 B3
Chieri I 119 B4
Chiesa in Valmalenco
I. 120 A2
Chieti I 169 A4
Chieti Scalo I 169 A4
Chiéuti I 171 B3
Chigwell GB. 45 B4
Chiliomodi GR. . . .184 B3
Chillarón de Cuenca
E 152 B1
Chillarón del Rey
E 151 B5

Chilleurs-aux-Bois
F. 103 A4
Chillón E 156 B3
Chilluevar E. 164 B1
Chiloeches E. 151 B4
Chimay B 91 A4
Chimeneas E. 163 A4
Chinchilla de Monte
Aragón E. 158 C2
Chinchón E 151 B4
Chingford GB. 45 B4
Chinon F 102 B2
Chióggia I 122 B1
Chiomonte I. 119 B3
Chipiona E 161 C3
Chippenham GB . . .43 A4
Chipping Campden
GB 44 A2
Chipping Norton
GB 44 B2
Chipping Ongar
GB 45 B4
Chipping Sodbury
GB 43 A4
Chirac F 130 A2
Chirbury GB 39 B3
Chirens F 118 B2
Chirivel E 164 B2
Chirk GB 38 B3
Chirnside GB 35 C5
Chişinău = Khisinev
MD. 17 B8
Chişineu Criş RO .113 C5
Chissey-en-Morvan
F. 104 B3
Chiusa I 108 C2
Chiusa di Pésio I . .133 A3
Chiusaforte I 122 A2
Chiusa Scláfani I . .176 B2
Chiusi I 135 B4
Chiva E 159 B3
Chivasso I 119 B4
Chlewiska PL 87 A4
Chludowo PL. 75 B5
Chlumec nad Cidlinou
CZ 84 B3
Chlum u Třeboně
CZ 96 C2
Chmielnik PL 87 B4
Chobienia PL 85 A4
Chobienice PL 75 B4
Choceň CZ. 97 A4
Choceń PL 77 B4
Chochołów PL 99 B3
Chocianów PL. 85 A3
Chociw PL. 86 A3
Chociwel PL. 75 A4
Choczewo PL. 68 A2
Chodaków PL. 77 B5
Chodecz PL. 77 B4
Chodov CZ 83 B4
Chodziez PL. 75 B5
Chojna PL 74 B3
Chojnice PL. 68 B2
Chojno
Kujawsko-Pomorskie
PL 77 B4
Wielkopolskie PL .75 B5
Chojnów PL 85 A3
Cholet F 114 A3
Chomérac F 117 C4
Chomutov CZ 83 B5
Chop UA. 12 D5
Chora GR. 184 B2
Chora Sfakion GR 185 D5
Chorges F 132 A2
Chorley GB 38 A4
Chornobyl = Chernobyl
UA 13 C9
Chortkiv UA. 13 D6
Chorzele PL 77 A5
Chorzew PL. 86 A2
Chorzów PL. 86 B2
Choszczno PL 75 A4
Chotěboř CZ 97 B3
Chouilly F 91 B4
Chouto P 154 B2
Chouzy-sur-Cisse
F. 103 B3
Chozas de Abajo
E 142 B1
Chrast CZ 97 B3
Chrást CZ. 96 B1
Chrastava CZ 84 B2
Chřibská CZ. 84 B2
Christchurch GB . . .44 C2
Christiansfeld DK . .59 C2
Chroberz PL 87 B4
Chropyně CZ. 98 B1
Chrzanów PL. 86 B3
Chtelnica SK 98 C1
Chudovo RUS 9 C7
Chueca E 157 A4
Chulmleigh GB 42 B3
Chur CH 107 C4
Church Stretton
GB 39 B4
Churriana E 163 B3
Churwalden CH. . .107 C4
Chvalšiny CZ. 96 C2
Chýnov CZ. 96 B2
Ciacova RO 126 B3
Ciadír-Lunga MD. .17 B8
Ciadoncha E 143 B3
Cianciana I. 176 B2
Ciano d'Enza I 134 A3
Ciążen PL 76 B2
Cibakhaza H 113 C4
Ciborro P 154 C2
Cicagna I 134 A2
Cicciano I 170 C2
Ciciliano I 169 B2
Cicognolo I 120 B3
Cidadelhe P 149 B2
Cide TR 23 A7
Cidones E 143 C4

Ciechanów
Dolnośląskie PL. . .85 A4
Mazowieckie PL. . .77 B5
Ciechocinek PL. . . .76 B3
Cieląadz PL. 87 A4
Ciemnik PL 75 A4
Ciempozuelos E . .151 B4
Ciepielów PL 87 A5
Cierny Balog SK . . .99 C3
Cierp-Gaud F. 145 B4
Cierpice PL 76 B3
Ciervana E. 143 A3
Cierznie PL. 68 B2
Cieslé PL. 77 B5
Cieszanów PL. 98 B2
Cieszyn PL. 98 B2
Cifer SK 98 C1
Çifteler TR 187 C6
Cifuentes E 151 B5
Cigales E 142 C2
Cigliano I 119 B5
Cihanbeyli TR 23 B7
Cillas E 152 B2
Cilleros E 149 B3
Cilleruelo de Arriba
E 143 C3
Cilleruelo de Bezana
E 143 B3
Cimalmotto CH . . .119 A5
Cimanes del Tejar
E 141 B5
Ciminna I 176 B2
Cimişlia MD 17 B8
Cimoláis I. 122 A1
Cîmpulung RO 17 C6
Çınarcık TR 186 B4
Cinctorres E 153 B3
Cinderford GB 39 C4
Çine TR 188 B3
Činěves CZ 84 B3
Cinfães P 148 A1
Cingia de Botti I . . .120 B3
Cíngoli I 136 B2
Cinigiano I 135 C4
Cinobaña SK 99 C3
Cinq-Mars-la-Pile
F. 102 B2
Cinquefrondí I 175 C2
Cintegabelle F 146 A2
Cintruénigo E 144 B2
Ciółkowo PL 77 B4
Ciperez E 149 B3
Cirat E 153 B3
Cirella I 174 B1
Cirey-sur-Vezouze
F. 92 C2
Ciria E 152 A2
Ciriè I 119 B4
Cirigliano I 174 A2
Ciró I 174 B3
Ciró Marina I 174 B3
Ciry-le-Noble F . . .104 C3
Cislău RO 17 C7
Cismon del Grappa
I. 121 B4
Cisneros E 142 B2
Cissac-Médoc F . .128 A2
Čista CZ 96 A1
Cisterna di Latina
I. 169 B2
Cistérniga E 150 A3
Cisternino I 173 B3
Cistierna E 142 B1
Čitluk BIH. 139 B3
Cítov CZ. 84 B2
Cittadella I 121 B4
Cittàdella Pieve I . .135 C5
Cittádel Vaticano =
Vatican City I . . .168 B2
Città di Castello I . .135 B5
Cittaducale I 169 A2
Cittanova I 175 C2
Città Sant'Angelo
I. 169 A4
Ciudadela de Menorca
E 167 B3
Ciudad Real E 157 B4
Ciudad Rodrigo E .149 B3
Ciutadilla E 147 C2
Cividale del Friuli
I. 122 A2
Cívita I 169 A3
Cívita Castellana I .168 A2
Civitanova Alta I . .136 B2
Civitanova Marche
I. 136 B2
Civitavécchia I. . . .168 A1
Civitella di Romagna
I. 135 A4
Civitella di Tronto
I. 136 C2
Civitella Roveto I . .169 B3
Civray F 115 B4
Çivril TR 189 A4
Cizur Mayor E 144 B2
Clabhach GB. 34 B1
Clachan GB. 31 B2
Clachan na Luib
GB 31 B1
Clacton-on-Sea GB 45 B5
Cladich GB 34 B2
Claggan GB 34 B2
Clairvaux-les-Lacs
F. 105 C4
Clamecy F 104 B2
Claonaig GB 34 C2
Clarecastle IRL 28 B3
Claregalway IRL . . .28 A3
Claremorris IRL. . . .28 A2
Clarinbridge IRL. . .28 A3
Clashmore
GB 32 D2
IRL 29 B4
Claudy GB 27 B3
Clausthal-Zellerfeld
D. 82 A2
Cláut I 122 A1

Clay Cross GB. 40 B2
Claye-Souilly F 90 C2
Cléder F 100 A1
Cleethorpes GB. . . .41 B3
Clefmont F 105 A4
Cléguérec F 100 A2
Clelles F 118 C2
Clenze D 73 B3
Cleobury Mortimer
GB 39 B4
Cléon-d'Andran F .117 C4
Cléré-les-Pins F . .102 B2
Clères F 89 A5
Clermont F 90 B2
Clermont-en-Argonne
F. 91 B5
Clermont-Ferrand
F. 116 B3
Clermont-l'Hérault
F. 130 B2
Clerval F 105 B5
Clervaux L 92 A2
Cléry-St André F . .103 B3
Cles I 121 A4
Clevedon GB 43 A4
Cleveleys GB. 38 A3
Cley GB 41 C5
Clifden IRL 28 A1
Clifford GB. 39 B3
Clisson F 101 B4
Clitheroe GB 40 B1
Clogh IRL 30 B1
Cloghan
Donegal IRL. 26 B3
Offaly IRL. 28 A4
Clogheen IRL. 29 B4
Clogher GB 27 B3
Cloghjordan IRL . . .28 B3
Clohars-Carnoët
F. 100 B2
Clonakilty IRL 29 C3
Clonaslee IRL 30 A1
Clondalkin IRL. 30 A2
Clones IRL 27 B3
Clonmany IRL 27 A3
Clonmel IRL. 29 B4
Clonmellon IRL 30 A1
Clonord IRL. 30 A1
Clonroche IRL 30 B2
Cloone IRL 26 C3
Cloppenburg D 71 B5
Closeburn GB. 36 A3
Clough GB. 27 B5
Clova GB 35 B4
Clovelly GB 42 B2
Clowne GB. 40 B2
Cloyes-sur-le-Loir
F. 103 B3
Cloyne IRL 29 C3
Cluis F 103 C3
Cluj-Napoca RO. . .17 B5
Clun GB 39 B3
Clunes GB. 34 B3
Cluny F 117 A4
Cluses F 118 A3
Clusone I 120 B2
Clydach GB 39 C3
Clydebank GB. 34 C3
Coachford IRL. 29 C3
Coagh GB 27 B4
Coalisland GB. 27 B4
Coalville GB. 40 C2
Coaña E 141 A4
Çobanlar TR 187 D5
Cobas E 140 A2
Cobertelade E 151 A5
Cobeta E 152 B1
Cóbh IRL 29 C3
Cobreces E 142 A2
Coburg D 82 B2
Coca E 150 A3
Cocentaina E 159 C3
Cochem D 80 B3
Cockburnspath GB 35 C5
Cockermouth GB . .36 B3
Codigoro I 121 C5
Codogno I 120 B2
Codos E 152 A2
Codróipo I 122 B1
Codrongianos I . . .178 B2
Coelhoso P 149 A3
Coesfeld D. 71 C4
Coevorden NL. 71 B3
Cofrentes E 159 B2
Cogeces del Monte
E 150 A3
Coggeshall GB 45 B4
Cognac F 115 C3
Cogne I 119 B4
Cognin F 118 B2
Cogolin F 132 B2
Cogollos de Guadix
E 164 B1
Cogollos-Vega E. .163 A4
Cogolludo E 151 B4
Coimbra P 148 B1
Coín E 163 B3
Coirós E 140 A2
Čoka SRB 126 B2
Col SLO 123 B3
Colares P 154 C1
Cölbe D. 81 B4
Colbitz D. 73 B4
Colchester GB 45 B4
Coldingham GB. . . .35 C5
Colditz D 83 A4
Coldstream GB. . . .35 C5
Colebrooke GB 43 B3
Colera E 146 B4
Coleraine GB. 27 A4
Colfiorito I 136 B1
Cólico I 120 A2
Coligny F 118 A2
Colindres E 143 A3
Collado-Mediano
E 151 B3
Collado Villalba E .151 B4

Collagna I 134 A3
Collanzo E 142 A1
Collat F 117 B3
Coll de Nargó E . . .147 B2
Collécchio I 120 C3
Colledimezzo I 169 B4
Colle di Val d'Elsa
I 135 B4
Colleferro I 169 B3
Colle Isarco I 108 C2
Collelongo I 169 B3
Collepasso I 173 B4
Collepepe I 136 C1
Collesalvetti I 134 B3
Colle Sannita I 170 B2
Collesano I 176 B2
Colli a Volturno I . . .169 B4
Collin GB 36 A3
Collinée F 101 A3
Collingham
  Nottinghamshire
  GB 40 B2
  West Yorkshire
  GB 40 B3
Collinghorst D 71 A4
Cóllio I 120 B3
Collobrières F 132 B2
Collon IRL 27 C4
Collooney IRL 26 B2
Colmar F 106 A2
Colmars F 132 A2
Colmenar E 163 B3
Colmenar de la Sierra
E 151 A4
Colmenar de Oreja
E 151 B4
Colmenar Viejo E . .151 B4
Colmonel GB 36 A2
Colne GB 40 B1
Colobraro I 174 A2
Cologna Véneta I . .121 B4
Cologne = Köln D . .80 D2
Cologne F 129 C3
Cologne al Serio I . .120 B2
Colombey-les-Belles
F 92 C1
Colombey-les-deux-
Églises F 105 A3
Colombres E 142 A2
Colomera E 163 A4
Colomers E 147 B3
Colomiers F 129 C4
Colònia de Sant Jordi
E 167 B3
Colorno I 120 C3
Colos P 160 B1
Cölpin D 74 A2
Colpy GB 33 D4
Colsterworth GB . . .40 C3
Coltishall GB 41 C5
Colunga E 142 A1
Colwell GB 37 A4
Colwyn Bay GB 38 A3
Colyford GB 43 B3
Comácchio I 121 C5
Coma-ruga E 147 C2
Combarros E 141 B4
Combeaufontaine
F 105 B4
Comber GB 27 B5
Comblain-au-Pont
B 80 B1
Combloux F 118 B3
Combourg F 88 B2
Combronde F 116 B3
Comeglians I 109 C3
Comillas E 142 A2
Comines F 78 B3
Cómiso I 177 C3
Comloşu Mare RO .126 B2
Commensacq F 128 B2
Commentry F 116 A2
Commerau D 84 A2
Commercy F 92 C1
Como I 120 B2
Cómpeta E 163 B4
Compiègne F 90 B2
Comporta P 154 C2
Comps-sur-Artuby
F 132 B2
Comrat MD 17 B8
Comrie GB 35 B4
Comunanza I 136 C2
Cona
  Emilia Romagna
  I 121 C4
  Veneto I 121 B5
Concarneau F 100 B2
Conceição P 160 B1
Conches-en-Ouche
F 89 B4
Concordia Sagittária
I 122 B1
Concordia sulla
Sécchia I 121 C3
Concots F 129 B4
Condat F 116 B2
Condeixa P 148 B1
Condemios de Abajo
E 151 A4
Condemios de Arriba
E 151 A4
Condé-sur-l'Escaut
F 79 B3
Conde-sur-Marne F .91 B4
Condé-sur-Noireau
F 88 B3
Condino I 121 B3
Condom F 129 C3
Condove I 119 B4
Condrieu F 117 B4
Conegliano I 122 B1
Conflans-sur-Lanterne
F 105 B5
Confolens F 115 B4
Conforto E 141 A3

Cong IRL 28 A2
Congleton GB 40 B1
Congosto E 141 B4
Congosto de Valdavia
E 142 B2
Congostrina E 151 A4
Conil de la Frontera
E 162 B1
Coningsby GB 41 B3
Coniston GB 36 B3
Conlie F 102 A1
Conliège F 105 C4
Conna IRL 29 B3
Connah's Quay GB .38 A3
Connantre F 91 C3
Connaugh IRL 28 B3
Connaux F 131 A3
Connel GB 34 B2
Connerré F 102 A2
Cononbridge GB . . .32 D2
Čonoplja SRB 126 B1
Conques F 116 C2
Conques-sur-Orbiel
F 146 A3
Conquista E 157 B3
Conquista de la Sierra
E 156 A2
Consándolo I 121 C4
Consélice I 135 A4
Conselve I 121 B4
Consenvoye F 91 B5
Consett GB 37 B5
Consolação P 154 B1
Constancia P 154 B2
Constanco E 140 A2
Constantí E 147 C2
Constantina E 162 A2
Constanţa RO 17 C8
Consuegra E 157 A4
Consuma I 135 B4
Contarina I 122 B1
Contay F 90 B2
Conthey CH 119 A4
Contigliano I 168 A2
Contis-Plage F 128 B1
Contrada I 170 C2
Contres F 103 B3
Contrexéville F 105 A4
Controne I 172 B1
Contursi Termi I 172 B1
Conty F 90 B2
Conversano I 173 B3
Conwy GB 38 A3
Cookstown GB 27 B4
Coole F 91 C4
Coolgreany IRL 30 B2
Cooneen GB 27 B3
Cootehill IRL 27 B3
Cope E 165 B3
Copenhagen =
  København DK . . .61 D2
Copertino I 173 B4
Copparo I 121 C4
Coppenbrugge D . . .72 B2
Corabia RO 17 D6
Córaci I 175 B2
Coralići BIH 124 C1
Corato I 171 B4
Coray F 100 A2
Corbeil-Essonnes
F 90 C2
Corbeny F 91 B3
Corbera E 159 B3
Corbère F 90 B2
Corbigny F 104 B2
Corbion B 91 B4
Corbridge GB 37 B4
Corby GB 40 C3
Corconte E 143 A3
Corcubión E 140 B1
Corcumello I 169 A3
Cordenòns I 122 B1
Cordes-sur-Ciel F . .129 B4
Córdoba E 156 C3
Cordobilla de Lácara
E 155 B4
Cordovado I 122 B1
Corella E 144 B2
Coreses E 150 A2
Corfe Castle GB . . .43 B4
Corga de Lobão
P 148 B1
Cori I 169 B2
Coria E 155 B4
Coria del Río E 162 A1
Corigliano Cálabro
I 174 B2
Corinaldo I 136 B1
Corinth = Korinthos
GR 184 B3
Cório I 119 B4
Coripe E 162 B2
Cork IRL 29 C3
Corlay F 100 A2
Corleone I 176 B2
Corleto Monforte I . .172 B1
Corleto Perticara I . .174 A2
Çorlu TR 186 A2
Cormainville F 103 A3
Cormatin F 104 C3
Cormeilles F 89 A4
Cormery F 102 B2
Cormòns I 122 B2
Cornago E 144 B2
Cornberg D 82 A1
Cornellana E 141 A4
Corníglio I 134 A3
Cornimont F 106 B1
Corniolo I 135 B4
Cornuda I 121 B5
Cornudella de
  Montsant E 147 C1
Cornudilla E 143 B3
Cornus F 130 B2
Çorovodë AL 182 C2
Corpach GB 34 B2
Corps F 118 C2
Corps Nuds F 101 B4

Corral de Almaguer
E 157 A4
Corral de Ayllon E .151 A4
Corral de Calatrava
E 157 B3
Corrales E 149 A4
Corral-Rubio E 158 C2
Corran GB 34 B2
Corredoiras E 140 A2
Corréggio I 121 C3
Corrèze F 116 B1
Corridónia I 136 B2
Corris GB 38 B3
Corrubedo E 140 B1
Córsico I 120 B2
Corsock GB 36 A3
Corte F 180 A2
Corteconceptión
E 161 B3
Cortegaca P 148 B1
Cortegada E 140 B2
Cortegana E 161 B3
Cortemaggiore I . . .120 B2
Cortemilia I 133 A4
Corte Pinto P 160 B2
Cortes E 144 C2
Cortes de Aragón
E 153 B3
Cortes de Arenoso
E 153 B3
Cortes de Baza E . .164 B2
Cortes de la Frontera
E 162 B2
Cortes de Pallás
E 159 B3
Cortiçadas P 154 C2
Cortico P 148 A2
Cortijo de Arriba
E 157 A3
Cortijos Nuevos E .164 A2
Cortina d'Ampezzo
I 108 C3
Corton GB 41 C5
Cortona I 135 B4
Coruche P 154 C2
Corullón E 141 B4
Çorum TR 23 A8
Corvara in Badia I . .108 C2
Corvera E 165 B3
Corwen GB 38 B3
Cosenza I 174 B2
Cosham GB 44 C2
Coslada E 151 B4
Cosne-Cours-sur-Loire
F 104 B1
Cosne d'Allier F . . .103 C4
Cospeito E 140 A3
Cossato I 119 B5
Cossaye F 104 C2
Cossé-le-Vivien F . .101 B5
Cossonay CH 105 C5
Costa da Caparica
P 154 C1
Costa de Santo André
P 160 A1
Costalpino I 135 B4
Costa Nova P 148 B1
Costaros F 117 C3
Costeşti RO 17 C6
Costigliole d'Asti
I 119 C5
Costigliole Saluzzo
I 133 A3
Coswig
  Sachsen D 83 A5
  Sachsen-Anhalt D .83 A4
Cotherstone GB . . .37 B5
Cotronei I 175 B2
Cottbus D 84 A2
Cottenham GB 45 A4
Cottingham GB 40 B3
Coublanc F 105 B4
Couches F 104 C3
Couço P 154 C2
Coucouron F 117 C3
Coucy-le-Château-
Auffrique F 90 B3
Couëron F 101 B4
Couflens F 146 B2
Couhé F 115 B4
Couiza F 146 B3
Coulags GB 31 B3
Coulanges F 104 C2
Coulanges-la-Vineuse
F 104 B2
Coulanges-sur-Yonne
F 104 B2
Couleuvre F 104 C1
Coulmier-le-Sec F .104 B3
Coulommiers F 90 C3
Coulonges-sur-l'Autize
F 114 B3
Coulounieix-Chamiers
F 129 A3
Coulport GB 34 B3
Coupar Angus GB . .35 B4
Coupéville F 91 C4
Couptrain F 89 B3
Coura P 140 C2
Courcelles B 79 B4
Courcelles-Chaussy
F 92 B2
Courchevel F 118 B3
Cour-Cheverny F . .103 B3
Courcôme F 115 C4
Courcon F 114 B3
Courgenay CH 106 B2
Courniou F 130 B1
Cournon-d'Auvergne
F 116 B3
Cournonterral F 130 B2
Courpière F 117 B3
Coursan F 130 B2
Courseulles-sur-Mer
F 89 A3
Cours-la-Ville F 117 A4

Courson-les-Carrières
F 104 B2
Courtalain F 103 A3
Courtenay F 104 A2
Courtomer F 89 B4
Courville
  Eure-et-Loire F . .89 B5
  Marne F 91 B3
Coussac-Bonneval
F 115 C5
Coutances F 88 A2
Couterne F 89 B3
Coutras F 128 A2
Couvet CH 106 C1
Couvin B 91 A4
Couzon F 104 C2
Covadonga E 142 A1
Covaleda E 143 C4
Covarrubias E 143 B3
Covas E 148 A1
Cove GB 31 B3
Coventry GB 44 A2
Coverack GB 42 B1
Covigliáio I 135 A4
Covilhã P 148 B2
Cowbridge GB 39 C3
Cowdenbeath GB . .35 B4
Cowes GB 44 C2
Cox F 129 C4
Cózar E 157 B4
Cozes F 114 C3
Cozzano F 180 B2
Craco I 174 A2
Cracow = Kraków
PL 99 A3
Craibstone GB 33 D4
Craighouse GB 34 C2
Craignure GB 34 B2
Crail GB 35 B5
Crailsheim D 94 B2
Craiova RO 17 C5
Cramlington GB 37 A5
Cranleigh GB 44 B3
Craon F 101 B5
Craonne F 91 B3
Craponne F 117 B4
Craponne-sur-Arzon
F 117 B3
Crathie GB 32 D3
Crato P 155 B3
Craughwell IRL 28 A3
Craven Arms GB . . .39 B4
Crawford GB 36 A3
Crawinkel D 82 B2
Crawley GB 44 B3
Creag Ghoraidh
GB 31 B1
Crecente E 140 B2
Crèches-sur-Saône
F 117 A4
Crécy-en-Ponthieu
F 78 B1
Crécy-la-Chapelle
F 90 C2
Crécy-sur-Serre F . .91 B3
Crediton GB 43 B3
Creeslough IRL 26 A3
Creetown GB 36 B2
Creeve GB 27 B4
Creglingen D 94 B2
Creil F 90 B2
Creissels F 130 A2
Crema I 120 B2
Cremeaux F 117 B3
Crémenes E 142 B1
Crémieu F 118 B2
Cremlingen D 73 B3
Cremona I 120 B3
Creney F 91 C4
Črenšovci SLO 111 C3
Créon F 128 B2
Crepaja SRB 127 B2
Crépey F 92 C1
Crépy F 91 B3
Crépy-en-Valois F . .90 B2
Cres HR 123 C3
Crescentino I 119 B5
Crespino I 121 C4
Crespos E 150 B3
Cressage GB 39 B4
Cressensac F 129 A4
Cressia F 105 C4
Crest F 117 C5
Cresta CH 107 C4
Créteil F 90 C2
Creully F 88 A3
Creussen D 95 B3
Creutzwald F 92 B2
Creuzburg D 82 A2
Crevalcore I 121 C4
Crèvecoeur-le-Grand
F 90 B2
Crevillente E 165 A4
Crévola d'Ossola
I 119 A5
Crewe GB 38 A4
Crewkerne GB 43 B4
Criales E 143 B3
Crianlarich GB 34 B3
Criccieth GB 38 B2
Crickhowell GB 39 C3
Cricklade GB 44 B2
Crieff GB 35 B4
Criel-sur-Mer F 90 A1
Crimond GB 33 D5
Crimmitschau D . . .83 B4
Crinitz D 84 A1
Cripán E 143 B4
Criquetot-l'Esneval
F 89 A4
Crispiano I 173 B3
Crissolo I 119 C4
Cristóbal E 149 B4
Crivitz D 73 A4
Crna SLO 110 C1
Crna Bara
  Srbija SRB 127 C1
  Vojvodina SRB . . .126 B2

Crnac HR 125 B3
Crnča SRB 127 C1
Crni Lug
  BIH 138 A2
  HR 123 B3
Crni Vrh SLO 123 B3
Crnjelovo Donje
  BIH 125 C5
Črnomelj SLO 123 B4
Crocketford GB 36 A3
Crocq F 116 B2
Crodo I 119 A5
Croglin GB 37 B4
Crolly IRL 26 A2
Cromarty GB 32 D2
Cromer GB 41 C5
Cronat F 104 C2
Crookhaven IRL . . .29 C2
Crookstown IRL . . .29 C3
Croom IRL 29 B3
Cropalati I 174 B2
Crópani I 175 C2
Crosbost GB 31 A2
Crosby GB 38 A3
Crósia I 174 B2
Crossakiel IRL 27 C3
Cross-Hands GB . . .39 C2
Crosshaven IRL . . .29 C3
Crosshill GB 36 A2
Crossmolina IRL . . .26 B1
Crotone I 175 B3
Crouy F 90 B3
Crowborough GB . .45 B4
Crowland GB 41 C3
Crowthorne GB 44 B3
Croyde GB 42 A2
Croydon GB 44 B3
Crozon F 100 A1
Cruas F 117 C4
Cruceni RO 126 A3
Crúcoli I 174 B3
Cruden Bay GB 33 D5
Crudgington GB . . .38 B4
Cruis F 132 A1
Crumlin GB 27 B4
Cruseilles F 118 A3
Crusheen IRL 28 B3
Cruz de Incio E 141 B3
Crvenka SRB 126 B1
Červeny Kamen SK. .98 B2
Csabacsüd H 113 C4
Csabrendek H 111 B4
Csákánydoroszló
H 111 C3
Csákvár H 112 B2
Csanádapáca H . . .113 C4
Csanádpalota H . . .126 A2
Csány H 113 B3
Csanytelek H 113 C4
Csapod H 111 B3
Császár H 112 B2
Császártöltés H 112 C3
Csávoly H 125 A5
Csemö H 113 B3
Csengöd H 112 C3
Csépa H 113 C4
Csepreg H 111 B3
Cserkeszölö H 113 C4
Csernely H 113 A4
Csesztreg H 111 C3
Csökmö H 113 B5
Csököly H 124 A3
Csokonyavisonta
H 124 A3
Csólyospálos H . . .113 C3
Csongrád H 113 C4
Csopak H 112 C1
Csorna H 111 B4
Csorvás H 113 C4
Csurgo H 124 A3
Cuacos de Yuste
E 150 B2
Cualedro E 140 C3
Cuanca de Campos
E 142 B1
Cuba H 112 B3
Cubel E 152 A2
Cubelles E 147 C2
Cubillos E 143 C4
Cubillos del Sil E . .141 B4
Cubjac F 129 A3
Cubo de la Solana
E 152 A1
Çubuk TR 23 A7
Cuckfield GB 44 B3
Cucuron F 131 B4
Cudillero E 141 A4
Cuéllar E 151 A3
Cuenca E 152 B1
Cuers F 132 B2
Cuerva E 157 A3
Cueva de Agreda
E 144 C2
Cuevas Bajas E . . .163 A3
Cuevas del Almanzora
E 164 B3
Cuevas del Becerro
E 162 B2
Cuevas del Campo
E 164 B2
Cuevas del Valle
E 150 B3
Cuevas de San
  Clemente E 143 B3
Cuevas de San Marcos
E 163 A3
Cuges-les-Pins F . .132 B1
Cúglieri I 178 B2
Cugnaux F 129 C4
Cuijk NL 80 A1
Cuinzier F 117 A4
Cuiseaux F 105 C4
Cuisery F 105 C4
Culan F 103 C4
Culemborg NL 79 A5
Cúllar E 164 B2
Cullaville IRL 27 B4
Cullera E 159 B3
Cullivoe GB 33 A5

Cullompton GB 43 B3
Cully CH 106 C1
Culoz F 118 B2
Cults GB 33 D4
Cumbernauld GB . .35 C4
Cumbres de San
  Bartolomé E 161 A3
Cumbres Mayores
  E 161 A3
Cumiana I 119 C4
Cumnock GB 36 A2
Cumra TR 23 C7
Cúneo I 133 A3
Cunlhat F 117 B3
Cuntis E 140 B2
Cuorgnè I 119 B4
Cupar GB 35 B4
Cupello I 170 A2
Cupra Maríttima I . .136 B2
Cupramontana I . . .136 B2
Čuprija SRB 127 D3
Curinga I 175 C2
Currelos E 140 B3
Currie GB 35 C4
Curtea de Argeş
  RO 17 C6
Curtici RO 126 A3
Curtis E 140 A2
Curtis Santa Eulalia
  E 140 A2
Čurug SRB 126 B2
Cusano Mutri I 170 B2
Cushendall GB 27 A4
Cusset F 117 A3
Cussy-les-Forges
  F 104 B3
Custines F 92 C2
Cutanda E 152 B2
Cutro I 175 B2
Cutrofiano I 173 B4
Cuts F 90 B3
Cuvilly F 90 B2
Cuxhaven D 64 C1
Cvikov CZ 84 B2
Cwmbran GB 39 C3
Cybinka PL 75 B3
Czacz PL 75 B5
Czajków PL 86 A2
Czaplinek PL 75 A5
Czarlin PL 69 A3
Czarna Woda PL . .68 B3
Czarnca PL 87 B3
Czarne PL 68 B1
Czarnków PL 75 B5
Czarnowo PL 76 A3
Czarnozyly PL 86 A2
Czarny Bór PL 85 B4
Czarny-Dunajec PL .99 B3
Czarny Las PL 86 A1
Czchow PL 99 B4
Czechowice-Dziedzice
  PL 98 B2
Czempiń PL 75 B5
Czermno PL 87 A4
Czernichów PL 99 B3
Czerniejewo PL 76 B2
Czernikowo PL 76 B3
Czersk PL 68 B2
Czerwieńsk PL 75 B4
Czerwionka-Leszczyny
  PL 86 B2
Częstochowa PL . . .86 B3
Czeszewo PL 76 B2
Człopa PL 75 A5
Człuchów PL 68 B2
Czołpino PL 68 A2

D

Dağ TR 189 B5
Daaden D 81 B3
Dabas H 112 B3
Dąbie PL 76 B3
Dąbki PL 67 B5
Dabo F 92 C3
Dąbrowa PL 76 B2
Dąbrowa Górnicza
  PL 86 B3
Dąbrowa Tarnowska
  PL 87 B4
Dąbrowice PL 77 B4
Dabromierz PL 85 B4
Dachau D 108 A2
Dačice CZ 97 B3
Daday TR 23 A7
Dagali N 47 B5
Dägebüll D 64 B1
Dagmersellen CH . .106 B2
Dahlen D 83 A4
Dahlenburg D 73 A3
Dahme D 83 A5
Dähre D 73 B3
Daikanvik S 195 E7
Dail bho Dheas GB .31 A2
Dailly GB 36 A2
Daimiel E 157 A4
Daingean IRL 30 A1
Dakovica KOS 16 D4
Đakovo HR 125 B4
Dal
  Akershus N 48 B3
  Telemark N 47 C5
Dalaas A 107 B5
Dalabrog GB 31 B1
Dala-Floda S 50 B1
Dala-Husby S 50 B2
Dala-Järna S 50 B1
Dalaman TR 188 C3
Dalarö S 57 A4
Dalbeattie GB 36 B3
Dalby
  DK 59 C3
  Skåne S 61 D3
  Uppsala S 57 A3

Dalby continued
  Värmland S 49 B5
Dale
  Pembrokeshire
  GB 39 C1
  Shetland GB 33 A5
  Hordaland N 46 B2
  Sogn og Fjordane
  N 46 A2
Dalen
  Akershus N 48 C3
  Telemark N 53 A4
Daleszyce PL 87 B4
Dalhalvaig GB 32 C3
Dalheim L 92 B2
Dalhem S 57 C4
Dalias E 164 C2
Dalj HR 125 B4
Dalkeith GB 35 C4
Dalkey IRL 30 A2
Dalmally GB 34 B3
Dalmellington GB . .36 A2
Dalmose DK 65 A4
Daløy N 46 A2
Dalry
  Dumfries & Galloway
  GB . . . . .34 C
  North Ayrshire GB .36 A
Dalrymple GB . . . . .36 A
Dalseter N . . . . .47 A
Dalsjöfors S . . . . . . .60 B
Dalskog S . . . . .54 B
Dals Långed S . . . .54 B
Dals Rostock S . . . .54 B
Dalston GB . . . . . . .36 B
Dalstorp S . . . . .60 B
Dalton-in-Furness
  GB . . . . .36 B
Daluis F . . . . .132 A
Dalum
  D . . . . .71 B
  S . . . . .60 B
Dalvík IS . . . . .191 B
Dalwhinnie GB . . . .32 E
Dalyan TR . . . . .188 C
Damasi GR . . . . . . .182 D
Damasławek PL . . . .76 B
Damazan F . . . . . . .129 B
Damgan F . . . . .101 B
Dammarie-les-Lys
  F . . . . .90 C
Dammartin-en-Goële
  F . . . . .90 B
Damme D . . . . .71 B
Dámnica PL . . . . . . .68 A
Dampierre F . . . . . .105 B
Dampierre-sur-Salon
  F . . . . .105 B
Damüls A . . . . .107 B
Damville F . . . . .89 B
Damvillers F . . . . . . .92 B
Damwoude NL . . . .70 A
Danasjö S . . . . .195 E
Danbury GB . . . . . .45 B
Dångebo S . . . . . . .63 B
Dangers F . . . . .89 B
Dangé-St Romain
  F . . . . .102 C
Dangeul F . . . . .89 B
Danilovgrad MNE . .16 D
Danischenhagen D .64 B
Daniszyn PL . . . . . .85 A
Danjoutin F . . . . . . .106 B
Dannas S . . . . .60 B
Dannemare F . . . . .106 B
Dannemora S . . . . .51 B
Dannenberg D . . . .73 A
Dánszentmiklós
  H . . . . .112 B
Dány H . . . . .112 B
Daoulas F . . . . .100 A
Darabani RO . . . . . .17 A
Darány H . . . . .125 B
Darda HR . . . . .125 B
Dardesheim D . . . .73 C
Darfeld D . . . . .71 B
Darfo I . . . . .120 B
Dargiń PL . . . . .68 A
Dargun D . . . . .66 C
Darlington GB . . . . .37 B
Darłowo PL . . . . . . .68 A
Darmstadt D . . . . . .93 B
Darney F . . . . .105 A
Daroca E . . . . .152 A
Darque P . . . . .148 A
Darragh IRL . . . . . .28 B
Dartford GB . . . . . . .45 B
Dartington GB . . . . .43 B
Dartmouth GB . . . . .43 B
Darton GB . . . . .40 B
Daruvar HR . . . . . .124 B
Darvas H . . . . .113 B
Darvel GB . . . . .36 A
Darwen GB . . . . . . .38 A
Dassel D . . . . .82 A
Dassow D . . . . .65 C
Datça TR . . . . .188 C
Datteln D . . . . .80 A
Dattenfeld D . . . . . .81 B
Daugard DK . . . . . .59 C
Daugavpils LV . . . . .8 E
Daumeray F . . . . . .102 B
Daun D . . . . .80 B
Daventry GB . . . . . .44 A
Davle CZ . . . . .96 B
Davor HR . . . . .124 B
Davos CH . . . . .107 C
Davutlar TR . . . . . .188 B
Davyd Haradok BY .13 B
Dawlish GB . . . . . . .43 B
Dax F . . . . .128 C
Dazkırı TR . . . . . . .189 B
Deal GB . . . . .45 B
Deauville F . . . . . . .89 A
Deba E . . . . .143 A
Debar MK . . . . .182 B
Dębe PL . . . . .77 B
Dębica PL . . . . .87 B
Dębnica Kaszubska
  PL . . . . .68 A

Dębno PL 74 B3
Dębołęka PL 86 A2
Dębowa Łąka PL 69 B4
Debrc SRB 127 C1
Debrecen H 113 B5
Debrznica PL 75 B4
Debrzno PL 68 B2
Debstedt D 72 A1
Decazeville F 130 A1
Dechtice SK 98 C1
Decima I 168 B2
Decimomannu I 179 C2
Děčín CZ 84 B2
Decize F 104 C2
De Cocksdorp NL . . .70 A1
Decollatura I 175 B2
Decs H 125 A4
Deddington GB 44 B2
Dedeler D 187 B5
Dedelow D 74 A2
Dedemli TR 189 B7
Dedemsvaart NL 71 B3
Dédestapolcsány
H 113 A4
Dedovichi RUS 9 D6
Deeping St Nicholas
GB 41 C3
Deftera CY 181 A2
Dég H 112 C2
Degaña E 141 B4
Degeberga S 61 D4
Degerfors S 55 A5
Degerhamn S 63 B4
Degernes N 54 A2
Deggendorf D 95 C4
Deggingen D 94 C1
Dego I 133 A4
Degolados P 155 B3
De Haan B 78 A3
Dehesas de Guadix
E 164 B1
Dehesas Viejas I 163 A4
Deia I 166 B2
Deining D 95 B3
Deinze B 79 B3
Déiva Marina I 134 A2
Dej RO 17 B5
Deje S 55 A4
De Koog NL 70 A1
Delabole GB 42 B2
Delary S 61 C3
Delbrück D 81 A4
Delčevo MK 182 B4
Delden NL 71 B3
Deleitosa E 156 A2
Delekovec HR 124 A2
Delémont CH 106 B2
Delft NL 70 B1
Delfzijl NL 71 A3
Délia I 176 B2
Delianuova I 175 C1
Deliblato SRB 127 C3
Delice TR 23 B7
Deliceto I 171 B3
Delitzsch D 83 A4
Dellach A 109 C4
Delle F 106 B2
Delme F 92 C2
Delmen-horst D 72 A1
Delnice HR 123 B3
Delsbo S 200 E2
Delvin IRL 30 A1
Delvinë AL 182 D2
Demandice SK 112 A2
Demen D 73 A4
Demigny F 105 C3
Demirci TR 186 C3
Demirköy TR 186 A2
Demirtaş TR 186 B4
Demmin D 66 C2
Demonte I 133 A3
Demyansk RUS 9 D8
Denain F 78 B3
Denbigh GB 38 A3
Den Burg NL 70 A1
Dender-monde B . . .79 A4
Denekamp NL 71 B4
Den Ham NL 71 B3
Den Helder NL 70 B1
Denholm GB 35 C5
Denia E 159 C4
Denizli TR 188 B4
Denkendorf D 95 C3
Denklingen D 81 B3
Denny GB 35 B4
Den Oever NL 70 B2
Denta RO 126 B3
Déols F 103 C3
De Panne B 78 A2
Derbent TR 188 A3
Derby GB 40 C2
Derecske H 113 B5
Dereköy TR 186 A2
Derenberg D 82 A2
Derinkuyu TR 23 B8
Dermbach D 82 B2
Dermulo I 121 A4
Deronje SRB 125 B5
Derrygonnelly GB . . .26 B3
Derrylin GB 27 B3
Derry/Londonderry
GB 27 B3
Dersingham GB 41 C4
Dervaig GB 34 B1
Derval F 101 B4
Derveni GR 184 A3
Derventa BIH 125 C3
Dervock GB 27 A4
Desana I 119 B5
Descartes F 102 C2
Desenzano del Garda
I 121 B3
Deset N 48 A3
Deševa BIH 139 B4
Desfina GR 184 A3
Desimirovac SRB . . .127 C2
Désio I 120 B2

Deskati GR 182 D3
Deskle SLO 122 A2
Desná CZ 84 B3
Dešov CZ 97 C3
Despotovac SRB . . .127 C3
Despotovo SRB 126 B1
Dessau D 83 A4
Deštná CZ 96 B2
Destriana E 141 B4
Désulo I 179 B3
Desvres F 78 B1
Deszk H 126 A2
Deta RO 126 B3
Detmold D 72 C1
Dětřichov CZ 98 B1
Dettelbach D 94 B2
Dettingen
Baden-Württemberg
D 94 C1
Baden-Württemberg
D 107 B4
Dettwiller F 93 C3
Detva SK 99 C3
Deurne NL 80 A1
Deutschkreutz A . . .111 B3
Deutschlandsberg
A 110 C2
Deutsch Wagram
A 111 A3
Deva RO 16 C5
Dévaványa H 113 B4
Devecser H 111 B4
Develi TR 23 B8
Deventer NL 70 B3
Devil's Bridge GB . . .39 B3
Devin BG 183 B6
Devinska Nova Ves
SK 111 A3
Devizes GB 43 A5
Devonport GB 42 B2
Devrek TR 187 A6
Devrekâni TR 23 A7
Ðevrske HR 137 B4
De Wijk NL 71 B3
Dewsbury GB 40 B2
Deza E 152 A1
Dežanovac HR 124 B3
Dhali CY 181 A2
Dherinia CY 181 A2
Diamante I 174 B1
Dianalund DK 61 D1
Diano d'Alba I 119 C5
Diano Marina I 133 B4
Dicomano I 135 B4
Didcot GB 44 B2
Didimoticho GR 186 A1
Die F 118 C2
Diebling F 92 B2
Dieburg D 93 B4
Diego del Carpio
E 150 B2
Diekirch L 92 B2
Diélette F 88 A2
Diémoz F 118 B2
Dienten am Hochkönig
A 109 B3
Diepenbeck B 79 B5
Diepholz D 71 B5
Dieppe F 89 A5
Dierberg D 74 A1
Dierdorf D 81 B3
Dieren NL 70 B3
Dierhagen D 66 B1
Diesdorf D 73 B3
Diessen D 108 B2
Diest B 79 B5
Dietenheim D 94 C2
Dietfurt D 95 B3
Dietikon CH 107 B3
Dietmannsried D . . .107 B5
Dietzenbach D 93 A4
Dieulefit F 131 A4
Dieulouard F 92 C2
Dieuze F 92 C2
Diever NL 71 B3
Diez D 81 B4
Diezma E 163 A4
Differdange L 92 B1
Digermulen N 194 B6
Dignac F 115 C4
Dignano I 122 A1
Digne-les-Bains F . . .132 A2
Digny F 89 B5
Digoin F 104 C2
Dijon F 105 B4
Dikanäs S 195 E7
Dikili TR 186 C1
Diksmuide B 78 A2
Dilar E 163 A4
Dillenburg D 81 B4
Dillingen
Bayern D 94 C2
Saarland D 92 B2
Dilsen B 80 A1
Dimaro I 121 A3
Dimitrovgrad BG . . .183 A7
Dimitsana GR 184 B3
Dinami I 175 C2
Dinan F 101 A3
Dinant B 79 B4
Dinar TR 189 A5
Dinard F 101 A3
Dinek TR 187 C6
Dingden D 80 A2
Dingelstädt D 82 A2
Dingle
IRL 29 B1
S 54 B2
Dingolfing D 95 C4
Dingtuna S 56 A2
Dingwall GB 32 D2
Dinkelsbühl D 94 B2
Dinkelscherben D . . .94 C2
Dinklage D 71 B5
Dinslaken D 80 A2
Dinxperlo NL 80 A2
Diö S 63 B2
Diósgyör H 113 A4

Diósjeno H 112 B3
Diou F 104 C2
Dippen GB 34 C2
Dipperz D 82 B1
Dippoldiswalde D . . .84 B1
Dirdal N 52 B2
Dirlewang D 108 B1
Dischingen D 94 C2
Disentis CH 107 C3
Diso I 173 B4
Diss GB 45 A5
Distington GB 36 B3
Ditzingen D 93 C5
Ditzum D 71 A4
Divača SLO 122 B2
Dives-sur-Mer F 89 A3
Divín SK 99 C3
Divion F 78 B2
Divišov CZ 96 B2
Divonne les Bains
F 118 A3
Dixmont F 104 A2
Dizy-le-Gros F 91 B4
Djúpivogur IS 191 C11
Djupvasshytta N 198 C4
Djura S 50 B1
Djuras S 50 B2
Djursa S 50 B2
Djurås S 62 A3
Djursdala S 62 A3
Dlouhá Loucka CZ . .98 B1
Długowola PL 87 A5
Dmitrov RUS 9 D10
Dno RUS 9 C6
Doade E 141 B3
Doğanhisar TR 189 A6
Dobanovci SRB 127 C2
Dobbertin D 73 A5
Dobbiaco I 108 C3
Dobczyce PL 99 B4
Dobele LV 8 D3
Döbeln D 83 A5
Doberlug-Kirchhain
D 83 A5
Dobern D 84 A2
Dobersberg A 97 C3
Dobiegniew PL 75 B4
Dobieszyn PL 87 A5
Doboj BIH 125 C4
Dobošnica BIH 125 C4
Doboz H 113 C5
Dobrá CZ 98 B2
Dobra
Wielkopolskie PL . . .76 C3
Zachodnio-Pomorskie
PL 74 A3
Zachodnio-Pomorskie
PL 75 A4
Dobrá Niva SK 99 C3
Dobřany CZ 96 B1
Dobre PL 76 B3
Dobre Miasto PL 69 B5
Dobreta-Turnu-Severin
RO 16 C5
Dobri H 111 C3
Dobrica SRB 126 B2
Dobrinishta BG 183 B5
Dobříš CZ 96 B2
Dobro E 143 B3
Dobrodzień PL 86 B2
Dobromierz PL 85 B4
Dobrosołowo PL 76 B3
Dobroszyce PL 85 A5
Dobrovnik SLO 111 C3
Dobrush BY 13 B9
Dobruška CZ 85 B4
Dobrzany PL 75 A4
Dobrzeń Wielki PL . . .86 B1
Dobrzyca
Wielkopolskie PL . . .75 A5
Wielkopolskie PL . . .85 A5
Zachodnio-Pomorskie
PL 67 B4
Dobrzyń nad Wisłą
PL 77 B4
Dobšiná SK 99 C4
Dobwalls GB 42 B2
Dochamps B 80 B1
Docking GB 41 C4
Docksta S 200 C4
Doddington GB 37 A4
Döderhult D 62 A4
Doesburg NL 70 B3
Doetinchem NL 71 C3
Dogliani I 133 A3
Dogueno P 160 B2
Doische B 91 A4
Dois Portos P 154 B1
Dojč SK 98 C1
Dokka N 48 B2
Dokkedal DK 58 B3
Dokkum NL 70 A2
Dokleżovje SLO 111 C3
Doksy CZ 84 B2
Dokuz TR 189 A7
Dolancourt F 104 A3
Dolceácqua I 133 B3
Dol-de-Bretagne F . .88 B2
Dole F 105 B4
Dolenja vas SLO . . .123 B3
Dolenjske Toplice
SLO 123 B4
Dolfor GB 39 B3
Dolgarrog GB 38 A3
Dolgellau GB 38 B3
Doliana GR 182 D2
Dolianova I 179 C3
Dolice PL 75 A4
Doljani HR 138 A2
Döllach im Mölltal
A 109 C3
Dolle D 73 B4
Dollnstein D 94 C3
Dollon F 104 A2
Döllstadt D 82 A2

Dolná Strehová
SK 99 C3
Dolné Saliby SK 111 A4
Dolni Benešov CZ . . .98 B2
Dolni Bousov CZ 84 B3
Dolní Kounice CZ . . .97 B4
Dolní Kralovice CZ . .97 B3
Dolni Újezd CZ 97 B4
Dolní Žandov CZ 95 A4
Dolný Kubín SK 99 B3
Dolo I 121 B5
Dolores E 165 A4
Dolovo SRB 127 C2
Dölsach A 109 C3
Dolsk PL 76 B2
Domažlice CZ 95 B4
Dombås N 198 C6
Dombasle-sur-Meurthe
F 92 C2
Dombegyház H 126 A3
Dombóvár H 112 C2
Domène F 118 B2
Domérat F 116 A2
Domfessel F 92 C3
Domfront F 88 B3
Domfront-en-
Champagne F 102 A2
Domingão P 154 B2
Domingo Pérez
Granada E 163 A4
Toledo E 150 C3
Dömitz D 73 A4
Dommartin F 91 C4
Dommartin-le-Franc
F 91 C4
Domme F 129 B4
Dommitzsch D 83 A4
Domodóssola I 119 A5
Domokos GR 182 D4
Domoszló H 113 B4
Dompaire F 105 A5
Dompierre-du-Chemin
F 101 A3
Dompierre-sur-Besbre
F 104 C2
Dompierre-sur-Mer
F 114 B2
Domrémy-la-Pucelle
F 92 C1
Dömsöd H 112 B3
Domsure F 118 A2
Domvena GR 184 A3
Domžale SLO 123 A3
Donado E 141 B4
Donaghadee GB 27 B5
Don Alvaro E 155 C4
Doña Mencía E 163 A3
Donaueschingen
D 106 B3
Donauwörth D 94 C2
Don Benito E 156 B2
Doncaster GB 40 B2
Donegal IRL 26 B2
Donestebe-
Santesteban E 144 A2
Donges F 101 B3
Dongo I 120 A2
Donington GB 41 C3
Doniños E 140 A2
Donja Bebrina HR . . .125 B4
Donja Brela HR 138 B2
Donja Dubica BIH . . .125 B4
Donja Dubrava
HR 124 A2
Donja Kupčina
HR 123 B4
Donja Šatornja
SRB 127 C2
Donja Stubica HR . . .124 B1
Donje Brišnik BIH . . .138 B3
Donje Stative HR . . .123 B4
Donji-Andrijevci
HR 125 B4
Donji Kazanci BIH . . .138 B2
Donji Koričáni
BIH 138 A3
Donji Lapac HR 124 C1
Donji Malovan
BIH 138 B3
Donji Miholjac HR . . .125 B4
Donji Mosti HR 124 A2
Donji Poloj HR 123 B4
Donji Rujani BIH 138 B2
Donji Srb HR 138 A2
Donji Svilaj BIH 125 B4
Donji Tovarnik
SRB 127 C1
Donji Vakuf BIH 138 A3
Donnalucata I 177 C3
Donnemarie-Dontilly
F 90 C3
Donnersbach A 110 B1
Donnersbachwald
A 109 B5
Donnerskirchen A . . .111 B3
Donorático I 134 B3
Donostia-San
Sebastián E 144 A2
Donovaly SK 99 C3
Donzenac F 129 A4
Donzère F 131 A3
Donzy F 104 B2
Doonbeg IRL 29 B2
Doorn NL 70 B2
Dor E 140 A1
Dorchester GB 43 B4
Dørdal N 53 B5
Dordrecht NL 79 A4

Dörenthe D 71 B4
Dores GB 32 D2
Dorfen D 95 C4
Dorfgastein A 109 B4
Dorfmark D 72 B2
Dorf Mecklenburg
D 65 C2
Dorgali I 178 B3
Dorking GB 44 B3
Dormagen D 80 A2
Dormánd H 113 B4
Dormans F 91 B3
Dornava SLO 124 A1
Dornbirn A 107 B4
Dornburg D 83 A3
Dorndorf D 82 B2
Dornecy F 104 B2
Dornes F 104 C2
Dornhan D 93 C4
Dornie GB 31 B3
Dornoch GB 32 D2
Dornum D 71 A4
Dorog H 112 B2
Dorohoi RO 17 B7
Dorotea S 200 B2
Dorotowo PL 69 B5
Dörpen D 71 B4
Dorsten D 80 A2
Dortan F 118 A2
Dortmund D 80 A3
Doruchów PL 86 A2
Dorum D 64 C1
Dörverden D 72 B2
Dörzbach D 94 B1
Dos Aguas E 159 B3
Dosbarrios E 151 C4
Döşemealtı TR 189 B5
Dos Hermanas E . . .162 A2
Dospat BG 183 B6
Dos-Torres E 156 B3
Dötlingen D 72 B1
Dottignies B 78 B3
Döttingen CH 106 B3
Douai F 78 B3
Douarnenez F 100 A1
Douchy F 104 B2
Douchy-les-Mines
F 78 B3
Doucier F 105 C4
Doudeville F 89 A4
Doué-la-Fontaine
F 102 B1
Douglas
Isle of Man GB 36 B2
South Lanarkshire
GB 36 A3
Doulaincourt-Saucourt
F 91 C5
Doulevant-le-Château
F 91 C4
Doullens F 90 A2
Dounby GB 33 B3
Doune GB 35 B3
Dounreay GB 32 C3
Dour B 79 B3
Dourdan F 90 C2
Dournazac F 115 C4
Douvaine F 118 A3
Douvres-la-Délivrande
F 89 A3
Douzy F 91 B5
Dover GB 45 B5
Dovje SLO 109 C4
Dovre N 198 D6
Downham Market
GB 41 C4
Downhill GB 27 A4
Downpatrick GB 27 B5
Dowra IRL 26 B2
Doxato GR 183 B6
Doyet F 116 A2
Dozule F 89 A3
Draga SLO 123 B3
Drăgăşani RO 17 C6
Dragatuš SLO 123 B4
Dragichyn BY 13 B6
Draginja SRB 127 C1
Dragocvet SRB 127 D3
Dragolovci BIH 125 C3
Dragoni I 170 B2
Dragør DK 61 D2
Dragotina HR 124 B2
Dragotinja BIH 124 B2
Dragozetići HR 123 B3
Draguignan F 132 B2
Drahnsdorf D 74 C2
Drahonice CZ 96 B2
Drahovce SK 98 C1
Drama GR 183 B6
Drammen N 54 A1
Drangedal N 53 A5
Drangsnes IS 190 B4
Dransfeld D 82 A1
Dranske D 66 B2
Draperstown GB 27 B4
Drassburg A 111 B3
Drávaszabolcs H . . .125 B4
Dravograd SLO 110 C2
Drawno PL 75 A4
Drawsko Pomorskie
PL 75 A4
Drayton GB 41 C5
Drążdżewo PL 77 A6
Draženov CZ 95 B4
Draževac SRB 127 C2
Dražice HR 123 B3
Drebkau D 84 A2
Dreieich D 93 A4
Dreisen D 93 B4
Drenovci HR 125 C4
Drensteinfurt D 81 A3
Dresden D 84 A1
Dretyń PL 68 A1

Dreux F 89 B5
Dřevohostice CZ 98 B1
Drevsjø N 199 D9
Drewitz D 73 B5
Drezdenko PL 75 B4
Drežnica HR 123 B4
Drežnik-Grad HR 123 C4
Drietona SK 98 C1
Driffield GB 40 A3
Drimnin GB 34 B2
Drimoleague IRL 29 C2
Dringenberg D 81 A5
Drinić BIH 138 A2
Drinjača BIH 139 A5
Drinovci BIH 138 B3
Driopida GR 185 B5
Drivstua N 198 C6
Drlače SRB 127 C1
Drnholec CZ 97 C4
Drniš HR 138 B2
Drnje HR 124 A2
Drnovice CZ 97 B4
Dro I 121 B3
Drøbak N 54 A1
Drobin PL 77 B5
Drochia MD 17 A7
Drochtersen D 64 C2
Drogheda IRL 30 A2
Drohobych UA 13 D5
Droitwich Spa GB . . .44 A1
Drołtowice PL 85 A5
Dromahair IRL 26 B2
Dromcolliher IRL 29 B3
Dromore
Down GB 27 B4
Tyrone GB 27 B3
Dromore West IRL . . .26 B2
Dronero I 133 A3
Dronfield GB 40 B2
Drongan GB 36 A2
Dronninglund DK 58 A3
Dronrijp NL 70 A2
Dronten NL 70 B2
Drosendorf A 97 C3
Drösing A 97 C4
Drottningholm S 57 A3
Droué F 103 A3
Drulingen F 92 C3
Drumbeg GB 32 C1
Drumcliff IRL 26 B2
Drumgask GB 32 D2
Drumkeeran IRL 26 B2
Drummore GB 36 B2
Drumnadrochit GB . . .32 D2
Drumquin GB 27 B3
Drumshanbo IRL 26 B2
Drumsna IRL 26 C2
Drunen NL 79 A5
Druten NL 80 A1
Druya BY 13 A7
Družetići SRB 127 C2
Drvar BIH 138 A2
Drvenik HR 138 B3
Drwalew PL 77 C6
Drymen GB 34 B3
Drynoch GB 31 B2
Drzewce PL 76 B2
Drzewiany PL 68 B1
Drzewica PL 87 A4
Duas Igrejas P 149 A3
Dub SRB 127 C2
Dubá CZ 84 B2
Dubăsari MD 17 B8
Duben D 74 C2
Dübendorf CH 107 B3
Dubi CZ 84 B1
Dubica HR 124 B2
Dublin IRL 30 A2
Dubna RUS 9 D10
Dubňany CZ 98 C1
Dubnica nad Váhom
SK 98 C2
Dubnik SK 112 B2
Dubno UA 13 C6
Dubodiel SK 98 C2
Dubona SRB 127 C2
Dubovac SRB 127 C3
Dubovic BIH 124 C2
Dubrava HR 124 B2
Dubrave BIH 125 C4
Dubravica
HR 123 B4
SRB 127 C2
Dubrovnik HR 139 C4
Dubrovytsya UA 13 C7
Ducey F 88 B2
Duchcov CZ 84 B1
Ducherow D 74 A2
Dučina SRB 127 C2
Duclair F 89 A4
Dudar H 112 B1
Duddington GB 40 C3
Duderstadt D 82 A2
Dudeştii Vechi RO . . .126 A2
Dudley GB 40 C1
Dueñas E 142 C2
Duesund N 46 B2
Dueville I 121 B4
Duffel B 79 A4
Duffield GB 40 C2
Dufftown GB 32 D3
Duga Resa HR 123 B4
Dugi Rat HR 138 B2
Dugny-sur-Meuse
F 92 B1
Dugo Selo HR 124 B2
Duino I 122 B2
Duisburg D 80 A2
Dukat AL 182 C1
Dukovany CZ 97 B4
Duleek IRL 30 A2
Dülken D 80 A2
Dülmen D 80 A3
Dulovo BG 17 D7
Dulpetorpet N 49 B4
Dulverton GB 43 A3

Dumbarton GB 34 C3
Dümerek TR 187 C6
Dumfries GB 36 A3
Dumlupınar TR 187 D4
Dümpelfeld D 80 B2
Dunaalmás H 112 B2
Dunabogdány H 112 B3
Dunafalva H 125 A4
Dunaföldvár H 112 B2
Dunaharaszti H 112 B3
Dunajská Streda
SK 111 B4
Dunakeszi H 112 B3
Dunakiliti H 111 B4
Dunakömlöd H 112 C2
Dunapataj H 112 C2
Dunaszekcső H 125 A4
Dunaszentgyorgy
H 112 C2
Dunatetétlen H 112 C3
Dunaújváros H 112 B2
Dunavecse H 112 C2
Dunbar GB 35 B5
Dunbeath GB 32 C3
Dunblane GB 35 B4
Dunboyne IRL 30 A2
Dundalk IRL 27 B4
Dundee GB 35 B5
Dundrennan GB 36 B3
Dundrum GB 27 B5
Dunfanaghy IRL 26 A3
Dunfermline GB 35 B4
Dungannon GB 27 B4
Dungarvan IRL 29 B4
Dungiven GB 27 B4
Dunglow IRL 26 B2
Dungourney IRL 29 C3
Duninowo PL 68 A1
Dunkeld GB 35 B4
Dunker S 56 A2
Dunkerque = Dunkirk
F 78 A2
Dunkineely IRL 26 B2
Dunkirk = Dunkerque
F 78 A2
Dun Laoghaire IRL . .30 A2
Dunlavin IRL 30 A2
Dunleer IRL 27 C4
Dun-le-Palestel F . . .116 A1
Dun-les-Places F . . .104 B3
Dunlop GB 36 A2
Dunloy GB 27 A4
Dunmanway IRL 29 C2
Dunmore IRL 28 A3
Dunmore East IRL . . .30 B2
Dunmurry GB 27 B4
Dunnet GB 32 C3
Dunningen D 107 A3
Dunoon GB 34 C3
Duns GB 35 C5
Dunscore GB 36 A3
Dunsford GB 43 B3
Dunshaughlin IRL . . .30 A2
Dunstable GB 44 B3
Dunster GB 43 A3
Dun-sur-Auron F 103 C4
Dun-sur-Meuse F . . .91 B5
Dunvegan GB 31 B2
Duplek SLO 110 C2
Dupnitsa BG 17 D5
Durağan TR 23 A8
Durach D 107 B5
Durak TR 186 C3
Durana E 143 B4
Durance F 128 B3
Durango E 143 A4
Durankulak BG 17 D8
Duras F 128 B3
Durban-Corbières
F 146 B3
Dürbheim D 107 A3
Durbuy B 79 B5
Dúrcal E 163 B4
Ðurdjenovac HR 125 B4
Ðurdjevac HR 124 A3
Ðurdjevik BIH 139 A4
Düren D 80 B2
Durham GB 37 B5
Ðurinci SRB 127 C2
Durlach D 93 C4
Ðurmanec HR 124 A1
Durness GB 32 C2
Dürnkrut A 97 C4
Dürrboden CH 107 C4
Dürrenboden CH 107 C3
Durrës AL 182 B1
Durrow IRL 30 B1
Durrus IRL 29 C2
Dursunbey TR 186 C3
Durtal F 102 B1
Durup DK 58 B1
Durusu TR 186 A4
Dusina BIH 139 B3
Dusnok H 112 C2
Dusocin PL 69 B3
Düsseldorf D 80 A2
Dusslingen D 93 C5
Duszniki PL 75 B5
Duszniki-Zdrój PL . . .85 B4
Dutovlje SLO 122 B2
Duved N 199 B9
Düzağac TR 187 D5
Düzce TR 187 B6
Dvärsätt S 199 B11
Dvor HR 124 B2
Dvorce CZ 98 B1
Dvorníky SK 98 C1
Dvory nad Žitavou
SK 112 B2
Dvůr Králvéné
Labem CZ 85 B3
Dybvad DK 58 A3
Dyce GB 33 D4
Dygowo PL 67 B4
Dykehead GB 35 B4
Dymchurch GB 45 B5

Dymer UA 13 C9
Dyrnes N 198 B4
Dywity PL 69 B5
Džaniċi BIH 139 B3
Dziadowa Kłoda PL 86 A1
Działdowo PL 77 A5
Działoszyce PL 87 B4
Działoszyn PL 86 A2
Dziemiany PL 68 A2
Dzierzążnia PL 77 B5
Dzierzgoń PL 69 B4
Dzierzgowo PL 77 A5
Dzierżoniów PL 85 B4
Dzisna BY 13 A8
Dziwnów PL 67 B3
Dźwierzuty PL 77 A5
Dzyarzhynsk BY 13 B7
Dzyatlava BY 13 B6

E

Ea E 143 A4
Eaglesfield GB 36 A3
Ealing GB 44 B3
Eardisley GB 39 B3
Earls Barton GB 44 A3
Earl Shilton GB 40 C2
Earlston GB 35 C5
Easington GB 41 B4
Easky IRL 26 B2
Eastbourne GB 45 C4
East Calder GB 35 C4
East Dereham GB 41 C4
Easter Skeld GB 33 A5
East Grinstead GB 45 B4
East Ilsley GB 44 B2
East Kilbride GB 36 A2
Eastleigh GB 44 C2
East Linton GB 35 C5
East Markham GB 40 B3
Easton GB 43 B4
East Wittering GB 44 C3
Eaton Socon GB 44 A3
Eaux-Bonnes F 145 B3
Eauze F 128 C3
Ebberup DK 59 C2
Ebbs A 108 B3
Ebbw Vale GB 39 C3
Ebeleben D 82 A2
Ebeltoft DK 59 B3
Ebene Reichenau A 109 C4
Eben im Pongau A 109 B4
Ebensee A 109 B4
Ebensfeld D 94 A2
Eberbach D 93 B4
Ebergötzen D 82 A2
Ebermann-Stadt D 94 B3
Ebern D 82 B2
Eberndorf A 110 C1
Ebersbach D 84 A2
Ebersberg D 108 A2
Ebersdorf
 Bayern D 82 B3
 Niedersachsen D 72 A2
Eberstein A 110 C1
Eberswalde D 74 B2
Ebnat-Kappel CH 107 B4
Éboli I 170 C3
Ebrach D 94 B2
Ebreichsdorf A 111 B3
Ebreuil F 116 A3
Ebstorf D 72 A3
Ecclefechan GB 36 A3
Eccleshall GB 40 C1
Eceabat TR 186 B1
Echallens CH 106 C1
Echauri E 144 B2
Echinos GR 183 B7
Echiré F 114 B3
Échirolles F 118 B2
Echourgnac F 128 A3
Echt NL 80 A1
Echte D 82 A2
Echternach L 92 B2
Ecija E 162 A2
Ečka SRB 126 B2
Eckartsberga D 82 A3
Eckelshausen D 81 B4
Eckental D 94 B3
Eckernförde D 64 B2
Eckerö FIN 51 B6
Eckington GB 40 B2
Éclaron F 91 C4
Écommoy F 102 B2
Écouché F 89 B3
Ecouis F 90 B1
Ecséd H 113 B3
Ecsegfalva H 113 B4
Écueillé F 103 B3
Ed S 54 B2
Eda S 49 C4
Eda glasbruk S 49 C4
Edam NL 70 B2
Edane S 55 A3
Edderton GB 32 D2
Ede NL 70 B2
Edebäck S 49 B5
Edebo S 51 B5
Edelény H 99 C4
Edelschrott A 110 B2
Edemissen D 72 B3
Edenbridge GB 45 B4
Edenderry IRL 30 A1
Edenkoben D 93 B4
Edesheim D 93 B4
Edessa GR 182 C4
Edewecht D 71 A4
Edgeworthstown IRL 30 A1
Edinburgh GB 35 C4
Edineţ MD 17 A7
Edirne TR 186 A1
Edland N 52 A3
Edolo I 120 A3
Edøy N 198 B5
Edremit TR 186 C2
Edsbro S 51 C5
Edsbruk S 56 B2
Edsbyn S 50 A2
Edsele S 200 C2
Edsleskog S 54 A3
Edsvalla S 55 A4
Eekloo B 79 A3
Eemshaven NL 71 A3
Eerbeek NL 70 B3
Eersel NL 79 A5
Eferding A 96 C2
Effiat F 116 A3
Efteløt N 53 A5
Egeln D 73 C4
Eger H 113 B4
Egerbakta H 113 B4
Egernsund DK 64 B2
Egersund N 52 B2
Egerszólát H 113 B4
Egervár H 111 C3
Egg
 A 107 B4
 D 107 A5
Eggby S 55 B4
Eggedal N 47 B6
Eggenburg A 97 C3
Eggenfelden D 95 C4
Eggesin D 74 A3
Eggum N 194 B4
Egham GB 44 B3
Éghezée B 79 B4
Egiertowo PL 68 A3
Egilsstaðir IS 191 B11
Egina GR 185 B4
Eginio GR 182 C4
Egio GR 184 A3
Égletons F 116 B2
Egling D 108 B2
Eglinton GB 27 A3
Eglisau CH 107 B3
Égliseneuve-d'Entraigues F 116 B2
Eglofs D 107 B4
Egmond aan Zee NL 70 B1
Egna I 121 A4
Egosthena GR 184 A4
Egremont GB 36 B3
Egtved DK 59 C2
Eguilles F 131 B4
Eguilly-sous-Bois F 104 A3
Éguzon-Chantôme F 103 C3
Egyek H 113 B4
Egyházasrádóc H 111 B3
Ehekirchen D 94 C3
Ehingen D 94 C1
Ehra-Lessien D 73 B3
Ehrang D 92 B2
Ehrenfriedersdorf D 83 B4
Ehrenhain D 83 B4
Ehrenhausen A 110 C2
Ehringshausen D 81 B4
Ehrwald A 108 B1
Eibar E 143 A4
Eibelstadt D 94 B2
Eibenstock D 83 B4
Eibergen NL 71 B3
Eibiswald A 110 C2
Eichenbarleben D 73 B4
Eichendorf D 95 C4
Eichstätt D 95 C3
Eickelborn D 81 A4
Eide
 Hordaland N 46 B3
 Møre og Romsdal N 198 C4
Eidet N 194 A9
Eidfjord N 46 B4
Eidsberg N 54 A2
Eidsbugarden N 47 A5
Eidsdal N 198 C4
Eidsfoss N 53 A6
Eidskog N 49 B4
Eidsvåg
 Hordaland N 46 B2
 Møre og Romsdal N 198 C5
Eidsvoll N 48 B3
Eikefjord N 46 A2
Eikelandsosen N 46 B2
Eiken N 52 B3
Eikesdal N 198 C5
Eikstrand N 53 A5
Eilenburg D 83 A4
Eilsleben D 73 B4
Eina N 48 B2
Einbeck D 82 A1
Eindhoven NL 79 A5
Einsiedeln CH 107 B3
Einville-au-Jard F 92 C2
Eisenach D 82 B2
Eisenberg
 Rheinland-Pfalz D 93 B4
 Thüringen D 83 B3
Eisenerz A 110 B1
Eisenhüttenstadt D 74 B3
Eisenkappel A 110 C1
Eisenstadt A 111 B3
Eisentratten A 109 C4
Eisfeld D 82 B2
Eisleben D 82 A3
Eislingen D 94 C1
Eitensheim D 95 C3
Eiterfeld D 82 B1
Eitorf D 80 B3
Eivindvik N 46 B1
Eivissa = Ibiza E 166 C1
Eixo P 148 B1
Ejby DK 59 C2
Ejea de los Caballeros E 144 B2
Ejstrupholm DK 59 C2
Ejulve E 153 B3
Eke B 79 B3
Ekeby
 Gotland S 57 C4
 Skåne S 61 D2
 Uppsala S 51 B5
Ekeby-Almby S 56 A1
Ekenäs S 55 B4
Ekenässjön S 62 A3
Ekerö S 57 A3
Eket S 61 C3
Eketorp S 63 B4
Ekevik S 56 B2
Ekkerøy N 193 B14
Ekshärad S 49 B5
Eksingedal N 46 B2
Eksjö S 62 A2
Eksta S 57 C4
Ekträsk S 200 B5
El Alamo
 Madrid E 151 B4
 Sevilla E 161 B3
El Algar E 165 B4
El Almendro E 161 B2
El Alquián E 164 C2
Élancourt F 90 C1
El Arahal E 162 A2
El Arenal E 150 B2
El Arguellite E 164 A2
Elassona GR 182 D4
El Astillero E 143 A3
Elati GR 182 D3
Żelazno PL 85 B4
El Ballestero E 158 C1
El Barco de Ávila E 150 B2
Elbasan AL 182 B2
El Berrón E 142 A1
El Berrueco E 151 B4
Elbeuf F 89 A4
Elbingerode D 82 A2
Elbląg PL 69 A4
El Bodón E 149 B3
El Bonillo E 158 C1
El Bosque E 162 B2
El Bullaque E 157 A3
Elburg NL 70 B2
El Burgo E 162 B3
El Burgo de Ebro E 153 A3
El Burgo de Osma E 151 A4
El Burgo Ranero E 142 B1
El Buste E 144 C2
El Cabaco E 149 B3
El Callejo E 143 A3
El Campillo E 161 B3
El Campillo de la Jara E 156 A2
El Cañavete E 158 B1
El Carpio E 157 C3
El Carpio de Tajo E 150 C3
El Casar E 151 B4
El Casar de Escalona E 150 B3
El Castillo de las Guardas E 161 B3
El Centenillo E 157 B4
El Cerro E 149 B4
El Cerro de Andévalo E 161 B3
Elche E 165 A4
Elche de la Sierra E 158 C1
Elchingen D 94 C2
El Comenar E 162 B2
El Coronil E 162 A2
El Crucero E 141 A4
El Cubo de Tierra del Vino E 149 A4
El Cuervo E 162 B1
Elda E 159 C3
Eldena D 73 A4
Eldingen D 72 B3
Elefsina GR 185 A4
El Ejido E 164 C2
Elek H 113 C5
Elemir SRB 126 B2
El Escorial E 151 B3
El Espinar E 151 B3
Eleutheroupoli GR 183 C6
El Frago E 144 B3
El Franco E 141 A4
El Frasno E 152 A2
Elgå N 199 C8
El Garrobo E 161 B3
El Gastor E 162 B2
Elgin GB 32 D3
Elgoibar E 143 A4
Elgol GB 31 B2
El Gordo E 150 C2
El Grado E 145 B4
El Granado E 161 B2
El Grao de Castelló E 159 B4
El Grau E 159 C3
Elgshøa N 49 A4
El Higuera E 163 A3
El Hijate E 164 B2
El Hontanar E 152 B2
El Hoyo E 157 B4
Elie GB 35 B5
Elizondo E 144 A2
Ełk PL 12 B5
Elkhovo BG 17 D7
Ellenberg D 94 B2
Ellesmere GB 38 B4
Ellesmere Port GB 38 A4
Ellezelles B 79 B3
Ellingen D 94 B2
Ellmau A 109 B3
Ellon GB 33 D4
Ellös S 54 B2
Ellrich D 82 A2
Ellwangen D 94 C2
Elm
 CH 107 C4
Elm *continued*
 D 72 A2
Elmadağ TR 23 B7
El Madroño E 161 B3
El Maillo E 149 B3
Elmalı TR 189 C4
El Masnou E 147 C3
El Mirón E 150 B2
El Molar E 151 B4
El Molinillo E 157 A3
El Morell E 147 C2
Elmshorn D 64 C2
Elmstein D 93 B3
El Muyo E 151 A4
Elne F 146 B3
Elnesvågen N 198 C4
El Olmo E 151 A4
Elorrio E 143 A4
Elöszállás H 112 C2
Elouda GR 185 D6
Éloyes F 105 A5
El Palo E 163 B3
El Pardo E 151 B4
El Payo E 149 B3
El Pedernoso E 158 B1
El Pedroso E 162 A2
El Peral E 158 B2
El Perelló
 Tarragona E 153 B4
 Valencia E 159 B3
Elphin GB 32 C1
El Picazo E 158 B1
El Pinell de Bray E 153 A4
El Piñero E 150 A2
El Pla de Santa Maria E 147 C2
El Pobo E 153 B3
El Pobo de Dueñas E 152 B2
El Pont d'Armentera E 147 C2
El Port de la Selva E 147 B4
El Port de Llançà E 146 B4
El Port de Sagunt E 159 B3
El Prat de Llobregat E 147 C3
El Provencio E 158 B1
El Puente E 143 A3
El Puente del Arzobispo E 150 C2
El Puerto E 141 A4
El Puerto de Santa María E 162 B1
El Real de la Jara E 161 B3
El Real de San Vincente E 150 B3
El Robledo E 157 A3
El Rocio E 161 B3
El Rompido E 161 B2
El Ronquillo E 161 B3
El Royo E 143 C4
El Rubio E 162 A3
El Sabinar E 164 A2
El Saler E 159 B3
El Salobral E 158 C2
El Saucejo E 162 A2
Els Castells E 147 B2
Elsdorf D 80 B2
Elsenfeld D 93 B5
El Serrat AND 146 B2
Elsfleth D 72 A1
Elspeet NL 70 B2
Elst NL 70 C2
Elstead GB 44 B3
Elster D 83 A4
Elsterberg D 83 B4
Elsterwerda D 83 A5
Elstra D 84 A2
El Temple E 144 C3
El Tiemblo E 150 B3
Eltmann D 94 B2
El Toboso E 157 A5
El Tormillo E 145 C3
El Torno E 149 B4
Eltville D 93 A4
El Valle de las Casas E 142 B1
Elvas P 155 C3
Elvebakken N 192 C7
El Vellón E 151 B4
Elven F 101 B3
El Vendrell E 147 C2
Elverum N 48 B3
El Villar de Arnedo E 144 B1
Elvington GB 40 B3
El Viso E 156 B3
El Viso del Alcor E 162 A2
Elxleben D 82 A2
Ely GB 45 A4
Elzach D 106 A3
Elze D 72 B2
Emådalen S 50 A1
Embleton GB 37 A5
Embonas GR 188 C2
Embrun F 132 A2
Embún E 144 B3
Emden D 71 A4
Emecik TR 188 C2
Emet TR 186 C4
Emirdağ TR 187 C6
Emlichheim D 71 B3
Emmaboda S 63 B3
Emmaljunga S 61 C3
Emmeloord NL 70 B2
Emmen
 CH 106 B3
 NL 71 B3
Emmendingen D 106 A2
Emmer-Compascuum NL 71 B4
Emmerich D 80 A2
Emmern D 72 B2
Emöd H 113 B4
Émpoli I 135 B3
Emsbüren D 71 B4
Emsdetten D 71 B4
Emsfors S 62 A4
Emskirchen D 94 B2
Emstek D 71 B5
Emsworth GB 44 C3
Emyvale IRL 27 B4
Enafors S 199 B9
Enånger S 51 A4
Encamp AND 146 B2
Encarnaçao P 154 C1
Encinas de Abajo E 150 B2
Encinas de Esgueva E 142 C2
Encinasola E 161 A3
Encinas Reales E 163 A3
Encio E 143 B3
Enciso E 144 B1
Enden N 199 D7
Endingen D 106 A2
Endrinal E 149 B4
Endröd H 113 C4
Enebakk N 54 A2
Eneryda S 63 B2
Enese H 111 B4
Enez TR 183 C8
Enfield IRL 30 A2
Eng A 108 B2
Engelberg CH 106 C3
Engelhartszell A 96 C1
Engelskirchen D 80 B3
Engen D 107 B3
Enger N 48 B2
Engerdal N 199 D8
Engerneset N 49 A4
Enge-sande D 64 B1
Engesvang DK 59 B2
Enghien B 79 B4
Engstingen D 94 C1
Engter D 71 B5
Enguera E 159 C3
Enguidanos E 158 B2
Enkenbach D 93 B3
Enkhuizen NL 70 B2
Enklinge FIN 51 B7
Enköping S 56 A3
Enna I 177 B3
Ennezat F 116 B3
Ennigerloh D 81 A4
Enningdal N 54 B2
Ennis IRL 28 B3
Enniscorthy IRL 30 B2
Enniskean IRL 29 C3
Enniskillen GB 27 B3
Ennistimon IRL 28 B2
Enns A 110 A1
Eno FIN 9 A7
Enontekiö FIN 196 A6
Ens NL 70 B2
Enschede NL 71 B3
Ensdorf D 95 B3
Ensisheim F 106 B2
Enstaberga S 56 B2
Enstone GB 44 B2
Entlebuch CH 106 B3
Entrácque I 133 A3
Entradas P 160 B1
Entrains-sur-Nohain F 104 B2
Entrambasaguas E 143 A3
Entrambasmestas E 143 A3
Entraygues-sur-Truyère F 116 C2
Entre-os-Rios P 148 A1
Entrevaux F 132 B2
Entrin Bajo E 155 C4
Entroncamento P 154 B2
Entzheim F 93 C3
Envermeu F 89 A5
Enviken S 50 B2
Enying H 112 C2
Enzingerboden A 109 B3
Enzklösterle D 93 C4
Épagny F 90 B3
Epalinges CH 106 C1
Epannes F 114 B3
Epanomi GR 182 C4
Epe
 D 71 B4
 NL 70 B2
Épernay F 91 B3
Épernon F 90 C1
Epfig F 93 C3
Épierre F 118 B3
Épila E 152 A2
Épinac F 104 C3
Épinal F 105 A5
Episcopia I 174 A2
Episkopi CY 181 B1
Epitalio GR 184 B2
Epoisses F 104 B3
Eppenbrunn D 93 B3
Eppendorf D 83 B5
Epping GB 45 B4
Eppingen D 93 B4
Epsom GB 44 B3
Epworth GB 40 B3
Eraclea I 122 B1
Eraclea Mare I 122 B1
Erba I 120 B2
Erbach
 Baden-Württemberg D 94 C1
 Hessen D 93 B4
Erbalunga F 180 A2
Erbendorf D 95 B4
Érchie I 173 B3
Ercolano I 170 C2
Ercsi H 112 B2
Érd H 112 B2
Erdek TR 186 B2
Erdemli TR 23 C8
Erdevik SRB 126 B1
Erding D 95 C3
Erdötelek H 113 B4
Erdut HR 125 B5
Erdweg D 95 C3
Ereğli
 Konya TR 23 C8
 Zonguldak TR 187 A6
Erenkaya TR 189 B7
Eresfjord N 198 C5
Eresos GR 183 D7
Eretria GR 185 A4
Erfde D 64 B2
Erfjord N 52 A2
Erfstadt D 80 B2
Erfurt D 82 B3
Ērgli LV 8 D4
Ergoldsbach D 95 C4
Eriboll GB 32 C2
Érice I 176 A1
Ericeira P 154 C1
Eğridir TR 189 B5
Eriksberg S 195 E6
Eriksmåla S 62 B3
Eringsboda S 63 B3
Eriswil CH 106 B2
Erithres GR 185 A4
Erkelenz D 80 A2
Erkner D 74 B2
Erkrath D 80 A2
Erla E 144 B3
Erlangen D 94 B3
Erli I 133 A4
Erlsbach A 109 C3
Ermelo NL 70 B2
Ermenak TR 23 C7
Ermenonville F 90 B2
Ermezinde P 148 A1
Ermidas P 160 A1
Ermioni GR 184 B4
Ermoupoli GR 185 B5
Ermsleben D 82 A3
Erndtebrück D 81 B4
Ernée F 88 B3
Ernestinovo HR 125 B4
Ernstbrunn A 97 C4
Erolzheim D 107 A5
Erquelinnes B 79 B4
Erquy F 101 A3
Erra P 154 C2
Erratzu E 144 A2
Errindlev DK 65 B4
Erro E 144 B2
Ersa F 180 A2
Érsekcsanád H 125 A4
Ersekë AL 182 C2
Érsekvadkert H 112 B3
Ersmark S 200 C6
Erstein F 93 C3
Erstfeld CH 107 C3
Ertebølle DK 58 B2
Ertingen D 107 A4
Ervedal
 Coimbra P 148 B1
 Portalegre P 154 B3
Ervenik HR 138 A1
Ervidel P 160 B1
Ervy-le-Châtel F 104 A2
Erwitte D 81 A4
Erxleben D 73 B4
Erzsébet H 125 A4
Esbjerg DK 59 C1
Esbly F 90 C2
Escacena del Campo E 161 B3
Escairón E 140 B3
Escalada E 143 B3
Escalante E 143 A3
Escalaplano I 179 C3
Escalona E 150 B3
Escalona del Prado E 151 A3
Escalonilla E 150 C3
Escalos de Baixo P 155 B3
Escalos de Cima P 155 B3
Escamilla E 152 B1
Es Caná E 166 B1
Escañuela E 157 C3
Es Castell E 167 B4
Escatrón E 153 A3
Eschach D 107 B4
Eschau D 94 B1
Eschede D 72 B3
Eschenau D 95 B3
Eschenbach D 95 B3
Eschenz CH 107 B3
Eschershausen D 72 C2
Esch-sur-Alzette L 92 B1
Esch-sur-Sûre L 92 B1
Eschwege D 82 A2
Eschweiler D 80 B2
Escobasa de Almazán E 152 A1
Escoeuilles F 78 B1
Escombreras E 165 B4
Escos F 144 A2
Escource F 128 B1
Escragnolles F 132 B2
Escrick GB 40 B2
Escurial E 156 A2
Escurial de la Sierra E 149 B4
Esens D 71 A4
Esgos E 140 B3
Esher GB 44 B3
Eskdalemuir GB 36 A3
Eskifjörður IS 191 B12
Eskilhem S 57 C4
Eskilsäter S 55 B4
Eskilstrup DK 65 B4
Eskilstuna S 56 A2
Eskipazar TR 187 B7
Eskişehir TR 187 C5
Eslarn D 95 B4
Eslava E 144 B2
Eslida E 159 B3
Eslohe D 81 A4
Eslöv S 61 D3
Eşme TR 188 A3
Es Mercadal E 167 B4
Es Migjorn Gran E 167 B4
Espa N 48 B3
Espalion F 130 A1
Esparragalejo E 155 C4
Esparragosa del Caudillo E 156 B2
Esparragossa de la Serena E 156 B2
Esparreguera E 147 C2
Esparron F 132 B1
Espe N 46 B3
Espedal N 52 B2
Espejo
 Alava E 143 B3
 Córdoba E 163 A3
Espeland N 46 B2
Espelkamp D 72 B1
Espeluche F 131 A3
Espeluy E 157 B4
Espera E 162 B2
Esperança P 155 B3
Espéraza F 146 B3
Espéria I 169 B3
Espevær N 52 A1
Espiel E 156 B2
Espinama E 142 A2
Espiñaredo E 140 A3
Espinasses F 132 A2
Espinelves E 147 C3
Espinhal P 154 A2
Espinho P 148 A1
Espinilla E 142 A2
Espinosa de Cerrato E 143 C3
Espinosa de los Monteros E 143 A3
Espinoso del Rey E 156 A3
Espirito Santo P 160 B2
Espluga de Francolí E 147 C2
Esplús E 145 C4
Espolla E 146 B3
Espoo FIN 8 B4
Esporles E 166 B2
Es Port d'Alcúdia E 167 B3
Esposende P 148 A1
Espot E 146 B2
Es Pujols E 166 C1
Esquedas E 145 B3
Esquivias E 151 B4
Essay F 89 B4
Essen
 B 79 A4
 Niedersachsen D 71 B4
 Nordrhein-Westfalen D 80 A3
Essenbach D 95 C4
Essertaux F 90 B2
Essingen D 94 C2
Esslingen D 94 C1
Es Soleràs E 153 A4
Essoyes F 104 A3
Estacas E 140 B2
Estadilla E 145 B4
Estagel F 146 B3
Estaires F 78 B2
Estang F 128 C2
Estarreja P 148 B1
Estartit E 147 B4
Estavayer-le-Lac CH 106 C1
Este I 121 B4
Esteiro E 140 A2
Estela P 148 A1
Estella E 144 B1
Estellencs E 166 B2
Estepa E 162 A3
Estépar E 143 B3
Estepona E 162 B2
Esternay F 91 C3
Esterri d'Aneu E 146 B2
Esterwegen D 71 B4
Estissac F 104 A2
Estivadas E 140 B3
Estivareilles F 116 A2
Estivella E 159 B3
Estói P 160 B2
Estopiñán E 145 C4
Estoril P 154 C1
Estoublon F 132 B2
Estrée-Blanche F 78 B2
Estrées-St Denis F 90 B2
Estrela P 155 C3
Estremera E 151 B4
Estremoz P 155 C3
Estuna S 51 C5
Esyres F 102 B2
Esztergom H 112 B2
Etables-sur-Mer F 100 A3
Étain F 92 B1
Étalans F 105 B5
Etalle B 92 B1
Étampes F 90 C2
Etang-sur-Arroux F 104 C3
Étaples F 78 B1
Etauliers F 128 A2
Etili TR 186 C1
Etna N 48 B1
Etne N 52 A1
Etoges F 91 C3
Etoliko GR 184 A2
Eton GB 44 B3
Etréaupont F 91 B3
Étréchy F 90 C2
Étrépagny F 90 B1
Étretat F 89 A4
Étroeungt F 91 A3
Étroubles I 119 B4
Ettal D 108 B2
Ettelbruck L 92 B2
Etten NL 79 A4
Ettenheim D 106 A2
Ettington GB 44 A2
Ettlingen D 93 C4
Ettringen D 108 A1
Etuz F 105 B4
Etxarri-Aranatz E 144 B1
Etyek H 112 B2
Eu F 90 A1

Euerdorf D 82 B2
Eulate E 144 B1
Eupen B 80 B2
Europoort NL 79 A4
Euskirchen D 80 B2
Eutin D 65 B3
Evanger N 46 B3
Évaux-les-Bains F 116 A2
Evciler
  Afyon TR 189 A4
  Çanakkale TR . . 186 C1
Evenskjær N 194 B7
Evenstad N 48 A3
Evercreech GB 43 A4
Evergem B 79 A3
Everöd S 61 D4
Eversberg D 81 A4
Everswinkel D 71 C4
Evertsberg S 49 A5
Evesham GB 44 A2
Évian-les-Bains F . .118 A3
Evisa F 180 A1
Evje N 53 B3
Evolène CH 119 A4
Évora P 154 C3
Evoramonte P 155 C3
Evran F 101 A4
Evrecy F 89 A3
Évreux F 89 A5
Évron F 102 A1
Évry F 90 C2
Ewell GB 44 B3
Ewersbach D 81 B4
Excideuil F 115 C5
Exeter GB 43 B3
Exmes F 89 B4
Exminster GB 43 B3
Exmouth GB 43 B3
Eydehamn N 53 B4
Eye
  Peterborough
    GB 41 C3
  Suffolk GB 45 A5
Eyemouth GB 35 C5
Eyguians F 132 A1
Eyguières F 131 B4
Eygurande F 116 B2
Eylie F 145 B4
Eymet F 129 B3
Eymoutiers F 116 B1
Eynsham GB 44 B2
Eyrarbakki IS 190 D4
Eystrup D 72 B2
Ezaro E 140 B1
Ezcaray E 143 B4
Ezcároz E 144 B2
Ezine TR 186 C1
Ezmoriz P 148 B1

F

Fabara E 153 A4
Fábbrico I 121 C3
Fåberg N 48 A2
Fabero E 141 B4
Fábiánsebestyén
  H 113 C4
Fåborg DK 64 A3
Fabrègues F 130 B2
Fabriano I 136 B1
Fabrizia I 175 C2
Facha P 148 A1
Facinas E 162 B2
Fačkov SK 98 B2
Fadagosa P 155 B3
Fadd H 112 C2
Faédis I 122 A2
Faenza I 135 A4
Fafe P 148 A1
Fagagna I 122 A2
Făgăraş RO 17 C6
Fågelberget S 199 A11
Fågelfors S 62 A3
Fågelmara S 63 B3
Fågelsta S 55 B6
Fagerås S 55 A4
Fagerheim N 47 B4
Fagerhøy N 48 A1
Fagerhult S 62 A3
Fagerlund N 48 B2
Fagernes
  Oppland N 47 B6
  Troms N . . . 192 C3
Fagersanna S 55 B5
Fagersta S 50 B2
Fåglavik S 55 B4
Fagnano Castello
  I 174 B2
Fagnières F 91 C4
Faido CH 107 C3
Fains-Véel F 91 C5
Fairford GB 44 B2
Fairlie GB 34 C3
Fajsz H 112 C2
Fakenham GB 41 C4
Fåker S 199 B11
Fakse DK 65 A5
Fakse Ladeplads
  DK 65 A5
Falaise F 89 B3
Falcade I 121 A4
Falcarragh IRL 26 A2
Falces E 144 B2
Fălciu RO 17 B8
Falconara I 177 B3
Falconara Marittima
  I 136 B2
Falcone I 177 A3
Faldingworth GB . . .40 B3
Falerum S 56 B2
Fălești MD 17 B7
Falkenberg
  Bayern D 95 B4
  Bayern D 95 C4
  Brandenburg D . .83 A5
  S 60 C2
Falkensee D 74 B2
Falkenstein
  Bayern D 95 B4

Falkenstein continued
  Sachsen D 83 B4
Falkenthal D 74 B2
Falkirk GB 35 B4
Falkland GB 35 B4
Falköping S 55 B4
Fall D 108 B2
Falla S 56 B1
Fallingbostel D 72 B2
Falmouth GB 42 B1
Falset E 147 C1
Fălticeni RO 17 B7
Falun S 50 B2
Famagusta CY 181 A2
Fammestad N 46 B2
Fanano I 135 A3
Fanjeaux F 146 A3
Fano I 136 B2
Fão P 148 A1
Fara in Sabina I 168 A2
Faramontanos de
  Tábara E 149 A4
Fara Novarese I 119 B5
Farasdues E 144 B2
Fårbo S 62 A4
Fareham GB 44 C2
Färentuna S 57 A3
Fårevejle DK 61 D1
Färgelanda S 54 B2
Färila S 200 E1
Faringdon GB 44 B2
Faringe S 51 C5
Farini I 120 C2
Fariza E 149 A3
Färjestaden S 63 B4
Farkadona GR 182 D4
Farkasfa H 111 C3
Farlete E 153 A3
Färlöv S 61 C4
Farmos H 113 B3
Färnäs S 50 B1
Farnborough GB 44 B3
Farnese I 168 A1
Farnham GB 44 B3
Farnroda D 82 B2
Faro P 160 B2
Fåro S 57 C5
Fårösund S 57 C5
Farra d'Alpago I 122 A1
Farranfore IRL 29 B2
Farre DK 59 B2
Farsala GR 182 D4
Farsø DK 58 B2
Farsund N 52 B2
Farum DK 61 D2
Fårup DK 58 B2
Fasana I 172 B1
Fasano I 173 B3
Fáskrúðsfjörður
  IS 191 C11
Fassberg D 72 B3
Fastiv UA 13 C8
Fastnäs S 49 B5
Fatmomakke S 195 E6
Fátima P 154 B2
Fättjaur S 195 E6
Faucogney-et-la-Mer
  F 105 B5
Faulenrost D 74 A1
Faulquemont F 92 B2
Fauquembergues F 78 B2
Fauske N 194 C6
Fauville-en-Caux F .89 A4
Fauvillers B 92 B1
Fåvang N 48 A2
Favara
  E 159 B3
  I 176 B2
Faverges F 118 B3
Faverney F 105 B5
Faversham GB 45 B4
Favignana I 176 B1
Fawley GB 44 C2
Fay-aux-Loges F .103 B4
Fayence F 132 B2
Fayet F 130 B1
Fayl-Billot F 105 B4
Fayón E 153 A4
Fearn GB 32 D3
Fécamp F 89 A4
Feda N 52 B2
Fedje N 46 B1
Feeny GB 27 B3
Fegen S 60 B3
Fegyvernek H 113 B4
Fehrbellin D 74 B1
Fehring A 111 C3
Feichten A 108 B1
Feiring N 48 B3
Feistritz im Rosental
  A 110 C1
Feketić SRB 126 B1
Felanitx E 167 B3
Feld am See A 109 C4
Feldbach A 110 C2
Feldberg D 74 A2
Feldkirch A 107 B4
Feldkirchen in Kärnten
  A 109 C5
Feldkirchen-Westerham
  D 108 B2
Felgueiras P 148 A1
Félix E 164 C2
Felixstowe GB 45 B5
Felizzano I 119 C5
Felletin F 116 B2
Fellingsbro S 56 A1
Felnac RO 126 A3
Felnémet H 113 B4
Felpéc H 111 B4
Fels am Wagram A .97 C3
Felsberg D 81 A5
Felsőnyék H 112 C2
Felsöszentiván H .126 A1

Felsöszentmárton
  H 125 B3
Felsözsolca H 113 A4
Felsted DK 64 B2
Feltre I 121 A4
Femsjö S 60 C3
Fene E 140 A2
Fenestrelle I 119 B4
Fénétrange F 92 C3
Feneu F 102 B1
Fengersfors S 54 B3
Fenit IRL 29 B2
Fensmark DK 65 A4
Fenwick GB 36 A2
Feolin Ferry GB 34 C1
Ferbane IRL 28 A4
Ferdinandovac
  HR 124 A3
Ferdinandshof D 74 A2
Fère-Champenoise
  F 91 C3
Fère-en-Tardenois
  F 91 B3
Ferentillo I 168 A2
Ferentino I 169 B3
Feres GR 183 C8
Feria E 155 C4
Feričanci HR 125 B3
Ferizli TR 187 B5
Ferla I 177 B3
Ferlach A 110 C1
Ferleiten A 109 B3
Fermil P 148 A2
Fermo I 136 B2
Fermoselle E 149 A3
Fermoy IRL 29 B3
Fernancabellero E 157 A4
Fernán Núñez E . . .163 A3
Fernán Peréz E 164 C2
Fernão Ferro P 154 C1
Fernay-Voltaire F . .118 A3
Ferndown GB 43 B5
Ferness GB 32 D3
Fernhurst GB 44 B3
Ferns IRL 30 B2
Ferpécle CH 119 A4
Ferrals-les-Corbières
  F 146 A3
Ferrandina I 172 B2
Ferrara I 121 C4
Ferrara di Monte Baldo
  I 121 B3
Ferreira E 141 A3
Ferreira do Alentejo
  P 160 A1
Ferreira do Zêzere
  P 154 B2
Ferreras de Abajo
  E 141 C4
Ferreras de Arriba
  E 141 C4
Ferreries E 167 B4
Ferreruela E 152 A2
Ferreruela de Tabara
  E 149 A3
Ferret CH 119 B4
Ferrette F 106 B2
Ferriere I 120 C2
Ferrière-la-Grande
  F 79 B3
Ferrières
  Hautes-Pyrénées
    F 145 A3
  Loiret F 103 A4
  Oise F 90 B2
Ferrières-sur-Sichon
  F 117 A3
Ferrol E 140 A2
Ferryhill GB 37 B5
Fertörakos H 111 B3
Fertöszentmiklós
  H 111 B3
Ferwerd NL 70 A2
Festieux F 91 B3
Festøy N 198 C3
Festvåg N 194 C5
Fetești RO 17 C7
Fethard
  Tipperary IRL . . .29 B4
  Wexford IRL 30 B2
Fethiye TR 188 C4
Fetsund N 48 C3
Fettercairn GB 35 B5
Feucht D 95 B3
Feuchtwangen D . . .94 B2
Feudingen D 81 B4
Feuges F 91 C4
Feuquières F 90 B1
Feurs F 117 B4
Fevik N 53 B4
Ffestiniog GB 38 B3
Fiamignano I 169 A3
Fiano I 119 B4
Ficarazzi I 176 A2
Ficarolo I 121 C4
Fichtelberg D 95 A3
Ficulle I 135 C5
Fidenza I 120 C3
Fidjeland N 52 B2
Fieberbrunn A 109 B3
Fier AL 182 C1
Fiera di Primiero I . .121 A4
Fiesch CH 119 A5
Fiesso Umbertiano
  I 121 C4
Figari F 180 B2
Figeac F 116 C2
Figeholm S 62 A4
Figgjo N 52 B1
Figline Valdarno I .135 B4
Figols E 145 B4
Figueira da Foz P .148 B1
Figueira de Castelo
  Rodrigo P 149 B3
Figueira dos Caveleiros
  P 160 A1
Figueiredo P 154 B3
Figueiredo de Alva
  P 148 B2

Figueiródos Vinhos
  P 154 B2
Figueres E 147 B3
Figueroles E 153 B3
Figueruela de Arriba
  E 141 C4
Filadélfia I 175 C2
Fil'akovo SK 99 C3
Filderstadt D 94 C1
Filey GB 41 A3
Filiași RO 17 C5
Filiates GR 182 D2
Filiatra GR 184 B2
Filipstad S 55 A5
Filisur CH 107 C4
Fillan N 198 B5
Filotio GR 185 B6
Filottrano I 136 B2
Filskov DK 59 C2
Filton GB 43 A4
Filtvet N 54 A1
Filzmoos A 109 B4
Finale Emilia I 121 C4
Finale Ligure I 133 A4
Fiñana E 164 B2
Finby FIN 51 B7
Fincham GB 41 C4
Finchingfield GB . . .45 B4
Findhorn GB 32 D3
Findochty GB 33 D4
Finike TR 189 C5
Finkenberg A 108 B2
Finnea IRL 27 C3
Finneidfjord N 195 D4
Finnerödja S 55 B5
Finnskog N 49 B4
Finnsnes N 194 A9
Finntorp S 54 A3
Finócchio I 168 B2
Finsjö S 62 A4
Finsland N 52 B3
Finspång S 56 B1
Finsterwalde D 84 A1
Finsterwolde NL 71 A4
Finstown GB 33 B3
Fintona GB 27 B3
Fionnphort GB 34 B1
Fiorenzuola d'Arda
  I 120 C2
Firenze = Florence
  I 135 B4
Firenzuola I 135 A4
Firmi F 130 A1
Firminy F 117 B4
Firmo I 174 B2
Fischamend Markt
  A 111 A3
Fischbach
  A 110 B2
  D 93 B3
Fischbeck D 73 B5
Fishbourne GB 44 C2
Fishguard GB 39 C2
Fiskardo GR 184 A1
Fiskebäckskil S 54 B2
Fiskebøl N 194 B5
Fismes F 91 B3
Fisterra E 140 B1
Fitero E 144 B2
Fitjar N 46 C2
Fiuggi I 169 B3
Fiumata I 169 A3
Fiumefreddo Brúzio
  I 174 B2
Fiumefreddo di Sicilia
  I 177 B4
Fiumicino I 168 B2
Fivemiletown GB . . .27 B3
Fivizzano I 134 A3
Fjälkinge S 63 B2
Fjällåsen S 196 B3
Fjällbacka S 54 B2
Fjæra N 46 C3
Fjärdhundra S 56 A2
Fjellerup DK 58 B3
Fjerritslev DK 58 A2
Fjordgard N 194 A8
Fjugesta S 55 A5
Flå N 47 B6
Flåbygd N 53 A4
Flaca E 147 B3
Flace F 117 A4
Fladungen D 82 B2
Flaine F 118 A3
Flaka FIN 51 B7
Flåm N 46 B4
Flamatt CH 106 C2
Flamborough GB . . .41 A3
Flammersfeld D 81 B3
Flassans-sur-Issole
  F 132 B2
Flatdal N 53 A4
Flatebø N 46 B3
Flateby N 48 C3
Flateland N 52 A3
Flateyri IS 190 A2
Flatøydegard N 47 B6
Flatråker N 46 C2
Flattach A 109 C4
Flatvarp S 62 A4
Flauenskjold DK 58 A3
Flavigny-sur-Moselle
  F 92 C2
Flavy-le-Martel F . . .90 B3
Flawil CH 107 B4
Flayosc F 132 B2
Flechtingen D 73 B4
Fleckeby D 64 B2
Fleetmark D 73 B4
Fleetwood GB 38 A3
Flehingen D 93 B4
Flekke N 46 A2
Flekkefjord N 52 B2
Flen S 56 A2
Flensburg D 64 B2
Fleringe S 57 C4
Flerohopp S 62 B3
Flers F 88 B3

Flesberg N 47 C6
Fleurance F 129 C3
Fleuré F 115 B4
Fleurier CH 105 C5
Fleurus B 79 B4
Fleury
  Hérault F 130 B2
  Yonne F 104 B2
Fleury-les-Aubrais
  F 103 B3
Fleury-sur-Andelle
  F 89 A5
Fleury-sur-Orne F . .89 A3
Flieden D 81 B5
Flimby GB 36 B3
Flims CH 107 C4
Flint GB 38 A3
Flirey F 92 C1
Flirsch A 108 B1
Flisa N 49 B4
Flisby S 62 A2
Fliseryd S 62 A4
Flix E 153 A4
Flixecourt F 90 A2
Flize F 91 B4
Flobecq B 79 B3
Floby S 55 B4
Floda S 60 B2
Flodden GB 37 A4
Flogny-la-Chapelle
  F 104 B2
Flöha D 83 B5
Flonheim D 93 B4
Florac F 130 A2
Floreffe B 79 B4
Florence = Firenze
  I 135 B4
Florennes B 79 B4
Florensac F 130 B2
Florentin F 129 C5
Florenville B 91 B5
Flores de Avila E . . .150 B2
Floresta I 177 B3
Floreşti MD 17 B8
Floridia I 177 B4
Florina GR 182 C3
Florø N 46 A2
Flörsheim D 93 A4
Floss D 95 B4
Fluberg N 48 B2
Flúðir IS 190 C5
Flühli CH 106 C3
Flumet F 118 B3
Fluminimaggiore I 179 C2
Flums CH 107 B4
Flyeryd S 63 B3
Flygsfors S 62 B3
Foča BIH 139 B4
Foça TR 186 D1
Fochabers GB 32 D3
Focşani RO 17 C7
Foeni RO 126 B2
Fogdö S 56 A2
Fóggia I 171 B3
Foglianise I 170 B2
Föglö FIN 51 B7
Fohnsdorf A 110 B1
Foiano della Chiana
  I 135 B4
Foix F 146 B2
Fojnica
  BIH 139 B3
  BIH 139 B4
Fokstua N 198 C6
Földeák H 126 A2
Foldereid N 199 A9
Földes H 113 B5
Folegandros GR . . .185 C6
Folelli F 180 A2
Folgaria I 121 B4
Folgosinho P 148 B2
Folgoso de la Ribera
  E 141 B4
Folgoso do Courel
  E 141 B3
Foligno I 136 C1
Folkärna S 50 B3
Folkestad N 198 C3
Folkestone GB 45 B5
Follafoss N 199 B8
Folldal N 198 C6
Follebu N 48 A2
Follina I 121 B5
Föllinge S 199 B11
Follónica I 135 C3
Fölsbyn S 54 A3
Foncebadón E 141 B4
Foncine-le-Bas F . .105 C5
Fondevila E 140 C2
Fondi I 169 B3
Fondo I 121 A4
Fonelas E 164 B1
Fonfría
  Teruel E 152 B2
  Zamora E 149 A3
Fonn N 46 A3
Fonnes N 46 B1
Fonni I 178 B3
Fontaine F 91 C4
Fontainebleau F 90 C2
Fontaine de Vaucluse
  F 131 B4
Fontaine-Française
  F 105 B4
Fontaine-le-Dun F . .89 A4
Fontan F 133 A3
Fontanarejo E 157 A3
Fontane I 133 A3
Fontanélice I 135 A4
Fontanières F 116 A2
Fontanosas E 157 B3
Fontblanca E 168 A1
Fontenay-le-Comte
  F 114 B3
Fontenay-Trésigny
  F 90 C2

Fontevrault-l'Abbaye
  F 102 B2
Fontiveros E 150 B3
Fontoy F 92 B1
Fontpédrouse F 146 B3
Font-Romeu F 146 B3
Fontstown IRL 30 A2
Fonz E 145 B4
Fonzaso I 121 A4
Fóppolo I 120 A2
Föra S 62 A4
Forbach
  D 93 C4
  F 92 B2
Forcall E 153 B3
Forcalquier F 132 B1
Forcarei E 140 B2
Forchheim D 94 B3
Forchtenau A 111 B3
Forchtenberg D 94 B1
Ford GB 34 B2
Førde
  Hordaland N 52 A1
  Sogn og Fjordane
    N 46 A2
Förderstedt D 83 A3
Førdesfjorden N 52 A1
Fordham GB 45 A4
Fordingbridge GB . .44 C2
Fordon PL 76 A3
Fordóngiánus I 179 C2
Forenza I 172 B1
Foresta di Búrgos
  I 178 B2
Forfar GB 35 B5
Forges-les-Eaux F . .90 B1
Foria I 172 B1
Forio I 170 C1
Forjães P 148 A1
Forl I I 135 A5
Forlimpopoli I 135 A5
Formazza I 119 A5
Formby GB 38 A3
Formerie F 90 B1
Formiga I 135 A3
Formigine I 135 A3
Formigliana I 119 B5
Formiguères F 146 B3
Fornalutx E 166 B2
Fornåsa S 56 B1
Fornelli I 178 B2
Fornells E 167 A4
Fornelos de Montes
  E 140 B2
Fornes E 163 B4
Forni Avoltri I 109 C3
Forni di Sopra I 122 A1
Forni di Sotto I 122 A1
Forno
  Piemonte I 119 B4
  Piemonte I 119 B5
Forno Alpi-Gráie I . .119 B4
Forno di Zoldo I 121 A5
Fornos de Algodres
  P 148 B2
Fornovo di Taro I . .120 C3
Foros do Arrão P . .154 B2
Forráskút H 126 A1
Forres GB 32 D3
Forriolo E 140 B3
Fors S 50 B3
Forsand N 52 B2
Forsbacka S 51 B3
Forserum S 62 A2
Forshaga S 55 A4
Forsheda S 60 B3
Forsinain GB 32 C3
Forslev DK 65 A4
Forsmark
  Uppsala S 51 B5
  Västerbotten S . .195 E6
Forsmo S 200 C3
Forsnäs S 195 D9
Forsnes N 198 B5
Forssa FIN 8 B3
Forst D 84 A2
Forsvik S 55 B5
Fort Augustus GB . .32 D2
Fortanete E 153 B3
Forte dei Marmi I . .134 B3
Fortezza I 108 C2
Forth GB 35 C4
Fort-Mahon-Plage
  F 78 B1
Fortrie GB 33 D4
Fortrose GB 32 D2
Fortun N 47 A4
Fortuna E 165 A3
Fortuneswell GB . . .43 B4
Fort William GB 34 B2
Forvik N 195 E3
Fos F 145 B4
Fosdinovo I 134 A3
Foss N 47 B6
Fossacésia I 169 A4
Fossano I 133 A3
Fossato di Vico I . . .136 B1
Fossbakken N 194 B8
Fosse-la-Ville B 79 B4
Fossombrone I 136 B1
Fos-sur-Mer F 131 B3
Fot H 112 B3
Fouchères F 104 A3
Fouesnant F 100 B1
Foug F 92 C1
Fougères F 88 B2
Fougerolles F 105 B5
Foulain F 105 A4
Fountainhall GB . . .35 C5
Fouras F 114 C2
Fourchambault F . . .104 B2
Fourmies F 91 A4
Fourna GR 182 D3
Fournels F 116 C3
Fourni GR 188 B1

Fournols F 117 B3
Fourques F 146 B3
Fourquevaux F 146 A2
Fours F 104 C2
Fowey GB 42 B2
Foxdale GB 36 B2
Foxford IRL 26 C1
Foyers GB 32 D2
Foynes IRL 29 B2
Foz E 141 A3
Foza I 121 B4
Foz do Arelho P 154 B1
Foz do Giraldo P . . .155 B3
Frabosa Soprana
  I 133 A3
Frades de la Sierra
  E 149 B4
Fraga E 153 A4
Fragagnano I 173 B3
Frailes E 163 A4
Fraire B 79 B4
Fraize F 106 A1
Framlingham GB . . .45 A5
Frammersbach D . . .94 A1
Framnes N 54 A1
França P 141 C4
Francaltroff F 92 C2
Francavilla al Mare
  I 169 A4
Francavilla di Sicília
  I 177 B4
Francavilla Fontana
  I 173 B3
Francavilla in Sinni
  I 174 A2
Francescas F 129 B3
Franco E 148 A2
Francofonte I 177 B3
Francos E 151 A4
Frändefors S 54 B3
Franeker NL 70 A2
Frangy F 118 A2
Frankenau D 81 A4
Frankenberg
  Hessen D 81 A4
  Sachsen D 83 B5
Frankenburg A 109 A4
Frankenfels A 110 B2
Frankenmarkt A 109 B4
Frankenthal D 93 B4
Frankfurt
  Brandenburg D . .74 B3
  Hessen D 81 B4
Frankrike S 199 B10
Fränsta S 200 D2
Františkovy Lázně
  CZ 83 B4
Franzburg D 66 B1
Frascati I 168 B2
Frasdorf D 109 B3
Fraserburgh GB 33 D4
Frashër AL 182 C2
Frasne F 105 C5
Frasnes-lez-Anvaing
  B 79 B3
Frasseto F 180 B2
Frastanz A 107 B4
Fratel P 155 B3
Fratta Todina I 135 C5
Frauenau D 96 C1
Frauenkirchen A . . .111 B3
Frauenstein D 83 B5
Frauental A 110 C2
Frayssinet F 129 B4
Frayssinet-le-Gélat
  F 129 B4
Frechas P 149 A2
Frechen D 80 B2
Frechilla E 142 B2
Freckenhorst D 71 C4
Fredeburg D 81 A4
Fredelsloh D 82 A1
Fredeng N 48 B2
Fredensborg DK 61 D2
Fredericia DK 59 C2
Frederiks DK 59 B2
Frederikshavn DK . .58 A3
Frederikssund DK . .61 D2
Frederiksværk DK . .61 D2
Fredrika S 200 B4
Fredriksberg S 50 B1
Fredriksdal S 62 A2
Fredrikstad N 54 A1
Fregenal de la Sierra
  E 161 A3
Fregene I 168 B2
Freiberg D 83 B5
Freiburg
  Baden-Württemberg
    D 106 B2
  Niedersachsen D . 64 C2
Freienhagen D 81 A5
Freienhufen D 84 A1
Freienstein D 81 B5
Freihung D 95 B3
Freila E 164 B2
Freisen D 92 B3
Freising D 95 C3
Freistadt A 96 C2
Freital D 84 A1
Freixedas P 149 B2
Freixo de Espada à
  Cinta P 149 A3
Fréjus F 132 B2
Fremdingen D 94 C2
Frenštát pod
  Radhoštěm CZ . .98 B2
Freren D 71 B4
Freshford IRL 30 B1
Freshwater GB 44 C2
Fresnay-sur-Sarthe
  F 89 B4
Fresneda de la Sierra
  E 152 B1
Fresneda de la Sierra
  Tiron E 143 B3

Fresnedillas E ... 151 B3
Fresnes-en-Woevre F ... 92 B1
Fresne-St Mamès F ... 105 B4
Fresno Alhandiga E ... 150 B2
Fresno de la Ribera E ... 150 A2
Fresno de la Vega E ... 142 B1
Fresno de Sayago E ... 149 A4
Fresnoy-Folny F ... 90 B1
Fresnoy-le-Grand F 91 B3
Fressenville F ... 90 A1
Fresvik N ... 46 A3
Fréteval F ... 103 B3
Fretigney F ... 105 B4
Freudenberg
Baden-Württemberg D ... 94 B1
Nordrhein-Westfalen D ... 81 B3
Freudenstadt D ... 93 C4
Freux B ... 92 B1
Frévent F ... 78 B2
Freyburg D ... 83 A3
Freyenstein D ... 73 A5
Freyming-Merlebach F ... 92 B2
Freystadt D ... 95 B3
Freyung D ... 96 C1
Frias de Albarracin E ... 152 B2
Fribourg CH ... 106 C2
Frick CH ... 106 B3
Fridafors S ... 63 B2
Fridaythorpe GB ... 40 A3
Friedberg
A ... 111 B3
Bayern D ... 94 C2
Hessen D ... 81 B4
Friedeburg D ... 71 A4
Friedewald D ... 82 B1
Friedland
Brandenburg D ... 74 B3
Mecklenburg-Vorpommern D ... 74 A2
Niedersachsen D ... 82 A1
Friedrichroda D ... 82 B2
Friedrichsdorf D ... 81 B4
Friedrichshafen D 107 B4
Friedrichskoog D ... 64 B1
Friedrichstadt D ... 64 B2
Friedrichswalde D ... 74 A2
Friesach A ... 110 C1
Friesack D ... 73 B5
Friesenheim D ... 93 C3
Friesoythe D ... 71 A4
Friggesund S ... 200 E2
Frigiliana E ... 163 B4
Frihetsli N ... 192 D3
Frillesås S ... 60 B2
Frinnaryd S ... 62 A2
Frinton-on-Sea GB ... 45 B5
Friockheim GB ... 35 B5
Friol E ... 140 A3
Fristad S ... 60 B2
Fritsla S ... 60 B2
Fritzlar D ... 81 A5
Frizington GB ... 36 B3
Frödinge S ... 62 A4
Froges F ... 118 B2
Frohburg D ... 83 A4
Frohnhausen D ... 81 B4
Frohnleiten A ... 110 B2
Froissy F ... 90 B2
Frombork PL ... 69 A4
Frome GB ... 43 A4
Frómista E ... 142 B2
Fröndenberg D ... 81 A3
Fronsac F ... 128 B2
Front I ... 119 B4
Fronteira P ... 155 B3
Frontenay-Rohan-Rohan F ... 114 B3
Frontenhausen D ... 95 C4
Frontignan F ... 130 B2
Fronton F ... 129 C4
Fröseke S ... 62 B3
Frosinone I ... 169 B3
Frosolone I ... 170 B2
Frosta N ... 199 B7
Frøstrup DK ... 58 A1
Frosunda S ... 57 A4
Frouard F ... 92 C2
Frövi S ... 56 A1
Frøyset N ... 46 B2
Fruges F ... 78 B2
Frutigen CH ... 106 C2
Frýdek-Místek CZ ... 98 B2
Frýdlant CZ ... 84 B3
Frydlant nad Ostravicí CZ ... 98 B2
Frygnowo PL ... 77 A5
Fryšták CZ ... 98 B1
Fucécchio I ... 135 B3
Fuencaliente
Ciudad Real E ... 157 A4
Ciudad Real E ... 157 B3
Fuencemillán E ... 151 B4
Fuendejalón E ... 144 C2
Fuengirola E ... 163 B3
Fuenlabrada E ... 151 B4
Fuenlabrada de los Montes E ... 156 A3
Fuensalida E ... 151 B3
Fuensanta E ... 164 B3
Fuensanta de Martos E ... 163 A4
Fuente-Álamo E ... 158 C2
Fuente-Álamo de Murcia E ... 165 B3
Fuentealbilla E ... 158 B2
Fuente al Olmo de Iscar E ... 150 A3
Fuentecén E ... 151 A4
Fuente Dé E ... 142 A2
Fuente de Cantos E ... 155 C4
Fuente del Arco E 156 B2
Fuente del Conde E ... 163 A3
Fuente del Maestre E ... 155 C4
Fuente de Santa Cruz E ... 150 A3
Fuente el Fresno E ... 157 A4
Fuente el Saz de Jarama E ... 151 B4
Fuente el Sol E ... 150 A3
Fuenteguinaldo E 149 B3
Fuentelapeña E ... 150 A2
Fuentelcésped E ... 151 A4
Fuentelespino de Haro E ... 158 B1
Fuentelespino de Moya E ... 158 B2
Fuentenovilla E ... 151 B4
Fuente Obejuna E 156 B2
Fuente Palmera E 162 A2
Fuentepelayo E ... 151 A3
Fuentepinilla E ... 151 A5
Fuenterroble de Salvatierra E ... 150 B2
Fuenterrobles E ... 158 B2
Fuentes E ... 158 B1
Fuentesaúco E ... 151 A3
Fuentesaúco E ... 150 A2
Fuentes de Andalucía E ... 162 A2
Fuentes de Ebro E ... 153 A3
Fuentes de Jiloca E ... 152 A2
Fuentes de la Alcarria E ... 151 B5
Fuentes de León E ... 161 A3
Fuentes de Nava E ... 142 B2
Fuentes de Oñoro E ... 149 B3
Fuentes de Ropel E ... 142 B1
Fuentespalda E ... 153 B4
Fuentespina E ... 151 A4
Fuente-Tójar E ... 163 A3
Fuente Vaqueros E ... 163 A4
Fuentidueña E ... 151 A4
Fuentidueña de Tajo E ... 151 B4
Fuerte del Rey E ... 157 C4
Fügen A ... 108 B2
Fuglebjerg DK ... 65 A4
Fuglevik N ... 54 A1
Fuhrberg D ... 72 B2
Fulda D ... 82 B1
Fulgatore I ... 176 B1
Fully CH ... 119 A4
Fulnek CZ ... 98 B1
Fülöpszállás H ... 112 C3
Fulpmes A ... 108 B2
Fulunäs S ... 49 A5
Fumay F ... 91 B4
Fumel F ... 129 B3
Funäsdalen S ... 199 C9
Fundão P ... 148 B2
Funzie GB ... 33 A6
Furadouro P ... 148 B1
Fure N ... 46 A2
Fürstenau D ... 71 B4
Furstenau D ... 81 A5
Fürstenberg D ... 74 A2
Fürstenfeld A ... 111 B3
Fürstenfeldbruck D ... 108 A2
Fürstenstein D ... 96 C1
Fürstenwalde D ... 74 B3
Fürstenwerder D ... 74 A2
Fürstenzell D ... 96 C1
Furta H ... 113 B5
Fürth
Bayern D ... 94 B2
Hessen D ... 93 B4
Furth im Wald D ... 95 B4
Furtwangen D ... 106 A3
Furuby S ... 62 B3
Furudal S ... 50 A2
Furuflaten N ... 192 C4
Furulund S ... 61 D3
Furusjö S ... 60 B3
Fusa N ... 46 B2
Fuscaldo I ... 174 B2
Fusch an der Grossglocknerstrasse A ... 109 B3
Fushë Arrëz AL ... 182 A2
Fushë-Krujë AL ... 182 B1
Fusina I ... 122 B1
Fusio CH ... 107 C3
Füssen D ... 108 B1
Fustiñana E ... 144 B2
Futog SRB ... 126 B1
Futrikelv N ... 192 C3
Füzesabony H ... 113 B4
Füzesgyarmat H ... 113 B5
Fužine HR ... 123 B3
Fyllinge S ... 61 C2
Fynshav DK ... 64 B2
Fyresdal N ... 53 A4

G

Gaaldorf A ... 110 B1
Gabaldón E ... 158 B2
Gabarret F ... 128 C2
Gabčíkovo SK ... 111 B4
Gąbin PL ... 77 B4
Gabriac F ... 130 A1
Gabrovo BG ... 17 D6
Gaby I ... 119 B4
Gacé F ... 89 B4
Gacko BIH ... 139 B4
Gäddede S ... 199 A11
Gadebusch D ... 65 C4
Gadmen CH ... 106 C3
Gádor E ... 164 C2
Gádoros H ... 113 C4
Gael F ... 101 A3
Găeşti RO ... 17 C6
Gaeta I ... 169 B3
Gafanhoeira P ... 154 C2
Gaflenz A ... 110 B1
Gagarin RUS ... 9 E9
Gaggenau D ... 93 C4
Gagliano Castelferrato I ... 177 B3
Gagliano del Capo I ... 173 C4
Gagnet S ... 50 B2
Gaibanella I ... 121 C4
Gaildorf D ... 94 B1
Gaillac F ... 129 C4
Gaillefontaine F ... 90 B1
Gaillon F ... 89 A5
Gainsborough GB ... 40 B3
Gairloch GB ... 31 B3
Gairlochy GB ... 34 B3
Gáiro I ... 179 C3
Gaj
HR ... 124 B3
SRB ... 127 C3
Gaja-la-Selve F ... 146 A2
Gajanejos E ... 151 B5
Gajary SK ... 97 C4
Gajdobra SRB ... 126 B1
Galan F ... 145 A4
Galanta SK ... 111 A4
Galapagar E ... 151 B3
Galápagos E ... 151 B4
Galaroza E ... 161 B3
Galashiels GB ... 35 C5
Galatas GR ... 185 B4
Galaţi RO ... 17 C8
Galatina I ... 173 B4
Galatista GR ... 183 C5
Galátone I ... 173 B4
Galaxidi GR ... 184 A3
Galdakao E ... 143 A4
Galeata I ... 135 B4
Galende E ... 141 B4
Galera E ... 164 B2
Galéria F ... 180 A1
Galgamácsa H ... 112 B3
Galgate GB ... 38 A4
Galgon F ... 128 B2
Galinduste E ... 150 B2
Galinoporni CY ... 181 A3
Galisteo E ... 155 B4
Galizes P ... 148 B2
Galków PL ... 87 A3
Gallarate I ... 120 B1
Gallardon F ... 90 C1
Gallegos de Argañán E ... 149 B3
Gallegos del Solmirón E ... 150 B2
Galleguillos de Campos E ... 142 B1
Galleno I ... 135 B3
Galliate I ... 120 B1
Gallicano I ... 134 A3
Gállio I ... 121 B4
Gallipoli = Gelibolu TR ... 186 B1
Gallípoli I ... 173 B3
Gällivare S ... 196 B3
Gallizien A ... 110 C1
Gallneukirchen A ... 96 C2
Gällö S ... 199 C12
Gallocanta E ... 152 B2
Gällstad S ... 60 B3
Gallur E ... 144 C2
Galmisdale GB ... 31 C2
Galmpton GB ... 43 B3
Galston GB ... 36 A2
Galta N ... 52 A1
Galtelli I ... 178 B3
Galten DK ... 59 B2
Galtür A ... 107 C5
Galve de Sorbe E ... 151 A4
Galveias P ... 154 B2
Gálvez E ... 157 A3
Galway IRL ... 28 A2
Gamaches F ... 90 B1
Gámbara I ... 120 B3
Gambárie I ... 175 C1
Gambassi Terme I ... 135 B3
Gambatesa I ... 170 B2
Gambolò I ... 120 B1
Gaming A ... 110 B2
Gamla Uppsala S ... 51 C4
Gamleby S ... 62 A4
Gamlingay GB ... 44 A3
Gammelgarn S ... 57 C4
Gammelstad S ... 196 D5
Gammertingen D ... 107 A4
Gams CH ... 107 B4
Gamvik
Finnmark N ... 192 B6
Finnmark N ... 193 A12
Gan F ... 145 A3
Gáname E ... 149 A3
Ganda di Martello I ... 108 C1
Gandarela P ... 148 A1
Ganddal N ... 52 B1
Ganderkesee D ... 72 A1
Gandesa E ... 153 A4
Gandía E ... 159 C3
Gandino I ... 120 B2
Gandrup DK ... 58 A3
Ganges F ... 130 B2
Gånghester S ... 60 B3
Gangi I ... 177 B3
Gangkofen D ... 95 C4
Gannat F ... 116 A3
Gannay-sur-Loire F ... 104 C2
Gänserdorf A ... 97 C4
Ganzlin D ... 73 A5
Gap F ... 132 A2
Gara H ... 125 A5
Garaballa E ... 158 B2
Garaguso I ... 172 B2
Garbayuela E ... 156 A2
Garbhallt GB ... 34 B2
Garbsen D ... 72 B2
Garching D ... 109 A3
Garciaz E ... 156 A2
Garcihernández E 150 B2
Garcillán E ... 151 B3
Garcinarro E ... 151 B5
Garcisobaco E ... 162 B2
Garda I ... 121 B3
Gardanne F ... 131 B4
Gärdås S ... 49 B5
Gårdby S ... 63 B4
Gardeja PL ... 69 B3
Gardelegen D ... 73 B4
Gardermoen N ... 48 B3
Gardiki GR ... 182 E3
Garding D ... 64 B1
Gardone Riviera I ... 121 B3
Gardone Val Trómpia I ... 120 B3
Gárdony H ... 112 B2
Gardouch F ... 146 A2
Gårdsjö S ... 55 B5
Gårdskär S ... 51 B4
Gards Köpinge S ... 63 C2
Garein F ... 128 B2
Garelochhead GB ... 34 B3
Garéoult F ... 132 B2
Garešnica HR ... 124 B2
Garéssio I ... 133 A4
Garforth GB ... 40 B2
Gargaliani GR ... 184 B2
Gargaligas E ... 156 A2
Gargallo E ... 153 B3
Garganta la Olla E 150 B2
Gargantiel E ... 156 B3
Gargellen A ... 107 C4
Gargilesse-Dampierre F ... 103 C3
Gargnano I ... 121 B3
Gargnäs S ... 195 E8
Gárgoles de Abajo E ... 152 B1
Gargrave GB ... 40 B1
Garitz D ... 73 C5
Garlasco I ... 120 B1
Garlieston GB ... 36 B2
Garlin F ... 128 C2
Garlitos E ... 156 B2
Garmisch-Partenkirchen D 108 B2
Garnat-sur-Engièvre F ... 104 C2
Garpenberg S ... 50 B3
Garphyttan S ... 55 A5
Garray E ... 143 C4
Garrel D ... 71 B5
Garriguella E ... 146 B4
Garrison GB ... 26 B2
Garrovillas E ... 155 B4
Garrucha E ... 164 B3
Gars-am-Kamp A ... 97 C3
Garsås S ... 50 B1
Garsdale Head GB 37 B4
Gärsnäs S ... 63 C2
Garstang GB ... 38 A4
Gartow D ... 73 A4
Gartz D ... 74 A3
Gærum DK ... 58 A3
Garvagh GB ... 27 B4
Garvão P ... 160 B1
Garve GB ... 32 D2
Garwolin PL ... 12 C4
Garz D ... 66 B2
Garzyn PL ... 85 A4
Gąsawa PL ... 76 B2
Gåsborn S ... 49 C6
Gaschurn A ... 107 C5
Gascueña E ... 152 B1
Gasny F ... 90 B1
Gąsocin PL ... 77 B5
Gastes F ... 128 B1
Gastouni GR ... 184 B2
Gastouri GR ... 182 D1
Gata
E ... 149 B3
HR ... 138 B2
Gata de Gorgos E 159 C4
Gătaia RO ... 126 B3
Gatchina RUS ... 9 C7
Gatehouse of Fleet GB ... 36 B2
Gátér H ... 113 C3
Gateshead GB ... 37 B5
Gátova E ... 159 B3
Gattendorf A ... 111 A3
Gatteo a Mare I ... 136 A1
Gattinara I ... 119 B5
Gattorna I ... 134 A2
Gaucín E ... 162 B2
Gaulstad N ... 199 B9
Gaupne N ... 47 A4
Gautefall N ... 53 A4
Gauting D ... 108 A2
Gauto S ... 195 D7
Gava E ... 147 C3
Gavardo I ... 121 B3
Gavarnie F ... 145 B3
Gávavencsello H ... 113 A5
Gavi I ... 120 C1
Gavião P ... 154 B3
Gavirate I ... 120 B1
Gävle S ... 51 B4
Gavoi I ... 178 B3
Gavorrano I ... 135 C3
Gavray F ... 88 B2
Gavrio GR ... 185 B5
Gävunda S ... 49 B6
Gaweinstal A ... 97 C4
Gaworzyce PL ... 85 A3
Gawroniec PL ... 75 A5
Gaydon GB ... 44 A2
Gayton GB ... 41 C4
Gazipaşa TR ... 189 C7
Gazoldo degli Ippoliti I ... 121 B3
Gazzuolo I ... 121 B3
Gbelce SK ... 112 B2
Gdańsk PL ... 69 A3
Gdinj HR ... 138 B2
Gdov RUS ... 8 C5
Gdów PL ... 99 B4
Gdynia PL ... 69 A3
Gea de Albarracin E ... 152 B2
Geary GB ... 31 B2
Géaudot F ... 91 C4
Geaune F ... 128 C2
Gebesee D ... 82 A2
Gebiz TR ... 189 B5
Gebze TR ... 187 B4
Géderlak H ... 112 C2
Gedern D ... 81 B5
Gedinne B ... 91 B4
Gediz TR ... 187 D4
Gèdre F ... 145 B4
Gedser DK ... 65 B4
Gedsted DK ... 58 B2
Geel B ... 79 A4
Geesthacht D ... 72 A3
Geetbets B ... 79 B5
Gefell D ... 83 B3
Gehrden D ... 72 B2
Gehren D ... 82 B3
Geilenkirchen D ... 80 B2
Geilo N ... 47 B5
Geinsheim D ... 93 B4
Geisa D ... 82 B1
Geiselhöring D ... 95 C4
Geiselwind D ... 94 B2
Geisenfeld D ... 95 C3
Geisenhausen D ... 95 C4
Geisenheim D ... 93 B4
Geising D ... 84 B1
Geisingen D ... 107 B3
Geislingen D ... 94 C1
Geistthal A ... 110 B2
Geiterygghytta N ... 47 B4
Geithain D ... 83 A4
Geithus N ... 48 C1
Gela I ... 177 B3
Geldermalsen NL ... 79 A5
Geldern D ... 80 A2
Geldrop NL ... 80 A1
Geleen NL ... 80 B1
Gelembe TR ... 186 C2
Gelendost TR ... 189 A6
Gelibolu = Gallipoli TR ... 186 B1
Gelida E ... 147 C2
Gelnhausen D ... 81 B5
Gelnica SK ... 99 C4
Gelsa E ... 153 A3
Gelse H ... 111 C3
Gelsenkirchen D ... 80 A3
Gelsted DK ... 59 C2
Geltendorf D ... 108 A2
Gelterkinden CH ... 106 B2
Gelting D ... 64 B2
Gelu RO ... 126 A3
Gelves E ... 162 A1
Gembloux B ... 79 B4
Gemeaux F ... 105 B4
Gémenos F ... 132 B1
Gemerská Poloma SK ... 99 C4
Gemerská Ves SK ... 99 C4
Gemert NL ... 80 A1
Gemla S ... 62 B2
Gemlik TR ... 186 B4
Gemmenich B ... 80 B1
Gemona del Friuli I ... 122 A2
Gémozac F ... 114 C3
Gemund D ... 80 B2
Gemünden
Bayern D ... 94 A1
Hessen D ... 81 B4
Rheinland-Pfalz D ... 93 B3
Genappe B ... 79 B4
Génave E ... 164 A2
Genazzano I ... 169 B2
Gençay F ... 115 B4
Gencsapáti H ... 111 B3
Gendringen NL ... 80 A2
Genelard F ... 104 C3
Genemuiden NL ... 70 B3
Generalski Stol HR ... 123 B4
Geneva = Genève CH ... 118 A3
Genevad S ... 61 C3
Genève = Geneva CH ... 118 A3
Genevriéres F ... 105 B4
Gengenbach D ... 93 C4
Genillé F ... 103 B3
Genk B ... 80 B1
Genlis F ... 105 B4
Gennep NL ... 80 A1
Genner DK ... 64 A2
Gennes F ... 102 B1
Genoa = Génova I 134 A1
Genola I ... 133 A3
Génova = Genoa I 134 A1
Genowefa PL ... 76 B3
Gensingen D ... 93 B3
Gent = Ghent B ... 79 A3
Genthin D ... 73 B5
Gentioux F ... 116 B1
Genzano di Lucánia I ... 172 B2
Genzano di Roma I ... 168 B2
Georgenthal D ... 82 B2
Georgsmarienhütte D ... 71 B5
Gera D ... 83 B4
Geraards-bergen B 79 B3
Gerace I ... 175 C2
Geraci Sículo I ... 177 B3
Geraki GR ... 184 C3
Gérardmer F ... 106 A1
Geras A ... 97 C3
Gerbéviller F ... 92 C2
Gerbini I ... 177 B3
Gerbstedt D ... 83 A3
Gerði IS ... 191 C9
Gerede TR ... 187 B7
Gerena E ... 161 B3
Geretsried D ... 108 B2
Gérgal E ... 164 B2
Gergy F ... 105 C3
Gerindote E ... 150 C3
Gerjen H ... 112 C2
Gerlos A ... 108 B3
Germay F ... 92 C1
Germencik TR ... 188 B2
Germering D ... 108 A2
Germersheim D ... 93 B4
Gernika-Lumo E ... 143 A4
Gernrode D ... 82 A3
Gernsbach D ... 93 C4
Gernsheim D ... 93 B4
Geroda D ... 82 B1
Gerola Alta I ... 120 A2
Geroldsgrun D ... 83 B3
Gerolsbach D ... 95 C3
Gerolstein D ... 80 B2
Gerolzhofen D ... 94 B2
Gerovo HR ... 123 B3
Gerpinnes B ... 79 B4
Gerrards Cross GB 44 B3
Gerri de la Sal E ... 147 B2
Gersfeld D ... 82 B1
Gerstetten D ... 94 C2
Gersthofen D ... 94 C2
Gerstungen D ... 82 B2
Gerswalde D ... 74 A2
Gerzat F ... 116 B3
Gerze TR ... 23 A8
Gerzen D ... 95 C4
Gescher D ... 71 C4
Geseke D ... 81 A4
Geslau D ... 94 B2
Gespunsart F ... 91 B4
Gesté F ... 101 B4
Gestorf D ... 72 B2
Gesualda I ... 170 C3
Gesunda S ... 50 B1
Gesztely H ... 113 A4
Geta FIN ... 51 B6
Getafe E ... 151 B4
Getinge S ... 60 C2
Getxo E ... 143 A4
Geversdorf D ... 64 C2
Gevgelija MK ... 182 B4
Gevora del Caudillo E ... 155 C4
Gevrey-Chambertin F ... 105 B3
Gex F ... 118 A3
Gey D ... 80 B2
Geyikli TR ... 186 C1
Geysir IS ... 190 C5
Geyve TR ... 187 B5
Gföhl A ... 97 C3
Ghedi I ... 120 B3
Ghent = Gent B ... 79 A3
Gheorgheni RO ... 17 B6
Ghigo I ... 119 C4
Ghilarza I ... 178 B2
Ghisonaccia F ... 180 A2
Ghisoni F ... 180 A2
Gialtra GR ... 182 E4
Gianitsa GR ... 182 C4
Giardinetto Vécchio I ... 171 B3
Giardini Naxos I ... 177 B4
Giarratana I ... 177 B3
Giarre I ... 177 B4
Giat F ... 116 B2
Giaveno I ... 119 B4
Giazza I ... 121 B4
Giba I ... 179 C2
Gibellina Nuova I ... 176 B1
Gibostad N ... 194 A9
Gibraleón E ... 161 B3
Gibraltar GBZ ... 162 B2
Gic H ... 111 B4
Gideå S ... 200 C5
Gideåkroken S ... 200 B3
Gidle PL ... 86 B3
Giebelstadt D ... 94 B1
Gieboldehausen D ... 82 A2
Gielniów PL ... 87 A4
Gielow D ... 74 A1
Gien F ... 103 B4
Giengen D ... 94 C2
Giens F ... 132 B2
Giera RO ... 126 B2
Gieselwerder D ... 81 A5
Giessen D ... 81 B4
Gieten NL ... 71 A3
Giethoorn NL ... 70 B3
Giffaumont-Champaubert F ... 91 C4
Gifford GB ... 35 C5
Gifhorn D ... 73 B3
Gige H ... 125 A3
Gignac F ... 130 B2
Gijón = Xixón E ... 142 A1
Gilena E ... 162 A3
Gilford GB ... 27 B4
Gillberga S ... 55 A3
Gilleleje DK ... 61 C2
Gilley F ... 105 B5
Gilley-sur-Loire F ... 104 C2
Gillingham
Dorset GB ... 43 A4
Medway GB ... 45 B4
Gilocourt F ... 90 B2
Gilserberg D ... 81 B5
Gilsland GB ... 37 B4
Gilze NL ... 79 A4
Gimåt S ... 200 C4
Gimo S ... 51 B5
Gimont F ... 129 C3
Ginasservis F ... 132 B1
Gingelom B ... 79 B5
Gingst D ... 66 B2
Ginosa I ... 171 C4
Ginzling A ... 108 B2
Giões P ... 160 B2
Gióia dei Marsi I ... 169 B3
Gióia del Colle I ... 173 B2
Gióia Sannitica I ... 170 B2
Gióia Táuro I ... 175 C1
Gioiosa Iónica I ... 175 C2
Gioiosa Marea I ... 177 A3
Giosla GB ... 31 A2
Giovinazzo I ... 171 B4
Girifalco I ... 175 C2
Giromagny F ... 106 B1
Girona E ... 147 C3
Gironcourt-sur-Vraine F ... 92 C1
Gironella E ... 147 B2
Gironville-sous-les-Côtes F ... 92 C1
Girvan GB ... 36 A2
Gislaved S ... 60 B3
Gislev DK ... 59 C3
Gisors F ... 90 B1
Gissi I ... 170 A2
Gistad S ... 56 B1
Gistel B ... 78 A2
Gistrup DK ... 58 B3
Giswil CH ... 106 C3
Githio GR ... 184 C3
Giugliano in Campania I ... 170 C2
Giulianova I ... 136 C2
Giulvăz RO ... 126 B2
Giurgiu RO ... 17 D6
Give DK ... 59 C2
Givet F ... 91 A4
Givors F ... 117 B4
Givry
B ... 79 B4
F ... 104 C3
Givry-en-Argonne F ... 91 C4
Givskud DK ... 59 C2
Giżalki PL ... 76 B2
Gizeux F ... 102 B2
Giżycko PL ... 12 A4
Gizzeria I ... 175 C2
Gizzeria Lido I ... 175 C2
Gjedved DK ... 59 C2
Gjegjan AL ... 182 B2
Gjendesheim N ... 47 A5
Gjerde N ... 46 B3
Gjerlev DK ... 58 B3
Gjermundshamn N 46 B2
Gjerrild DK ... 58 B3
Gjerstad N ... 53 B5
Gjesås N ... 49 B4
Gjesvær N ... 193 A9
Gjirokastër AL ... 182 C2
Gjøfjell N ... 54 A1
Gjøl DK ... 58 A2
Gjøra N ... 198 C6
Gjøvik N ... 48 B2
Gladbeck D ... 80 A2
Gladenbach D ... 81 B4
Gladstad N ... 195 E2
Glamis GB ... 35 B4
Glamoč BIH ... 138 A2
Glamsbjerg DK ... 59 C3
Gland CH ... 105 C5
Glandorf D ... 71 B4
Glanegg A ... 110 C1
Glanshammar S ... 56 A1
Glarus CH ... 107 B4
Glasgow GB ... 35 C3
Glashütte
Bayern D ... 108 B2
Sachsen D ... 84 B1
Glastonbury GB ... 43 A4
Glatzau A ... 110 C2
Glauchau D ... 83 B4
Glava S ... 54 A3
Glavatičevo BIH ... 139 B4
Glavičice BIH ... 127 C1
Gŭlŭbovo BG ... 183 A7
Glein
A ... 110 B1
N ... 195 D3
Gleinstätten A ... 110 C2
Gleisdorf A ... 110 B2
Glenamoy IRL ... 26 B1
Glenarm GB ... 27 B5
Glenavy GB ... 27 B4
Glenbarr GB ... 34 C2
Glenbeigh IRL ... 29 B2
Glenbrittle GB ... 31 B2
Glencoe GB ... 34 B2
Glencolumbkille IRL ... 26 B2
Glendalough IRL ... 30 A2
Glenealy IRL ... 30 B2
Glenelg GB ... 31 B3
Glenfinnan GB ... 34 B2
Glengarriff IRL ... 29 C2
Glenluce GB ... 36 B2
Glennamaddy IRL ... 28 A3
Glenrothes GB ... 35 B4
Glenties IRL ... 26 B2
Glesborg DK ... 58 B3
Glesien D ... 83 A4
Gletsch CH ... 106 C3
Glewitz D ... 66 B1
Glifada GR ... 185 B4
Glimåkra S ... 63 B2
Glin IRL ... 29 B2
Glina HR ... 124 B2
Glinde D ... 72 A3
Glinojeck PL ... 77 B5
Glinsk IRL ... 28 A2
Gliwice PL ... 86 B2
Glödnitz A ... 109 C5
Gloggnitz A ... 110 B2
Głogoczów PL ... 99 B3
Glogonj SRB ... 127 C2
Glogovac SRB ... 127 C3
Głogów PL ... 85 A4
Głogówek PL ... 86 B1
Glomel F ... 100 A2
Glomfjord N ... 195 D4
Glommen S ... 60 C2
Glommersträsk S ... 196 D2
Glonn D ... 108 B2
Glorenza I ... 108 C1
Gloria P ... 154 B2
Glosa GR ... 183 D5

Glossop GB 40 B2
Gloucester GB. . . .39 C4
Głowaczów PL 87 A5
Główczyce PL 68 A2
Głowen D 73 B5
Głowno PL 77 C4
Gložan SRB 126 B1
Głubczyce PL 86 B1
Głuchołazy PL 85 B5
Głuchów PL 87 A4
Głuchowo PL 75 B4
Glücksburg D 64 B2
Glückstadt D 64 C2
Glumina BIH 139 A5
Glumsø DK 65 A4
Glušci SRB 127 C1
Glusk BY 13 B8
Głuszyca PL 85 B4
Glyngøre DK 58 B1
Glyn Neath GB. 39 C3
Gmünd
 Karnten A 109 C4
 Nieder Österreich
 A 96 C2
Gmund D 108 B2
Gmunden A 109 B4
Gnarp S 200 D3
Gnarrenburg D 72 A2
Gnesau A 109 C4
Gnesta S 56 A3
Gnięchowice PL 85 A4
Gniew PL 69 B3
Gniewkowo PL 76 B3
Gniezno PL 76 B2
Gnoien D 66 C1
Gnojnice BIH 139 B3
Gnojno PL 87 B4
Gnosall GB 40 C1
Gnosjö S 60 B3
Göbel TR 186 B3
Göçbeyli TR 186 C2
Goch D 80 A2
Gochsheim D 94 A2
Göd H 112 B3
Godalming GB. 44 B3
Godby FIN 51 B6
Goðdalir IS 190 B6
Goddelsheim D 81 A4
Gódega di Sant'Urbano
 I 122 B1
Godegård S 56 B1
Godelheim D 81 A5
Goderville F 89 A4
Godiasco I 120 C2
Godič SLO 123 A3
Godkowo PL 69 A4
Godmanchester
 GB 44 A3
Gödöllö H 112 B3
Gödre H 125 A3
Godshill GB. 44 C2
Godzikowice PL 85 B5
Godziszewo PL 69 A3
Goes NL 79 A3
Goetzenbrück F 93 C3
Góglio I 119 A5
Gogolin PL 86 B2
Göhren D 66 B2
Goirle NL 79 A5
Góis P 148 B1
Góito I 121 B3
Goizueta E 144 A2
Gojna Gora SRB 127 D2
Gójsk PL 77 B4
Gökçedağ TR 186 C3
Gökçen TR 188 A2
Gökçeören TR 188 A3
Gökçeyazı TR 186 C2
Göktepe TR 188 B3
Gol N 47 B5
Gola
 HR 124 A3
 N 48 A1
Gołańcz PL 76 B2
Gölbaşı TR 23 B7
Gölby FIN 51 B6
Gölcük
 Kocaeli TR 187 B4
 Niğde TR 23 B8
Golčův Jenikov CZ . .97 B3
Goldach D 107 B4
Goldbach D 93 A5
Goldbeck D 73 B4
Goldberg D 73 A5
Goldelund D 64 B2
Goldenstedt D 72 B1
Gołębiewo PL 69 A3
Golegã P 154 B2
Goleniów PL 75 A3
Golfo Aranci I 178 B3
Gölhisar TR 189 B4
Golina PL 76 B3
Gölle H 112 C2
Göllersdorf A 97 C4
Golling an der Salzach
 A 109 B4
Gölmarmara TR 186 D2
Golnice PL 84 A3
Golnik SLO 123 A3
Gölova TR 189 C5
Gölpazarı TR 187 B5
Gols A 111 B3
Golspie GB 32 D3
Golssen D 74 C2
Golub-Dobrzyń PL . .77 A4
Golubinci SRB 127 C2
Goluchów PL 86 A1
Golymin-Ośrodek
 PL 77 B5
Golzow D 73 B5
Gomagoi I 108 C1
Gómara E 152 A1
Gomaringen D 93 C5
Gömbe TR 189 C4
Gömeç TR 186 C1
Gomel = Homyel
 BY 13 B9
Gomes Aires P 160 B1
Gómezserracin E .150 A3

Gommern D 73 B4
Gomulin PL 86 A3
Gonäs S 50 B2
Goncelin F 118 B2
Gończyce PL 87 A5
Gondomar
 E 140 B2
 P 148 A1
Gondrecourt-le-
 Château F 92 C1
Gondrin F 128 C3
Gönen
 Balıkesir TR 186 B2
 Isparta TR 189 B5
Gonfaron F 132 B2
Goñi E 144 B2
Goni
 GR 182 D4
 I 179 C3
Gonnesa I 179 C2
Gonnosfanádiga I .179 C2
Gonzaga I 121 C3
Goodrich GB 39 C4
Goodwick GB 39 B1
Gooik B 79 B4
Goole GB 40 B3
Goor NL 71 B3
Göpfritz an der Wild
 A 97 C3
Goppenstein CH . .119 A4
Göppingen D 94 C1
Gor E 164 B2
Góra
 Dolnośląskie PL . .85 A4
 Mazowieckie PL . .77 B5
Gorafe E 164 B1
Gorawino PL 67 C4
Goražde BIH 139 B4
Gőrbeháza H 113 B5
Gordaliza del Pino
 E 142 B1
Gördes TR 186 D3
Gørding DK 59 C1
Górdola CH 120 A1
Gordon GB 35 C5
Gordoncillo E 142 B1
Gorebridge GB 35 C4
Gorenje Jelenje
 HR 123 B3
Gorenji Jelenje
 . . . . .123 B3
Gorey
 GB 88 A1
 IRL 30 B2
Gorgonzola I 120 B2
Gorica HR 137 A4
Gorican HR 124 A2
Gorinchem NL 79 A4
Goring GB 44 B2
Gorizia = Görz
 I 122 B2
Górki PL 77 B4
Gorleben D 73 A4
Gorleston-on-sea
 GB 41 C5
Gørlev DK 61 D1
Görlitz D 84 A2
Görmin D 66 C2
Górna Grupa PL 69 B3
Gorna Oryakhovitsa
 BG 17 D6
Gornja Gorevnica
 SRB 127 D2
Gornja Ploča HR . . .137 A4
Gornja Radgona
 SLO 110 C2
Gornja Sabanta
 SRB 127 D3
Gornja Trešnjevica
 SRB 127 C2
Gornja Tuzla BIH . .125 C4
Gornja Vas SLO 123 B3
Gornje Polje MNE .139 C4
Gornje Ratkovo
 BIH 124 C2
Gornji Grad SLO . . .123 A3
Gornji Humac HR .138 B2
Gornji Jasenjani
 BIH 139 B3
Gornji Kamengrad
 BIH 124 C2
Gornji Kneginec
 HR 124 A2
Gornji Kosinj HR . .123 C4
Gornji Milanovac
 SRB 127 C2
Gornji Podgradci
 BIH 124 B3
Gornji Ravno BIH .138 B3
Gornji Sjenicak
 HR 124 B1
Gornji Vakuf BIH .138 B3
Górno PL 87 B4
Görömböly H 113 A4
Górowo Iławeckie
 PL 69 A5
Gorran Haven GB . . .42 B2
Gorredijk NL 70 A3
Gorron F 88 B3
Gorseinon GB 39 C2
Gort IRL 28 A3
Gortin GB 27 B3
Görzke D 73 B5
Górzno
 Kujawsko-Pomorskie
 PL 77 A4
 Zachodnio-Pomorskie
 . . . . .75 A4
Gorzów Śląski PL . .86 A2
Gorzów Wielkopolski
 PL 75 B4
Górzyca PL 74 B3
Gorzyce PL 98 B2
Górzyn PL 84 A2
Gorzyń PL 75 B4
Gorzyno PL 68 A2
Gosaldo I 121 A4
Gosau A 109 B4

Gosberton GB 41 C3
Gościcino PL 68 A3
Gościęcin PL 86 B2
Gościm PL 75 B4
Gościno PL 67 B4
Gosforth GB 36 B3
Goslar D 82 A2
Goslice PL 77 B4
Gospić HR 137 A4
Gosport GB 44 C2
Gössäter S 55 B4
Goss Ilsede D 72 B3
Gössnitz D 83 B4
Gössweinstein D. 95 B3
Gostivar MK. 182 B2
Gostków PL 77 C4
Göstling an der Ybbs
 A 110 B1
Grandson CH 106 C1
Grandvillars F 106 B1
Grandvilliers F 90 B1
Grañén E 145 C3
Grangärde S 50 B1
Grange IRL 26 B2
Grangemouth GB . . .35 B4
Grange-over-Sands
 . . . . .36 B4
Grängesberg S 50 B1
Granges-de Crouhens
 F 145 B4
Granges-sur-Vologne
 F 106 A1
Gräningen D 73 B5
Granitola-Torretta
 I 176 B1
Granja
 Évora P 155 C3
 Porto P 148 A1
Granja de Moreruela
 E 142 C1
Granja de
 Torrehermosa E 156 B2
Gränna S 55 B5
Grannäs
 Västerbotten S . .195 E7
 Västerbotten S . .195 E8
Granö S 200 B5
Granollers E 147 C3
Granowiec PL 85 A5
Granowo PL 75 B5
Gransee D 74 A2
Gransherad N 53 A5
Grantham GB 40 C3
Grantown-on-Spey
 GB 32 D3
Grantshouse GB 35 C5
Granville F 88 B2
Grærup Strand DK .59 C1
Gräsås S 60 C2
Grasbakken N . . .193 B12
Grasberg D 72 A2
Grasmere GB 36 B3
Grassano I 172 B2
Grassau D 109 B3
Grasse F 132 B2
Grassington GB 40 A2
Græsted DK 61 C2
Gråsten DK 64 B2
Grästorp S 54 B3
Gratkorn A 110 B2
Gråträsk S 196 D2
Gratwein A 110 B2
Graus E 145 C4
Grávalos E 144 B2
Gravberget N 49 B4
Grave NL 80 A1
Gravedona I 120 A2
Gravelines F 78 A2
Gravellona Toce I . .119 B5
Gravendal S 50 B1
Gravens DK 59 C2
Gravesend GB 45 B4
Graveson F 131 B3
Gravina in Púglia
 I 172 B2
Gray F 105 B4
Grayrigg GB 37 B4
Grays GB 45 B4
Grayshott GB 44 B3
Graz A 110 B2
Grazalema E 162 B2
Grazzano Visconti
 I 120 C2
Greåker N 54 A2
Great Dunmow GB .45 B4
Great Malvern GB . . .39 B4
Great Torrington
 GB 42 B2
Great Waltham GB .45 B4
Great Yarmouth
 GB 41 C5
Grebbestad S 54 B2
Grebenstein D 81 A5
Grębocice PL 85 A4
Grębocin PL 76 A3
Greding D 95 B3
Gredstedbro DK 59 C1
Greencastle IRL 27 A4
Greenhead GB. 37 B4
Greenlaw GB 35 C5
Greenock GB 34 C3
Greenway GB 39 C2
Greenwich GB 45 B4
Grefrath D 80 A2
Greifenburg A 109 C4
Greiffenberg D 74 A2
Greifswald D 66 B2
Grein A 110 A1
Greipstad N 53 B3
Greiz D 83 B4
Grenaa DK 58 B3
Grenade F 129 C4

Gran N 48 B2
Granada E 163 A4
Granard IRL 27 C3
Grañas E 140 A3
Granátula de Calatrava
 E 157 B4
Grancey-le-Château
 F 105 B4
Grandas de Salime
 E 141 A4
Grandcamp-Maisy
 F 88 A2
Grand-Champ F .100 B3
Grand Couronne F .89 A5
Grand-Fougeray F 101 B4
Grândola P 160 A1
Grandpré F 91 B4
Grandrieu
 B 79 B4
 F 117 C3
Grenade-sur-l'Adour
 F 128 C2
Grenchen CH 106 B2
Grendi N 53 B3
Grenivik IS 191 B7
Grenoble F 118 B2
Gréoux-les-Bains
 F 132 B1
Gresenhorst D 66 B1
Gressoney-la-Trinité
 I 119 B4
Gressoney-St.-Jean
 I 119 B4
Gressthal D 82 B2
Gressvik N 54 A1
Gresten A 110 B2
Gretna GB 36 B3
Greussen D 82 A2
Greve in Chianti I .135 B4
Greven
 Mecklenburg-
 Vorpommern D . . .73 A3
 Nordrhein-Westfalen
 . . . . .71 B4
Grevena GR 182 C3
Grevenbroich D 80 A2
Grevenmacher L 92 B2
Grevesmühlen D 65 C4
Grevestrand DK 61 D2
Grevie S 61 C2
Greystoke GB 36 B4
Greystones IRL 30 A2
Grez-Doiceau B 79 B4
Grèzec F 129 B4
Grez-en-Bouère F .102 B1
Grezzana I 121 B4
Grgar SLO 122 A2
Grgurevci SRB 127 B1
Griesbach D 96 C1
Griesheim D 93 B4
Gries in Sellrain A 108 B2
Grieskirchen A 109 A4
Griffen A 110 C1
Grignan F 131 A3
Grignano I 122 B2
Grigno I 121 A4
Grignols F 128 B2
Grignon F 118 B3
Grijota E 142 B2
Grijpskerk NL 71 A3
Grillby S 56 A3
Grimaud F 132 B2
Grimbergen B 79 B4
Grimma D 83 A4
Grimmen D 66 B2
Grimmialp CH 106 C2
Grimsås S 60 B3
Grimsby GB 41 B3
Grímsstaðir IS 191 B9
Grimstad N 53 B4
Grímstorp S 62 A2
Grindavik IS 190 D3
Grindelwald CH 106 C3
Grindheim N 52 B3
Grindsted DK 59 C1
Griñón E 151 B4
Gripenberg S 62 A2
Gripsholm S 56 A3
Grisolles F 129 C4
Grisslehamn S 51 B5
Gritley GB 33 C4
Grizebeck GB 36 B3
Grndina BIH 124 C2
Gröbming A 109 B4
Gröbzig D 83 A3
Grocka SRB 127 C2
Gröditz D 83 A5
Gródki PL 77 A5
Grodków PL 85 B5
Grodziec PL 76 B3
Grodzisk Mazowiecki
 PL 77 B5
Grodzisk Wielkoposki
 PL 75 B5
Groenlo NL 71 B3
Groesbeek NL 80 A1
Grohote HR 138 B2
Groitzsch D 83 A4
Groix F 100 B2
Grójec PL 77 C5
Grom PL 77 A5
Gromiljca BIH 139 B4
Grömitz D 65 B3
Gromnik PL 99 B4
Gromo I 120 B2
Gronau
 Niedersachsen D .72 B2
 Nordrhein-Westfalen
 . . . . .71 B4
Grønbjerg DK 59 B1
Grönenbach D 107 B5
Grong N 199 A9
Grönhögen S 63 B4
Groningen
 D 73 C4
 NL 71 A3
Grønnestrand DK . . .58 A2
Grono CH. 120 A2
Grönskåra S 62 A3
Grootegast NL 71 A3
Gropello Cairoli I . .120 B1
Grorud N 48 B2
Grósio I 120 A3
Grossa SRB 127 D2
Grossalmerode D . . .82 A1
Grossarl A 109 B4
Grossalupe E 156 A2
Grossarma E 151 B3
Gross-Bieberau D . . .93 B4
Gross Berkel D 72 B2
Gross-Bodungen D .82 A2
Gross-börnecke D . . .82 A3
Grossburgwedel D . .72 B2
Grossschönau D 84 B2
Gross-Dölln D 74 B2
Grossenbrode D 65 B4
Grossenehrich D 82 A2
Grossengottern D . . .82 A2
Grossenhain D 83 A5

Grossenkneten D . .71 B5
Grossenlüder D 81 B5
Grossensee D 72 A3
Grossenzersdorf
 A 111 A3
Grosseto I 135 C4
Gross-Gerau D 93 B4
Grossgerungs A 96 C2
Grossglobnitz A 97 C3
Grosshabersdorf D 94 B2
Grossharras A 97 C4
Grosshartmansdorf
 D 83 B5
Grosshöchstetten
 CH 106 C2
Grosskrut A 97 C4
Gross Lafferde D . . .72 B3
Gross Leutheb D . . .74 B3
Grosslohra D 82 A2
Gross Muckrow D . . .74 B3
Gross Oesingen D . .72 B3
Grossostheim D 93 B5
Grosspertholz A 96 C2
Grosspetersdorf
 A 111 B3
Grosspostwitz D 84 A2
Grossraming A 110 B1
Grossräschen D 84 A2
Gross Reken D 80 A3
Grossrinderfeld D . . .94 B1
Grossröhrsdorf D 84 A2
Gross Sarau D 65 C3
Gross Särchen D 84 A2
Grossschirma D 83 B5
Gross Schönebeck
 D 74 B2
Grossschweinbarth
 A 97 C4
Grosssieglharts A . . .97 C3
Grosssölk A 109 B4
Gross Umstadt D . . .93 B4
Grosswarasdorf A 111 B3
Gross Warnow D 73 A4
Gross-Weikersdorf
 A 97 C3
Gross-Welle D 73 A5
Grosswilfersdorf
 A 110 B2
Gross Wokern D 65 C5
Grostenquin F 92 C2
Grosuplje SLO 123 B3
Grotli N 198 C4
Grötlingbo S 57 C4
Grottáglie I 173 B3
Grottaminarda I 170 B3
Grottammare I 136 C2
Grotte di Castro I .168 A1
Grotteria I 175 C2
Gróttole I 172 B2
Grouw NL 70 A2
Grov N 194 B8
Grova N 53 A4
Grove E 140 B2
Grua N 48 B2
Grube D 65 B4
Grubišno Polje
 HR 124 B3
Grude BIH 138 B3
Grudusk PL 77 A5
Grudziądz PL 69 B3
Grue N 49 B4
Gruissan F 130 B2
Grullos E 141 A4
Grumo Áppula I 171 B4
Grums S 55 A4
Grünau im Almtal
 A 109 B4
Grünberg D 81 B4
Grünburg A 110 B1
Grundarfjörður IS 190 C2
Gründau D 81 B5
Gründelhardt D 94 B1
Grundforsen S 49 A4
Grundlsee A 109 B4
Grundsund S 54 B2
Grunewald D 84 A1
Grungedal N 53 A3
Grunow D 74 B3
Grünstadt D 93 B4
Gruvberget S 50 A3
Gruyères CH 106 C2
Gruža SRB 127 D2
Grybów PL 99 B4
Grycksbo S 50 B2
Gryfice PL 67 C4
Gryfino D 74 A3
Gryfów Śląski PL . . .84 A3
Gryllefjord N 194 A8
Grymyr N 48 B2
Gryt S 56 B2
Grytgöl S 56 B1
Grythyttan S 55 A5
Grytnäs S 57 B3
Grzmiąca PL 68 B1
Grzybno PL 74 A3
Grzywna PL 76 A3
Gschnitz A 108 B2
Gschwend D 94 C1
Gstaad CH 106 C2
Gsteig CH 119 A4
Gstadt D 109 B3
Guadahortuna E . . .163 A4
Guadalajara E 151 B4
Guadalaviar E 152 B2
Guadalcanal E 156 B2
Guadalcázar E 162 A3
Guadalix de la Sierra
 E 151 B4
Guadálmez E 156 B3
Guadalupe E 156 A2
Guadamur E 151 C3
Guadarrama E 151 B3
Guadiaro E 162 B2
Guadix E 164 B1
Guagnano I 173 B3
Guagno F 180 A1
Guajar-Faragüit E 163 B4
Gualchos E 163 B4
Gualdo Tadino I . . .136 B1

Gualtieri I 121 C3
Guarcino I 169 B3
Guarda P 149 B2
Guardamar del Segura
 E 165 A4
Guardão P 148 B1
Guardavalle I 175 C2
Guardea I 168 A2
Guárdia I 172 B1
Guardiagrele I 169 A4
Guardiarégia I 170 B2
Guárdia Sanframondi
 I 170 B2
Guardias Viejas E 164 C2
Guardiola de Bergueda
 E 147 B2
Guareña E 156 B1
Guaro E 162 B3
Guarromán E 157 B4
Guasila I 179 C3
Guastalla I 121 C3
Gubbhögen S 199 A12
Gúbbio I 136 B1
Guben D 74 C3
Gubin PL 74 C3
Gudå N 199 B8
Gudavac BIH 124 C2
Guddal N 46 A2
Gudhem S 55 B4
Gudhjem DK 67 A3
Gudow D 73 A3
Güdül TR 187 B7
Gudvangen N 46 B3
Guebwiller F 106 C2
Guéjar-Sierra E . . .163 A4
Guémené-Penfao
 F 101 B4
Guémené-sur-Scorff
 F 100 A2
Güeñes E 143 A3
Guer F 101 B3
Guérande F 101 B3
Guéret F 116 A1
Guérigny F 104 B2
Guesa E 144 B2
Gueugnon F 104 C3
Guglionesi I 170 B2
Gühlen Glienicke
 D 74 A1
Guia P 154 B2
Guichen F 101 B4
Guidizzolo I 121 B3
Guidónia-Montecélio
 I 168 B2
Guglia I 135 A3
Guignes F 90 C2
Guijo E 156 B3
Guijo de Coria E . .149 B3
Guijo de Santa Bábera
 E 150 B2
Guijuelo E 150 B2
Guildford GB 44 B3
Guillaumes F 132 A2
Guillena E 162 A1
Guillestre F 118 C3
Guillos E 128 B2
Guilsfield GB 38 B3
Guilvinec F 100 B1
Guimarães P 148 A1
Guincho P 154 C1
Guînes F 78 B1
Guingamp F 100 A2
Guipavas F 100 A1
Guisborough GB 37 B5
Guiscard F 90 B3
Guiscriff F 100 A2
Guise F 91 B3
Guisona E 147 C2
Guitiriz E 140 A3
Guîtres F 128 A2
Gujan-Mestras F . .128 B1
Gulbene LV 8 D5
Gulçayır TR 187 C6
Guldborg DK 65 B4
Gullabo S 63 B3
Gullane GB 35 B5
Gullbrå N 46 B3
Gullbrandstorp S . . .61 C2
Gulleråsen S 50 A2
Gullhaug N 53 A6
Gullringen S 62 A3
Gullspång S 55 B5
Gullstein N 198 B5
Güllük TR 188 B2
Gülnar TR 23 C7
Gülpınar TR 186 C1
Gülşehir TR 23 B8
Gulsvik N 48 B1
Gumiel de Hizán
 E 143 C3
Gummersbach D 81 A3
Gümüldür TR 188 A2
Gümüşhacıköy TR . 23 A8
Gümüşova TR 187 B5
Gundelfingen D 94 C2
Gundel-fingen D . . .106 A2
Gundelsheim D 93 B5
Gundershausen F . .93 C3
Gundinci HR 125 B4
Gündoğmuş TR 189 C7
Güney
 Burdur TR 189 B4
 Denizli TR 188 A4
Gunja HR 125 C4
Günlüce TR 188 B3
Gunnarn S 195 E8
Gunnarskog S 49 C4
Gunnarn S 196 C4
Gunnebo S 62 A4
Gunnislake GB 42 B2
Günselsdorf A 111 B3
Guntersblum D 93 B4
Guntersdorf A 97 C4
Guntersdorf A 109 A4
Güntersleben D 94 B1
Guntín E 140 B3

Guntersdorf A 97 C4
Guntin E. 140 B3
Günyüzü TR. 187 C6
Günzburg D 94 C2
Gunzenhausen D . .94 B2
Güre
  Balıkesir TR . . . 186 C1
  Uşak TR. 186 D4
Gurk A 110 C1
Gurrea de Gállego
  E 144 B3
Gürsu TR 186 B4
Gušće HR 124 B2
Gusev RUS. 12 A5
Gúspini I 179 C2
Gusselby S 56 A1
Güssing A 111 B3
Gusswerk A 110 B2
Gustav Adolf S . . .49 B5
Gustavsberg S 57 A4
Gustavsfors S 54 A3
Güstrow D 65 C5
Gusum S 56 B2
Gutcher GB 33 A5
Gutenstein A 110 B2
Gütersloh D 81 A4
Guttannen CH . . .106 C3
Guttaring A 110 C1
Guttau D 84 A2
Güttingen CH . . .107 B4
Gützkow D 66 C2
Guzów PL. 77 B5
Gvardeysk RUS. . . .12 A4
Gvarv N 53 A5
Gvozd MNE 139 C5
Gvozdansko HR . .124 B2
Gwda Wielka PL . .68 B1
Gwennap GB. 42 B1
Gy F 105 B4
Gyál H 112 B3
Gyarmat H 111 B4
Gyékényes H. . . .124 A3
Gyé-sur-Seine F . .104 C3
Gyljen S 196 C5
Gylling DK. 59 C3
Gyoma H 113 C4
Gyömöre H 111 B4
Gyömrö D 112 B3
Gyón H. 112 B3
Gyöngyfa H 125 B3
Gyöngyös H 113 B3
Gyöngyöspata H .113 B3
Gyönk H. 112 C2
Györ H 111 B4
Györszemere H . .111 B4
Gypsera CH 106 C2
Gysinge S 51 B3
Gyttorp S 55 A5
Gyula H 113 C5
Gyulafirátót H . . .112 B1
Gyulaj H 112 C2

H

Haacht B 79 B4
Haag
  Nieder Österreich
  A 110 A1
  Ober Österreich A 109 A4
  D 108 A3
Haaksbergen NL . .71 B3
Haamstede NL 79 A3
Haan D 80 A3
Haapajärvi FIN 3 E9
Haapsalu EST 8 C3
Haarlem NL 70 B1
Habas F 128 C2
Habay B 92 B1
Habo S 62 A2
Håbol S 54 B3
Habry CZ 97 B3
Habsheim F 106 B2
Hachenburg D 81 B3
Hacıbektaş TR 23 B8
Hacılar TR 23 C7
Hacinas E 143 C3
Hackås S 199 C11
Hacketstown IRL . . .30 B2
Hackthorpe GB . . .37 B4
Hadamar D. 81 B4
Hädanberg S 200 C4
Haddington GB . . .35 C5
Hadersdorf am Kamp
  A. 97 C3
Haderslev DK 59 C2
Haderup DK. 59 B1
Hadım TR. 23 C7
Hadleigh
  Essex GB. 45 B4
  Suffolk GB 45 A4
Hadlow GB. 45 B4
Hadmersleben D . .73 B4
Hadsten DK 59 B3
Hadsund DK 58 B3
Hadžići BIH 139 B4
Hafnarfjörður IS . .190 C4
Hafnir IS. 190 D3
Hafslo N 47 A4
Haganj HR 124 B2
Hagby S 63 B4
Hage D 71 A4
Hægebostad N 52 B3
Hægeland N 53 B3
Hagen
  Niedersachsen D . 72 A1
  Nordrhein-Westfalen
  D. 80 A3
Hagenbach D. 93 B4
Hagenow D 73 A4
Hagetmau F 128 C2
Hagfors S. 49 B5
Häggenås S 199 B11
Hagondange F. . . .92 B2
Hagsta S 51 B4
Haguenau F 93 C3
Hahnbach D. 95 B3

Hahnslätten D 81 B4
Hahót H 111 C3
Haiger D. 81 B4
Haigerloch D 93 C4
Hailsham GB 45 C4
Hainburg A. 111 A3
Hainfeld A 110 A2
Hainichen D. 83 B5
Hajdúböszörmény
  H 113 B5
Hajdučica SRB . . .126 B2
Hajdúdorogo H . .113 B5
Hajdúnánás H . . .113 B5
Hajdúszoboszló
  H 113 B5
Hajnáčka SK 113 A3
Hajnówka PL 13 B5
Hajós H 112 C3
Håkafot S 199 A11
Hakkas S 196 C4
Håksberg S 50 B2
Halaszi H 111 B4
Halberstadt D 82 A3
Halberton GB 43 B3
Hald Ege DK 58 B2
Haldem D 71 B5
Halden N 54 A2
Haldensleben D . . .73 B4
Halenbeck D 73 A5
Halesowen GB. . . .40 C1
Halesworth GB 45 A5
Halfing D 109 B3
Halhjem N 46 B2
Häljelöt S 56 B2
Halkirk GB 32 C3
Hall S 57 C4
Hälla S 200 C3
Hallabro S 63 B3
Hällabrottet S 56 A1
Halland GB 45 C4
Hälleryd S 63 B2
Hallaryd S 61 C3
Hällberga S 56 A2
Hällbybrunn S 56 A2
Halle
  D 79 B4
  Nordrhein-Westfalen
  D. 72 B1
  Sachsen-Anhalt D .83 A3
Hålleberga S 62 B3
Hällefors S 55 A5
Hälleforsnäs S 56 A2
Hallein A 109 B4
Hällekis S 55 B4
Hallen S 199 B11
Hallen S 51 B4
Hallenberg D 81 A4
Hällestad S 56 B1
Hällevadsholm S . .54 B2
Hällevik S 63 B2
Hälleviksstrand S . .54 B2
Hallingby N 48 B2
Hallingeberg S 62 A4
Hallingen N 47 B6
Hall in Tirol A 108 B2
Hällnäs S 195 D9
Hällnäs S 51 B4
Hällnäs S 200 B5
Hallormsstaður
  IS 191 B11
Hallsberg S 56 A1
Hållsta S 56 A2
Hallstahammar S . .56 A2
Haro E 143 B4
Haroldswick GB . . .33 A6
Háromfa H 124 A3
Haroué F 92 C2
Harpenden GB. . . .44 B3
Harplinge S 60 C2
Harpstedt D 72 B1
Harrogate GB 40 A2
Harrow GB 44 B3
Härryda S 60 B2
Haydon Bridge GB .37 B4
Hayle GB. 42 B1
Haymana TR 187 C7
Hay-on-Wye GB. . .39 B3
Hayrabolu TR 186 A2
Haysyn UA. 13 D8
Hayvoron UA. 13 D8
Haywards Heath
  GB. 44 C3
Hazebrouck F 78 B2
Hazlov CZ 83 B4
Heacham GB. 41 C4
Headcorn GB. 45 B4
Headford IRL 28 A2
Heanor GB. 40 B2
Héas F 145 B4
Heathfield GB. 45 C4
Hebden Bridge GB .40 B1
Heberg S 60 C2
Heby S 51 C3
Hechingen D 93 C4
Hechlingen D. 94 C2
Hecho E. 144 B3
Hechtel B 79 A5
Hechthausen D . . .72 A2
Heckelberg D. 74 B2
Heckington GB . . .41 C3
Hecklingen D 82 A3
Hed S 56 A1
Hedalen N. 48 B1
Hedared S 60 B2
Heddal N 53 A5
Hédé F 101 A4
Hede S 199 C10
Hedekas S 54 B2
Hedemora S 50 B2
Hedensted DK 59 C2
Hedersleben D 82 A3
Hedesunda S. 51 B4
Hedge End GB. . . .44 C2
Hedon GB 41 B3
Heede D 71 B4
Heek D 71 B4
Heemstede NL. . . .70 B1
Heerde NL 70 B3
Heerenveen NL. . . .70 B2

Hamont B. 80 A1
Hámor H. 113 A4
Hamra
  Gävleborg S. . . .199 D12
  Gotland S. 57 D4
Hamrångefjärden
  S 51 B4
Hamstreet GB 45 B4
Hamsund N 194 B6
Han TR. 187 C5
Hanaskog S 61 C4
Hanau D. 81 B4
Händelöp S 62 A4
Handlová SK. 98 C2
Hanerau-
  Hademarschen D 64 B2
Hånger S 60 B3
Hanhimaa FIN . . .197 B8
Hankensbüttel D . .73 B3
Han Knežica BIH . .124 B2
Hanko FIN 8 C3
Hannover D 72 B2
Hannut B 79 B5
Han Pijesak BIH. . .139 A4
Hansnes N 192 C3
Hanstedt D. 72 A3
Hanstholm DK. 58 A1
Hantsavichy BY. . . .13 B7
Hanušovice CZ . . .85 B4
Haparanda S 196 D7
Haradok BY 13 A8
Harads S 196 C4
Häradsbäck S 63 B2
Häradsbygden S . .50 B2
Harbo S 51 B4
Harboør DK 58 B1
Harburg
  Bayern D 94 C2
  Hamburg D 72 A2
Hårby DK 59 C3
Harc H 112 C2
Hardegarijp NL . . .70 A2
Hardegsen D 82 A1
Hardelot Plage F . .78 B1
Hardenbeck D 74 A2
Hardenberg NL . . .71 B3
Harderwijk NL 70 B2
Hardheim D. 94 B1
Hardt D. 106 A3
Hareid N 198 C3
Haren
  D. 71 B4
  NL 71 A3
Harestua N 48 B2
Harfleur F 89 A4
Harg S 51 B5
Hargicourt F 90 B3
Hargnies F 91 A4
Hargshamn S 51 B5
Härja S 55 B4
Harkány H. 125 B4
Härkeberga S 56 A3
Harkebrügge D 71 A4
Harlech GB 38 B2
Harleston GB 45 A5
Hårlev DK. 65 A5
Harlingen NL 70 A2
Harlösa S 61 D3
Harlow GB. 45 B4
Harmancık TR . . .186 C4
Harmånger S 200 E3
Härnevi S 56 A3
Härnösand S 200 D3
Hamstreet...

Hastigrow GB 32 C3
Hastings GB 45 C4
Hästveda S 61 C3
Hasvik N 192 B6
Hatfield
  Hertfordshire GB . .44 B3
  South Yorkshire
  GB. 40 B3
Hatherleigh GB. . . .42 B2
Hathersage GB . . .40 B2
Hatlestrand N 46 B2
Hattem NL 70 B3
Hatten
  D 71 A4
  F. 93 C3
Hattfjelldal N 195 E4
Hatting DK 59 C2
Hattingen D 80 A3
Hattstedt D 64 B2
Hatvan H 112 B3
Hatvik N 46 B2
Hau D. 80 A2
Haudainville F 92 B1
Hauganes IS 191 B7
Haugastøl N 47 B4
Hauge N 52 B2
Haugesund N 52 A1
Haughom N 52 B2
Haugsdal N 46 B2
Haugsdorf A 97 C4
Haukedal N 46 A3
Haukeland N 46 B2
Haukeligrend N . . .52 A3
Haukeliseter N 52 A3
Haukipudas FIN . . .3 D9
Haulerwijk NL 71 A3
Haunersdorf D 95 C4
Haus
  A. 110 C2
Hausach D 106 A3
Hausham D 108 B2
Hausmannstätten
  A. 110 C2
Hausvik N 52 B2
Hautajärvi FIN . . .197 C12
Hautefort F 129 A4
Hauterives F 117 B5
Hauteville-Lompnès
  F. 118 B2
Haut-Fays B. 91 A5
Hautmont F 79 B3
Hautrage B. 79 B3
Hauzenberg D 96 C1
Havant GB. 44 C3
Havdhem S 57 C4
Havdrup DK. 61 D2
Havelange B 79 B5
Havelberg D 73 B5
Havelte NL 70 B3
Haverfordwest GB .39 C2
Haverhill GB 45 A4
Havering GB 45 B4
Håverud S 54 B3
Havířov CZ. 98 B2
Havixbeck D 71 C4
Havlíčkův Brod CZ .97 B3
Havndal DK. 58 B3
Havneby DK. 64 A1
Havnebyen DK 61 D1
Havnsø DK. 61 D1
Havøysund N 193 A8
Havran TR. 186 C2
Havrebjerg DK. . . .61 D1
Havsa TR. 186 A1
Havstenssund S . . .54 B2
Hawes GB 37 B4
Hawick GB. 35 C5
Hawkhurst GB. . . .45 B4
Hawkinge GB. 45 B5
Haxey GB. 40 B3
Hayange F 92 B2
Haydarlı TR 189 A5

Heerhugowaard NL 70 B1
Heerlen NL. 80 B1
Heeze NL. 80 A1
Heggenes N. 47 A6
Hegra N 199 B8
Hegyeshalom H. . .111 B4
Hegyközség H . . .111 B3
Heia N 199 A9
Heide D 64 B2
Heidelberg D 93 B4
Heiden D 80 A2
Heidenau D 84 B1
Heidenheim D 94 C2
Heidenreichstein A .97 C3
Heikendorf D 64 B3
Heikkilä FIN 197 C12
Heilam GB 32 C2
Heiland N 53 B4
Heilbad Heiligenstadt
  D 82 A2
Heilbronn D 93 B5
Heiligenblut A . . .109 B3
Heiligendamm D . .65 B4
Heiligendorf D 73 B3
Heiligengrabe D . .73 A5
Heiligenhafen D . . .65 B3
Heiligenhaus D . . .80 A2
Heiligenkreuz A . .111 C3
Heiligenstadt D . . .94 B3
Heiloo NL 70 B1
Heilsbronn D 94 B2
Heim N 198 B6
Heimburg D 82 A2
Heimdal N 199 B7
Heinersdorf D 74 B3
Heining D 96 C1
Heiningen D 94 C1
Heinola FIN 8 B5
Heinsberg D 80 A2
Heist-op-den-Berg
  B. 79 A4
Hejde S 57 C4
Hejdeby S 57 C4
Hejls DK. 59 C2
Hejnice CZ. 84 B3
Hel PL. 69 A3
Helchteren B 79 A5
Heldburg D 82 B2
Heldrungen D 82 A3
Helechosa E 156 A3
Helensburgh GB . . .34 B3
Helfenberg A 96 C2
Helgen N 53 A5
Helgeroa N 53 B5
Hella
  IS 190 D5
  N. 46 A3
Helland N 194 B7
Hellas S 55 B3
Helle N 52 B2
Helleland N 52 B2
Hellendoorn NL . . .71 B3
Hellenthal D. 80 B2
Hellesøy N 46 B1
Hellesylt N 198 C3
Hellevoetsluis NL . .79 A4
Helligskogen N . . .192 C4
Hellín E 158 C2
Hellissandur IS . . .190 C2
Hellum DK 58 A3
Hellvi S 57 C4
Hellvik N 52 B1
Helm-brechts D. . . .83 B3
Helmond NL 80 A1
Helmsdale GB 32 C3
Helmsley GB. 37 B5
Helmstedt D. 73 B3
Hel'pa SK 99 C3
Helsa D 82 A1
Helsby GB 38 A4
Helsingborg S. 61 C2
Helsinge DK. 61 C2
Helsingør DK. 61 C2
Helsinki FIN 8 B4
Helston GB 42 B1
Hemau D 95 B3
Hemavan S 195 E6
Hemel Hempstead
  GB. 44 B3
Hemer D. 81 A3
Héming F 92 C2
Hemmet DK 59 C1
Hemmingstedt D . .64 B2
Hemmoor D 64 C2
Hemnes N 54 A2
Hemnesberget N . .195 D4
Hemse S 57 C4
Hemsedal N 47 B5
Hemslingen D 72 A2
Hemsworth GB . . .40 B2
Hen N 48 B2
Henån S 54 B2
Hendaye F 144 A2
Hendek TR. 187 B5
Hendungen D 82 B2
Henfield GB. 44 C3
Hengelo
  Gelderland NL . . .71 B3
  Overijssel NL . . .71 B3
Hengersberg D 95 C5
Hengoed GB 39 C3
Hénin-Beaumont F .78 B2
Henley-on-Thames
  GB. 44 B3
Hennan S 200 D1
Henneberg D. 82 B2
Hennebont F 100 B2
Henne Strand DK . .59 C1
Hennigsdorf D 74 B2
Hennset N 198 B5
Hennstedt
  Schleswig-Holstein
  D. 64 B2
  Schleswig-Holstein
  D. 64 B2
Henrichemont F . .103 B4
Henryków PL. 85 B5
Henrykowo PL. . . .69 A5

Hensås N 47 A5
Henstedt-Ulzburg
  D 64 C2
Heppenheim D 93 B4
Herad
  Buskerud N 47 B6
  Vest-Agder N . . .52 B2
Heradsbygd N 48 B3
Heraklion = Iraklio
  GR 185 D6
Herálec CZ. 97 B4
Herand N 46 B3
Herbault F 103 B3
Herbern D 81 A3
Herbertstown IRL . .29 B3
Herbeumont B. 91 B5
Herbignac F. 101 B3
Herbisse F 91 C4
Herbitzheim F 92 B3
Herbolzheim D . . .106 A2
Herborn D 81 B4
Herbrechtingen D . .94 C2
Herby PL 86 B2
Herceg-Novi MNE . .16 D3
Hercegovać HR. . .124 B3
Hercegszántó H . .125 B4
Herchen D 80 B3
Heréd H 112 B3
Hereford GB 39 B4
Herefoss N 53 B4
Hereke TR 187 B4
Herencia E 157 A4
Herend H 111 B4
Herent B. 79 B4
Herentals B 79 A4
Hérépian F 130 B2
Herfølge DK. 61 D2
Herford D 72 B1
Herguijuela E 156 A2
Héric F 101 B4
Héricourt F. 106 B1
Héricourt-en-Caux
  F. 89 A4
Hérimoncourt F. . .106 B1
Heringsdorf D 65 B4
Herisau CH 107 B4
Hérisson F 103 C4
Herk-de-Stad B . . .79 B5
Herlufmagle DK. . .65 A4
Hermagor A 109 C4
Hermannsburg D . .72 B3
Hermansverk N . . .46 A3
Heřmanův Městec
  CZ 97 B3
Herment F 116 B2
Hermeskeil D 92 B2
Hermisende E 141 C4
Hermonville F 91 B3
Hermsdorf D 83 B3
Hernani E 144 A2
Hernansancho E . .150 B3
Herne D 80 A3
Herne Bay GB 45 B5
Hernes N 48 B3
Herning DK 59 B1
Herøya N 53 A5
Herramelluri E . . .143 B3
Herräng S 51 B5
Herre N. 53 A5
Herrenberg D 93 C4
Herrera E 162 A2
Herrera de Alcántara
  E 155 B3
Herrera del Duque
  E 156 A2
Herrera de los Navarros
  E 152 A2
Herrera de Pisuerga
  E 142 B2
Herreros del Suso
  E 150 B2
Herrestad S 54 B2
Herrhamra S 57 B3
Herritslev DK. 65 B4
Herrlisheim F. 93 C3
Herrljunga S 55 B4
Herrnhut D. 84 A2
Herrsching D 108 A2
Hersbruck D. 95 B3
Hersby S 57 A4
Herscheid D. 81 A3
Herselt B 79 A4
Herso GR 182 B4
Herstal B 80 B1
Herstmonceux GB .45 C4
Herten D 80 A3
Hertford GB 44 B3
Hervás E 149 B4
Hervik N. 52 A1
Herxheim D 93 B4
Herzberg
  Brandenburg D . .74 B1
  Brandenburg D . .83 A5
  Niedersachsen D .82 A2
Herzbrock D 81 A4
Herzfelde D 74 B2
Herzlake D 71 B4
Herzogenaurach D .94 B2
Herzogenbuchsee
  CH 106 B2
Herzogenburg A . .110 A2
Herzsprung D 73 A5
Hesby N 52 A1
Hesdin F 78 B2
Hesel D 71 A4
Heskestad N 52 B2
Hessdalen S 199 C8
Hesselager DK 65 A3
Hesseng N 193 C13
Hessisch Lichtenau
  D 82 A1
Hessisch-Oldendorf
  D 72 B2
Hestra S 60 B3
Heswall GB 38 A3
Hetlevik N 46 B2
Hettange-Grande F 92 B2
Hetton-le-Hole GB .37 B5
Hettstedt D 82 A3
Heuchin F 78 B2

Heudicourt-sous-les-
  Côtes F 92 C1
Heunezel F. 105 A5
Heuqueville F 89 A4
Heves H 113 B4
Héviz H. 111 C4
Hexham GB. 37 B4
Heysham GB. 36 B4
Heytesbury GB. . . .43 A4
Hidas H 125 A4
Hieflau A 110 B1
Hiendelaencina E .151 A5
Hiersac F 115 C4
High Bentham GB . .37 B4
Highclere GB. 44 B2
High Hesket GB. . . .37 B4
Highley GB. 39 B4
High Wycombe GB .44 B3
Higuera de Arjona
  E 157 C4
Higuera de Calatrava
  E 163 A3
Higuera de la Serena
  E 156 B2
Higuera de la Sierra
  E 161 B3
Higuera de Vargas
  E 155 C4
Higuera la Real E .161 A3
Higuers de Llerena
  E 156 B1
Higueruela E 158 C2
Híjar E 153 A3
Hilchenbach D. . . .81 A4
Hildburghausen D. .82 B2
Hilden D 80 A2
Hilders D 82 B1
Hildesheim D 72 B2
Hilgay GB. 41 C4
Hillared S 60 B3
Hille D 72 B1
Hillegom NL. 70 B1
Hillerød DK 61 D2
Hillerstorp S 60 B3
Hillesheim D 80 B2
Hillestad N. 53 A6
Hillmersdorf D 83 A5
Hillsborough GB. . .27 B4
Hillswick GB. 33 A5
Hilpoltstein D 95 B3
Hiltpoltstein D 94 B3
Hilvarenbeek N . . .79 A5
Hilversum NL. 70 B2
Himarë AL 182 C1
Himbergen D 73 A3
Himesháza H 125 A4
Himmelberg A . . .109 C5
Himmelpforten D . .72 A2
Himod N. 111 B4
Hinckley GB. 40 C2
Hindås S 60 B2
Hindelang D 108 B1
Hindelbank CH . . .106 B2
Hinderavåg N 52 A1
Hindhead GB 44 B3
Hinojosa del Valle
  E 156 B1
Hinnerup DK 59 B3
Hinneryd S. 61 C3
Hinojal E 155 B4
Hinojales E 161 B3
Hinojos E 161 B3
Hinojosa del Duque
  E 156 B2
Hinojosas de Calatrava
  E 157 B3
Hinterhornbach A .108 B1
Hinterriss A 108 B2
Hintersee
  A 109 B4
  D 74 A3
Hinterstoder A . . .110 B1
Hintertux A. 108 B2
Hinterweidenthal D 93 B3
Hinwil CH. 107 B3
Hios GR 185 A7
Hippolytushoef NL .70 B1
Hirschaid D 94 B2
Hirschau D. 95 B3
Hirschfeld D 83 A5
Hirschhorn D. 93 B4
Hirsingue F 106 B2
Hirson F 91 B4
Hirtshals DK 58 A2
Hirvaskoski FIN. . .197 D10
Hirzenhain D 81 B5
Hisarcık TR 186 C4
Hishult S 61 C3
Hissjön S 200 C6
Hitchin GB 44 B3
Hitra N 198 B5
Hittarp S. 61 C2
Hittisau A 107 B4
Hittun N 46 A1
Hitzacker D 73 A4
Hjallerup DK 58 A3
Hjällstad S 49 B5
Hjältevad S 62 A3
Hjärnarp S. 61 C2
Hjartdal N. 53 A4
Hjellestad N 46 B2
Hjelmeland N. 52 A2
Hjelset N 198 C4
Hjerkinn N 198 C6
Hjerm DK 58 B1
Hjerpsted DK 64 A1
Hjerting DK. 59 C1
Hjo S 55 B5
Hjordkær DK 64 A2
Hjørring DK 58 A2
Hjorted S. 62 A4
Hjortkvarn S. 56 B1
Hjortnäs S 50 B1
Hjortsberga S 62 B2
Hjukse N 53 A5
Hjuksebø N 53 A5
Hjulsjö S 55 A5
Hliník nad Hronom
  SK 98 C2
Hlinsko CZ. 97 B3

Hlío IS 191 A10
Hlohovec SK 98 C1
Hlubokánad Vltavou
CZ 96 B2
Hlučín CZ 98 B2
Hlyboka UA 17 A6
Hlybokaye BY 13 A7
Hniezdne SK 99 B4
Hnilec SK 99 C4
Hnúšťa SK 99 C3
Hobol H 125 A3
Hobro DK 58 B2
Hobscheid L 92 B1
Hocalar TR 189 A4
Hochdonn D 64 B2
Hochdorf CH 106 B3
Hochfelden F 93 C3
Hochspeyer D 93 B3
Höchstadt D 94 B2
Höchstädt D 94 C2
Hochstenbach D 81 B3
Höchst im Odenwald
D 93 B5
Höckendorf D 83 B5
Hockenheim D 93 B4
Hoddesdon GB 44 B3
Hodejov SK 99 C3
Hodenhagen D 72 B2
Hodkovice CZ 84 B3
Hódmezövásárhely
H 113 C4
Hodnet GB 38 B4
Hodonín CZ 98 C1
Hodslavice CZ 98 B2
Hoedekenskerke
NL 79 A3
Hoegaarden B 79 B4
Hoek van Holland
NL 79 A4
Hoenderlo NL 70 B2
Hof
D 83 B3
N 53 A6
Hofbieber D 82 B1
Hoff GB 37 B4
Hofgeismar D 81 A5
Hofheim
Bayern D 82 B2
Hessen D 93 A4
Hofkirchen im
Mühlkreis A 96 C1
Höfn IS 191 C10
Hofors S 50 B3
Hofsós IS 190 B6
Hofstad N 199 A7
Höganäs S 61 C2
Högbo S 51 B3
Hogdal S 54 A2
Høgebru N 46 A4
Högfors S 50 C2
Högklint S 57 C4
Högsäter S 54 B3
Högsby S 62 A4
Högsjö S 56 A1
Hogstad S 55 B6
Högyész H 112 C2
Hohenau A 97 C4
Hohenberg A 110 B2
Hohenbucko D 83 A5
Hohenburg D 95 B3
Hohendorf D 66 B1
Hohenems A 107 B4
Hohenhameln D 72 B3
Hohenhausen D 72 B1
Hohenkirchen D 71 A4
Hohenlinden D 108 A2
Hohenlockstedt D 64 C2
Hohenmölsen D 83 A4
Hohennauen D 73 B5
Hohen Neuendorf
D 74 B2
Hohenseeden D 73 B5
Hohentauern A 110 B1
Hohentengen D 106 B3
Hohenwepel D 81 A5
Hohenwestedt D 64 B2
Hohenwutzen D 74 B3
Hohenzieritz D 74 A2
Hohn D 64 B2
Hohne D 72 B3
Hohnstorf D 73 A3
Højer DK 64 B1
Højslev Stby DK 58 B2
Hok S 62 A2
Hökerum S 60 B3
Hökhuvud S 51 B5
Hokksund N 53 A5
Hökön S 63 B2
Hol N 47 B5
Hólar IS 190 B6
Holašovice CZ 96 C2
Holbæk
Aarhus Amt. DK 58 B3
Vestsjællands Amt.
DK 61 D1
Holbeach GB 41 C4
Holdenstedt D 73 B3
Holdhus N 46 B2
Holdorf D 71 B5
Holeby DK 65 B4
Hølen N 54 A1
Hølervasseter N 47 B6
Holešov CZ 98 B1
Holguera E 155 B4
Holič SK 98 C1
Holice
CZ 97 A3
SK 111 B4
Höljes S 49 B4
Hollabrunn A 97 C4
Hollandstoun GB 33 B4
Høllen N 53 B3
Hollfeld D 95 B3
Hollókő H 112 B3
Hollstadt D 82 B2
Hollum NL 70 A2
Höllviksnäs S 66 A1
Holm N 195 E3
Hólmavík IS 190 B4
Holmbukt N 192 B5
Holmedal S 54 A2
Holmegil N 54 A2
Holmen N 48 B2
Holme-on-Spalding-
Moor GB 40 B3
Holmes Chapel GB 38 A4
Holmestrand N 54 A1
Holmfirth GB 40 B2
Holmfoss N 193 C14
Holmsbu N 54 A1
Holmsjö S 63 B3
Holmsund S 200 C6
Holmsveden S 50 A3
Holmudden S 57 C5
Hölö S 57 A3
Holøydal N 199 C8
Holsbybrunn S 62 A3
Holseter N 48 A1
Holsljunga S 60 B2
Holstebro DK 59 B1
Holsted DK 59 C1
Holsworthy GB 42 B2
Holt
D 64 B2
Norfolk GB 41 C5
Wrexham GB 38 A4
IS 190 D6
N 53 B4
Holten NL 71 B3
Holtwick D 71 B4
Holum N 52 B3
Holwerd NL 70 A2
Holycross IRL 29 B4
Holyhead GB 38 A2
Holýšov CZ 95 B5
Holywell GB 38 A3
Holywood GB 27 B5
Holzdorf D 83 A5
Holzhausen D 72 B1
Holzheim D 94 C2
Holzkirchen D 108 B2
Holzminden D 81 A5
Holzthaleben D 82 A2
Homberg
Hessen D 81 A5
Hessen D 81 B5
Homburg D 93 B3
Hommelstø N 195 E3
Hommersåk N 52 B1
Homokmegy H 112 C3
Homokszentgyörgy
H 124 A3
Homyel = Gomel
BY 13 B9
Honaz TR 188 B4
Hondarribia E 144 A2
Hondón de los Frailes
E 165 A4
Hondschoote F 78 B2
Hönebach D 82 B1
Hønefoss N 48 B2
Honfleur F 89 A4
Høng DK 61 D1
Honiton GB 43 B3
Hönningen D 80 B2
Honningsvåg N 193 B9
Hönö S 60 B1
Honrubia E 158 B1
Hontalbilla E 151 A3
Hontheim D 92 A2
Hontianske-Nemce
SK 98 C2
Hontoria de la Cantera
E 143 B3
Hontoria del Pinar
E 143 C3
Hontoria de
Valdearados E 143 C3
Hoofddorp NL 70 B1
Hoogerheide NL 79 A4
Hoogeveen NL 71 B3
Hoogezand-Sappemeer
NL 71 A3
Hoogkarspel NL 70 B2
Hoogkerk NL 71 A3
Hoogstede D 71 B3
Hoogstraten B 79 A4
Hook GB 44 B3
Hooksiel D 71 A5
Höör S 61 D3
Hoorn NL 70 B2
Hope GB 38 A3
Hopen N 194 C6
Hope under Dinmore
GB 39 B4
Hopfgarten A 108 B3
Hopfgarten in
Defereggen A 109 C3
Hopseidet N 193 B11
Hopsten D 71 B4
Hoptrup DK 59 C2
Hora Svatého
Sebestiána CZ 83 B5
Horažďovice CZ 96 B1
Horb am Neckar D 93 C4
Horbelev DK 65 B5
Hørby DK 58 A3
Hörby S 61 D3
Horcajada de la Torre
E 158 A1
Horcajo de los Montes
E 156 A3
Horcajo de Santiago
E 151 C4
Horcajo-Medianero
E 150 B2
Horche E 151 B4
Horda S 62 A2
Hordabø N 46 B1
Hordalia N 52 A2
Hordvik N 46 B2
Hořesedly CZ 83 B5
Horezu RO 17 C6
Horgen CH 107 B3
Horgoš SRB 126 A1
Horia RO 126 A3
Hořice CZ 84 B3
Horjul SLO 123 A3
Horka D 84 A2
Hörken S 50 B1
Horki BY 13 A9
Hörle S 60 B4
Horn
A 97 C3
D 81 A4
N 48 B2
S 62 A3
Horna E 158 C2
Hornachos E 156 B1
Hornachuelos E 162 A2
Horná Mariková
SK 98 B2
Hornanes N 46 C2
Horná Streda SK 98 C1
Horná Štrubna SK 98 C2
Horná Súča SK 98 C1
Hornbæk
Aarhus Amt. DK 58 B2
Frederiksværk DK 61 C2
Hornberg D 106 A3
Hornburg D 73 B3
Horncastle GB 41 B3
Horndal S 50 B3
Horndean GB 44 C2
Horne
Fyns Amt. DK 64 A3
Ribe Amt. DK 59 C1
Hörnebo S 55 B5
Horneburg D 72 A2
Hörnefors S 200 C5
Horní Bečva CZ 98 B2
Horni Benešov CZ 98 B1
Horni Cerekev CZ 97 B3
Horní Jiřetín CZ 83 B5
Horní Lomná CZ 98 B2
Horni Maršov CZ 85 B3
Hornindal N 198 D3
Hørning DK 59 B3
Hörningsholm S 57 A3
Horní Planá CZ 96 C2
Horni Slavkov CZ 83 B4
Horni Vltavice CZ 96 C1
Hornnes N 53 B3
Horno D 84 A2
Hornos E 164 A2
Hornoy-le-Bourg F 90 B1
Hornsea GB 41 B3
Hornsjø N 48 A2
Hornslet DK 59 B3
Hornstein A 111 B3
Hörnum D 64 B1
Hornum DK 58 B2
Horný Tisovník SK 99 C3
Horodenka UA 13 D6
Horodnya UA 13 C9
Horodok
Khmelnytskyy
UA 13 D7
Lviv UA 13 D5
Horokhiv UA 13 C6
Horovice CZ 96 B1
Horred S 60 B2
Hörröd S 61 D4
Hörsching A 110 A1
Horsens DK 59 C2
Horsham GB 44 B3
Hørsholm DK 61 D2
Horslunde DK 65 B4
Horšovský Týn CZ 95 B4
Horst NL 80 A2
Horstel D 71 B4
Horsten D 71 A4
Horstmar D 71 B4
Hort H 113 B3
Horta P 148 A2
Horten N 54 A1
Hortezuela E 151 A5
Hortiguela E 143 B3
Hortobágy H 113 B5
Horton in Ribblesdale
GB 37 B4
Hørve DK 61 D1
Hörvik S 63 B2
Horwich GB 38 A4
Hosanger N 46 B2
Hösbach D 93 A5
Hosena D 84 A2
Hosenfeld D 81 B5
Hosingen L 92 A2
Hosio FIN 197 D8
Hospental CH 107 C3
Hospital IRL 29 B3
Hossegor F 128 C1
Hosszuhetény H 125 A4
Hostal de Ipiés E 145 B3
Hošťálkova CZ 98 B1
Hostalric E 147 C3
Hostens F 128 B2
Hostěradice CZ 97 C4
Hostinné CZ 85 B3
Hostomice CZ 96 B2
Hostouň CZ 95 B4
Hotagen S 199 B11
Hoting S 200 B2
Hotolisht AL 182 B2
Hotton B 79 B5
Houdain F 78 B2
Houdan F 90 C1
Houdelaincourt F 92 C1
Houeillès F 128 B3
Houffalize B 92 A1
Houghton-le-Spring
GB 37 B5
Houlberg DK 59 B2
Houlgate F 89 A3
Hounslow GB 44 B3
Hourtin F 128 A1
Hourtin-Plage F 128 A1
Houthalen B 79 A5
Houyet B 79 B4
Hov
DK 59 C3
N 48 B2
Hova S 55 B5
Høvåg N 53 B4
Hovborg DK 59 C1
Hovda N 47 B6
Hovden N 52 A3
Hove GB 44 C3
Hovedgård DK 59 C2
Hovelhof D 81 A4
Hoven DK 59 C1
Hovet N 47 B5
Hovingham GB 40 A3
Hovmantorp S 62 B3
Hovsta S 56 A1
Howden GB 40 B3
Howe D 72 A3
Höxter D 81 A5
Hoya D 72 B2
Hoya de Santa Maria
E 161 B3
Hoya-Gonzalo E 158 C2
Høyanger N 46 A3
Hoyerswerda D 84 A2
Høyjord N 53 A6
Hoylake GB 38 A3
Høylandet N 199 A9
Hoym D 82 A3
Høymyr N 47 C6
Hoyocasero E 150 B3
Hoyo de Manzanares
E 151 B4
Hoyo de Pinares
E 150 B3
Hoyos E 149 B3
Hoyos del Espino
E 150 B2
Hrabusiče SK 99 C4
Hradec Králové CZ 85 B3
Hradec nad Moravicí
CZ 98 B1
Hrádek CZ 97 C4
Hrádek nad Nisou
CZ 84 B2
Hradište SK 98 C2
Hrafnagil IS 191 B7
Hrafnseyri IS 190 B2
Hranice
Severomoravsky
CZ 98 B1
Západočeský CZ 83 B4
Hranovnica SK 99 C4
Hrasnica BIH 139 B4
Hrastnik SLO 123 A4
Hřensko CZ 84 B2
Hriňová SK 99 C3
Hrisoupoli GR 183 C6
Hrochov CZ 97 B4
Hrochův Tynec CZ 97 B3
Hrodna BY 13 B5
Hrodzyanka BY 13 B8
Hronov CZ 85 B4
Hronský Beňadik
SK 98 C2
Hrotovice CZ 97 B4
Hrtkovci SRB 127 C1
Hrun IS 190 A5
Hrušov SK 112 A3
Hrušovany nad
Jevišovkou CZ 97 C4
Hřuštin SK 99 B3
Hrvaćani BIH 124 C3
Hrvace HR 138 B2
Hrymayliv UA 13 D7
Huben A 109 C3
Hückel-hoven D 80 A2
Hückeswagen D 80 A3
Hucknall GB 40 B2
Hucqueliers F 78 B1
Huddersfield GB 40 B2
Huddinge S 57 A3
Huddunge S 51 B3
Hude D 72 A1
Hudiksvall S 200 E3
Huélago E 163 A4
Huélamo E 152 B2
Huelgoat F 100 A2
Huelma E 163 A4
Huelva E 161 B3
Huéneja E 164 B2
Huércal de Almeria
E 164 C2
Huércal-Overa E 164 B3
Huerta de Abajo E 143 B3
Huerta del Rey E 143 C3
Huerta de
Valdecarabanos
E 151 C4
Huertahernando E 152 B1
Huesa E 164 B1
Huesca E 145 B3
Huéscar E 164 B2
Huete E 151 B5
Huétor Tájar E 163 A3
Hüfingen D 106 B3
Hufthamar N 46 B2
Hugh Town GB 42 B1
Huglfing D 108 B2
Huissen NL 70 C2
Huittinen FIN 8 B3
Huizen NL 70 B2
Hulín CZ 98 B1
Hüls D 80 A2
Hulsig DK 58 A3
Hulst NL 79 A4
Hult S 62 A3
Hulta S 56 B2
Hulteby S 55 A5
Hulterstad S 63 B4
Hultsfred S 62 A3
Humanes E 151 B4
Humberston GB 41 B3
Humble DK 65 B3
Humenné SK 12 D4
Humilladero E 163 A3
Humlebæk DK 61 D2
Humlum DK 58 B1
Hummelsta S 56 A2
Humpolec CZ 97 B3
Humshaugh GB 37 A4
Hundåla N 195 E3
Hundested DK 61 D1
Hundorp N 48 A1
Hundvåg N 52 A1
Hundvin N 46 B2
Hunedoara RO 17 C5
Hünfeld D 82 B1
Hungen D 81 B4
Hungerford GB 44 B2
Hunndalen N 48 B2
Hunnebostrand S 54 B2
Hunstanton GB 41 C4
Huntingdon GB 44 A3
Huntley GB 39 C4
Huntly GB 33 D4
Hünxe D 80 A2
Hurbanovo SK 112 B2
Hürbel D 107 A4
Hurdal N 48 B3
Hurezani RO 17 C5
Hurlford GB 36 A2
Hurstbourne Tarrant
GB 44 B2
Hurstpierpoint GB 44 C3
Hürth D 80 B2
Hurum N 47 A5
Hurup DK 58 B1
Húsafell IS 190 C5
Húsavík IS 191 A8
Husbands Bosworth
GB 44 A2
Husby
D 64 B2
DK 59 B1
Husey IS 191 B11
Huşi RO 17 B8
Husina BIH 139 A4
Husinec CZ 96 B1
Husinish GB 31 B1
Huskvarna S 62 A2
Husnes N 46 C2
Husøy N 194 A8
Hustad N 198 C4
Hüsten D 81 A3
Hustopeče CZ 97 C4
Hustopeče nad Bečvou
CZ 98 B1
Husum
D 64 B2
S 200 C5
Husvika N 195 E3
Huta PL 75 B5
Hutovo BIH 139 C3
Hüttenberg A 110 C1
Hüttlingen D 94 C2
Huttoft GB 41 B4
Hutton Cranswick
GB 40 B3
Hüttschlag A 109 B4
Huttwil CH 106 B2
Huy B 79 B5
Hüyük TR 189 B6
Hval N 48 B2
Hvåle N 47 B6
Hvaler N 54 A2
Hvalpsund DK 58 B2
Hvammstangi IS 190 B5
Hvammur IS 190 B6
Hvanneyri IS 190 C4
Hvar HR 138 B2
Hvarnes N 53 A5
Hveragerði IS 190 D4
Hvidbjerg DK 58 B1
Hvide Sande DK 59 C1
Hvittingfoss N 53 A6
Hvolsvöllur IS 190 D5
Hybe SK 99 B3
Hycklinge S 62 A3
Hydra GR 185 B4
Hyen N 198 D2
Hyères F 132 B2
Hyères Plage F 132 B2
Hylestad N 52 A3
Hylke DK 59 C2
Hyllestad N 46 A2
Hyllstofta S 61 C3
Hyltebruk S 60 B3
Hynnekleiv N 53 B4
Hythe
Hampshire GB 44 C2
Kent GB 45 B5
Hyvinkää FIN 8 B4

I

Iam RO 127 B3
Iaşi RO 17 B7
Iasmos GR 183 B7
Ibahernando E 156 A2
Ibarranguelua E 143 A4
Ibbenbüren D 71 B4
Ibeas de Juarros
E 143 B3
Ibestad N 194 B8
Ibi E 159 C3
Ibiza = Eivissa E 166 C1
İbradı TR 189 B6
İbriktepe TR 186 A1
Ibros E 157 B4
Ibstock GB 40 C2
İçel TR 23 C8
Ichenhausen D 94 C2
Ichtegem B 78 A3
Ichtershausen D 82 B2
Idanha-a-Novo P 155 B3
Idar-Oberstein D 93 B3
Idd N 54 A2
Idiazábal E 144 B1
Idivuoma S 196 A4
Idkerberget S 50 B2
Idön S 51 B5
Idre S 199 D9
Idrija SLO 123 A3
Idritsa RUS 9 D6
Idstein D 81 B4
Idvor SRB 126 B2
Iecca Mare RO 126 B2
Ielsi I 170 B2
Ieper = Ypres B 78 B2
Ierapetra GR 185 D6
Ierissos GR 183 C5
Ifjord N 193 B11
Ig SLO 123 B3
Igal H 112 C1
Igea E 144 B1
Igea Marina I 136 A1
Igelfors S 56 B1
Igersheim D 94 B1
Iggesund S 200 E3
Iglesias E 143 B3
Iglésias I 179 C2
Igls A 108 B2
Igny-Comblizy F 91 B3
Igorre E 143 A4
Igoumenitsa GR 182 D2
Igries E 145 B3
Igualada E 147 C2
Igüeña E 141 B4
Iguerande F 117 A4
Iharosberény H 124 A3
Ihl'any SK 99 B4
Ihlienworth D 64 C1
Ihringen D 106 A2
Ihrlerstein D 95 C3
İhsaniye TR 187 C5
Ii FIN 197 D8
Iijärvi FIN 193 C11
Iisalmi FIN 3 E10
IJmuiden NL 70 B1
IJsselmuiden NL 70 B2
IJzendijke NL 79 A3
Ikast DK 59 B2
Ikervár H 111 B3
Ilandža SRB 126 B2
Ilanz CH 107 C4
Ilava SK 98 C2
Iława PL 69 B4
il Castagno I 135 B3
Ilche E 145 C4
Ilchester GB 43 B4
Ilfeld D 82 A2
Ilfracombe GB 42 A2
Ilgaz TR 23 A7
Ilgın TR 189 A6
Ílhavo P 148 B1
Ilica TR 186 C2
Ilidža BIH 139 B4
Ilijaš BIH 139 B4
Ilirska Bistrica
SLO 123 B3
Ilkeston GB 40 C2
Ilkley GB 40 B2
Illana E 151 B5
Illano E 141 A4
Illar E 164 C2
Illas E 141 A5
Illats F 128 B2
Illertissen D 94 C2
Illescas E 151 B4
Ille-sur-Têt F 146 B3
Illfurth F 106 B2
Illichivsk UA 17 B9
Illiers-Combray F 89 B5
Illkirch-Graffenstaden
F 93 C3
Illmersdorf D 74 C2
Illmitz A 111 B3
Íllora E 163 A4
Illueca E 152 A2
Ilmajoki FIN 8 A3
Ilmenau D 82 B2
Ilminster GB 43 B4
Ilok HR 126 B1
Ilomantsi FIN 9 A7
Iłow PL 77 B5
Iłowa PL 84 A3
Iłowo-Osada PL 77 A5
Ilsenburg D 82 A2
Ilshofen D 94 B1
Ilz A 110 B2
Iłża PL 87 A5
Imatra FIN 9 B6
Imielin PL 86 B3
Imingen N 47 B5
Immeln S 63 B2
Immenhausen D 81 A5
Immenstadt D 107 B5
Immingham GB 41 B3
Ímola I 135 A4
Imon E 151 A5
Imotski HR 138 B3
Impéria I 133 B4
Imphy F 104 C2
İmroz TR 183 C7
Imsland N 52 A1
Imst A 108 B1
Inagh IRL 28 B2
Inari FIN 193 D10
Inca E 167 B2
Inchnadamph GB 32 C2
Incinillas E 143 B3
Indal S 200 D3
Indjija SRB 127 B2
Indre Arna N 46 B2
Indre Billefjord N 193 B9
Indre Brenna N 193 B9
İğneada TR 186 A2
İnebolu TR 23 A7
İnecik TR 186 B2
İnegöl TR 187 B4
Inerthal CH 107 B3
Infiesto E 142 A1
Ingatorp S 62 A3
Ingedal N 54 A2
Ingelheim D 93 B4
Ingelmunster B 78 B3
Ingelstad S 62 B2
Ingleton GB 37 B4
Ingolfsland N 47 C5
Ingolstadt D 95 C3
Ingrandes
Maine-et-Loire
F 101 B5
Vienne F 102 C2
Ingwiller F 93 C3
Inhisar TR 187 B5
Iniesta E 158 B2
Inishannon IRL 29 C3
Inishcrone IRL 26 B1
Inke H 124 A3
Inndyr N 195 C5
Innellan GB 34 C3
Innerleithen GB 35 C4
Innermessan GB 36 B2
Innertkirchen CH 106 C3
Innervillgraten A 109 C3
Innsbruck A 108 B2
Innset N 194 B9
Innvik N 198 D3
İnönü TR 187 C5
Inowłódz PL 87 A4
Inowrocław PL 76 B3
Ins CH 106 B2
Insch GB 33 D4
Insjön S 50 B2
Ińsko PL 75 A4
Instow GB 42 A2
İntepe TR 186 B1
Interlaken CH 106 C2
Intragna CH 120 A1
Introbio I 120 B2
Inverallochy GB 33 D5
Inveran
GB 32 D2
IRL 28 A2
Inveraray GB 34 B2
Inverbervie GB 35 B5
Invergarry GB 32 D2
Invergordon GB 32 D2
Invergowrie GB 35 B4
Inverkeilor GB 35 B5
Inverkeithing GB 35 B4
Invermoriston GB 32 D2
Inverness GB 32 D2
Inveruno I 120 B1
Inverurie GB 33 D4
Ioannina GR 182 D2
Iolanda di Savoia
I 121 C4
Ion Corvin RO 17 C7
Ióppolo I 175 C1
Ios GR 185 C6
Ipati GR 182 E4
İpsala TR 186 B1
Ipswich GB 45 A5
Iraklia GR 183 B5
Iraklio = Heraklion
GR 185 D6
Irdning A 110 B1
Iregszemcse H 112 C2
Irgoli I 178 B3
Irig SRB 127 B1
Ironbridge GB 39 B4
Irpin UA 13 C9
Irrel D 92 B2
Irsina I 172 B2
Irsta S 56 A2
Irthlingborough GB 44 A3
Iruela E 141 B4
Irún E 144 A2
Irurita E 144 A2
Irurzun E 144 B2
Irvine GB 36 A2
Irvinestown GB 27 B3
Isaba E 144 B3
Isabela E 157 B4
Ísafjörður IS 190 A2
Isane N 198 D2
Isaszeg H 112 B3
Isbister GB 33 A5
Íscar E 150 A3
İscehisar TR 187 D5
Ischgl A 107 B5
Íschia I 170 C1
Ischia di Castro I 168 A1
Ischitella I 171 B3
Isdes F 103 B4
Ise N 54 A2
Iselle I 119 A5
Iseltwald CH 106 C2
Isen D 108 A3
Isenbüttel D 73 B3
Iseo I 120 B3
Iserlohn D 81 A3
Isérnia I 170 B2
Isfjorden N 198 C4
Ishëm AL 182 B1
Isigny-sur-Mer F 88 A2
Işıklı TR 189 A4
Ísili I 179 C3
İskilip TR 23 A8
Isla Canela E 161 B2
Isla Cristina E 161 B2
Islares E 143 A3
Isleham GB 45 A4
Isle of Whithorn
GB 36 B2
Ismaning D 108 A2
Isna P 154 B3
Isnestoften N 192 B6
Isny D 107 B5
Isoba E 142 A1
Isokylä
FIN 197 C10
S 196 B5
Isola F 132 A3
Isola d'Asti I 119 C5
Isola del Gran Sasso
d'Itália I 169 A3
Isola della Scala I 121 B4
Isola delle Fémmine
I 176 A2
Ísola del Liri I 169 B3
Ísola di Capo Rizzuto
I 175 C3
Isona E 147 B2
İspagnac F 130 A2
Isparta TR 189 B5
Isperikh BG 17 D7
Íspica I 177 C3
Isselburg D 80 A2
Issigeac F 129 B3
Issogne I 119 B4
Issoire F 116 B3
Issoncourt F 91 C5
Issoudun F 103 C4
Issum D 80 A2
Is-sur-Tille F 105 B4
Issy-l'Evêque F 104 C2
Istán E 162 B3
İstanbul TR 186 A3
Istebna PL 98 B2
Ístia d'Ombrone I 135 C4
Istiea GR 183 E5
Istres F 131 B3

Istvándi H 125 A3
Itea GR 184 A3
Ithaki GR 184 A1
Itoiz E 144 B2
Itrabo E 163 B4
Itri I 169 B3
Ittireddu I 178 B2
Ittiri I 178 B2
Itzehoe D 64 C2
Ivalo FIN. 193 D11
Iván H. 111 B3
Ivanava BY. 13 B6
Ivančice CZ 97 B4
Ivančna Gorica
SLO 123 B3
Iváncsa H. 112 B2
Ivanec HR 124 A2
Ivanić Grad HR . . .124 B2
Ivanjska BIH 124 C3
Ivanka SK. 98 C2
Ivankovo HR 125 B4
Ivano-Frankivsk
UA 13 D6
Ivanovice na Hané
CZ 98 B1
Ivanska HR 124 B2
Ivatsevichy BY. 13 B6
Ivaylovgrad BG . . .183 B8
Iveland N 53 B3
Ivoz Ramet B 79 B5
Ivrea I 119 B4
Ivrindi TR 186 C2
Ivry-en-Montagne
F. 104 B3
Ivry-la-Bataille F . . .90 C1
Ivybridge GB. 42 B3
Iwaniska PL. 87 B5
Iwiny PL. 85 A3
Iwuy F 78 B3
Ixworth GB. 45 A4
Izarra E. 143 B4
Izbica Kujawska PL 76 B3
Izbište SRB 127 B3
Izeda P 149 A3
Izegem B 78 B3
Izernore F 118 A2
Izmayil UA 17 C8
İzmir TR 188 A2
İzmit = Kocaeli
TR 187 B4
Iznájar E. 163 A3
Iznalloz E. 163 A4
Iznatoraf E 164 A1
İznik TR 187 B4
Izola SLO 122 B2
Izsák H. 112 C3
Izsófalva H. 99 C4
Izyaslav UA 13 C7

J

Jabalquinto E . . .157 B4
Jablanac HR 123 C3
Jablanica BIH 139 B3
Jablonec nad Jizerou
CZ 84 B3
Jablonec nad Nisou
CZ 84 B3
Jablonka PL. 99 B3
Jablonica SK. 98 C1
Jabłonna PL. 77 B5
Jablonnénad Orlicí
CZ 97 A4
Jablonne Podještědi
CZ 84 B2
Jablonov nad Turňou
SK 99 C4
Jabłonowo Pomorskie
PL. 69 B4
Jablúnka CZ 98 B1
Jablunkov CZ 98 B2
Jabučje SRB 127 C2
Jabugo E 161 B3
Jabuka SRB. 127 C2
Jabukovac HR. . . .124 B2
Jaca E 145 B3
Jáchymov CZ 83 B4
Jacobidrebber D . . .72 B1
Jade D 71 A4
Jäderfors S 50 B3
Jädraås S. 50 B3
Jadraque E 151 B5
Jaén E 163 A4
Jagare BIH 124 C3
Jagel D. 64 B2
Jagenbach A 96 C3
Jægerspris DK 61 D1
Jagodina SRB 127 C3
Jagodnjak HR 125 B4
Jagodzin PL. 84 A3
Jagstheim D 94 B2
Jagstzell D. 94 B2
Jahodna SK. 111 A4
Jajce BIH 138 A3
Ják H 111 B3
Jakabszállás H. . . .112 C3
Jäkkvik S. 195 D8
Jakobsnes N 193 C14
Jakovlje HR 124 B1
Jakšic HR 125 B3
Jakubany SK. 99 B4
Jalance E. 159 B2
Jalasjärvi FIN 8 A3
Jalhay B. 80 B1
Jaligny-sur-Besbre
F. 117 A3
Jallais F 102 B1
Jalón E. 159 C3
Jâlons F. 91 C4
Jamena SRB 125 C5
Jamilena E. 163 A4
Jämjö S 63 B3
Jamnička Kiselica
HR 124 B1
Jamno PL. 67 B5
Jamoigne B 92 B1

Jämsä FIN 8 B4
Jämshög S 63 B2
Jamu Mare RO. . . .126 B3
Janakkala FIN 8 B4
Jandelsbrunn D . . .96 C1
Jänickendorf D 74 B2
Janikowo PL 76 B3
Janja BIH 125 C5
Janjina HR 138 C3
Janki
Łódzkie PL. 86 A3
Mazowieckie PL. . .77 B5
Jankov CZ 96 B2
Jankowo Dolne PL .76 B2
Jánoshalma H 126 A1
Jánosháza H 111 B4
Jánoshida H 113 B4
Jánossomorja H . .111 B4
Janovice nad Uhlavou
CZ 96 B1
Janów PL. 86 B3
Janowiec Wielkopolski
PL. 76 B2
Janowo PL 77 A5
Jänsmässholmen
S. 199 B10
Janville F 103 A3
Janzé F 101 B4
Jarabá SK 99 C3
Jaraczewo PL 76 C2
Jarafuel E 159 B2
Jaraicejo E 156 A2
Jaraíz de la Vera
E 150 B2
Jarak SRB 127 C1
Jarandilla de la Vera
E 150 B2
Jaray E 152 A1
Jard-sur-Mer F . . .114 B2
Jaren N 48 B2
Jargeau F. 103 B4
Jarkovac SRB 126 B2
Järlåsa S 51 C4
Jarmen D 66 C2
Järna S. 57 A3
Jarnac F 115 C3
Järnäs S. 200 C5
Järnforsen S 62 A3
Jarny F 92 B1
Jarocin PL 76 C2
Jaroměř CZ 85 B3
Jaroměřice nad
Rokytnou CZ . . .97 B3
Jaroslav CZ 97 A4
Jaroslavice CZ 97 C4
Jarosław PL 12 C5
Jarosławiec PL 68 A1
Jarošov nad Nežarkou
CZ 96 B3
Järpås S. 55 B3
Järpen S 199 B10
Jarrow GB 37 B5
Järso FIN 51 B6
Järvenpää FIN. 8 B4
Jarvorník CZ 85 B4
Järvsö S. 200 E2
Jarzé F 102 B1
Jaša Tomic SRB . .126 B2
Jasenak HR 123 B4
Jasenica BIH 124 C2
Jasenice HR 137 A4
Jasenovac HR 124 B2
Jasenovo SRB . . .127 C3
Jasień PL. 84 A3
Jasienica PL 84 A2
Jasło PL 12 D4
Jásova SK 112 B2
Jasseron F 118 A2
Jastarnia PL 69 A3
Jastrebarsko HR . .123 B4
Jastrowie PL 68 B1
Jastrzębia-Góra PL 68 A3
Jastrzębie Zdrój
PL. 98 B2
Jászals-
Lószentgyörgy
H 113 B4
Jászapáti H 113 B4
Jászárokszállás
H 113 B3
Jászberény H 113 B3
Jászdózsa H 113 B4
Jászfényszaru H . .113 B3
Jászjakóhalma H. .113 B4
Jászkarajenö H . . .113 B4
Jászkisér H 113 B4
Jászladány H 113 B4
Jászszentlászló
H 113 C3
Jásztelek H 113 B4
Játar E 163 B4
Jättendal S 200 E3
Jatznick D 74 A2
Jaun CH. 106 C2
Jausiers F 132 A2
Jávea E 159 C4
Jävenitz D 73 B4
Javerlhac F 115 C4
Javier E 144 B2
Javorani BIH 124 C3
Javorina SK. 99 B4
Javron F. 89 B3
Jawor PL 85 A4
Jaworzno PL. 86 B3
Jaworzyna Śl. 85 B4
Jayena E 163 B4
Jażow PL 84 A2

Jeesiö FIN 197 B9
Jegłownik PL. 69 A4
Jegun F 129 C3
Jēkabpils LV 8 D4
Jektevik N 46 C2
Jektvik N 195 D4
Jelcz-Laskowice
PL. 85 A5
Jelenec SK. 98 C2
Jelenia Góra PL. . . .85 B3
Jelgava LV 8 D3
Jelka SK. 111 A4
Jelling DK 59 C2
Jels DK. 59 C2
Jelsa
HR 138 B2
N 52 A2
Jelšava SK. 99 C4
Jemgum D 71 A4
Jemnice CZ 97 B3
Jena D 82 B3
Jenaz CH 107 C4
Jenbach A 108 B2
Jenikow PL 75 A4
Jennersdorf A 111 C3
Jenny S 62 A4
Jerchel D 73 B4
Jeres del Marquesado
E 164 B1
Jerez de la Frontera
E 162 B1
Jerez de los Caballeros
E 155 C4
Jerica E 159 B3
Jerichow D 73 B5
Jerka PL 75 B5
Jermenovci SRB . .126 B3
Jerslev DK 58 A3
Jerte E 150 B2
Jerup DK 58 A3
Jerxheim D 73 B3
Jerzmanowice PL . .87 B3
Jerzu I 179 C3
Jerzwałd PL. 69 B4
Jesberg D 81 B5
Jesenice
Středočeský CZ .83 B5
Středočeský CZ .96 B2
SLO 109 C5
Jeseník CZ 85 B5
Jesenké SK 99 C4
Jesi I 136 B2
Jésolo I 122 B1
Jessen D 83 A4
Jessenitz D 73 A4
Jessheim N 48 B3
Jessnitz D 83 A4
Jesteburg D 72 A2
Jeumont F 79 B4
Jeven-stedt D 64 B2
Jever D 71 A4
Jevíčko CZ. 97 B4
Jevišovice CZ 97 C3
Jevnaker N 48 B2
Jezerane HR 123 B4
Jezero
BIH 138 A3
HR 123 B4
Jeżów PL. 87 A3
Jičín CZ. 84 B3
Jičíněves CZ 84 B3
Jihlava CZ 97 B3
Jijona E 159 C3
Jilemnice CZ 84 B3
Jilové CZ 84 B2
Jílové u Prahy CZ. .96 B2
Jimbolia RO. 126 B2
Jimena E 163 A4
Jimena de la Frontera
E 162 B2
Jimera de Libar E .162 B2
Jimramov CZ 97 B4
Jince CZ. 96 B1
Jindřichovice CZ. . .83 B4
Jindřichův Hradec
CZ 96 B3
Jirkov CZ 83 B5
Jistebnice CZ 96 B2
Joachimsthal D. . . .74 B2
João da Loura P . .154 C2
Jobbágyi H 112 B3
Jochberg A 109 B3
Jockfall S. 196 C5
Jódar E 163 A4
Jodoigne B 79 B4
Joensuu FIN 9 A6
Joesjö S. 195 E5
Joeuf F 92 B1
Jõgeva EST. 8 C5
Johanngeorgenstadt
D 83 B4
Johannishus S 63 B3
Johanniskirchen D 95 C4
Johansfors S 63 B3
John o'Groats GB. .32 C3
Johnshaven GB . . .35 B5
Johnstone GB. 34 C3
Johnstown IRL 30 B1
Jõhvi EST. 8 C5
Joigny F 104 B2
Joinville F 91 C5
Jokkmokk S. 196 C2
Jöllenbeck D 72 B1
Jomala FIN 51 B6
Jönåker S 56 B2
Jonava LT. 13 A6
Joncy F 104 C3
Jondal N 46 B3
Jondalen N 53 A5
Joniškis LT. 8 D3
Jönköping S 60 B3
Jonkowo PL. 69 B5
Jønnbu N 53 A5
Jonsberg S 56 B2
Jonsered S 60 B2
Jonstorp S 61 C2
Jonzac F 114 C3
Jorba E 147 C2
Jordanów PL. 99 B3

Jordanowo PL 75 B4
Jordanów Ślaski
PL. 85 B4
Jordbro S. 57 A4
Jordbrua N 195 D5
Jördenstorf D 66 C1
Jordet N 49 A4
Jordøse DK 59 C3
Jork D 72 A2
Jörlanda S 60 B1
Jormlien S 199 A10
Jormvattnet S . . .199 A11
Jörn S 200 A6
Jørpeland N 52 A2
Jorquera E 158 B2
Jošan HR 123 C4
Jošavka BIH 124 C3
Josipdol HR 123 B4
Josipovac HR 125 B4
Jössefors S 54 A3
Josselin F 101 B3
Jøssund N 199 A7
Jostedal N 47 A4
Jósvafő H 99 C4
Jou P 148 A2
Jouarre F 90 C3
Joué-lès-Tours F . .102 B2
Joué-sur-Erdre F . .101 B4
Joure NL 70 B2
Joutsa FIN. 8 B5
Joutseno FIN. 9 B6
Joutsijärvi FIN . .197 C10
Joux-la-Ville F . . .104 B2
Jouy F 90 C1
Jouy-le-Châtel F . . .90 C3
Jouy-le-Potier F . .103 B3
Joyeuse F 131 A3
Joze F 116 B3
Juankoski FIN. 9 A6
Juan-les-Pins F . . .132 B3
Jübek D 64 B2
Jubera E 144 B1
Jubrique E 162 B2
Jüchsen D 82 B2
Judaberg N 52 A1
Judenburg A 110 B1
Juelsminde DK 59 C3
Jugon-les-Lacs F . .101 A3
Juillac F 129 A4
Juillan F. 145 A4
Juist D 71 A4
Jukkasjärvi S. . . .196 B3
Jule N. 199 A10
Julianadorp NL 70 B1
Julianstown IRL . . .30 A2
Jülich D 80 B2
Jullouville F 88 B2
Jumeaux F 117 B3
Jumièges F 89 A4
Jumilhac-le-Grand
F. 115 C5
Jumilla E 159 C2
Jumisko FIN 197 C11
Juncosa E 153 A4
Juneda E 147 C1
Jung S 55 B4
Jungingen D 93 C5
Junglingster L. 92 B2
Juniville F. 91 B4
Junosuando S . . .196 B5
Junqueira P 149 A2
Junsele S. 200 C2
Juoksengi S 196 C6
Juoksenki FIN . . .196 C6
Juprelle B 80 B1
Jurata PL 69 A3
Jurbarkas LT 12 A5
Jurjevo HR. 123 C3
Jürmala LV. 8 D3
Jurmu FIN 197 D10
Jursla S. 56 B2
Jussac F 116 C2
Jussey F 105 B4
Jussy F 90 B3
Juta H 125 A3
Jüterbog D 74 C2
Juuka FIN 3 E11
Juuma FIN 197 C12
Juvigny-le-Terte F. .88 B2
Juvigny-sous-Andaine
F. 89 B3
Juzennecourt F . . .105 A3
Jyderup DK 61 D1
Jyrkänkoski FIN .197 C12
Jyväskylä FIN 8 A4

K

Kaamanen FIN. . .193 C11
Kaamasmukka
FIN. 193 C10
Kaaresuvanto FIN 192 D6
Kaarssen D 73 A4
Kaatscheuvel NL. . .79 A5
Kaba H. 113 B5
Kåbdalis S 196 C3
Kačarevo SRB 127 C2
Kács H 113 B4
Kadan CZ 83 B5
Kadarkút H 125 A3
Kadınhanı TR 189 A7
Kaduy RUS 9 C10
Kåfalla S 56 A1
Kåfjord N 192 B7
Kåfjordbotn N . . .192 C4
Kågeröd S 61 D3
Kahl D 93 A5
Kahla D 82 B3
Kainach bei Voitsberg
A. 110 B2
Kaindorf A 110 B2
Kainulasjärvi S . . .196 C5
Kairala FIN. 197 B10
Kaisepakte S 192 D3
Kaisersesch D 80 B3
Kaiserslautern D . . .93 B3
Kaisheim D 94 C2
Kajaani FIN 3 D10
Kajárpéc H 111 B4

Kajdacs H 112 C2
Kakanj BIH. 139 A4
Kakasd H 125 A4
Kaklik TR 189 B4
Kakolewo PL. 85 A4
Kál H 113 B4
Kalajoki FIN. 3 D8
Kalak N 193 B11
Kalamata GR 184 B3
Kalambaka GR . . .182 D3
Kalamria GR 182 C4
Kalandra GR 183 D5
Kälarne S 200 D2
Kalavrita GR 184 A3
Kalbe D 73 B4
Kalce SLO 123 B3
Káld H 111 B4
Kale
Antalya TR 189 C4
Denizli TR 188 B3
Kalecik TR 23 A7
Kalefeld D 82 A2
Kalesija BIH 139 A4
Kalety PL. 86 B2
Kalevala RUS 3 D12
Kalholvn N 47 B5
Kalí HR. 137 A4
Kalimnos GR 188 B1
Kaliningrad RUS. . .69 A5
Kalinkavichy BY . . .13 B8
Kalinovac HR 124 A3
Kalinovik BIH. 139 B4
Kalinovo SK. 99 C3
Kalirachi GR 183 C6
Kaliska
Pomorskie PL. . .68 A3
Pomorskie PL. . .68 B3
Kalisko PL 86 A3
Kalisz PL 86 A2
Kalisz Pomorski PL 75 A4
Kaljord N 194 B6
Kalkan TR 189 C4
Kalkar D 80 A2
Kalkım TR 186 C2
Kall
D 80 B2
S 199 B10
Källby S 55 B4
Kållered S 60 B2
Kållerstad S 60 B3
Kallinge S 63 B3
Kallmünz D 95 B3
Kallo FIN 196 B7
Kallsedet S 199 B9
Källvik S. 56 B3
Kalmar S 63 B4
Kalmthout B 79 A4
Kalná SK 112 A2
Kalocsa H 112 C2
Kalokhorio CY. . . .181 B2
Kalo Nero GR 184 B2
Kaloni GR 186 C1
Káloz H 112 C2
Kals A. 109 B3
Kalsdorf A 110 C2
Kaltbrunn CH 107 B4
Kaltenbach A 108 B2
Kaltenkirchen D . . .64 C2
Kaltennordheim D. .82 B2
Kalundborg DK 61 D1
Kalush UA 13 D6
Kalv S. 60 B3
Kalvåg N 198 D1
Kalvehave DK 65 A5
Kalwang A 110 B1
Kalwaria-Zebrzydowska
PL. 99 B3
Kalyazin RUS 9 D10
Kam H 111 B3
Kaman TR 23 B7
Kamares CY 185 C5
Kambos CY 181 A1
Kamen D 81 A3
Kamenice CZ. 97 B3
Kamenice nad Lipou
CZ 96 B3
Kamenná SK. 112 B2
Kamenný Most
SK 112 B2
Kamenska HR. . . .124 B3
Kamensko HR 138 B2
Kamenz D 84 A2
Kamičak BIH 124 C2
Kamień PL. 87 A4
Kamieniec Zabk PL 85 B4
Kamienka SK. 99 B4
Kamień Krajeński
PL. 76 A2
Kamienna Góra PL 85 B4
Kamień Pomorski
PL. 67 C3
Kamiros Skala
GR 188 C2
Kamnik SLO 123 A3
Kampen NL 70 B2
Kampinos PL. 77 B5
Kamp-Lintfort D . . .80 A2
Kampor HR 123 C3
Kamyanets-Podil's'kyy
UA 13 D7
Kamyanka-Buz'ka
UA. 13 C6
Kamýk nad Vltavou
CZ 96 B2
Kanal SLO 122 A2
Kanalia GR 182 D4
Kandalaksha RUS. .3 C13
Kandanos GR . . .185 D4
Kandel D 93 B4
Kandern D. 106 B2
Kandersteg CH . . .106 C2
Kandila GR 184 B3
Kandıra TR 187 A5
Kandyty PL. 69 A5
Kanfanar HR 122 B2
Kangasala FIN. 8 B4
Kangos S 196 B5
Kangosjärvi FIN . .196 B6

Kaniów PL 75 C3
Kanjiža SRB 126 A2
Kankaanpää FIN 8 B3
Kannus FIN 3 E8
Kanturk IRL 29 B3
Kapaklı TR 186 A2
Kapellen
A 110 B2
B 79 A4
Kapellskär S 57 A5
Kapfenberg A 110 B2
Kapfenstein A 110 C2
Kaplice CZ 96 C2
Kapljuh BIH 124 C2
Kápolna H 113 B4
Kápolnásnyék H . .112 B2
Kaposfö H 125 A3
Kaposfüred H 125 A3
Kaposszekcsö H . .125 A4
Kaposvár H 125 A3
Kapp N. 48 B2
Kappel D 93 C3
Kappeln D 64 B2
Kappelshamn S . . .57 C4
Kappl A. 107 B5
Kappstad S 55 A4
Kaprun A 109 B3
Kaptol HR 125 B3
Kapuvár H 111 B4
Karaadilli TR 189 A5
Karabiğa TR 186 B2
Karabük TR 187 A7
Karaburun TR 186 D1
Karacabey TR 186 B3
Karacaköy TR 186 A3
Karacaören TR . . .189 A5
Karacasu TR 188 B3
Karácsond H 113 B4
Karád H 112 C1
Karahallı TR 189 A4
Karaisali TR 23 C8
Karaman
Balıkesir TR . . .186 C3
Karaman TR 23 C7
Karamanlı TR. . . .189 B4
Karamürsel TR . . .187 B4
Karan SRB 127 D1
Karancslapujto H . .113 A3
Karaova TR 188 B2
Karapınar TR 23 C7
Karasjok N 193 C9
Karasu TR 187 A5
Karataş
Adana TR 23 C8
Manisa TR 188 A3
Karatoprak TR . . .188 B2
Karavostasi CY . . .181 A1
Karbenning S 50 B3
Kårberg S 55 B5
Karby
D 64 B2
DK 58 B1
Kårby S 62 A4
Karby S 57 A4
Karcag H 113 B4
Karczów PL 86 B1
Karczowiska PL. . . .85 A4
Kardamena GR . .188 C2
Kardamila GR . . .185 A7
Kardamili GR 184 C3
Kardašova Rečice
CZ 96 B2
Kardis S 196 C6
Karditsa GR 182 D3
Kärdla EST. 8 C3
Kardoskút H 113 C4
Karesuando S . . .192 D6
Kargı TR 23 A8
Kargopol RUS 9 B11
Kargowa PL. 75 B4
Karigasniemi FIN .193 C9
Karise DK. 65 A5
Karistos GR. 185 A5
Karkkila FIN 8 B4
Karlholmsbruk S . .51 B4
Karlino PL 67 C4
Karlobag HR 137 A4
Karlovac HR 123 B4
Karlovasi GR 188 B1
Karlovčic SRB 127 C2
Karlovice CZ 85 B5
Karlovo BG 17 D6
Karlovy Vary CZ . . .83 B4
Karłowice PL. 86 B1
Karlsborg S 55 B5
Karlshamn S 63 B2
Karlshöfen D 72 A2
Karlshus N. 54 A1
Karlskoga S 55 A5
Karlskrona S 63 B3
Karlsrud N 47 B5
Karlstad S 55 A4
Karlstadt D 94 B1
Karlstetten A 110 A2
Karlstift A 96 C2
Karlstorp S 62 A3
Karmacs H 111 C4
Karmin PL 85 A5
Kärna S 60 B1
Karnobat BG 17 D7
Karojba HR 122 B2
Karow D. 73 A5
Karpacz PL 85 B3
Karpathos GR . . .188 D2
Karpenisi GR 182 E3
Karpuzlu TR 188 B2
Kärrbo S 56 A2
Karrebaeksminde
DK 65 A4
Karshult S 60 B3
Karsin PL. 68 B2
Kårsta S. 57 A4
Karstädt D 73 A4
Karsin TR 189 A4
Kartal TR 186 B4
Kartitsch A 109 C3
Kartuzy PL. 68 A3
Karungi S. 196 C6
Karunki FIN 196 C7

Karup DK 59 B2
Karviná CZ. 98 B2
Kås DK. 58 A2
Kaş TR 189 C4
Kasaba TR 189 C4
Kašava CZ 98 B1
Kåseberga S 66 A3
Kasejovice CZ. 96 B1
Kasfjord N 194 B7
Kashin RUS 9 D10
Kašina HR 124 B2
Kasina-Wielka PL . .99 B4
Kaskinen FIN. 8 A2
Kašperské Hory
CZ 96 B1
Kassandrino GR . .183 C5
Kassel D. 81 A5
Kassiopi GR 182 D1
Kastamonu TR 23 A7
Kastav HR 123 B3
Kasteli GR 185 D6
Kastellaun D 93 A3
Kastelli GR 185 D6
Kaštel-Stari HR . .138 B2
Kaštel Zegarski
HR 138 A1
Kasterlee B 79 A4
Kastl D. 95 B3
Kastlösa S 63 B4
Kastorf D 65 C3
Kastoria GR 182 C3
Kastorio GR 184 B3
Kastraki GR 185 C6
Kastrosikia GR . . .182 D2
Kastsyukovichy
BY 13 B10
Kaszaper H 113 C4
Katakolo GR 184 B2
Katapola GR 185 C6
Katastari GR 184 B1
Katerbow D 74 B1
Katerini GR 182 C4
Kathikas CY. 181 B1
Kätkesuando S . .196 A6
Katlenburg-Lindau
D. 82 A2
Káto Achaia GR. . .184 A2
Káto Pyrgos CY. . .181 A1
Katouna GR. 182 E3
Katovice CZ 96 B1
Katowice PL. 86 B3
Katrineberg S 50 A3
Katrineholm S. 56 B2
Kattarp S 61 C2
Kattavia GR 188 D2
Katthammarsvik S .57 C4
Kattilstorp S 55 B4
Katwijk NL 70 B1
Katymár H 125 A5
Katy Wrocławskie
PL. 85 A4
Katzenelnbogen D .81 B3
Katzhütte D 82 B3
Kaub D. 93 A3
Kaufbeuren D 108 B1
Kauhajoki FIN. 8 A3
Kauhava FIN 3 E8
Kaukonen FIN . . .196 B7
Kauliranta FIN . . .196 C6
Kaulsdorf D 82 B3
Kaunas LT. 13 A5
Kaunisvaara S . . .196 B6
Kaupanger N 47 A4
Kautokeino N 192 C7
Kautzen A. 97 C3
Kavadarci MK 182 B4
Kavajë E. 182 B1
Kavakköy TR 186 B1
Kavaklı TR 186 A2
Kavaklıdere TR . . .188 B3
Kavala BG 183 C6
Kavarna BG 17 D8
Kävlinge S 61 D3
Kawcze PL. 68 A1
Kaxås S 199 B10
Kaxholmen S 62 A2
Käylä FIN. 197 C12
Kaymakçı TR 188 A3
Kaymaz TR 187 C6
Kaynarca TR 187 A5
Käyrämö FIN 197 C9
Kayseri TR 23 B8
Kaysersberg F . . .106 A2
Kazanlŭk BG 17 D6
Kazár H 113 A3
Kazimierza Wielka
PL. 87 B4
Kazincbarcika H . .113 A4
Kaźmierz PL. 75 B5
Kcynia PL. 76 B2
Kdyně CZ 95 B5
Kea GR. 185 B5
Keadew IRL 26 B2
Keady GB. 27 B4
Kecel H 112 C3
Keçiborlu TR 189 B5
Kecskemét H 113 C3
Kédainiai LT 13 A5
Kędzierzyn-Koźle
PL. 86 B2
Keel IRL 28 A1
Keenagh IRL 28 A4
Keerbergen B 79 A4
Kefalos GR 188 C1
Kefken TR 187 A5
Keflavík IS 190 C3
Kegworth GB. 40 C2
Kehl D 93 C3
Kehrigk D. 74 B2
Keighley GB 40 B2
Keila EST. 8 C4
Keillmore GB. 34 C2
Keiss GB 32 C3
Keith GB 33 D4
Kelankylä FIN .197 D10
Kelberg D 80 B2
Kelbra D 82 A3
Kelč CZ 98 B1
Kelchsau A 108 B3
Kělcyrë AL. 182 C2

Keld GB 37 B4
Kelebia H 126 A1
Kelekçi TR 188 B4
Kelemér H 99 C4
Keles TR 186 C4
Kelheim D 95 C3
Kell D 92 B2
Kellas GB 32 D3
Kellinghusen D 64 C2
Kelloselkä FIN . . .197 C11
Kells
  GB 27 B4
  IRL 27 C4
Kelmis B 80 B2
Kelokedhara CY . .181 B1
Kelottijärvi FIN . .192 D6
Kelsall GB 38 A4
Kelso GB 35 C5
Kelsterbach D 93 A4
Keltneyburn GB . . .35 B3
Kelujärvi FIN 197 B10
Kemaliye TR 188 A3
Kemalpaşa TR 188 A2
Kematen A 108 B2
Kemberg D 83 A4
Kemer
  Antalya TR 189 C5
  Burdur TR 189 B5
  Muğla TR 189 C4
Kemerkaya TR 187 D6
Kemeten A 111 B3
Kemi FIN 196 D7
Kemijärvi FIN . . .197 C10
Keminmaa FIN . . .196 D7
Kemnath D 95 B3
Kemnay GB 33 D4
Kemnitz
  Brandenburg D . . .74 B1
  Mecklenburg-
  Vorpommern D . . .66 B2
Kempen D 80 A2
Kempsey GB 39 B4
Kempten D 107 B5
Kemptthal CH 107 B3
Kendal GB 37 B4
Kenderes H 113 B4
Kengyel H 113 B4
Kenilworth GB 44 A2
Kenmare IRL 29 C2
Kenmore GB 35 B4
Kennacraig GB 34 C2
Kenyeri H 111 B4
Kenzingen D 106 A2
Kepez TR 186 B1
Kępice PL 68 A1
Kępno PL 86 A2
Kepsut TR 186 C3
Keramoti GR 183 C6
Keräntöjärvi S . . .196 B6
Keratea GR 185 B4
Kerecsend H 113 B4
Kerekegyhaza H . .112 C3
Kerepestarcsa H . .112 B3
Keri GR 184 B1
Kérien F 100 A2
Kerkafalva H 111 C3
Kerken D 80 A2
Kerkrade NL 80 B2
Kerkyra GR 182 D1
Kerlouan F 100 A1
Kernascléden F . . .100 A2
Kernhof A 110 B2
Kerns CH 106 C3
Kerpen D 80 B2
Kerrysdale GB 31 B3
Kerta H 111 B4
Kerteminde DK 59 C3
Kerzers CH 106 C2
Keşan TR 186 B1
Kesgrave GB 45 A5
Kesh GB 26 B3
Keskin TR 23 B7
Kesselfall A 109 B3
Kestenga RUS 3 D12
Keswick GB 36 B3
Keszthely H 111 C4
Kétegyháza H 113 C5
Kéthely H 111 C4
Kętrzyn PL 12 A4
Kettering GB 44 A3
Kettlewell GB 40 A1
Kéty PL 99 B3
Ketzin D 74 B1
Keula D 82 A2
Keuruu FIN 8 A4
Kevelaer D 80 A2
Kevermes H 113 C5
Kevi SRB 126 B1
Keyingham GB 41 B3
Keynsham GB 43 A4
Kežmarok SK 99 B4
Kharmanli BG 183 B7
Khaskovo BG 183 B7
Khimki RUS 9 E10
Khisinev = Chişinău
  MD 17 B8
Khmelnik UA 13 D7
Khmelnytskyy UA . .13 D7
Khodoriv UA 13 D6
Kholm RUS 9 D7
Khotyn UA 13 D7
Khoyniki BY 13 C8
Khvoynaya RUS . . .9 C9
Kiato GR 184 A3
Kibæk DK 59 B1
Kiberg N 193 B14
Kicasalih TR 186 A1
Kičevo MK 182 B2
Kidderminster GB . .39 B4
Kidlington GB 44 B2
Kidsgrove GB 40 B1
Kidwelly GB 39 C2
Kiefersfelden D . . .108 B3
Kiel D 64 B3
Kielce PL 87 B4
Kielczygłów PL 86 A3
Kielder GB 37 A4
Kiełpino PL 68 A3

Kielpiny PL 77 A4
Kierinki FIN 197 B8
Kiernozia PL 77 B4
Kierspe D 81 A3
Kietrz PL 86 B2
Kietz D 74 B3
Kiev = Kyyiv UA . . .13 C9
Kiezmark PL 69 A3
Kiffisia GR 185 A4
Kifino Selo BIH . . .139 B4
Kihlanki
  FIN 196 B6
  S 196 B6
Kiistala FIN 197 B8
Kije PL 87 B4
Kijevo HR 138 B2
Kikallen N 46 B2
Kikinda SRB 126 B2
Kil
  N 53 B5
  Örebro S 55 A6
  Värmland S 55 A4
Kila S 55 A3
Kilafors S 50 A3
Kilbaha IRL 29 B2
Kilbeggan IRL 30 A1
Kilberry GB 34 C2
Kilbirnie GB 34 C3
Kilboghamn N 195 D4
Kilbotn N 194 B7
Kilb Rabenstein A .110 A2
Kilchattan GB 34 C2
Kilchoan GB 34 B1
Kilconnell IRL 28 A3
Kilcormac IRL 28 A4
Kilcreggan GB 34 C3
Kilcrow IRL 27 B4
Kildare IRL 30 A2
Kildinstroy RUS 3 B13
Kildonan GB 32 C3
Kildorrery IRL 29 B3
Kilegrend N 53 A4
Kilen N 53 A4
Kilgarvan IRL 29 C2
Kilia UA 17 C8
Kilioni GR 184 A1
Kiparissia GR 184 B2
Kipfenburg D 95 C3
Kippen GB 35 B3
Kiraz TR 188 A3
Kirazlı TR 186 B1
Kirberg D 81 B4
Kirchbach in
  Steiermark A 110 C2
Kirchberg
  CH 106 B2
  Baden-Württemberg
  D 94 B1
  Rheinland-Pfalz D .93 B3
Kirchberg am Wechsel
  A 110 B2
Kirchberg an der
  Pielach A 110 A2
Kirchberg in Tirol
  A 109 B3
Kirchbichl A 108 B3
Kirchdorf
  Bayern D 96 C1
  Mecklenburg-
  Vorpommern D . . .65 C4
  Niedersachsen D . .72 B1
Kirchdorf an der Krems
  A 109 B5
Kirchdorf in Tirol
  A 109 B3
Kirchenlamitz D . . .83 B3
Kirchenthumbach
  D 95 B3
Kirchhain D 81 B4
Kirchheim
  Baden-Württemberg
  D 94 C1
  Bayern D 108 A1
  Hessen D 81 B5
Kirchheimbolanden
  D 93 B4
Kirchhundem D 81 A4
Kirchlintein D 72 B2
Kirchschlag A 111 B3
Kirchweidach D . . .109 A3
Kirchzarten D 106 B2
Kircubbin GB 27 B5
Kireç TR 186 C3
Kırıkkale TR 23 B7
Kirillov RUS 9 C11
Kirishi RUS 9 C8
Kırka TR 187 C5
Kırkağaç TR 186 C2
Kirkbean GB 36 B3
Kirkbride GB 36 B3
Kirkby GB 38 A4
Kirkby Lonsdale
  GB 37 B4
Kirkby Malzeard
  GB 40 A2
Kirkbymoorside
  GB 37 B6
Kirkby Stephen GB .37 B4
Kirkcaldy GB 35 B4
Kirkcolm GB 36 B1
Kirkconnel GB 36 A2
Kirkcowan GB 36 B2
Kirkcudbright GB . . .36 B2
Kirkehamn N 52 B2
Kirke Hyllinge DK . .61 D1
Kirkenær N 49 B4
Kirkenes N 193 C14
Kirkham GB 38 A4
Kirkintilloch GB 35 C3
Kirkjubæjarklaustur
  IS 191 D7
Kirkkonummi FIN . . .8 B4
Kırklareli TR 186 A2
Kirkmichael GB 35 B4
Kirk Michael GB . . .36 B2
Kirkoswald GB 36 A2
Kirkpatrick Fleming
  GB 36 A3
Kirkton of Glenisla
  GB 35 B4
Kirkwall GB 33 C4
Kirkwhelpington
  GB 37 A5
Kirn D 93 B3
Kirovsk RUS 3 C13
Kirriemuir GB 35 B5
Kırşehir TR 23 B8
Kirton GB 41 C3
Kirton in Lindsey
  GB 40 B3
Kirtorf D 81 B5
Kiruna S 196 B3
Kisa S 62 A3
Kisač SRB 126 B1
Kisbér H 112 B2
Kiseljak BIH 139 B4
Kisielice PL 69 B4
Kiskőre H 113 B4
Kisköros H 112 C3
Kiskunfélegyháza
  H 113 C3

Kinloch continued
  Highland GB 32 C2
Kinlochbervie GB . .32 C1
Kinlochewe GB 32 D1
Kinlochleven GB . . .34 B3
Kinlochmoidart GB .34 B2
Kinloch Rannoch
  GB 35 B3
Kinloss GB 32 D3
Kinlough IRL 26 B2
Kinn N 48 B2
Kinna S 60 B2
Kinnared S 60 B3
Kinnarp S 55 B4
Kinnegad IRL 30 A1
Kinne-Kleva S 55 B4
Kinnitty IRL 28 A4
Kinrooi B 80 A1
Kinross GB 35 B4
Kinsale IRL 29 C3
Kinsarvik N 46 B3
Kintarvie GB 31 A2
Kintore GB 33 D4
Kinvarra IRL 28 A3
Kioni GR 184 A1
Kiparissia GR 184 B2
Kirby Hylie DK 61 D1
Kippel GB 35 B3
Kiraz TR 188 A3
Kirazlı TR 186 B1

Kiskunhalas H 112 C3
Kiskunlacháza H . .112 B2
Kiskunmajsa H . . .113 C3
Kislång H 112 C2
Kisslegg D 107 B4
Kissolt H 112 C3
Kissónerga CY 181 B1
Kist D 94 B1
Kistanje HR 138 B1
Kistelek H 113 C3
Kisterenye H 113 A3
Kisújszállás H 113 B4
Kisvárda H 16 A5
Kisvejke H 112 C2
Kiszkowo PL 76 B2
Kiszombor H 126 A2
Kitee FIN 9 A7
Kithnos GR 185 B5
Kiti CY 181 B2
Kitkiöjärvi S 196 B6
Kitkiöjoki S 196 B6
Kittelfjäll S 195 E6
Kittendorf D 74 A1
Kittilä FIN 196 B7
Kittlitz D 84 A2
Kittsee A 111 A4
Kitzbühel A 109 B3
Kitzingen D 94 B2
Kiuruvesi FIN 3 E10
Kivertsi UA 13 C6
Kividhes CY 181 B1
Kivik S 63 C2
Kivotos GR 182 C3
Kıyıköy TR 186 A3
Kızılcabölük TR . . .188 B4
Kızılcadağ TR 189 B4
Kızılcahamam TR . .23 A7
Kızılırmak TR 23 A7
Kızılkaya TR 189 B5
Kızılkuyu TR 187 D6
Kızılören
  Afyon TR 189 A5
  Konya TR 189 B7
Kjeldebotn N 194 B7
Kjellerup DK 59 B2
Kjellmyra N 49 B4
Kjøllefjord N 193 B11
Kjøpmannskjaer N .54 A1
Kjøpsvik N 194 B7
Kl'ačno SK 98 C2
Kladanj BIH 139 A4
Kläden D 73 B4
Klädesholmen S . . .60 B1
Kladnice HR 138 B2
Kladno CZ 84 B2
Kladruby CZ 95 B4
Klagenfurt A 110 C1
Klågerup S 61 D3
Klagstorp S 66 A2
Klaipėda LT 8 E2
Klaistow D 74 B1
Klaksvik FO 4 A3
Klana HR 123 B3
Klanac HR 123 C4
Klanjec HR 123 A4
Klardorf D 95 B4
Klarup DK 58 A3
Klašnice BIH 124 C3
Klässbol S 55 A3
Klášterec nad Ohří
  CZ 83 B5
Klášter pod Znievom
  SK 98 C2
Klatovy CZ 96 B1
Klaus an der
  Pyhrnbahn A 110 B1
Klazienaveen NL . . .71 B3
Klecko PL 76 B2
Kleczew PL 76 B3
Klein Plasten D 74 A1
Klein Sankt Paul
  A 110 C1
Kleinsölk A 109 B4
Kleinzell A 110 B2
Klejtrup DK 58 B2
Klek SRB 126 B2
Klemensker DK 67 A3
Klenak SRB 127 C1
Klenci pod Cerchovem
  CZ 95 B4
Klenica PL 75 C4
Klenje SRB 127 C1
Klenoec MK 182 B2
Klenovec SK 99 C3
Klenovica HR 123 B3
Klenovnik HR 124 A2
Kleppe N 52 B1
Kleppestø N 46 B2
Kleptow D 74 A2
Kleszewo PL 77 B6
Kleve D 80 A2
Klevshult S 60 B4
Klewki PL 77 A5
Kličevac SRB 127 C3
Kliening A 110 C1
Klietz D 73 B5
Klikuszowa PL 99 B3
Klimkovice CZ 98 B2
Klimontów PL 87 B5
Klimovichi BY 13 B9
Klimpfjäll S 195 E5
Klin RUS 9 D10
Klinča Sela HR . . .123 B4
Klingenbach A 111 B3
Klingenberg D 93 B5
Klingenmunster D . .93 B4
Klingenthal D 83 B4
Klinken D 73 A4
Klintehamn S 57 C4
Kliny PL 87 A4
Kliplev DK 64 B2
Klippan S 61 C3
Klis HR 138 B2
Klitmøller DK 58 A1
Klitten D 84 A6
Klixbüll D 64 B1
Kljajićevo SRB . . .126 B1
Ključ BIH 138 A2
Klobouky CZ 97 C4
Kłobuck PL 86 B2

Klockestrand S . . .200 D3
Kłodawa
  Lubuskie PL 75 B4
  Wielkopolskie PL .76 B3
Kłodzko PL 85 B4
Kløfta N 48 B3
Klokkarvik N 46 B2
Klokkerholm DK . . .58 A3
Klokočov SK 98 B2
Klomnice PL 86 B3
Klonowa PL 86 A2
Kloosterzande NL . .79 A4
Klopot PL 74 B3
Klos AL 182 B2
Kloštar Ivanić HR .124 B2
Kloster
  D 66 B2
  DK 59 B1
Klosterfelde A 74 B2
Klostermansfeld D .82 A3
Klosterneuburg A . .97 C4
Klosters CH 107 C4
Kloten CH 107 B3
Klötze D 73 B4
Klövsjö S 199 C11
Klövträsk S 196 D4
Kluczbork PL 86 B2
Kluczewo PL 75 A5
Kluisbergen B 79 B3
Klundert NL 79 A4
Klutz D 65 C4
Klyetsk BY 13 B7
Knaben N 52 B2
Knaften S 200 B4
Knapstad N 54 A2
Knäred S 61 C3
Knaresborough GB .40 A2
Knarvik N 46 B2
Knebel DK 59 B3
Knebworth GB 44 B3
Knesebeck D 73 B3
Knesselare B 78 A3
Knežak SLO 123 B3
Kneževi Vinogradi
  HR 125 B4
Kneževo HR 125 B4
Knić SRB 127 D2
Knighton GB 39 B3
Knin HR 138 A2
Knislinge S 61 C4
Knittelfeld A 110 B1
Knivsta S 57 A3
Knock IRL 28 A3
Knocktopher IRL . . .30 B1
Knokke-Heist B 78 A3
Knowle GB 44 A2
Knurów PL 86 B2
Knutby S 51 C5
Knutsford GB 38 A4
Kobarid SLO 122 A2
København =
  Copenhagen DK . .61 D2
Kobenz A 110 B1
Kobersdorf A 111 B3
Kobiernice PL 99 B3
Kobierzyce PL 85 B4
Kobilje SLO 111 C3
Kobiór PL 86 B2
Koblenz
  CH 106 B3
  D 81 B3
Kobryn BY 13 B6
Kobylanka PL 75 A3
Kobylin PL 85 A5
Kobylniki PL 77 B5
Kocaali TR 187 A5
Kocaaliler TR 189 B5
Kocaeli = İzmit
  TR 187 B4
Kočani MK 182 B4
Koçarlı TR 188 B2
Koceljevo SRB . . .127 C1
Kočerin BIH 138 B3
Kočevje SLO 123 B3
Kočevska Reka
  SLO 123 B3
Kochel am See D . .108 B2
Kocs H 112 B2
Kocsér H 113 B3
Kocsola H 112 C2
Kodal N 53 A6
Kode S 60 B1
Kodersdorf D 84 A2
Kodrab PL 86 A3
Kodrovnik HR 124 A2
Köflach A 110 B2
Kofçaz TR 186 A2
Köflach A 110 B2
Køge DK 61 D2
Kohlberg D 95 B4
Kohtla-Järve EST . . .8 C5
Köinge S 60 B2
Kojetín CZ 98 B1
Kökar FIN 51 C7
Kokava SK 99 C3
Kokkinotrimithia . .181 A2
Kokkola FIN 3 E8
Kokoski PL 69 A3
Koksijde B 78 A2
Kola
  BIH 124 C3
  RUS 3 B13
Köla S 54 A3
Kołacin PL 87 A3
Kolari FIN 196 B6
Kolárovo SK 112 B1
Kolašin MNE 16 D3
Kolbäck S 56 A2
Kołbacz PL 75 A3
Kołbaskowo PL 74 A3
Kolbeinsstaðir IS .190 C3
Kolbermoor D 108 B3
Kolbnitz A 109 C4
Kolbotn N 54 A1
Kolbu N 48 B2
Kolby Kås DK 59 C3
Kolczewo PL 67 C3
Kolczygłowy PL 68 A2
Kolding DK 59 C2

Kolesd H 112 C2
Kolgrov N 46 A1
Kolín CZ 97 A3
Kolind DK 59 B3
Kolinec CZ 96 B1
Koljane HR 138 B2
Kølkær DK 59 B2
Kölleda D 82 A3
Kollum NL 70 A3
Köln = Cologne D . .80 B2
Koło PL 76 B3
Kołobrzeg PL 67 B4
Kolochau D 83 A5
Kolomyya UA 13 D6
Kolonowskie PL 86 B2
Koloveč CZ 95 B5
Kolpino RUS 9 C7
Kolrep D 73 A5
Kölsillre S 199 C12
Kolsko PL 75 C4
Kolsva S 56 A1
Kolta SK 112 A2
Kolunič BIH 138 A2
Koluszki PL 87 A3
Kolut SRB 125 B4
Kolvereid N 199 A8
Kølvrå DK 59 B2
Komadi H 113 B5
Komagvær N 193 B14
Komarica BIH 125 C3
Kómárno SK 112 B2
Komárom H 112 B2
Komatou Yialou
  CY 181 A3
Komboti GR 182 D3
Komen SLO 122 B2
Komin HR 138 B3
Komiža HR 138 B2
Komját H 99 C4
Komjatice SK 112 A2
Komletinci HR 125 B4
Komló H 125 A4
Komoča SK 112 B2
Komorniki PL 75 B5
Komorzno PL 86 A2
Komotini GR 183 B7
Konak SRB 126 B2
Konakovo RUS 9 D10
Konarzyny PL 68 B2
Kondias GR 183 D7
Kondopaga RUS . . .9 A9
Kondorfa H 111 C3
Kondoros H 113 C4
Konevo RUS 9 A11
Køng DK 65 A4
Konga S 63 B3
Köngäs FIN 196 B7
Kongerslev DK 58 B3
Kongsberg N 53 A5
Kongshamn N 53 B4
Kongsmark DK 64 A1
Kongsmoen N 199 A9
Kongsvik N 194 B7
Kongsvinger N 48 B3
Konice CZ 97 B4
Konie PL 77 C5
Koniecpol PL 86 B3
Königsberg D 82 B2
Königsbronn D 94 C2
Königsbrück D 84 A1
Königsbrunn A 94 C2
Königsdorf D 108 B2
Königsee D 82 B3
Königshorst D 74 B1
Königslutter D 73 B3
Königssee D 109 B3
Königstein
  Hessen D 81 B4
  Sachsen D 84 B2
Königstetten A 97 C4
Königswartha D . . .84 A2
Königswiesen A . . .96 C2
Königswinter D 80 B3
Königs Wusterhausen
  D 74 B2
Konin PL 76 B3
Konispol AL 182 D2
Konitsa GR 182 C2
Köniz CH 106 C2
Konjevići BIH 139 A5
Konjevrate HR 138 B2
Konjic BIH 139 B3
Konjščina HR 124 A2
Könnern D 83 A3
Konnerud N 53 A6
Konopiska PL 86 B2
Konotop PL 75 C4
Końskie PL 87 A4
Konsmo N 52 B3
Konstancin-Jeziorna
  PL 77 B6
Konstantynów Łódzki
  PL 86 A3
Konstanz D 107 B4
Kontich B 79 A4
Kontiolahti FIN 9 A6
Konya TR 189 B7
Konz D 92 B2
Kópasker IS 191 A9
Kópavogur IS 190 C4
Kopčany SK 98 C1
Koper SLO 122 B2
Kopervik N 52 A1
Kópháza H 111 B3
Kopice PL 85 B5
Kopidlno CZ 84 B3
Köping S 56 A1
Köpingebro S 66 A2
Köpingsvik S 62 B4
Kopmanholmen
  S 200 C4
Koppang N 48 A3
Koppangen N 192 C4
Kopparberg S 50 C1
Koppelo FIN 193 D11
Koppom S 54 A3
Koprivlen BG 183 B5
Koprivna BIH 125 C4
Koprivnica HR 124 A2

Kopřivnice CZ 98 B2
Köprübaşı TR 186 D3
Koprzywnica PL 87 B5
Kopstal L 92 B2
Kopychyntsi UA . . .13 D6
Kopytkowo PL 69 B3
Korbach D 81 A4
Körbecke D 81 A4
Korçë AL 182 C2
Korčula HR 138 C3
KorczycÓw PL 75 B3
Korenita SRB 127 C1
Korets UA 13 C7
Korfantów PL 85 B5
Körfez TR 187 B4
Korgen N 195 D4
Korinth DK 64 A3
Korinthos = Corinth
  GR 184 B3
Korita
  BIH 138 A2
  HR 139 C3
Korithi GR 184 B1
Korkuteli TR 189 B5
Körmend H 111 B3
Korne D 68 A2
Korneuburg A 97 C4
Kornevo RUS 69 A5
Kórnik PL 76 B2
Kornsjø N 54 B2
Környe H 112 B2
Koromačno HR 123 C3
Koroni GR 184 C2
Koronos GR 185 B6
Koronowo PL 76 A2
Körösladány H 113 C5
Köröstarcsa H 113 C5
Korosten UA 13 C8
Korostyshev UA . . .13 C8
Korpikä S 196 D6
Korpikylä FIN 196 C6
Korpilombolo S . . .196 C6
Korsberga
  Jönköping S 62 A3
  Skaraborg S 55 B5
Korshavn N 54 A1
Korskrogen S 200 E1
Korsnäs S 50 B2
Korsør DK 65 A4
Korsun
  Shevchenkovskiy
  UA 13 D9
Korträsk S 196 D3
Kortrijk B 78 B3
Korucu TR 186 C2
Koryčany CZ 98 B1
Korzeńsko PL 85 A4
Korzybie PL 68 A1
Kos GR 188 C2
Kosakowo PL 69 A3
Kosanica MNE 139 B5
Kösching D 95 C3
Kościan PL 75 B5
Kościelec PL 76 B3
Kościerzyna PL 68 A2
Koserow D 66 B2
Košetice CZ 97 B3
Košice SK 12 D4
Kosjerić SRB 127 D1
Koška HR 125 B4
Koskullskulle S . . .196 B3
Kosovska Mitrovica
  KOS 16 D4
Kosta S 62 B3
Kostajnica HR 124 B2
Kostajnik SRB 127 C1
Kostanjevica SLO .123 B4
Kostelec nad Černými
  Lesy CZ 96 B2
Kostelec na Hané
  CZ 97 B5
Kostice CZ 84 B1
Kostkowo PL 68 A3
Kostojevići SRB . .127 C1
Kostolac SRB 127 C3
Kostomłoty PL 85 A4
Kostopil UA 13 C7
Kostów PL 86 A2
Kostrzyn
  Lubuskie PL 74 B3
  Wielkopolskie PL .76 B2
Koszalin PL 67 B5
Koszęcin PL 86 B2
Kőszeg H 111 B3
Koszwaly PL 69 A3
Koszyce PL 87 B4
Kot SLO 123 B4
Kotala FIN 197 B11
Kötelek H 113 B4
Köthen D 83 A3
Kotka FIN 8 B5
Kotomierz PL 76 A3
Kotor MNE 16 D3
Kotoriba HR 124 A2
Kotorsko BIH 125 C4
Kotor Varoš BIH . .124 C3
Kotovsk UA 17 B8
Kotronas GR 184 C3
Kötschach D 109 C3
Kötzting D 95 B4
Koudum NL 70 B2
Kouřim CZ 96 A2
Kout na Šumave
  CZ 95 B5
Kouvola FIN 8 B5
Kovačevac SRB . .127 C2
Kovdor RUS 197 B13
Kovel' UA 13 C6
Kovilj SRB 126 B2
Kovin SRB 127 C3
Kowal PL 77 B4
Kowalewo Pomorskie
  PL 69 B3
Kowalów PL 75 B3
Kowary PL 85 B3
Köyceğiz TR 188 C3

Kozani GR 182 C3
Kozarac
  BIH 124 C2
  HR 124 B1
Kozárovce SK 98 C2
Kozelets UA. 13 C9
Kozica HR 138 B3
Kozięgłowy PL. 86 B3
Kozienice PL. 87 A5
Kozina SLO 122 B2
Kozje SLO 123 A4
Kozlu TR 187 A6
Kozluk BIH. 139 A5
Koźmin PL. 85 A5
Kozolupy CZ. 96 B1
Kożuchów PL 84 A3
Kožuhe BIH 125 C4
Kozyatyn UA. 13 D8
Kozyürük TR. 186 A1
Kräckelbräken S . . .49 A6
Krackow D. 74 A3
Kraddsele S. 195 E7
Krąg PL 68 A1
Kragenæs DK 65 B4
Kragerø N 53 B5
Krągi PL 68 B1
Kragujevac SRB .127 C2
Kraiburg D 109 A3
Krajenka PL. 68 B1
Krajišnik SRB 126 B2
Krajková CZ. 83 B4
Krajné SK. 98 C1
Krajnik Dolny PL. . .74 A3
Krakača BIH. 124 B1
Kräklingbo S 57 C4
Kraków = Cracow
  PL. 99 A3
Krakow am See D . .73 A5
Králíky CZ. 85 B4
Kraljevica HR 123 B3
Kraljevo SRB. 16 C1
Kral'ovany SK 99 B3
Král'ov Brod SK . .111 A4
Kralovice CZ 96 B1
Kralupy nad Vltavou
  CZ. 84 B2
Králův Dvůr CZ . . .96 B2
Kramfors S 200 D3
Kramsach A 108 B2
Kramsk PL 76 B3
Kråmvik N 53 A4
Kranenburg D 80 A2
Krania GR 182 D3
Krania Elasonas
  GR. 182 D4
Kranichfeld D 82 B3
Kranidi GR 184 B4
Kranj SLO 123 A3
Kranjska Gora
  SLO 109 C4
Krapanj HR 138 B1
Krapina HR 124 A1
Krapje HR 124 B2
Krapkowice PL. 86 B1
Kraselov CZ. 96 B1
Krašić HR 123 B4
Kråslava LV 8 E5
Kraslice CZ. 83 B4
Krasna PL 87 A4
Krasna Lipa CZ . . .84 B2
Krasne PL 77 B5
Krašnik PL. 12 C5
Krašnja SLO 123 A3
Krásno SK 98 B2
Krásnohorské
  Podhradie SK . . .99 C4
Krasno Polje HR . .123 C4
Krasnozavodsk
  RUS. 9 D11
Krasnystaw PL 13 C5
Krasnyy RUS. 13 A9
Krasnyy Kholm
  RUS. 9 C10
Krasocin PL. 87 B4
Kraszewice PL. 86 A2
Kraszkowice PL. . . .86 A2
Kratigos GR. 186 C1
Kratovo MK 182 A4
Kraubath A. 110 B1
Krausnick D. 74 B2
Krautheim D 94 B1
Kravaře CZ. 84 B2
Kraváre CZ 98 B2
Kravarsko HR 124 B2
Kraznějov CZ. 96 B1
Krčedin SRB 126 B2
Kŭrdzhali BG. 183 B7
Krefeld D 80 A2
Kregme DK 61 D2
Krembz D 73 A4
Kremenets UA. 13 C6
Kremmen D 74 B2
Kremna SRB 127 D1
Kremnica SK. 98 C2
Krempe D. 64 C2
Krems A 97 C3
Kremsbrücke A . . .109 C4
Kremsmünster A . .110 A1
Křemže CZ. 96 C2
Křenov CZ. 97 B4
Krepa PL 76 C3
Krępa Krajeńska
  PL. 75 A5
Krepsko PL 68 B1
Kresevo BIH 139 B4
Kressbronn D 107 B4
Krestena GR 184 B2
Kretinga LT 8 E2
Krettsy RUS. 9 C8
Kreuth D 108 B2
Kreuzau D 80 B2
Kreuzlingen CH. . .107 B4
Kreuztal D 81 B3
Krewelin D 74 B2
Krezluk BIH. 138 A3
Krichem BG. 183 A6

Krieglach A 110 B2
Kriegsfeld D 93 B3
Kriens CH 106 B3
Krimml A 108 B3
Krimpen aan de IJssel
  NL. 79 A4
Křinec CZ. 84 B3
Kristdala S 62 A4
Kristiansand N 53 B4
Kristianstad S 61 C4
Kristiansund N . . .198 B4
Kristiinankaupunki
  FIN. 8 A2
Kristinefors S 49 B4
Kristinehamn S 55 A5
Kriváň SK. 99 C3
Kriva Palanka MK .182 A4
Křivoklát CZ 96 A1
Křižanov CZ. 97 B4
Križevci HR 124 A2
Krk HR 123 B3
Krka SLO 123 B3
Krnjača SRB 127 C2
Krnjak HR 123 B4
Krnjeuša BIH 124 C2
Krnjevo SRB 127 C3
Krnov CZ. 98 A1
Krobia PL. 85 A4
Kroczyce PL. 86 B3
Krøderen N 48 B1
Krokees GR. 184 C3
Krokek S 56 B2
Krokom S 199 B11
Krokowa PL. 68 A3
Krokstad-elva N . . .53 A5
Kroksund N 54 A2
Kroměříž CZ 98 B1
Krommenie NL 70 B1
Krompachy SK 99 C4
Kronach D 82 B3
Kronshagen D 64 B3
Kronshtadt RUS . . .9 C6
Kröpelin D 65 B4
Kropp D 64 B2
Kroppenstedt D. . . .73 C4
Kropstädt D. 74 C1
Krościenko nad
  Dunajcem PL 99 B4
Kröslin D 66 B2
Krośnice PL. 85 A5
Krośniewice PL. . . .77 B4
Krosno PL 12 D4
Krosno Odrzańskie
  PL. 75 B4
Krostitz D. 83 A4
Krotoszyn PL 85 A5
Krottendorf A. 110 B2
Krouna CZ. 97 B4
Krowiarki PL. 86 B2
Krrabë AL. 182 B1
Kršan HR 123 B3
Krško SLO. 123 B4
Krstac MNE 139 B4
Krstur SRB 126 A2
Křtiny CZ. 97 B4
Kruft D 80 B3
Kruishoutem B 79 B3
Krujë AL. 182 B1
Krulyewshchyna
  BY 13 A7
Krumbach
  A. 111 B3
  D 94 C2
Krumovgrad BG . .183 B7
Krün D 108 B2
Krupá CZ. 84 B1
Krupa na Vrbasu
  BIH. 124 C3
Krupanj SRB 127 C1
Krupina SK 99 C3
Krupka CZ. 84 B1
Krupki BY. 13 A8
Krusá DK 64 B2
Kruščica BIH 139 A3
Kruševac SRB. 16 D4
Kruševo MK. 182 B3
Kruszwica PL 76 B3
Kruszyn PL 77 B4
Krychaw BY. 13 B9
Krynica PL. 99 B4
Krynica Morska PL .69 A4
Krzęcin PL 75 A4
Krzelów PL. 85 A4
Krzepice PL. 86 B2
Krzepielów PL. 85 A4
Krzeszowice PL. . . .86 B3
Krzeszyce PL. 75 B4
Krzynowłaga Mała
  PL. 77 A5
Krzywiń PL. 75 C5
Krzyżanowice PL. . .98 B2
Krzyżowa PL 99 B3
Krzyż Wielkopolski
  PL. 75 B5
Ksiaz Wielkopolski
  PL. 87 B4
Książ Wielkopolski
  PL. 76 B2
Kętbowiec PL 75 A5
Kübekháza H. 126 A2
Küblis CH 107 C4
Kuchary PL. 86 A1
Kuchl A. 109 B4
Kucice PL. 77 B5
Kuciste HR 138 C3
Kuçovë AL 182 C1
Küçükbahçe TR. . .188 A1
Küçükköy TR. 186 C1
Küçükkuyu TR. . . .186 C1
Kucura SRB. 126 B1
Kuczbork-Osada
  PL. 77 A5
Kuddby S 56 B2
Kudowa-Zdrój PL .85 B4
Kufstein A 108 B3
Kuggeboda S 63 B3
Kuggörana S 200 E3
Kühbach D. 95 C3
Kuhmo FIN 3 D11

Kuhmoinen FIN 8 B4
Kuhnsdorf A 110 C1
Kuhstedt D 72 A1
Kuinre NL. 70 B2
Kuivaniemi FIN . . .197 D8
Kuivastu EST. 8 C3
Kukës AL 182 A2
Kuklin PL. 77 A5
Kukljica HR 137 A4
Kukujevci SRB . . .127 B1
Kula
  Srbija SRB 127 C3
  Vojvodina SRB. .126 B1
  TR. 188 A3
Kuldīga LV 8 D2
Kulen Vakuf BIH . .124 C2
Kulina BIH 125 C4
Kullstedt D. 82 A2
Kulmain D. 95 B3
Kulmbach D. 82 B3
Kuloharju FIN 197 D11
Kulu TR 23 B7
Kumachevo RUS. . .69 A5
Kumafşarı TR 189 B4
Kumane SRB 126 B2
Kumanovo MK. . . .182 A3
Kumbağ TR 186 B2
Kumdanlı TR 189 A5
Kumkale TR. 186 C1
Kumla
  S. 56 A1
  S. 50 C3
Kumlinge FIN 51 B7
Kumluca TR. 189 C5
Kumrovec HR 123 A4
Kunadacs H 112 C3
Kunágota H 113 C5
Kunbaja H 126 A1
Kunda EST. 8 C5
Kundl A 108 B2
Kunes N. 193 B10
Kunfehértó H 126 A1
Kungälv S 60 B1
Kungsängen S 57 A3
Kungsäter S. 60 B2
Kungsbacka S. 60 B2
Kungsgården S. . . .50 B3
Kungshamn S 54 B2
Kungs-Husby S . . .56 A3
Kungsör S. 56 A2
Kunhegyes H. 113 B4
Kunmadaras H . . .113 B4
Kunovice CZ. 98 B1
Kunów PL 87 B5
Kunowo
  Wielkopolskie PL. .76 C2
  Zachodnio-Pomorskie
  PL. 74 A3
Kunštát CZ 97 B4
Kunszállás H 113 C3
Kunszentmárton
  H 113 C4
Kunszentmiklós
  H 112 B3
Kunžak CZ. 97 B3
Künzelsau D 94 B1
Kuolayarvi RUS. . .197 C12
Kuolio FIN. 197 D11
Kuopio FIN 8 A5
Kuosku FIN. 197 B11
Kup
  H. 111 B4
  PL. 86 B1
Kupferzell D. 94 B1
Kupinec HR 123 B4
Kupinečki Kraljevac
  HR 124 B1
Kupinovo SRB. . . .127 C2
Kupirovo HR. 138 A2
Kupjak HR 123 B3
Kuppenheim D 93 C4
Kupres BIH 138 B3
Küps D 82 B3
Kurd H 112 C2
Küre TR. 23 A7
Kuressaare EST 8 C3
Kurikka FIN 8 A3
Kuřim CZ. 97 B4
Kuřivody CZ. 84 B2
Kurki PL. 77 A5
Kurort Oberwiesenthal
  D. 83 B4
Kurort Schmalkalden
  D. 82 B2
Kurort Stolberg D .82 A2
Kurort Wippra D . .82 A3
Kurów PL 12 C5
Kurowice PL. 86 A3
Kurravaara S 196 B3
Kursu FIN. 197 C11
Kurşunlu
  Bursa TR 187 B4
  Çankırı TR. 23 A7
Kurtakko FIN 196 B7
Kürten D. 80 A3
Kurvinen FIN 197 D12
Kurzelów PL. 87 B3
Kusadak SRB 127 C2
Kuşadası TR 188 B2
Kusel D 93 B3
Küsnacht CH. 106 B3
Küssnacht CH. . . .106 B3
Kütahya TR 187 C4
Kutenholz D. 72 A2
Kutina HR 124 B2
Kutjevo HR 125 B3
Kutná Hora CZ. 97 B3
Kutno PL 77 B4
Kuttara FIN 193 D10
Küttingen CH. 106 B3
Kúty SK 98 C1
Kuusamo FIN 197 D12
Kuusankoski FIN . . .8 B5
Kuvshinovo RUS . . .9 D9
Kuyucak TR. 188 B3
Kuzmin SRB 127 B1
Kuźnia Raciborska
  PL. 86 B2
Kuźnica Czarnkowska
  PL. 75 B5

Kuźnica Żelichowska
  PL. 75 B5
Kvaløysletta N 192 C2
Kvalsund N 192 B7
Kvam
  Nord-Trøndelag
  N 199 A8
  Oppland N 198 D6
Kvamsøy N 46 A3
Kvænangsbotn N .192 C6
Kvanndal N. 46 B3
Kvänum S 55 B4
Kværndrup DK 59 C3
Kvås N 52 B3
Kvasice CZ. 98 B1
Kvelde N 53 A5
Kvenna N. 198 C5
Kvernaland N 52 B1
Kvibille S 60 C2
Kvicksund S 56 A2
Kvidinge S 61 C3
Kvikkjokk S 195 D8
Kvikne
  Hedmark N 199 C7
  Oppland N 47 A6
Kvilda CZ. 96 B1
Kville S. 54 B2
Kvillsfors S 62 A3
Kvinesdal N 52 B2
Kvinlog N. 52 B2
Kvinnherad N 46 C3
Kvissel DK 58 A3
Kvisvik N 198 B5
Kviteseid N. 53 A4
Kvitsøy N. 52 A1
Kwakowo PL. 68 A2
Kwidzyn PL. 69 B3
Kwilcz PL 75 B5
Kyakhta GB. 31 B3
Kyjov CZ. 98 C1
Kyleakin GB. 31 B3
Kyle of Lochalsh
  GB. 31 B3
Kylerhea GB. 31 B3
Kylestrome GB 32 C1
Kyllburg D 92 A2
Kyllini GR 184 B2
Kynšperk nad Ohří
  CZ. 83 B4
Kyperounda CY. . .181 B1
Kyrenia CY. 181 A2
Kyritz D 73 B5
Kyrkesund S. 60 A1
Kyrkhult S 63 B2
Kyrksæterøra N. . .198 B6
Kyrkhult S. 63 B2
Kysucké Nové Mesto
  SK 98 B2
Kythira GR. 184 C3
Kythréa CY 181 A2
Kyustendil BG. 16 D5
Kyyiv = Kiev UA. . .13 C9
Kyyjärvi FIN. 8 A4

L

Laa an der Thaya A .97 C4
La Adrada E. 150 B3
Laage D 65 C5
La Alameda E 157 B4
La Alberca E 149 B3
La Alberca de Záncara
  E 158 B1
La Albergueria de
  Argañán E. 149 B3
La Albuera E 155 C4
La Aldea del Portillo del
  Busto E. 143 B3
La Algaba E 162 A1
La Aliseda de Tormes
  E 150 B2
La Almarcha E 158 B1
La Almolda E 153 A3
La Almunia de Doña
  Godina E. 152 A2
Laanila FIN 193 D11
La Antillas E 161 B2
La Arena E 141 A4
Laatzen D. 72 B2
La Aulaga E 161 B3
La Balme-de-Sillingy
  F 118 B3
Laban IRL. 28 A3
La Bañeza E 141 B5
La Barca de la Florida
  E 162 B2
La Barre-de-Monts
  F 114 B1
La Barre-en-Ouche
  F 89 B4
La Barrosa E 162 B1
La Barthe-de-Neste
  F 145 A4
La Bassée F 78 B2
La Bastide-de-Sérou
  F 146 A2
La Bastide-des-
  Jourdans F 132 B1
Labastide-Murat F .129 B4
La Bastide-Puylaurent
  F 117 C4
Labastide-Rouairoux
  F 130 B1
Labastide-St Pierre
  F 129 C4
La Bathie F 118 B3
Lábatlan H. 112 B2
La Baule-Escoublac
  F 101 B3
La Bazoche-Gouet
  F 102 A2
La Bégude-de-Mazenc
  F 131 A3
Labenne F. 128 C1
La Bernerie-en-Retz
  F 114 A1
Labin HR 123 B3
La Bisbal d'Empordà
  E 147 C4
Łabiszyn PL. 76 B2
Lad H 125 A3
Ładbergen D 71 B4
Lablachère F. 131 A3

Lábod H 124 A3
Laboe D 64 B3
La Boissière F. 89 A4
Labouheyre F. 128 B2
La Bourboule F . . .116 B2
La Bóveda de Toro
  E 150 A2
La Brède F. 128 B2
La Bresse F 106 A1
La Bridoire F 118 B2
La Brillanne F 132 B1
Labrit F. 128 B2
Labros E 152 A2
La Bruffière F. 114 A2
Labruguière F. 130 B1
La Bussière F 103 B4
Laç AL 182 B1
La Caillère F 114 B3
Lacalahorra E. 164 B1
Lacanau F 128 B1
Lacanau-Océan F .128 A1
Lacanche F 104 B3
La Canourgue F . . .130 A2
La Capelle F. 91 B3
Lacapelle-Marival
  F. 129 B4
Laćarak SRB 127 B1
La Cardanchosa
  E 156 B2
La Caridad E 141 A4
La Carlota E 162 A3
La Carolina E 157 B4
Lacaune F 130 B1
La Cava E. 153 B4
La Cavalerie F. 130 A2
Laceby GB 41 B3
Lacedónia I 172 A1
La Celle-en-Moravan
  F 104 B3
La Celle-St Avant
  F 102 B2
La Cerca E 143 B3
Láces I 108 C1
La Chaise-Dieu F .117 B3
La Chaize-Giraud
  F 114 B2
La Chaize-le-Vicomte
  F 114 B2
La Chambre F 118 B3
Lachania GR 188 D2
La Chapelaude F . .116 A2
La Chapelle-d'Angillon
  F 103 B4
La Chapelle-en-
  Aalgaudémar F . .118 C3
La Chapelle-en-Vercors
  F 118 C2
La Chapelle-Glain
  F 101 B4
La Chapelle-la-Reine
  F 90 C2
La Chapelle-Laurent
  F 116 B3
La Chapelle-St Luc
  F 91 C4
La Chapelle-sur-Erdre
  F 101 B4
La Chapelle-
  Vicomtesse F . . .103 B3
La Charce F 132 A1
La Charité-sur-Loire
  F 104 B2
La Chartre-sur-le-Loir
  F 102 B2
La Châtaigneraie
  F 114 B3
La Châtre F 103 C3
La Chaussée-sur-
  Marne F 91 C4
La Chaux-de-Fonds
  CH 106 B1
Lachen CH 107 B3
Lachendorf D 72 B3
La Cheppe F 91 B4
La Chèze F 101 A3
Lachowice PL 99 B3
La Ciotat F 132 B1
Łąck PL 77 B4
Läckeby S 62 B4
Läckö S 55 B4
La Clayette F 117 A4
La Clusaz F 118 B3
Lacock GB. 43 A4
La Codosera E 155 B3
La Concha E 143 A3
La Condamine-
  Châtelard F. 132 A2
Láconi I 179 C3
La Contienda E . . .161 A3
La Coquille F 115 C4
La Coronada E. . . .156 B2
La Côte-St André
  F 118 B2
La Cotinière F 114 C2
La Courtine F 116 B2
Lacq F 145 A3
La Crau F. 132 B2
La Crèche F 115 B3
La Croix F. 102 B2
Lacroix-Barrez F . .116 C2
Lacroix-St Ouen F. .90 B2
Lacroix-sur-Meuse
  F 92 C1
La Croix-Valmer F .132 B2
La Cumbre E 156 A2
Łączna PL. 87 B4
Łącznik PL. 86 B1
Lad H 125 A3
Ladbergen D 71 B4
Ladek-Zdrój PL. . . .85 B4

Ladelund D 64 B2
Ladendorf A. 97 C4
Ladignac-le-Long
  F. 115 C5
Ladispoli I 168 B2
Ladoeiro P. 155 B3
Ladon F 103 B4
Łabowa PL. 99 B4
La Douze F 129 A3
Ladushkin RUS. . . .69 A5
Ladybank GB. 35 B4
Laer D 71 B4
La Espina E 141 A4
La Estrella E 156 A2
La Farga de Moles
  E 146 B2
La Fatarella E 153 A4
La Felipa E 158 B2
La Fère F 90 B3
La Ferrière
  Indre-et-Loire F .102 B2
  Vendée F 114 B2
La Ferrière-en-
  Parthenay F 115 B3
La-Ferté-Alais F . . .90 C2
La Ferté-Bernard
  F. 102 A2
La Ferté-Frênel F. . .89 B4
La Ferté-Gaucher
  F. 90 C3
La Ferté-Imbault
  F. 103 B3
La Ferté-Macé F . . .89 B3
La Ferté-Milon F . . .90 B3
La Ferté-sous-Jouarre
  F. 90 C3
La Ferté-St-Aubin
  F. 103 B3
La Ferté-St-Cyr F . .103 B3
La Ferté-Vidame F. .89 B4
La Ferté Villeneuil
  F. 103 B3
La Feuillie F. 90 B1
La Flèche F 102 B1
La Flotte F 114 B2
La Font de la Figuera
  E 159 C3
La Fouillade F 130 A1
Lafrançaise F 129 B4
La Fregeneda E . . .149 B3
La Fresneda E 153 B4
La Fuencubierta E .162 A3
La Fuente de San
  Esteban E 149 B3
La Fulioala E 147 C2
La Gacilly F 101 B3
La Galera E 153 B4
Lagan S 60 C3
Laganadi I 175 C1
Lagarde F 146 A2
La Garde-Freinet
  F. 132 B2
Lagares
  Coimbra P 148 B2
  Porto P 148 A1
La Garnache F. . . .114 B2
Lagaro I 135 A4
La Garriga E 147 C3
La Garrovilla E. . . .155 C4
Lagartera E 150 C2
La Gaubretière F . .114 B2
Lågbol S 51 B5
Lage D 72 C1
Lägerdorf D 64 C2
Lagg GB. 34 C2
Laggan GB. 32 D2
Laggartorp S 55 A5
Łagiewniki PL 85 B4
La Gineta E 158 B1
Láglio I 120 B2
Lagnieu F 118 B2
Lagny-sur-Marne F .90 C2
Lago
  Calábria I. 175 B2
  Veneto I. 121 B5
Lagôa P 160 B1
Lagoaça P 149 A3
Lagonegro I 174 A1
Lagos
  GR 183 B7
  P 160 B1
Lagosanto I 121 C5
Łagów
  Lubuskie PL. 75 B4
  Świętokrzyskie PL. .87 B5
La Granadella
  Alicante E 159 C4
  Lleida E 153 A4
La Grand-Combe
  F. 131 A3
La Grande-Croix
  F. 117 B4
La Grande-Motte
  F. 131 B3
La Granja d'Escarp
  E 153 A4
La Granjuela E 156 B2
La Grasse F 146 A3
La Grave F 118 B3
La Gravelle F 101 A4
La Guardia E 151 C4
La Guardia de Jaén
  E 163 A4
Laguarres E 145 B4
Laguenne F. 116 B1
Laguépie F. 129 B4
Laguiole F. 116 C2
Laguna de Duera
  E 150 A3
Laguna del
  Marquesado E .152 B2
Laguna de Negrillos
  E 142 B1

Lagundo I 108 C2
Lagunilla E 149 B3
La Haba E 156 B2
Laharie F. 128 B1
La Haye-du-Puits F .88 A2
La Haye-Pesnel F . .88 B2
Lahden D. 71 B4
La Herlière F 78 B2
La Hermida E 142 A2
La Herrera E 158 C1
Laheycourt F. 91 C5
La Higuera E 158 C2
La Hiniesta E 149 A4
Lahnstein D. 81 B3
Laholm S 61 C3
La Horcajada E . . .150 B2
La Horra E 143 C3
Lahr D. 93 C3
Lahti FIN 8 B4
La Hulpe B 79 B4
La Hutte F 89 B4
Laichingen D. 94 C1
L'Aigle F. 89 B4
La Iglesuela E 150 B3
La Iglesuela del Cid
  E 153 B3
Laignes F 104 B3
Laiguéglia I 133 B4
L'Aiguillon-sur-Mer
  F 114 B2
Laimbach am Ostrong
  A. 97 C3
Laina E. 152 A1
Lainio S 196 B5
Lairg GB. 32 C2
La Iruela E 164 B2
Laissac F 130 A1
Laisvall S 195 D8
Láives I 121 A4
La Javie F 132 A2
Lajkovac SRB 127 C2
La Jonchère-St
  Maurice F 116 A1
La Jonquera E 146 B3
Lajoskomárom H .112 C2
Lajosmizse H 112 B3
Lak H 99 C4
Lakenheath GB . . .45 A4
Lakitelek H. 113 C4
Lakki GR. 185 D4
Lakolk DK 64 A1
Łąkorz PL. 69 B4
Lakšárska Nová Ves
  SK 98 C1
Lakselv N 193 B8
Laksfors N. 195 E4
Laktaši BIH 124 C3
La Lantejuela E . . .162 A2
Lalapaşa TR. 186 A1
L'Albagès E. 153 A4
Lalbenque F 129 B4
L'Alcudia E 159 B3
L'Aldea E 153 B4
Lalín E 140 B2
La Línea de la
  Concepción E. . .162 B2
Lalizolle F 116 A3
La Llacuna E 147 C2
Lalley F 118 C2
Lalling D 95 C5
Lalm N 198 D6
La Londe-les-Maures
  F 132 B2
La Loupe F. 89 B5
La Louvière B 79 B4
L'Alpe-d'Huez F . .118 B3
La Luisiana E 162 A2
Laluque F. 128 C1
Lam D. 95 B5
La Machine F. 104 C2
la Maddalena I . . .178 A3
Lama dei Peligni I .169 A4
Lamadrid E 142 A2
Lamagistère F 129 B3
La Mailleraye-sur-Seine
  F. 89 A4
La Malène F 130 A2
Lama Mocogno I . .135 A3
La Mamola E 163 B4
La Manresana dels
  Prats E 147 C2
Lamarche F 105 A4
Lamarche-sur-Saône
  F. 105 B4
Lamargelle F 105 B3
Lamarosa P 154 B2
Lamarque F 128 A2
Lamas E. 148 B1
La Masadera E 145 C3
Lamas de Moaro
  P 140 B2
Lamastre F. 117 C4
La Mata E 150 C3
La Mata de Ledesma
  E 149 A4
La Mata de
  Monteagudo E . .142 B1
Lambach D. 109 A4
Lamballe F. 101 A3
Lamberhurst GB. . .45 B4
Lambesc F 131 B4
Lambia GR. 184 B2
Lambley GB. 37 B4
Lambourn GB 44 B2
Lamego P 148 A2
La Meilleraye-de-
  Bretagne F 101 B4
La Ménitré F. 102 B1
L'Ametlla de Mar
  E 153 B4
Lamia GR. 182 E4
Lammhult S. 62 A2
La Mojonera E 164 C2
La Mole F 132 B2
La Molina E 147 B2
La Monnerie-le-Montel
  F. 117 B3
La Morera E 155 C4

La Mothe-Achard F 114 B2
Lamothe-Cassel F 129 B4
Lamothe-Montravel F 128 B3
La Mothe-St Héray F 115 B3
Lamotte-Beuvron F 103 B4
La Motte-Chalançon F 131 A4
La Motte-du-Caire F 132 A2
La Motte-Servolex F 118 B2
Lampertheim D . . . 93 B4
Lampeter GB 39 B2
L'Ampolla E 153 B4
Lamprechtshausen A 109 B3
Lamsfeld D 74 C3
Lamspringe D 72 C3
Lamstedt D 72 A2
La Mudarra E 142 C2
La Muela E 152 A2
La Mure F 118 C2
Lamure-sur-Azergues F 117 A4
Lana I 108 C2
Lanaja E 145 C3
Lanarce F 117 C3
Lanark GB 36 A3
La Nava E 161 B3
La Nava de Ricomalillo E 156 A3
La Nava de Santiago E 155 B4
Lancaster GB 37 B4
Lanchester GB . . . 37 B5
Lanciano I 169 A4
Lancing GB 44 C3
Lançon-Provence F 131 B4
Lancova Vas SLO .124 A1
Landau
Bayern D 95 C4
Rheinland-Pfalz D .93 B4
Landeck A 108 B1
Landen B 79 B5
Landerneau F 100 A1
Landeryd S 60 B3
Landesbergen D . .72 B2
Landete F 158 B2
Landévant F 100 B2
Landévennec F . . .100 A1
Landeyjahöfn 190 D5
Landivisiau F 100 A1
Landivy F 88 B2
Landl A 108 B3
Landön S 199 B11
Landos F 117 C3
Landouzy-le-Ville F 91 B4
Landquart CH 107 C4
Landrecies F 91 A3
Landreville F 104 A3
Landriano I 120 B2
Landsberg D 108 A1
Lands-berg D 83 A4
Landsbro S 62 A2
Landscheid D 92 B2
Landshut D 95 C4
Landskrona S 61 D2
Landstuhl D 93 B3
Lanesborough IRL .28 A4
Lanester F 100 B2
Lanestosa E 143 A3
La Neuve-Lyre F . .89 B4
La Neuve VILLE CH . .106 B2
Langå DK 59 B2
Langada GR 185 A7
Langadas GR 183 C5
Langa de Duero E 151 A4
Langadia GR 184 B3
Langangen N 53 A5
Långared S 60 A2
Långaröd S 61 D3
Långaryd S 60 B3
Långås S 60 C2
Långasjö S 63 B3
Langau A 97 C3
Langeac F 117 B3
Langeais F 102 B2
Langedijk NL 70 B1
Langeln D 73 C3
Langelsheim D . . .72 C3
Langemark-Poelkapelle B 78 B2
Langen
Hessen D 93 B4
Niedersachsen D .72 A1
Langenau D 94 C2
Langenberg D 81 A4
Langenbruck CH . .106 B2
Langenburg D 94 B1
Längenfeld A 108 B1
Langenfeld D 80 A2
Langenhorn D 64 B1
Langenlois A 97 C3
Langenlonsheim D 93 B3
Langennaundorf D .83 A5
Langennufnach D 94 C2
Langenthal CH . . .106 B2
Langenzenn D 94 B2
Langeoog D 71 A4
Langesund N 53 A5
Langewiesen D . . .82 B2
Långflon S 49 A4
Langförden D 71 B5
Langhagen D 73 A4
Länghem S 60 B3
Langhirano I 120 C3
Langholm GB 36 A4
Langholt IS 191 D7
Långlöt S 62 B4
Langnau CH 106 C2
Langø DK 65 B4
Langogne F 117 C3
Langon F 128 B2
Langquaid D 95 C4

Långrådna S 56 B2
Langreo E 142 A1
Langres F 105 B4
Långsele S 200 C3
Långserud S 54 A3
Langset N 48 B3
Långshyttan S 50 B3
Langstrand N 192 B7
Långträsk S 196 D3
Langueux F 101 A3
Languidic F 100 B2
Längvik S 57 A4
Langwarden D 71 A5
Langwathby GB . .37 B4
Langwedel D 72 B2
Langweid D 94 C2
Langwies CH 107 C4
Lanheses P 148 A1
Lanięta PL 77 B4
Lanildut F 100 A1
Lanjarón E 163 B4
Lanmeur F 100 A2
Lanna
Jönköping S 60 B3
Örebro S 55 A5
Lännaholm S 51 C4
Lannavaara S 196 A4
Lannéanou F 100 A2
Lannemezan F . . . 145 A4
Lanneuville-sur-Meuse F 91 B5
Lannilis F 100 A1
Lannion F 100 A2
La Nocle-Maulaix F 104 C2
Lanouaille F 115 C5
Lansjärv S 196 C5
Lanškroun CZ 97 B4
Lanslebourg-Mont-Cenis F 119 B3
Lanta F 129 C4
Lantadilla E 142 B2
Lanton F 128 B1
Lantosque F 133 B3
La Nuez de Arriba E 143 B3
Lanusei I 179 C3
Lanúvio I 168 B2
Lanvollon F 100 A3
Lánycsók H 125 A4
Lanz D 73 A4
Lanza E 140 A2
Lanzada I 120 B2
Lanzahita E 150 B3
Lanžhot CZ 97 C4
Lanzo Torinese I . . 119 B4
Laole SRB 127 C3
Laon F 91 B3
Laons F 89 B5
La Paca E 164 B3
La Pacaudière F . .117 A3
Lapalisse F 117 A3
La Palma d'Ebre E 153 A4
La Palma del Condado E 161 B3
La Palme F 146 B4
La Palmyre F 114 C2
La Parra E 155 C4
Łapczyna Wola PL .87 B3
La Pedraja de Portillo E 150 A3
La Peraleja E 152 B1
La Petit-Pierre F . .93 C3
Lapeyrade F 128 B2
Lapeyrouse F 116 A2
Lapford GB 42 B3
La Pinilla E 165 B3
Lapithos CY 181 A2
La Plagne F 118 B3
La Plaza E 141 A4
Laplume F 129 B3
La Pobla de Lillet E 147 B2
La Pobla de Vallbona E 159 B3
La Pobla Llarga E .159 B3
La Pola de Gordón E 142 B1
la Porta F 180 A2
La Pouèze F 102 B1
Lapoutroie F 106 A2
La Póveda de Soria E 143 B4
Lapovo SRB 127 C3
Läppe S 56 A1
Lappeenranta FIN .8 B6
Lappoluobbal N . . 192 C7
Lappträsk S 196 C6
La Preste F 146 B3
La Primaube F . . . 130 A1
Lapseki TR 186 B1
Lapua FIN 8 A3
La Puebla de Almoradie E 157 A4
La Puebla de Cazalla E 162 A2
La Puebla de los Infantes E 162 A2
La Puebla del Río E 162 A1
La Puebla de Montalbán E 150 C3
La Puebla de Roda E 145 B4
La Puebla de Valdavia E 142 B2
La Puebla de Valverde E 152 B3
La Pueblanueva E 150 C3
La Puerta de Segura E 164 A2
La Punt CH 107 C4
L'Áquila I 169 A3
La Quintana E . . . 162 A3
La Quintera E 162 A2
La Rábita
Granada E 164 C1
Jaén E 163 A3
Laracha E 140 A2

Laragh IRL 30 A2
Laragne-Montéglin F 132 A1
La Rambla E 163 A3
l'Arboç E 147 C2
L'Arbresle F 117 B4
Larceveau F 144 A2
Larche
Alpes-de-Haute-Provence F . . . 132 A2
Corrèze F 129 A4
Lårdal N 53 A4
Lærdalsøyri N 47 A4
Lardosa P 155 B3
La Reale I 178 A2
Laredo E 143 A3
La Redondela E . . 161 B2
La Réole F 128 B2
Largentière F 131 A3
L'Argentière-la-Bessée F 118 C3
Largs GB 34 C3
Lari I 134 B3
La Riera E 141 A4
La Riera de Gaià E 147 C2
La Rinconada E . . 162 A1
Lariño E 140 B1
Larino I 170 B2
Larisa GR 182 D4
La Rivière-Thibouville F 89 A4
Larkhall GB 36 A3
Larkollen N 54 A1
Larmor-Plage F . . 100 B2
Larnaca CY 181 B2
Larne GB 27 B5
La Robla E 142 B1
La Roca de la Sierra E 155 B4
La Roche I 106 C2
La Rochebeaucourt-Argentine F . . . 115 C4
La Roche-Bernard F 101 B3
La Roche-Canillac F 116 B1
La Roche-Chalais F 128 A3
La Roche Derrien F 100 A2
La Roche-des-Arnauds F 132 A1
La Roche-en-Ardenne B 80 B1
La Roche-en-Brénil F 104 B3
La Rochefoucauld F 115 C4
La Roche-Guyon F .90 B1
La Rochelle F 114 B2
La Roche-Posay F 115 B4
La Roche-sur-Foron F 118 A3
La Roche-sur-Yon F 114 B2
Larochette L 92 B2
La Rochette F 131 A4
La Roda
Albacete E 158 B1
Oviedo E 141 A4
La Roda de Andalucía E 162 A3
Laroquebrou F . . . 116 C2
La Roquebrussanne F 132 B1
Laroque d'Olmes F 146 B2
La Roque-Gageac F 129 B4
La Roque-Ste Marguerite F . . . 130 A2
Laroque-Timbaut F 129 B3
Larouco E 141 B3
Larraga E 144 B2
Larrau F 144 A3
Larrazet F 129 C4
Larsnes N 198 C2
La Rubia E 143 C4
Laruns F 145 A3
Larva E 164 B1
La Sagrada E 149 B3
La Salceda E 151 A4
Lasalle F 131 A2
La Salle F 118 C3
Lasarte E 144 A1
Låsby DK 59 B2
Las Cabezadas E .151 A4
Las Cabezas de San Juan E 162 B2
Las Correderas E .157 B4
Las Cuevas de Cañart E 153 B3
La Seca E 150 A2
La Selva del Camp E 147 C2
La Senia E 153 B4
La Serra E 147 C2
La Seu d'Urgell E .146 B2
La Seyne-sur-Mer F 132 B1
Las Gabias E 163 A4
Las Herencias E . .150 C3
Las Herrerías E . . 161 B2
Łasin PL 69 B4
Łask PL 86 A3
Laska PL 68 B2
Łaskarzew PL 87 A5
Laško SLO 123 A4

Laskowice PL 76 A3
Las Labores E 157 A4
Las Mesas E 158 B1
Las Minas E 164 A3
Las Navas E 163 A3
Las Navas de la Concepción E . . 156 C2
Las Navas del Marqués E 150 B3
Las Navillas E . . . 157 A3
Las Negras E 164 C3
La Solana E 157 B4
La Souterraine F . .116 A1
Las Pajanosas E . .161 B3
Laspaules E 145 B4
Las Pedroñas E . . 158 B1
La Spézia I 134 A2
Las Planes d'Hostoles E 147 B3
Las Rozas
Cantabria E 142 B2
Madrid E 151 B4
Lassan D 66 C2
Lassay-les-Châteaux F 89 B3
Lasseube F 145 A3
Lassigny F 90 B2
La Storta I 168 B2
Lastovo HR 138 C2
Lastras de Cuéllar E 151 A3
Lästringe S 56 B3
Lastrup D 71 B4
Las Uces E 149 A3
La Suze-sur-Sarthe F 102 B2
Las Veguillas E . . 149 B4
Las Ventas con Peña Aguilera E 157 A3
Las Ventas de San Julián E 150 B2
Las Villes E 153 B4
Latasa E 144 B2
Látera I 168 A1
Laterza I 171 C4
La Teste F 128 B1
Lathen D 71 B4
Latheron GB 32 C3
La Thuile I 119 B3
Latiano I 173 B3
Latina I 169 B2
Latisana I 122 B2
Látky SK 99 C3
La Toba E 152 B2
La Toledana E . . . 157 A3
La Torre de Cabdella E 146 B1
La Torre de Esteban Hambrán E 151 B3
La Torre del l'Espanyol E 153 A4
La Torresaviñán E 152 B1
La Tour d'Aigues F 132 B1
La Tour de Peilz CH 106 C1
La Tour-du-Pin F . .118 B2
La Tranche-sur-Mer F 114 B2
La Tremblade F . . . 114 C2
La Trimouille F . . . 115 B5
La Trinité F 100 B2
La Trinité-Porhoët F 101 A3
Latrónico I 174 A2
Latronquière F . . . 116 C2
Latterbach CH . . . 106 C2
La Turballe F 101 B3
Laubach D 81 B4
Laubert F 117 C3
Laucha D 83 A3
Lauchhammer D . .84 A1
Lauchheim D 94 C2
Lauda-Königshofen D 94 B1
Laudal N 52 B3
Lauder GB 35 C5
Lauenau D 72 B2
Lauenburg D 73 A3
Lauf D 95 B3
Laufach D 94 A1
Laufen
CH 106 B2
D 109 B3
Lauffen D 93 B5
Laugar IS 191 B8
Laugarbakki IS . . . 190 B5
Laugarvatn IS . . . 190 C5
Laugharne GB 39 C2
Laujar de Andarax E 164 C2
Laukaa FIN 8 A4
Lauker S 196 D2
Laukvik N 194 C5
La Uña E 142 A1
Launceston GB . . . 42 B2
La Unión E 165 B4
Launois-sur-Vence F 91 B4
Laupheim D 94 C1
Lauragh IRL 29 C2
Laureana di Borrello I 175 C2
Laurencekirk GB . .35 B5
Laurencetown IRL .28 A3
Laurenzana I 172 B1
Lauria I 174 A1
Laurière F 116 A1
Laurieston GB 36 B2
Lauris F 172 B1
Lausanne CH 106 C1
Lauta D 84 A2
Lautenthal D 82 A2
Lauterach A 107 B4
Lauterbach D 81 B5

Lauterbrunnen CH 106 C2
Lauterecken D 93 B3
Lauterhofen D 95 B3
Lautrec F 130 B1
Lauvsnes N 199 A7
Lauvvlk N 52 B2
Lauzerte F 129 B4
Lauzès F 129 B4
Lauzun F 129 B3
Lavagna I 134 A2
Laval F 102 A1
La Vall d'Uixó E . . 159 B3
Lavamünd A 110 C1
Lavara GR 186 A1
Lavardac F 129 B3
Lavaris P 148 B1
Lavarone I 121 B4
Lavau F 104 B1
Lavaur F 129 C4
La Vecilla de Curueño E 142 B1
La Vega
Asturias E 141 A5
Asturias E 142 A1
Cantabria E 142 A2
Lavelanet F 146 B2
La Velilla E 151 A4
La Velles E 150 A2
Lavello I 172 A1
Lavelsloh D 72 B1
Laveno I 120 B1
La Ventosa E 152 B1
Lavezzola I 135 A4
Laviano I 172 B1
La Victoria E 162 A3
La Vid E 151 A4
Lavik N 46 A2
La Vilavella E 159 B3
La Vilella Baixa E .147 C1
La Villa de Don Fadrique E 157 A4
Lavilledieu F 131 A3
La Villedieu F 115 B3
La Ville Dieu-du-Temple F 129 B4
Lavinio-Lido di Enea I 168 B2
Lav is I 121 A4
Lavit F 129 C3
Lavoncourt F 105 B4
Lavos P 148 B1
La Voulte-sur-Rhône F 117 C4
Lavoûte-Chilhac F 117 B3
Lavradio P 154 C1
Lavre P 154 C2
Lavrio GR 185 B5
La Wantzenau F . .93 C3
Lawers GB 35 B3
Ławy PL 75 B3
Laxå S 55 B5
Laxamýri IS 191 B8
Laxe E 140 A2
Laxey GB 36 B2
Laxford Bridge GB .32 C1
Laxhall S 55 B4
Laxsjö S 199 B11
Laxtjarn S 49 B6
Laxvik S 61 C2
Laxviken S 199 B11
Laza E 141 B3
Lazarevac SRB . . 127 C2
Lazarevo SRB . . . 126 B2
Lazise I 121 B3
Łaziska Grn. PL . . . 86 B2
Lazkao E 144 A1
Lázně Bělohrad CZ 84 B3
Lázně Bohdaneč CZ 97 A3
Lázně Kynžvart CZ 95 B4
Lazonby GB 37 B4
La Zubia E 163 A4
Łazy PL 67 B5
Lazzaro I 175 D1
Lea GB 40 B3
Leadburn GB 35 C4
Leadhills GB 36 A3
Leap IRL 29 C2
Leatherhead GB . .44 B3
Łeba PL 68 A2
Lebach D 92 B2
Lauffen D 93 B5
Le Bar-sur-Loup F 132 B2
Le Béage F 117 C4
Le Beausset F . . . 132 B1
Lebekke B 79 A4
Le Bessat F 117 B4
Le Blanc F 115 B5
Le Bleymard F . . . 130 A2
Łebno PL 68 A3
Leboreiro E 140 B3
Le Boulou F 146 B3
Le Bourg-d'Oisans F 118 B3
Le Bourget-du-Lac F 118 B2
Le Bourgneuf-la-Forêt F 101 A5
Le Bousquet d'Orb F 130 B2
Le Brassus CH . . . 105 C5
Le Breuil F 117 A3
Le Breuil-en-Auge F 89 A4
Lebring A 110 C2
Le Brusquet F . . . 132 A2
Le Bry CH 106 C2
Le Bugue F 129 B3
Le Buisson F 129 B3

Lebus D 74 B3
Lebusa D 83 A5
Leca da Palmeira P 148 A1
Le Caloy F 128 C2
Le Cap d'Agde F . .130 B2
Le Cateau Cambrésis F 91 A3
Le Caylar F 130 B2
Le Cayrol F 116 C2
Lecce I 173 B4
Lecco I 120 B2
Lécera E 153 A3
Lećevica HR 138 B2
Lech A 107 B5
Le Chambon-Feugerolles F . . 117 B4
Le Chambon-sur-Lignon F 117 B4
Le Château d'Oléron F 114 C2
Le Châtelard F . . . 118 B3
Le Châtelet F 103 C4
Le Chatelet-en-Brie F 90 C2
Lechbruck D 108 B1
Lechena GR 184 B2
Le Chesne F 91 B4
Le Cheylard F 117 C4
Lechlade GB 44 B2
Lechovice CZ 97 C4
Leciñena E 145 C3
Leck D 64 B1
Le Collet-de-Deze F 131 A2
Le Conquet F 100 A1
Le Creusot F 104 C3
Le Croisic F 101 B3
Le Crotoy F 78 B1
Lectoure F 129 C3
Łęczyca
Łódzkie PL 77 B4
Zachodnio-Pomorskie PL 75 A4
Ledaña E 158 B2
Ledbury GB 39 B4
Lede B 79 B3
Ledečnad Sazavou CZ 97 B3
Ledenice CZ 96 C2
Le Deschaux F . . . 105 C4
Ledesma E 149 A3
Lédignan F 131 B3
Lédigos E 142 B2
Ledmore GB 32 C2
Lednice CZ 97 C4
Lednicke-Rovné SK 98 B2
Le Donjon F 117 A3
Le Dorat F 115 B5
Lędyczek PL 68 B1
Lędziny PL 86 B3
Leeds GB 40 B2
Leek
GB 40 B1
NL 71 A3
Leenaun IRL 28 A2
Leens NL 71 A3
Leer D 71 A4
Leerdam NL 79 A5
Leerhafe D 71 A4
Leese D 72 B2
Leeuwarden NL . . . 70 A2
Leeuwarden NL . . . 70 A2
Leezen D 64 C3
Le Faou F 100 A1
Le Faouët F 100 A2
Lefka CY 181 A1
Lefkada GR 182 E2
Lefkimis GR 182 D2
Lefkoniko CY 181 A2
Le Folgoet F 100 A1
Le Fossat F 146 A2
Le Fousseret F . . . 146 A2
Le Fugeret F 132 A2
Leganés E 151 B4
Legau D 107 B5
Le Gault-Soigny F .91 C3
Legbąd PL 68 B2
Legé F 114 B2
Le Grand-Bornand F 118 B3
Legionowo PL 77 B5
Léglise B 92 B1
Legnago I 121 B4
Legnano I 120 B1
Legnaro I 121 B4
Legnica PL 85 A4
Łęgowo PL 69 A3
Legrad HR 124 A2
Le Grand-Bourg F 116 A1
Le Grand-Lucé F .102 B2
Le Grand-Pressigny F 102 C2
Le Grand-Quevilly F 89 A5
Le Grau-du-Roi F .131 B3
Léguevin F 129 C4
Legutiano E 143 B4
Le Havre F 89 A4
Le Hohwald F 93 C3
Le Houga F 128 C2
Léhon F 101 A3
Lehrberg D 94 B2
Lehre D 73 B3
Lehrte D 72 B2
Lehsen D 73 A4
Leibnitz A 110 C2
Leicester GB 40 C2
Leiden NL 70 B1
Leidschendam NL . 70 B1
Leigh GB 38 A4
Leighlinbridge IRL .30 B2
Leighton Buzzard GB 44 B3
Leignon B 79 B5
Leikanger N 198 C2

Leimen D 93 B4
Leinefelde D 82 A2
Leinesfjord N 194 C6
Leintwardine GB . .39 B4
Leipojärvi S 196 B4
Leipzig D 83 A4
Leira
Nordland N 195 D4
Oppland N 47 B6
Leiramoen N 195 D5
Leiria P 154 B2
Leirvassbu N 47 A5
Leirvik
Hordaland N 52 A1
Sogn og Fjordane N 46 A2
Leisach A 109 C3
Leisnig D 83 A4
Leiston GB 45 A5
Leitholm GB 35 C5
Leitrim IRL 26 C2
Leitza E 144 A2
Leitzkau D 73 B4
Lejkowo PL 68 A1
Lekani GR 183 B6
Łekawa PL 86 A3
Łękawica PL 99 B3
Lekeitio E 143 A4
Lekenik HR 124 B2
Lekeryd S 62 A2
Leknes N 194 B4
Łęknica PL 84 A2
Leksand S 50 B1
Leksvik N 199 B7
Lekunberri E 144 A2
Lekvattnet S 49 B4
Le Lardin-St Lazare F 129 A4
Le Lauzet-Ubaye F 132 A2
Le Lavandou F . . . 132 B2
Le Lion-d'Angers F 102 B1
Lelkowo PL 69 A5
Le Locle CH 106 B1
Le Loroux-Bottereau F 101 B4
Le Louroux-Béconnais F 101 B5
Lelów PL 86 B3
Le Luc F 132 B2
Le Lude F 102 B2
Lelystad NL 70 B2
Lem
Ringkøbing DK . .59 B1
Viborg Amt. DK . .58 B1
Le Malzieu-Ville F .116 C3
Le Mans F 102 A2
Le Mas-d'Azil F . . 146 A2
Le Massegros F . .130 A2
Le Mayet-de-Montagne F 117 A3
Lembach F 93 B3
Lemberg F 93 B3
Lembèye F 145 A3
Lemelerveld NL . . .71 B3
Le Mêle-sur-Sarthe F 89 B4
Le Ménil F 105 A5
Le Merlerault F . . . 89 B4
Le Mesnil-sur-Oger F 91 C4
Lemförde D 71 B5
Lemgo D 72 B1
Le Miroir F 105 C4
Lemland FIN 51 B7
Lemmer NL 70 B2
Le Molay-Littry F . .88 A3
Le Monastier-sur-Gazeille F 117 C3
Le Monêtier-les-Bains F 118 C3
Le Mont-Dore F . . 116 B2
Le Montet F 116 A3
Le Mont-St Michel F 88 B2
Lempdes F 116 B3
Le Muret F 128 B2
Le Muy F 132 B2
Lemvig DK 58 B1
Lemwerder D 72 A1
Lena N 48 B2
Lenart SLO 110 C2
Lenartovce SK 99 C4
Lenauheim RO . . . 126 B2
Lencloître F 102 C2
Lend A 109 B4
Lendalfoot GB . . . 36 A2
Lendava SLO . . . 111 C3
Lendery RUS 3 E12
Lendinara I 121 B4
Lendorf A 109 C4
Lendum DK 58 A3
Le Neubourg F . . . 89 A4
Lengefeld D 83 B5
Lengerich
Niedersachsen D .71 B4
Nordrhein-Westfalen D 71 B4
Lenggries D 108 B2
Lengyeltóti H 111 C4
Lenhovda S 62 B3
Lennartsfors S . . . 54 A2
Lennestadt D 81 A4
Lennoxtown GB . . 35 C3
Leno I 120 B3
Lénola I 169 B3
Le Nouvion-en-Thiérache F 91 A3
Lens
B 79 B3
F 78 B2
Lensahn D 65 B3
Lens Lestang F . . 117 B5
Lensvik N 198 B6

Lentellais E 141 B3
Lentföhrden D 64 C2
Lenti H 111 C3
Lentini I 177 B3
Lenungshammar S 54 A3
Lenzburg CH 106 B3
Lenzen D 73 A4
Lenzerheide CH 107 C4
Leoben A 110 B2
Leogang A 109 B3
Leominster GB 39 B4
León E 142 B1
Léon F 128 C1
Leonberg D 93 C5
Léoncel F 118 C2
Leonding A 96 C2
Leonessa I 169 A2
Leonforte I 177 B3
Leonidio GR 184 B3
Leopoldsburg B 79 A5
Leopoldsdorf im Marchfeld A 111 A3
Leopoldshagen D 74 A2
Leova MD 17 B8
Le Palais F 100 B2
Le Parcq F 78 B2
Lepe E 161 B2
Le Péage-de-Roussillon F 117 B4
Le Pellerin F 101 B4
Lepenou GR 182 E3
Le Perthus F 146 B3
Le Pertuis F 117 B4
Le Petit-Bornand F 118 B3
Lephin GB 31 B2
L'Epine F 132 A1
Le Poët F 132 A1
Lepoglava HR 124 A2
Le Poirè-sur-Vie F 114 B2
Le Pont CH 105 C5
Le Pont-de-Montvert F 130 A2
Le Porge F 128 B1
Le Porge-Océan F 128 B1
Le Portel F 78 B1
Le Pouldu F 100 B2
Le Pouliguen F 101 B3
Leppäjärvi FIN 192 D7
Leppävirta FIN 8 A5
Leppin D 73 B4
le Prese I 120 A3
Lepsény H 112 C2
Le Puy-en-Velay F 117 B3
Le Puy-Ste Réparade F 131 B4
Le Quesnoy F 79 B3
Léquile I 173 B4
Le Rayol F 132 B2
Lercara Friddi I 176 B2
Lerdal S 54 B2
Leré F 103 B4
Lérici I 134 A2
Lerin E 144 B2
Lerma E 143 B3
Lerm-et-Musset F 128 B2
Lermoos A 108 B1
Le Roeulx B 79 B4
Le Rouget F 116 C2
Lérouville F 92 C1
Le Rozier F 130 A2
Lerum S 60 B2
Le Russey F 106 B1
Lervik N 54 A1
Lerwick GB 33 A5
Lés E 145 B4
Les Abrets F 118 B2
Les Aix-d'Angillon F 103 B4
Lesaka E 144 A2
Les Ancizes-Comps F 116 B2
Les Andelys F 90 B1
Les Arcs
Savoie F 119 B3
Var F 132 B2
Les-Aubiers F 102 C1
Les Baux-de-Provence F 131 B3
Les Bézards F 103 B4
Les Bois CH 106 B1
Les Bordes F 103 B4
Les Borges Blanques E 147 C1
Les Borges del Camp E 147 C2
Les Brunettes F 104 C2
Lesbury GB 37 A5
Les Cabannes F 146 B2
L'Escala E 147 B4
Lescar F 145 A3
L'Escarène F 133 B3
Lesce SLO 123 A3
Lescheraines F 118 B3
Lesconil F 100 B1
Les Contamines-Montjoie F 118 B3
les Coves de Vinroma E 153 B4
Les Déserts F 118 B2
Les Deux-Alpes F 118 C3
Les Diablerets CH 119 A4
Lesdins F 90 B3
Les Echelles F 118 B2
Le Sel-de-Bretagne F 101 B4
Le Sentier CH 105 C5
Les Escaldes AND 146 B2
Les Essarts F 114 B2
Les Estables F 117 C4
Les Eyzies-de-Tayac F 129 B4
Les Gets F 118 A3
Les Grandes-Ventes F 89 A5
Les Haudères CH 119 A4
Les Herbiers F 114 B2
Les Hôpitaux-Neufs F 105 C5
Lesično SLO 123 A4
Lésina I 171 B3
Lesjaskog N 198 C5
Lesjöfors S 49 C6
Leskovac SRB 16 D4
Leskova Dolina SLO 123 B3
Leskovec
CZ 98 B1
SLO 123 B4
Leskovice CZ 97 B3
Leskovik AL 182 C2
Leslie GB 35 B4
Les Lucs-sur-Boulogne F 114 B2
Les Mages F 131 A3
Lesmahagow GB 36 A3
Les Mazures F 91 B4
Les Mées F 132 A1
Lesmont F 91 C4
Les Mureaux F 90 C1
Leśna PL 84 A3
Lesneven F 100 A1
Leśnica PL 86 B2
Lešnica SRB 127 C1
Leśniów Wielkoplski PL 75 C4
Lesnoye RUS 9 C9
Les Omergues F 132 A1
Les Ormes-sur-Voulzie F 90 C3
Les Orres F 132 A2
Le Souquet F 128 C1
Lesparre-Médoc F 128 A2
l'Espérance F 91 B3
l'Esperou F 130 A2
Les Pieux F 88 A2
Lesponne F 145 A4
Les Ponts-de-Cé F 102 B1
Les Ponts-de-Martel CH 106 C1
Les Praz F 119 B3
L'Espunyola E 147 B2
Les Riceys F 104 B3
Les Roches F 117 B4
Les Rosaires F 101 A3
Les Rosiers F 102 B1
Les Rousses F 105 C5
Les Sables-d'Olonne F 114 B2
Lessach A 109 B4
Lessay F 88 A2
Lessebo S 62 B3
Les Settons F 104 B3
Lessines B 79 B3
L'Estany E 147 C3
Les Ternes F 116 B2
Lesterps F 115 B4
Les Thilliers en-Vexin F 90 B1
Les Touches F 101 B4
Les Trois Moûtiers F 102 B2
Les Vans F 131 A3
Les Verrières CH 105 C5
Les Vignes F 130 A2
Leswalt GB 36 B1
Leszno
Mazowieckie PL 77 B5
Wielkopolskie PL 85 A4
Leszno Górne PL 84 A3
Letchworth GB 44 B3
Le Teil F 131 A3
Le Teilleul F 88 B3
Le Temple-de-Bretagne F 101 B4
Letenye H 111 C3
Le Theil F 89 B4
Le Thillot F 106 B1
Letino I 170 B2
Letohrad CZ 97 A4
Le Touquet-Paris-Plage F 78 B1
Le Touvet F 118 B2
Letovice CZ 97 B4
Le Translay F 90 B1
Le Tréport F 90 A1
Letschin D 74 B3
Letterfrack IRL 28 A2
Letterkenny IRL 26 B3
Lettermacaward IRL 26 B2
Lettoch GB 32 D3
Letur E 164 A2
Letux E 153 A3
Letzlingen D 73 B4
Leucate F 146 B4
Leuchars GB 35 B5
Leuglay F 105 B3
Leuk CH 119 A4
Leukerbad CH 119 A4
Leumrabhagh GB 31 A2
Leuna D 83 A4
Leusden NL 70 B2
Leutenberg D 82 B3
Leuterschach D 108 B1
Leutershausen D 94 B2
Leutkirch D 107 B5
Leuven B 79 B4
Leuze-en-Hainaut B 79 B3
Le Val F 132 B2
Le Val-André F 101 A3
Le Val-d'Ajol F 105 B5
Levan AL 182 C1
Levanger N 199 B8
Levanjska Varoš HR 125 B4
Lévanto I 134 A2
Levaré F 88 B3
Levata I 120 B3
Leveld N 47 B5
Leven
East Yorkshire GB 41 B3
Leven *continued*
Fife GB 35 B5
Leverano I 173 B3
Le Verdon-sur-Mer F 114 C2
Leverkusen D 80 A2
Levern D 72 B1
Le Vernet F 132 A2
Levet F 103 C4
Levice SK 112 A2
Lévico Terme I 121 A4
Levie F 180 B2
Levier F 105 C5
Le Vigan F 130 B2
Lévignen F 90 B2
le Ville I 135 B5
Levinovac HR 124 B3
Le Vivier-sur-Mer F 88 B2
Levoča SK 99 B4
Levroux F 103 C3
Lewes GB 45 C4
Lewin Brzeski PL 85 B5
Lewisham GB 44 B3
Leyburn GB 37 B5
Leyland GB 38 A4
Leysdown-on-Sea GB 45 B4
Leysin CH 119 A4
Lezajsk PL 12 C5
Lézardrieux F 100 A2
Lézat-sur-Léze F 146 A2
Lezay F 115 B3
Lezhë AL 182 B1
Lézignan-Corbières F 130 B1
Lezignan-la-Cèbe F 130 B2
Ležimir SRB 126 B1
Lézinnes F 104 B3
Lezoux F 117 B3
Lezuza E 158 C1
Lhenice CZ 96 C2
Lherm F 146 A2
Lhommaizé F 115 B4
L'Hospitalet F 146 B2
L'Hospitalet de l'Infant E 147 D1
L'Hospitalet de Llobregat E 147 C3
L'Hospitalet-du-Larzac F 130 B2
Lhuître F 91 C4
Liancourt F 90 B2
Liart F 91 B4
Liatorp S 63 B2
Liatrie GB 32 D2
Libáň CZ 84 B3
Libceves CZ 84 B1
Liběchov CZ 84 B2
Liber E 141 B3
Liberec CZ 84 B3
Libiąż PL 86 B3
Libina CZ 98 B1
Libochovice CZ 84 B2
Libohovë AL 182 C2
Libourne F 128 B2
Libramont B 92 B1
Librazhd AL 182 B2
Librilla E 165 B3
Libros E 152 B2
Licata I 176 B2
Licciana Nardi I 134 A3
Licenza I 169 A2
Liceros E 151 A4
Lich D 81 B4
Lichères-près-Aigremont F 104 B2
Lichfield GB 40 C2
Lichtenau
A 97 C3
D 81 A4
Lichtenberg D 83 B3
Lichtenfels D 82 B3
Lichtensteig CH 107 B4
Lichtenstein D 83 B4
Lichtenvoorde NL 71 C3
Lichtervelde B 78 A3
Lička Jesenica HR 123 B4
Lickershamn S 57 C4
Lički Osik HR 123 C4
Ličko Lešce HR 123 C4
Licodía Eubéa I 177 B3
Licques F 78 B1
Lida BY 13 B6
Lidar N 47 A6
Lidečko CZ 98 B2
Liden S 200 D2
Lidhult S 60 C3
Lidköping S 55 B4
Lido I 122 B1
Lido Azzurro I 173 B3
Lido degli Estensi I 122 C1
Lido degli Scacchi I 122 C1
Lido della Nazioni I 122 C1
Lido di Camaiore I 134 B3
Lido di Casalbordino I 169 A4
Lido di Castél Fusano I 168 B2
Lido di Cincinnato I 168 B2
Lido di Classe I 135 A5
Lido di Fermo I 136 B2
Lido di Fondi I 169 B3
Lido di Jésolo I 122 B1
Lido di Licola I 170 C2
Lido di Metaponto I 174 A2
Lido di Óstia I 168 B2
Lido di Policoro I 174 A2
Lido di Pomposa I 122 C1
Lido di Savio I 135 A5
Lido di Scanzano I 174 A2
Lido di Siponto I 171 B3
Lido di Squillace I 175 C2
Lido di Volano I 122 C1
Lido Riccio I 169 A4
Lidoriki GR 184 A3
Lido Silvana I 173 B3
Lidsjöberg S 199 A12
Lidzbark PL 77 A4
Lidzbark Warmiński PL 69 A5
Liebenau
A 96 C2
D 72 B2
Liebenwalde D 74 B2
Lieberose D 74 C3
Liebling RO 126 B3
Lieboch A 110 C2
Liège B 80 B1
Lieksa FIN 3 E12
Lienen D 71 B4
Lienz A 109 C3
Liepāja LV 8 D2
Lier B 79 A4
Lierbyen N 54 A1
Liernais F 104 B3
Liesing A 109 C3
Liestal CH 106 B2
Liétor E 158 C2
Lieurac F 146 B2
Lieurey F 89 A4
Liévin F 78 B2
Liezen A 110 B1
Liffol-le-Grand F 92 C1
Lifford IRL 27 B3
Liffré F 101 A4
Ligardes F 129 B3
Lignano Sabbiadoro I 122 B2
Ligne F 101 B4
Lignières F 103 C4
Ligny-en-Barrois F 92 C1
Ligny-le-Châtel F 104 B2
Ligoła Polska PL 85 A5
Ligourio GR 184 B4
Ligowo PL 77 B4
Ligueil F 102 B2
Likavka SK 99 B3
Likenäs S 49 B5
Likhoslavl RUS 9 D9
Lild Strand DK 58 A1
L'Île-Bouchard F 102 B2
l'Île-Rousse F 180 A1
Lilienfeld A 110 A2
Lilienthal D 72 A1
Lilla Edet S 54 B3
Lilla Tjärby S 61 C3
Lille
B 79 A4
F 78 B3
Lillebonne F 89 A4
Lillehammer N 48 A2
Lillerød DK 61 D2
Lillers F 78 B2
Lillesand N 53 B4
Lillestrøm N 48 C3
Lillhärdal S 199 D11
Lillkyrka S 56 A3
Lillo E 157 A4
Lillögda S 200 B3
Lillpite S 196 D4
Lima S 49 B5
Limanowa PL 99 B4
Limassol CY 181 B2
Limavady GB 27 A4
Limbach-Oberfrohna D 83 B4
Limbaži LV 8 D4
Limbourg B 80 B1
Limburg D 81 B4
Lime DK 58 B3
Limedsforsen S 49 B5
Limenaria GR 183 C6
Limenas Chersonisou GR 185 D6
Limerick IRL 29 B3
Limes I 121 B3
Limésy F 89 A4
Limmared S 60 B3
Limni GR 183 E5
Limoges F 115 C5
Limogne-en-Quercy F 129 B4
Limoise F 104 C2
Limone Piemonte I 133 A3
Limone sul Garda I 121 B3
Limons F 117 B3
Limours F 90 C2
Limoux F 146 A3
Linares E 157 B4
Linares de Mora E 153 B3
Linares de Riofrio E 149 B4
Linaria GR 183 E6
Linas de Broto E 145 B3
Lincoln GB 40 B3
Lind DK 59 B1
Lindås N 46 B2
Lindau D 107 B4
Lindberget N 48 A3
Lindelse DK 65 B3
Lindenberg D 74 B3
Lindenberg im Allgäu D 107 B4
Lindern D 71 B4
Linderöd S 61 D3
Lindesberg S 56 A1
Lindesnäs S 50 B1
Lindesnes N 52 C3
Lindholmen S 57 A4
Lindknud DK 59 C2
Lindlar D 80 A3
Lindö S 56 B2
Lindome S 60 B2
Lindos GR 188 C3
Lindoso P 148 A1
Lindow D 74 B1
Lindsdal S 62 B4
Lindshammar S 62 A3
Lindstedt D 73 B4
Lindved DK 59 C2
Linë CZ 96 B1
Lingbo S 50 A3
Lingen D 71 B4
Linghed S 50 B2
Linghem S 56 B1
Linguaglossa I 177 B4
Linia PL 68 A2
Linie PL 74 A3
Liniewo PL 68 A3
Linkenheim D 93 B4
Linköping S 56 B1
Linksness GB 33 C3
Linlithgow GB 35 C4
Linneryd S 63 B3
Linnes Hammarby S 51 C4
Linnich D 80 B2
Linsell S 199 C10
Linslade GB 44 B3
Linthal CH 107 C4
Linyola E 147 C1
Linz
A 96 C2
D 80 B3
Liomseter N 47 A6
Lionárisso CY 181 A3
Lioni I 172 B1
Lion-sur-Mer F 89 A3
Lipany SK 99 B4
Lipar SRB 126 B1
Lípari I 177 A3
Lipcani MD 17 A7
Liperi FIN 9 A6
Liphook GB 44 B3
Lipiany PL 75 A3
Lipik HR 124 B3
Lipka PL 68 B2
Lipki Wielkie PL 75 B4
Lipnica PL 68 B2
Lipnica Murowana PL 99 B4
Lipnik PL 87 B5
Lipník nad Bečvou CZ 98 B1
Lipno
Kujawsko-Pomorskie PL 77 B4
Łódzkie PL 86 A2
Liposthey F 128 B2
Lipovac HR 125 B5
Lipovec CZ 97 B4
Lipovets UA 13 D8
Lipovljani HR 124 B2
Lipowiec PL 77 A6
Lipowina PL 69 A4
Lippborg D 81 A4
Lippó H 125 B4
Lippoldsberg D 81 A5
Lippstadt D 81 A4
Lipsko PL 87 A5
Liptál CZ 98 B1
Liptovská-Lúžna SK 99 C3
Liptovská Osada SK 99 C3
Liptovská-Teplička SK 99 C4
Liptovský Hrádok SK 99 B3
Liptovský Milkuláš SK 99 B3
Lipusz PL 68 A2
Lipůvka CZ 97 B4
Liré F 101 B4
Lisac BIH 139 A3
Lisbellaw GB 27 B3
Lisboa = Lisbon P 154 C1
Lisbon = Lisboa P 154 C1
Lisburn GB 27 B4
Liscannor IRL 28 B2
Lisdoonvarna IRL 28 A2
Lisewo PL 69 B3
Lisia Góra PL 87 B5
Lisięcice PL 86 B1
Lisieux F 89 A4
Lisjö S 56 A2
Liskeard GB 42 B2
L'Isle CH 105 C5
L'Isle-Adam F 90 B2
L'Isle-de-Noé F 129 C3
L'Isle-en-Dodon F 145 A4
L'Isle-Jourdain
Gers F 129 C4
Vienne F 115 B4
L'Isle-sur-la-Sorgue F 131 B4
L'Isle-sur-le Doubs F 105 B5
L'Isle-sur-Serein F 104 B3
Lisle-sur-Tarn F 129 C4
Lismore IRL 29 B4
Lisnaskea GB 27 B3
Lišov CZ 96 B2
Lisów
Lubuskie PL 74 B3
Śląskie PL 86 B2
Lisse NL 70 B1
Lissycasey IRL 28 B2
List D 64 A1
Listerby S 63 B3
Listowel IRL 29 B2
Listrac-Médoc F 128 A2
Liszki PL 99 A3
Liszkowo PL 76 A2
Lit S 199 B11
Litava SK 99 C3
Litcham GB 41 C4
Lit-et-Mixe F 128 B1
Litija SLO 123 A3
Litke H 112 A3
Litlabø N 52 A1
Litochoro GR 182 C4
Litoměřice CZ 84 B2
Litomyšl CZ 97 B4
Litovel CZ 98 B1
Litschau A 96 C3
Littlehampton GB 44 C3
Littleport GB 45 A4
Littleton IRL 29 B4
Little Walsingham GB 41 C4
Litvinov CZ 83 B5
Livadero GR 182 C3
Livadhia CY 181 B2
Livadi GR 182 C4
Livadia GR 184 A3
Livarot F 89 B4
Liveras CY 181 A1
Livernon F 129 B4
Liverovici MNE 139 C5
Liverpool GB 38 A4
Livigno I 107 C5
Livingston GB 35 C4
Livno BIH 138 B2
Livo FIN 197 D9
Livold SLO 123 B3
Livorno I 134 B3
Livorno Ferraris I 119 B5
Livron-sur-Drôme F 117 C4
Livry-Louvercy F 91 B4
Lixheim F 92 C3
Lixouri GR 184 A1
Lizard GB 42 C1
Lizy-sur-Ourcq F 90 B3
Lizzano I 173 B3
Lizzano in Belvedere I 135 A3
Ljig SRB 127 C2
Ljørdalen N 49 A4
Ljosland N 52 B3
Ljubija BIH 124 C2
Ljubinje BIH 139 C4
Ljubljana SLO 123 A3
Ljubno ob Savinji SLO 123 A3
Ljubovija SRB 127 C1
Ljubuški BIH 138 B3
Ljugarn S 57 C4
Ljung S 60 B3
Ljunga S 56 B2
Ljungaverk S 200 D2
Ljungby S 60 C3
Ljungbyhed S 61 C3
Ljungbyholm S 63 B4
Ljungdalen S 199 C9
Ljungsarp S 60 B3
Ljungsbro S 56 B1
Ljungskile S 54 B2
Ljusdal S 200 E2
Ljusfallshammar S 56 B1
Ljusne S 51 A4
Ljusterö S 57 A4
Ljutomer SLO 111 C3
Lŭki BG 183 B6
Lladurs E 147 B2
Llafranc E 147 C4
Llagostera E 147 C3
Llanaelhaiarn GB 38 B2
Llanarth GB 39 B2
Llanbedr GB 38 B2
Llanbedrog GB 38 B2
Llanberis GB 38 A2
Llanbister GB 39 B3
Llanbrynmair GB 39 B3
Llançà E 146 B4
Llandeilo GB 39 C3
Llandissilio GB 39 C2
Llandovery GB 39 C3
Llandrillo GB 38 B3
Llandrindod Wells GB 39 B3
Llandudec F 100 A1
Llandudno GB 38 A3
Llandysul GB 39 B2
Llanelli GB 39 C2
Llanerchymedd GB 38 A2
Llanes E 142 A2
Llanfair Caereinion GB 38 B3
Llanfairfechan GB 38 A3
Llanfyllin GB 38 B3
Llangadog GB 39 C3
Llangefni GB 38 A2
Llangollen GB 38 B3
Llangrannog GB 39 B2
Llangurig GB 39 B3
Llanidloes GB 39 B3
Llanilar GB 39 B2
Llanrhystud GB 39 B2
Llanrwst GB 38 A3
Llansannan GB 38 A3
Llansawel GB 39 B2
Llanstephan GB 39 C2
Llanteno E 143 A3
Llanthony GB 39 C3
Llantrisant GB 39 C3
Llantwit-Major GB 39 C3
Llanuwchllyn GB 38 B3
Llanwddyn GB 38 B3
Llanwrda GB 39 C3
Llanwrtyd Wells GB 39 B3
Llanybydder GB 39 B2
Llanymynech GB 38 B3
Llavorsí E 146 B2
Lleida E 153 A4
Llera E 156 B1
Llerena E 156 B1
Lles E 146 B2
Llessui E 146 B2
Llinars E 147 B2
Lliria E 159 B3
Llivia E 146 B2
Llodio E 143 A4
Lloret de Mar E 147 C3
Llosa de Ranes E 159 B3
Lloseta E 167 B2
Llucena del Cid E 153 B3
Llucmajor E 167 B2
Llutxent E 159 C3
Llwyngwril GB 38 B2
Llyswen GB 39 B3
Lnáře CZ 96 B1
Lniano PL 76 A3
Loanhead GB 35 C4
Loano I 133 A4
Loarre E 145 B3
Löbau D 84 A2
Löbejün D 83
Löberöd S 61
Łobez PL 75
Löbnitz D 66
Lobón E 155
Loburg D 73
Łobżenica PL 76
Locana I 119
Locarno CH 120
Loccum D 72
Loče SLO 123
Lochailort GB 34
Lochaline GB 34
Lochans GB 36
Locharbriggs GB 36
Lochau A 107
Loch Baghasdail GB 31
Lochcarron GB 31
Lochearnhead GB 34
Lochem NL 71
Loches F 102
Lochgelly GB 35
Lochgilphead GB 34
Lochgoilhead GB 34
Lochinver GB 32
Loch nam Madadh GB 31
Lochranza GB 34
Ločika SRB 127
Lockenhaus A 111
Lockerbie GB 36
Löcknitz D 74
Locmaria F 100
Locmariaquer F 100
Locminé F 100
Locorotondo I 173
Locquirec F 100
Locri I 175
Locronan F 100
Loctudy F 100
Lodares de Osma E 151
Lodé I 178
Lodeinoye Pole RUS 9
Lodève F 130
Lodi I 120
Løding N 194
Lødingen N 194
Lodosa E 144
Lödöse S 54
Łódź PL 86
Loeches E 151
Løfallstrand N 46
Lofer A 109
Lofsdalen S 199
Loftahammar S 62
Lofthus N 46
Loftus GB 37
Loga N 52
Logatec SLO 123
Lögdeå S 200
Lograto I 120
Logroño E 143
Logrosán E 156
Løgstør DK 58
Løgumgårde DK 64
Løgumkloster DK 64
Lohals DK 65
Lohiniva FIN 197
Lohja FIN 8
Löhlbach D 81
Lohmen
Mecklenburg-Vorpommern D 65
Sachsen D 84
Löhnberg D 81
Lohne D 71
Löhne D 72
Lohr D 94
Lohra D 81
Lohsa D 84
Loiano I 135
Loimaa FIN 8
Lóiri I 178
Loitz D 66
Loivos P 148
Loivos do Monte P 148
Loja E 163
Lojanice SRB 127
Lojsta S 57
Løjt Kirkeby DK 64
Lok SK 112
Lokca SK 99
Løken N 54
Lokeren B 79
Loket CZ 83
Lokka FIN 197 B1
Løkken
DK 58
N 198
Loknya RUS 9
Lökösháza H 113
Lokve SRB 126
Lollar D 81
L'Olleria E 159
Lölling-Graben A 110
Lom
BG 17
N 198
SK 99
Lombez F 146
Lomello I 120
Łomianki PL 77
Lomma S 61
Lommaryd S 62
Lommatzsch D 83
Lommel B 79
Lommersum D 80
Lomnice CZ 97
Lomnice nad Lužnicí CZ 96
Lomnice-nad Popelkou CZ 84
Lompolo FIN 196
Łomza PL 12
Lönashult S 63
Lønborg DK 59
Londerzeel B 79

Londinières F 89 A5
London GB 44 B3
Lonevåg N 46 B2
Longa GR 184 C2
Longare I 121 B4
Longares E 152 A4
Longarone I 122 A1
Longastrino I 135 A5
Long Bennington
GB 40 C3
Longbenton GB 37 A5
Longchamp-sur-Aujon
F 105 A3
Longchaumois F . . .118 A2
Long Eaton GB 40 C2
Longeau F 105 B4
Longecourt-en-Plaine
F 105 B4
Longeville-les-St Avold
F 92 B2
Longeville-sur-Mer
F 114 B2
Longford IRL 28 A4
Longframlington
GB 37 A5
Longhope GB 33 C3
Longhorsley GB 37 A5
Longhoughton GB . .37 A5
Longi I 177 A3
Long Melford GB . . .45 A4
Longny-au-Perche
F 89 B4
Longobucco I 174 B2
Long Preston GB . . .40 A1
Longré F 115 B3
Longridge GB 38 A4
Longroiva P 149 B2
Long Sutton GB 41 C4
Longtown
Cumbria GB 36 A4
Herefordshire GB . 39 C4
Longueau F 90 B2
Longué-Jumelles
F 102 B1
Longuyon F 92 B1
Longvic F 105 B4
Longvilly B 92 A1
Longwy F 92 B1
Lonigo I 121 B4
Löningen D 71 B4
Lonja HR 124 B2
Lönneberga S 62 A3
Lönsboda S 63 B2
Lønset N 198 C6
Lons-le-Saunier F . .105 C4
Lønstrup DK 58 A2
Looe GB 42 B2
Loone-Plage F 78 A2
Loon op Zand NL . . .79 A5
Loosdorf A 110 A2
Lo Pagán E 165 B4
Lopar HR 123 C3
Lopare BIH 125 C4
Lopera E 157 C3
Lopigna F 180 A1
Loppersum NL 71 A3
Łopuszna PL 99 B4
Łopuszno PL 87 B4
Lor F 91 B4
Lora N 198 C5
Lora de Estepa E . .162 A3
Lora del Río E 162 A2
Loranca del Campo
E 151 B5
Lorbé E 140 A2
Lörby S 63 B2
Lorca E 164 B3
Lorch D 93 A3
Lørenfallet N 48 B3
Lørenskog N 48 C2
Loreo I 122 B1
Loreto I 136 B2
Lorgues F 132 B2
Lorica I 174 B2
Lorient F 100 B2
Lorignac F 114 C3
Lőrinci H 112 B3
Loriol-sur-Drôme
F 117 C4
Lormes F 104 B2
Loro Ciuffenna I . . .135 B4
Lorqui E 165 A3
Lörrach D 106 B2
Lorrez-le-Bocage
F 103 A4
Lorris F 103 B4
Lorup D 71 B4
Łoś PL 77 C5
Los S 199 D12
Losacino E 149 A3
Los Alcázares E . . .165 B4
Los Arcos E 144 B1
Losar de la Vera E . 150 B2
Los Barios de Luna
E 141 B5
Los Barrios E 162 B2
Los Caños de Meca
E 162 B1
Los Cerricos E 164 B2
Los Corrales E 162 A2
Los Corrales de Buelna
E 142 A2
Los Dolores E 165 B3
Losenstein A 110 B1
Los Gallardos E . . .164 B3
Losheim
Nordrhein-Westfalen
D 80 B2
Saarland D 92 B2
Los Hinojosos E . . .158 B1
Los Isidros E 159 B2
Los Molinos E 151 B3
Los Morales E 162 A2
Los Navalmorales
E 156 A3
Los Navalucillos
E 156 A3
Losne F 105 B4
Los Nietos E 165 B4
Løsning DK 59 C2

Los Palacios y
Villafranca E 162 A2
Los Pozuelos de
Calatrava E 157 B3
Los Rábanos E 143 C4
Los Santos E 149 B4
Los Santos de la
Humosa E 151 B4
Los Santos de
Maimona E 155 C4
Lossburg D 93 C4
Losse F 128 B2
Losser NL 71 B4
Lossiemouth GB . . .32 D3
Lössnitz D 83 B4
Loštice CZ 97 B4
Los Tijos E 142 A2
Lostwithiel GB 42 B2
Los Villares E 163 A4
Los Yébenes E 157 A4
Løten N 48 B3
Lotorp S 56 B1
Lottefors S 50 A3
Löttorp S 62 A5
Lotyń PL 68 B1
Lotzorai I 179 C3
Louargat F 100 A2
Loudéac F 101 A3
Loudun F 102 B2
Loué F 102 B1
Loughborough GB . .40 C2
Loughbrickland GB 27 B4
Loughrea IRL 28 A3
Louhans F 105 C4
Louisburgh IRL 28 A2
Loukhi RUS 3 C13
Loulay F 114 B3
Loulé P 160 B1
Louny CZ 84 B1
Lourdes F 145 A3
Lourenzá E 141 A3
Loures P 154 C1
Loures-Barousse
F 145 A4
Louriçal P 154 A2
Lourinhã P 154 B1
Lourmarin F 131 B4
Loury F 103 B4
Lousa
Bragança P 149 A2
Castelo Branco P 155 B3
Lousã P 148 B1
Lousada
E 140 B3
P 148 A1
Louth GB 41 B3
Loutra Edipsou
GR 183 E5
Loutraki GR 184 B3
Loutropoli Thermis
GR 186 C1
Louverné F 102 A1
Louvie-Juzon F . . .145 A3
Louviers F 89 A5
Louvigné-du-Désert
F 88 B2
Louvois F 91 B4
Lova I 121 B5
Lovasberény H 112 B2
Lövåsen S 49 C5
Lovászpatona H . . .111 B4
Lövberga S 200 C1
Lovech BG 17 D6
Lövenich D 80 A2
Lövere I 120 B3
Lövestad S 61 D3
Loviisa FIN 8 B5
Lovikka S 196 B5
Lovinobaňa SK 99 C3
Loviste HR 138 B3
Lovke HR 123 B3
Lovnäs S 49 A5
Lövö H 111 B3
Lovosice CZ 84 B2
Lovozero RUS 3 C14
Lovran HR 123 B3
Lovreć HR 138 B2
Lovrenc na Pohorju
SLO 110 C2
Lovrin RO 126 B2
Lövstabruk S 51 B4
Löwenberg D 74 B2
Löwenstein D 94 B1
Lowick GB 37 A5
Łowicz PL 77 B4
Loxstedt D 72 A1
Loyew BY 13 C9
Loż SLO 123 B3
Loza CZ 96 B1
Łozina PL 85 A5
Loznica SRB 127 C1
Ložnicko Polje
SRB 127 C1
Lozorno SK 111 A4
Lozovik SRB 127 C3
Lozoyuela E 151 B4
Lozzo di Cadore I . .109 C3
Luanco E 141 A5
Luarca E 141 A4
Lubaczów PL 13 C5
Lubań PL 84 A3
Lubanie PL 76 B3
Lubanów PL 86 A3
Lubars D 73 B5
Lubasz PL 75 B5
Lubawa PL 69 B4
Lubawka PL 85 B4
Lübbecke D 72 B1
Lübben D 74 C2
Lübbenau D 84 A1
Lubczyna PL 74 A3
Lübeck D 65 C3
Lubenec CZ 83 B5
Lubenia PL 76 B3

Lubiatowo PL 75 A4
Lubichowo PL 69 B3
Lubicz Dolny PL . . .76 A3
Lubień PL 99 B3
Lubienia PL 87 A5
Lubień Kujawski
PL 77 B4
Lubieszewo PL 75 A4
Lubin
Dolnośląskie PL . .85 A4
Zachodnio-Pomorskie
PL 67 C3
Lublin PL 12 C5
Lubliniec PL 86 B2
Lubmin D 66 B2
Lubniewice PL 75 B4
Lubochnia PL 87 A4
Lubomierz
Dolnośląskie PL . .84 A3
Małopolskie PL . .99 B4
Luboń PL 76 B1
L'ubotín SK 99 B4
Lubowidz PL 77 A4
Łubowo
Wielkopolskie PL .76 B2
Zachodnio-Pomorskie
PL 68 B1
Lubraniec PL 76 B3
Lubrin E 164 B2
Lubrza PL 85 B5
Lubsko PL 84 A2
Lübtheen D 73 A4
Lubuczewo PL 68 A2
Luby CZ 83 B4
Lübz D 73 A5
Luc F 117 C3
Lucainena de las
Torres E 164 B2
Lucan IRL 30 A2
Lučani SRB 127 D2
Lúcar E 164 B2
Luçay-le-Mâle F . . .103 B3
Lucca I 134 B3
Lucciana F 180 A2
Lucé F 90 C1
Luče SLO 123 A3
Lucena
Córdoba E 163 A3
Huelva E 161 B3
Lucena-les-Aix F 104 C2
Lucenay-l'Evéque
F 104 B3
Lučenec SK 99 C3
Luceni E 144 C2
Lucens CH 106 C1
Lucera I 171 B3
Luceram F 133 B3
Lüchow D 73 B4
Luciana E 157 B3
Lucignano I 135 B4
Lucija SLO 122 B2
Lucka D 83 A4
Luckau D 84 A1
Luckenwalde D 74 B2
Lückstedt D 73 B4
Luco dei Marsi I . . .169 B3
Luçon F 114 B2
Luc-sur-Mer F 89 A3
Ludanice SK 98 C2
Ludbreg HR 124 A2
Lüdenscheid D 81 A3
Lüderitz D 73 B4
Lüdersdorf D 65 C3
Ludgershall GB 44 B2
Ludgo S 56 B3
Lüdinghausen D 80 A3
Ludlow GB 39 B4
Ludomy PL 75 B5
Ludvika S 50 B2
Ludweiler Warndt
D 92 B2
Ludwigsburg D 94 C1
Ludwigsfelde D 74 B2
Ludwigshafen D . . .93 B4
Ludwigslust D 73 A4
Ludwigsstadt D 82 B3
Ludza LV 8 D5
Luesia E 144 B2
Luftkurort Arendsee
D 73 B4
Lug
BIH 139 C4
HR 125 B4
Luga RUS 9 C7
Lugagnano Val d'Arda
I 120 C2
Lugano CH 120 A1
Lugau D 83 B4
Lugnas S 55 B4
Lúgnola I 168 A2
Lugny F 105 C3
Lugo
E 140 A3
I 135 A4
Lugoj RO 16 C4
Lugones E 141 A5
Lugros E 163 A4
Luhačovice CZ 98 B1
Luhe D 95 B4
Luino I 120 B1
Luintra E 140 B3
Lújar E 163 B4

Luleå S 196 D5
Lüleburgaz TR 186 A2
Lumbarda HR 138 C3
Lumbier E 144 B2
Lumbrales E 149 B3
Lumbreras E 143 B4
Lumbres F 78 B2
Lummelunda S 57 C4
Lummen B 79 B5
Lumparland FIN 51 B7
Lumpiaque E 152 A2
Lumsas DK 61 D1
Lumsden GB 33 D4
Lumsheden S 50 B3
Lun HR 123 C3
Luna E 144 B3
Lunamatrona I 179 C2
Lunano I 136 B1
Lunas F 130 B2
Lund
N 199 A8
Skåne S 61 D3
Västra Götaland
S 54 A3
Lundamo N 199 B7
Lunde
DK 59 C1
Sogn og Fjordane
N 46 A3
Sogn og Fjordane
N 46 A3
Telemark N 53 A5
S 200 D3
Lundebyvollen N . . .49 B4
Lunden D 64 B2
Lunderseter N 49 B4
Lunderskov DK 59 C2
Lundsberg S 55 A5
Lüneburg D 72 A3
Lunel F 131 B3
Lünen D 81 A3
Lunéville F 92 C2
Lungern CH 106 C3
Lungro I 174 B2
Luninyets BY 13 B6
Lunz am See A 110 B2
Luogosanto I 178 A3
Łupawa PL 68 A2
Lupión E 157 B4
Lupoglav HR 123 B3
Luppa D 83 A4
Luque E 163 A3
Lurago d'Erba I . . .120 B2
Luras I 178 B3
Lurcy-Lévis F 104 C1
Lure F 105 B5
Lurgan GB 27 B4
Luri F 180 A2
Lury-sur-Arnon F . .103 B4
Lušci Palanka BIH 124 C2
Lusévera I 122 A2
Lushnjë AL 182 C1
Lusignan F 115 B4
Lusigny-sur-Barse
F 104 A3
Lusnić BIH 138 B2
Luso P 148 B1
Lüsów PL 75 B5
Luspebryggan S . . .196 B2
Luss GB 34 B3
Lussac F 128 B2
Lussac-les-Châteaux
F 115 B4
Lussac-les-Eglises
F 115 B5
Lussan F 131 A3
Lüssow D 65 C5
Lustenau A 107 B4
Lüstnice CZ 84 B2
Luster N 47 A4
Lutago I 108 C2
Lutherstadt Wittenberg
D 83 A4
Lütjenburg D 65 B3
Lutnes N 49 A4
Lutocin PL 77 B4
Lutomiersk PL 86 A3
Luton GB 44 B3
Lutry CH 106 C1
Lutsk UA 13 C6
Lutter am Barenberge
D 72 C3
Lutterworth GB 40 C2
Lututów PL 86 A2
Lützen D 83 A4
Lutzow D 73 A4
Luusua FIN 197 C10
Luvos S 196 C1
Luxembourg L 92 B2
Luxeuil-les-Bains
F 105 B5
Luxey F 128 B2
Luz
Évora P 155 C3
Faro P 160 B1
Faro P 160 B2
Luzarches F 90 B2
Luže CZ 97 B4
Luzech F 129 B4
Luzern CH 106 B3
Luzino PL 68 A3
Luz-St Sauveur F . .145 B3
Luzy F 104 C2
Luzzi I 174 B2
L'viv UA 13 D6
Lwówek PL 75 B5
Lwówek Śląski PL . .84 A3
Lyakhavichy BY . . .13 B7
Lybster GB 32 C3
Lychen D 74 A2
Lychkova RUS 9 D8
Lyckeby S 63 B3
Lycksele S 200 B4
Lydd GB 45 C4
Lydford GB 42 B2
Lydney GB 39 C4
Lyepyel BY 13 A8
Lygna N 48 B2
Lygna N 47 B5
Lykling N 52 A1
Lyme Regis GB 43 B4
Lymington GB 44 C2
Lympne GB 45 B5
Lyndhurst GB 44 C2
Lyneham GB 43 A5
Lyness GB 33 C3
Lyngdal
Buskerud N 47 C6
Vest-Agder N 52 B3
Lyngør N 53 B5
Lyngsa DK 58 A3
Lyngseidet N 192 C4
Lyngsnes N 199 A8
Lynmouth GB 42 A3
Lynton GB 42 A3
Lyntupy BY 13 A7
Lyon F 117 B4
Lyons-la-Forêt F . . .90 B1
Lyozna BY 13 A9
Lyrestad S 55 B5
Lysánad Labem
CZ 84 B2
Lysápod Makytou
SK 98 B2
Lysebotn N 52 A2
Lysekil S 54 B2
Lysice CZ 97 B4
Lysomice PL 76 A3
Lysøysund N 198 B6
Lyss CH 106 B2
Lystrup DK 59 B3
Lysvik S 49 B5
Łyszkowice PL 77 C4
Lytham St Anne's
GB 38 A3
Lyuban RUS 9 C7
Lyubertsy RUS 9 E10
Lyubimets BG 183 B8
Lyuboml' UA 13 C6
Lyubytino RUS 9 C8

M

Maaninkavaara
FIN 197 C11
Maarheeze NL 80 A1
Maaseik B 80 A1
Maastricht NL 80 B1
Mablethorpe GB . . .41 B4
Mably F 117 A4
Macael E 164 B2
Maçanet de Cabrenys
E 146 B3
Mação P 154 B2
Macau F 128 A2
Maccagno-Agra I . .120 A1
Maccarese I 168 B2
Macchiagódena I . .170 B2
Macclesfield GB . . .40 B1
Macduff GB 33 D4
Maceda E 140 B3
Macedo de Cavaleiros
P 149 A3
Maceira
Guarda P 148 B2
Leiria P 154 B2
Macël HR 124 A1
Macerata I 136 B2
Macerata Féltria I . .136 B1
Machault F 91 B4
Machecoul F 114 B2
Mchowo PL 77 A5
Machrihanish GB . . .34 C2
Machynlleth GB 39 B3
Macieira P 148 A1
Maciejowice PL 87 A5
Macinaggio F 180 A2
Mackenrode D 82 A2
Mačkovci SLO 111 C3
Macomer I 178 B2
Mâcon B 91 A4
Mâcon F 117 A4
Macotera E 150 B2
Macroom IRL 29 C3
Macugnaga I 119 B4
Madan BG 183 B6
Madängsholm S 55 B4
Madaras H 126 A1
Maddaloni I 170 B2
Made NL 79 A4
Madeley GB 38 B4
Maderuelo E 151 A4
Madetkoski FIN . . .197 B9
Madley GB 39 B4
Madocsa H 112 C2
Madona LV 8 D5
Madonna di Campíglio
I 121 A3
Madrid E 151 B4
Madridejos E 157 A4
Madrigal de las Altas
Torres E 150 A2
Madrigal de la Vera
E 150 B2
Madrigalejo E 156 A2
Madrigalejo de Monte
E 143 B3
Madrigueras E 158 B2
Madroñera E 156 A2
Maël-Carhaix F . . .100 A2
Maella E 153 A4
Maello E 150 B3
Mafra P 154 C1
Magacela E 156 B2
Magallón E 144 C2
Magaluf E 166 B2
Magán E 151 C4
Magaña E 144 C1
Magasa I 121 B3
Magaz E 142 C2
Magdeburg D 73 B4
Magensc q F 128 C2
Maghera GB 27 B4

Lygna N 48 B2
Magherafelt GB 27 B4
Maghull GB 38 A4
Magilligan GB 27 A4
Magione I 135 B5
Magiot o P 154 C1
Maglaj BIH 125 C4
Maglehem S 63 C2
Magliano de'Marsi
I 169 A3
Magliano Sabina I . .168 A2
Magliano in Toscana
I 168 A1
Maglić SRB 126 B1
Máglie I 173 B4
Maglód H 112 B3
Magnac-Bourg F . .115 C5
Magnac-Laval F . . .115 B5
Magnières F 92 C2
Magnor N 49 C4
Magny-Cours F 104 C2
Magny-en-Vexin F . .90 B1
Mágocs H 125 A4
Maguilla E 156 B2
Maguiresbridge GB 27 B3
Magyarbóly H 125 B4
Magyarkeszi H 112 C2
Magyarszék H 125 A4
Mahide E 141 C4
Mahilyow BY 13 B9
Mahmudiye TR 187 C5
Mahora E 158 B2
Mahovo HR 124 B2
Mähring D 95 B4
Maia
E 144 A2
P 148 A1
Maiaelrayo E 151 A4
Maials E 153 A4
Maîche F 106 B1
Maida I 175 C2
Maiden Bradley GB 43 A4
Maidenhead GB 44 B3
Maiden Newton GB 43 B4
Maidstone GB 45 B4
Maienfeld CH 107 B4
Maignelay Montigny
F 90 B2
Maijanen FIN 197 B8
Maillezais F 114 B3
Mailly-le-Camp F . . .91 C4
Mailly-le-Château
F 104 B2
Mainar E 152 A2
Mainbernheim D . . .94 B2
Mainburg D 95 C3
Mainhardt D 94 B1
Maintal D 81 B4
Maintenon F 90 C1
Mainvilliers F 90 C1
Mainz D 93 A4
Maiori I 170 C2
Mairena de Aljarafe
E 162 A1
Mairena del Alcor
E 162 A2
Maisach D 108 A2
Maishofen A 109 B3
Maison-Rouge F . . .90 C3
Maissau A 97 C3
Maisse F 90 C2
Maizières-lès-Vic F 92 C2
Maja HR 124 B2
Majadahonda E . . .151 B4
Majadas E 150 C2
Majavatn N 195 E4
Majs H 125 B4
Majšperk SLO 123 A4
Makarska HR 138 B3
Makkum NL 70 A2
Maklár H 113 B4
Makó H 126 A2
Makoszyce PL 85 B5
Makov SK 98 B2
Makovac SRB 16 D4
Mąkowarsko PL 76 A2
Maków Mazowiecki
PL 77 B6
Maków Podhalański
PL 99 B3
Makrakomi GR 182 E4
Maksniemi FIN 196 D7
Malá S 195 E9
Malacky SK 97 C3
Maladzyechna BY . .13 A7
Malå Bosna SRB . .126 A1
Malagón E 157 A4
Malaguilla E 151 B4
Malahide IRL 30 A2
Malaja Kladuša BIH 124 B1
Malá Krsna SRB . .127 C3
Malá Lehota SK 98 C2
Malanów PL 76 C3
Mala Pijace SRB . .126 A1
Malá Subotica HR 124 A2
Malaucène F 131 A4
Malaunay F 89 A5
Malaya Vishera RUS 9 C8
Malborghetto I 109 C4
Malbork PL 69 A4
Malborn D 92 B2
Malbuisson F 105 C5
Malcésine I 121 B3
Malchin D 74 A1
Malching D 96 C1
Malchow D 73 A5
Malcocinado E 156 B2
Malczyce PL 85 A4
Maldegem B 79 A3
Maldon GB 45 B4
Małdyty PL 69 B4
Malemort F 129 A4
Malente D 65 B3
Målerås S 62 B3
Males GR 185 D6
Malesherbes F 90 C2
Malesina GR 183 E5
Malestroit F 101 B3

Maletto I 177 B3
Malexander S 56 B1
Malgrat de Mar E . .147 C3
Malhadas P 149 A3
Malia
CY 181 B1
GR 185 D6
Malicorne-sur-Sarthe
F 102 B1
Malijai F 132 A2
Malildjoš SRB 126 B1
Málilla S 62 A3
Mali Lošinj HR 123 C3
Malin IRL 27 A3
Málinec SK 99 C3
Malingsbo S 50 C2
Maliniec PL 76 B3
Malinska HR 123 B3
Maliq AL 182 C2
Malkara TR 186 B1
Małki PL 69 B4
Malko Tǔrnovo BG .17 D7
Mallaig GB 34 A2
Mallaranny IRL 28 A2
Mallemort F 131 B4
Mallén E 144 C2
Malléon F 146 A2
Mallersdorf-Pfaffenberg
D 95 C4
Málles Venosta I . .108 C1
Malling DK 59 B3
Mallnitz A 109 C4
Mallow IRL 29 B3
Mallwyd GB 38 B3
Malm N 199 A8
Malmbäck S 62 A2
Malmberget S 196 B3
Malmby S 56 A3
Malmédy B 80 B2
Malmesbury GB 43 A4
Malmköping S 56 A2
Malmö S 61 D3
Malmon S 54 B2
Malmslätt S 56 B1
Malnate I 120 B1
Malo I 121 B4
Małogoszcz PL 87 B4
Maloja CH 120 A2
Małomice PL 84 A3
Måløy N 198 D2
Malpartida E 155 B4
Malpartida de la Serena
E 156 B2
Malpartida de Plasencia
E 150 C1
Malpas
E 145 B4
GB 38 A4
Malpica P 155 B3
Malpica de Bergantiños
E 140 A2
Malpica de Tajo E .150 C3
Malsch D 93 C4
Malšice CZ 96 B2
Malta A 109 C4
Maltat F 104 C2
Maltby GB 40 B2
Malung S 49 B5
Malungsfors S 49 B5
Maluszów PL 75 B4
Maluszyn PL 87 B3
Malva E 142 C1
Malvaglia CH 120 A1
Malveira P 154 C1
Malvik N 199 B7
Malyn UA 13 C8
Mamarrosa P 148 B1
Mamer L 92 B2
Mamers F 89 B4
Mamirolle F 105 B5
Mammendorf D 108 A2
Mámmola I 175 C2
Mamoiada I 178 B3
Mamonovo RUS 69 A4
Mamuras AL 182 B1
Manacor E 167 B3
Manavgat TR 189 C6
Mancera de Abajo
E 150 B2
Mancha Real E 163 A4
Manchester GB 40 B1
Manching D 95 C3
Manchita E 156 B1
Manciano I 168 A1
Manciet F 128 C2
Mandal N 52 B3
Mandanici I 177 A4
Mándas I 179 C3
Mandatoríccio I . . .174 B2
Mandayona E 151 B5
Mandelieu-la-Napoule
F 132 B2
Mandello del Lário
I 120 B2
Mandelsloh D 72 B2
Manderfeld B 80 B2
Manderscheid D . . .80 B2
Mandino Selo BIH 138 B2
Mandoudi GR 183 E5
Mandra GR 185 A4
Mandraki GR 188 C2
Mandúria I 173 B3
Mane
Alpes-de-Haute-
Provence F 132 B1
Haute-Garonne F 145 A4
Manérbio I 120 B3
Mañeru E 144 B2
Manetin CZ 96 B1
Manfredónia I 171 B3
Mangalia RO 17 D8
Manganeses de la
Lampreana E . . .149 A4
Manganeses de la
Polvorosa E 141 B5

Mangen N 48 C3
Manger N 46 B2
Mangiennes F 92 B4
Mangotsfield GB . .43 A4
Mångsbodarna S. .49 A5
Mangualde P 148 B2
Maniago I 122 A1
Manilva E 162 B2
Manisa TR 186 D2
Manises E 159 B3
Mank A 110 A2
Månkarbo S 51 B4
Manlleu E 147 C3
Manna DK 58 A2
Männedorf CH 107 B3
Mannersdorf am
  Leithagebirge A .111 B3
Mannheim D 93 B4
Manningtree GB . .45 B5
Manoppello I 169 A4
Manorbier GB 39 C2
Manorhamilton IRL 26 B2
Manosque F 132 B1
Manowo PL 67 B5
Manresa E 147 C2
Månsarp S 62 A2
Månsåsen S 199 B11
Manschnow D 74 B3
Mansfeld D 82 A3
Mansfield GB 40 B2
Mansilla de Burgos
  E 143 B3
Mansilla de las Mulas
  E 142 B1
Manskog S 55 A3
Mansle F 115 C4
Manso F 180 A1
Manteigas P 148 B2
Mantel D 95 B4
Mantes-la-Jolie F . .90 C1
Mantes-la-Ville F . .90 C1
Manthelan F 102 B2
Mantorp S 56 B1
Mántova I 121 B3
Mänttä FIN 197 B9
Mäntyjärvi FIN . . .197 C10
Manuel E 159 B3
Manyas TR 186 B2
Manzanal de Arriba
  E 141 B4
Manzanares E . . .157 A4
Manzanares el Real
  E 151 B4
Manzaneda
  León E 141 B4
  Orense E 141 B3
Manzanedo E 143 B3
Manzaneque E . . .157 A4
Manzanera E 153 B3
Manzanilla E 161 B3
Manzat F 116 B2
Manziana I 168 A2
Manziat F 117 A4
Maó E 167 B4
Maoča BIH 125 C4
Maqueda E 150 B3
Mara E 152 A2
Maramaraereğlisi
  TR 186 B2
Maraña E 142 A1
Maranchón E 152 A1
Maranello I 135 A3
Marano I 170 C2
Marano Lagunare
  I 122 B2
Marans F 114 B2
Maratea I 174 B1
Marateca P 154 C2
Marathokambos
  GR 188 B1
Marathonas GR . .185 A4
Marathóvouno
  CY 181 A2
Marazion GB 42 B1
Marbach
  Baden-Württemberg
  D. 94 C1
  Hessen D. 82 B1
  F 92 C2
Marbäck S 60 B3
Mårbacka S 55 A4
Marbella E 162 B3
Marboz F 118 A2
Marburg D 81 B4
Marcali H 111 C4
Marčana HR. 122 C2
Marcaria I 121 B3
Marcelová SK 112 B2
Marcenat F 116 B2
March GB 41 C4
Marchamalo E . . .151 B4
Marchaux F 105 B5
Marche-en-Famenne
  B 79 B5
Marchegg A 111 A3
Marchena E 162 A2
Marchenoir F 103 B3
Marcheprime F . . .128 B2
Marciac F 128 C2
Marciana Marina I 134 C3
Marcianise I 170 B2
Marcigny F 117 A4
Marcilla E 144 B2
Marche-la-Croisille
  F 116 B2
Marcillac-Vallon F 130 A1
Marcillat-en-Combraille
  F 116 A2
Marcille-sur-Seine
  F 91 C3
Marcilloles F 118 B2
Marcilly-le-Hayer F .91 C3
Marcinkowice PL . .75 A5
Marciszów PL 85 B4
Marck F 78 B1
Marckolsheim F . .106 A2

Marco de Canevezes
  P. 148 A1
Mårdsele S. 200 B5
Mårdsjö S 200 C1
Mareham le Fen
  GB 41 B3
Marek S 62 A3
Marennes F 114 C2
Maresquel F. 78 B1
Mareuil F 115 C4
Mareuil-en-Brie F . .91 C3
Mareuil-sur-Arnon
  F. 103 C4
Mareuil-sur-Lay F .114 B2
Mareuil-sur-Ourcq
  F. 90 B3
Margam GB 39 C3
Margariti GR 182 D2
Margate GB 45 B5
Margaux F 128 A2
Margerie-Hancourt
  F. 91 C4
Margès F 117 B5
Margherita di Savóia
  I. 171 B4
Margita SRB 126 B3
Margone I 119 B4
Margonin PL 76 B2
Margut F 91 B5
Maria E. 164 B2
Mariager DK. 58 B2
Mariana E 152 B1
Maria Neustift A . .110 B1
Marianelund S 62 A3
Mariánopoli I 176 B2
Mariánské Lázně
  CZ 95 B4
Mariapfarr A. 109 B4
Maria Saal A 110 C1
Mariazell A 110 B2
Maribo DK 65 B4
Maribor SLO 110 C2
Marieberg S 56 A1
Mariehamn FIN . . .51 B6
Marieholm S 61 D3
Mariembourg B 91 A4
Marienbaum D 80 A2
Marienberg D. 83 B5
Marienheide D 81 A3
Marienthal D 73 B3
Mariestad S 55 B4
Marieux F. 90 A2
Marigliano I 170 C2
Marignane F 131 B4
Marigny
  Jura F 105 C4
  Manche F. 88 A2
Marigny-le-Châtel
  F. 91 C3
Marija Bistrica HR 124 A2
Marijampolė LT . . .13 A5
Marín E. 140 B2
Marina HR 138 B2
Marina del Cantone
  I. 170 C2
Marina di Acquappesa
  I. 174 B1
Marina di Alberese
  I. 168 A1
Marina di Amendolara
  I. 174 B2
Marina di Árbus I .179 C2
Marina di Campo I 134 C3
Marina di Carrara
  I. 134 A3
Marina di Castagneto-
  Donorático I 134 B3
Marina di Cécina I 134 B3
Marina di Gáiro I . .179 C3
Marina di Ginosa I 173 B2
Marina di Gioiosa
  Iónica I 175 C2
Marina di Grosseto
  I. 135 C3
Marina di Léuca I .173 C4
Marina di Massa I .134 A3
Marina di Nováglie
  I. 173 C4
Marina di Pisa I . .134 B3
Marina di Ragusa
  I. 177 C3
Marina di Ravenna
  I. 135 A5
Marina di Torre Grande
  I. 179 C2
Marinaleda E 162 A3
Marina Romea I . .135 A5
Marine de Sisco F 180 A2
Marinella I 176 B1
Marinella di Sarzana
  I. 134 A3
Marineo I 176 B2
Marines F. 90 B1
Maringues F 116 B3
Marinha das Ondas
  P 154 A2
Marinha Grande P 154 B2
Marinhas P. 148 A1
Marino I. 168 B2
Marjaliza E 157 A4
Markabygd N 199 B8
Markaryd S 61 C3
Markelo NL 71 B3
Market Deeping GB 40 C3
Market Drayton GB 38 B4
Market Harborough
  GB 40 C3
Markethill GB 27 B4
Market Rasen GB .40 B3
Market Warsop GB .40 B2
Market Weighton
  GB 40 B3
Markgröningen D . .93 C5
Markhausen D 71 B4
Marki PL 77 B6
Markina-Xemein E 143 A4
Markinch GB 35 B4

Märkische Buchholz
  D. 74 B2
Markitta S 196 B4
Markkleeberg D. . .83 A4
Marklohe D 72 B2
Marknesse NL 70 B2
Markneukirchen D .83 B4
Markopoulo GR. . .185 B4
Markovac
  Srbija SRB 127 C3
  Vojvodina SRB. .126 B3
Markowice PL. 86 B2
Markranstädt D . . .83 A4
Marksuhl D 82 B2
Markt Allhau A . . .111 B3
Markt Bibart D 94 B2
Marktbreit D. 94 B2
Markt Erlbach D . . .94 B2
Markt-heidenfeld D .94 B1
Markt Indersdorf D .95 C3
Marktl D. 95 C4
Marktleuthen D . . .83 B3
Marktoberdorf D . .108 B1
Marktredwitz D . . .95 A4
Markt Rettenbach
  D. 108 B1
Markt Schwaben
  D. 108 A2
Markt-Übelbach A .110 B2
Markusica HR 125 B4
Markušovce SK. . . .99 C4
Marl D. 80 A3
Marlborough
  Devon GB 42 B3
  Wiltshire GB. 44 B2
Marle F. 91 B3
Marlieux F 117 A5
Marlow
  D. 66 B1
  GB 44 B3
Marma S 51 B4
Marmagne F 104 C3
Marmande F 128 B3
Marmara TR. 186 B2
Marmaris TR 188 C3
Marmelete P. 160 B1
Marmolejo E 157 B3
Marmoutier F 93 C3
Marnay F 105 B4
Marne D 64 C2
Marnheim D 93 B4
Marnitz D 73 A4
Maroldsweisach D .82 B2
Marolles-les-Braults
  F. 89 B4
Maromme F 89 A5
Marone I. 120 B3
Maroslele H 126 A2
Maróstica I 121 B4
Marotta I 136 B2
Marpisa GR 185 B6
Marquion F 78 B3
Marquise F 78 B1
Marradi I 135 A4
Marrasjärvi FIN . .197 C8
Marraskoski FIN . .197 C8
Marratxi E 166 B2
Marrúbiu I 179 C2
Marrum NL. 70 A2
Marrupe E 150 B3
Marsac F 129 C5
Marsac-en-Livradois
  F. 117 B3
Marságlia I 120 C2
Marsala I 176 B1
Marsberg D 81 A4
Marsciano I 135 C5
Marseillan F 130 B2
Marseille = Marseilles
  F. 131 B4
Marseille en Beauvaisis
  F. 90 B1
Marseilles = Marseille
  F. 131 B4
Mársico Nuovo I . .172 B1
Marske-by-the-Sea
  GB 37 B5
Mars-la-Tours F . . .92 B1
Marsliden S 195 E6
Marson F 91 C4
Märsta S. 57 A3
Marstal DK 65 B3
Marstrand S 60 B1
Marta I 168 A1
Martano I 173 B4
Martel F 129 B4
Martelange B 92 B1
Martfeld D 72 B2
Martfű H. 113 B4
Martham GB 41 C5
Marthon F 115 C4
Martiago E 149 B3
Martigné-Briand F 102 B1
Martigné-Ferchaud
  F. 101 B4
Martigne-sur-Mayenne
  F. 102 A1
Martigny CH 119 A4
Martigny-les-Bains
  F. 105 A4
Martigues F 131 B4
Martim-Longo P . .160 B2
Martin SK 98 B2
Martina CH. 108 C1
Martina Franca I . .173 B3
Martinamor E 150 B2
Martin de la Jara
  E 162 A3
Martinengo I 120 B2
Martin Muñoz de las
  Posadas E 150 A3
Martinsberg A 97 C3
Martinščica HR . . .123 C3
Martinsicuro I 136 C2
Martinszell D 107 B5
Mártis I 178 B2
Martofte DK 59 C3
Martonvásár H . . .112 B2

Martorell E. 147 C2
Martos E 163 A4
Martres Tolosane
  F. 146 A1
Martti FIN. 197 B11
Marugán E. 150 B3
Marúggio I 173 B3
Marvão P 155 B3
Marvejols F 130 A2
Marville F 92 B1
Marwałd PL 77 A4
Marykirk GB. 35 B5
Marypark GB 32 D3
Maryport GB 36 B3
Marytavy GB 42 B2
Marzabotto I 135 A4
Marzahna D 74 C1
Marzahne D 73 B5
Marzamemi I 177 C4
Marzocca I 136 B2
Masa E 143 B3
Mas-Cabardès I . .146 A3
Máscali I 177 B4
Mascaraque E . . .157 A4
Mascarenhas P . .149 A2
Mascioni I 169 A3
Mas de Barberáns
  E 153 B4
Mas de las Matas
  E 153 B3
Masegoso E. 158 C1
Masegoso de Tajuña
  E 151 B5
Masera I 119 A5
Masevaux F 106 B1
Masfjorden N 46 B2
Masham GB. 37 B5
Masi N 192 C7
Maside E 140 B2
Maslacq F 144 A3
Maslinica HR 138 B2
Masloc RO. 126 B3
Maslovare BIH . . .138 A3
Masone I 133 A4
Massa I 134 A3
Massa Fiscáglia I .121 C5
Massafra I 173 B3
Massa Lombarda
  I. 135 A4
Massa Lubrense I 170 C2
Massamagrell E . .159 B3
Massa Maríttima I .135 B3
Massa Martana I . .136 C1
Massanassa E . . .159 B3
Massarosa I 134 B3
Massat F 146 B2
Massay F 103 B3
Massbach D. 82 B2
Masseret F 116 B1
Masseube F 145 A4
Massiac F 116 B3
Massignac F 115 C4
Massing D 95 C4
Massmechelen B. .80 B1
Masterud N 49 B4
Mästocka S 61 C3
Masty BY 13 B6
Masúa I 179 C2
Masueco E 149 A3
Masugnsbyn S . . .196 B5
Mašun SLO 123 B3
Maszewo
  Lubuskie PL. 75 B3
  Zachodnio-Pomorskie
  PL. 75 A4
Mata de Alcántara
  E 155 B4
Matala GR 185 E5
Matalebreras E . .144 C1
Matallana de Torio
  E 142 B1
Matamala E 151 A5
Mataporquera E . .142 B2
Matapozuelos E . .150 A3
Mataró E 147 C3
Matarocco I 176 B1
Matélica I 136 B2
Matera I 172 B2
Mátészalka H 16 B5
Matet E 159 B3
Matfors S 200 D3
Matha F 115 C3
Mathay F 106 B1
Matignon F 101 A3
Matilla de los Caños
  del Rio E 149 B4
Matlock GB 40 B2
Matosinhos P 148 A1
Matour F 117 A4
Matrei am Brenner
  A 108 B2
Matrei in Osttirol
  A 109 B3
Matrice I 170 B2
Matsdal S 195 E6
Mattarello I 121 A4
Mattersburg A . . .111 B3
Mattighofen A 109 A4
Mattinata I 171 B4
Mattos P 154 B2
Mattsee A. 109 B4
Mattsmyra S 50 A2
Måttsund S 196 D5
Matulji HR 123 B3
Maubert-Fontaine
  F. 91 B4
Maubeuge F 79 B3
Maubourguet F . . .145 A4
Mauchline GB 36 A2
Maud GB 33 D4
Mauer-kirchen A . .109 A4
Mauern D 95 C3
Mauguio F 131 B3
Maulbronn D 93 C4
Maule F. 90 C1

Mauléon F 114 B3
Mauléon-Barousse
  F. 145 B4
Mauléon-Licharre
  F. 144 A3
Maulévrier F 114 A3
Maum IRL 28 A2
Maurach A 108 B2
Maure-de-Bretagne
  F. 101 B4
Maureilhan F 130 B2
Måureni RO. 126 B3
Mauriac F 116 B2
Mauron F 101 A3
Maurs F 116 C2
Maury F 146 B3
Maussane-les-Alpilles
  F. 131 B3
Mautern A 97 C3
Mauterndorf A . . .109 B4
Mautern im Steiermark
  A. 110 B1
Mauthausen A 110 A1
Mauthen A 109 C3
Mauvezin F 129 C3
Mauzé-sur-le-Mignon
  F. 114 B3
Maxent F 101 B3
Maxey-sur-Vaise F .92 C1
Maxial P. 154 B1
Maxieira P 154 B2
Maxwellheugh GB. .35 C5
Mayalde E 149 A4
Maybole GB 36 A2
Mayen D. 80 B3
Mayenne F 88 B3
Mayet F 102 B2
Mayorga E 142 B1
Mayres F 117 C4
Mayrhofen A 108 B2
Mazagón E 161 B3
Mazaleón E 153 A4
Mazamet F 130 B1
Mazan F 131 A4
Mazara del Vallo I 176 B1
Mazarambroz E . .157 A3
Mazarete E 152 B1
Mazaricos E 140 B2
Mazarrón E 165 B3
Mažeikiai LT 8 D3
Mazères F 146 A2
Mazères-sur-Salat
  F. 145 A4
Mazières-en-Gâtine
  F. 115 B3
Mazin HR 138 A1
Mazuelo E 143 B3
Mazyr BY 13 B8
Mazzarino I 177 B3
Mazzarrà Sant'Andrea
  I. 177 A4
Mazzo di Valtellina
  I. 120 A3
Mdzewo PL. 77 B5
Mealabost GB 31 A2
Mealhada P. 148 B1
Méan B 79 B5
Meana Sardo I . . .179 C3
Meaulne F 103 C4
Meaux F. 90 C2
Mebonden N 199 B8
Mecerreyes E . . .143 B3
Mechelen B. 79 A4
Mechernich D 80 B2
Mechnica PL. 86 B2
Mechowo PL 67 C4
Mechterstädt D . . .82 B2
Mecidiye TR. 186 B1
Mecikal PL 68 B2
Mecina-Bombarón
  E 164 C1
Meckenbeuren D .107 B4
Meckenheim
  Rheinland-Pfalz
  D. 80 B3
  Rheinland-Pfalz D .93 B4
Meckesheim D. . . .93 B4
Mecseknádasd H .125 A4
Meda
  I. 120 B2
  P 149 B2
Medak HR 137 A4
Medanı́ı 120 B1
Medebach D 81 A4
Medelim P 155 A3
Medemblik NL. . . .70 B2
Medena Selista
  BIH. 138 A2
Medesano I 120 C3
Medevi S 55 B5
Medgidia RO. 17 C8
Medgyesháza H . .113 C5
Medhamn S 55 A4
Mediaş RO 17 B6
Medicina I 135 A4
Medinaceli E 152 A1
Medina de las Torres
  E 155 C4
Medina del Campo
  E 150 A3
Medina de Pomar
  E 143 B3
Medina de Ríoseco
  E 142 C1
Medina Sidonia E 162 B2
Medinilla E 150 B2
Medja SRB. 126 B2
Medjedja BIH. 139 B5
Medulin HR 122 C2
Meduno I 122 A1
Medveda SRB. . . .127 C3
Medvedov SK 111 B4
Medvezhyegorsk
  RUS. 9 A9
Medvide HR. 137 A4
Medvode SLO . . .123 A3
Medzev SK. 99 C4
Medžitlija MK. 182 C3
Maule F 90 C1

Meerle B 79 A4
Meersburg D 107 B4
Meeuwen B 79 A5
Megalo Horio GR .188 C2
Megalopoli GR . . .184 B3
Megara GR. 185 A4
Megève F 118 B3
Meggenhofen A . .109 A4
Megra RUS 9 B10
Megyaszó H. 113 A5
Mehamn N 193 A11
Mehedeby S. 51 B4
Méhkerék H 113 C5
Mehun-sur-Yèvre
  F. 103 B4
Meigle GB 35 B4
Meijel NL 80 A1
Meilen CH 107 B3
Meilhan F 128 C2
Meimôa P. 149 B2
Meina I 119 B5
Meine D 73 B3
Meinersen D 72 B3
Meinerzhagen D . .81 A3
Meiningen D 82 B2
Meira E 141 A3
Meix-devant-Virton
  B 92 B1
Meka PL 86 A2
Meka Gruda BIH . .139 B4
Mel I 121 A5
Melbu N 194 B5
Melč CZ 98 B1
Meldal N 198 B6
Méldola I 135 A5
Meldorf D. 64 B2
Melegnano I 120 B2
Melenci SRB 126 B2
Melendugno I 173 B4
Melfi I 172 B1
Melfjordbotn N . . .195 D4
Melgaço P 140 B2
Melgar de Arriba
  E 142 B1
Melgar de Fernamental
  E 142 B2
Melgar de Yuso E .142 B2
Melhus N 199 B7
Meliana E 159 B3
Melide
  CH 120 B1
  E 140 B2
Melides P. 160 A1
Meligales GR. . . .184 B2
Melilli I 177 B4
Melinovac HR 124 C1
Melisenda I 179 C3
Melisey F 105 B5
Mélito di Porto Salvo
  I. 175 D1
Melk A. 110 A2
Melksham GB 43 A4
Mellakoski FIN. . .196 C7
Mellanström S . . .195 E9
Mellansel S 61 C2
Melle
  B 79 A3
  D 71 B5
  F 115 B3
Mellendorf D 72 B2
Mellerud S 54 B3
Mellieha M 175 C3
Mellösa S 56 A2
Mellrichstadt D . . .82 B2
Melnice I 124 B2
Mělnické Vtelno
  CZ 84 B2
Mělník CZ. 84 B2
Melón E 140 B2
Melrose GB 35 C5
Mels CH 107 B4
Meltaus FIN. 197 C8
Meltham GB. 40 B2
Melton Mowbray
  GB 40 C3
Meltosjärvi FIN . .196 C7
Melun F 90 C2
Melvaig GB 31 B3
Melvich GB 32 C3
Mélykút H. 126 A1
Melzo I 120 B2
Memaliaj AL. 182 C1
Membrilla E 157 B4
Membrio E. 155 B3
Memer F 129 B4
Memmelsdorf D. . .94 B2
Memmingen D. . . .107 B5
Memória P 154 B2
Menággio I 120 A2
Menai Bridge GB . .38 A2
Menasalbas E . . .157 A3
Menat F 116 A2
Mendavia E 144 B1
Mendaza E 144 B1
Mende F 130 A2
Menden D 81 A3
Menderes TR 188 A2
Mendig D 80 B3
Mendiga P 154 B2
Mendrisio CH 120 B1
Ménéac F 101 A3
Menemen TR 188 A2
Menen B 78 B3
Menesjärvi FIN . .193 D10
Menetou-Salon F .103 B4
Menfi I. 176 B1
Ménföcsanak H . .111 B4
Mengamuñoz E . .150 B3
Mengen
  D 107 A4
  TR. 187 B7
Mengeš SLO 123 A3
Mengíbar E 157 C4
Mengkofen D. 95 C4
Menou F. 104 B2
Mens F. 118 C2

Menslage D 71 B4
Mensträsk S 200 A5
Mentana I 168 A2
Menton F 133 B3
Méntrida E. 151 B3
Méobecq F 115 B5
Méounes-les-Montrieux
  F. 132 B1
Meppel NL 70 B3
Meppen D 71 B4
Mequinenza E . . .153 A4
Mer F 103 B3
Mera
  Coruña E 140 A2
  Coruña E 140 A3
Meråker N 199 B8
Merano I 108 C2
Merate I 120 B2
Mercadillo E 143 A3
Mercatale I 135 B5
Mercatino Conca I 136 B1
Mercato San Severino
  I 170 C2
Mercato Saraceno
  I 135 B5
Merching D 108 A1
Merchtem B. 79 B4
Merdrignac F. 101 A3
Merdžanići BIH . .139 B3
Meré E 142 A2
Mere GB. 43 A4
Meréville F. 90 C2
Merfeld D. 80 A3
Méribel F 118 B3
Méribel Motraret
  F. 118 B3
Meriç TR 186 A1
Mérida E. 155 C4
Mérignac F. 128 B2
Měřín CZ 97 B3
Mering D 94 C2
Merkendorf D 94 B2
Merklín CZ. 96 B1
Merksplas B. 79 A4
Merlánna S 56 A2
Merlimont Plage F. .78 B1
Mern DK. 65 A5
Mernye H 111 C4
Mersch L 92 B2
Merseburg D 83 A3
Mers-les-Bains F. .90 A1
Merthyr Tydfil GB .39 C3
Mertingen D. 94 C2
Mértola P 160 B2
Méru F 90 B2
Merufe P. 140 B2
Mervans F 105 C4
Merville F 78 B2
Méry-sur-Seine F . .91 C3
Merzen D 71 B4
Merzifon TR. 23 A8
Merzig D. 92 B2
Mesagne I 173 B3
Mesão Frio P 148 A2
Mesas de Ibor E . .156 A2
Meschede D. 81 A4
Meschers-sur-Gironde
  F. 114 C3
Meslay-du-Maine
  F. 102 B1
Mesna N. 48 A2
Mesnalien N. 48 A2
Mesocco CH 120 A2
Mésola I. 122 C1
Mesologi GR 184 A2
Mesopotamo GR .182 D2
Mesoraca I 175 B2
Messac F 101 B4
Messancy B. 92 B1
Messdorf D 73 B4
Messei F 88 B3
Messejana P 160 B1
Messelt N. 48 A3
Messina I 177 A4
Messingen D 71 B4
Messini GR 184 B3
Messkirch D 107 B4
Messlingen S 199 C9
Messstetten D. . . .107 A4
Mesta GR 185 A6
Mestanza E 157 B3
Městec Králové CZ 84 B3
Mestlin D 73 A4
Město Albrechtice
  CZ 85 B5
Město Libavá CZ . .98 B1
Město Touškov CZ .96 B1
Mestre I 122 B1
Mesvres F 104 C3
Mesztegnyő H . . .111 C4
Meta I 170 C2
Metajna HR 137 A4
Metelen D 71 B4
Methana GR. 185 B4
Methlick GB. 33 D4
Methven GB 35 B4
Methwold GB. 41 C4
Metković HR 139 B3
Metlika SLO 123 B4
Metnitz A 110 C1
Metsäkylä FIN . .197 D11
Metslawier NL. . . .70 A3
Metsovo GR. 182 D3
Metten D 95 C4
Mettendorf D 92 B2
Mettet B 79 B4
Mettingen D. 71 B4
Mettlach D 92 B2
Mettlen CH. 106 C2
Mettmann D 80 A2
Metz F 92 B2
Metzervisse F 92 B2
Metzingen D 94 C1
Meulan F 90 B1
Meung-sur-Loire
  F. 103 B3
Meuselwitz D. 83 A4
Meuzac F 115 C5
Mevagissey GB . . .42 B2
Mexborough GB . .40 B2

Meximieux F 118 B2
Mey GB 32 C3
Meyenburg D 71 B5
Meyerhöfen D 71 B5
Meylan F 118 B2
Meymac F 116 B2
Meyrargues F 132 B1
Meyrueis F 130 A2
Meyssac F 129 A4
Meysse F 117 C4
Meyzieu F 117 B4
Mèze F 130 B2
Mézériat F 117 A5
Mežica SLO 110 C1
Mézidon-Canon F 89 A3
Mézières-en-Brenne F 115 B5
Mézières-sur-Issoire F 115 B4
Mézilhac F 117 C4
Mézilles F 104 B2
Mézin F 128 B3
Mezőberény H 113 C5
Mezőcsát H 113 B4
Mezőfalva H 112 C2
Mezőhegyes H 126 A2
Mezőkeresztes H 113 B4
Mezőkomárom H 112 C2
Mezőkövácsháza H 113 C4
Mezőkövesd H 113 B4
Mezőörs H 111 B4
Mézos F 128 B1
Mezőszilas H 112 C2
Mezőtúr H 113 B4
Mezquita de Jarque E 153 B3
Mezzano
Emilia Romagna I 135 A5
Trentino Alto Adige I 121 A4
Mezzojuso I 176 B2
Mezzoldo I 120 A2
Mezzolombardo I 121 A4
Mgarr M 175 C3
Miajadas E 156 A2
Miały PL 75 B5
Mianowice PL 68 A2
Miasteczko Krajeńskie PL 76 A2
Miasteczko Sł. PL 86 B2
Miastko PL 68 A1
Michalovce SK 12 D4
Michałowice PL 87 B3
Michelau D 94 B2
Michelbach D 94 B2
Micheldorf A 110 B1
Michelhausen A 110 A2
Michelsneukirchen D 95 B4
Michelstadt D 93 B5
Michendorf D 74 B2
Mickleover GB 40 C2
Midbea GB 33 B4
Middelburg NL 79 A3
Middelfart DK 59 C2
Middelharnis NL 79 A4
Middelkerke B 78 A2
Middelstum NL 71 A3
Middlesbrough GB 37 B5
Middleton Cheney GB 44 A2
Middleton-in-Teesdale GB 37 B4
Middletown GB 27 B4
Middlewich GB 38 A4
Middlezoy GB 43 A4
Midhurst GB 44 C3
Midleton IRL 29 C3
Midlum D 64 C1
Midsomer Norton GB 43 A4
Midtgulen N 198 D2
Midtskogberget N 49 A4
Midwolda NL 71 A4
Mid Yell GB 33 A5
Miechów PL 87 B4
Miedes de Aragón E 152 A2
Miedes de Atienza E 151 A4
Międzybodzie Bielskie PL 99 B3
Międzybórz PL 85 A5
Międzychód PL 75 B4
Międzylesie PL 85 B4
Międzyrzec Podlaski PL 12 C5
Międzyrzecz PL 75 B4
Międzywodzie PL 67 B3
Międzyzdroje PL 67 C3
Miejska Górka PL 85 A4
Miélan F 145 A4
Mielec PL 87 B5
Mielęcin PL 75 A3
Mielno
Warmińsko-Mazurskie PL 77 A5
Zachodnio-Pomorskie PL 67 B5
Miengo E 143 A3
Mieraslompolo FIN 193 C11
Miercurea Ciuc RO 17 B6
Mieres
Asturias E 141 A5
Girona E 147 B3
Mieroszów PL 85 B4
Mierzyn PL 86 A3
Miesau D 93 B3
Miesbach D 108 B2
Mieścisko PL 76 B2
Mieste D 73 B4
Miesterhorst D 73 B4
Mieszków PL 76 B2
Mieszkowice PL 74 B3
Mietków PL 85 B4
Migennes F 104 B2
Miggiano I 173 C4
Migliánico I 169 A4
Migliarino I 121 C4
Migliónico I 172 B2
Mignano Monte Lungo I 169 B3
Migné F 115 B5
Miguel Esteban E 157 A4
Miguelturra E 157 B4
Mihajlovac SRB 127 C2
Miháld H 111 C4
Mihalgazi TR 187 B5
Mihalıççık TR 187 C6
Mihályi H 111 B4
Mihla D 82 A2
Mihohnić HR 123 B3
Miholjsko HR 123 B4
Mihovljan HR 124 A1
Mijares E 150 B3
Mijas E 163 B3
Mike H 124 A3
Mikines GR 184 B3
Mikkeli FIN 8 B5
Mikkelvik N 192 B3
Mikleuš HR 125 B3
Mikołajki Pomorskie PL 69 B4
Mikołów PL 86 B2
Mikonos GR 185 B6
Mikorzyn PL 86 A2
Mikro Derio GR 183 B8
Mikstat PL 86 A1
Mikulášovice CZ 84 B2
Mikulov CZ 97 C4
Mikulovice CZ 85 B5
Milagro E 144 B2
Miłakowo PL 69 A5
Milan = Milano I 120 B2
Miland N 47 C5
Milano = Milan I 120 B2
Milano Marittima I 135 A5
Milas TR 188 B2
Milazzo I 177 A4
Mildenhall GB 45 A4
Milejewo PL 69 A4
Milelín CZ 85 B3
Miletić SRB 125 B5
Miletićevo SRB 126 B3
Mileto I 175 C2
Milevsko CZ 96 B2
Milford IRL 26 A3
Milford Haven GB 39 C1
Milford on Sea GB 44 C2
Milhão P 149 A3
Milići BIH 139 A5
Miličín CZ 96 B2
Milicz PL 85 A5
Milín CZ 96 B2
Militello in Val di Catánia I 177 B3
Miljevina BIH 139 B4
Milkowice PL 85 A4
Millançay F 103 B3
Millares E 159 B3
Millas F 146 B3
Millau F 130 A2
Millesimo I 133 A4
Millevaches F 116 B2
Millom GB 36 B3
Millport GB 34 C3
Millstatt A 109 C4
Millstreet
Cork IRL 29 B2
Waterford IRL 29 B4
Milltown
Galway IRL 28 A3
Kerry IRL 29 B1
Milltown Malbay IRL 28 B2
Milly-la-Forêt F 90 C2
Milmarcos E 152 A2
Milmersdorf D 74 A2
Milna HR 138 B2
Milnthorpe GB 37 B4
Milogórze PL 69 A5
Miłomłyn PL 69 B4
Milos GR 185 C5
Miloševo SRB 127 C3
Miłosław PL 76 B2
Milot AL 182 B1
Milówka PL 99 B3
Miltach D 95 B4
Miltenberg D 94 B1
Milton Keynes GB 44 A3
Miltzow D 66 B2
Milverton GB 43 A3
Milzyn PL 76 B3
Mimice HR 138 B2
Mimizan F 128 B1
Mimizan-Plage F 128 B1
Mimoň CZ 84 B2
Mina de Juliana P 160 B1
Mina de São Domingos P 160 B2
Minas de Riotinto E 161 B3
Minateda E 158 C2
Minaya E 158 B1
Minde P 154 B2
Mindelheim D 108 A1
Mindelstetten D 95 C3
Minden D 72 B1
Mindszent H 113 C4
Minehead GB 43 A3
Mineo I 177 B3
Minerbe I 121 B4
Minérbio I 121 C4
Minervino Murge I 171 B4
Minglanilla E 158 B2
Mingorria E 150 B3
Minnesund N 48 B3
Miño E 140 A2
Miño de San Esteban E 151 A4
Minsen D 71 A4
Minsk BY 13 B7
Mińsk Mazowiecki PL 12 B4
Minsterley GB 39 B4
Mintlaw GB 33 D4
Minturno I 169 B3
Mionica
BIH 125 C4
SRB 127 C2
Mios F 128 B2
Mira
E 158 B2
I 121 B5
P 148 B1
Mirabel E 155 B4
Mirabel-aux-Baronnies F 131 A4
Mirabella Eclano I 170 B3
Mirabella Imbáccari I 177 B3
Mirabello I 121 C4
Miradoux F 129 B3
Miraflores de la Sierra E 151 B4
Miralrio E 151 B5
Miramar P 148 A1
Miramare I 136 A1
Miramas F 131 B3
Mirambeau F 114 C3
Miramont-de-Guyenne F 129 B3
Miranda de Arga E 144 B2
Miranda de Ebro E 143 B4
Miranda do Corvo P 148 B1
Miranda do Douro P 149 A3
Mirande F 129 C3
Mirandela P 149 A2
Mirandilla E 155 C4
Mirándola I 121 C4
Miranje HR 137 A4
Mirano I 121 B5
Miras AL 182 C2
Miravet E 153 A4
Miré F 102 B1
Mirebeau F 102 C2
Mirebeau-sur-Bèze F 105 B4
Mirecourt F 105 A5
Mirepoix F 146 A2
Mires GR 185 D5
Miribel F 117 B4
Miričina BIH 125 C4
Mirina GR 183 D7
Mirna SLO 123 B4
Miroslav CZ 97 C4
Mirosławice PL 85 B4
Mirosławiec PL 75 A5
Mirošov CZ 96 B1
Mirotice CZ 96 B2
Mirovice CZ 96 B2
Mirow D 74 A1
Mirsk PL 84 B3
Mirzec PL 87 A5
Misi FIN 197 C9
Misilmeri I 176 A2
Miske H 112 C3
Miskolc H 113 A4
Mislinja SLO 110 C2
Missanello I 174 A2
Missillac F 101 B3
Mistelbach
A 97 C4
D 95 B3
Misten N 194 C5
Misterbianco I 177 B4
Misterhult S 62 A4
Mistretta I 177 B3
Misurina I 109 C3
Mitchelstown IRL 29 B3
Mithimna GR 186 C1
Mithoni GR 184 C2
Mitilini GR 186 C1
Mitilinii GR 188 B1
Mittelberg
Tirol A 108 C1
Vorarlberg A 107 B5
Mittenwald D 108 B2
Mittenwalde D 74 B2
Mitterback A 110 B2
Mitterdorf im Mürztal A 110 B2
Mitter-Kleinarl A 109 B4
Mittersheim F 92 C2
Mittersill A 109 B3
Mitterskirchen D 95 C4
Mitterteich D 95 B4
Mitton F 128 B2
Mittweida D 83 B4
Mitwitz D 82 B3
Mizhhir'ya UA 13 D5
Mjällby S 63 B2
Mjåvatn N 53 B4
Mjöbäck S 60 B2
Mjölby S 56 B1
Mjølfjell N 46 B3
Mjøndalen N 53 A6
Mjørlund N 48 B2
Mladá Boleslav CZ 84 B2
Mladá Vožice CZ 96 B2
Mladé Buky CZ 85 B3
Mladenovac SRB 127 C2
Mladenovo SRB 126 B1
Mladikovine BIH 139 A3
Mława PL 77 A5
Mlinište BIH 138 A2
Młodzieszyn PL 77 B5
Młogoszyn PL 77 B4
Młynary PL 69 A4
Mnichóvice CZ 96 B2
Mnichovo Hradiště CZ 84 B2
Mniów PL 87 A4
Mnisek nad Hnilcom SK 99 C4
Mníšek pod Brdy CZ 96 B2
Mniszek PL 87 A4
Mniszków PL 87 A4
Mo
Hedmark N 48 B3
Hordaland N 46 B2
Mo *continued*
Møre og Romsdal N 198 C5
Telemark N 53 A3
Gävleborg S 51 A3
Västra Götaland S 54 B2
Moaña E 140 B2
Moate IRL 28 A4
Mocejón E 151 C4
Močenok SK 111 A4
Mochales E 152 A1
Mochowo PL 77 B4
Mochy PL 75 B5
Mockern D 73 B4
Mockfjärd S 50 B1
Möckmühl D 94 B1
Mockrehna D 83 A4
Moclin E 163 A4
Mocsa H 112 B2
Mőcsény H 125 A4
Modane F 118 B3
Modbury GB 42 B3
Módena I 121 C3
Módica I 177 C3
Modigliana I 135 A4
Modlin PL 77 B5
Mödling A 111 A3
Modliszewice PL 87 A4
Modliszewko PL 76 B2
Modogno I 171 B4
Modra SK 98 C1
Modran BIH 125 C3
Modriča BIH 125 C4
Möðrudalur IS 191 B10
Modrý Kamen SK 99 C3
Moëlan-sur-Mer F 100 B2
Moelfre GB 38 A2
Moelv N 48 B2
Moen N 194 A9
Moena I 121 A4
Moerbeke B 79 A3
Moers D 80 A2
Móes P 148 B2
Moffat GB 36 A3
Mogadouro P 149 A3
Mogata S 56 B2
Móggio Udinese I 122 A2
Mogielnica PL 87 A4
Mogilany PL 99 B3
Mogilno PL 76 B2
Mogliano I 136 B2
Mogliano Véneto I 122 B1
Mogor E 140 B2
Mógoro I 179 C2
Moguer E 161 B3
Mohács H 125 B4
Moheda S 62 A2
Mohedas E 149 B3
Mohedas de la Jara E 156 A2
Mohelnice CZ 97 B4
Mohill IRL 26 C3
Möhlin CH 106 B2
Moholm S 55 B5
Mohorn D 83 A5
Mohyliv-Podil's'kyy UA 13 D7
Moi N 52 B2
Moià E 147 C3
Móie I 136 B2
Moimenta da Beira P 148 B2
Mo i Rana N 195 D5
Moirans F 118 B2
Moirans-en-Montagne F 118 A2
Moisaküla EST 8 C4
Moisdon-la-Rivière F 101 B4
Moissac F 129 B4
Moita
Coimbra P 148 B1
Guarda P 149 B2
Santarém P 154 B2
Setúbal P 154 C1
Moita dos Ferreiros P 154 B1
Moixent E 159 C3
Mojacar E 164 B3
Mojados E 150 A3
Mojmírovce SK 112 A2
Mojtin SK 98 C2
Möklinta S 50 B3
Mokošica HR 139 C4
Mokronog SLO 123 B4
Mokro Polje HR 138 A2
Mokrzyska PL 99 A4
Møkster N 46 B2
Mol
B 79 A5
SRB 126 B2
Mola di Bari I 173 A3
Molai GR 184 C3
Molare I 133 A4
Molaretto I 119 B4
Molas F 145 A4
Molassano I 134 A1
Molbergen D 71 B4
Mold GB 38 A3
Molde N 198 C4
Møldrup DK 58 B2
Moledo do Minho P 148 A1
Molfetta I 171 B4
Molfsee D 64 B3
Moliden S 200 C4
Molières F 129 B4
Molina de Aragón E 152 B2
Molina de Segura E 165 A3
Molinar E 143 A3
Molinaseca E 141 B4
Molinella I 121 C4
Molinet F 104 C2
Molinicos E 158 C1
Molini di Tures I 108 C2
Molinos de Duero E 143 C4
Molins de Rei E 147 C3
Moliterno I 174 A1
Molkom S 55 A4
Möllbrücke A 109 C4
Mölle S 61 C2
Molledo E 142 A2
Möllenbeck D 74 A2
Mollerussa E 147 C1
Mollet de Perelada E 146 B3
Mollina E 163 A3
Mölln D 73 A3
Molló E 146 B3
Mollösund S 54 B2
Mölltorp S 55 B5
Mölnbo S 56 A3
Mölndal S 60 B2
Mölnlycke S 60 B2
Molompize F 116 B3
Moloy F 105 B3
Molsheim F 93 C3
Moltzow D 73 A5
Molve HR 124 A3
Molveno I 121 A3
Molvizar E 163 B4
Molzbichl A 109 C4
Mombaróccio I 136 B1
Mombeltrán E 150 B2
Mombris D 93 A5
Mombuey E 141 B4
Momchilgrad BG 183 B7
Mommark DK 64 B3
Momo I 119 B5
Monaghan IRL 27 B4
Monar Lodge GB 32 D2
Monasterace Marina I 175 C2
Monasterevin IRL 30 A1
Monasterio de Rodilla E 143 B3
Monastir I 179 C3
Monbahus F 129 B3
Monbazillac F 129 B3
Moncada E 159 B3
Moncalieri I 119 B4
Moncalvo I 119 B5
Monção P 140 B2
Moncarapacho P 160 B2
Moncel-sur-Seille F 92 C2
Monchegorsk RUS 3 C13
Mönchengladbach = Munchen-Gladbach D 80 A2
Mónchio della Corti I 134 A3
Monchique P 160 B1
Monclar-de-Quercy F 129 C4
Moncofa E 159 B3
Moncontour F 101 A3
Moncoutant F 114 B3
Monda E 162 B3
Mondariz E 140 B2
Mondavio I 136 B1
Mondéjar E 151 B4
Mondello I 176 A2
Mondim de Basto P 148 A2
Mondolfo I 136 B2
Mondoñedo E 141 A3
Mondorf-les-Bains L 92 B2
Mondoubleau F 102 B2
Mondovì I 133 A3
Mondragon F 131 A3
Mondragone I 170 B1
Mondsee A 109 B4
Monéglia I 134 A2
Monegrillo E 153 A3
Monein F 145 A3
Monemvasia GR 184 C4
Monési I 133 A3
Monesiglio I 133 A4
Monesterio E 161 A3
Monestier-de-Clermont F 118 C2
Monestiés F 130 A1
Monéteau F 104 B2
Moneygall IRL 28 B4
Moneymore GB 27 B4
Monfalcone I 122 B2
Monfero E 140 A2
Monflanquin F 129 B3
Monflorite E 145 B3
Monforte P 155 B3
Monforte da Beira
E 155 B3
P 155 B3
Monforte d'Alba I 133 A3
Monforte del Cid E 165 A4
Monforte de Lemos E 140 B3
Monforte de Moyuela E 152 A2
Monghidoro I 135 A4
Mongiana I 175 C2
Monguelfo I 108 C3
Monheim D 94 C2
Moniaive GB 36 A3
Monifieth GB 35 B5
Monikie GB 35 B5
Monistrol-d'Allier F 117 C3
Monistrol de Montserrat E 147 C2
Monistrol-sur-Loire F 117 B4
Mönkebude D 74 A2
Monkton GB 36 A2
Monmouth GB 39 C4
Monnaie F 102 B2
Monnerville F 90 C2
Monnickendam NL 70 B2
Monolithos GR 188 C2
Monópoli I 173 B3
Monor H 112 B3
Monóvar E 159 C3
Monpazier F 129 B3
Monreal
D 80 B3
E 144 B2
Monreal del Campo E 152 B2
Monreale I 176 A2
Monroy E 155 B4
Monroyo E 153 B3
Mons B 79 B3
Monsaraz P 155 C3
Monschau D 80 B2
Monségur F 128 B3
Monsélice I 121 B4
Mønshaug N 46 B3
Monster NL 70 B1
Mönsterås S 62 A4
Monsummano Terme I 135 B3
Montabaur D 81 B3
Montafia I 119 C5
Montagnac F 130 B2
Montagnana I 121 B4
Montaigu F 114 B2
Montaigu-de-Quercy F 129 B4
Montaiguët-en-Forez F 117 A3
Montaigut F 116 A2
Montaigut-sur-Save F 129 C4
Montainville F 90 C1
Montalbán E 153 B3
Montalbán de Córdoba E 163 A3
Montalbano Elicona I 177 A4
Montalbano Iónico I 174 A2
Montalbo E 158 B1
Montalcino I 135 B4
Montaldo di Cósola I 120 C2
Montalegre P 148 A2
Montalieu-Vercieu F 118 B2
Montalivet-les-Bains F 114 C2
Montallegro I 176 B2
Montalto delle Marche I 136 C2
Montalto di Castro I 168 A1
Montalto Pavese I 120 C2
Montalto Uffugo I 174 B2
Montalvão P 155 B3
Montamarta E 149 A4
Montana BG 17 D5
Montana-Vermala CH 119 A4
Montánchez E 156 A1
Montanejos E 153 B3
Montano Antilia I 172 B1
Montans F 129 C4
Montargil P 154 B2
Montargis F 103 B4
Montastruc-la-Conseillère F 129 C4
Montauban F 129 B4
Montauban-de-Bretagne F 101 A3
Montbard F 104 B3
Montbarrey F 105 B4
Montbazens F 130 A1
Montbazon F 102 B2
Montbéliard F 106 B1
Montbenoit F 105 C5
Montbeugny F 104 C2
Montblanc E 147 C2
Montbozon F 105 B5
Montbrison F 117 B4
Montbron F 115 C4
Montbrun-les-Bains F 131 A4
Montceau-les-Mines F 104 C3
Montcenis F 104 C3
Montchanin F 104 C3
Montcornet F 91 B4
Montcuq F 129 B4
Montdardier F 130 B2
Mont-de-Marsan F 128 C2
Montdidier F 90 B2
Monteagudo E 165 A3
Monteagudo de las Vicarias E 152 A1
Montealegre E 142 C2
Montealegre del Castillo E 159 C2
Montebello Iónico I 175 D1
Montebello Vicentino I 121 B4
Montebelluna I 121 B5
Montebourg F 88 A2
Montebruno I 134 A2
Monte-Carlo MC 133 B3
Montecarotto I 136 B2
Montecassiano I 136 B2
Montecastrilli I 168 A2
Montecatini Terme I 135 B3
Montécchio I 136 B1
Montécchio Emilia I 121 C3
Montécchio Maggiore I 121 B4
Montech F 129 C4
Montechiaro d'Asti I 119 B5
Monte Clara P 155 B3
Monte Clérigo P 160 B1
Montecórice I 170 C2
Montecorvino Rovella I 170 C2
Monte da Pedra P 155 B3
Monte de Goula P 155 B3
Montederramo E 141 B3
Montedoro I 176 B2
Monte do Trigo P 155 C3
Montefalco I 136 C1
Montefalcone di Val Fortore I 170 B3
Montefalcone nel Sánnio I 170 B2
Montefano I 136 B2
Montefiascone I 168 A2
Montefiorino I 134 A3
Montefortino I 136 C2
Montefranco I 168 A2
Montefrío E 163 A4
Montegiordano Marina I 174 A2
Montegiórgio I 136 B2
Monte Gordo P 160 B2
Montegranaro I 136 B2
Montehermoso E 149 B3
Montejicar E 163 A4
Montejo de la Sierra E 151 A4
Montejo de Tiermes E 151 A4
Monte Juntos P 155 C3
Montel-de-Gelat F 116 B2
Monteleone di Púglia I 171 B3
Monteleone di Spoleto I 169 A2
Monteleone d'Orvieto I 135 C5
Montelepre I 176 A2
Montelibretti I 168 A2
Montelier F 117 C5
Montélimar F 131 A3
Montella
E 146 B2
I 170 C3
Montellano E 162 A2
Montelupo Fiorentino I 135 B4
Montemaggiore Belsito I 176 B2
Montemagno I 119 C5
Montemayor E 163 A3
Montemayor de Pinilla E 150 A3
Montemésola I 173 B3
Montemilleto I 170 B2
Montemilone I 172 A1
Montemolin E 161 A3
Montemónaco I 136 C2
Montemor-o-Novo P 154 C2
Montemor-o-Velho P 148 B1
Montemurro I 174 A1
Montendre F 128 A2
Montenegro de Cameros E 143 B4
Montenero di Bisáccia I 170 B2
Monteneuf F 101 B3
Monteparano I 173 B3
Montepescali I 135 C4
Montepiano I 135 A4
Monte Porzio I 136 B2
Montepulciano I 135 B4
Monte Real P 154 B2
Montereale I 169 A3
Montereale Valcellina I 122 A1
Montereau-Faut-Yonne F 90 C2
Monte Redondo P 154 B2
Monterénzio I 135 A4
Monte Romano I 168 A1
Monteroni d'Arbia I 135 B4
Monteroni di Lecce I 173 B4
Monterosso al Mare I 134 A2
Monterosso Almo I 177 B3
Monterosso Grana I 133 A3
Monterotondo I 168 A2
Monterotondo Maríttimo I 135 B3
Monterrey E 141 C3
Monterroso E 140 B3
Monterrubio de la Serena E 156 B2
Monterubbiano I 136 B2
Montesa E 159 C3
Montesalgueiro E 140 A2
Monte San Giovanni Campano I 169 B3
Montesano sulla Marcellana I 174 A1
Monte San Savino I 135 B4
Monte Sant'Ángelo I 171 B3
Montesárchio I 170 B2
Montescaglioso I 171 C4
Montesclaros E 150 B3
Montesilvano I 169 A4
Montespértoli I 135 B4
Montesquieu-Volvestre F 146 A2
Montesquiou F 129 C3
Montestruc-sur-Gers F 129 C3
Montes Velhos P 160 B1
Montevarchi I 135 B4
Montéveglio I 135 A4
Monte Vilar P 154 B1
Montfaucon F 101 B4
Montfaucon-d'Argonne F 91 B5
Montfaucon-en-Velay F 117 B4
Montferrat
Isère F 118 B2
Var F 132 B2
Montfort-en-Chalosse F 128 C2

Montfort-l'Amaury F 90 C1
Montfort-le-Gesnois F 102 A2
Montfort-sur-Meu F 101 A4
Montfort-sur-Risle F 89 A4
Montgai E 147 C1
Montgaillard F 145 A4
Montgenèvre F 118 C3
Montgiscard F 146 A2
Montgomery GB 39 B3
Montguyon F 128 A2
Monthermé F 91 B4
Monthey CH 119 A3
Monthois F 91 B4
Monthureux-sur-Saône F 105 A4
Monti I 178 B3
Monticelli d'Ongina I 120 B2
Montichiari I 120 B3
Monticiano I 135 B4
Montiel E 158 C1
Montier-en-Der F 91 C4
Montieri I 135 B4
Montiglio I 119 B5
Montignac F 129 A4
Montigny-le-Roi F 105 B4
Montigny-lès-Metz F 92 B2
Montigny-sur-Aube F 105 B3
Montijo
E 155 C4
P 154 C2
Montilla E 163 A3
Montillana E 163 A4
Montilly F 104 C2
Montivilliers F 89 A4
Montjaux F 130 A1
Montjean-sur-Loire F 102 B1
Montlhéry F 90 C2
Montlieu-la-Garde F 128 A2
Mont-Louis F 146 B3
Montlouis-sur-Loire F 102 B2
Montluçon F 116 A2
Montluel F 117 B5
Montmarault F 116 A2
Montmartin-sur-Mer F 88 B2
Montmédy F 92 B1
Montmélian F 118 B3
Montmeyan F 132 B2
Montmeyran F 117 C4
Montmirail
Marne F 91 C3
Sarthe F 102 A2
Montmiral F 118 B2
Montmirat F 131 B3
Montmirey-le-Château F 105 B4
Montmoreau-St Cybard F 115 C4
Montmorency F 90 C2
Montmorillon F 115 B4
Montmort-Lucy F 91 C3
Montoir-de-Bretagne F 101 B3
Montoire-sur-le-Loir F 102 B2
Montoito P 155 C3
Montolieu F 146 A3
Montório al Vomano I 169 A3
Montoro E 157 B3
Montpellier F 131 B2
Montpezat-de-Quercy F 129 B4
Montpezat-sous-Bouzon F 117 C4
Montpon-Ménestérol F 128 A3
Montpont-en-Bresse F 105 C4
Montréal
Aude F 146 A3
Gers F 128 C3
Montredon-Labessonnié F 130 B1
Montréjeau F 145 A4
Montrésor F 103 B3
Montresta I 178 B2
Montret F 105 C4
Montreuil
Pas de Calais F 78 B1
Seine St Denis F 90 C2
Montreuil-aux-Lions F 90 B3
Montreuil-Bellay F 102 B1
Montreux CH 106 C1
Montrevault F 101 B4
Montrevel-en-Bresse F 118 A2
Montrichard F 103 B3
Montricoux F 129 B4
Mont-roig del Camp E 147 C1
Montrond-les-Bains F 117 B4
Montrose GB 35 B5
Montroy E 159 B3
Montsalvy F 116 C2
Montsauche-les-Settons F 104 B3
Montseny E 147 C3
Montsoreau F 102 B2
Mont-sous-Vaudrey F 105 C4
Monts-sur-Guesnes F 102 C2
Mont-St Aignan F 89 A5
Mont-St Vincent F 104 C3
Montsûrs F 102 A1
Montuenga E 150 A3
Montuïri E 167 B3
Monturque E 163 A3
Monza I 120 B2
Monzón E 145 C4
Monzón de Campos E 142 B2
Moorbad Lobenstein D 83 B3
Moordorf D 71 A4
Moorslede B 78 B3
Moos D 107 B3
Moosburg D 95 C3
Moosburg im Kärnten A 110 C1
Mór H 112 B2
Mora E 157 A4
Móra P 154 C2
Mora S 50 A1
Moraby S 50 B2
Móra d'Ebre E 153 A4
Mora de Rubielos E 153 B3
Moradillo de Roa E 151 A4
Morąg PL 69 B4
Mórahalom H 126 A1
Moraime E 140 A1
Morais P 149 A3
Mòra la Nova E 153 A4
Moral de Calatrava E 157 B4
Moraleda de Zafayona E 163 A4
Moraleja E 149 B3
Moraleja del Vino E 150 A2
Morales del Vino E 150 A2
Morales de Toro E 150 A2
Morales de Valverde E 141 C5
Moralina E 149 A3
Morano Cálabro I 174 B2
Mörarp S 61 C2
Morasverdes E 149 B3
Morata de Jalón E 152 A2
Morata de Jiloca E 152 A2
Morata de Tajuña E 151 B4
Moratalla E 164 A3
Moravče SLO 123 A3
Moravec CZ 97 B4
Moraviţa RO 126 B3
Morávka CZ 98 B2
Moravská Třebová CZ 97 B4
Moravské Budějovice CZ 97 B3
Moravské Lieskové SK 98 C1
Moravske Toplice SLO 111 C3
Moravský-Beroun CZ 98 B1
Moravský Krumlov CZ 97 B4
Moravský Svätý Ján SK 98 C1
Morawica PL 87 B4
Morawin PL 86 A2
Morbach D 92 B3
Morbegno I 120 A2
Morbier F 105 C5
Mörbisch am See A 111 B3
Mörbylånga S 63 B4
Morcenx F 128 B2
Morciano di Romagna I 136 B1
Morcone I 170 B2
Morcuera E 151 A4
Mordelles F 101 A4
Mordoğan TR 188 A1
Moréac F 100 B3
Morebattle GB 35 C5
Morecambe GB 36 B4
Moreda
Granada E 163 A4
Oviedo E 142 A1
Morée F 103 B3
Moreles de Rey E 141 B5
Morella E 153 B3
Moreruela de los Infanzones E 149 A4
Morés E 152 A2
Móres I 178 B2
Morestel F 118 B2
Moretonhampstead GB 43 B3
Moreton-in-Marsh GB 44 B2
Moret-sur-Loing F 90 C2
Moretta I 119 C4
Moreuil F 90 B2
Morez F 105 C5
Mörfelden D 93 B4
Morgat F 100 A1
Morges CH 105 C5
Morgex I 119 B4
Morgongåva S 51 C3
Morhange F 92 C2
Morhet B 92 B1
Mori I 121 B3
Morialmé B 79 B4
Morianes P 160 B2
Moriani Plage F 180 A2
Mórichida H 111 B4
Moriles E 163 A3
Morille E 150 B2
Moringen D 82 A1
Morjärv S 196 C5
Morkarla S 51 B4
Mørke DK 59 B3
Mørkøv DK 61 D1
Morkovice-Slížany CZ 98 B1
Morlaàs F 145 A3
Morlaix F 100 A2
Morley F 91 C5
Mörlunda S 62 A3
Mormanno I 174 B1
Mormant F 90 C2
Mornant F 117 B4
Mornay-Berry F 103 B4
Morón de Almazán E 152 A1
Morón de la Frontera E 162 A2
Morović SRB 125 B5
Morozzo I 133 A3
Morpeth GB 37 A5
Morphou CY 181 A1
Mörrum S 63 B2
Morsbach D 81 B3
Mörsch D 93 C4
Mörsil S 199 B10
Morsum D 64 B1
Mørsvikbotn N 194 C6
Mortagne-au-Perche F 89 B4
Mortagne-sur-Gironde F 114 C3
Mortagne-sur-Sèvre F 114 B3
Mortágua P 148 B1
Mortain F 88 B3
Mortara I 120 B1
Morteau F 105 B5
Mortegliano I 122 B2
Mortelle I 177 A4
Mortemart F 115 B4
Mortimer's Cross GB 39 B4
Mortrée F 89 B4
Mörtschach A 109 C3
Mortsel B 79 A4
Morud DK 59 C3
Morwenstow GB 42 B2
Moryń PL 74 B3
Morzeszczyn PL 69 B3
Morzewo PL 69 B4
Morzine F 118 A3
Mosbach D 93 B5
Mosbjerg DK 58 A3
Mosby N 53 B3
Mosca P 149 A3
Moscavide P 154 C1
Moščenica HR 124 B2
Mošćenice HR 123 B3
Moščenicka Draga HR 123 B3
Mosciano Sant'Ángelo I 136 C2
Mościsko PL 85 B4
Moscow = Moskva RUS 9 E10
Mosina PL 75 B5
Mosjøen N 195 E4
Moskog N 46 A3
Moskorzew PL 87 B3
Moskosel S 196 D2
Moskuvarra FIN 197 B9
Moskva = Moscow RUS 9 E10
Moslavina Podravska HR 125 B3
Moşniţa Nouă RO 126 B3
Moso in Passíria I 108 C2
Mosonmagyaróvár H 111 B4
Mošorin SRB 126 B2
Mošovce SK 98 C2
Mosqueruela E 153 B3
Moss N 54 A1
Mossfellsbær IS 190 C4
Mössingen D 93 C5
Møsstrand N 47 C5
Most CZ 83 B5
Mosta M 175 C3
Mostar BIH 139 B3
Mosterhamn N 52 A1
Mostki PL 75 B4
Most na Soči SLO 122 A2
Móstoles E 151 B4
Mostová SK 111 A4
Mostowo PL 68 A1
Mostuéjouls F 130 A2
Mosty PL 75 A3
Mostys'ka UA 13 D5
Mosvik N 199 B7
Mota del Cuervo E 158 B1
Mota del Marqués E 150 A2
Motala S 55 B6
Motherwell GB 35 C4
Möthlow D 74 B1
Motilla del Palancar E 158 B2
Motnik SLO 123 A3
Motovun HR 122 B2
Motril E 163 B4
Motta I 121 B4
Motta di Livenza I 122 B1
Motta Montecorvino I 170 B3
Motta Visconti I 120 B1
Mottisfont GB 44 B2
Móttola I 173 B3
Mou DK 58 B3
Mouchard F 105 C4
Moudon CH 106 C1
Moudros GR 183 D7
Mougins F 132 B2
Mouilleron en-Pareds F 114 B3
Mouliherne F 102 B2
Moulinet F 133 B3
Moulins F 104 C2
Moulins-Engilbert F 104 C2
Moulins-la-Marche F 89 B4
Moulismes F 115 B4
Moult F 89 A3
Mountain Ash GB 39 C3
Mountbellew IRL 28 A3
Mountfield GB 27 B3
Mountmellick IRL 30 A1
Mountrath IRL 30 A1
Mountsorrel GB 40 C2
Moura P 160 A2
Mourão P 155 C3
Mourenx F 145 A3
Mouriés F 131 B3
Mourmelon-le-Grand F 91 B4
Mouronho P 148 B1
Mourujärvi FIN 197 C11
Mouscron B 78 B3
Mousehole GB 42 B1
Moussac F 131 B3
Moussey F 92 C2
Mousteru F 100 A2
Moustey F 128 B2
Moustiers-Ste Marie F 132 B2
Mouthe F 105 C5
Mouthier-Haute-Pierre F 105 B5
Mouthoumet F 146 B3
Moutier CH 106 B2
Moûtiers F 118 B3
Moutiers-les-Mauxfaits F 114 B2
Mouy F 90 B2
Mouzaki GR 182 D3
Mouzon F 91 B5
Møvik N 46 B2
Moville IRL 27 A3
Moy
Highland GB 32 D2
Tyrone GB 27 B4
Moycullen IRL 28 A2
Moyenmoutier F 92 C2
Moyenvic F 92 C2
Moylough IRL 28 A3
Mózar E 141 C5
Mozhaysk RUS 9 E10
Mozirje SLO 123 A3
Mözs H 112 C2
Mozzanica I 120 B2
Mramorak SRB 127 C2
Mrčajevci SRB 127 D2
Mrkonjić Grad BIH 138 A3
Mrkopalj HR 123 B3
Mrocza PL 76 A2
Mroczeń PL 86 A1
Mroczno PL 69 B4
Mrzezyno PL 67 B4
Mšec CZ 84 B1
Mšeno CZ 84 B2
Mstów PL 86 B3
Mstsislaw BY 13 A9
Mszana Dolna PL 99 B4
Mszczonów PL 77 C5
Muć HR 138 B2
Múccia I 136 B2
Much D 80 B3
Mücheln D 83 A3
Much Marcle GB 39 C4
Muchów PL 85 A4
Much Wenlock GB 39 B4
Mucientes E 142 C2
Muckross IRL 29 B2
Mucur TR 23 B8
Muda P 160 B1
Mudanya TR 186 B3
Mudau D 93 B5
Müden D 72 B3
Mudersbach D 81 B3
Mudurnu TR 187 B6
Muel E 152 A2
Muelas del Pan E 149 A4
Muess D 73 A4
Muff IRL 27 A3
Mugardos E 140 A2
Muge P 154 B2
Mügeln
Sachsen D 83 A5
Sachsen-Anhalt D 83 A5
Múggia I 122 B2
Mugnano I 135 B5
Mugron F 128 C2
Mugueimes E 140 C3
Muhi H 113 B4
Mühlacker D 93 C4
Mühlbach am Hochkönig A 109 B4
Mühlberg
Brandenburg D 83 A5
Thüringen D 82 B2
Mühldorf
A 109 C4
D 95 C4
Muhleberg CH 106 C2
Mühleim D 107 A3
Muhlen-Eichsen D 65 C4
Mühlhausen
Bayern D 94 B2
Thüringen D 82 A2
Mühltroff D 83 B3
Muhos FIN 3 D10
Muhr A 109 B4
Muine Bheag IRL 30 B2
Muirkirk GB 36 A2
Muir of Ord GB 32 D2
Muirteira P 154 B1
Mukacheve UA 12 D5
Muker GB 37 B4
Mula E 165 A3
Muğla TR 188 B3
Mulben GB 32 D3
Mulegns CH 107 C4
Mules I 108 C2
Mülheim D 80 A2
Mulhouse F 106 B2
Muljava SLO 123 B3
Mullanys Cross IRL 26 B2
Müllheim D 106 B2
Mullhyttan S 55 A5
Mullinavat IRL 30 B1
Mullingar IRL 30 A1
Mullion GB 42 B1
Müllrose D 74 B3
Mullsjö S 60 B3
Mulseryd S 60 B3
Munaðarnes IS 190 A4
Munana E 150 B2
Muñás E 141 A4
Münchberg D 83 B3
Müncheberg D 74 B3
München = Munich D 108 A2
Munchen-Gladbach = Mönchengladbach D 80 A2
Münchhausen D 81 B4
Mundaka E 143 A4
Münden D 82 A1
Munderfing A 109 A4
Munderkingen D 107 A4
Mundesley GB 41 C5
Munera E 158 B1
Mungia E 143 A4
Munich = München D 108 A2
Muñico E 150 B2
Muniesa E 153 A3
Munka-Ljungby S 61 C2
Munkebo DK 59 C3
Munkedal S 54 B2
Munkflohögen S 199 B11
Munkfors S 49 C5
Munktorp S 56 A2
Münnerstadt D 82 B2
Muñopepe E 150 B3
Muñotello E 150 B3
Münsingen
CH 106 C2
D 94 C1
Munsö S 57 A3
Münster
CH 106 C3
Hessen D 93 B4
Munster D 72 B3
Münster D 71 C4
Munster F 106 A2
Muntibar E 143 A4
Münzkirchen A 96 C1
Muodoslompolo S 196 B6
Muonio FIN 196 B6
Muotathal CH 107 C3
Muradiye TR 186 D2
Murakeresztúr H 124 A2
Murán SK 99 C4
Murano I 122 B1
Muras E 140 A3
Murat F 116 B2
Muratlı TR 186 A2
Murato F 180 A2
Murat-sur-Vèbre F 130 B1
Murau A 109 B5
Muravera I 179 C3
Murazzano I 133 A4
Murça P 148 A2
Murchante E 144 B2
Murchin D 66 C2
Murcia E 165 B3
Murczyn PL 76 B2
Mur-de-Barrez F 116 C2
Mur-de-Bretagne F 100 A2
Mur-de-Sologne F 103 B3
Mureck A 110 C2
Mürefte TR 186 B2
Muret F 146 A2
Murg CH 107 B4
Murguia E 143 B4
Muri CH 106 B3
Murias de Paredes E 141 B4
Muriedas E 143 A3
Muriel Viejo E 143 C4
Murillo de Rio Leza E 143 B4
Murillo el Fruto E 144 B2
Murjek S 196 C3
Murlaggan GB 34 B2
Murmansk RUS 3 B13
Murmashi RUS 3 B13
Murnau D 108 B2
Muro
E 167 B3
F 180 A1
Muro de Alcoy E 159 C3
Murol F 116 B2
Muro Lucano I 172 B1
Muron F 114 B3
Muros E 140 B1
Muros de Nalón E 141 A4
Murowana Goślina PL 76 B2
Mürren CH 106 C2
Murrhardt D 94 C1
Murska Sobota SLO 111 C3
Mursko Središce HR 111 C3
Murtas E 164 C1
Murten CH 106 C2
Murter HR 137 B4
Murtiçi TR 189 C6
Murtosa P 148 B1
Murtovaara FIN 197 D12
Murvica HR 137 A4
Murviel-lès-Béziers F 130 B2
Mürzsteg A 110 B2
Murzynowo PL 75 B4
Mürzzuschlag A 110 B2
Musculdy F 144 A3
Muskö S 57 A4
Mušov CZ 97 C4
Musselburgh GB 35 C4
Musselkanaal NL 71 B4
Mussidan F 129 A3
Mussomeli I 176 B2
Musson B 92 B1
Mussy-sur-Seine F 104 B3
Mustafakemalpaşa TR 186 B3
Muszaki PL 77 A5
Muszyna PL 99 B4
Mut TR 23 C7
Muta SLO 110 C2
Muthill GB 35 B4
Mutné SK 99 B3
Mutriku E 143 A4
Muttalip TR 187 C5
Mutterbergalm A 108 B2
Muurola FIN 197 C8
Muxía E 140 A1
Muxilka-Ugarte E 143 A4
Muzillac F 101 B3
Mužla SK 112 B2
Muzzano del Turgnano I 122 B2
Mybster GB 32 C3
Myckelgensjö S 200 C3
Myennes F 104 B1
Myjava SK 98 C1
Myking N 46 B2
Mykland N 53 B4
Myra N 53 B5
Myrdal N 46 B4
Myre
Nordland N 194 A6
Nordland N 194 B6
Myresjö S 62 A2
Mýri IS 191 B8
Myrtou CY 181 A2
Mysen N 54 A2
Mysłakowice PL 85 B3
Myślenice PL 99 B3
Myślibórz PL 75 B3
Mysłowice PL 86 B3
Myszków PL 86 B3
Mytishchi RUS 9 E10
Mýtna SK 99 C3
Mýtne Ludany SK 112 A2
Mýto CZ 96 B1

N

Nå N 46 B3
Naaldwijk NL 79 A4
Naantali FIN 8 B2
Naas IRL 30 A2
Nabais P 148 B2
Nabbelund S 62 A5
Nabburg D 95 B4
Načeradec CZ 96 B2
Náchod CZ 85 B4
Nacław PL 68 A1
Nadarzyce PL 75 A5
Nadarzyn PL 77 B5
Nádasd H 111 C3
Nădlac RO 126 A2
Nádudvar H 113 B5
Nadvirna UA 13 D6
Näfels CH 107 B4
Nafpaktos GR 184 A2
Nafplio GR 184 B3
Nagel D 95 B3
Nagele NL 70 B2
Naggen S 200 D2
Nagłowice PL 87 B4
Nagold D 93 C4
Nagore E 144 B2
Nagyatád H 124 A3
Nagybajom H 124 A3
Nagybaracska H 125 A4
Nagybátony H 113 B3
Nagyberény H 112 C2
Nagybörzsöny H 112 B2
Nagycenk H 111 B3
Nagycserkesz H 113 B5
Nagydorog H 112 C2
Nagyfüged H 113 B4
Nagyhersány H 125 B4
Nagyigmánd H 112 B2
Nagyiván H 113 B4
Nagykanizsa H 111 C3
Nagykáta H 113 B3
Nagykonyi H 112 C2
Nagykörös H 113 B3
Nagykörü H 113 B4
Nagylóc H 112 A3
Nagymágocs H 113 C4
Nagymányok H 125 A4
Nagymaros H 112 B2
Nagyoroszi H 112 A3
Nagyrábé H 113 B5
Nagyréde H 113 B3
Nagyszékely H 112 C2
Nagyszénás H 113 C4
Nagyszokoly H 112 C2
Nagytöke H 113 C4
Nagyvázsony H 111 C4
Nagyvenyim H 112 C2
Naharros E 152 B1
Nahe D 64 C3
Naila D 83 B3
Nailloux F 146 A2
Nailsworth GB 43 A4
Naintré F 115 B4
Nairn GB 32 D3
Najac F 129 B4
Nájera E 143 B4
Nak H 112 C2
Nakksjø N 53 A5
Nakło nad Notecią PL 76 A2
Nakskov DK 65 B4
Nalda E 143 B4
Nälden S 199 B11
Nálepkovo SK 99 C4
Nalliers F 114 B2
Nallıhan TR 187 B6
Nalzen F 146 B2
Nalžouské Hory CZ 96 B1
Namdalseid N 199 A8
Náměšť nad Oslavou CZ 97 B4
Námestovo SK 99 B3
Namnå N 49 B4
Namsos N 199 A8
Namsskogan N 199 A10
Namur B 79 B4
Namysłów PL 86 A1
Nançay F 103 B4
Nanclares de la Oca E 143 B4
Nancy F 92 C2
Nangis F 90 C3
Nannestad N 48 B3
Nant F 130 A2
Nanterre F 90 C2
Nantes F 101 B4
Nanteuil-le-Haudouin F 90 B2
Nantiat F 115 B5
Nantua F 118 A2
Nantwich GB 38 A4
Naoussa
Cyclades GR 185 B6
Imathia GR 182 C4
Napajedla CZ 98 B1
Napiwoda PL 77 A5
Naples = Nápoli I 170 C2
Nápoli = Naples I 170 C2
Nar S 57 C4
Nara N 46 A1
Naraval E 141 A4
Narberth GB 39 C2
Nærbø N 52 B1
Narbonne F 130 B1
Narbonne-Plage F 130 B2
Narbuvollen N 199 C8
Narcao I 179 C2
Nardò I 173 B4
Narkaus FIN 197 C9
Narken S 196 C5
Narmo N 48 B3
Narni I 168 A2
Naro I 176 B2
Naro Fominsk RUS 9 E10
Narón E 140 A2
Narros del Castillo E 150 B2
Narta HR 124 B2
Naruszewo PL 77 B5
Narva EST 8 C6
Narvik N 194 B8
Narzole I 133 A3
Näs FIN 51 B7
Nås S 50 B1
Näs S 57 C4
Näsåker S 200 C2
Năsăud RO 17 B6
Nasavrky CZ 97 B3
Nasbinals F 116 C3
Næsbjerg DK 59 C1
Näshull S 62 A3
Našice HR 125 B4
Nasielsk PL 77 B5
Naso I 177 A3
Nassau D 81 B3
Nassenfels D 95 C3
Nassenheide D 74 B2
Nassereith A 108 B1
Nässjö S 62 A2
Nastätten D 81 B3
Næstved DK 65 A4
Näsum S 63 B2
Näsviken S 199 B12
Natalinci SRB 127 C2
Naters CH 119 A5
Nater-Stetten D 108 A2
Nattavaara S 196 C3
Natters A 108 B2
Nattheim D 94 C2
Nättraby S 63 B3
Naturno I 108 C1
Naucelle F 130 A1
Nauders A 108 C1
Nauen D 74 B1
Naul IRL 30 A2
Naumburg D 83 A3
Naundorf D 83 B5
Naunhof D 83 A4
Naustdal N 46 A2
Nautijaur S 196 C2
Nautsi RUS 193 D13
Nava E 142 A1
Navacerrada E 151 B3
Navaconcejo E 149 B4
Nava de Arévalo E 150 B3
Nava de la Asunción E 150 A3
Nava del Rey E 150 A2
Navafriá E 151 A4
Navahermosa E 157 A3
Navahrudak BY 13 B6
Naval E 145 B4
Navalacruz E 150 B3
Navalcán E 150 B2
Navalcarnero E 151 B3
Navaleno E 143 C3
Navalmanzano E 151 A3
Navalmoral E 150 B3
Navalmoral de la Mata E 150 C2
Naválón E 159 C3
Navalonguilla E 150 B2
Navalperal de Pinares E 150 B3
Navalpino E 157 A3
Navaltalgordo E 150 B3
Navaltoril E 156 A3
Navaluenga E 150 B3
Navalvillar de Pela E 156 A2
Navan IRL 30 A2
Navaperal de Tormes E 150 B2
Navapolatsk BY 13 A8
Navarclés E 147 C2
Navarredonda de Gredos E 150 B2
Navarrenx F 144 A3
Navarrés E 159 B3
Navarrete E 143 B4
Navarrevisca E 150 B3
Navás E 147 C2
Navascués E 144 B2
Navas del Madroño E 155 B
Navas del Rey E 151 B

Navas del Sepillar
E 163 A3
Navas de Oro E . . .150 A3
Navas de San Juan
E 157 B4
Navasfrias E 149 B3
Nave I. 120 B3
Nave de Haver F . .149 B3
Nävekvarn S 56 B2
Navelli I 169 A3
Navenby GB 40 B3
Näverkärret S 56 A1
Naverstad S 54 B2
Navès E 147 C2
Navezuelas E. 156 A2
Navia E. 141 A4
Navia de Suarna
E 141 B4
Navilly F 105 C4
Năvodari RO 17 C8
Naxos GR 185 B6
Nay F 145 A3
Nazaré P. 154 B1
Nazarje SLO. 123 A3
Nazilli TR 188 B3
Nazza D 82 A2
Nea Anchialos
GR. 182 D4
Nea Epidavros
GR. 184 B4
Nea Flippias GR . .182 D2
Nea Kalikratia GR 183 C5
Nea Makri GR 185 A4
Nea Moudania GR 183 C5
Neap GB 33 A5
Nea Peramos GR. .183 C6
Neapoli
Kozani GR 182 C3
Kriti GR 185 D6
Lakonia GR 184 C4
Nea Stira GR 185 A5
Neath GB 39 C3
Nea Visa GR 186 A1
Nea Zichni GR 183 B5
Nebljusi HR. 124 C1
Neblo SLO. 122 A2
Nebolchy RUS. 9 C8
Nebra D 82 A3
Nebreda E 143 C3
Nechanice CZ. 84 B3
Neckargemünd D .93 B4
Neckarsulm D 94 B1
Neda E 140 A2
Neded SK. 112 A1
Nedelišće HR. . . .124 A1
Nederweert NL. . . .80 A1
Nedreberg N. 48 B3
Nedre Gärdsjö S . .50 B2
Nedre Soppero S .196 A4
Nedstrand N 52 A1
Nedvědice CZ. 97 B4
Nedza PL. 86 B2
Neede NL 71 B3
Needham Market
GB 45 A5
Needingworth GB . .44 A3
Neermoor D 71 A4
Neeroeteren B. 80 A1
Neerpelt B 79 A5
Neesen D 72 B1
Neetze D 73 A3
Nefyn GB 38 B2
Negotin SRB 16 C5
Negotino MK 182 B4
Negrar I 121 B3
Negredo E 151 A5
Negreira E 140 B2
Nègrepelisse F . . .129 B4
Negru Vodă RO. . . .17 D8
Negueira de Muñiz
E 141 A4
Neheim D. 81 A4
Neila E 143 B4
Néive I 119 C5
Nejdek CZ. 83 B4
Nekla PL. 76 B2
Neksø DK. 67 A4
Nelas P. 148 B2
Nelaug N 53 B4
Nelidovo RUS 9 D8
Nelim FIN 193 D12
Nellingen D 94 C1
Nelson GB 40 B1
Neman RUS 12 A5
Nemea GR 184 B3
Nemesgörzsöny
H 111 B4
Nemeskér H. 111 B3
Nemesnádudvar
H 125 A5
Nemesszalók H . . .111 B4
Németkér H 112 C2
Nemours F 103 A4
Nemška Loka
SLO. 123 B4
Nemšová SK 98 C2
Nenagh IRL 28 B3
Nenince SK 112 A3
Nenita GR 185 A7
Nenzing A 107 B4
Neochori GR 182 D3
Neo Chori GR 184 A2
Neon Petritsi GR . .183 B5
Nepi I 168 A2
Nepomuk CZ 96 B1
Nérac F 129 B3
Neratovice CZ 84 B2
Nerchau D 83 A4
Néré F 115 C3
Neresheim D 94 C2
Nereto I 136 C2
Nerezine HR 123 C3
Nerežišća HR. 138 B2
Neringa LT 12 A4
Néris-les Bains F . .116 A2
Nerito I 169 A3
Nerja E 163 B4
Néronde F 117 B4
Nérondes F 103 C4
Nerpio E. 164 A2

Nersingen D 94 C2
Nerva E 161 B3
Nervesa della Battáglia
I 121 B5
Nervi I. 134 A2
Nes
Buskerud N 48 B1
Hedmark N 48 B2
NL. 70 A2
Sogn og Fjordane
N. 46 A3
Sør-Trøndelag N .198 B6
Nesbyen N 47 B6
Neset N 199 D7
Nesflaten N 52 A2
Nesjahverfi IS 191 C10
Neskaupstaður
IS 191 B12
Nesland N 53 A3
Neslandsvatn N. . . .53 B5
Nesle F 90 B2
Nesna N 195 D4
Nesoddtangen N. . .48 C2
Nesovice CZ. 98 B1
Nesselwang D 108 B1
Nesslau CH 107 B4
Nessmersiel D. . . .71 A4
Nesso I 120 B2
Nesterov UA 13 C5
Nestorio GR. 182 C3
Nesttun N. 46 B2
Nesvady SK. 112 B2
Nesvatnstemmen
N 53 B4
Nether Stowey GB. .43 A3
Netland N 52 B2
Netolice CZ 96 B2
Netphen D 81 B4
Netstal CH 107 B4
Nettancourt F 91 C4
Nettetal D 80 A2
Nettlingen D 72 B3
Nettuno I. 168 B2
Neualbenreuth D . .95 B4
Neubeckum D 81 A4
Neubrandenburg D 74 A2
Neubruchhausen D 72 B1
Neubukow D 65 B4
Neuburg D 94 C3
Neuchâtel CH 106 C1
Neu Darchau D . . .73 A3
Neudau A 111 B3
Neudietendorf D . . .82 B2
Neudorf D 93 B4
Neuenbürg D 93 C4
Neuenburg D 71 A4
Neuendorf D 66 B2
Neuenhagen D 74 B2
Neuenhaus D. 71 B3
Neuenkirchen
Niedersachsen D .71 B5
Niedersachsen D . 72 A2
Nordrhein-Westfalen
D 71 B4
Nordrhein-Westfalen
D 81 B3
Neuenrade D 81 A3
Neuenwalde D 64 C1
Neuerburg D. 92 A2
Neufahrn
Bayern D 95 C3
Bayern D 95 C4
Neuf-Brisach F . . .106 A2
Neufchâteau
B. 92 B1
F 92 C1
Neufchâtel-en-Bray
F. 90 B1
Neufchâtel-sur-Aisne
F. 91 B4
Neuflize F 91 B4
Neugersdorf D 84 B2
Neuhardenberg D . .74 B3
Neuharlingersiel D .71 A4
Neuhaus
Bayern D 95 B3
Bayern D 96 C1
Niedersachsen D . 64 C2
Niedersachsen D . 73 A3
Niedersachsen D . .81 A5
Neuhaus a Rennweg
D 82 B3
Neuhausen
CH 107 B3
D 83 B5
Neuhausen ob Eck
D 107 B3
Neuhof
Bayern D 94 B2
Hessen D 82 B1
Neuhofen an der Krems
A 110 A1
Neuillé-Pont-Pierre
F. 102 B2
Neuilly-en-Thelle F .90 B2
Neuilly-le-Réal F . .104 C2
Neuilly-l'Évêque
F. 105 B4
Neuilly-St Front F . .90 B3
Neu-Isenburg D . . .93 A4
Neukalen D 66 C1
Neu Kaliss D 73 A4
Neukirch D 84 A2
Neukirchen
A 109 A4
Hessen D 81 B5
Schleswig-Holstein
D 64 B1
Neukirchen am
Grossvenediger
A. 109 B3
Neukirchen bei Heiligen
Blut D 95 B4
Neukloster D 65 C4
Neulengbach A . . .110 A2
Neulise F 117 B4
Neu Lübbenau D . .74 B2
Neum BIH. 139 C3
Neumagen D 92 B2
Neumarkt D 95 B3

Neumarkt am Wallersee
A. 109 B4
Neumarkt im
Hausruckkreis A 109 A4
Neumarkt im Mühlkreis
A. 96 C2
Neumarkt im
Steiermark A 110 B1
Neumarkt Sankt Veit
D 95 C4
Neumünster D 64 B2
Neunburg vorm Wald
D 95 B4
Neung-sur-Beuvron
F. 103 B3
Neunkirch
Luzern CH 106 B3
Schaffhausen CH 107 B3
Neunkirchen
A 111 B3
Nordrhein-Westfalen
D 80 B3
Saarland D 92 B3
Neunkirchen am Brand
D 94 B3
Neuötting D 95 C4
Neupetershain D . . .84 A2
Neuravensburg D .107 B4
Neureut D 93 B4
Neuruppin D 74 B1
Neusäss D 94 C2
Neusiedl A 111 B3
Neuss D 80 A2
Neussargues-Moissac
F. 116 B2
Neustadt
Bayern D 94 B2
Bayern D 95 B4
Bayern D 95 C3
Brandenburg D . .73 B5
Hessen D 81 B5
Niedersachsen D . 72 B2
Rheinland-Pfalz D .93 B4
Sachsen D 84 A2
Schleswig-Holstein
D 65 B3
Thüringen D. 82 B3
Thüringen D. 83 B3
Neustadt-Glewe D .73 A4
Neustift im Stubaital
A. 108 B2
Neustrelitz D 74 A2
Neutal A 111 B3
Neutrebbin D 74 B3
Neu-Ulm D 94 C2
Neuves-Maisons F .92 C2
Neuvic
Corrèze F 116 B2
Dordogne F. 129 A3
Neuville-aux-Bois
F. 103 A4
Neuville-de-Poitou
F. 115 B4
Neuville-les-Dames
F. 117 A5
Neuville-sur-Saône
F. 117 B4
Neuvy-le-Roi F . . .102 B2
Neuvy-Santour F . .104 A2
Neuvy-St Sépulchre
F. 103 C3
Neuvy-sur-Barangeon
F. 103 B4
Niederaula D 82 B1
Niederbipp CH. . . .106 B2
Niederbronn-les-Bains
F. 93 C3
Niederfischbach D .81 B3
Niedergörsdorf D . .74 C1
Niederkrüchten D . .80 A2
Niederndorf A 108 B3
Nieder-Olm D. 93 B4
Niederösterreich . . . . .
Niedersachswerfen
D 82 A2
Niederstetten D . . .94 B1
Niederurnen CH . .107 B4
Niederwölz A 110 B1
Niedoradz PL. 85 A3
Niedzica PL 99 B4
Niegosławice PL. . .85 A3
Niehl D 81 A5
Niemcza PL. 85 B4
Niemegk D 74 B1
Niemisel S 196 C5
Niemodlin PL. 85 B5

New Milton GB. . . .44 C2
New Pitsligo GB . . .33 D4
Newport
Isle of Wight GB. . 44 C2
Newport GB. 39 C4
Pembrokeshire GB 39 B2
Telford & Wrekin
GB. 38 B4
Mayo IRL 28 A2
Tipperary IRL 29 B3
Newport-on-Tay
GB 35 B5
Newport Pagnell
GB 44 A3
Newquay GB 42 B1
New Quay GB 39 B2
New Radnor GB. . . .39 B3
New Romney GB. . .45 C4
New Ross IRL 30 B2
New Scone GB 35 B4
Newton Abbot GB .43 B3
Newton Arlosh GB .36 B3
Newton Aycliffe GB 37 B5
Newton Ferrers GB 42 B2
Newtonhill GB. 33 D4
Newtonmore GB . . .32 D2
Newton Stewart GB 36 B2
Newtown
Herefordshire
GB. 39 B4
Powys GB 39 B3
Newtownabbey GB 27 B5
Newtownards GB . .27 B5
Newtownbutler GB .27 B3
Newtown Cunningham
IRL 27 B3
Newtownhamilton
GB 27 B4
Newtownmountkennedy
IRL 30 A2
Newtown St Boswells
GB 35 C5
Newtown Sands
IRL 29 B2
Newtownstewart
GB 27 B3
Nexon F 115 C5
Neyland GB 39 C2
Nibbiano I. 120 C2
Nibe DK. 58 B2
Nicastro I 175 C2
Niccone I 135 B5
Nice F. 133 B3
Nickelsdorf A. 111 B4
Nicolosi I 177 B4
Nicosia
CY. 181 A2
I. 177 B3
Nicótera I 175 C1
Nidda D 81 B5
Nidge TR. 23 C8
Nidzica PL 77 A5
Niebla E 161 B3
Nieborów PL 77 B5
Niebüll D 64 B1
Niechanowo PL. . . .76 B2
Niechorze PL. 67 B4
Niedalino PL. 67 B5
Niederaula D 82 B1
Niederbipp CH. . . .106 B2
Niederbronn-les-Bains
F. 93 C3
Niederfischbach D .81 B3
Niedergörsdorf D . .74 C1
Niederkrüchten D . .80 A2
Niederndorf A 108 B3
Nieder-Olm D. 93 B4
Niedersachswerfen
D 82 A2
Niederstetten D . . .94 B1
Niederurnen CH . .107 B4
Niederwölz A 110 B1
Niedoradz PL. 85 A3
Niedzica PL 99 B4
Niegosławice PL. . .85 A3
Niehl D 81 A5
Niemcza PL. 85 B4
Niemegk D 74 B1
Niemisel S 196 C5
Niemodlin PL. 85 B5

Nilivaara S 196 B4
Nîmes F 131 B3
Nimis I 122 A2
Nimtofte DK 58 B3
Nin HR 137 A4
Nindorf D 64 B2
Ninemilehouse IRL .30 B1
Ninove B 79 B4
Niort F 114 B3
Niš SRB 16 D4
Nisa P. 155 B3
Niscemi I 177 B3
Niskala FIN 197 D10
Nissafors S 60 B3
Nissan-lez-Ensérune
F. 130 B2
Nissedal N 53 A4
Nissumby DK 58 B1
Nisterud N 53 A5
Niton GB 44 C2
Nitra SK 98 C2
Nitrianske-Pravno
SK. 98 C2
Nitrianske Rudno
SK. 98 C2
Nitry F 104 B2
Nittedal N. 48 B2
Nittenau D 95 B4
Nittendorf D 95 B3
Nivala FIN 3 E9
Nivelles B 79 B4
Nivnice CZ. 98 C1
Nižná SK 99 B3
Nižná Boca SK. . . .99 C3
Nižne Repaše SK. .99 B4
Nizza Monferrato I 119 C5
Njarðvík IS. 190 D3
Njegǔševo SRB. . .126 B1
Njivice HR 123 B3
Njurundabommen
S 200 D3
Njutånger S 200 E3
Noailles F 90 B2
Noain E. 144 B2
Noale I. 121 B5
Noalejo E. 163 A4
Nobber IRL 27 C4
Noblejas E 151 C4
Noceda E 141 B4
Nocera Inferiore I .170 C2
Nocera Terinese I .175 C2
Nocera Umbra I . . .136 B1
Noceto I. 120 C3
Noci I 173 B3
Nociglia I 173 B4
Nodeland N 53 B3
Nödinge S 60 B2
Nods F 105 B5
Noé F 146 A2
Noépoli I 174 A2
Noeux-les-Mines F .78 B2
Noez E 157 A3
Nogales E 155 C4
Nogara I. 121 B4
Nogarejas E 141 B4
Nogaro F 128 C2
Nogent F 105 A4
Nogent l'Artaud F .90 C3
Nogent-le-Roi F . . .90 C2
Nogent-le-Rotrou F 89 B4
Nogent-sur-Seine
F. 91 C3
Nogent-sur-Vernisson
F. 103 B4
Nogersund S 63 B2
Noguera E 152 B2
Nogueirones E . . .163 A3
Nohfelden D 92 B3
Nohn D 80 B2
Noia E 140 B2
Noicáttaro I 173 A2
Noirétable F 117 B3
Noirmoutier-en-l'Île
F. 114 A1
Noja E 143 A3
Nojewo PL. 75 B5
Nokia FIN. 8 B3
Nol S 60 B2
Nola I 170 C2
Nolay F. 104 C3
Noli I 133 A4
Nolnyra S 51 B4
Nombela E 150 B3
Nomeny F 92 C2
Nomexy F 92 C2
Nonancourt F 89 B5
Nonant-le-Pin F . . .89 B4
Nonántola I 121 C4
Nonaspe E 153 A4
None I. 119 C4
Nontron F 115 C4
Nonza F 180 A2
Noordhorn NL 71 A3
Noordwijk NL. 70 B1
Nieuw-Amsterdam
NL 71 B3
Noordwijkerhout
NL 70 B1
Noordwolde NL. . . .70 B2
Noppikoski S. 50 A1
Nora S 55 A6
Nørager DK 58 B2
Norberg S 50 B2
Norboda S 51 B5
Nórcia I 136 C2
Nordagutu N 53 A5
Nordanås S 200 B4
Nordausques F 78 B2
Nordborg DK 64 B2
Nordby
Aarhus Amt. DK . .59 C3
Ribe Amt. DK 59 C1
Norddeich D 71 A4
Norddorf D 64 B1
Norden D 71 A4
Nordenham D 72 A1
Norderhov N. 48 B2
Norderney D 71 A4
Norderstapel D 64 B2
Norderstedt D 64 C3
Nordfjord N 193 B14
Nordfjordeid N 198 D3
Nordfold N 194 C6

Nordhalben D 82 B3
Nordhausen D 82 A2
Nordheim vor der Rhön
D 82 B2
Nordholz D 64 C1
Nordhorn D 71 B4
Nordingrå S 200 D4
Nordkjosbotn N. . .192 C3
Nordli N 199 A10
Nördlingen D. 94 C2
Nordmaling S 200 C5
Nordmark S 49 C6
Nordmela N 194 A6
Nordråker S 200 B1
Nordre Osen N 48 A3
Nordsinni N 48 B1
Nørdstedalsseter
N 198 D4
Nordstemmen D . . .72 B2
Nordvågen N 193 B10
Nordwalde D 71 B4
Noreña E 142 A1
Noresund N 48 B1
Norg NL 71 A3
Norheimsund N 46 B3
Norie S 63 B2
Norma I 169 B2
Nornäs S 49 A5
Norrahammar S . . .62 A2
Norråker S 200 B1
Norrala S 51 A3
Norra Vi S 62 A3
Nørre Aby DK. 59 C2
Nørre Alslev DK. . . .65 B4
Nørre Lyndelse DK .59 C3
Nørre Nebel DK 59 C1
Norrent-Fontes F . . .78 B2
Nørre Snede DK . . .59 C2
Nørresundby DK. . .58 A2
Nørre Vorupør DK. .58 B1
Norrfjärden S 196 D4
Norrhed S 196 C3
Norrhult Klavreström
S 62 A3
Norrköping S 56 B2
Norrkédika S 51 B5
Norrsundet S 51 B4
Norrtälje S 57 A4
Nors DK 58 A1
Norsbron S 55 A4
Norsholm S 56 B1
Norsjö S 200 B5
Nörten-Hardenberg
D 82 A1
Northallerton GB. . .37 B5
Northam GB 42 A2
Northampton GB . . .44 A3
North Berwick GB. .35 B5
North Charlton GB .37 A5
Northeim D 82 A2
Northfleet GB 45 B4
North Frodingham
GB 40 B3
North Kessock GB .32 D2
Northleach GB. 44 B2
North Molton GB. . .42 A3
North Petherton
GB 43 A4
North Tawton GB. . .42 B3
North Thoresby GB 41 B3
North Walsham GB 41 C5
Northwich GB 38 A4
Norton GB 40 A3
Nortorf D 64 B2
Nort-sur-Erdre F . .101 B4
Nörvenich D 80 B2
Norwich GB 41 C5
Norwick GB 33 A6
Nøsen N 47 B5
Nossa Senhora do
Cabo P. 154 C1
Nossebro S 55 B3
Nössemark S 54 A2
Nossen D 83 A5
Notaresco I 169 A3
Noto I. 177 C4
Notodden N 53 A5
Nottingham GB 40 C2
Nottuln D 71 C4
Nouan-le-Fuzelier
F. 103 B4
Nouans-les-Fontaines
F. 103 B3
Nougaroulet F 129 C3
Nouvion F 78 B1
Nouzonville F 91 B4
Nova I 111 C3
Nová Baňa SK 98 C2
Nová Bystrica SK. .99 B3
Nová Bystřice CZ . .97 B3
Nova Crnja SRB . .126 B2
Nováféltria I 135 B5
Nova Gorica SLO .122 B2
Nova Gradiška
HR. 124 B3
Novák SK 98 C2
Novalaise F 118 B2
Novales E 145 B3
Nova Levante I . . .108 C2
Novalja HR. 137 A3
Nová Paka CZ 84 B3
Nova Pazova SRB 127 C2
Nová Pec CZ 96 C1
Novara I 120 B1
Novara di Sicília I .177 A4
Nova Siri I 174 A2
Novate Mezzola I . .120 A2
Nova Topola BIH . .124 B3
Novaya Ladoga RUS 9 B8
Nova Zagora BG . . .17 D6
Nové Hrady CZ 96 C2
Nové Město D 71 B4
Nové Mesto nad Váhom
SK. 98 C1
Nové Město nad Metují
CZ. 85 B4
Nové Město na Moravě
CZ. 97 B4

Nové Město pod
Smrkem CZ. 84 B3
Nové Mitrovice CZ .96 B1
Noventa di Piave I 122 B1
Noventa Vicentina
I 121 B4
Novés F 151 B3
Noves F 131 B3
Nové Sady SK 98 C1
Novés de Segre E 147 B2
Nové Strašeci CZ . .84 B1
Nové Zámky SK. . .112 B2
Novgorod RUS 9 C7
Novi Bečej SRB . .126 B2
Novi di Módena I . .121 C3
Novigrad
Istarska HR. 122 B2
Zadarsko-Kninska
HR. 137 A4
Novigrad Podravski
HR. 124 A2
Novi Kneževac
SRB. 126 A2
Novi Lígure I 120 C1
Noville B 92 A1
Novi Marof HR. . . .124 A2
Novion-Porcien F . .91 B4
Novi Pazar
BG 17 D7
SRB 16 D4
Novi Sad SRB 126 B1
Novi Slankamen
SRB. 126 B2
Novi Travnik BIH . .139 A3
Novi Vinodolski
HR. 123 B3
Novohrad-Volynskyy
UA 13 C7
Novo Mesto SLO. .123 B4
Novo Miloševo
SRB. 126 B2
Novorzhev RUS. . . .9 D6
Novo Selo BIH. . . .125 B3
Novoselytsya UA. . .13 A7
Novosokolniki RUS .9 D6
Novoveská Huta
SK. 99 C4
Novovolynsk UA. . .13 C6
Novska HR. 124 B2
Nový Bor CZ 84 B2
Nový Bydžov CZ . . .84 B3
Nový-Chevrières F .91 B4
Novy Dwór Mazowiecki
PL. 77 B5
Nový-Hrozenkov
CZ. 98 B2
Nový Jičín CZ 98 B2
Novy Knin CZ 96 B2
Nowa Cerekwia PL .86 B1
Nowa Dęba PL. 87 B5
Nowa Karczma PL. .68 A3
Nowa Kościoł PL. . .85 A3
Nowa Ruda PL. 85 B4
Nowa Słupia PL . . .87 B5
Nowa Sól PL 85 A3
Nowa Wieś PL 69 B4
Nowa-Wieś Wielka
PL. 76 B3
Nowe PL. 69 B3
Nowe Brzesko PL . .87 B4
Nowe Grudze PL. . .77 B4
Nowe Kiejkuty PL . .77 A6
Nowe Miasteczko
PL. 85 A3
Nowe Miasto
Mazowieckie PL. .77 B5
Mazowieckie PL. .87 A4
Nowe Miasto
Lubawskie PL. . . .69 B4
Nowe Miasto nad Wartą
PL. 76 B2
Nowe Skalmierzyce
PL. 86 A2
Nowe Warpno PL. . .74 A3
Nowica PL. 69 A4
Nowogard PL. 75 A4
Nowogród Bobrzanski
PL. 84 A3
Nowogrodziec PL . .84 A3
Nowosolna PL. 86 A3
Nowy Dwór Gdański
PL. 69 A4
Nowy Korczyn PL . .87 B4
Nowy Sącz PL. 99 B4
Nowy Staw PL 69 A4
Nowy Targ PL. 99 B4
Nowy Tomyśl PL . . .75 B5
Nowy Wiśnicz PL. . .99 B4
Noyalo F 101 B3
Noyal-Pontivy F . . .100 A3
Noyant F 102 B2
Noyelles-sur-Mer F 78 B1
Noyen-sur-Sarthe
F. 102 B1
Noyers F 104 B2
Noyers-sur-Cher
F. 103 B3
Noyers-sur-Jabron
F. 132 A1
Noyon F 90 B2
Nozay F 101 B4
Nuaillé F 102 B1
Nuaillé-d'Aunis F .114 B3
Nubledo E 141 A5
Nueno E 145 B3
Nuestra Señora Sa
Verge des Pilar
E 166 C1
Nueva E 142 A2
Nueva Carteya E . .163 A3
Nuevalos E 152 A2
Nuits F 104 B3
Nuits-St Georges
F. 105 B3
Nule I 178 B3
Nules E 159 B3

Nulvi I 178 B2
Numana I 136 B2
Numansdorp NL . . .79 A4
Nümbrecht D 81 B3
Nunchritz D 83 A5
Nuneaton GB 40 C2
Nunnanen FIN 196 A7
N Unnaryd S 60 B3
Nuñomoral E 149 B3
Nunspeet NL 70 B2
Nuorgam FIN 193 B11
Núoro I 178 B3
Nurallao I 179 C3
Nuremberg = Nürnberg
D 94 B3
Nurmes FIN 3 E11
Nürnberg = Nuremberg
D 94 B3
Nurri I 179 C3
Nürtingen D 94 C1
Nus I 119 B4
Nusnäs S 50 B1
Nusplingen D 107 A3
Nuštar HR 125 B4
Nuupas FIN 197 C9
Nyåker S 200 C5
Nyáregyháza H 112 B3
Nyarlörinc H 113 C3
Nyasvizh BY 13 B7
Nybble S 55 A5
Nybergsund N 49 A4
Nyborg DK 64 B2
Nyborg
    DK 59 C3
    S 196 D6
Nybro S 62 B3
Nybster GB 32 C3
Nyby DK 65 B5
Nye S 62 A3
Nyékládháza H 113 B4
Nyergesujfalu H . . .112 B2
Nyhammar S 50 B1
Nyhyttan S 55 A5
Nyirád H 111 B4
Nyirbátor H 16 B5
Nyíregyháza H 16 B4
Nyker DK 67 A3
Nykil S 56 B1
Nykirke N 48 B2
Nykøbing
    Falster DK 65 B4
    Vestsjællands Amt.
    DK 61 D1
Nykøbing Mors DK .58 B1
Nyköping S 56 B3
Nykroppa S 55 A5
Nykvarn S 56 A3
Nykyrke S 55 B5
Nyland S 200 C3
Nylars DK 67 A3
Nymburk CZ 84 B3
Nynäshamn S 57 B3
Nyon CH 118 A3
Nyons F 131 A4
Nýřany CZ 96 B1
Nýrsko CZ 95 B5
Nyrud N 193 C13
Nysa PL 85 B5
Nysäter S 55 A3
Nyseter N 198 C5
Nyskoga S 49 B4
Nysted DK 65 B4
Nystrand N 53 A5
Nyúl H 111 B4
Nyvoll N 192 B7

O

Oadby GB 40 C2
Oakengates GB 38 B4
Oakham GB 40 C3
Oanes N 52 B2
Obalj BIH 139 B4
Oban GB 34 B2
O Barco E 141 B4
Obbola S 200 C6
Obdach A 110 B1
Obejo E 156 B3
Oberammergau D 108 B2
Oberasbach D 94 B2
Oberau D 108 B2
Oberaudorf D 108 B3
Oberbruck F 106 B1
Oberdiessbach
    CH 106 C2
Oberdorf CH 106 B2
Oberdrauburg A . . .109 C3
Oberelsbach D 82 B2
Obere Stanz A 110 B2
Ober Grafendorf
    A 110 A2
Obergünzburg D . .108 B1
Obergurgl A 108 C2
Oberhausen D 80 A2
Oberhof D 82 B2
Oberkirch D 93 C4
Oberkirchen D 81 A4
Oberkochen D 94 C2
Obermassfeld-
    Grimmenthal D . .82 B2
Ober-Morlen D 81 B4
Obermünchen D 95 C3
Obernai F 93 C3
Obernberg A 96 C1
Obernburg D 93 B5
Oberndorf D 93 C4
Oberndorf bei Salzburg
    A 109 B3
Obernkirchen D 72 B2
Oberort A 110 B2
Oberriet CH 107 B4
Oberröblingen D . . .82 A3
Oberrot D 94 B1
Oberstaufen D 107 B5
Oberstdorf D 107 B5

Obertauern A 109 B4
Obertilliach A 109 C3
Obertraubling D 95 C4
Obertraun A 109 B4
Obertrubach D 95 B3
Obertrum A 109 B4
Oberursel D 81 B4
Obervellach A 109 C4
Oberviechtach D 95 B4
Oberwart A 111 B3
Oberwesel D 93 A3
Oberwinter D 80 B3
Oberwölzstadt A . . .110 B1
Oberzell D 96 C1
Obice PL 87 B4
Óbidos E 154 B1
Obing D 109 B3
Objat F 129 A4
Objazda PL 68 A2
Öblarn A 109 D5
Obninsk RUS 9 E10
Oborniki PL 75 B5
Oborniki Śląskie
    PL 85 A4
Obornjača SRB . . .126 B1
Obrenovac SRB . . .127 C2
Obrež SRB 127 C1
Obrigheim D 93 B5
Obrov SLO 123 B3
Obrovac
    HR 137 A4
    SRB 126 B1
Obrovac Sinjski
    HR 138 B2
Obruk TR 23 B7
Obrzycko PL 75 B5
Obudovac BIH 125 C4
Ocaña E 151 C4
O Carballiño E 140 B2
Occhiobello I 121 C4
Occimiano I 119 B5
Očevlja BIH 139 A4
Ochagavía E 144 B2
Ochiltree GB 36 A2
Ochla PL 84 A3
Ochotnica-Dolna
    PL 99 B4
Ochotnica-Górna
    PL 99 B4
Ochsenfurt D 94 B2
Ochsenhausen D . .107 A4
Ochtendung D 80 B3
Ochtrup D 71 B4
Ocieka PL 87 B5
Ockelbo S 50 B3
Öckerö S 60 B1
Ocniţa MD 17 A7
O Corgo E 141 B3
Očová SK 99 C3
Ócsa H 112 B3
Öcseny H 125 A4
Öcsöd H 113 C4
Octeville F 88 A2
Ocypel PL 69 B3
Ödåkra S 61 C2
Odby DK 58 B1
Odda N 46 B3
Odder DK 59 C3
Ödeborg S 54 B2
Odeceixe P 160 B1
Odechów PL 87 A5
Odeleite P 160 B2
Odemira P 160 B1
Ödemiş TR 188 A2
Odensbacken S 56 A1
Odense DK 59 C3
Odensjö
    Jönköping S 62 A2
    Kronoberg S 60 C3
Oderberg D 74 B3
Oderzo I 122 B1
Odesa = Odessa
    UA 17 B9
Ödeshög S 55 B5
Odessa = Odesa
    UA 17 B9
Odiáxere P 160 B1
Odie GB 33 B4
Odiham GB 44 B3
Odintsovo RUS 9 E10
Odivelas P 160 A1
Odolanów PL 85 A5
Odón E 152 B2
Odorheiu Secuiesc
    RO 17 B6
Odrowaz PL 87 A4
Odry CZ 98 B1
Odrzywół PL 87 A4
Ødsted DK 59 C2
Odžaci SRB 126 B1
Odžak BIH 125 B4
Oebisfelde D 73 B3
Oederan D 83 B5
Oeding D 71 C3
Oegstgeest NL 70 B1
Oelde D 81 A4
Oelsnitz D 83 B4
Oer-Erkenschwick
    D 80 A3
Oerlinghausen D . . .72 C1
Oettingen D 94 C2
Oetz A 108 B1
Oeventrop D 81 A4
Offanengo I 120 B2
Offenbach D 81 B4
Offenburg D 93 C3
Offida I 136 C2
Offingen D 94 C2
Offranville F 89 A5
Ofte N 53 A4
Ofterschwang D . . .107 B5
Oggiono I 120 B2
Ogihares I 163 A4
Ogliastro Cilento 170 C3
Ogliastro Marina I . .170 C2
Ogmore-by-Sea GB 39 C3
Ogna N 52 B1
Ogre LV 8 D4
Ogrodzieniec PL . . .86 B3

Ogulin HR 123 B4
Ögur IS 190 A3
Ohanes E 164 B2
Ohey B 79 B5
Ohlstadt D 108 B2
Ohrdorf D 73 B3
Ohrdruf D 82 B2
Ohrid MK 182 B2
Öhringen D 94 B1
Oia E 140 B2
Oiã P 148 B1
Oiartzun E 144 A2
Oijärvi FIN 197 D8
Oilgate IRL 30 B2
Oimbra E 148 A2
Oiselay-et-Grachoux
    F 105 B4
Oisemont F 90 B1
Oisterwijk NL 79 A5
Öja S 57 C4
Ojén E 162 B3
Ójrzeń PL 77 B5
Ojuelos Altos E . . .156 B2
Okány H 113 C5
Okehampton GB 42 B2
Oklaj HR 138 B2
Økneshamn N 194 B6
Okoč SK 111 B4
Okoličné SK 99 B3
Okonek PL 68 B1
Okonin PL 69 B3
Okříšky CZ 97 B3
Oksa PL 87 B4
Øksfjord N 192 B6
Øksna N 48 B3
Okučani HR 124 B3
Okulovka RUS 9 C8
Ólafsfjörður IS 191 A7
Ólafsvík IS 190 C2
ÖLagnö S 57 A4
Olagüe E 144 B2
Öland N 53 B4
Olargues F 130 B1
Oława PL 85 B5
Olazagutia E 144 B1
Olbernhau D 83 B5
Ólbia I 178 B3
Olching D 108 A2
Oldbury GB 43 A4
Oldcastle IRL 27 C3
Old Deer GB 33 D4
Oldeberkoop NL 70 B3
Oldeboorn NL 70 A2
Olden N 198 D3
Oldenbrok D 71 A5
Oldenburg
    Niedersachsen D .71 A5
    Schleswig-Holstein
    D 65 B3
Oldenzaal NL 71 B3
Olderdalen N 192 C4
Olderfjord N 193 B9
Oldersum D 71 A4
Oldervik N 192 C2
Oldham GB 40 B1
Oldisleben D 82 A3
Oldmeldrum GB 33 D4
Olea E 142 B2
Oleby S 49 B5
Olechów PL 85 A5
Oledo P 155 B3
Oléggio I 120 B1
Oleiros
    Coruña E 140 A2
    Coruña E 140 B1
    P 154 B3
Oleksandriya UA . . .13 C7
Olen B 79 A4
Ølen N 52 A1
Olenegorsk RUS 3 B13
Olenino RUS 9 D8
Olesa de Montserrat
    E 147 C2
Oleśnica E 85 A5
Oleśnice CZ 97 B4
Oleśno PL 86 B2
Olestende B 78 A2
Olesterhout NL 79 A4
Oleszno PL 87 B4
Oletta F 180 A2
Olette F 146 B3
Olevsk UA 13 C7
Olfen D 80 A3
Olgiate Comasco
    I 120 B1
Olginate I 120 B2
Ølgod DK 59 C1
Olginmore GB 32 C3
Olhão P 160 B2
Olhava FIN 197 D8
Olhavo P 154 B1
Oliana E 147 B2
Olias del Rey E . . .151 C4
Oliena I 178 B3
Oliete E 153 A3
Olimbos GR 188 D2
Olite E 144 B2
Oliva E 159 C3
Oliva de la Frontera
    E 155 C4
Oliva de Mérida E .156 B1
Oliva de Plasencia
    E 149 B3
Olivadi I 175 C2
Olival P 154 B2
Olivares E 161 B3
Olivares de Duero
    E 142 C2
Olivares de Júcar
    E 158 B1
Oliveira de Azeméis
    P 148 B1
Oliveira de Frades
    P 148 B1
Oliveira do Conde
    P 148 B2
Oliveira do Douro
    P 148 A1

Oliveira do Hospital
    P 148 B2
Olivenza E 155 C3
Olivet F 103 B3
Olivone CH 107 C3
Öljehult S 63 B3
Olkusz PL 86 B3
Ollerton GB 40 B2
Ollerup DK 65 A3
Olliergues F 117 B3
Ölmbrotorp S 56 A1
Olme S 55 A4
Olmedilla de Alarcón
    E 158 B1
Olmedillo de Roa
    E 143 C3
Olmedo
    E 150 A3
    I 178 B2
Olmeto F 180 B1
Olmillos de Castro
    E 149 A3
Olmos de Ojeda E 142 B2
Olney GB 44 A3
Olocau del Rey E .153 B3
Olofström S 63 B2
Olomouc CZ 98 B1
Olonets RUS 9 B8
Olonne-sur-Mer F .114 B2
Olonzac F 130 B1
Oloron-Ste Marie
    F 145 A3
Olost E 147 C3
Olot E 147 B3
Olovo BIH 139 A4
Olpe D 81 A3
Olsberg D 81 A4
Olsene B 79 B3
Olserud S 55 A4
Olshammar S 55 B5
Olshanka UA 13 D9
Olszanica PL 85 A3
Olsztyn
    Śląskie PL 86 B3
    Warmińsko-Mazurskie
    PL 69 B5
Olsztynek PL 77 A5
Olszyna PL 84 A3
Olszyny PL 77 A6
Oltedal N 52 B2
Olten CH 106 B2
Olteniţa RO 17 C7
Olula del Río E 164 B2
Ølve N 46 B2
Olvega E 144 C2
Olvera E 162 B2
Olympia GR 184 B2
Olzai I 178 B3
Omagh GB 27 B3
Omalos GR 185 D4
Omegna I 119 B5
Omiš HR 138 B2
Omišalj HR 123 B3
Ommen NL 71 B3
Omodhos CY 181 B1
Omoljica SRB 127 C2
On B 79 B5
Oña E 143 B3
Onano I 168 A1
Onarup S 49 B5
Oñati E 143 A4
Onda E 159 B3
Ondara E 159 C4
Ondarroa E 143 A4
Onesse-et-Laharie
    F 128 B1
Oneşti RO 17 B7
Onhaye B 79 B4
Onich GB 34 B2
Onil E 159 C3
Onis E 142 A2
Önnestad S 61 C4
Onsala S 60 B2
Ontinyent E 159 C3
Ontur E 158 C2
Onzain F 103 B3
Onzonilla E 142 B1
Oostburg NL 79 A3
Oostende B 78 A2
Oosterend NL 70 A2
Oosterhout NL 79 A4
Oosterwolde NL 71 B3
Oosterzele B 79 B3
Oosthuizen NL 70 B2
Oostkamp B 78 A3
Oostmalle B 79 A4
Oost-Vlieland NL . . .70 A2
Oostvoorne NL 79 A4
Ootmarsum NL 71 B3
Opalenica PL 75 B5
O Páramo E 140 B3
Opařany CZ 96 B2
Opatija HR 123 B3
Opatów
    Śląskie PL 86 B2
    Świętokrzyskie PL .87 B5
    Wielkopolskie PL .86 A2
Opatówek PL 86 A2
Opatowiec PL 87 B4
Opava CZ 98 B1
O Pedrouzo E 140 B2
Opeinde NL 70 A3
Oper Thalkirchdorf
    D 107 B5
Opglabbeek B 80 A1
Opicina I 122 B2
O Pino E 140 B2
Oplotnica SLO 123 A4
Opmeer NL 70 B1
Opochka RUS 9 D6
Opočno CZ 85 B4
Opoczno PL 87 A4
Opole PL 86 B1
Oporów PL 77 B4
O Porriño E 140 B2
Opovo SRB 127 B2
Oppach D 84 A2
Oppdal N 198 C6

Oppeby
    Östergötland S . .56 B1
    Södermanland S .56 B2
Oppedal N 46 A2
Oppegård N 54 A1
Oppenau D 93 C4
Oppenberg A 110 B1
Oppenheim D 93 B4
Óppido Lucano I . .172 B1
Óppido Mamertina
    I 175 C1
Opponitz A 110 B1
Oppstad N 48 B3
Oprtalj HR 122 B2
Opsaheden S 49 B5
Opuzen HR 138 B3
Ora
    CY 181 B2
    I 121 A4
Orada P 155 C3
Oradea RO 16 B4
Oradour-sur-Glane
    F 115 C5
Oradour-sur-Vayres
    F 115 C4
Oragonja SLO 122 B2
Orah BIH 139 C4
Orahova BIH 138 A3
Orahovica HR 125 B3
Orahovo BIH 124 B3
Oraison F 132 B1
Orajärvi FIN 196 C7
Orange F 131 A3
Orani I 178 B3
Oranienbaum D 83 A4
Oranienburg D 74 B2
Oranmore IRL 28 A3
Orašac SRB 127 C2
Orašje BIH 125 B4
Oravská Lesná SK .99 B3
Oravská Polhora
    SK 99 B3
Oravské Veselé SK 99 B3
Oravsky-Podzámok
    SK 99 B3
Orba E 159 C3
Orbacém P 148 A1
Orbais F 91 C3
Ørbæk DK 59 C3
Orbassano I 119 B4
Orbe CH 105 C5
Orbec F 89 A4
Orbetello I 168 A1
Orbetello Scalo I . .168 A1
Orbigny F 103 B3
Ørby DK 59 B3
Örbyhus S 51 B4
Orce E 164 B2
Orcera E 164 A2
Orchamps-Vennes
    F 105 B5
Orches F 102 C2
Orchete E 159 C3
Orchies F 78 B3
Orchowo PL 76 B3
Orcières F 118 C3
Ordes E 140 A2
Ordhead GB 33 D4
Ordino AND 146 B2
Ordizia E 144 A1
Orduña E 143 B4
Ore S 50 A2
Orea E 152 B2
Orebić HR 138 C3
Örebro S 56 A1
Öregcsertő H 112 C3
Öregrund S 51 B5
Os
    Hedmark N 48 B3
    Hedmark N 199 C8
Osann-Monzel D . . .92 B2
Osbruk S 62 A2
Øsby DK 59 C2
Osby S 61 C3
Oščadnica SK 98 B2
Oschatz D 83 A5
Oschersleben D 73 B4
Óschiri I 178 B3
Oscilowo PL 77 B5
Osdorf D 64 B3
Osečina SRB 127 C1
Osečná CZ 84 B2
Oseja de Sajambre
    E 142 A1
Osek CZ 84 B1
Osen N 199 A7
Osera de Ebro E . .153 A3
Osidda I 178 B3
Osie PL 69 B3
Osieczna
    Pomorskie PL . . .68 B3
    Wielkopolskie PL .75 C5
Osieczno PL 75 A4
Osiek
    Kujawsko-Pomorskie
    PL 76 B3
    Kujawsko-Pomorskie
    PL 77 A4
    Pomorskie PL . . .69 B3
    Świętokrzyskie PL .87 B5
Osiek nad Notecią
    PL 76 A2
Osielsko PL 76 A3
Osijek HR 125 B4
Osilnica SLO 123 B3
Ósilo I 178 B2
Ósimo I 136 B2
Osinja BIH 125 C3
Osintorf BY 13 A9
Osipaonica SRB . . .127 C3
Osjaków PL 86 A2
Oskamull GB 34 B1
Oskarshamn S 62 A4
Oskarström S 60 C2
Oslany SK 98 C2
Oslavany CZ 97 B4
Ošlje HR 139 C3
Oslo N 48 C2
Øsløs DK 58 A1
Osmancık TR 23 A8

Osmaneli TR 187 B4
Ösmo S 57 B3
Osmolin PL 77 B4
Osnabrück D 71 B5
Ośno Lubuskie PL .75 B3
Osoblaha CZ 85 B5
Osor HR 123 C3
Osorno E 142 B2
Ósoyra N 46 A2
Øsøyro N 46 B2
Óspakseyri IS 190 B4
Os Peares E 140 B3
Ospedaletti I 133 B3
Ospitaletto I 120 B3
Oss NL 80 A1
Ossa de Montiel E 158 C1
Ossi I 178 B2
Ossjøen N 47 A5
Ossun F 145 A3
Ostanå S 61 C4
Ostanvik S 50 A2
Östashkov RUS 9 D8
Östavall S 200 D1
Ostbevern D 71 B4
Østborg N 199 A10
Østby N 49 A4
Osted DK 61 D1
Ostenfeld D 64 B2
Oster UA 13 C9
Øster Assels DK . . .58 B1
Osterburg D 73 B4
Osterburken D 94 B1
Österbybruk S 51 B4
Österbyhavn DK . . .58 A4
Österbymo S 62 A3
Ostercappeln D 71 B5
Österfärnebo S 51 B3
Osterfeld D 83 A3
Österforse S 200 C3
Osterhever D 64 B1
Osterhofen D 95 C5
Osterholz-Scharmbeck
    D 72 A1
Øster Hornum DK . .58 B2
Øster Hurup DK . . .58 B3
Østerild DK 58 A1
Øster Jølby DK 58 B1
Österlövsta S 51 B4
Øster-marie DK 67 A4
Ostermiething A . . .109 A3
Osterode am Harz
    D 82 A2
Ostersiel D 64 B1
Östersund S 199 B11
Øster Tørslev DK . . .58 B3
Östervåla S 51 B4
Östervallskog S 54 A2
Østervrå S 58 A3
Osterwieck D 73 C3
Osterzell D 108 B1
Ostffyasszonyfa
    H 111 B4
Östfora S 51 C4
Östhammar S 51 B5
Ostheim F 106 A2
Ostheim vor der Rhön
    D 82 B2
Osthofen D 93 B4
Ostiano I 120 B3
Ostíglia I 121 B4
Ostiz E 144 B2
Östmark S 49 B4
Ostnor S 50 A1
Ostojićevo SRB . . .126 B2
Ostra I 136 B2
Östra Amtervik S . .55 A4
Östra Husby S 56 B2
Östra Ljungby S 61 C3
Östra Ryd S 56 B2
Ostrau D 83 A5
Ostrava CZ 98 B2
Østre Halsen N 53 A6
Osthrauderfehn D . .71 A4
Ostritz D 84 A2
Ostróda PL 69 B4
Ostroh UA 13 C7
Ostrołęka PL 12 B4
Ostropole PL 68 B1
Ostroróg PL 75 B5
Ostrošovac BIH . . .124 C1
Ostrov
    CZ 83 B4
    RUS 8 D6
Ostrov nad Oslavou
    CZ 97 B3
Ostrówek PL 86 A2
Ostrowiec PL 68 A1
Ostrowiec-
    Świętokrzyski PL .87 B5
Ostrowite PL 77 A4
Ostrów Mazowiecka
    PL 12 B4
Ostrowo PL 76 B3
Ostrów Wielkopolski
    PL 86 A1
Ostrożac BIH 139 B3
Ostrzeszów PL 86 A1
Ostseebad
    Kühlungsborn D . .65 B4
Ostuni I 173 B3
Osuna E 162 A2
Osvětimany CZ 98 B1
Oswestry GB 38 B3
Oświęcim PL 86 B3
Osztopán H 111 C4
Oteiza E 144 B2
Otelec RO 126 B2
Oteo E 143 A3
Oterbekk N 54 A1
Otero de Herreros
    E 151 B3
Otero de O Bodas
    E 141 C4
Othem S 57 C4
Otley GB 40 B2
Otmuchów PL 85 B5
Otočac HR 123 C4

Otok
Splitsko-Dalmatinska
HR. 138 B2
Vukovarsko-Srijemska
HR. 125 B4
Otoka BIH 124 C2
Otranto I. 173 B4
Otrić HR. 138 A2
Otríčoli I. 168 A2
Otrokovice CZ. 98 B1
Otta N. 198 D6
Ottana I 178 B3
Ottaviano I 170 C2
Ottenby S. 63 B4
Ottendorf-Okrilla D 84 A1
Ottenhöfen D. 93 C4
Ottenschlag A. 97 C3
Ottensheim A. 96 C2
Otterbach D. 93 B3
Otterbäcken S. 55 B5
Otterberg D. 93 B3
Otterburn GB. 37 A4
Otter Ferry GB. . . .34 B2
Otterndorf D. 64 C1
Ottersweier D 93 C4
Otterup DK. 59 C3
Ottery St Mary GB. .43 B3
Ottignies B. 79 B4
Ottmarsheim F. . . .106 B2
Ottobeuren D. 107 B5
Öttömös H 126 A1
Ottone I 120 C2
Ottsjö S 199 B10
Ottweiler D. 92 B3
Otveşti RO. 126 B3
Ötvöskónyi H 124 A3
Otwock PL 12 B4
Ouanne F. 104 B2
Ouarville F. 90 C1
Oucques F. 103 B3
Oud-Beijerland NL .79 A4
Ouddorp NL. 79 A3
Oudemirdum NL. . . .70 B2
Oudenaarde B. 79 B3
Oudenbosch NL. . . .79 A4
Oudenburg B. 78 A3
Oude-Pekela NL 71 A4
Oude-Tonge NL. . . .79 A4
Oudewater NL. 70 B1
Oud Gastel NL. 79 A4
Oudon F. 101 B4
Oue DK. 58 B2
Oughterard IRL. . . .28 A2
Ouguela P 155 B3
Ouistreham F. 89 A3
Oulainen FIN 3 D9
Oulchy-le-Château
F. 91 B3
Oullins F 117 B4
Oulmes F. 114 B3
Oulton GB 41 C5
Oulton Broad GB. . .41 C5
Oulu FIN. 3 D9
Oulx I 119 B3
Oundle GB 40 C3
Ouranopoli GR 183 C6
Ourém P. 154 B2
Ourense E 140 B3
Ourique P. 160 B1
Ourol E 140 A3
Ouroux-en-Morvan
F. 104 B2
Ousdale GB 32 C3
Oust F 146 B2
Outakoski FIN 193 C10
Outeiro P. 148 B1
Outeiro de Rei E . .140 A3
Outes E 140 B2
Outokumpu FIN. 9 A6
Outreau F. 78 B1
Outwell GB 41 C4
Ouzouer-le-Marché
F. 103 B3
Ouzouer-sur-Loire
F. 103 B4
Ovada I 133 A4
Ovar P 148 B1
Ovelgönne D 72 A1
Overath D. 80 B3
Overbister GB 33 B4
Øverbygd N 192 D3
Overdinkel NL. 71 B4
Överenhörna S 56 A3
Overhalla N 199 A8
Overijse B 79 B4
Over-jerstal DK 59 C2
Overlade DK 58 B2
Överlida S 60 B2
Överö FIN 51 B7
Overpelt B 79 A5
Overton GB 38 B4
Övertorneå S. 196 C6
Överum S. 62 A4
Ovidiopol UA. 17 B9
Oviedo E 141 A5
Oviglio I 119 C5
Ovíndoli I 169 A3
Ovodda I 178 B3
Øvre Årdal N 47 A4
Øvrebygd N 52 B2
Øvre Rendal N 199 D8
Øvre Sirdal N 52 B2
Øvre Soppero S . . .196 A4
Övre Ullerud S 55 A4
Ovruch UA. 13 C8
Ovtrup DK 59 C1
Owińska PL. 76 B1
Oxaback S. 60 B2
Oxberg S. 49 A6
Oxelösund S 56 B3
Oxenholme GB 37 B4
Oxford GB 44 B2
Oxie S 61 D3
Oxted GB. 45 B4
Oyaca TR 187 C7
Øye N 47 A5
Øyenkilen N. 54 A1
Øyer N 48 A2

Øyeren N 49 B4
Oyfiell N. 53 A4
Øygärdslia N 53 B4
Oykel Bridge GB . . .32 D2
Øymark N. 54 A2
Oyonnax F 118 A2
Øyslebø N. 52 B3
Øystese N 46 B3
Oyten D 72 A2
Øyuvsbu N. 52 A3
Ozaeta E 143 B4
Ozalj HR. 123 B4
Ożarów PL. 87 B5
Ożarów Maz PL 77 B5
Ozd H 113 A4
Ożd'any SK 99 C3
Ozieri I 178 B3
Ozimek PL. 86 B2
Ozimica BIH. 139 A4
Ozora H 112 C2
Ozorków PL. 77 C4
Ozzano Monferrato
I. 119 B5

P

Paakkola FIN. 196 D7
Paal B. 79 A5
Pabianice PL. 86 A3
Pacanów PL. 87 B5
Paceco I. 176 B1
Pachino I. 177 C4
Pačir SRB. 126 B1
Pack A 110 B2
Paços de Ferreira
P 148 A1
Pacov CZ. 96 B3
Pacsa H 111 C4
Pacy-sur-Eure F 89 A5
Paczków PL. 85 B5
Padany RUS 3 E13
Padborg DK. 64 B2
Padej SRB 126 B2
Padene HR. 138 A2
Paderborn D 81 A4
Paderne P. 160 B1
Padiham GB 40 B1
Padina SRB. 126 B2
Padinska Skela
SRB. 127 C2
Padornelo P. 148 A1
Pádova I. 121 B4
Padragkút H 111 B4
Padria I 178 B2
Padrón E 140 B2
Padru I. 178 B3
Padstow GB. 42 B2
Padul E 163 A4
Padula I 172 B1
Paduli I 170 B2
Paesana I 119 C4
Paese I 121 B5
Pag HR. 137 A4
Pagani I 170 C2
Pagánica I 169 A3
Pagánico I 135 C4
Pagl ieta I. 169 A4
Pagny-sur-Moselle
F. 92 C2
Páhi H 112 C3
Pahkakumpu
FIN. 197 C11
Pahl D 108 B2
Paide EST 8 C4
Paignton GB 43 B3
Pailhès F 146 A2
Paimboeuf F. 101 B3
Paimpol F 100 A2
Paimpont F 101 A3
Painswick GB 43 A4
Painten D. 95 C3
Paisley GB. 34 C3
Pajala S 196 B6
Pajares E 141 A5
Pajares de los Oteros
E 142 B1
Pajęczno PL. 86 A2
Pâka H 111 C3
Pakość PL. 76 B3
Pakosławice PL. 85 B5
Pakoštane HR 137 B4
Pakrac HR 124 B3
Paks H 112 C2
Palacios de la Sierra
E 143 C3
Palaciòs de la
Valduerna E 141 B5
Palacios del Sil E .141 B4
Palacios de Sanabria
E 141 B4
Palaciosrubios E. . .150 A2
Palafrugell E. 147 C4
Palagiano I 173 B3
Palagonia I 177 B3
Paláia I 135 B3
Palaiokastritsa
GR 182 D1
Palaiseau F 90 C2
Palamas GR. 182 D4
Palamòs E 147 C4
Påläng S 196 D5
Palanga LT. 8 E2
Palanzano I 134 A3
Palárikovo SK 112 A2
Palas de Rei E 140 B3
Palata I 170 B2
Palau I. 178 A3
Palavas-les-Flots
F 131 B2
Palazuelos de la Sierra
E 143 B3
Palazzo Adriano I . .176 B2
Palazzo del Pero I .135 B4
Palazzolo Acréide
I 177 B3
Palazzolo sull'Oglio
I 120 B2

Palazzo San Gervásio
I. 172 B1
Palazzuolo sul Senio
I 135 A4
Paldiski EST 8 C4
Pale BIH 139 B4
Palekastro GR 185 D7
Palena I 169 B4
Palencia E 142 B2
Palenciana E. 163 A3
Paleochora GR 185 D4
Paleometokho CY .181 A2
Palermo I 176 A2
Paleros GR 182 E2
Palestrina I 169 B2
Pálfa H 112 C2
Palfau A 110 B1
Palhaça P. 148 B1
Palheiros da Tocha
P 148 B1
Palheiros de Quiaios
P 148 B1
Paliaopoli GR 185 B5
Palić SRB. 126 A1
Palidoro I. 168 B2
Palinuro I 172 B1
Paliouri GR 183 D5
Paliseul B. 91 B5
Pallanza I. 119 B5
Pallares E 161 A3
Palluaruelo de Monegros
E 153 A3
Pallas Green IRL . . .29 B3
Pallerols E 146 B2
Palling D 109 A3
Palluau F 114 B2
Palma P. 154 C2
Palma Campánia
I. 170 C2
Palma del Río E . . .162 A2
Palma de Mallorca
E 166 B2
Palma di Montechiaro
I 176 B2
Palmádula I 178 B2
Palmanova I 122 B2
Palma Nova E 166 B2
Palmela P. 154 C2
Palmerola E 147 B3
Palmi I 175 C1
Pälmonostora H . . .113 C3
Palo del Colle I 171 B4
Palojärvi FIN 192 D7
Palojoensuu FIN . . .196 A6
Palomares E 164 B3
Palomares del Campo
E 158 B1
Palomas E 156 B1
Palombara Sabina
I. 168 A2
Palos de la Frontera
E 161 B3
Palotaboszok H. . . .125 A4
Palotás H 112 B3
Pals E 147 C4
Pålsboda S. 56 A1
Paluzza I 109 C4
Pamhagen A 111 B3
Pamiers F 146 A2
Pamiętowo PL. 76 A2
Pampaneira E. 163 B4
Pamparato I. 133 A3
Pampilhosa
Aveiro P. 148 B1
Coimbra P. 148 B2
Pamplona E. 144 B2
Pampow D 73 A4
Pamukçu TR 186 C2
Pamukkale TR 188 B4
Pamukova TR 187 B5
Panagyurishte BG. .17 D6
Pancalieri I 119 C4
Pančevo SRB. 127 C2
Pancey F 91 C5
Pancorvo E 143 B3
Pancrudo E 152 B2
Pandino I 120 B2
Pandrup DK. 58 A2
Panenský-Týnec
CZ. 84 B1
Panes E 142 A2
Panevėžys LT. 8 E4
Pangbourne GB 44 B2
Panissières F 117 B4
Panki PL. 86 B2
Panningen NL. 80 A1
Pannonhalma H . . .111 B4
Pano Lefkara CY . . .181 B2
Pano Panayia CY .181 B1
Panormos GR 185 B6
Panschwitz-Kuckau
D. 84 A2
Pansdorf D. 65 C3
Pantano de Cíjara
E 156 A3
Panticosa E 145 B3
Pantín E 140 A2
Pantoja E 151 B4
Pantón E 140 B3
Panxon E. 140 B2
Páola I 174 B2
Paola M 175 C3
Pápa H 111 B4
Papasídero I 174 B1
Pápateszér H 111 B4
Papenburg D. 71 A4
Paphos CY. 181 B1
Pappenheim D. 94 C2
Paprotnia PL. 77 B5
Parábita I 173 B4
Paracin SRB 127 D3
Parád H 113 B4
Parada
Bragança P 149 A3
Viseu P. 148 B1
Paradas E 162 A2
Paradela P 148 B1

Parades de Rubiales
E 150 A2
Paradinas de San Juan
E 150 B2
Paradiso di Cevadale
I 108 C1
Paradyż PL. 87 A4
Parainen FIN 8 B3
Parakhino Paddubye
RUS. 9 C8
Parakka S 196 B4
Paralimni CY. 181 A2
Parallo Astros GR 184 B3
Paramé F. 88 B2
Paramithia GR. 182 D2
Páramo I 141 A4
Páramo del Sil E . . .141 B4
Parandaça P. 148 A2
Paravadella E 141 A3
Paray-le-Monial F .104 C3
Parceiros P. 154 B2
Parcey F 105 B4
Parchim D 73 A4
Parciaki PL. 77 A6
Parcice PL. 86 A2
Pardilla E 151 A4
Pardubice CZ 97 A3
Paredes
E 151 B5
P 148 A1
Paredes de Coura
P 140 C2
Paredes de Nava
E 142 B2
Paredes de Siguenza
E 151 A5
Pareja E 151 B5
Parennes F 102 A1
Parenti I 175 B2
Parentis-en-Born
F. 128 B1
Parey D 73 B4
Parfino RUS. 9 D7
Parga GR. 182 D2
Pargny-sur-Saulx F 91 C4
Pari-Gagné F 117 A4
Parigné-l'Évêque
F. 102 B2
Parikkala FIN. 9 B6
Paris F 90 C2
Parkalompolo S . . .196 B5
Parkano FIN. 8 A3
Parknasilla IRL. 29 C2
Parla E 151 B4
Parlavá E 147 B4
Parma I 120 C3
Parndorf A 111 B3
Párnica SK. 99 B3
Parnu EST. 8 C4
Parolis E 164 A2
Paros GR. 185 B6
Parrillas E 150 B2
Parsberg D. 95 B3
Parstein D 74 B3
Partakko FIN 193 C11
Partanna I 176 B1
Parthenay F 102 C1
Partinico I. 176 A2
Partizani SRB 127 C2
Partizánske SK 98 C2
Partney GB 41 B4
Páryd S 63 B3
Parzymiechy PL. . . .86 A2
Paşcani RO. 17 B7
Pasewalk D 74 A2
Pašina Voda MNE .139 B5
Påskallavik S. 62 A4
Pasłęk PL. 69 A4
Pašman HR 137 B4
Passage East IRL. . .30 B1
Passail A 110 B2
Passais F. 88 B3
Passau D 96 C1
Passegueiro P. 148 B1
Passignano sul
Trasimeno I. 136 B2
Passo di Tréia I 136 B2
Passopisciaro I. . . .177 B4
Passow D. 74 A3
Passy F 118 B3
Pastavy BY 13 A7
Pástena I 170 B2
Pastrana E 151 B5
Pastrengo I 121 B3
Pasym PL. 77 A5
Pásztó H 113 B3
Pata SK 98 C1
Patay F 103 A3
Pateley Bridge GB .40 A2
Paterek PL. 76 A2
Paterna E 159 B3
Paterna del Campo
E 161 B3
Paterna del Madera
E 158 C1
Paterna de Rivera
E 162 B2
Paternion A. 109 C4
Paternò I 177 B3
Paternópoli I 170 C3
Patersdorf D 95 B4
Paterswolde NL. . . .71 A3
Patitiri GR 183 D5
Patmos GR 188 B1
Patna GB 36 A2
Patnow PL. 76 B3
Patoniva FIN. 193 C11
Patopirtti FIN. 197 B12
Patos AL 182 C1
Patra = Patras GR 184 A2
Patras = Patra GR 184 A2
Patreksfjörður IS. .190 B2
Patrickswell IRL. . . .29 B3
Patrimonio F 180 A2
Patrington GB 41 B3
Pattada I 178 B3
Pattensen
Niedersachsen D. .72 A3
Niedersachsen D. .72 B2

Patterdale GB 36 B4
Patti I 177 A3
Páty H 112 B2
Pau F 145 A3
Pauillac F. 128 A2
Paularo I 109 C4
Paulhaguet F 117 B3
Paulhan F 130 B2
Paulilátino I 178 B2
Paullo I 120 B2
Paulstown IRL. 30 B1
Pausa D 83 B3
Pauträsk S. 200 B3
Pavia
I 120 B2
P 154 C2
Pavias E 159 B3
Pavilly F. 89 A4
Pāvilosta LV. 8 D2
Pavullo nel Frignano
I 135 A3
Pawłowice PL. 86 A1
Pawłowice PL. 98 B2
Paxi GR 182 D2
Payallar TR 189 C6
Payerne CH 106 C1
Paymogo E. 161 B2
Payrac F 129 B4
Pazardzhik BG. . . .183 A6
Pazaryeri TR 187 B4
Pazin HR 122 B2
Paziols F 146 B3
Pčelić HR. 124 B3
Peal de Becerro E .164 B1
Peasmarsh GB. 45 C4
Peć KOS. 16 D4
Péccioli I. 135 B3
Pécel H. 112 B3
Pechao P. 160 B2
Pechenga RUS 3 B12
Pechenizhyn UA. . . .13 D6
Pecica RO. 126 A3
Pečínci SRB. 127 C1
Pecka SRB. 127 C1
Peckelsheim D 81 A5
Pečory RUS 8 D5
Pécs H 125 A4
Pécsvárad H 125 A4
Peczniew PL. 86 A2
Pedaso I 136 B2
Pedavena I. 121 A4
Pederobba I 121 B4
Pedersker DK 67 A3
Pedescala I 121 B4
Pedrafita E 141 B3
Pedrajas de San
Esteban E 150 A3
Pedralba E. 159 B3
Pedralba de la Praderia
E 141 B4
Pedraza E 151 A4
Pedreguer E 159 C4
Pedrera E 162 A3
Pedro Abad E 157 C3
Pedro Bernardo E 150 B3
Pedroche E 156 B3
Pedrógão P 160 A2
Pedrogao P 149 B2
Pedrógão P 154 B2
Pedrógão Grande
P 154 B2
Pedrola E 144 C2
Pedro-Martinez E .164 B1
Pedro Muñoz E . . .158 B1
Pedrosa del Rey
E 150 A2
Pedrosa del Rio Urbel
E 143 B3
Pedrosa de Tobalina
E 143 B3
Pedrosillo de los Aires
E 149 B4
Pedrosillo el Ralo
E 150 A2
Pędzewo PL. 76 A3
Peebles GB 35 C4
Peel GB 36 B2
Peenemünde D 66 B2
Peer B 79 A5
Pega P 149 B2
Pegalajar E 163 A4
Pegau D 83 A4
Peggau A. 110 B2
Pegli I. 133 A4
Pegnitz D. 95 B3
Pego E 159 C3
Pegões-Estação
P 154 C2
Pegões Velhos P . .154 C2
Pęgów PL. 85 A4
Pegswood GB 37 A5
Pehlivanköy TR. . . .186 A1
Peine D 72 B3
Peisey-Nancroix F 118 B3
Peissenberg D. 108 B2
Peiting D. 108 B1
Peitz D 84 A2
Péjo I. 121 A3
Pelagićevo BIH. . . .125 C4
Pelahustán E. 150 B3
Pełczyce PL. 75 A4
Pelhřimov CZ 97 B3
Pélissanne F 131 B4
Pelkosenniemi
FIN. 197 B10
Pellegrino Parmense
I 120 C2
Pellegrue F. 128 B3
Pellérd H 125 A4
Pellestrina I 122 B1
Pellevoisin F 103 C3
Pellizzano I 121 A3
Pello
FIN 196 C7
S 196 C6
Peloche E. 156 A2
Pelplin PL. 69 B3
Pelussin F 117 B4

Pély H. 113 B4
Pembroke GB 39 C2
Pembroke Dock
GB. 39 C2
Pernek SK. 98 C1
Pernes P 154 B2
Pernes-les-Fontaines
F. 131 A4
Pernik BG 17 D5
Pernink CZ. 83 B4
Pernitz A. 110 B2
Pernu FIN. 197 C10
Peroguarda P 160 A1
Pérols F. 131 B2
Péronne F 90 B2
Péronnes B 79 B4
Pero Pinheiro P . . .154 C1
Perorrubio E 151 A4
Perosa Argentina
I 119 C4
Perozinho P. 148 A1
Perpignan F 146 B3
Perranporth GB 42 B1
Perranzabuloe GB. .42 B1
Perrecy-les-Forges
F. 104 C3
Perrero I. 119 C4
Perrignier F 118 A3
Perros-Guirec F . . .100 A2
Persan F 90 B2
Persberg S. 55 A5
Persenbeug A 110 A2
Pershore GB. 44 A1
Persön S 196 D5
Perstorp S 61 C3
Perth GB 35 B4
Pertisau A 108 B2
Pertoča SLO. 111 C3
Pertuis F 131 B4
Perućac SRB. 127 D1
Perúgia I 136 B1
Perušić HR 123 C4
Péruwelz B. 79 B3
Pervomaysk UA. . . .13 D9
Perwez B 79 B4
Pesadas de Burgos
E 143 B3
Pesaguero E 142 A2
Pésaro I 136 B1
Pescantina I 121 B3
Pescara I 169 A4
Pescasséroli I 169 B3
Peschici I. 171 B4
Peschiera del Garda
I 121 B3
Péscia I 135 B3
Pescina I 169 A3
Pescocostanzo I. . .169 B4
Pescopagano I 172 B1
Pesco Sannita I . . .170 B2
Peshkopi AL. 182 B2
Peshtera BG 183 A6
Pesmes F 105 B4
Pesnica SLO. 110 C2
Peso da Régua P . .148 A2
Pesquera de Duero
E 142 C2
Pessac F 128 B2
Pestovo RUS 9 C9
Petäjäskoski FIN. . .197 C8
Petalidi GR. 184 C2
Pétange L 92 B1
Petas GR 182 D3
Peteranec HR 124 A2
Peterborough GB . .41 C3
Peterculter GB. 33 D4
Peterhead GB 33 D5
Peterlee GB. 37 B5
Petersfield GB. 44 B3
Petershagen
Brandenburg D . .74 B2
Brandenburg D . .74 B3
Nordrhein-Westfalen
D. 72 B1
Petershausen D. . . .95 C3
Peterswell IRL. 28 A3
Pétervására H 113 A4
Petília Policastro I 175 B2
Petín E 141 B3
Pětipsy CZ. 83 B5
Petkus D 74 B2
Petlovac HR. 125 B4
Petlovača SRB 127 C1
Petöfiszállás H 113 C3
Petra E 167 B3
Petralia Sottana I . .177 B3
Petrčane HR 137 A4
Petrella Tifernina I 170 B2
Petrer E 159 C3
Petreto-Bicchisano
F. 180 B1
Petrich BG. 183 B5
Petrijevci HR 125 B4
Petrinja HR 124 B2
Petrodvorets RUS. . .9 C6
Pétrola E 158 C2
Petronà I 175 B2
Petronell A 111 A3
Petroşani RO. 17 C5
Petrovac RUS. 69 A5
Petrovaradin SRB 126 B1
Petrovice
BIH 139 A4
CZ. 84 B1
Petrovo RUS. 69 A5
Petrozavodsk RUS . .9 B9
Petsmo FIN . . . . . .3 E8 ?
Pettigo IRL. 26 B3
Petworth GB 44 C3
Peuerbach A. 96 C1
Peuntenansa E 142 A2
Peurasuvanto FIN 197 B9
Pevensey Bay GB . .45 C4
Peveragno I 133 A3
Pewsey GB 44 B2
Peymeinade F . . . . .132 B2 ?
Peyrat-le-Château
F. 116 B1
Peyrehorade F 128 C1

Peyriac-Minervois
F 146 A3
Peyrins F 117 B5
Peyrissac F 116 B1
Peyrolles-en-Provence
F 132 B1
Peyruis F 132 A1
Pézarches F 90 C2
Pézenas F 130 B2
Pezinok SK 111 A4
Pezuls F 129 B3
Pfaffenhausen D . .108 A1
Pfaffenhofen
Bayern D 94 C2
Bayern D 95 C3
Pfaffenhoffen F 93 C3
Pfäffikon CH 107 B3
Pfarrkirchen D 95 C4
Pfeffenhausen D . . .95 C3
Pfetterhouse F . . .106 B2
Pforzheim D 93 C4
Pfreimd D 95 B4
Pfronten D 108 B1
Pfullendorf D 107 B4
Pfullingen D 94 C1
Pfunds A 108 C1
Pfungstadt D 93 B4
Pfyn CH 107 B3
Phalsbourg F 92 C3
Philippeville B 79 B4
Philippsreut D 96 C1
Philippsthal D 82 B1
Piacenza I 120 B2
Piacenza d'Adige
I 121 B4
Piádena I 120 B3
Piana F 180 A1
Piana Crixia I 133 A4
Piana degli Albanesi
I 176 B2
Piana di Monte Verna
I 170 B2
Piancastagnáio I . .135 C4
Piandelagotti I 134 A3
Pianella
Abruzzi I 169 A4
Toscana I 135 B4
Pianello Val Tidone
I 120 C2
Pianoro I 135 A4
Pians A 108 B1
Pías E 141 B4
Pias P 160 A2
Piaseczno PL 77 B6
Piasek PL 74 B3
Piaski PL 69 A4
Piastów PL 77 B5
Piaszcyna PL 68 A2
Piątek PL 77 B4
Piatra Neamţ RO . . .17 B7
Piazza al Sérchio
I 134 A3
Piazza Armerina I .177 B3
Piazza Brembana
I 120 B2
Piazze I 135 C4
Piazzola sul Brenta
I 121 B4
Picassent E 159 B3
Piccione I 136 B1
Picerno I 172 B1
Picher D 73 A4
Pickering GB 40 A3
Pico I 169 B3
Picón E 157 A3
Picquigny F 90 B2
Piechowice PL 84 B3
Piecnik PL 75 A5
Piedicavallo I 119 B4
Piedicroce F 180 A2
Piedimonte Etneo
I 177 B4
Piedimonte Matese
I 170 B2
Piedimulera I 119 A5
Piedipaterno I 136 C1
Piedrabuena E 157 A3
Piedraescrita E . . .156 A3
Piedrafita E 142 A1
Piedrahita E 150 B2
Piedralaves E 150 B3
Piedras Albas E . . .155 B4
Piedras Blancas E 141 A5
Piegaro I 135 C5
Piekary Śl. PL 86 B2
Piekoszów PL 87 B4
Pieksämäki FIN 8 A5
Pielenhofen D 95 B3
Pielgrzymka PL 85 A3
Pieniężno PL 69 A5
Pieńsk PL 84 A3
Pienza I 135 B4
Piera E 147 C2
Pieranie PL 76 B3
Pierowall GB 33 B4
Pierre-Buffière F . .115 C5
Pierrecourt F 105 B4
Pierre-de-Bresse
F 105 C4
Pierrefeu-du-Var
F 132 B2
Pierrefitte-Nestalas
F 145 B3
Pierrefitte-sur-Aire
F 92 C1
Pierrefonds F 90 B2
Pierrefontaine-les-
Varans F 105 B5
Pierrefort F 116 C2
Pierrelatte F 131 A3
Pierrepont
Aisne F 91 B3
Meurthe-et-Moselle
F 92 B1
Piesendorf A 109 B3
Piešťany SK 98 C1
Pieszkowo PL 69 A5
Pieszyce PL 85 B4
Pietarsaari FIN 3 E8
Pietragalla I 172 B1
Pietra Ligure I 133 A4
Pietralunga I 136 B1
Pietramelara I 170 B2
Pietraperzía I 177 B3
Pietrasanta I 134 B3
Pietravairano I 170 B2
Pieve del Cáiro I . .120 B1
Pieve di Bono I . . .121 B3
Pieve di Cadore I . .122 A1
Pieve di Cento I . . .121 C4
Pieve di Soligo I . .121 B5
Pieve di Teco I 133 A3
Pievepélago I 134 A3
Pieve Santo Stefano
I 135 B5
Pieve Torina I 136 B2
Piges GR 182 D3
Píglio I 169 B3
Pigna I 133 B3
Pignan F 130 B2
Pignataro Maggiore
I 170 B2
Piittisjärvi FIN 197 C9
Pijnacker NL 70 B1
Pikalevo RUS 9 C9
Piła PL 75 A5
Pilar de la Horadada
E 165 B4
Pilas E 161 B3
Pilastri I 121 C4
Piława Górna PL . . .85 B4
Piławki PL 69 B4
Pilchowice PL 86 B2
Pilea GR 183 C5
Pilgrimstad S 199 C12
Pili
Dodekanisa GR . 188 C2
Trikala GR 182 D3
Pilica PL 86 B3
Pilis H 112 B3
Piliscaba H 112 B2
Pilisszántó H 112 B2
Pilisvörösvár H . . .112 B2
Pilos GR 184 C2
Pilsting D 95 C4
Pilszcz PL 98 A1
Pilterud N 48 C2
Pilu RO 113 C5
Pina de Ebro E . . .153 A3
Piñar E 163 A4
Pınarbaşı TR 186 C1
Pınarhisar TR 186 A2
Pinas F 145 A4
Pincehely H 112 C2
Pinchbeck GB 41 C3
Pińczów PL 87 B4
Pineda de la Sierra
E 143 B3
Pineda de Mar E . .147 C3
Pinerella I 135 A5
Pinerolo I 119 C4
Pineta Grande I . . .170 C1
Pineto I 169 A4
Piney F 91 C4
Pinggau A 111 B3
Pinhal Novo P 154 C2
Pinhão P 148 A2
Pinheiro
Aveiro P 148 A1
Aveiro P 148 B1
Pinheiro Grande
P 154 B2
Pinhel P 149 B2
Pinhoe GB 43 B3
Pinilla E 158 C2
Pinilla de Toro E . .150 A2
Pinkafeld A 111 B3
Pinneberg D 72 A2
Pinnow D 74 C3
Pino F 180 A2
Pino del Rio E 142 B2
Pino de Val E 140 B2
Pinofranqueado E 149 B3
Pinols F 117 B3
Piñor E 140 B2
Pinos del Valle E . .163 B4
Pinoso E 159 C2
Pinos Puente E . . .163 A4
Pinsk BY 13 B7
Pintamo FIN 197 D10
Pinto E 151 B4
Pinzano al Tagliamento
I 122 A1
Pinzio P 149 B2
Pinzolo I 121 A3
Pióbbico I 136 B1
Piombino I 134 C3
Pionki PL 87 A5
Pionsat F 116 A2
Pióraco I 136 B1
Piornal E 150 B2
Piotrkowice PL 87 B4
Piotrków-Kujawski
PL 76 B3
Piotrków Trybunalski
PL 86 A3
Piotrowo PL 75 B5
Piove di Sacco I . .121 B5
Piovene I 121 B4
Piperskärr S 62 A4
Pipriac F 101 B4
Piraeus = Pireas
GR 185 B4
Piran SLO 122 B2
Pireas = Piraeus
GR 185 B4
Piré-sur-Seiche F .101 A4
Pirgi GR 185 A6
Pirgos
Ilia GR 184 B2
Kriti GR 185 D6
Piriac-sur-Mer F . .101 B3
Piringsdorf A 111 B3
Pirmasens D 93 B3
Pirna D 84 B1
Pirnmill GB 34 C2
Pirot SRB 16 D5
Pirovac HR 137 B4
Pirttivuopio S 196 B2
Pisa I 134 B3
Pisany F 114 C3
Pisarovina HR 124 B1
Pischelsdorf in der
Steiermark A 110 B2
Pişchia RO 126 B3
Pisciotta I 172 B1
Písek CZ 96 B2
Pisogne I 120 B3
Pissos F 128 B2
Pissouri CY 181 B1
Pisticci I 174 A2
Pistóia I 135 B3
Piteå S 196 D4
Piteşti RO 17 C6
Pithiviers F 103 A4
Pitigliano I 168 A1
Pitkyaranta RUS 9 B7
Pitlochry GB 35 B4
Pitomača HR 124 B3
Pitres E 163 B4
Pittentrail GB 32 D2
Pitvaros H 126 A2
Pivka SLO 123 B3
Pivnice SRB 126 B1
Piwniczna PL 99 B4
Pizarra E 163 B3
Pizzano I 121 A3
Pizzighettone I . . .120 B2
Pizzo I 175 C2
Pízzoli I 169 A3
Pizzolungo I 176 A1
Pjätteryd S 61 C4
Plabennec F 100 A1
Placencia E 143 A4
Plaffeien CH 106 C2
Plaisance
Gers F 128 C3
Haute-Garonne F 129 C4
Tarn F 130 B1
Plaka GR 183 D7
Plan E 145 B4
Planá CZ 95 B4
Planánad Lužnici
CZ 96 B2
Plaňany CZ 96 A3
Planchez F 104 B3
Plancoët F 101 A3
Plancy-l'Abbaye F . .91 C3
Plan-de-Baix F 118 C2
Plandište SRB 126 B3
Plan-d'Orgon F . . .131 B3
Plánice CZ 96 B1
Planina
SLO 123 A4
SLO 123 B3
Plankenfels D 95 B3
Plasencia E 149 B3
Plasenzuela E 156 A1
Plaški HR 123 B4
Plassen
Buskerud N 47 B4
Hedmark N 49 A4
Plášť'ovce SK 112 A3
Plasy CZ 96 B1
Platamona Lido I . .178 B2
Platania I 175 B2
Platanos GR 185 D4
Platí I 175 C2
Platičevo SRB 127 C1
Platja d'Aro E 147 C4
Plattling D 95 C4
Plau D 73 A5
Plaue
Brandenburg D . . .73 B5
Thüringen D 82 B2
Plauen D 83 B4
Plavecký Mikuláš
SK 98 C1
Plavinas LV 8 D4
Plavna SRB 125 B5
Plavnica SK 99 B4
Plavno HR 138 A2
Playben F 100 A2
Pléaux F 116 B2
Pleine-Fourgères F 88 B2
Pleinfeld D 94 B2
Pleinting D 95 C5
Plélan-le-Grand F .101 B3
Plémet F 101 A3
Pléneuf-Val-André
F 101 A3
Plentzia E 143 A4
Plérin F 101 A3
Plešivec SK 99 C4
Plessa D 83 A5
Plessé F 101 B4
Plestin-les-Grèves
F 100 A2
Pleszew PL 76 C2
Pleternica HR 125 B3
Plettenberg D 81 A3
Pleubian F 100 A2
Pleumartin F 115 B4
Pleumeur-Bodou
F 100 A2
Pleurs F 91 C3
Pleven BG 17 D6
Plevnik-Drienové
SK 98 B2
Pleyber-Christ F . .100 A2
Pliego E 165 B3
Pliešovce SK 99 C3
Plitvička Jezera
HR 123 C4
Plitvički Ljeskovac
HR 123 C4
Ploaghe I 178 B2
Ploče HR 138 B3
Plochingen D 94 C1
Płock PL 77 B4
Ploemeur F 100 B2
Ploërmel F 101 B3
Ploeuc-sur-Lie F . .101 A3
Plogastel St Germain
F 100 B1
Plogoff F 100 A1
Ploieşti RO 17 C7
Plomari GR 186 D1
Plombières-les-Bains
F 105 B5
Plomin HR 123 B3
Plön D 65 B3
Plonéour-Lanvern
F 100 B1
Płonia PL 74 A3
Płoniawy PL 77 B6
Płońsk PL 77 B5
Płoskinia PL 69 A4
Plössberg D 95 B4
Płoty PL 67 C4
Plouagat F 100 A2
Plouaret F 100 A2
Plouarzel F 100 A1
Plouay F 100 B2
Ploubalay F 101 A3
Ploubazlanec F . . .100 A2
Ploudalmézeau F .100 A1
Ploudiry F 100 A1
Plouescat F 100 A1
Plouézec F 100 A3
Plougasnou F 100 A2
Plougastel-Daoulas
F 100 A1
Plougonven F 100 A2
Plougonver F 100 A2
Plougrescant F . . .100 A2
Ploguenast F 101 A3
Plouguerneau F . .100 A1
Plouha F 100 A3
Plouhinec F 100 A1
Plouigneau F 100 A2
Ploumanach F 100 A2
Plounévez-Quintin
F 100 A2
Plouray F 100 A2
Plouzévédé F 100 A1
Plovdiv BG 183 A6
Plozévet F 100 B1
Plumbridge GB 27 B3
Pluméliau F 100 B3
Plumlov CZ 97 B5
Plungė LT 8 E2
Pluty PL 69 A5
Pluvigner F 100 B3
Plužine
BIH 139 B4
MNE 139 B4
Płuznica PL 69 B3
Plymouth GB 42 B2
Plymstock GB 42 B2
Płytnica PL 68 B1
Plyusa RUS 9 C6
Plzeň CZ 96 B1
Pniewy PL 75 B5
Pobes E 143 B4
Poběžovice CZ 95 B4
Pobiedziska PL 76 B2
Pobierowo PL 67 B3
Pobla de Segur E .145 B4
Pobladura del Valle
E 142 B1
Pobla-Tornesa E . .153 B4
Pobra de Trives E .141 B3
Pobra do Brollón
E 141 B3
Pobra do Caramiñal
E 140 B2
Pobudje BIH 139 A5
Počátky CZ 97 B3
Poceirão P 154 C2
Pöchlarn A 110 A2
Pociecha PL 87 A4
Pockau D 83 B5
Pocking D 96 C1
Pocklington GB 40 B3
Podbořany CZ 83 B5
Podbrdo SLO 122 A2
Podbrezová SK 99 C3
Podčetrtek SLO . . .123 A4
Poddębice PL 76 C3
Poděbrady CZ 84 B3
Podence P 149 A3
Podensac F 128 B2
Podenzano I 120 C2
Podersdorf am See
A 111 B3
Podgaje PL 68 B1
Podgora HR 138 B3
Podgóra PL 87 A5
Podgorač HR 125 B4
Podgorica MNE 16 D3
Podgorie AL 182 C2
Podgrad SLO 123 B3
Podhájska SK 112 A2
Podkova BG 183 B7
Podlapača HR 123 C4
Podlejki PL 69 B5
Podlužany SK 98 C2
Podnovlje BIH 125 C4
Podolie SK 98 C1
Podolínec SK 99 B4
Podolsk RUS 9 E10
Podporozhy RUS . . .9 B9
Podromanija BIH . .139 B4
Podturen HR 111 C3
Podvín CZ 97 C4
Podwilk PL 99 B3
Poetto I 179 C3
Poggendorf D 66 B2
Poggiardo I 173 B4
Poggibonsi I 135 B4
Póggio a Caiano I .135 B4
Poggio Imperiale I 171 B3
Póggio Mirteto I . . .168 A2
Póggio Moiano I . . .169 A2
Póggio Renatico I 121 C4
Póggio Rusco I . . .121 C4
Pöggstall A 97 C3
Pogny F 91 C4
Pogorzela PL 85 A5
Pogorzelice PL 68 A2
Pogradec AL 182 C2
Pogrodzie PL 69 A4
Pohorelá SK 99 C4
Pohořelice CZ 97 C4
Pohronská Polhora
SK 99 C3
Poiares P 148 B1
Poio E 140 B2
Poirino I 119 C4
Poisson F 117 A4
Poissons F 91 C5
Poissy F 90 C2
Poitiers F 115 B4
Poix-de-Picardie F .90 B1
Poix-Terron F 91 B4
Pokka FIN 197 A8
Pokój PL 86 B1
Pokupsko HR 124 B1
Pol E 141 A3
Pola RUS 9 D7
Pol a Charra GB . . .31 B1
Pola de Allande E .141 A4
Pola de Laviana E 142 A1
Pola de Lena E 141 A5
Pola de Siero E . . .142 A1
Pola de Somiedo
E 141 A4
Polaincourt-et-
Clairefontaine F .105 B5
Połajewo PL 75 B5
Polán E 151 C3
Polanica-Zdrój PL . .85 B4
Połaniec PL 87 B5
Polanów PL 68 A1
Polatlı TR 187 C7
Polatsk BY 13 A8
Polch D 80 B3
Polcirkeln S 196 C4
Pólczno PL 68 A2
Połczyn-Zdrój PL . . .67 C5
Polegate GB 45 C4
Poleñino E 145 C3
Polesella I 121 C4
Polessk RUS 12 A4
Polgár H 113 B5
Polgárdi H 112 B2
Polhov Gradec
SLO 123 A3
Police PL 74 A3
Police nad Metují
CZ 85 B4
Polichnitos GR 186 C1
Polička CZ 97 B4
Poličnik HR 137 A4
Policoro I 174 A2
Policzna PL 87 A5
Poligiros GR 183 C5
Polignano a Mare
I 173 B3
Poligny F 105 C4
Polis CY 181 A1
Polistena I 175 C2
Polizzi Generosa I 176 B3
Poljana SRB 127 C3
Poljanák HR 123 C4
Poljčane SLO 123 A4
Polje BIH 125 C3
Poljice
BIH 138 A2
BIH 139 A4
Polkowice PL 85 A4
Polla I 172 B1
Pollas E 150 A2
Pöllau A 110 B2
Polleben D 82 A3
Pollença E 167 B3
Pollenfeld D 95 C3
Pollfoss N 198 D4
Póllica I 170 C3
Polminhac F 116 C2
Polná CZ 97 B3
Polna RUS 8 C6
Polne PL 75 A5
Polomka SK 99 C3
Polonne UA 13 C7
Polperro GB 42 B2
Polruan GB 42 B2
Pöls A 110 B1
Polska Cerekiew
PL 86 B2
Poltár SK 99 C3
Põltsamaa EST 8 C4
Polyarny RUS 3 B13
Polyarnyye Zori
RUS 3 C13
Polzela SLO 123 A4
Pomarance I 135 B3
Pomarez F 128 C2
Pomárico I 172 B2
Pomáz H 112 B3
Pombal P 154 B2
Pomeroy GB 27 B4
Pomézia I 168 B2
Pommard F 105 B3
Pommelsbrunn D . . .95 B3
Pomonte I 134 C3
Pomorie BG 17 D7
Pomos CY 181 A1
Pompei I 170 C2
Pompey F 92 C2
Pomposa I 122 C1
Poncin F 118 A2
Pondorf D 95 C3
Ponferrada E 141 B4
Poniec PL 85 A4
Ponikva SLO 123 A4
Poniky SK 99 C3
Pons F 114 C3
Ponsacco I 134 B3
Pont I 119 B4
Pont-a-Celles B 79 B4
Pontacq F 145 A3
Pontailler-sur-Saône
F 105 B4
Pont-a-Marcq F 78 B3
Pont-à-Mousson F .92 C2
Pontão P 154 B2
Pontardawe GB 39 C3
Pontarddulais GB . .39 C2
Pontarion F 116 B1
Pontarlier F 105 C5
Pontassieve I 135 B4
Pontaubault F 88 B2
Pont-Audemer F . . .89 A4
Pontaumur F 116 B2
Pont-Aven F 100 B2
Pont Canavese I . .119 B4
Pontcharra F 118 B3
Pontcharra-sur-Turdine
F 117 B4
Pontchâteau F 101 B3
Pont-Croix F 100 A1
Pont-d'Ain F 118 A2
Pont-de-Beauvoisin
F 118 B2
Pont-de-Buis-lès-
Quimerch F 100 A1
Pont-de-Chéruy F 118 B2
Pont de Dore F . . .117 B3
Pont-de-Labeaume
F 117 C4
Pont-de-l'Arche F . .89 A5
Pont de Molins E . .147 B3
Pont-de-Roide F . .106 B1
Pont-de-Salars F . .130 A1
Pont-d'Espagne F 145 B3
Pont de Suert E . . .145 B4
Pont-de-Vaux F . . .117 A4
Pont-de-Veyle F . . .117 A4
Pont d'Ouilly F 89 B3
Pont-du-Château
F 116 B3
Pont-du-Navoy F . .105 C4
Ponte a Moriano I .134 B3
Ponte Arche I 121 A3
Ponteareas E 140 B2
Pontebba I 109 C4
Ponte Cáffaro I . . .121 B3
Pontecagnano I . . .170 C2
Ponte-Caldelas E .140 B2
Ponteceso E 140 A2
Pontecesures E . . .140 B2
Pontecorvo I 169 B3
Ponte da Barca P .148 A1
Pontedássio I 133 B4
Pontedécimo I 133 A4
Ponte de Lima P . .148 A1
Ponte dell'Ólio I . .120 C2
Pontedera I 134 B3
Ponte de Sor P . . .154 B2
Pontedeume E 140 A2
Ponte di Barbarano
I 121 B4
Ponte di Legno I . .121 A3
Ponte di Nava I . . .133 A3
Ponte di Piave I . . .122 B1
Ponte Felcino I . . .136 B1
Pontefract GB 40 B2
Ponte Gardena I . .108 C2
Ponteginori I 135 B3
Pontelagoscuro I .121 C4
Ponteland GB 37 A5
Pontelandolfo I . . .170 B2
Ponte-Leccia F . . .180 A2
Pontelongo I 121 B5
Ponte nelle Alpi I . .122 A1
Pont-en-Royans F 118 B2
Pontenure I 120 C2
Pontenx-les-Forges
F 128 B1
Ponterwyd GB 39 B3
Ponte San Giovanni
I 136 B1
Ponte San Pietro I 120 B2
Pontevedra E 140 B2
Pontevico I 120 B3
Pont Farcy F 88 B2
Pontfaverger-
Moronvillers F . . .91 B4
Pontgibaud F 116 B2
Ponticino I 135 B4
Pontigny F 104 B2
Pontijou F 103 B3
Pontínia I 169 B3
Pontinvrea I 133 A4
Pontivy F 100 A3
Pont-l'Abbé F 100 B1
Pont-l'Évêque F . . .89 A4
Pontlevoy F 103 B3
Pontoise F 90 B2
Pontones E 164 A2
Pontonx-sur-l'Abour
F 128 C2
Pontoon IRL 26 C1
Pontorson F 88 B2
Pontrémoli I 134 A2
Pont-Remy F 90 A1
Pontresina CH 107 C4
Pontrhydfendigaid
GB 39 B3
Pontrieux F 100 A2
Ponts E 147 C2
Ponts-aux-Dames
F 90 C2
Pont Scorff F 100 B2
Pöntsö FIN 196 B7
Pont-Ste Maxence
F 90 B2
Pont-St Esprit F . .131 A3
Pont-St Mamet F . .129 B3
Pont-St Martin
F 101 B4
I 119 B4
Pont-St Vincent F . .92 C2
Pont-sur-Yonne F .104 A2
Pontvallain F 102 B2
Pontypool GB 39 C3
Pontypridd GB 39 C3
Ponza I 169 C2
Poo E 142 A2
Poole GB 43 B5
Poolewe GB 31 B3
Poperinge B 78 B2
Pópoli I 169 A3
Popovac SRB 127 D3
Popovača HR 124 B2
Popow PL 77 B4
Poppel B 79 A5
Poppenhausen
Bayern D 82 B2
Hessen D 82 B1
Poppi I 135 B4
Poprad SK 99 B4
Popučke SRB 127 C1
Pópulo P 148 A2
Populónia I 134 C3
Pörböly H 125 A4
Porcuna E 163 A3
Pordenone I 122 B1
Pordic F 100 A3
Poręba PL 86 B3
Poreč HR 122 B2
Pori FIN 8 B2
Porjus S 196 C2
Porkhov RUS 9 D6
Porlezza I 120 A2
Porlock GB 43 A3
Pörnbach D 95 C3
Pornic F 101 B3
Pornichet F 101 B3
Porodin SRB 127 C3
Poronin PL 99 B3
Poros
Attiki GR 185 B4
Kefalonia GR 184 A1
Poroszló H 113 B4
Porozina HR 123 B3
Porquerolles F . . .132 C2
Porrentruy CH 106 B2
Porreres E 167 B3
Porretta Terme I . .135 A3
Porsgrunn N 53 A5
Porspoder F 100 A1
Port-a-Binson F 91 B3
Portacloy IRL 26 B1
Portadown GB 27 B4
Portaferry GB 27 B5
Portaje E 155 B4
Portalegre P 155 B3
Portarlington IRL . . .30 A1
Port Askaig GB 34 C1
Portavadie GB 34 C2
Portavogie GB 27 B5
Portbail F 88 A2
Port Bannatyne GB 34 C2
Port-Barcarès F . . .146 B4
Portbou E 146 B4
Port-Camargue F .131 B3
Port Charlotte GB . .34 C1
Port d'Andratx E . .166 B2
Port-de-Bouc F . . .131 B3
Port-de-Lanne F . .128 C1
Port de Pollença
E 167 B3
Port-des-Barques
F 114 C2
Port de Sóller E . . .166 B2
Portegrandi I 122 B1
Portel P 155 C3
Portela P 148 B1
Port Ellen GB 34 C1
Portelo P 141 C4
Portemouro E 140 B2
Port-en-Bessin F . . .88 A3
Port'Ercole I 168 A1
Port Erin GB 36 B2
Portes-lès-Valence
F 117 C4
Portets F 128 B2
Port Eynon GB 39 C2
Portezuelo E 155 B4
Port Glasgow GB . .34 C3
Portglenone GB . . .27 B4
Porthcawl GB 39 C3
Port Henderson GB 31 B3
Porthleven GB 42 B1
Porthmadog GB . . .38 B2
Porticcio F 180 B1
Portici I 170 C2
Portico di Romagna
I 135 A4
Portilla de la Reina
E 142 A2
Portillo E 150 A3
Portimao P 160 B1
Portinatx E 166 B1
Portinho da Arrabida
P 154 C1
Port Isaac GB 42 B2
Portishead GB 43 A4
Port-Joinville F . . .114 B1
Portknockie GB 33 D4
Port-la-Nouvelle F 130 B2
Portlaoise IRL 30 A1
Portlethen GB 33 D4
Port Logan GB 36 B2
Port Louis F 100 B2
Portmagne IRL 29 C1
Portmahomack GB 32 D3
Portman E 165 B4
Port Manech F 100 B2
Portnacroish GB . . .34 B2
Portnahaven GB . . .34 C1
Port Nan Giuran
GB 31 A2
Port-Navalo F 100 B3
Port Nis GB 31 A2
Porto
F 180 A1
P 148 A1
Porto-Alto P 154 C2
Porto Azzurro I . . .134 C3
Portocannone I . . .170 B3
Porto Cerésio I . . .120 B1
Porto Cervo I 178 A3
Porto Cesáreo I . . .173 B3
Porto Colom E 167 B3
Porto Covo P 160 B1
Porto Cristo E 167 B3
Porto d'Áscoli I . . .136 C2
Porto de Lagos P .160 B1
Porto de Mos P . . .154 B2
Porto de Rei P 154 C2
Porto do Son E . . .140 B2
Porto Empédocle
I 176 B2
Portoferráio I 134 C3
Portofino I 134 A2
Porto Garibaldi I . .122 C1
Portogruaro I 122 B1
Portokhelion GR . .184 B4
Portomaggiore I . .121 C4
Portomarin E 140 B3
Porton GB 44 B2
Portonovo E 140 B2

Portopalo di Capo
Passero I 177 C4
Porto Petro E 167 B3
Porto Pino I 179 D2
Porto Potenza Picena
I 136 B2
Portør N 53 B5
Porto Recanati I 136 B2
Porto San Giórgio
I 136 B2
Porto Sant'Elpídio
I 136 B2
Porto Santo Stéfano
I 168 A1
Portoscuso I 179 C2
Porto Tolle I 122 C1
Porto Tórres I 178 B2
Porto-Vécchio F . . .180 B2
Portovénere I 134 A2
Portpatrick GB 36 B1
Portreath GB 42 B1
Portree GB 31 B2
Portroe IRL 28 B3
Portrush GB 27 A4
Port St Mary GB 36 B2
Portsall F 100 A1
Portsmouth GB 44 C2
Portsoy GB 33 D4
Port-Ste Marie F . . .129 B3
Portstewart GB 27 A4
Port-St-Louis-du-
Rhône F 131 B3
Port-sur-Saône F . .105 B5
Port Talbot GB 39 C3
Portugalete E 143 A4
Portumna IRL 28 A3
Port-Vendres F 146 B4
Port William GB 36 B2
Porvoo FIN 8 B4
Porzuna E 157 A3
Posada
Oviedo E 141 A5
Oviedo E 142 A2
I 178 B3
Posada de Valdeón
E 142 A2
Posadas E 162 A2
Poschiavo CH 120 A3
Posedarje HR 137 A4
Posio FIN 197 C11
Positano I 170 C2
Possagno I 121 B4
Posseck D 83 B4
Possesse F 91 C4
Pössneck D 83 B3
Posta I 169 A3
Postal I 108 C2
Posta Piana I 172 A1
Postbauer-Heng D . .95 B3
Posterholt NL 80 A2
Postioma I 121 B5
Postira HR 138 B2
Postojna SLO 123 B3
Postoloprty CZ 84 B1
Postomino PL 68 A1
Posušje BIH 138 B3
Potamos
Attiki GR 184 C3
Attiki GR 184 D4
Potegowo PL 68 A2
Potenza I 172 B1
Potenza Picena I . . .136 B2
Potes E 142 A2
Potigny F 89 B3
Potočari BIH 127 C1
Potoci
BIH 138 A2
BIH 139 B3
Potony H 125 B3
Potries E 159 C3
Potsdam D 74 B2
Potštát CZ 98 B1
Pottenbrunn A 110 A2
Pottendorf A 111 B3
Pottenstein
A 111 B3
D 95 B3
Potters Bar GB 44 B3
Pöttmes D 94 C3
Pöttsching A 111 B3
Potworów PL 87 A4
Pouancé F 101 B4
Pougues-les-Eaux
F 104 B2
Pouilly-en-Auxois
F 104 B3
Pouilly-sous Charlieu
F 117 A4
Pouilly-sur-Loire
F 104 B1
Poujol-sur-Orb F . .130 B2
Poullaouen F 100 A2
Poulton-le-Fylde
GB 38 A4
Poundstock GB 42 B2
Pourcy F 91 B3
Pourrain F 104 B2
Poussu FIN 197 D12
Pouyastruc F 145 A4
Pouy-de-Touges
F 146 A2
Pouzauges F 114 B3
Pova de Santa Iria
P 154 C1
Považská Bystrica
SK 98 B2
Povedilla E 158 C1
Povenets RUS 9 A9
Povlja HR 138 B2
Povljana HR 137 A4
Póvoa
Beja P 161 A2
Santarém P 154 B2
Póvoa de Lanhoso
P 148 A1
Póvoa de Varzim
P 148 A1
Póvoa e Meadas
P 155 B3
Powidz PL 76 B2

Poyales del Hoyo
E 150 B2
Poynton GB 40 B1
Poyntz Pass GB 27 B4
Poysdorf A 97 C4
Poza de la Sal E . . .143 B3
Pozaldez E 150 A3
Pozán de Vero E . . .145 B4
Pozanti TR 23 C8
Požarevac SRB 127 C3
Požega
HR 125 B3
SRB 127 D2
Poznań PL 76 B1
Pozo Alcón E 164 B2
Pozoantiguo E 150 A2
Pozoblanco E 156 B3
Pozo Cañada E 158 C2
Pozo de Guadalajara
E 151 B4
Pozo de la Serna
E 157 B4
Pozohondo E 158 C2
Pozondón E 152 B2
Pożrzadło Wielkie
PL 75 A4
Pozuel del Campo
E 152 B2
Pozuelo de Alarcón
E 151 B4
Pozuelo de Calatrava
E 157 B4
Pozuelo del Páramo
E 142 B1
Pozuelo de Zarzón
E 149 B3
Pozzallo I 177 C3
Pozzomaggiore I . . .178 B2
Pozzo San Nicola
I 178 B2
Pozzuoli I 170 C2
Pozzuolo I 135 B4
Prabuty PL 69 B4
Prača BIH 139 B4
Prachatice CZ 96 B1
Prada E 141 B3
Pradelle F 118 C2
Pradelles F 117 C3
Prades
E 147 C1
F 146 B3
Pradła PL 86 B3
Prado
E 142 A1
P 148 A1
Prado del Rey E . . .162 B2
Pradoluengo E 143 B3
Pragelato I 119 B3
Pragersko SLO 123 A4
Prägraten A 109 B3
Prague = Praha CZ .84 B2
Praha = Prague CZ .84 B2
Prahecq F 115 B3
Praia P 154 B1
Práia a Mare I 174 B1
Praia da Rocha P . .160 B1
Praia da Viera P . . .154 B2
Praia de Mira P 148 B1
Praiano I 170 C2
Pralboino I 120 B3
Pralognan-la-Vanoise
F 118 B3
Pramanda GR 182 D3
Pranjani SRB 127 C2
Prapatnica HR 138 B2
Præstø DK 65 A5
Praszka PL 86 A2
Prat F 146 A1
Prata I 135 B3
Prata di Pordenone
I 122 B1
Pratau D 83 A4
Prat de Compte E . .153 B4
Pratdip E 147 C1
Pratella I 170 B2
Prato I 135 B4
Prátola Peligna I . . .169 A3
Pratola Serra I 170 C2
Prats-de-Mollo-la-
Preste F 146 B3
Prauthoy F 105 B4
Pravia E 141 A4
Praxmar A 108 B2
Prayssac F 129 B4
Prazzo I 132 A3
Prebold SLO 123 A4
Préchac F 128 B2
Précy-sur-Thil F . . .104 B3
Predappio I 135 A4
Predazzo I 121 A4
Předín CZ 97 B3
Preding A 110 C2
Predjame SLO 123 B3
Predlitz A 109 B4
Predmeja SLO 122 B2
Predoi I 108 B3
Pré-en-Pail F 89 B3
Prees GB 38 B4
Preetz D 64 B3
Préfailles F 101 B3
Pregarten A 96 C2
Pregrada HR 123 A4
Preignan F 129 C3
Preili LV 8 D5
Preitenegg A 110 C1
Prekaja BIH 138 A2
Preko HR 137 B4
Preločac CZ 97 B4
Prelošćica HR 124 B2
Prem SLO 123 B3
Premantura HR 122 C2
Prémery F 104 B2
Prémia I 119 A5
Premià de Mar E . . .147 C3
Premnitz D 73 B5
Prémont F 91 A3
Prenzlau D 74 A2
Preodac BIH 138 A2

Přerov CZ 98 B1
Prerow D 66 B1
Presencio E 143 B3
Presicce I 173 C4
Presly F 103 B4
Pressac F 115 B4
Pressath D 95 B3
Pressbaum A 111 A3
Prestatyn GB 38 A3
Prestebakke N 54 B2
Presteigne GB 39 B3
Přeštice CZ 96 B1
Preston
Lancashire GB . . .38 A4
Scottish Borders
GB 35 C5
Prestonpans GB 35 C5
Prestwick GB 36 A2
Prettin D 83 A4
Preturo I 169 A3
Pretzchendorf D 83 B5
Pretzier D 73 B4
Pretzsch D 83 A4
Preuilly-sur-Claise
F 115 B4
Prevalje SLO 110 C1
Prevenchères F 131 A2
Préveranges F 116 A2
Preveza GR 182 E2
Prevršac HR 124 B2
Prezid HR 123 B3
Priaranza del Bierzo
E 141 B4
Priay F 118 A2
Pribeta SK 112 B2
Priboj
BIH 125 C4
SRB 16 D3
Příbor CZ 98 B2
Příbram CZ 96 B2
Pribylina SK 99 B3
Přibyslav CZ 97 B3
Pričević SRB 127 C1
Pridjel BIH 125 C4
Priego E 152 B1
Priego de Córdoba
E 163 A3
Priekule LV 8 D2
Prien D 109 B3
Prienai LT 13 A5
Prievidza SK 98 C2
Prigradica HR 138 C2
Prigrevica SRB 125 B5
Prijeboj HR 123 C4
Prijedor BIH 124 C2
Prijepolje SRB 16 D3
Prilep MK 182 B3
Priluka BIH 138 B2
Primda CZ 95 B4
Primel-Trégastel
F 100 A2
Primišje HR 123 B4
Primorsk
Kaliningrad RUS . .69 A5
Severo-Zapadnyy
RUS 9 B6
Primošten HR 138 B1
Primstal D 92 B2
Princes Risborough
GB 44 B3
Princetown GB 42 B2
Principina a Mare
I 135 C4
Priolo Gargallo I . . .177 B4
Prioro E 142 B2
Priozersk RUS 9 B7
Prirechnyy RUS .193 C14
Prisoje BIH 138 B3
Priština KOS 16 D4
Pritzerbe D 73 B5
Pritzier D 73 A4
Pritzwalk D 73 A5
Privas F 117 C4
Priverno I 169 B3
Privlaka
Vukovarsko-
Srijemska HR . . .125 B4
Zadarska HR 137 A4
Prizna HR 123 C3
Prizren KOS 16 D4
Prizzi I 176 B2
Prnjavor
BIH 125 C3
HR 124 B1
SRB 127 C1
Proaza E 141 A4
Probstzella D 82 B3
Probus GB 42 B2
Prócchio I 134 C3
Prochowice PL 85 A4
Prócida I 170 C2
Prodhromos CY 181 B1
Prodo I 135 C5
Proença-a-Nova P 154 B3
Proença-a-Velha
P 155 A3
Profondeville B 79 B4
Prokuplje SRB 16 D4
Propriano F 180 B1
Prosec CZ 97 B4
Prösen D 83 A5
Prosenjakovci
SLO 111 C3
Prosotsani GR 183 B5
Prostějov CZ 98 B1
Prószków PL 86 B1
Proszowice PL 87 B4
Protić BIH 138 A2
Protivanov CZ 97 B4
Protivín CZ 96 B2
Prötzel D 74 B2
Provins F 90 C3
Prozor BIH 139 B3
Prrenjas AL 182 B2
Prudhoe GB 37 B5
Prudnik PL 85 B5
Pruggern A 109 B4
Prügy H 113 A5
Prüm D 80 B2

Pruna E 162 B2
Prunelli-di-Fiumorbo
F 180 A2
Prunetta I 135 A3
Pruniers F 103 C4
Prusice PL 85 A4
Pruské SK 98 B2
Pruszcz Gdański
PL 69 A3
Pruszków PL 77 B5
Prutz A 108 B1
Prüzen D 65 C5
Pruzhany BY 13 B6
Pružina SK 98 B2
Pürvomay BG 183 A7
Przasnysz PL 77 A5
Przechlewo PL 68 B2
Przecław PL 87 B5
Przedbórz PL 87 A3
Przedecz PL 76 B3
Przejęslav PL 84 A3
Przemków PL 85 A3
Przemocze PL 75 A3
Przemyśl PL 12 D5
Przerąb PL 87 A3
Przewodnik PL 69 B3
Przewodowo Parcele
PL 77 B5
Przewóz PL 84 A2
Przezmark PL 69 B4
Przodkowo PL 68 A3
Przybiernów PL 75 A3
Przyborowice PL . . .77 B5
Przybyszew PL 87 A4
Przybyszów PL 86 A3
Przylęg PL 75 B4
Przysucha PL 87 A4
Przytoczna PL 75 B4
Przytyk PL 87 A4
Przywidz PL 68 A3
Psachna GR 185 A4
Psara GR 185 A6
Psary PL 76 C3
Pskov RUS 8 C6
Pszczew PL 75 B4
Pszczółki PL 69 A3
Pszczyna PL 98 B2
Pszów PL 86 B2
Pteleos GR 182 D4
Ptolemaida GR 182 C3
Ptuj SLO 124 A1
Ptusza PL 68 B1
Puch A 109 B4
Puchberg am
Schneeberg A . . .110 B2
Puchevillers F 90 A2
Puchheim D 108 A2
Púchov SK 98 B2
Pučišća HR 138 B2
Puck PL 69 A3
Puçol E 159 B3
Puconci SLO 111 C3
Pudasjärvi FIN 197 D10
Puderbach D 81 B3
Pudozh RUS 9 B10
Puebla de Albortón
E 153 A3
Puebla de Alcocer
E 156 B2
Puebla de Beleña
E 151 B4
Puebla de Don
Fadrique E 164 B2
Puebla de Don Rodrigo
E 156 A3
Puebla de Guzmán
E 161 B2
Puebla de la Calzada
E 155 C4
Puebla de la Reina
E 156 B1
Puebla de Lillo E . . .142 A1
Puebla del Maestre
E 161 A3
Puebla del Principe
E 158 C1
Puebla de Obando
E 155 B4
Puebla de Sanabria
E 141 B4
Puebla de Sancho
Pérez E 155 C4
Puente Almuhey
E 142 B2
Puente de Domingo
Flórez E 141 B4
Puente de Génave
E 164 A2
Puente del Congosto
E 150 B2
Puente de Montañana
E 145 B4
Puente Duero E 150 A3
Puente-Genil E 162 A3
Puente la Reina E .144 B2
Puente la Reina de
Jaca E 144 B3
Puentelarrá E 143 B4
Puente Mayorga E .162 B2
Puente Viesgo E . . .143 A3
Puertas
Asturias E 142 A2
Salamanca E 149 A3
Puerto de Mazarrón
E 165 B3
Puerto de Santa Cruz
E 156 A2
Puerto de San Vicente
E 156 A2
Puerto-Lápice E . . .157 A4
Puertollano E 157 B3
Puerto Lumbreras
E 164 B3
Puerto Moral E 161 B3
Puerto Real E 162 B1
Puerto Rey E 157 A4
Puerto Seguro E . . .149 B3
Puerto Serrano E . .162 B2

Puget-Sur-Argens
F 132 B2
Puget-Théniers F .132 B2
Puget-ville F 132 B2
Pugnochiuso I 171 B4
Puigcerdà E 146 B2
Puig Reig E 147 C2
Puillon F 128 C2
Puimichel F 132 B2
Puimoisson F 132 B2
Puiseaux F 103 A4
Puisieux F 90 A2
Puisserguier F 130 B2
Puivert F 146 B3
Pujols E 128 B2
Pukanec SK 98 C2
Pukavik S 63 B2
Pukë AL 182 A1
Pula
HR 122 C2
I 179 C2
Puławy PL 12 C4
Pulborough GB 44 C3
Pulfero I 122 A2
Pulgar E 157 A3
Pulheim D 80 A2
Pulkau A 97 C3
Pulpi E 164 B3
Pulsano I 173 B3
Pulsnitz D 84 A2
Pułtusk PL 77 B6
Pumpsaint GB 39 B3
Punat HR 123 B3
Punta Marina I 135 A5
Punta Prima E 167 B4
Punta Sabbioni I . . .122 B1
Puntas de Calnegre
E 165 B3
Punta Umbria E 161 B3
Puolanka FIN 3 D10
Puoltikasvaara S .196 B4
Puoltsa S 196 B2
Puračić BIH 125 C4
Purbach am Neusiedler
See A 111 B3
Purchena E 164 B2
Purfleet GB 45 B4
Purgstall A 110 A2
Purkersdorf A 111 A3
Purmerend NL 70 B1
Purullena E 164 B1
Pushkin RUS 9 C7
Pushkino RUS 9 D10
Püspökladány H . . .113 B5
Pusté Ulany SK 111 A4
Pustoshka RUS 9 D6
Puszcza Mariańska
PL 77 C5
Puszczykowo PL . . .76 B1
Pusztamagyaród
H 111 C3
Pusztamonostor
H 113 B3
Pusztaszabolcs H 112 B2
Pusztavám H 112 B2
Putanges-Pont-Ecrepin
F 89 B3
Putbus D 66 B2
Putignano I 173 B3
Putlitz D 73 A5
Putnok H 99 C4
Putte B 79 A4
Puttelange-aux-Lacs
F 92 B2
Putten NL 70 B2
Puttgarden D 65 B4
Püttlingen D 92 B2
Putzu Idu I 179 B2
Puy-Guillaume F . . .117 B3
Puylaroque F 129 B4
Puylaurens F 146 A3
Puy-l'Évêque F 129 B4
Puymirol F 129 B3
Puyôo F 128 C2
Puyrolland F 114 B3
Pwllheli GB 38 B2
Pyetrikaw BY 13 B8
Pyhäjärvi FIN 3 E9
Pyhäkylä FIN 197 D11
Pyla CY 181 A2
Pyla-sur-Mer F 128 B1
Pyrzyce PL 75 A3
Pysely CZ 96 B2
Pyskowice PL 86 B2
Pytalovo RUS 8 D5
Pyzdry PL 76 B2

Quakenbrück D 71 B4
Quargnento I 119 C5
Quarré-les-Tombes
F 104 B2
Quarteira P 160 B1
Quartu Sant'Elena
I 179 C3
Quatre-Champs F . .91 B4
Quedlinburg D 82 A3
Queensferry
Edinburgh GB . . .35 C4
Flintshire GB 38 A3
Queige F 118 B3
Queipo E 161 B3
Queixans E 146 B2
Quel E 144 B1
Quelaines-St-Gault
F 102 B1
Queljada E 148 A1
Quemada E 143 C3
Queralbs E 147 B3
Quercianella I 134 B3
Querfurt D 82 A3
Quérigut F 146 B3
Querndorf D . . . .
Radicófani I 135 C4
Radicóndoli I 135 B4
Radışeni BIH 138 B3
Radizel SLO 110 C2
Radków PL 85 B4

Pruna E . . . .
Questembert F . . .101 B3
Quettehou F 88 A2
Quevauvillers F 90 B2
Quevy B 79 B4
Quiaios P 148 B1
Quiberon F 100 B2
Quiberville F 89 A4
Quickborn D 64 C2
Quiévrain B 79 B3
Quillan F 146 B3
Quillebeuf F 89 A4
Quimper F 100 A1
Quimperlé F 100 B2
Quincampoix F 89 A5
Quincoces de Yuso
E 143 B3
Quincy F 103 B4
Quinéville F 88 A2
Quingey F 105 B4
Quinson F 132 B2
Quinssaines F 116 A2
Quinta-Grande P . . .154 C2
Quintana de la Serena
E 156 B2
Quintana del Castillo
E 141 B4
Quintana del Marco
E 141 B5
Quintana del Puenta
E 142 B2
Quintana-Martin
Galindez E 143 B3
Quintanaortuño E 143 B3
Quintanapalla E . . .143 B3
Quintanar de la Orden
E 157 A4
Quintanar de la Sierra
E 143 C3
Quintanar del Rey
E 158 B2
Quintanilla de la Mata
E 143 C3
Quintanilla del Coco
E 143 C3
Quintanilla de Onésimo
E 150 A3
Quintanilla de Somoza
E 141 B4
Quintas de Valdelucio
E 142 B2
Quintela P 148 B2
Quintin F 100 A3
Quinto E 153 A3
Quinzano d'Oglio
I 120 B3
Quiroga E 141 B3
Quismondo E 150 B3
Quissac F 131 B2
Quistello I 121 B3

Raab A 96 C1
Raabs an der Thaya
A 97 C3
Raahe FIN 3 D9
Raajärvi FIN 197 C9
Raalte NL 71 B3
Raamsdonksveer
NL 79 A4
Raanujarvi FIN 196 C7
Raattama FIN 196 A7
Rab HR 123 C3
Rabac HR 123 B3
Rábade E 140 A3
Rábafüzes H 111 C3
Rábahidvég H 111 B3
Rabanales E 149 A3
Rabapatona H 111 B4
Rabapordány H 111 B4
Rabastens F 129 C4
Rabastens-de-Bigorre
F 145 A4
Rabat = Victoria
M 175 C3
Rabat M 175 C3
Rabča SK 99 B3
Rabe SRB 126 A2
Rabi CZ 96 B1
Rabino PL 67 C4
Rabka PL 99 B3
Rabrovo SRB 127 C3
Rača SRB 127 C2
Rácale I 173 C4
Rácalmás H 112 B2
Racalmuto I 176 B2
Race SLO 110 C2
Rachecourt-sur-Marne
F 91 C5
Raciąż PL 77 B5
Racibórz PL 86 B2
Račinovci HR 125 C4
Ráckeve H 112 B2
Racławice PL 87 B4
Racławice Śląskie
PL 86 B1
Racot PL 75 B5
Råda
Skaraborg S 55 B4
Värmland S 49 B5
Radalj SRB 127 C1
Rădăuţi RO 17 B6
Radda in Chianti I .135 B4
Raddusa I 177 B3
Radeberg D 84 A1
Radeburg D 84 A1
Radeče SLO 123 A4
Radekhiv UA 13 C6
Radenci SLO 111 C3
Radenthein A 109 C4
Radevormwald D . . .80 A3
Radicófani I 135 C4
Radicóndoli I 135 B4
Radišići BIH 138 B3
Radizel SLO 110 C2
Radków PL 85 B4

Radlje ob Dravi
SLO 110 C2
Radlów PL 87 B4
Radmer an der Stube
A 110 B1
Radnejaur S 195 E9
Radnice CZ 96 B1
Radohova BIH 138 A3
Radojevo SRB 126 B2
Radolfzell D 107 B3
Radom PL 87 A5
Radomice PL 77 B4
Radomin PL 77 A4
Radomsko PL 86 A3
Radomyshl UA 13 C8
Radomyśl Wielki
PL 87 B5
Radošina SK 98 C1
Radošovce SK 98 C1
Radotin CZ 96 B2
Radovets BG 186 A1
Radoviš MK 182 B4
Radovljica SLO 123 A3
Radowo Wielkie PL 75 A4
Radstadt A 109 B4
Radstock GB 43 A4
Raduc HR 137 A4
Raduša MK 182 A3
Radviliškis LT 8 E3
Radzanów
Mazowieckie PL . .77 B5
Mazowieckie PL . .87 A4
Radziejów PL 76 B3
Radziejowice PL . . .77 B5
Radzovce SK 113 A3
Radzyń Chełmiński
PL 69 B3
Raeren B 80 B2
Raesfeld D 80 A2
Raffadali I 176 B2
Rafina GR 185 A4
Rafsbotn N 192 B7
Ragachow BY 13 B9
Ragály H 99 C4
Rageleje DK 61 C2
Raglan GB 39 C4
Ragnitz A 110 C2
Ragusa I 177 C3
Rahden D 72 B1
Råholt N 48 B3
Raiano I 169 A3
Raigada E 141 B3
Rain D 94 C2
Rainbach im Mühlkreis
A 96 C2
Rainham GB 45 B4
Rairiz de Veiga E . .140 B3
Raisdorf D 64 B3
Raisio FIN 8 B3
Raiskio FIN 197 D9
Raiva
Aveiro P 148 A1
Coimbra P 148 B1
Raja-Jooseppi
FIN 193 D12
Rajala FIN 197 B9
Rajcza PL 99 B3
Rajec SK 98 B2
Rájec-Jestřebí CZ . .97 B4
Rajecké Teplice SK .98 B2
Rajevo Selo HR 125 C4
Rajhrad CZ 97 B4
Rajić HR 124 B3
Rajka H 111 B4
Rakaca H 99 C4
Rakamaz H 113 A5
Rakek SLO 123 B3
Rakhiv UA 17 A6
Rakitna SLO 123 B3
Rakitovo BG 183 B6
Rakkestad N 54 A2
Rákóczifalva H 113 B4
Rakoniewice PL 75 B5
Rakoszyce PL 85 A4
Raková SK 98 B2
Rakovac BIH 125 B3
Rakovica HR 123 C4
Rakovník CZ 96 A1
Rakow D 66 B2
Raków PL 87 B5
Rakvere EST 8 C5
Ralja SRB 127 C2
Rälla S 62 B4
Ramacastañas E . .150 B2
Ramacca I 177 B3
Ramales de la Victoria
E 143 A3
Ramberg N 194 B4
Rambervillers F 92 C2
Rambouillet F 90 C1
Rambucourt F 92 C1
Ramdala S 63 B3
Ramerupt F 91 C4
Ramingstein A 109 B4
Ramirás E 140 B2
Ramiswil CH 106 B2
Ramkvilla S 62 A2
Ramme DK 58 B1
Rämmen S 49 B6
Ramnäs S 56 A2
Ramnes N 54 A1
Râmnicu Vâlcea
RO 17 C6
Ramonville-St Agne
F 129 C4
Rampside GB 36 B3
Ramsau D 109 B3
Ramsbeck D 81 A4
Ramsberg S 56 A1
Ramsele S 200 C2
Ramsey
Cambridgeshire
GB 44 A3
Isle of Man GB . . .36 B2
Ramseycleuch GB .36 A3

Ramsgate GB 45 B5
Ramsjö S 200 D1
Ramstein-Meisenbach
D 93 B3
Ramsund N 194 B7
Ramundberget S . .199 C9
Ramvik S 200 D3
Ranalt A 108 B2
Rånäs S 51 C5
Rånåsfoss N 48 B3
Rance B 91 A4
Rânchio I 135 B5
Randaberg N 52 A1
Randalstown GB . . .27 B4
Randan F 117 A3
Randazzo I 177 B3
Randegg A 110 A1
Randers DK 58 B3
Randijaur S 196 C2
Randin E 140 C3
Randsverk N 198 D6
Råneå S 196 D5
Rânes F 89 B3
Rångedala S 60 B3
Ranis D 82 B3
Rankweil A 107 B4
Rånnaväg S 60 B3
Ränneslöv S 61 C3
Rannoch Station
GB 34 B3
Ranovac SRB 127 C3
Ransäter S 55 A4
Ransbach-Baumbach
D 81 B3
Ransta S 56 A2
Ranttila FIN 193 C9
Ranua FIN 197 D9
Ranum DK 58 B2
Ranvalhal P 154 B1
Raon-l'Étape F 92 C2
Ráossi I 121 B4
Rapallo I 134 A2
Rapla EST 8 C4
Rapness GB 33 B4
Rapolano Terme I . .135 B4
Rapolla I 172 B1
Raposa P 154 B2
Rapperswil CH 107 B3
Raša HR 123 B3
Rasal E 145 B3
Rascafria E 151 B4
Rasdorf D 82 B1
Raseiniai LT 13 A5
Rašica SLO 123 B3
Rasines E 143 A3
Rasquera E 153 A4
Rássina I 135 B4
Rastatt D 93 C4
Rastede D 71 A5
Rastenberg D 82 A3
Rastošnica BIH 125 C4
Rastovac MNE 139 C4
Rasueros E 150 A2
Rasy PL 86 A3
Raszków PL 86 A1
Rätan S 199 C11
Rateče SLO 109 C4
Ratekau D 65 C3
Ratež SLO 123 B4
Rathangan IRL 30 A2
Rathcoole IRL 30 A2
Rathcormack IRL . .29 B3
Rathdrum IRL 30 B2
Rathebur D 74 A2
Rathenow D 73 B5
Rathfriland GB 27 B4
Rathkeale IRL 29 B3
Rathmelton IRL 27 A3
Rathmolyon IRL . . .30 A2
Rathmore IRL 29 B2
Rathmullan IRL 27 A3
Rathnew IRL 30 B2
Rathvilly IRL 30 B2
Ratibořské Hory
CZ 96 B2
Ratingen D 80 A2
Ratková SK 99 C4
Ratkovo SRB 126 B1
Ratne UA 13 C6
Rattelsdorf D 94 A2
Ratten A 110 B2
Rattosjärvi FIN . . .196 C7
Rattray GB 35 B4
Rättvik S 50 B2
Ratvika N 199 B7
Ratzeburg D 65 C3
Rätzlingen D 73 B4
Raucourt-et-Flaba
F 91 B4
Raudeberg N 198 D2
Raufarhöfn IS 191 A10
Raufoss N 48 B2
Rauhala FIN 196 B7
Rauland N 53 A4
Raulhac F 116 C2
Raulia N 195 E6
Rauma FIN 8 B2
Raundal N 46 B3
Raunds GB 44 A3
Rauris A 109 B4
Rautas S 196 B2
Rautavaara FIN 3 E11
Rauville-la-Bigot F .88 A2
Rauzan F 128 B2
Ravanusa I 176 B2
Rava-Rus'ka UA . . .13 C5
Ravča HR 138 B3
Ravels B 79 A4
Rävemåla S 63 B3
Ravenglass GB 36 B3
Ravenna I 135 A5
Ravensburg D 107 B4
Rävlanda S 60 B2
Ravna Gora HR 123 B3
Ravne na Koroškem
SLO 110 C1

Ravnje SRB 127 C1
Ravno BIH 139 C3
Ravno Selo SRB . . .126 B1
Rawa Mazowiecka
PL 87 A4
Rawicz PL 85 A4
Rawtenstall GB 40 B1
Rayleigh GB 45 B4
Ražana SRB 127 C1
Ražanac HR 137 A4
Razboj BIH 124 B3
Razes F 115 B5
Razgrad BG 17 D7
Razkrižje SLO 111 C3
Razlog BG 183 B5
Razo E 140 A2
Reading GB 44 B3
Réalmont F 130 B1
Rebais F 90 C3
Reboly RUS 3 E12
Rebordelo P 149 A2
Recanati I 136 B2
Recas E 151 B4
Recco I 134 A2
Recess IRL 28 A2
Recey-sur-Ource
F 105 B3
Recezinhos P 148 A1
Rechnitz A 111 B3
Rechytsa BY 13 B9
Recke D 71 B4
Recklinghausen D .80 A3
Recoaro Terme I . . .121 B4
Recogne B 92 B1
Recoules-
  Prévinquières F .130 A1
Recsk H 113 B4
Recz PL 75 A4
Reda PL 69 A3
Redalen N 48 B2
Redange L 92 B1
Redcar GB 37 B5
Redditch GB 44 A2
Redefin D 73 A4
Redhill GB 44 B3
Redkino RUS 9 D10
Redland GB 33 B3
Redlin D 73 A5
Redondela E 140 B2
Redondo P 155 C3
Red Point GB 31 B3
Redruth GB 42 B1
Redzikowo PL 68 A2
Reepham GB 41 C5
Rees D 80 A2
Reeth GB 37 B5
Reetz D 73 A4
Reftele S 60 B3
Regalbuto I 177 B3
Regen D 95 C5
Regensburg D 95 B4
Regenstauf D 95 B4
Reggello I 135 B4
Réggio di Calábria
I 175 C1
Reggiolo I 121 C3
Réggio nell'Emília
I 121 C3
Reghin RO 17 B6
Régil E 144 A1
Regna S 56 B1
Regniéville F 92 C1
Regny F 117 B4
Rego da Leirosa
P 154 A2
Regöly H 112 C2
Regueiro E 140 B2
Reguengo
  Portalegre P 155 B3
  Santarém P 154 B2
Reguengos de
  Monsaraz P 155 C3
Rehau D 83 B4
Rehburg D 72 B2
Rehden D 72 B1
Rehna D 65 C4
Reichelsheim D 93 B4
Reichelshofen D . . .94 B2
Reichenau A 110 B2
Reichenbach
  Sachsen D 83 B4
  Sachsen D 84 A2
Reichenfels A 110 B1
Reichensachsen D .82 A2
Reichertshofen D . .95 C3
Reichshoffen F 93 C3
Reiden CH 106 B2
Reigada
  E 141 A4
  P 149 B3
Reigate GB 44 B3
Reillanne F 132 B1
Reillo E 158 B2
Reims F 91 B4
Reinach CH 106 B3
Reinbek D 72 A3
Reinberg D 66 B2
Reine N 194 C4
Reinfeld D 65 C3
Reinheim D 93 B4
Reinli N 47 B6
Reinosa E 142 A2
Reinstorf D 65 C4
Reinsvoll N 48 B2
Reisach A 109 C4
Reiss GB 32 C3
Reitan N 199 C8
Reit im Winkl D 109 B3
Rejmyre S 56 B1
Rekavice BIH 124 C3
Rekovac SRB 127 D3
Relleu E 159 C3
Rém H 125 A5
Remagen D 80 B3
Rémalard F 89 B4
Rembercourt-aux-Pots
F 91 C5
Remedios P 154 B1

Remels D 71 A4
Remetea Mare RO .126 B3
Remich L 92 B2
Rémilly F 92 B2
Remiremont F 105 A5
Remolinos E 144 C2
Remoulins F 131 B3
Remscheid D 80 A3
Rémuzat F 131 A4
Rena N 48 A3
Renaison F 117 A3
Renazé F 101 B4
Renchen D 93 C4
Rencurel F 118 B2
Rende I 174 B2
Rendina GR 182 D3
Rendsburg D 64 B2
Renedo E 150 A3
Renens CH 105 C5
Renfrew GB 34 C3
Rengsjö S 50 A3
Reni UA 17 C8
Rennebu N 198 C6
Rennerod D 81 B4
Rennertshofen D . . .94 C3
Rennes F 101 A4
Rennes-les-Bains
F 146 B3
Rennweg A 109 B4
Rens DK 64 B2
Rensjön S 196 A2
Rentería E 144 A2
Rentjärn S 200 A4
Répcelak H 111 B4
Repojoki FIN 193 D9
Repvåg N 193 B9
Requena E 159 B2
Réquista F 130 A1
Rerik D 65 B4
Resana I 121 B4
Resarö S 57 A4
Reschen = Résia I .108 C1
Resen MK 182 B3
Resende P 148 A2
Résia = Reschen I .108 C1
Resita
  RO 16 C4
  RO 126 B3
Resko PL 67 C4
Resnik SRB 127 C2
Ressons-sur-Matz
F 90 B2
Restábal E 163 B4
Resuttano I 177 B3
Retamal E 155 C4
Retford GB 40 B3
Rethel F 91 B4
Rethem D 72 B2
Rethymno GR 185 D5
Retie B 79 A5
Retiers F 101 B4
Retortillo E 149 B3
Retortillo de Soria
E 151 A4
Retournac F 117 B4
Rétság H 112 B3
Rettenegg A 110 B2
Retuerta del Bullaque
E 157 A3
Retz A 97 C3
Retzbach D 94 B1
Reuden D 73 B5
Reuilly F 103 B4
Reus E 147 C2
Reusel NL 79 A5
Reuterstadt
  Stavenhagen D . .74 A1
Reuth D 83 B4
Reutlingen D 94 C1
Reutte A 108 B1
Reuver NL 80 A2
Revel F 146 A2
Revello I 119 C4
Revenga E 151 B3
Revest-du-Bion F . .132 A1
Révfülöp H 111 C4
Revigny-sur-Ornain
F 91 C4
Revin F 91 B4
Řevnice CZ 96 B2
Řevničov CZ 84 B1
Revo I 121 A4
Revsnes N 47 A4
Revúca SK 99 C4
Rewa PL 69 A3
Rewal PL 67 B4
Rexbo S 50 B2
Reyðarfjörður IS .191 B11
Reyero E 142 B1
Reykhólar IS 190 B3
Reykholt
  Árnessýsla IS . . .190 C5
  Borgarfjarðarsýsla
  IS 190 C4
Reykjahlið IS 191 B9
Reykjavík IS 190 C4
Rezé F 101 B4
Rēzekne LV 8 D5
Rezovo BG 17 E8
Rezzato I 120 B3
Rezzoáglio I 134 A2
Rhade D 72 A2
Rhaunen D 93 B3
Rhayader GB 39 B3
Rheda-Wiedenbrück
D 81 A4
Rhede
  Niedersachsen D .71 A4
  Nordrhein-Westfalen
  D 80 A2
Rheinau D 93 C3
Rheinbach D 80 B2
Rheinberg D 80 A2
Rheine D 71 B4
Rheinfelden D 106 B2
Rheinsberg D 74 A1
Rhêmes-Notre-Dame
I 119 B4
Rhenen NL 70 C2
Rhens D 81 B3

Rheydt D 80 A2
Rhiconich GB 32 C2
Rhinow D 73 B5
Rhiw GB 38 B2
Rho I 120 B2
Rhoden D 81 A5
Rhondda GB 39 C3
Rhosllanerchrugog
GB 38 A3
Rhosneigr GB 38 A2
Rhossili GB 39 C2
Rhubodach GB 34 C2
Rhuddlan GB 38 A3
Rhyl GB 38 A3
Rhynie GB 33 D4
Riala S 57 A4
Riallé F 101 B4
Riaño E 142 B1
Riano I 168 A2
Rians F 132 B1
Rianxo E 140 B2
Riaza E 151 A4
Riba E 143 A3
Ribadavia E 140 B2
Ribadeo E 141 A3
Riba de Saelices
E 152 B1
Ribadesella E 142 A1
Ribaflecha E 143 B4
Ribaforada E 144 C2
Ribare SRB 127 C3
Riba-roja d'Ebre E .153 A4
Riba-Roja de Turia
E 159 B3
Ribe DK 59 C1
Ribeauvillé F 106 A2
Ribécourt-Dreslincourt
F 90 B2
Ribeira da Pena P .148 A2
Ribeira de Piquín
E 141 A3
Ribemont F 91 B3
Ribera I 176 B2
Ribérac F 129 A3
Ribera de Cardós
E 146 B2
Ribera del Fresno
E 156 B1
Ribesalbes E 159 A3
Ribes de Freser E .147 B3
Ribiers F 132 A1
Ribnica
  BIH 139 A4
  SLO 123 B3
Ribnica na Potorju
  SLO 110 C2
Ribnik HR 123 B4
Ribnița MD 17 B8
Ribnitz-Damgarten
  D 66 B1
Ribolla I 135 C4
Řicany CZ 97 B4
Říčany CZ 96 B2
Riccia I 170 B2
Riccione I 136 A1
Ricco del Golfo I . . .134 A2
Richebourg F 105 A4
Richelieu F 102 B2
Richisau CH 107 B3
Richmond
  Greater London
  GB 44 B3
  North Yorkshire
  GB 37 B5
Richtenberg D 66 B1
Richterswil CH 107 B3
Rickling D 64 B3
Rickmansworth GB .44 B3
Ricla E 152 A2
Riddarhyttan S 50 C2
Ridderkerk NL 79 A4
Riddes CH 119 A4
Ridjica SRB 125 B5
Riec-sur-Bélon F . .100 B2
Ried A 109 A4
Riedenburg D 95 C3
Ried im Oberinntal
  A 108 B1
Riedlingen D 107 A4
Riedstadt D 93 B4
Riegersburg A 110 C2
Riego de la Vega
  E 141 B5
Riego del Camino
  E 149 A4
Riello E 141 B5
Riemst B 80 B1
Rienne B 91 B4
Riénsena E 142 A2
Riesa D 83 A5
Riese Pio X I 121 B4
Riesi I 177 B3
Riestedt D 82 A3
Rietberg D 81 A4
Rieti I 169 A2
Rietschen D 84 A2
Rieumes F 146 A2
Rieupeyroux F 130 A1
Rieux-Volvestre F .146 A2
Riez F 132 B2
Rīga LV 8 D4
Riggisberg CH 106 C2
Rignac F 130 A1
Rignano Gargánico
I 171 B3
Rigolato I 109 C3
Rigside GB 36 A3
Rigutino I 135 B4
Riihimäki FIN 8 B4
Rijeka HR 123 B3
Rijen NL 79 A4
Rijkevorsel B 79 A4
Rijssen NL 71 B3
Rila BG 183 A5
Rilić BIH 138 B3
Rilievo I 176 B1
Rillé F 102 B2
Rillo de Gallo E 152 B2
Rimavská Baňa SK .99 C3

Rimavská Seč SK . .99 C4
Rimavská Sobota
  SK 99 C4
Rimbo S 57 A4
Rimforsa S 56 B1
Rímini I 136 A1
Rimogne F 91 B4
Rimpar D 94 B1
Rimske Toplice
  SLO 123 A4
Rincón de la Victoria
  E 163 B3
Rincón de Soto E . .144 B2
Rindal N 198 B6
Rinde N 46 A3
Ringarum S 56 B2
Ringaskiddy IRL . . .29 C3
Ringe DK 59 C3
Ringebu N 48 A2
Ringkøbing DK 59 B1
Ringoes B 63 C2
Ringsaker N 48 B2
Ringsted DK 61 D1
Ringwood GB 44 C2
Rinkaby S 63 C2
Rinkabyholm S 63 B4
Rinlo E 141 A3
Rinn A 108 B2
Rinteln D 72 B2
Rio E 140 A2
Riobo E 140 B2
Riodeva E 152 B2
Riofrio E 150 B3
Rio frío de Riaza
  E 151 A4
Riofrio de Aliste E .149 A3
Riogordo E 163 B3
Rioja E 164 C2
Riola I 135 A4
Riola Sardo I 179 C2
Riolobos E 155 B4
Riom F 116 B3
Riomaggiore I 134 A2
Rio Maior P 154 B2
Rio Marina I 134 C3
Riom-ès-Montagnes
  F 116 B2
Rion-des-Landes
  F 128 C2
Rionegro del Puente
  E 141 B4
Rionero in Vúlture
  I 172 B1
Riopar E 158 C1
Riós E 141 C3
Rioseco E 142 A1
Rioseco de Tapia
  E 141 B5
Rio Tinto P 148 A1
Riotord F 117 B4
Riotorto E 141 A3
Rioz F 105 B5
Ripač BIH 124 C1
Ripacándida I 172 B1
Ripanj SRB 127 C2
Ripatransone I 136 C2
Ripley GB 40 B2
Ripoll E 147 B3
Ripon GB 40 A2
Riposto I 177 B4
Ripsa S 56 B2
Risan MNE 16 D3
Risbäck S 200 B1
Risca GB 39 C3
Rischenau D 81 A5
Riscle F 128 C2
Risebo S 56 B2
Risnes N 46 A2
Rišňovce SK 98 C1
Risør N 53 B5
Risøyhamn N 194 B6
Rissna S 199 B12
Ritsem S 194 C8
Ritterhude D 72 A1
Riutula FIN 193 D10
Riva del Garda I . . .121 B3
Riva Lígure I 133 B3
Rivanazzano I 120 C2
Rivarolo Canavese
  I 119 B4
Rivarolo Mantovano
  I 121 B3
Rive-de-Gier F 117 B4
Rivedoux-Plage F . .114 B2
Rivello I 174 A1
Rivergaro I 120 C2
Rives F 118 B2
Rivesaltes F 146 B3
Rivignano I 122 B2
Rivne UA 13 C7
Rívoli I 119 B4
Rivolta d'Adda I . . .120 B2
Rixheim F 106 B2
Rixo S 54 B2
Riza GR 183 C5
Rizokarpaso CY . . .181 A3
Rjukan N 47 C5
Rø DK 67 A3
Rö S 57 A4
Roa
  E 143 C3
  N 48 B2
Roade GB 44 A3
Roager DK 59 C1
Roaldkvam N 52 A2
Roanne F 117 A4
Röbäck S 200 C6
Robakowo PL 69 B3
Róbbio I 120 B1
Roberton GB 35 C5
Robertsfors S 200 B6
Robertville B 80 B2
Robleda E 149 B3

Robledillo de Trujillo
  E 156 A2
Robledo
  Albacete E 158 C1
  Orense E 141 B4
Robledo de Chavela
  E 151 B3
Robledo del Buey
  E 156 A3
Robledo del Mazo
  E 156 A3
Robledollano E 156 A2
Robles de la Valcueva
  E 142 B1
Robliza de Cojos
  E 149 B4
Robres E 145 C3
Robres del Castillo
  E 144 B1
Rocafort de Queralt
  E 147 C2
Rocamadour F 129 B4
Roccabernarda I . . .175 B2
Roccabianca I 120 B3
Roccadáspide I 172 B1
Rocca di Mezzo I . .169 A3
Rocca di Papa I . . .168 B2
Roccagorga I 169 B3
Rocca Imperiale I . .174 A2
Roccalbegna I 135 C4
Roccalumera I 177 B4
Roccamena I 176 B2
Roccamonfina I 170 B1
Roccanova I 174 A2
Roccapalumba I . . .176 B2
Roccapassa I 169 A3
Rocca Priora I 136 B2
Roccaraso I 169 B4
Rocca San Casciano
  I 135 A4
Roccasecca I 169 B3
Rocca Sinibalda I . .169 A2
Roccastrada I 135 B4
Roccatederighi I . . .135 B4
Roccella Iónica I . . .175 C2
Rocchetta
  Sant'António I . . .172 A1
Rocester GB 40 C2
Rochdale GB 40 B1
Rochechouart F . . .115 C4
Rochefort
  B 79 B5
  F 114 C3
Rochefort-en-Terre
  F 101 B3
Rochefort-Montagne
  F 116 B2
Rochefort-sur-Nenon
  F 105 B4
Roche-lez-Beaupré
  F 105 B5
Rochemaure F 131 A3
Rocheservière F . . .114 B2
Rochester
  Medway GB 45 B4
  Northumberland
  GB 37 A4
Rochlitz D 83 A4
Rociana del Condado
  E 161 B3
Rockenhausen D . . .93 B3
Rockhammar S 56 A1
Rockneby S 62 B4
Ročko Polje HR 123 B3
Ročov CZ 84 B1
Rocroi F 91 B4
Rodach D 82 B2
Roda de Bara E . . .147 C2
Roda de Ter E 147 C3
Rodalben D 93 B3
Rødberg N 47 B5
Rødby DK 65 B4
Rødbyhavn DK 65 B4
Rødding
  Sønderjyllands Amt.
  DK 59 C2
  Viborg Amt. DK . .58 B1
Rödeby S 63 B3
Rodeiro E 140 B3
Rødekro DK 64 A2
Roden NL 71 A3
Rödenas E 152 B2
Rodenkirchen D . . .72 A1
Rödental D 82 B3
Rödermark D 93 B4
Rodewisch D 83 B4
Rodez F 130 A1
Roding D 95 B4
Rödjebro S 51 B4
Rødkærsbro DK . . .59 B2
Rodolivos GR 183 C5
Rodonà E 147 C2
Rødvig DK 65 A5
Roermond NL 80 A1
Roesbrugge B 78 B2
Roeschwoog F 93 C4
Roeselare B 78 B3
Roetgen D 80 B2
Roffiac F 116 B3
Röfors S 55 B5
Rofrano I 172 B1
Rogač HR 138 B2
Rogačica SRB 127 C1
Rogalinek PL 76 B1
Rogaška Slatina
  SLO 123 A4
Rogatec SLO 123 A4
Rogatica BIH 139 B5
Rogatyn UA 13 D6
Rogätz D 73 B4
Roggendorf D 65 C4
Roggiano Gravina
  I 174 B2
Roghadal GB 31 B2
Rogliano
  F 180 A2
  I 175 B2
Rognan N 195 C6
Rogne N 47 A6

Rognes F 131 B4
Rogny-les-7-Ecluses
  F 103 B4
Rogowo PL 76 B2
Rogoznica HR 138 B1
Rogoźnica PL 85 A4
Rogoźno PL 76 B1
Rohan F 101 A3
Röhlingen D 94 C2
Rohožník SK 98 C1
Rohr D 82 B2
Rohrbach A 96 C1
Rohrbach-lès-Bitche
  F 92 B3
Rohrberg D 73 B4
Rohr im Gebirge
  A 110 B2
Röhrnbach D 96 C1
Roisel F 90 B3
Roja LV 8 D3
Rojales E 165 A4
Röjeråsen S 50 B1
Rojewo PL 76 B3
Rokciny PL 87 A3
Rokietnica PL 75 B5
Rokiškis LT 8 E4
Rokitki PL 85 A4
Rokycany CZ 96 B1
Rolampont F 105 B4
Rold DK 58 B2
Røldal N 52 A2
Rolde NL 71 B3
Rolfs S 196 D6
Rollag N 47 B6
Rollán E 149 B4
Rolle CH 105 C5
Roma = Rome I . . .168 B2
Roma S 57 C4
Romagnano Sésia
  I 119 B5
Romagné F 88 B2
Romakloster S 57 C4
Roman RO 17 B7
Romana I 178 B2
Romanèche-Thorins
  F 117 A4
Romano di Lombardia
  I 120 B2
Romanshorn CH . . .107 B4
Romans-sur-Isère
  F 118 B2
Rombas F 92 B2
Rome = Roma I . . .168 B2
Romeán E 141 B3
Romenay F 105 C4
Romeral E 157 A4
Römerstein D 94 C1
Rometta I 177 A4
Romford GB 45 B4
Romhány H 112 B3
Römhild D 82 B2
Romilly-sur-Seine
  F 91 C3
Romont CH 106 C1
Romorantin-Lanthenay
  F 103 B3
Romrod D 81 B5
Romsey GB 44 C2
Rømskog N 54 A2
Rønbjerg DK 58 B1
Roncal E 144 B3
Ronce-les-Bains
  F 114 C2
Ronchamp F 106 B1
Ronchi dei Legionari
  I 122 B2
Ronciglione I 168 A2
Ronco Canavese I .119 B4
Ronco Scrivia I 120 C1
Ronda E 162 B2
Rønde DK 59 B3
Rone S 57 C4
Ronehamn S 57 C4
Rong N 46 B1
Rönnäng S 60 B1
Rønne DK 67 A3
Ronneburg D 83 B4
Ronneby S 63 B3
Rönneshytta S 55 B6
Rönninge S 57 A3
Rönnöfors S 199 B10
Rönö S 56 B2
Ronov nad Doubravou
  CZ 97 B3
Ronse B 79 B3
Roosendaal NL 79 A4
Roosky IRL 26 C3
Ropczyce PL 87 B5
Ropeid N 52 A2
Ropinsalmi FIN 192 D5
Ropuerelos del Páramo
  E 141 B5
Roquebilière F 133 A3
Roquebrun F 130 B2
Roquecourbe F 130 B1
Roquefort F 128 B2
Roquemaure F 131 A3
Roquesteron F 132 B3
Roquetas de Mar
  E 164 C2
Roquetes E 153 B4
Roquevaire F 132 B1
Røra N 199 B8
Rørbæk DK 58 B2
Rore BIH 138 B2
Röro S 60 B1
Røros N 199 C8
Rorschach CH 107 B4
Rørvig DK 61 D1
Rørvik N 199 A8
Rörvik S 62 A2
Rosà I 121 B4
Rosal de la Frontera
  E 161 B2
Rosalina Mare I . . .122 B1
Rosans F 132 A1
Rosário P 160 B1
Rosarno I 175 C1

Rosbach D 81 B3
Rosche D 73 B3
Rościszewo PL . . .77 B4
Roscoff F 100 A2
Roscommon IRL . .28 A3
Roscrea IRL . . .28 A4
Rosdorf D 82 A1
Rose I 174 B2
Rosegg A 109 C5
Rosehall GB 32 D2
Rosehearty GB . .33 D4
Rosel D 88 A1
Rosell E 153 B4
Roselló E 153 A4
Rosendal N 46 C3
Rosenfeld D 93 C4
Rosenfors S 62 A3
Rosenheim D . . .108 B3
Rosenow D 74 A2
Rosenthal D 81 A4
Rosersberg S 57 A3
Roses E 147 B4
Roseto degli Abruzzi
I 169 A4
Roseto Valfortore
I 170 B3
Rosheim F 93 C3
Rosia I 135 B4
Rosice CZ 97 B4
Rosières-en-Santerre
F 90 B2
Rosignano Maríttimo
I 134 B3
Rosignano Solvay
I 134 B3
Roşiori-de-Vede
RO 17 C6
Roskhill GB 31 B2
Roskilde DK 61 D2
Roskovec AL 182 C1
Röslau D 83 B3
Roslev DK 58 B1
Rosmaninhal P . . .155 B3
Rosnowo PL 67 B5
Rosolini I 177 C3
Rosova MNE 139 B5
Rosoy F 104 A2
Rosporden F 100 B2
Rosquete P 154 B2
Rosrath D 80 B3
Rossa CH 120 A2
Rossano I 174 B2
Rossas
Aveiro P 148 B1
Braga P 148 A1
Rossdorf D 82 B2
Rossett GB 38 A4
Rosshaupten D . . .108 B1
Rossiglione I 133 A4
Rossignol B 92 B1
Rossla D 82 A3
Rosslare IRL 30 B2
Rosslare Harbour
IRL 30 B2
Rosslau D 83 A4
Rosslea GB 27 B3
Rossleben D 82 A3
Rossön S 200 C2
Ross-on-Wye GB . .39 C4
Rossoszyca PL . . .86 A2
Rosswein D 83 A5
Röstånga S 61 C3
Roştár SK 99 C4
Rostock D 65 B5
Rostrenen F 100 A2
Røsvik N 194 C6
Rosvik S 196 D4
Rosyth GB 35 B4
Röszke H 126 A2
Rot S 49 A6
Rota E 161 C3
Rota Greca I 174 B2
Rot am See D 94 B2
Rotella I 136 C2
Rotenburg
Hessen D 82 B1
Niedersachsen D . .72 A2
Roth
Bayern D 94 B3
Rheinland-Pfalz D .81 B3
Rothbury GB 37 A5
Rothemühl D 74 A2
Röthenbach D 95 B3
Rothenburg D 84 A2
Rothenburg ob der
Tauber D 94 B2
Rothéneuf F 88 B2
Rothenklempenow
D 74 A3
Rothenstein D 94 C3
Rotherham GB 40 B2
Rothes GB 32 D3
Rothesay GB 34 C2
Rothwell GB 44 A3
Rotnes N 48 B2
Rotonda I 174 B2
Rotondella I 174 A2
Rotova E 159 C3
Rott
Bayern D 108 B1
Bayern D 108 B3
Rottach-Egern D . .108 B2
Röttenbach D 94 B3
Rottenbuch D 108 B1
Rottenburg
Baden-Württemberg
D 93 C4
Bayern D 95 C4
Rottenmann A . . .110 B1
Rotterdam NL 79 A4
Rotthalmünster D . .96 C1
Rottingdean GB . . .44 C3
Röttingen D 94 B1
Rottleberode D 82 A3
Rottne S 62 A2
Rottneros S 55 A4
Rottofreno I 120 B2
Rottweil D 107 A3
Rötz D 95 B4

Roubaix F 78 B3
Roudnice nad Labem
CZ 84 B2
Roudouallec F . . .100 A2
Rouen F 89 A5
Rouffach F 106 B2
Rougé F 101 B4
Rougemont F 105 B5
Rougemont le-Château
F 106 B1
Rouillac F 115 C3
Rouillé F 115 B4
Roujan F 130 B2
Roulans F 105 B5
Roundwood IRL . .30 A2
Rousínov CZ 97 B4
Roussac F 115 B5
Roussennac F . . .130 A1
Rousses F 130 A2
Roussillon F 117 B4
Rouvroy-sur-Audry
F 91 B4
Rouy F 104 B2
Rovanieman
maalaiskunta
FIN 197 C8
Rovaniemi FIN. . . .197 C8
Rovato I 120 B2
Rovensko pod
Troskami CZ 84 B3
Roverbella I 121 B3
Rovereto I 121 B4
Rövershagen D . . .65 B5
Roverud N 49 B4
Rovigo I 121 B4
Rovinj HR 122 B2
Rovišče HR 124 B2
Rów PL 74 B3
Rowy PL 68 A2
Royal Leamington Spa
GB 44 A2
Royal Tunbridge Wells
GB 45 B4
Royan F 114 C2
Royat F 116 B3
Roybon F 118 B2
Roybridge GB 34 B3
Roye F 90 B2
Royère-de-Vassivière
F 116 B1
Røykenvik N 48 B2
Royos S 164 B2
Røyrvik N 199 A10
Royston GB 44 A3
Rozadas E 141 A4
Rozalén del Monte
E 151 C5
Rózańsko PL 75 B3
Rozay-en-Brie F . . .90 C2
Roždalovice CZ. . . .84 B3
Rozdilna UA 17 B9
Rozental PL 69 B4
Rozhyshche UA . . .13 C6
Rožmitál pod
Třemšínem CZ . .96 B1
Rožňava SK 99 C4
Rožnov pod
Radhoštěm CZ. . .98 B2
Rozoy-sur-Serre F .91 B4
Rozprza PL 86 A3
Roztoky CZ 84 B2
Rozvadov CZ 95 B4
Rozzano I 120 B2
Rrëshen AL 182 B1
Rrogozhine AL . . .182 B1
Ruanes E 156 A2
Rubbestadnesset
N 46 C2
Rubi E 147 C3
Rubiá E 141 B4
Rubiacedo de Abajo
E 143 B3
Rubielos Bajos E .158 B1
Rubielos de Mora
E 153 B3
Rubiera I 121 C3
Rubik AL 182 B1
Rucandio E 143 B3
Rud
Akershus N 48 B3
Buskerud N 48 B2
Ruda
PL 86 A2
S 62 A4
Rudabánya H 99 C4
Ruda Maleniecka
PL 87 A4
Ruda Pilczycka PL .87 A4
Ruda Śl. PL 86 B2
Ruden D 110 C1
Rudersberg D 94 C1
Rudersdorf A 111 B3
Rüdersdorf D 74 B2
Ruderting D 96 C1
Rüdesheim D 93 B3
Rudkøbing DK 65 B3
Rudmanns A 97 C3
Rudna
CZ 96 A2
PL 85 A4
Rudnik SRB 127 C2
Rudniki
Opolskie PL 86 A2
Śląskie PL 86 B3
Rudno
Dolnośląskie PL. . .85 A4
Pomorskie PL 69 B3
Rudnya RUS 13 A9
Rudolstadt D 82 B3
Rudowica PL 84 A3
Rudozem BG 183 B6
Rudskoga S 55 A5
Rudston GB 40 A3
Ruds Vedby DK . . .61 D1
Rudzica PL 98 B2
Rue F 78 B1
Rueda E 150 A3
Rueda de Jalón E .152 A2

Ruelle-sur-Touvre
F 115 C4
Ruerrero E 143 B3
Ruffano I 173 C4
Ruffec F 115 B4
Rufina I 135 B4
Rugby GB 44 A2
Rugeley GB 40 C2
Ruggstrop S 62 B4
Rugles F 89 B4
Rugozero RUS 3 D13
Rühen D 73 B3
Ruhla D 82 B2
Ruhland D 84 A1
Ruhle D 71 B4
Ruhpolding D . . .109 B3
Ruhstorf D 96 C1
Ruidera E 158 C1
Ruillé-sur-le-Loir
F 102 B2
Ruinen NL 71 B3
Ruiselede B 78 A3
Ruka FIN 197 C12
Rulles B 92 B1
Rülzheim D 93 B4
Rum H 111 B3
Ruma SRB 127 B1
Rumboci BIH 138 B3
Rumenka SRB . . .126 B1
Rumia PL 69 A3
Rumigny F 91 B4
Rumilly F 118 B2
Rumma S 56 B2
Rumney GB 39 C3
Rumont F 91 C5
Runa P 154 B1
Runcorn GB 38 A4
Rundmoen N 195 D5
Rundvik S 200 C5
Runhällen S 51 B3
Runowo PL 69 A5
Runtuna S 56 B3
Ruokojärvi FIN . . .196 B7
Ruokolahti FIN 9 B6
Ruokto S 196 B2
Ruoms F 131 A3
Ruoti I 172 B1
Rupa HR 123 B3
Ruppichteroth D . .80 B3
Rupt-sur-Moselle
F 106 B1
Rus E 157 B4
Ruse BG 17 D7
Ruše SLO 110 C2
Rusele S 200 B4
Ruševo HR 125 B4
Rush IRL 30 A2
Rushden GB 44 A3
Rusiec PL 86 A2
Rusinowo
Zachodnio-Pomorskie
PL 67 C4
Zachodnio-Pomorskie
PL 75 A5
Ruskele S 200 B4
Ruski Krstur SRB .126 B1
Ruskington GB . . .40 B3
Rusovce SK 111 A4
Rüsselsheim D . . .93 B4
Russelv N 192 C4
Russi I 135 A5
Rust A 111 B3
Rustefjelbma N . .193 B12
Rustrel F 131 B4
Ruszki PL 77 B5
Ruszów PL 84 A3
Rute E 163 A3
Rüthen D 81 A4
Ruthin GB 38 A3
Ruthven GB 32 D2
Ruthwell GB 36 B3
Rüti CH 107 B3
Rutigliano I 173 A3
Rutledal N 46 A2
Rutvik S 196 D5
Ruurlo NL 71 B3
Ruuvaoja FIN 197 B11
Ruvo del Monte I .172 B1
Ruvo di Púglia I . .171 B4
Ruynes-en-Margeride
F 116 C3
Ružic HR 138 B2
Ružomberok SK . .99 B3
Ruzsa H 126 A1
Ry DK 59 B2
Rybany SK 98 C2
Rybina PL 69 A4
Rybnik PL 86 B2
Rychliki PL 69 B4
Rychlocice PL . . .86 A2
Rychnov nad Kněžnou
CZ 85 B4
Rychnowo PL 77 A5
Rychtal PL 86 A1
Rychwał PL 76 B3
Ryczów PL 87 A5
Ryczywół PL 75 B5
Ryd S 63 B2
Rydaholm S 62 B2
Rydal S 60 B2
Rydbo S 57 A4
Rydboholm S 60 B2
Ryde GB 44 C2
Rydöbruk S 60 C3
Rydsgård S 66 A2
Rydsnäs S 62 A3
Rydultowy PL 86 B2
Rydzyna PL 85 A4
Rye GB 45 C4
Rygge N 54 A1
Ryjewo PL 69 B3
Rykene N 53 B4
Rymań PL 67 C4
Rýmařov CZ 98 B1
Rynarzewo PL 76 A2
Ryomgård DK 59 B3
Rypefjord N 192 B7
Rypin PL 77 A4

Rysjedalsvika N . . .46 A2
Ryssby S 60 C4
Rytel PL 68 B2
Rytinki FIN 197 D10
Rytro PL 99 B4
Rywociny PL 77 A5
Rzeczenica PL 68 B2
Rzeczniów PL 87 A5
Rzeczyca PL 87 A4
Rzegnowo PL 77 A5
Rzejowice PL 87 A3
Rzemień PL 87 B5
Rzepin PL 75 B3
Rzesznikowo PL . .67 C4
Rzeszów PL 12 C4
Rzgów PL 86 A3
Rzhev RUS 9 D9

S

Saal
Bayern D 82 B2
Bayern D 95 C3
Saalbach A 109 B3
Saalburg D 83 B3
Saales F 92 C3
Saalfeld D 82 B3
Saalfelden am
Steinernen Meer
A 109 B3
Saanen CH 106 C2
Saarbrücken D . . .92 B2
Saarburg D 92 B2
Saarijärvi FIN 8 A4
Saari-Kämä FIN . .197 C9
Saarlouis D 92 B2
Saas-Fee CH 119 A4
Šabac SRB 127 C1
Sabadell E 147 C3
Sabáudia I 169 B3
Sabbioneta I 121 C3
Sabero E 142 B1
Sabiñánigo E 145 B3
Sabiote E 157 B4
Sables-d'Or-les-Pins
F 101 A3
Sabóia P 160 B1
Saborsko HR 123 B4
Sæbøvik N 52 A1
Sæby DK 58 A3
Sabres F 128 B2
Sabrosa P 148 A2
Sabugal P 149 B2
Sabuncu TR 187 C5
Sada E 140 A2
Sádaba E 144 B2
Saddell GB 34 C2
Sadernes E 147 B3
Sadki PL 76 A2
Sadków PL 85 A4
Sadkowice PL 87 A4
Sadlinki PL 69 B3
Sadów PL 75 B3
Sadská CZ 84 B2
Saelices E 151 C5
Saelices de Mayorga
E 142 B1
Sælvig DK 59 C3
Saerbeck D 71 B4
Saeul L 92 B1
Safaalan TR 186 A3
Safara P 161 A2
Säffle S 55 A3
Saffron Walden GB .45 A4
Safranbolu TR . . .187 A7
Säfsnäs S 50 B1
Şag RO 126 B3
Sagard D 66 B2
S'Agaro E 147 C4
Sågmyra S 50 B2
Sagone F 180 A1
Sagres P 160 C1
Ságújfalu H 113 A3
Sagunt E 159 B3
Sagvåg N 52 A1
Ságvár H 112 C2
Sagy F 105 C4
Sahagún E 142 B1
Šahy SK 112 A2
Saignelégier CH . .106 B1
Saignes F 116 B2
Saija FIN 197 B11
Saillagouse F . . .146 B3
Saillans F 118 C2
Sains Richaumont
F 91 B3
St Abb's GB 35 C5
St Affrique F 130 B1
St Agnan F 104 C2
St Agnant F 114 C3
St Agnes GB 42 B1
St Agrève F 117 B4
St Aignan F 103 B3
St Aignan-sur-Roë
F 101 B4
St Albans GB 44 B3
St Alban-sur-Limagnole
F 117 C3
St Amand-en-Puisaye
F 104 B2
St Amand-les-Eaux
F 79 B3
St Amand-Longpré
F 103 B3
St Amand-Montrond
F 103 C4
St Amans F 117 C3
St Amans-Soult F .130 B1

St Amant-Roche-Savine
F 117 B3
St Amarin F 106 B1
St Ambroix F 131 A3
St Amé F 106 A1
St Amour F 118 A2
St André-de-Corcy
F 117 B4
St André-de-Cubzac
F 128 B2
St André-de-l'Eure
F 89 B5
St André-de-
Roquepertuis F .131 A3
St André-de-Sangonis
F 130 B2
St Andre-de-Valborgne
F 130 A2
St André-les-Alpes
F 132 B2
St Andrews GB . . .35 B5
St Angel F 116 B2
St Anthème F 117 B3
St Antoine F 180 A2
St Antoine-de-Ficalba
F 129 B3
St Antönien CH . .107 C4
St Antonin-Noble-Val
F 129 B4
St Août F 103 C3
St Armant-Tallende
F 116 B3
St Arnoult F 90 C1
St Asaph GB 38 A3
St Astier F 129 A3
St Athan GB 39 C3
St Auban F 132 B2
St Aubin
CH 106 C1
F 105 B4
GB 88 A1
St Aubin-d'Aubigne
F 101 A4
St Aubin-du-Cormier
F 101 A4
St Aubin-sur-Mer F .89 A5
St Aulaye F 128 A3
St Austell GB 42 B2
St Avit F 116 B2
St Avold F 92 B2
St Aygulf F 132 B2
St Bauzille-de-Putois
F 130 B2
St Béat F 145 B4
St Beauzély F . . .130 A1
St Bees GB 36 B3
St Benim-d'Azy F .104 C2
St Benoît-du-Sault
F 115 B5
St Benoit-en-Woëvre
F 92 C1
St Berthevin F . . .102 A1
St Blaise-la-Roche
F 92 C3
St Blazey GB 42 B2
St Blin F 105 A4
St Bonnet F 118 C3
St Bonnet Briance
F 115 C5
St Bonnet-de-Joux
F 104 C3
St Bonnet-le-Château
F 117 B4
St Bonnet-le-Froid
F 117 B4
St Brévin-les-Pins
F 101 B3
St Briac-sur-Mer F 101 A3
St Brice-en-Coglès
F 88 B2
St Brieuc F 101 A3
St Bris-le-Vineux
F 104 B2
St Broladre F 88 B2
St Calais F 102 B2
St Cannat F 131 B4
St Cast-le-Guildo
F 101 A3
St Céré F 129 B4
St Cergue CH . . .118 A3
St Cergues F 118 A3
St Cernin F 116 B2
St Chamant F . . .116 B1
St Chamas F 131 B4
St Chamond F . . .117 B4
St Chély-d'Apcher
F 116 C3
St Chély-d'Aubrac
F 116 C2
St Chinian F 130 B1
St Christol F 131 A4
St Christol-lès-Alès
F 131 A3
St Christoly-Médoc
F 114 C3
St Christophe-du-
Ligneron F 114 B2
St Christophe-en-
Brionnais F 117 A4
St Ciers-sur-Gironde
F 128 A2
St Clair-sur-Epte F .90 B1
St Clar F 129 C3
St Claud F 115 C4
St Claude F 118 A2
St Clears GB 39 C2
St Columb Major
GB 42 B2
St Come-d'Olt F . .130 A1
St Cosme-en-Vairais
F 89 B4
St Cyprien
Dordogne F 129 B4
Pyrénées-Orientales
F 146 B4
St Cyr-sur-Loire F .102 B2
St Cyr-sur-Mer F .132 B1
St Cyr-sur-Methon
F 117 A4

St David's GB 39 C1
St Denis F 90 C2
St Denis-d'Oléron
F 114 B2
St Denis d'Orques
F 102 A1
St Didier F 117 A4
St Didier-en-Velay
F 117 B4
St Dié F 92 C2
St Dier-d'Auvergne
F 117 B3
St Dizier F 91 C4
St Dizier-Leyrenne
F 116 A1
St Dogmaels GB . .39 B2
Ste Adresse F 89 A4
Ste Anne F 89 B4
Ste Anne-d'Auray
F 100 B3
Ste Croix CH 105 C5
Ste Croix-Volvestre
F 146 A2
Ste Engrâce F . . .144 A3
Ste Enimie F 130 A2
St Efflam F 100 A2
Ste Foy-de-Peyrolières
F 146 A2
Ste Foy-la-Grande
F 128 B3
Ste Foy l'Argentiere
F 117 B4
Ste Gauburge-Ste
Colombe F 89 B4
Ste Gemme la Plaine
F 114 B2
Ste Geneviève F . .90 B2
Ste Égrève F 118 B2
Ste Hélène F 128 B2
Ste Hélène-sur-Isère
F 118 B3
Ste Hermine F . . .114 B2
Ste Jalle F 131 A4
Ste Livrade-sur-Lot
F 129 B3
St Eloy-les-Mines
F 116 A2
Ste Marie-aux-Mines
F 106 A2
Ste Marie-du-Mont
F 88 A2
Ste Maure-de-Touraine
F 102 B2
Ste Maxime F 132 B2
Ste Ménéhould F . .91 B4
Ste Mère-Église F .88 A2
St Émiland F 104 C3
St Émilion F 128 B2
St Enoder GB 42 B2
Sainteny F 88 A2
Ste Ode B 92 A1
Saintes F 114 C3
Ste Savine F 91 C4
Ste Sévère-sur-Indre
F 103 C4
Ste Sigolène F . . .117 B4
St Esteben F 144 A2
Ste Estèphe F . . .128 A2
Ste Suzanne F . . .102 A1
St Étienne F 117 B4
St Étienne-de-Baigorry
F 144 A2
St Étienne-de-Cuines
F 118 B3
St Etienne-de-Fursac
F 116 A1
St Etienne-de-Montluc
F 101 B4
St Etienne-de-St Geoirs
F 118 B2
St Étienne-de-Tinée
F 132 A2
St Étienne-du-Bois
F 118 A2
St Étienne-du-Rouvray
F 89 A5
St Etienne-les-Orgues
F 132 A1
Ste Tulle F 132 B1
St Fargeau F 104 B2
St Félicien F 117 B4
St Felix-de-Sorgues
F 130 B1
St Fillans GB 35 B3
St Firmin F 118 C3
St Florent F 180 A2
St Florentin F 104 B2
St Florent-le-Vieil
F 101 B4
St Florent-sur-Cher
F 103 C4
St Flour F 116 B3
St Flovier F 103 C3
St Fort-sur-le-Né
F 115 C3
St Fulgent F 114 B2
St Galmier F 117 B4
St Gaudens F 145 A4
St Gaultier F 115 B5
St Gély-du-Fesc F .130 B2
St Genest-Malifaux
F 117 B4
St Geniez F 132 A2
St Geniez-d'Olt F . .130 A1
St Genis-de-Saintonge
F 114 C3
St Genix-sur-Guiers
F 118 B2
St Gengoux-le-National
F 104 C3
St Georges Buttavent
F 88 B3
St Georges-d'Aurac
F 117 B3
St Georges-de-
Commiers F 118 B2

St Georges-de-Didonne
F 114 C3
St Georges-de-
Luzençon F 130 A1
St Georges-de Mons
F 116 B2
St Georges-de-Reneins
F 117 A4
St Georges d'Oléron
F 114 C2
St Georges-en-Couzan
F 117 B3
St Georges-lès-
Baillargeaux F .115 B4
St Georges-sur-Loire
F 102 B1
St Georges-sur-Meuse
B 79 B5
St Geours-de-Maremne
F 128 C1
St Gérand-de-Vaux
F 117 A3
St Gérand-le-Puy
F 117 A3
St Germain F 105 B5
St Germain-Chassenay
F 104 C2
St Germain-de-Calberte
F 130 A2
St Germain-de-
Confolens F 115 B4
St Germain-de-Joux
F 118 A2
St Germain-des-Fossés
F 117 A3
St Germain-du-Bois
F 105 C4
St Germain-du-Plain
F 105 C3
St Germain-du Puy
F 103 B4
St Germain-en-Laye
F 90 C2
St Germain-Laval
F 117 B4
St Germain-Lembron
F 116 B3
St Germain-les-Belles
F 116 B1
St Germain-l'Herm
F 117 B3
St Gervais-d'Auvergne
F 116 A2
St Gervais-les-Bains
F 118 B3
St Gervais-sur-Mare
F 130 B2
St Gildas-de-Rhuys
F 100 B3
St Gildas-des-Bois
F 101 B3
St Gilles
Gard F 131 B3
Ille-et-Vilaine F . .101 A4
St Gilles-Croix-de-Vie
F 114 B2
St Gingolph F 119 A3
St Girons
Ariège F 146 B2
Landes F 128 C1
St Girons-Plage F .128 C1
St Gobain F 91 B3
St Gorgon-Main F .105 B5
St Guénolé F 100 B1
St Harmon GB 39 B3
St Helens GB 38 A4
St Helier GB 88 A1
St Herblain F 101 B4
St Hilaire
Allier F 104 C2
Aude F 146 A3
St Hilaire-de-Riez
F 114 B2
St Hilaire-des-Loges
F 114 B3
St Hilaire-de-
Villefranche F . .114 C3
St Hilaire-du-Harcouët
F 88 B2
St Hilaire-du-Rosier
F 118 B2
St Hippolyte
Aveyron F 116 C2
Doubs F 106 B1
St Hippolyte-du-Fort
F 130 B2
St Honoré-les-Bains
F 104 C2
St Hubert B 92 A1
St Imier CH 106 B2
St Issey GB 42 B2
St Ives
Cambridgeshire
GB 44 A3
Cornwall GB 42 B1
St Izaire F 130 B1
St Jacques-de-la-Lande
F 101 A4
St Jacut-de-la-Mer
F 101 A3
St James F 88 B2
St Jaume d'Enveja
E 153 B4
St Jean-Brévelay
F 101 B3
St Jean-d'Angély
F 114 C3
St Jean-de-Belleville
F 118 B3
St Jean-de-Bournay
F 118 B2
St Jean-de-Braye
F 103 B3
St Jean-de-Côle F .115 C4
St Jean-de-Daye F . .88 A2

St Jean de Losne
F 105 B4
St Jean-de-Luz F . .144 A2
St Jean-de-Maurienne
F 118 B3
St Jean-de-Monts
F 114 B1
St Jean-d'Illac F . .128 B2
St Jean-du-Bruel
F 130 A2
St Jean-du-Gard F 131 A2
St Jean-en-Royans
F 118 B2
St Jean-la-Riviere
. . . . .133 B3
St Jean-Pied-de-Port
. . . . .144 A2
St Jean-Poutge F .129 C3
St Jeoire F 118 A3
St Joachim F 101 B3
St Johnstown IRL . .27 B3
St Jorioz F 118 B3
St Joris Winge B . .79 B4
St Jouin-de-Marnes
F 102 C1
St Juéry F 130 B1
St Julien F 118 A2
St Julien-Chapteuil
F 117 B4
St Julien-de-Vouvantes
F 101 B4
St Julien-du-Sault
. . . . .104 A2
St Julien-du-Verdon
F 132 B2
St Julien-en-Born
F 128 B1
St Julien-en-Genevois
F 118 A3
St Julien-l'Ars F . .115 B4
St Julien la-Vêtre
. . . . .117 B3
St Julien-Mont-Denis
F 118 B3
St Julien-sur-
Reyssouze F. . . .118 A2
St Junien F 115 C4
St Just
F 131 A3
GB 42 B1
St Just-en-Chaussée
F. 90 B2
St Just-en-Chevalet
. . . . .117 B3
St Justin F 128 C2
St Just-St Rambert
. . . . .117 B4
St Keverne GB. . . .42 B1
St Lary-Soulan F .145 B4
St Laurent-d'Aigouze
F 131 B3
St Laurent-de-
Chamousset F . .117 B4
St Laurent-de-Condel
F. 89 A3
St Laurent-de-la-
Cabrerisse F 146 A3
St Laurent-de-la-
Salanque F 146 B3
St Laurent-des-Autels
F 101 B4
St Laurent-du-Pont
F 118 B2
St Laurent-en-Caux
F. 89 A4
St Laurent-en-
Grandvaux F. . . .105 C4
St Laurent-Médoc
F 128 A2
St Laurent-sur-Gorre
F 115 C4
St Laurent-sur-Mer
F 88 A3
St Laurent-sur-Sèvre
F 114 B3
St Leger B 92 B1
St Léger-de-Vignes
F 104 C2
St Léger-sous-Beuvray
F 104 C3
St Léger-sur-Dheune
. . . . .104 C2
St Léonard-de-Noblat
. . . . .116 B1
St Leonards GB. . .45 C4
St Lô F 88 A2
St Lon-les-Mines
. . . . .128 C1
St Louis F 106 B2
St Loup F 117 A3
St Loup-de-la-Salle
. . . . .105 C3
St Loup-sur-Semouse
F 105 B5
St Lunaire F 101 A3
St Lupicin F 118 A2
St Lyphard F 101 B3
St Lys F 146 A2
St Macaire F. 128 B2
St Maclou F 89 A4
St Maixent-l'École
F. 115 B3
St Malo F 88 B1
St Mamet-la-Salvetat
F. 116 C2
St Mandrier-sur-Mer
F 132 B1
St Marcel
Drôme F. 117 C4
Saône-et-Loire F 105 C3
St Marcellin F 118 B2
St Marcellin sur Loire
F 117 B4
St Marcet F 145 A4
St Mards-en-Othe
F. 104 A2

St Margaret's-at-Cliffe
GB 45 B5
St Margaret's Hope
GB 33 C4
St Mars-la-Jaille F 101 B4
St Martin-d'Ablois
F. 91 C3
St Martin-d'Auxigny
F. 103 B4
St Martin-de-Belleville
F 118 B3
St Martin-de-Bossenay
F. 91 C3
St Martin-de-Crau
F. 131 B3
St Martin-de-Londres
. . . . .130 B2
St Martin-d'Entraunes
F 132 A2
St Martin-de-
Queyrières F 118 C3
St Martin-de-Ré F .114 B2
St Martin des Besaces
F. 88 A3
St Martin-d'Estreaux
. . . . .117 A3
St Martin-de-Valamas
. . . . .117 C4
St Martin-d'Hères
. . . . .118 B2
St Martin-du-Frêne
. . . . .118 A2
St Martin-en-Bresse
. . . . .105 C4
St Martin-en-Haut
. . . . .117 B4
St Martin-la-Méanne
. . . . .116 B1
St Martin-Osmonville
. . . . .90 B1
St Martin-sur-Ouanne
. . . . .104 B2
St Martin-Valmeroux
. . . . .116 A3
St Martin-Vésubie
. . . . .133 A3
St Martory F 145 A4
St Mary's GB 33 C4
St Mathieu F 115 C4
St Mathieu-de-Tréviers
. . . . .131 B2
St Maurice CH . . .119 A3
St Maurice-Navacelles
. . . . .130 B2
St Maurice-sur-Moselle
. . . . .106 B1
St Mawes GB. 42 B1
St Maximin-la-Ste
Baume F 132 B1
St Méard-de-Gurçon
. . . . .128 B3
St Médard-de-
Guizières F 128 A2
St Médard-en-Jalles
. . . . .128 B2
St Méen-le-Grand
. . . . .101 A3
St Menges F. 91 B4
St Merløse DK 61 D1
St Mĕsto CZ. 85 B4
St M'Hervé F 101 A4
St Michel
Aisne F. 91 B4
Gers F 145 A4
St Michel-Chef-Chef
. . . . .101 B4
St Michel-de-Castelnau
. . . . .128 B2
St Michel-de-Maurienne
F 118 B3
St Michel-en-Grève
F. 100 A2
St Michel-enl'Herm
F. 114 B2
St Michel-Mont-Mercure
. . . . .114 B3
St Mihiel F 92 C1
St Monance GB . . .35 B5
St Montant F 131 A3
St Moritz CH 107 C4
St Nazaire F 101 B3
St Nazaire-en-Royans
. . . . .118 B2
St Nazaire-le-Désert
F. 131 A4
St Nectaire F 116 B2
St Neots GB. 44 A3
St Nicolas-de-Port
. . . . .92 C2
St Nicolas-de-Redon
. . . . .101 B3
St Nicolas-du-Pélem
. . . . .100 A2
St Niklaas B 79 A4
St Omer F 78 B2
St Pair-sur-Mer F. .88 B2
St Palais F 144 A2
St Palais-sur-Mer
. . . . .114 C2
St Pardoux-la-Rivière
. . . . .115 C4
St Paul-Cap-de-Joux
. . . . .129 C4
St Paul-de-Fenouillet
F. 146 B3
St Paul-de-Varax
. . . . .118 A2
St Paulien F 117 B3
St Paul-le-Jeune F 131 A3
St Paul-lès-Dax F .128 C1
St Paul-Trois-Châteaux
. . . . .131 A3
St Pé-de-Bigorre
. . . . .145 A3
St Pée-sur-Nivelle
F. 144 A2
St Péravy-la-Colombe
. . . . .103 B3
St Péray F 117 C4
St Père-en-Retz F .101 B3

St Peter Port GB . . .88 A1
St Petersburg = Sankt-
Peterburg RUS . . .9 C7
St Philbert-de-Grand-
Lieu F 114 A2
St Pierre F 130 B1
St Pierre-d'Albigny
F 118 B3
St Pierre-d'Allevard
F 118 B3
St Pierre-de-Chartreuse
F 88 A2
St Pierre-de-Chignac
. . . . .129 A3
St Pierre-de-la-Fage
F 130 B2
St Pierre-d'Entremont
F 118 B2
St Pierre-d'Oléron
. . . . .114 C2
St Pierre-Eglise F . .88 A2
St Pierre-en-Port F .89 A4
St Pierre-le-Moûtier
. . . . .104 C2
St Pierre Montlimart
. . . . .101 B4
St Pierre-Quiberon
. . . . .100 B2
St Pierre-sur-Dives
. . . . .89 A3
St Pierreville F . . .117 C4
St Pieters-Leeuw B 79 B4
St Plancard F 145 A4
St Poix F 101 B4
St Pol-de-Léon F . .100 A2
St Polgues F 117 B3
St Pol-sur-Ternoise
. . . . .78 B2
St Pons-de-Thomières
. . . . .130 B1
St Porchaire F 114 C3
St Pourçain-sur-Sioule
. . . . .116 A3
St Priest F 117 B4
St Privat F 116 B2
St Quay-Portrieux
. . . . .100 A3
St Quentin F 90 B3
St Quentin-la-Poterie
. . . . .131 A3
St Quentin-les-Anges
. . . . .102 B1
St Rambert-d'Albon
. . . . .117 B4
St Rambert-en-Bugey
. . . . .118 B2
St Raphaël F 132 B2
St Rémy-de-Provence
. . . . .131 B3
St Rémy-du-Val F .89 B4
St Remy-en-Bouzemont
F 91 C4
St Renan F 100 A1
St Révérien F 104 B2
St Riquier F 90 A1
St Romain-de-Colbosc
F. 89 A4
St Rome-de-Cernon
F 130 A1
St Rome-de-Tarn
F 130 A1
St Sadurní-d'Anoia
E 147 C2
St Saëns F 89 A5
St Sampson GB. . .88 A1
St Samson-la-Poterie
F. 90 B1
St Saturnin-de-Lenne
F 130 A2
St Saturnin-lès-Apt
. . . . .131 B4
St Sauflieu F 90 B2
St Saulge F 104 B2
St Sauveur
Finistère F 100 A2
Haute-Saône F .105 B5
St Sauveur-de-
Montagut F 117 C4
St Sauveur-en-Puisaye
. . . . .104 B2
St Sauveur-en-Rue
. . . . .117 B4
St Sauveur-Lendelin
F. 88 A2
St Sauveur-le-Vicomte
F. 88 A2
St Sauveur-sur-Tinée
. . . . .132 A3
St Savin
Gironde F 128 A2
Vienne F. 115 B4
St Savinien F 114 C3
St Savournin F . . .131 B4
St Seine-l'Abbaye
F 105 B3
St Sernin-sur-Rance
F 130 B1
St Sevan-sur-Mer F 88 B1
St Sever F 128 C2
St Sever-Calvados
F. 88 B2
St Sorlin-d'Arves
. . . . .118 B3
St Soupplets F 90 B2
St Sulpice F 129 C4
St Sulpice-Laurière
. . . . .116 A1
St Sulpice-les-Feuilles
F. 115 B5
St Symphorien F. .128 B2
St Symphoriende-Lay
F. 117 B4
St Symphorien d'Ozon
. . . . .117 B4
St Symphoriensur-
Coise F 117 B4
St Teath GB 42 B2
St Thégonnec F . .100 A2
St Thiébault F . . .105 A4

St Trivier-de-Courtes
. . . . .118 A2
St Trivier sur-Moignans
. . . . .117 A4
St Trojan-les-Bains
. . . . .114 C2
St Tropez F 132 B2
St Truiden B 79 B5
St Vaast-la-Hougue
F. 88 A2
St Valérien F 104 A2
St Valery-en-Caux
F. 89 A4
St Valéry-sur-Somme
. . . . .78 B1
St Vallier
Drôme F. 117 B4
Saône-et-Loire F 104 C3
St Vallier-de-Thiey
. . . . .132 B2
St Varent F 102 C1
St Vaury F 116 A1
St Venant F 78 B2
St Véran F 119 C3
St Vincent I 119 B4
St Vincent-de-Tyrosse
. . . . .128 C1
St Vit F 105 B4
St Vith B 80 B2
St Vivien-de-Médoc
. . . . .114 C2
St Yan F 117 A4
St Ybars F 146 A2
St Yorre F 117 A3
St Yrieix-la-Perche
. . . . .115 C5
Saissac F 146 A3
Saja E 142 A2
Sajan SRB 126 B2
Sajókaza H. 99 C4
Sajószentpéter H .113 A4
Sajóvámos H 113 A4
Sakarya TR 187 B5
Šakiai LT 13 A5
Sakskøbing DK . . .65 B4
Sakule SRB 126 B2
Sala S 50 C3
Šaľa SK 111 A4
Sala Baganza I . . .120 C3
Sala Consilina I . . .172 B1
Salakovac SRB . .127 C3
Salamanca E 150 B2
Salamina GR 185 B4
Salandra I 172 B2
Salaparuta I 176 B1
Salar E 163 A3
Salardú E 145 B4
Salas E 141 A4
Salas de los Infantes
E 143 B3
Salau F 146 B2
Salavaux CH 106 C2
Salbertrand I 119 B3
Salbohed S 50 C3
Salbris F 103 B4
Salbu N 46 A2
Salce E 141 B4
Salching D 95 C4
Salcombe GB 43 B3
Saldaña E 142 B2
Saldus LV 8 D3
Sale I 120 C1
Saleby S 55 B4
Salem D 107 B4
Salemi I 176 B1
Salen
Argyll & Bute GB .34 B2
Highland GB 34 B2
N. 199 A8
Sälen S. 49 A5
Salernes F 132 B2
Salerno I 170 C2
Salers F 116 B2
Salford GB 40 B1
Salgótarján H 113 A3
Salgueiro P 155 B3
Salhus N 46 B2
Sali HR. 137 B4
Sálice Salentino I .173 B3
Salientes E 141 B4
Salies-de-Béarn F 144 A3
Salies-du-Salat F .145 A4
Salignac-Eyvigues
F 129 B4
Saligney-sur-Roudon
. . . . .104 C2
Salihli TR 188 A3
Salihorsk BY 13 B7
Salinas
Alicante E 159 C3
Huesca E 145 B4
Salinas de Medinaceli
E 152 A1
Salinas de Pisuerga
E 142 B2
Salindres F 131 A3
Saline di Volterra
I 135 B3
Salins-les-Bains F 105 C4
Salir P. 160 B1
Salisbury GB 44 B2
Salla
A. 110 B1
FIN 197 C11
Sallachy GB. 32 C2
Sallanches F 118 B3
Sallent E 147 C2
Sallent de Gállego
E 145 B3
Salles F 128 B2
Salles-Curan F . . .130 A1
Salles-sur-l'Hers
. . . . .146 A2
Sallins IRL 30 A2
Sällsjö S. 199 B10
Salmerón E 152 B1
Salmiech F 130 A1
Salmivaara FIN . .197 C11
Salmoral E 150 B2

Salo FIN 8 B3
Salò I 121 B3
Salobreña E 163 B4
Salon-de-Provence
F 131 B4
Salonica = Thessaloniki
GR 182 C4
Salonta RO 16 B4
Salorino E 155 B3
Salornay-sur-Guye
. . . . .104 C3
Salorno I 121 A4
Salou E 147 C2
Šalovci SLO. 111 C3
Salsbruket N 199 A8
Salses-le-Chateau
F 146 B3
Salsomaggiore Terme
I 120 C2
Salt E 147 C3
Saltaire GB 40 B2
Saltara I 136 B1
Saltash GB. 42 B2
Saltburn-by-the-Sea
GB 37 B6
Saltcoats GB. 34 C3
Saltfleet GB 41 B4
Salto P 148 A2
Saltrød N 53 B4
Saltsjöbaden S . . .57 A4
Saltvik
FIN 51 B7
S. 62 A4
Saludécio I 136 B1
Salussola I 119 B5
Saluzzo I 119 C4
Salvacañete E 152 B2
Salvada P. 160 B2
Salvagnac F 129 C4
Salvaleón E 155 C4
Salvaterra de Magos
P 154 B2
Salvaterra do Extremo
P 155 B4
Salvatierra
Avila E 143 B4
Badajoz E 155 C4
Salvatierra de Santiago
E 156 A1
Salviac F 129 B4
Salzburg A 109 B4
Salzgitter D 72 B3
Salzgitter Bad D . .72 B3
Salzhausen D 72 A3
Salzhemmendorf D 72 B2
Salzkotten D 81 A4
Salzmünde D 83 A3
Salzwedel D 73 B4
Samadet F 128 C2
Samandıra TR . . .186 B4
Samassi I 179 C2
Samatan F 146 A1
Sambiase I 175 C2
Sambir UA 13 D5
Samborowo PL . . .69 B4
Sambuca di Sicília
I 176 B2
Samedan CH 107 C4
Samer F 78 B1
Sami GR. 184 A1
Şamlı TR 186 C2
Sammichele di Bari
I 173 B2
Samnaun CH 107 C5
Samobor HR 123 B4
Samoëns F 118 A3
Samogneux F 92 B1
Samokov BG 17 D5
Samora Correia P .154 C2
Šamorín SK 111 A4
Samos
E 141 B3
GR 188 B1
Samoš SRB 126 B2
Samothraki GR . .183 C7
Samper de Calanda
E 153 A3
Sampéyre I 133 A3
Sampieri I 177 C3
Sampigny F 92 C1
Samplawa PL. 69 B4
Samproniano I . . .168 A1
Samtens D 66 B2
Samugheo I 179 C2
San Adrián E 144 B2
San Agustin E . . .164 C2
San Agustin de
Guadalix E 151 B4
Sanaigmore GB. . .34 C1
San Alberto I 135 A5
San Amaro E 140 B2
Sânandrei RO 126 B3
San Andrès del
Rabanedo E 142 B1
San Antanio di Santadi
I 179 C2
San Antolin de Ibias
E 141 A4
San Arcángelo I . .174 A2
Sanary-sur-Mer F .132 B1
San Asensio E . . .143 B4
San Bartoloméde las
Abiertas E 150 C3
San Bartoloméde la
Torre E 161 B2
San Bartolomée
Pinares E 150 B3
San Bartolomeo in
Galdo I 170 B3
San Benedetto del
Tronto I 136 C2
San Benedetto in Alpe
I 135 B4
San Benedetto Po
I 121 B3
San Benito E 156 B3
San Benito de la
Contienda E 155 C3
San Biágio Plátani
I 176 B2

San Biágio Saracinisco
I 169 B3
San Bonifacio I . . .121 B4
San Calixto E 156 C2
San Cándido I 109 C3
San Carlo
CH 119 A5
I 176 B2
San Carlos del Valle
E 157 B4
San Casciano dei Bagni
I 135 C4
San Casciano in Val di
Pesa I 135 B4
San Cataldo
Puglia I 173 B4
Sicilia I 176 B2
San Cebrián de Castro
E 149 A4
Sancergues F 104 B1
Sancerre F 103 B4
San Cesário di Lecce
I 173 B4
Sancey-le-Long F .105 B5
Sanchiorian E 150 B3
San Chírico Raparo
I 174 A2
San Cipirello I 176 B2
San Ciprián E 141 A3
San Clemente E . .158 B1
San Clodio E 141 B3
Sancoins F 104 C1
San Colombano al
Lambro I 120 B2
San Costanzo I . . .136 B2
San Crisóbal de
Entreviñas E 142 B1
San Cristóbal de la
Polantera E 141 B5
San Cristóbal de la
Vega E 150 A3
San Cristovo E . . .141 C3
Sancti-Petri E 162 B1
Sancti-Spiritus E . .149 B3
Sand
Hedmark N 48 B3
Rogaland N 52 A2
Sanda S 57 C4
San Damiano d'Asti
I 119 C5
San Damiano Macra
I 133 A3
Sandane N 198 D3
San Daniele del Friuli
I 122 A2
Sandanski BG 183 B5
Sandared S 60 B2
Sandarne S 51 A4
Sandau D. 73 B5
Sandbach
D. 96 C1
GB 38 A4
Sandbank GB 34 C3
Sandbanks GB . . .43 B5
Sandbukt N 192 C5
Sandby DK. 65 B4
Sande
D. 71 A5
Sogn og Fjordane
N. 46 A2
Vestfold N 54 A1
Sandefjord N 54 A1
Sandeid N. 52 A1
San Demétrio Corone
I 174 B2
San Demétrio né
Vestini I 169 A3
Sandersleben D . . .82 A3
Sanderstølen N . . .47 B6
Sandes N 53 B3
Sandesneben D. . .65 C3
Sandhead GB 36 B2
Sandhem S 60 B3
Sandhorst D 71 A4
Sandhurst GB 44 B3
Sandıklı TR 189 A5
Sandillon F 103 B4
Sandl A. 96 C2
Sandnes
GB 33 A5
N 52 B1
Sandness GB 33 A5
Sandnessjøen N . .195 D3
Sando E 149 B3
Sandomierz PL . . .87 B5
San Dónaci I 173 B3
San Donàdi Piave
I 122 B1
San Donato Val di
Comino I 169 B3
Sándorfalva H 126 A2
Sandown GB 44 C2
Sandøysund N 54 A1
Sandrigo I 121 B4
Sandsele S 195 E8
Sandset N 194 B5
Sandsjöfors S 62 A2
Sandstad N 198 B6
Sandvatn N 52 B2
Sandvig-Allinge DK 67 A3
Sandvika
Akershus N 48 C2
Hedmark N 48 B3
Nord-Trøndelag
N. 199 B9
Sandviken S 51 B3
Sandvikvåg N 46 C2
Sandwich GB. 45 B5
Sandy GB. 44 A3
San Emiliano E . . .141 B5
San Enrique E . . .162 B2
San Esteban E . . .141 A4
San Esteban de
Gormaz E 151 A4
San Esteban de la
Sierra E 149 B4
San Esteban de Litera
E 145 C4

San Esteban del Molar
E 142 C1
San Esteban del Valle
E 150 B3
San Esteban de
Valdueza E 141 B4
San Fele I 172 B1
San Felice Circeo
I 169 B3
San Felices E 143 B3
San Felices de los
Gallégos E 149 B3
San Felice sul Panaro
I 121 C4
San Ferdinando di
Púglia I 171 B4
San Fernando E . .162 B1
San Fernando de
Henares E 151 B4
San Fili I 174 B2
San Foca I 173 B4
San Fratello I 177 B3
Sangatte F 78 B1
San Gavino Monreale
I 179 C2
San Gémini Fonte
I 168 A2
Sangerhausen D . .82 A3
San Germano
Vercellese I 119 B5
San Giácomo
Trentino Alto Adige
I 108 C2
Umbria I 136 C1
San Gimignano I . .135 B4
San Ginésio I 136 B2
Sangineto Lido I . .174 B1
San Giórgio a Liri
I 169 B3
San Giorgio della
Richinvelda I 122 A1
San Giórgio del Sánnio
I 170 B2
San Giórgio di
Lomellina I 120 B1
San Giórgio di Nogaro
I 122 B2
San Giorgio di Piano
I 121 C4
San Giórgio Iónico
I 173 B3
San Giovanni a Piro
I 172 B1
San Giovanni Bianco
I 120 B2
San Giovanni di Sinis
I 179 C2
San Giovanni in Croce
I 120 B3
San Giovanni in Fiore
I 174 B2
San Giovanni in
Persiceto I. 121 C4
San Giovanni Reatino
I 169 A2
San Giovanni Rotondo
I 171 B3
San Giovanni Suérgiu
I 179 C2
San Giovanni Valdarno
I 135 B4
Sangis S 196 D6
San Giuliano Terme
I 134 B3
San Giustino I 135 B5
San Godenzo I . . .135 B4
Sangonera la Verde
E 165 B3
San Gregorio Magno
I 172 B1
Sangüesa E 144 B2
Sanguinet F 128 B1
San Guiseppe Jato
I 176 B2
Sanica BIH. 124 C2
Sanitz D. 65 B5
San Javier E 165 B4
San Jorge E 154 B2
San José E 164 C2
San Juan E 143 B3
San Juan de Alicante
E 165 A4
San Juan de la Nava
E 150 B3
San Justo de la Vega
E 141 B4
Sankt Aegyd am
Neuwalde A. 110 B2
Sankt Andrä A 110 C1
Sankt Andreasberg
D 82 A2
Sankt Anna S 56 B2
Sankt Anna am Aigen
A. 110 C2
Sankt Anton am
Arlberg A. 107 B5
Sankt Anton an der
Jessnitz A. 110 B2
Sankt Augustin D . .80 B3
Sankt Blasien D. . .106 B3
Sankt Englmar D. . .95 B4
Sankt Gallen
A. 110 B1
CH 107 B4
Sankt Gallenkirch
A. 107 B4
Sankt Georgen
A. 96 C2
D. 106 A3
Sankt Georgen am
Reith A. 110 B1
Sankt Georgen ob
Judenburg A. . . .110 B1
Sankt Georgen ob
Murau A. 109 B5
Sankt Gilgen A. . . .109 B4
Sankt Goar D 81 B3
Sankt Goarshausen
D 81 B3
Sankt Ingbert D. . . .92 B3

Sankt Jacob A 109 C5
Sankt Jakob in Defereggen A 109 C3
Sankt Johann am Tauern A 110 B1
Sankt Johann am Wesen A 109 A4
Sankt Johann im Pongau A 109 B4
Sankt Johann in Tirol A 109 B3
Sankt Katharein an der Laming A 110 B2
Sankt Kathrein am Hauenstein A 110 B2
Sankt Lambrecht A 110 B1
Sankt Leonhard am Forst A 110 A2
Sankt Leonhard im Pitztal A 108 B1
Sankt Lorenzen A 109 C3
Sankt Marein
  Steiermark A 110 B2
  Steiermark A 110 B2
Sankt Margarethen im Lavanttal A 110 C1
Sankt Margrethen CH 107 B4
Sankt Michael A 110 B2
Sankt Michael im Burgenland A 111 B3
Sankt Michael im Lungau A 109 B4
Sankt Michaelisdonn D 64 C2
Sankt Niklaus CH 119 A4
Sankt Nikolai im Sölktal A 109 B5
Sankt Olof S 63 C2
Sankt Oswald D 96 C1
Sankt Paul
  A 110 C1
  F 132 A2
Sankt Peter D 106 A3
Sankt Peter am Kammersberg A 110 B1
Sankt-Peterburg = St Petersburg RUS 9 C7
Sankt Peter-Ording D 64 B1
Sankt Pölten A 110 A2
Sankt Radegund A 110 B2
Sankt Ruprecht an der Raab A 110 B2
Sankt Salvator A 110 C1
Sankt Stefan A 110 C1
Sankt Stefan an der Gail A 109 C4
Sankt Stefan im Rosental A 110 C2
Sankt Valentin A 110 A1
Sankt Veit an der Glan A 110 C1
Sankt Veit an der Gölsen A 110 A2
Sankt Veit in Defereggen A 109 C3
Sankt Wendel D 92 B3
Sankt Wolfgang
  A 109 B4
  D 108 A3
San Lazzaro di Sávena I 135 A4
San Leo I 135 B5
San Leonardo de Yagüe E 143 C3
San Leonardo in Passiria I 108 C2
San Lorenzo al Mare I 133 B3
San Lorenzo a Merse I 135 B4
San Lorenzo Bellizzi I 174 B2
San Lorenzo de Calatrava E 157 B4
San Lorenzo de El Escorial E 151 B3
San Lorenzo de la Parrilla E 158 B1
San Lorenzo di Sebato I 108 C2
San Lorenzo in Campo I 136 B1
San Lorenzo Nuovo I 168 A1
San Lourenco P 160 A1
San Luca I 175 C2
Sanlúcar de Barrameda E 161 C3
Sanlúcar de Guadiana E 160 B2
Sanlúcar la Mayor E 161 B3
San Lúcido I 174 B2
Sanluri I 179 C2
San Marcello I 136 B2
San Marcello Pistoiese I 135 A3
San Marcial E 149 A4
San Marco I 170 C2
San Marco Argentano I 174 B2
San Marco dei Cavoti I 170 B2
San Marco in Lámis I 171 B3
San Marino RSM 136 B1
San Martín de Castañeda E 141 B4
San Martín de la Vega E 151 B4
San Martín de la Vega del Alberche E 150 B2
San Martín del Tesorillo E 162 B2
San Martín de Luiña E 141 A4
San Martín de Montalbán E 157 A3
San Martín de Oscos E 141 A4
San Martín de Pusa E 150 C3
San Martín de Unx E 144 B2
San Martín de Valdeiglesias E 150 B3
San Martino di Campagna I 122 A1
San Martino di Castrozza I 121 A4
San-Martino-di-Lota F 180 A2
San Martino in Pénsilis I 170 B3
San Mateo de Gallego E 144 C3
San Máuro Forte I 172 B2
San Michele all'Adige I 121 A4
San Michele di Ganzaria I 177 B3
San Michele Mondov i I 133 A3
San Miguel de Aguayo E 142 A2
San Miguel de Bernuy E 151 A4
San Miguel del Arroyo E 150 A3
San Miguel de Salinas E 165 B4
Sânmihaiu Roman RO 126 B3
San Millán de la Cogolla E 143 B4
San Miniato I 135 B3
San Muñoz E 149 B3
Sänna S 55 B5
Sannazzaro de'Burgondi I 120 B1
Sanne D 73 B4
Sannicandro di Bari I 171 B4
Sannicandro Gargánico I 171 B3
San Nicola del'Alto I 174 B2
San Nicolás del Puerto E 156 C2
Sânnicolau Mare RO 126 A2
San Nicolò I 121 C4
San Nicolò Gerrei I 179 C3
Sannidal N 53 B5
Sanniki PL 77 B4
Sanok PL 12 D5
San Pablo de los Montes E 157 A3
San Pancrázio Salentino I 173 B3
San Pantaleo I 178 A3
San Páolo di Civitate I 171 B3
San Pawl il-Bahar M 175 C3
San Pedro
  Albacete E 158 C1
  Oviedo E 141 A4
San Pedro de Alcántara E 162 B3
San Pedro de Ceque E 141 B4
San Pedro del Arroyo E 150 B3
San Pedro de Latarce E 142 C1
San Pedro del Pinatar E 165 B4
San Pedro del Romeral E 143 A3
San Pedro de Merida E 156 B1
San Pedro de Valderaduey E 142 B2
San Pedro Manrique E 144 B1
San Pellegrino Terme I 120 B2
San Piero a Sieve I 135 B4
San Piero in Bagno I 135 B4
San Piero Patti I 177 A3
San Pietro I 177 B3
San Pietro in Casale I 121 C4
San Pietro in Gu I 121 B4
San Pietro in Palazzi I 134 B3
San Pietro in Volta I 122 B1
San Pietro Vara I 134 A2
San Pietro Vernótico I 173 B3
San Polo d'Enza I 121 C3
Sanquhar GB 36 A3
San Quírico d'Órcia I 135 B4
San Rafael del Rio E 153 B4
San Remo I 133 B3
San Román de Cameros E 143 B4
San Roman de Hernija E 150 A2
San Román de la Cuba E 142 B2
San Roman de los Montes E 150 B3
San Romao P 155 C3
San Roque E 162 B2
San Roque de Riomera E 143 A3
San Rufo I 172 B1
San Sabastián de los Ballesteros E 162 A3
San Salvador de Cantamuda E 142 B2
San Salvo I 170 A2
San Salvo Marina I 170 A2
San Sebastián de los Reyes E 151 B4
San Sebastiano Curone I 120 C2
San Secondo Parmense I 120 C3
Sansepolcro I 135 B5
San Serverino Marche I 136 B2
San Severino Lucano I 174 A2
San Severo I 171 B3
San Silvestre de Guzmán E 161 B2
Sanski Most BIH 124 C2
San Sosti I 174 B2
San Stéfano di Cadore I 109 C3
San Stino di Livenza I 122 B1
Santa Agnès E 166 B1
Santa Amalia E 156 A1
Santa Ana
  Cáceres E 156 A2
  Jaén E 163 A4
Santa Ana de Pusa E 150 C3
Santa Barbara E 153 B4
Santa Bárbara P 160 B1
Santa Barbara de Casa E 161 B2
Santa Bárbara de Padrões P 160 B2
Santacara E 144 B2
Santa Catarina P 160 B2
Santa Caterina di Pittinuri I 178 B2
Santa Caterina Villarmosa I 177 B3
Santa Cesárea Terme I 173 B4
Santa Clara-a-Nova P 160 B1
Santa Clara-a-Velha P 160 B1
Santa Clara de Louredo P 160 B2
Santa Coloma de Farners E 147 C3
Santa Coloma de Gramenet E 147 C3
Santa Coloma de Queralt E 147 C2
Santa Colomba de Curueño E 142 B1
Santa Colomba de Somoza E 141 B4
Santa Comba E 140 A2
Santa Comba Dáo P 148 B1
Santa Comba de Rossas P 149 A3
Santa Cristina I 120 B2
Santa Cristina de la Polvorosa E 141 B5
Santa Croce Camerina I 177 C3
Santa Croce di Magliano I 170 B2
Santa Cruz
  E 140 A2
  P 154 B1
Santa Cruz de Alhama E 163 A4
Santa Cruz de Campezo E 143 B4
Santa Cruz de Grio E 152 A2
Santa Cruz de la Salceda E 151 A4
Santa Cruz de la Sierra E 156 A2
Santa Cruz de la Zarza E 151 C4
Santa Cruz del Retamar E 151 B3
Santa Cruz del Valle E 150 B2
Santa Cruz de Moya E 159 B2
Santa Cruz de Mudela E 157 B4
Santa Cruz de Paniagua E 149 B3
Santadi I 179 C2
Santa Doménica Talao I 174 B1
Santa Doménica Vittória I 177 B3
Santa Elena E 157 B4
Santa Elena de Jamuz E 141 B5
Santaella E 162 A3
Santa Eufemia E 156 B3
Santa Eufémia d'Aspromonte I 175 C1
Santa Eulalia E 152 B2
Santa Eulália P 155 C3
Santa Eulalia de Oscos E 141 A3
Santa Eulàlia des Riu E 166 C1
Santa Fe E 163 A4
Santa Fiora I 135 C4
Sant'Ágata dei Goti I 170 B2
Sant'Ágata di Ésaro I 174 B1
Sant'Ágata di Puglia I 171 B3
Sant'Agata Feltria I 135 B5
Sant'Ágata Militello I 177 A3
Santa Gertrude I 108 C1
Santa Giustina I 121 A5
Sant Agust ide Lluçanès E 147 B3
Santa Iria P 160 B2
Santa Leocadia P 148 A1
Santa Lucia del Mela I 177 A4
Santa Lucia-de-Porto-Vecchio F 180 B2
Santa Luzia P 160 B1
Santa Maddalena Vallalta I 108 C3
Santa Magdalena de Polpis E 153 B4
Santa Margalida E 167 B3
Santa Margarida P 154 B2
Santa Margarida do Sado P 160 A1
Santa Margaridao de Montbui E 147 C2
Santa Margherita I 179 D2
Santa Margherita di Belice I 176 B2
Santa Margherita Ligure I 134 A2
Santa Maria
  CH 108 C1
  E 144 B3
Santa Maria al Bagno I 173 B3
Santa Maria Cápua Vétere I 170 B2
Santa Maria da Feira P 148 B1
Santa Maria de Cayón E 143 A3
Santa Maria de Corco E 147 B3
Santa Maria de Huerta E 152 A1
Santa Maria de la Alameda E 151 B3
Santa Maria de las Hoyas E 143 C3
Santa Maria del Camí E 167 B2
Santa Maria del Campo E 143 B3
Santa Maria del Campo Rus E 158 B1
Santa Maria della Versa I 120 C2
Santa Maria del Páramo E 142 B1
Santa Maria del Taro I 134 A2
Santa Maria de Mercadillo E 143 C3
Santa Maria de Nieva E 164 B3
Santa Maria de Trassierra E 156 C3
Santa Maria di Licodia I 177 B3
Santa Maria-di-Rispéscia I 168 A1
Santa Maria la Palma I 178 B2
Santa María la Real de Nieva E 150 A3
Santa Maria Maggiore I 119 A5
Santa Maria Ribarredonda E 143 B3
Santa Marina del Rey E 141 B5
Santa Marinella I 168 A1
Santa Marta
  Albacete E 158 B1
  Badajoz E 155 C4
Santa Marta de Magasca E 156 A1
Santa Marta de Penaguião P 148 A2
Santa Marta de Tormes E 150 B2
Santana
  Évora P 154 C2
  Setúbal P 154 C1
Sântana RO 126 A3
Santana da Serra P 160 B1
Sant'Ana de Cambas P 160 B2
Santana do Mato P 154 C2
Sant'Anastasia I 170 C2
Santander E 143 A3
Sant'Andrea Frius I 179 C3
Sant'Ángelo dei Lombardi I 172 B1
Sant'Angelo in Vado I 136 B1
Sant'Angelo Lodigiano I 120 B2
Santa Ninfa I 176 B1
Sant'Antíoco I 179 C2
Sant Antoni de Calonge E 147 C4
Sant Antoni de Portmany E 166 C1
Sant'Antonio-di-Gallura I 178 B3
Santanyí E 167 B3
Santa Olalla
  Huelva E 161 B3
  Toledo E 150 B3
Santa Pau E 147 B3
Santa Pola E 165 A4
Santa Ponça E 166 B2
Santarcángelo di Romagna I 136 A1
Santarém P 154 B2
Santa Severa
  F 180 A2
  I 168 A1
Santa Severina I 175 B2
Santas Martas E 142 B1
Santa Sofia I 135 B4
Santa Susana P 154 C2
Santa Suzana P 155 C3
Santa Teresa di Riva I 177 B4
Santa Teresa Gallura I 178 A3
Santa Uxía E 140 B2
Santa Valburga I 108 C1
Santa Vittória in Matenano I 136 B2
Sant Boi de Llobregat E 147 C3
Sant Carles de la Ràpita E 153 B4
Sant Carlos E 166 B1
Sant'Caterina I 135 C4
Sant Celoni E 147 C3
Sant Climent E 167 B4
Santed E 152 A2
Sant'Egídio alla Vibrata I 136 C2
Sant'Elia a Pianisi I 170 B2
Sant'Elia Fiumerapido I 169 B3
Santelices E 143 A3
San Telmo E 161 B3
Sant'Elpídio a Mare I 136 B2
Santéramo in Colle I 171 C4
Santervas de la Vega E 142 B2
Sant' Eufemia Lamezia 175 C2
Sant Feliu E 147 C3
Sant Feliu de Codines E 147 C3
Sant Feliu de Guíxols E 147 C4
Sant Feliu Sasserra E 147 C3
Sant Ferran E 166 C1
Sant Francesc de Formentera E 166 C1
Sant Francesc de ses Salines E 166 C1
Santhià I 119 B5
Sant Hilari Sacalm E 147 C3
Sant Hipòlit de Voltregà E 147 B3
Santiago de Alcántara E 155 B3
Santiago de Calatrava E 163 A3
Santiago de Compostela E 140 B2
Santiago de la Espade E 164 A2
Santiago de la Puebla E 150 B2
Santiago de la Ribera E 165 B4
Santiago del Campo E 155 B4
Santiago de Litem P 154 B2
Santiago do Cacém P 160 B1
Santiago do Escoural P 154 C2
Santiago Maior P 155 C3
Santibáñez de Béjar E 150 B2
Santibáñez de la Peña E 142 B2
Santibáñez de Murias E 142 A1
Santibáñez de Vidriales E 141 B4
Santibáñez el Alto E 149 B3
Santibáñez el Bajo E 149 B3
Santillana E 142 A2
Santiponce E 162 A1
San Tirso de Abres E 141 A3
Santisteban del Puerto E 157 B4
Santiuste de San Juan Bautiste E 150 A3
Santiz E 149 A4
Sant Jaume dels Domenys E 147 C2
Sant Joan Baptista E 166 B1
Sant Joan de les Abadesses E 147 B3
Sant Jordi E 153 B4
Sant Josep de sa Talaia E 166 C1
Sant Juliáde Loria AND 146 B2
Sant'Ilario d'Enza I 121 C3
Sant Llorençde Morunys E 147 B2
Sant Llorençdes Carctassar E 167 B3
Sant Llorenç Savall E 147 C3
Sant Luis E 167 B4
Sant Mart ìde Llemaná E 147 B3
Sant Marti de Maldá E 147 C2
Sant Marti Sarroca E 147 C2
Sant Mateu E 153 B4
Sant Miquel E 166 B1
Santo Aleixo P 161 A2
Santo Amado P 161 A2
Santo Amaro P 155 C3
Santo André P 160 A1
Santo Domingo E 155 C3
Santo Domingo de la Calzada E 143 B4
Santo Domingo de Silos E 143 C3
Santo Estêvão
  Faro P 160 B2
  Santarém P 154 C2
Santok PL 75 B4
Santomera E 165 A3
Santoña E 143 A3
Santo-Pietro-di Tenda F 180 A2
Sant'Oreste I 168 A2
Santo Spirito I 171 B4
Santo Stefano d'Aveto I 134 A2
Santo Stéfano di Camastra I 177 A3
Santo Stefano di Magra I 134 A2
Santo Stéfano Quisquina I 176 B2
Santo Tirso P 148 A1
Santotis E 142 A2
Santo Tomé E 164 A1
Santovenia
  Burgos E 143 B3
  Zamora E 142 C1
Sant Pau de Seguries E 147 B3
Santpedor E 147 C2
Sant Pere de Riudebitles E 147 C2
Sant Pere Pescador E 147 B4
Sant Pere Sallavinera E 147 C2
Sant Quirze de Besora E 147 B3
Sant Rafel E 166 C1
Sant Ramon E 147 C2
Santu Lussurgiu I 178 B2
Santutzi E 143 A3
Sant Vincençde Castellet E 147 C2
San Valentino alla Muta I 108 C1
San Venanzo I 135 C5
San Vicente de Alcántara E 155 B3
San Vicente de Arana E 144 B1
San Vicente de la Barquera E 142 A2
San Vicente de la Sonsierra E 143 B4
San Vicente de Toranzo E 143 A3
San Vietro E 149 A3
San Vigilio I 108 C2
San Vincente del Raspeig E 165 A4
San Vincenzo I 134 B3
San Vito I 179 C3
San Vito al Tagliamento I 122 B1
San Vito Chietino I 169 A4
San Vito dei Normanni I 173 B3
San Vito di Cadore I 108 C3
San Vito lo Capo I 176 A1
San Vito Romano I 169 B2
Sanxenxo E 140 B2
Sanza I 172 B1
São Aleixo P 155 C3
São Barnabé P 160 B1
São Bartoloméda Serra P 160 A1
São Bartolomeu de Messines P 160 B1
São Bento P 140 C2
São Brás P 160 B2
São Brás de Alportel P 160 B2
São Braz do Reguedoura P 154 C2
São Cristóvão P 154 C2
São Domingos P 160 B1
São Geraldo P 154 C2
São Jacinto P 148 B1
São João da Madeira P 148 B1
São João da Pesqueira P 148 A2
São João da Ribeira P 154 B2
São João da Serra P 148 B1
São João da Venda P 160 B2
São João dos Caldeireiros P 160 B2
São Julião P 155 B3
São Leonardo P 155 C3
São Luis P 160 B1
São Manços P 155 C3
São Marcos da Ataboeira P 160 B2
Saõ Marcos da Serra P 160 B1
São Marcos de Campo P 155 C3
São Martinho da Cortiça P 148 B1
São Martinho das Amoreiras P 160 B1
São Martinho do Porto P 154 B1
São Matias
  Beja P 160 A2
  Évora P 154 C2
São Miguel d'Acha P 155 A3
São Miguel de Machede P 155 C3
São Pedro da Torre P 140 C2
São Pedro de Cadeira P 154 B1
São Pedro de Moel P 154 B1
São Pedro de Solis P 160 B2
São Pedro do Sul P 148 B1
Saorge F 133 B3
São Romão P 154 C2
São Sebastião dos Carros P 160 B2
São Teotónio P 160 B1
São Torcato P 148 A1
Sapataria P 154 C1
Sapes GR 183 B7
Sapiãos P 148 A2
Sa Pobla E 167 B3
Sappada I 109 C3
Sappen N 192 C5
Sapri I 174 A1
Sarajärvi FIN 197 D10
Sarajevo BIH 139 B4
Saramon F 129 C3
Sarandë AL 182 D2
Saranovo SRB 127 C2
Saraorci SRB 127 C3
Sa Rapita E 167 B3
Saray TR 186 A2
Saraycık TR 187 C4
Sarayköy TR 188 B3
Saraylar TR 186 B2
Sarayönü TR 189 A7
Sarbia PL 75 B5
Sarbinowo
  Zachodnio-Pomorskie PL 67 B4
  Zachodnio-Pomorskie PL 74 B3
Sárbogárd H 112 C2
Sarcelles F 90 B2
Sarche I 121 A3
Sardara I 179 C2
Sardoal P 154 B2
Sardón de Duero E 150 A3
Sare F 144 A2
S'Arenal E 166 B2
Šarengrad HR 125 B5
Sarentino I 108 C2
Sarezzo I 120 B3
Sargans CH 107 B4
Sári H 112 B3
Sarıbeyler TR 186 C2
Sarıcakaya TR 187 B5
Sari-d'Orcino F 180 A1
Sarıgöl TR 188 A3
Sarıkaya TR 23 B8
Sarıköy TR 186 B2
Sarilhos Grandes P 154 C2
Sariñena E 145 C3
Sarıoba TR 187 C7
Sárisáp H 112 B2
Sarıyer TR 186 A4
Sarkad H 113 C5
Sárkeresztes H 112 B2
Sárkeresztúr H 112 B2
Särkijärvi FIN 196 B6
Şarkikaraağaç TR 189 A6
Şarköy TR 186 B2
Sarlat-la-Canéda F 129 B4
Sarliac-sur-l'Isle F 129 A3
Sármellék H 111 C4
Särna S 199 D10
Sarnadas P 155 B3
Sarnano I 136 B2
Sarnen CH 106 C3
Sarnesfield GB 39 B4
Sárnico I 120 B2
Sarno I 170 C2
Sarnonico I 121 A4
Sarnow D 74 A2
Sarny UA 13 C7
Särö S 60 B1
Saronno I 120 B2
Sárosd H 112 B2
Šarovce SK 112 A2
Sarpoil F 117 B3
Sarpsborg N 54 A2
Sarracín E 143 B3
Sarral E 147 C2
Sarralbe F 92 B3
Sarrancolin F 145 B4
Sarras F 117 B4
Sarre I 119 B4
Sarreaus E 140 B3
Sarrebourg F 92 C3
Sarreguemines F 92 B3
Sárrétudvari H 113 B5
Sarre-Union F 92 C3
Sarria E 141 B3
Sarriàde Ter E 147 B3
Sarrión E 153 B3
Sarroca de Lleida E 153 A4
Sarroch I 179 C3
Sarron F 128 C2
Sársina I 135 B5
Særslev DK 59 C3
Sarstedt D 72 B2
Sárszentlörinc H 112 C2
Sárszentmihaly H 112 B2
Sárszentmiklós H 112 C2
Sarteano I 135 C4
Sartène F 180 B1
Sartilly F 88 B2
Sartirana Lomellina I 120 B1
Saruhanlı TR 186 D2
Sárvár H 111 B3

Sarvisvaara S	196 C4
Sarzana I	134 A2
Sarzeau F	101 B3
Sarzedas P	155 B3
Sasalli TR	188 A1
Sasamón E	142 B2
Sa Savina E	166 C1
Sásd H	125 A4
Sasino PL	68 A2
Sássari I	178 B2
Sassello I	133 A4
Sassenberg D	71 C5
Sassetta I	134 B3
Sassnitz D	66 B2
Sassocorvaro I	136 B1
Sasso d'Ombrone I	135 C4
Sassoferrato I	136 B1
Sassoleone I	135 A4
Sasso Marconi I	135 A4
Sassuolo I	135 A3
Sástago E	153 A3
Šaštinske Stráže SK	98 C1
Sas van Gent NL	79 A3
Såtåhaugen N	199 C7
Satão P	148 B2
Såtenäs S	55 B3
Säter S	50 B2
Sätila S	60 B2
Satillieu F	117 B4
Satnica Đakovačka HR	125 B4
Sátoraljaújhely H	16 A4
Satow D	65 C4
Sätra-brunn S	50 C3
Sætre N	54 A1
Satrup D	64 B2
Satteins A	107 B4
Satu Mare RO	17 B5
Saturnia I	168 A1
Saucats F	128 B2
Saucelle E	149 A3
Sauda N	52 A2
Sauðárkrókur IS	190 B6
Saudasjøen N	52 A2
Sauerlach D	108 B2
Saugues F	117 C3
Sauherad N	53 A5
Saujon F	114 C3
Sauland N	53 A4
Saulces Monclin F	91 B4
Saulgau D	107 A4
Saulgrub D	108 B2
Saulieu F	104 B3
Saulnot F	106 B1
Sault F	131 A4
Sault-Brénaz F	118 B2
Sault-de-Navailles F	128 C2
Saulx F	105 B5
Saulxures-sur-Moselotte F	106 B1
Saulzais-le-Potier F	103 C4
Saumos F	128 B1
Saumur F	102 B1
Saunavaara FIN	197 B10
Saundersfoot GB	39 C2
Saurat F	146 B2
Saurbær	
Borgarfjarðarsýsla IS	190 C4
Dalasýsla IS	190 B4
Eyjafjarðarsýsla IS	191 B7
Sáuris I	109 C3
Sausset-les-Pins F	131 B4
Sauteyrargues F	131 B2
Sauvagnat F	116 B2
Sauve F	131 B2
Sauveterre-de-Béarn F	144 A3
Sauveterre-de-Guyenne F	128 B2
Sauviat-sur-Vige F	116 B1
Sauxillanges F	117 B3
Sauzet	
Drôme F	117 C4
Lot F	129 B4
Sauzé-Vaussais F	115 B4
Sauzon F	100 B2
Sava I	173 B3
Sävar S	200 C6
Savarsin RO	16 B5
Sävast S	196 D4
Savaştepe TR	186 C2
Savci SLO	111 C3
Säve S	60 B1
Savelletri I	173 B3
Savelli I	174 B2
Savenay F	101 B4
Saverdun F	146 A2
Saverne F	93 C3
Savières F	91 C3
Savigliano I	119 C4
Savignac-les-Eglises F	129 A3
Savignano Irpino I	171 B3
Savignano sul Rubicone I	136 A1
Savigny-sur-Braye F	102 B2
Saviñán E	152 A2
Savines-le-lac F	132 A2
Savino Selo SRB	126 B1
Savio I	135 A5
Sävja S	51 C4
Šavnik MNE	139 C5
Savognin CH	107 C4
Savona I	133 A4
Savonlinna FIN	9 B6
Savournon F	132 A1
Sævråsvåg N	46 B2

Sävsjö S	62 A2
Savsjön S	50 C1
Sävsjöström S	62 A3
Savudrija HR	122 B2
Savukoski FIN	197 B11
Sawbridgeworth GB	45 B4
Sawtry GB	44 A3
Sax E	159 C3
Saxdalen S	50 B1
Saxilby GB	40 B3
Saxmundham GB	45 A5
Saxnäs S	195 F6
Saxthorpe GB	41 C5
Sayalonga E	163 B3
Sayatón E	151 B5
Sayda D	83 B5
Šäytsjärvi FIN	193 C11
Šazava CZ	97 B3
Sázava CZ	96 B2
Scaër F	100 A2
Scafa I	169 A4
Scalasaig GB	34 B1
Scalby GB	40 A3
Scalea I	174 B1
Scaletta Zanclea I	177 A4
Scalloway GB	33 A5
Scambleby GB	41 B3
Scandale I	175 B2
Scandiano I	121 C3
Scandicci I	135 B4
Scandolara Ravara I	120 B3
Scanno I	169 B3
Scansano I	168 A1
Scanzano Jónico I	174 A2
Scarborough GB	40 A3
Scardovari I	122 C1
Scardoy GB	32 C2
Scarperia I	135 B4
Scarriff IRL	28 B3
Scey-sur-Saône et St Albin F	105 B4
Schachendorf A	111 B3
Schaffhausen CH	107 B3
Schafstädt D	83 A3
Schafstedt D	64 B2
Schäftlarn D	108 B2
Schagen NL	70 B1
Schalkau D	82 B3
Schangnau CH	106 C2
Schapbach D	93 C4
Scharbeutz D	65 B3
Schärding A	96 C1
Scharnitz A	108 B2
Scharrel D	71 A4
Schattendorf A	111 B3
Scheemda NL	71 A3
Scheessel D	72 A2
Schéggia I	136 B1
Scheibbs A	110 A2
Scheibenberg D	83 B4
Scheidegg D	107 B4
Scheifling A	110 B1
Scheinfeld D	94 B2
Schelklingen D	94 C1
Schenefeld	
Schleswig-Holstein D	64 B2
Schleswig-Holstein D	72 A2
Schenklengsfeld D	82 B1
Scherfede D	81 A5
Schermbeck D	80 A2
Scherpenzeel NL	70 B2
Schesslitz D	94 B3
Scheveningen NL	70 B1
Schieder-Schwalenberg D	72 C2
Schierling D	95 C4
Schiers CH	107 C4
Schildau D	83 A4
Schillingen D	92 B2
Schillingsfürst D	94 B2
Schilpário I	120 A3
Schiltach D	93 C4
Schiltigheim F	93 C3
Schio I	121 B4
Schirmeck F	92 C3
Schirnding D	83 B4
Schkeuditz D	83 A4
Schkölen D	83 A3
Schladen D	73 B3
Schladming A	109 B4
Schlangen D	81 A4
Schleiden D	80 B2
Schleiz D	83 B3
Schleswig D	64 B2
Schleusingen D	82 B2
Schlieben D	83 A5
Schliengen D	106 B2
Schliersee D	108 B2
Schlitz D	81 B5
Schloss Neuhaus D	81 A4
Schlossvippach D	82 A3
Schlotheim D	82 A2
Schluchsee D	106 B3
Schlüchtern D	81 B5
Schmallenberg D	81 A4
Schmelz D	92 B2
Schmidmühlen D	95 B3
Schmiedeberg D	84 B1
Schmiedefeld D	82 B2
Schmirn A	108 B2
Schmölln	
Brandenburg D	74 A3
Sachsen D	83 B4
Schnackenburg D	73 B4
Schneeberg D	83 B4
Schneizlreuth D	109 B3
Schneverdingen D	72 A2
Schöder A	109 B5
Schoenburg B	80 B2
Schollene D	73 B5
Schöllkrippen D	81 B5
Schomberg D	107 A3

Schönach D	95 C4
Schönau	
Baden-Württemberg D	106 B2
Bayern D	95 C4
Schönbeck D	74 A2
Schönberg	
Bayern D	96 C1
Mecklenburg-Vorpommern D	65 C3
Schleswig-Holstein D	65 B3
Schönebeck D	73 B4
Schöneck D	83 B4
Schönecken- D	80 B2
Schönermark D	74 A2
Schönewalde D	83 A5
Schongau D	108 B1
Schönhagen D	81 A5
Schönhausen D	73 B5
Schöningen D	73 B3
Schönkirchen D	64 B3
Schönsee D	95 B4
Schöntal D	94 B1
Schönthal D	95 B4
Schonungen D	94 A2
Schönwald D	65 B3
Schönwalde D	65 C3
Schoondijke NL	79 A3
Schoonebeek NL	71 B3
Schoonhoven NL	79 A4
Schopfheim D	106 B2
Schöppenstedt D	73 B3
Schörfling A	109 B4
Schorndorf D	94 C1
Schortens D	71 A4
Schotten D	81 B5
Schramberg D	106 A3
Schrattenbach A	107 B5
Schrecksbach D	81 B5
Schrems A	96 C3
Schrobenhausen D	95 C3
Schröcken A	107 B5
Schrozberg D	94 B1
Schruns A	107 B4
Schüpfheim CH	106 C3
Schüttorf D	71 B4
Schwaan D	65 C5
Schwabach D	94 B3
Schwäbisch Gmünd D	94 C1
Schwäbisch Hall D	94 B1
Schwabmünchen D	108 A1
Schwadorf A	111 A3
Schwagstorf D	71 B4
Schwaigern D	93 B5
Schwalmstadt D	81 B5
Schwanberg A	110 C2
Schwanden CH	107 C4
Schwandorf D	95 B4
Schwanebeck D	73 C4
Schwanenstadt A	109 A4
Schwanewede D	72 A1
Schwanfeld D	94 B2
Schwangau D	108 B1
Schwarmstedt D	72 B2
Schwarza D	82 B2
Schwarzach im Pongau A	109 B4
Schwarzau im Gebirge A	110 B2
Schwarzenau A	97 C3
Schwarzenbach D	83 B3
Schwarzenbach am Wald D	83 B3
Schwarzenbek D	72 A3
Schwarzenberg D	83 B4
Schwarzenburg CH	106 C2
Schwarzenfeld D	95 B4
Schwarz-heide D	84 A1
Schwaz A	108 B2
Schwechat A	111 A3
Schwedt D	74 A3
Schwei D	71 A5
Schweich D	92 B2
Schweighausen D	106 A2
Schweinfurt D	94 A2
Schweinitz D	83 A5
Schweinrich D	74 A1
Schwelm D	80 A3
Schwemsal D	83 A4
Schwendt A	109 B3
Schwenningen D	107 A3
Schwepnitz D	84 A1
Schwerin D	73 A4
Schwerte D	81 A3
Schweskau D	73 B4
Schwetzingen D	93 B4
Schwyz CH	107 B3
Sciacca I	176 B2
Sciara I	176 B2
Scicli I	177 C3
Ściechów PL	75 B3
Scigliano I	175 B2
Scilla I	175 C1
Ścinawa PL	85 A4
Scionzier F	118 A3
Scoglitti I	177 C3
Scole GB	45 A5
Sconser GB	31 B2
Scopello	
Piemonte I	119 B5
Sicilia I	176 A1
Scordia I	177 B3
Scorzè I	121 B5
Scotch Corner GB	37 B5
Scotter GB	40 B3
Scourie GB	32 C1
Scousburgh GB	33 B5
Scrabster GB	32 C3
Screeb IRL	28 A2
Scremerston GB	37 A5
Scritto I	136 B1
Scunthorpe GB	40 B3
Scuol CH	107 C5
Scúrcola Marsicana I	169 A3
Seaford GB	45 C4

Seaham GB	37 B5
Seahouses GB	37 A5
Seascale GB	36 B3
Seaton GB	43 B3
Sebazac-Concourès F	130 A1
Seben TR	187 B6
Sebersdorf A	110 B2
Sebezh RUS	8 D6
Sebnitz D	84 B2
Seborga I	133 B3
Seby S	63 B4
Seč	
Vychodočeský CZ	97 B3
Západočeský CZ	96 B1
Sečanj SRB	126 B2
Secemin PL	87 B3
Séchault F	91 B4
Seckau A	110 B1
Seclin F	78 B3
Secondigny F	114 B3
Seda P	155 B3
Sedan F	91 B4
Sedano E	143 B3
Sedbergh GB	37 B4
Sedella E	163 B3
Séderon F	131 A4
Sedgefield GB	37 B5
Sédico I	121 A5
Sédilo I	178 B2
Sédini I	178 B2
Sedlarica HR	124 B3
Sedlčany CZ	96 B2
Sedlec-Prčice CZ	96 B2
Sedlice CZ	96 B1
Sędziejowice PL	86 A3
Sędziszów PL	87 B4
Sędziszów Małopolski PL	87 B5
Seebach F	93 C3
Seeboden A	109 C4
Seefeld	
Brandenburg D	74 B2
Niedersachsen D	71 A5
Seefeld in Tirol A	108 B2
Seeg D	108 B1
Seehausen	
Bayern D	94 C2
Nordrhein-Westfalen D	80 A1
Seeheim-Jugenheim D	93 B4
Seelbach D	93 C3
Seelow D	74 B3
Seelze D	72 B2
Seerhausen D	83 A5
Sées F	89 B4
Seesen D	82 A2
Seeshaupt D	108 B2
Seewalchen A	109 B4
Seewiesen A	110 B2
Seferihisar TR	188 A1
Sefkerin SRB	127 B2
Segård N	48 B2
Segerstad S	55 A4
Segesd H	124 A3
Seglinge FIN	51 B7
Segmon S	55 A4
Segonzac F	115 C3
Segorbe E	159 B3
Segovia E	151 B3
Segré F	101 B5
Segura	
E	144 B1
P	155 B3
Segura de León E	161 A3
Segura de los Baños E	152 B3
Ségur-les-Villas F	116 B2
Segurrilla E	150 B3
Sehnde D	72 B2
Seia P	148 B2
Seiches-sur-le-Loir F	102 B1
Seifhennersdorf D	84 B2
Seignelay F	104 B2
Seijo E	140 C2
Seilhac F	116 B1
Seilles B	79 B5
Seim N	46 B2
Seinäjoki FIN	8 A3
Seissan F	145 A4
Seitenstetten Markt A	110 A1
Seixal P	154 C1
Seiz A	110 B1
Seizthal A	110 B1
Sejerslev DK	58 B1
Seksna RUS	9 C11
Selárdalur IS	190 B1
Selárgius I	179 C3
Selb D	83 B4
Selby GB	40 B2
Selca HR	138 B2
Selce HR	123 B3
Selçuk TR	188 B2
Selde DK	58 B2
Selenča SRB	126 B1
Selendi	
Manisa TR	186 D2
Manisa TR	186 D3
Selenicë AL	182 C1
Sélestat F	106 A2
Seleuš SRB	126 B2
Selevac SRB	127 C2
Selfoss IS	190 D5
Selgua E	145 C4
Selice SK	112 A1
Selje N	198 C2
Seljelvnes N	192 C3
Seljord N	53 A4
Selkirk GB	35 C5
Sellano I	136 C1
Selles-St Denis F	103 B3
Selles-sur-Cher F	103 B3

Sellières F	105 C4
Sellin D	66 B2
Sellye H	125 B3
Selm D	80 A3
Selnica ob Dravi SLO	110 C2
Selongey F	105 B4
Selonnet F	132 A2
Selow D	65 C4
Selsey GB	44 C3
Selsingen D	72 A2
Selters D	81 B3
Seltz F	93 C4
Selva E	167 B2
Selva di Cadore E	108 A3
Selva di Val Gardena I	108 C2
Selvik	
Sogn og Fjordane N	46 A2
Vestfold N	54 A1
Selvino I	120 B2
Sem N	54 A1
Semeljci HR	125 B4
Semič SLO	123 B4
Semide	
F	91 B4
P	148 B1
Semily CZ	84 B3
Seminara I	175 C1
Semlac RO	126 A2
Semlacu Mare RO	126 B3
Semmen-stedt D	73 B3
Šempeter SLO	123 A4
Semriach A	110 B2
Semur-en-Auxois F	104 B3
Sena E	145 C3
Sena de Luna E	141 B5
Senarpont F	90 B1
Sénas F	131 B4
Senčur SLO	123 A3
Senden	
Bayern D	94 C2
Nordrhein-Westfalen D	80 A3
Sendenhorst D	81 A3
Sendim P	149 A3
Senec SK	111 A4
Seneffe B	79 B4
Séneghe I	178 B2
Senés E	164 B2
Senez F	132 B2
Senftenberg D	84 A1
Sengouagnet F	145 B4
Sengwarden D	71 A5
Senica SK	98 C1
Senice na Hané CZ	98 B1
Senigállia I	136 B2
Senio	127 D3
Senirkent TR	189 A5
Sénis I	179 C2
Senise I	174 A2
Senj HR	123 C3
Senje SRB	127 D3
Senjehopen N	194 B8
Senjski Rudnik SRB	127 D3
Senlis F	90 B2
Sennan S	60 C2
Sennecey-le-Grand F	105 C3
Sennen GB	42 B1
Senno BY	13 A8
Sénnori I	178 B2
Sennwald CH	107 B4
Sennybridge GB	39 C3
Senohrad SK	99 C3
Senonches F	89 B5
Senones F	92 C2
Senovo SLO	123 A4
Senožeče SLO	123 B3
Senožeti SLO	123 A3
Sens F	104 A2
Sens-de-Bretagne F	101 A4
Senta SRB	126 B2
Senterada E	145 B4
Šentilj SLO	110 C2
Šentjernej SLO	123 B4
Šentjur SLO	123 A4
Senumstad N	53 B4
Seoane E	141 B3
Seon CH	106 B3
Sépeaux F	104 B2
Sépey CH	119 A4
Sepino I	170 B2
Sępólno Krajeńskie PL	76 A2
Seppenrade D	80 A3
Seppois F	106 B2
Septemvri BG	183 A6
Septeuil F	90 C1
Sepúlveda E	151 A4
Sequals I	122 A1
Sequeros E	149 B3
Seraincourt F	91 B4
Seraing B	80 B1
Seravezza I	134 B3
Sered' SK	98 C1
Seredka RUS	8 C6
Şereflikoçhisar TR	23 B7
Seregélyes H	112 B2
Seregno I	120 B2
Sérent F	101 B3
Serfaus A	108 B1
Sergiev Posad RUS	9 D11
Sergines F	104 A2
Seriate I	120 B2
Sérifontaine F	90 B1
Serifos GR	185 B5
Sérignan F	130 B2
Serik TR	189 C6
Serina I	120 B2
Serinhisar TR	188 B4
Sermaises F	90 C2

Sermaize-les-Bains F	91 C4
Sérmide I	121 C4
Sermoneta I	169 B2
Sernache de Bonjardim P	154 B2
Sernancelhe P	148 B2
Serock PL	77 B6
Serón E	164 B2
Serón de Najima E	152 A1
Serooskerke NL	79 A3
Seròs E	153 A4
Serpa P	160 B2
Serracapriola I	171 B3
Serrada E	150 A3
Serra de Outes E	140 B2
Serradifalco I	176 B2
Serradilla E	155 B4
Serradilla del Arroyo E	149 B3
Serradilla del Llano E	149 B3
Serramanna I	179 C2
Serramazzoni I	135 A4
Serranillos E	150 B3
Serrapetrona I	136 B2
Serra San Bruno I	175 C2
Serra San Quírico I	136 B2
Serrastretta I	175 B2
Serravalle	
Piemonte I	119 B5
Umbria I	136 C2
Serravalle di Chienti I	136 B1
Serravalle Scrivia I	120 C1
Serre I	172 B1
Serrejón E	150 C2
Serres	
F	132 A1
GR	183 B5
Serrières F	117 B4
Serrières-de-Briord F	118 B2
Sersale I	175 B2
Sertã P	154 B2
Sertig Dörfli CH	107 C4
Servance F	106 B1
Serverette F	117 C3
Servia GR	182 C4
Servian F	130 B2
Serviers F	131 A3
Servigliano I	136 B2
Sesa E	145 B3
Seseña Nuevo E	151 B4
Sesimbra P	154 C1
Seskarö S	196 D6
Seskinore GB	27 B3
Sesma E	144 B1
Sessa Aurunca I	170 B1
Ses Salines E	167 B3
Sesta Godano I	134 A2
Šestanovac HR	138 B2
Sestao E	143 A4
Sestino I	135 B5
Sesto I	109 C3
Sesto Calende I	120 B1
Sesto Fiorentino I	135 B4
Sesto San Giovanni I	120 B2
Sestola I	135 A3
Sestriere I	119 C3
Sestri Levante I	134 A2
Sestroretsk RUS	9 B7
Sestu I	179 C3
Sesvete HR	124 B2
Setcases E	146 B3
Sète F	130 B2
Setenil E	162 B2
Setermoen N	194 B9
Setonje SRB	127 C3
Setskog N	54 A2
Settalsjølia N	199 C7
Séttimo Torinese I	119 B4
Settimo Vittone I	119 B4
Settle GB	40 A1
Setúbal P	154 C2
Seubersdorf D	95 B3
Seui I	179 C3
Seúlo I	179 C3
Seurre F	105 C4
Sevel DK	58 B1
Sevenoaks GB	45 B4
Sévérac-le-Château F	130 A2
Sever do Vouga P	148 B1
Severin HR	123 B4
Severomorsk RUS	3 B13
Séveso I	120 B2
Ševětín CZ	96 B2
Sévigny F	91 B4
Sevilla E	162 A2
Sevilla la Nueva E	151 B3
Sevilleja de la Jara E	156 A3
Sevlievo BG	17 D6
Sevnica SLO	123 A4
Sevojno SRB	127 D1
Sevrier F	118 B3
Sexdrega S	60 B3
Seyches F	129 B3
Seyda D	83 A4
Seydişehir TR	189 B6
Seyðisfjörður IS	191 B12
Seyitgazi TR	187 C5
Seyitömer TR	187 C4
Seymen TR	186 A2
Seyne F	132 A2
Seynes F	131 A3
Seyssel F	118 B2
Sézanne F	91 C3
Sezulfe P	149 A2
Sezze I	169 B3

Sfântu Gheorghe RO	17 C6
Sforzacosta I	136 B2
Sgarasta Mhor GB	31 B1
's-Gravendeel NL	79 A4
's-Gravenhage = The Hague NL	70 B1
's-Gravenzande NL	79 A4
Shaftesbury GB	43 B4
Shaldon GB	43 B3
Shalskiy RUS	9 B9
Shanagolden IRL	29 B2
Shanklin GB	44 C2
Shap GB	37 B4
Sharpness GB	43 A4
Shawbury GB	38 B4
's-Heerenberg NL	80 A2
Sheerness GB	45 B4
Sheffield GB	40 B2
Shefford GB	44 A3
Shëmri AL	182 A2
Shenfield GB	45 B4
Shëngjergj AL	182 B2
Shepetivka UA	13 C7
Shepshed GB	40 C2
Shepton Mallet GB	43 A4
Sherborne GB	43 B4
Shercock IRL	27 C4
Sheringham GB	41 C5
's-Hertogenbosch NL	79 A5
Shiel Bridge GB	32 D1
Shieldaig GB	31 B3
Shijak AL	182 B1
Shillelagh IRL	30 B2
Shimsk RUS	9 C7
Shipston-on-Stour GB	44 A2
Shklow BY	13 A9
Shkodër AL	182 A1
Shoeburyness GB	45 B4
Shoreham-by-Sea GB	44 C3
Shotley Gate GB	45 B5
Shrewsbury GB	38 B4
Shugozero RUS	9 C9
Shumen BG	17 D7
Siabost GB	31 A2
Siamanna I	179 C2
Sianów PL	67 B5
Siatista GR	182 C3
Siauges-St Romain F	117 B3
Šiauliai LT	8 E3
Sibari I	174 B2
Sibbhult S	63 B2
Šibenik HR	138 B1
Siberstedt D	64 B2
Sibinj HR	125 B3
Sibiu RO	17 C6
Sibnica SRB	127 C2
Sibsey GB	41 B4
Siculiana I	176 B2
Šid SRB	125 B5
Sidari GR	182 D1
Siddeburen NL	71 A3
Sidensjö S	200 C4
Siderno I	175 C2
Sidirokastro GR	183 B5
Sidmouth GB	43 B3
Sidzina PL	99 B3
Siebe N	192 D7
Siebenlehn D	83 A5
Siedlce PL	12 B5
Siedlice PL	75 A4
Siedlinghausen D	81 A4
Siedlisko PL	75 B5
Siegburg D	80 B3
Siegen D	81 B4
Siegenburg D	95 C3
Sieghartskirchen A	111 A3
Siegsdorf D	109 B3
Siekierki PL	74 B3
Sielpia PL	87 A4
Siemiany PL	69 B4
Siena I	135 B4
Sieniawka PL	84 B2
Sienno PL	87 A5
Sieppijärvi FIN	196 B7
Sieradz PL	86 A2
Sieraków	
Śląskie PL	86 B2
Wielkopolskie PL	75 B5
Sierakowice PL	68 A2
Sierck-les-Bains F	92 B2
Sierentz F	106 B2
Sierning A	110 A1
Sierpc PL	77 B4
Sierra de Fuentes E	155 B4
Sierra de Luna E	144 B3
Sierra de Yeguas E	162 A3
Sierre CH	119 A4
Siestrzeń PL	77 B5
Sietamo E	145 B3
Siewierz PL	86 B3
Sigdal N	48 B1
Sigean F	130 B1
Sigerfjord N	194 B6
Sighetu-Marmatiei RO	17 B5
Sighişoara RO	17 B6
Sigillo I	136 B1
Siglufjörður IS	191 A7
Sigmaringen D	107 A4
Signa I	135 B4
Signes F	132 B1
Signy-l'Abbaye F	91 B4
Signy-le-Petit F	91 B4
Sigogne F	115 C3
Sigri GR	183 D7
Sigtuna S	57 A3
Sigueiro E	140 B2
Sigüenza E	151 A5
Sigües E	144 B2
Sigulda LV	8 D4
Siilinjärvi FIN	9 A5
Sikenica SK	112 A1

Sikfors S 196 D4
Sikia GR 183 C5
Sikinos GR 185 C6
Sikkilsdalseter N. . .47 A6
Siklós H 125 B4
Sikórz PL 77 B4
Sikselet S 195 D8
Silandro I 108 C1
Silánus I 178 B2
Silbaš SRB 126 B1
Şile TR 187 A4
Siles E 164 A2
Silgueiros P 148 B2
Silifke TR 23 C7
Silíqua I 179 C2
Silistra BG 17 C7
Silivri TR 186 A3
Siljan N 53 A5
Siljansnäs S 50 B1
Silkeborg DK 59 B2
Silla E 159 B3
Sillamäe EST 8 C5
Silleda E 140 B2
Sillé-le-Guillaume
F 102 A1
Sillenstede D 71 A4
Sillerud S 54 A3
Sillian A 109 C3
Silloth GB 36 B3
Silno PL 68 B2
Silnowo PL 68 B1
Silo HR 123 B3
Sils E 147 C3
Silsand N 194 A8
Silte S 57 C4
Šilute LT 12 A4
Silvalen N 195 E3
Silvaplana CH . . .107 C4
Silvares P 148 B2
Silvberg S 50 B2
Silverdalen S 62 A3
Silvermines IRL . . .28 B3
Silverstone GB . . .44 A2
Silverton GB 43 B3
Silves P 160 B1
Silvi Marina I . . .169 A4
Simandre F 105 C3
Šimanovci SRB . . .127 C2
Simard F 105 C4
Simat de Valldigna
E 159 B3
Simav TR 186 C3
Simbach
Bayern D 95 C4
Bayern D 95 C5
Simbário I 175 C2
Simeonovgrad BG 183 A7
Simeria RO 17 C5
Simi GR 188 C2
Simićevo SRB . . .127 C3
Simitli BG 183 B5
Simlångsdalen S . .60 C3
Simmerath D 80 B2
Simmerberg D . . .107 B4
Simmern D 93 B3
Šimonovce SK 99 C4
Simonsbath GB . . .43 A3
Simonstorp S 56 B2
Simontornya H . . .112 C2
Simplon CH 119 A5
Simrishamn S 63 C2
Sinaia RO 17 C6
Sinalunga I 135 B4
Sinarcas E 159 B2
Sincan TR 187 C7
Sincanlı TR 187 D5
Sindal DK 58 A3
Sindelfingen D . . .93 C5
Sindia I 178 B2
Sındırgı TR 186 C3
Sinekli TR 186 A3
Sines P 160 B1
Sinetta FIN 197 C8
Sineu E 167 B3
Singen D 107 B3
Singleton GB 44 C3
Singsås N 199 C7
Siniscóla I 178 B3
Sinj HR 138 B2
Sinlabajos E 150 A3
Sinn D 81 B4
Sínnai I 179 C3
Sinnes N 52 B2
Sinop TR 23 A8
Sins CH 106 B3
Sinsheim D 93 B4
Sint Annaland NL . .79 A4
Sint Annaparochie
NL 70 A2
Sint Athonis NL . . .80 A1
Sint Nicolaasga NL 70 B2
Sint Oedenrode NL 79 A5
Sintra P 154 C1
Sinzheim D 93 C4
Sinzig D 80 B3
Siófok H 112 C2
Sion CH 119 A4
Sion Mills GB. 27 B3
Siorac-en-Périgord
F 129 B3
Šipanska Luka HR 139 C3
Šipovo BIH. 138 A3
Sira N 52 B2
Siracusa I 177 B4
Siret RO 17 B7
Sirevåg N 52 B1
Sirig SRB 126 B1
Sirkka FIN 196 B7
Sirmione I 121 B3
Sirniö FIN. 197 D11
Široki 113 B4
Široké SK 99 C4
Široki Brijeg BIH . .139 B3
Sirolo I 136 B2
Siruela E 156 B2
Sisak HR 124 B2
Šišante E 158 B1
Šišljavić HR. 123 B4
Sissach CH 106 B2

Sissonne F 91 B3
Sistelo P 140 C2
Sisteron F 132 A1
Sistiana I 122 B2
Sistranda N 198 B5
Sitasjaurestugorna
S 194 C8
Sitges E 147 C2
Sitia GR 185 D7
Sittard NL. 80 A1
Sittensen D 72 A2
Sittingbourne GB .45 B4
Sitzenroda D 83 A4
Sivac SRB 126 B1
Sivasli TR 189 A4
Siverić HR 138 B2
Sivrihisar TR 187 C6
Sixt-Fer-á-Cheval
F 119 A3
Siziano I 120 B2
Sizun F 100 A1
Sjenica SRB 16 D3
Sjoa N 198 D6
Sjøåsen N 199 A8
Sjöbo S 61 D3
Sjøenden
Hedmark N 48 A3
Hedmark N 48 B3
Sjøholt N 198 C3
Sjøli N 48 A3
Sjølstad N 199 A9
Sjölunda S 56 A1
Sjømarken S 60 B2
Sjørring DK 58 B1
Sjötofta S 60 B3
Sjötorp S 55 B4
Sjoutnäset S 199 A11
Sjøvegan N 194 B8
Sjuntorp S 54 B3
Skåbu N 47 A6
Skafså N 53 A4
Skaftafell IS 191 D9
Skagaströnd IS . . .190 B5
Skagen DK 58 A3
Skagersvik S 55 B5
Skaiå N 53 B3
Skaidi N 193 B8
Skala GR 184 A1
Skała PL 87 B3
Skaland N 194 A8
Skala Oropou GR .185 A4
Skala-Podilska UA .13 D7
Skalat UA. 13 D6
Skalbmierz PL 87 B4
Skålevik N 53 B4
Skalica SK 98 C1
Skällinge S 60 B2
Skalná CZ 83 B4
Skals DK 58 B2
Skælskør DK 65 A4
Skalstugan S 199 B9
Skanderborg DK . . .59 B2
Skånes-Fagerhult
S 61 C3
Skåne-Tranås S . . .61 D3
Skånevik N 52 A1
Skänninge S 55 B6
Skanör med Falsterbo
S 66 A1
Skåpafors S 54 A3
Skåpe PL 75 B4
Skara S 55 B4
Skærbæk DK 64 A1
Skarberget N 194 B7
Skärblacka S 56 B1
Skarð IS 190 B3
Skarda S 200 B4
Skåre N 46 C3
Skåre S 55 A4
Skärhamn S 60 B1
Skarnes N 48 B3
Skärplinge S 51 B4
Skarp Salling DK . .58 B2
Skarrild DK 59 C1
Skarstad N 194 B7
Skärstad S 62 A2
Skarsvåg N 193 A9
Skarszewy PL 69 A3
Skårup DK 65 A3
Skärvången S 199 B11
Skarvsjöby S 195 F8
Skaryszew PL 87 A5
Skarżysko-Kamienna
PL. 87 A4
Skarżysko Ksiazece
PL. 87 A4
Skatøy N 53 B5
Skattkärr S 55 A4
Skattungbyn S 50 A1
Skatval N 199 B7
Skaulo S 196 B4
Skave DK 59 B1
Skawina PL 99 B3
Skebobruk S 51 C5
Skebokvarn S 56 A2
Skedala S 61 C2
Skedovi S 56 B1
Skedsmokorset N . .48 B3
Skee S 54 B2
Skegness GB. 41 B4
Skei N 46 A3
Skela SRB 127 C2
Skelani BIH 127 D1
Skellefteå S 2 D7
Skelleftehamn S . . .2 D7
Skelmersdale GB . .38 A4
Skelmorlie GB. 34 C3
Skelund DK 58 B3
Skender Vakuf
BIH 138 A3
Skene S 60 B2
Skępe PL 77 B4
Skepplanda S 60 B2
Skeppshult S 60 B3
Skerries IRL. 30 A2
Ski N 54 A1
Skiathos GR 183 D5
Skibbereen IRL . . .29 C2

Skibotn N. 192 C4
Skidra GR 182 C4
Skien N 53 A5
Skierniewice PL. . . .77 C5
Skillingaryd S 60 B4
Skillinge S 63 C2
Skillingmark S 49 C4
Skilloura CY. 181 A2
Skinnardai S 57 A4
Skinnskatteberg S .50 C2
Skipmannvik N . . .195 C6
Skipness GB 34 C2
Skipsea GB 41 B3
Skipton GB 40 B1
Skiptvet N 54 A2
Skíros GR 183 E6
Skivarp S 66 A2
Skive DK 58 B2
Skjánes N 193 B12
Skjærhalden N 54 A2
Skjeberg N 54 A2
Skjeggedal N 46 B3
Skjeljanger N 46 B1
Skjellavik N 46 C2
Skjern DK 59 C1
Skjervøy N. 192 B4
Skjold
Rogaland N 52 A1
Troms N 192 C3
Skjoldastraumen N 52 A1
Skjolden N 47 A4
Skjønhaug N 54 A2
Skjøtningsberg
N 193 A11
Škocjan SLO 123 B4
Skoczów PL 98 B2
Skodborg DK 59 C2
Škofja Loka SLO . .123 A3
Škofljica SLO 123 B3
Skog
Halland S 60 C2
Södermanland S .56 A2
Skoganvarre N . . .193 C9
Skogen S 54 A2
Skogfoss N 193 C13
Skoghall S 55 A4
Skogly N 193 C13
Skognes N 192 C3
Skogstorp
Halland S 60 C2
Södermanland S .56 A2
Skoki PL. 76 B2
Skokloster S 57 A3
Sköldinge S 56 A2
Skole UA 13 D5
Skollenborg N 53 A5
Sköllersta S 56 A1
Skomlin PL 86 A2
Skonseng N 195 D5
Skopelos GR 183 D5
Skopje MK 182 A3
Skoppum N 54 A1
Skórcz PL 69 B3
Skorogoszcz PL . . .86 B1
Skoroszów PL 85 A5
Skorovatn N 199 A10
Skorped S 200 C3
Skørping DK 58 B2
Skotfoss N 53 A5
Skotniki PL 87 A3
Skotselv N 48 C1
Skotterud N 49 C4
Skottorp S 61 C2
Skovby DK 64 B2
Skövde S 55 B4
Skovsgård DK 58 A2
Skrad HR 123 B3
Skradin HR 138 B1
Skradnik HR 123 B4
Skråmestø N 46 B1
Skredswik S 54 B2
Skreia N 48 B2
Skrolsvik N 194 A7
Skruv S 63 B3
Skrwilno PL 77 A4
Skrydstrup DK 59 C2
Skucani BIH 138 B2
Skudeneshavn N . . .52 A1
Skui N 48 C2
Skulsk PL 76 B3
Skultorp S 55 B4
Skultuna S 56 A2
Skuodas LT 8 D2
Skurup S 66 A2
Skute N 48 B2
Skuteč CZ 97 B3
Skutskär S 51 B4
Skutvik N 194 B6
Skvyra UA 13 D8
Skwierzyna PL. . . .75 B4
Skýcov SK 98 C2
Skyllberg S 55 B5
Skyttmon S 200 C1
Skyttorp S 51 B4
Sládkovičovo SK . .111 A4
Slagelse DK 61 D1
Slagharen NL. 71 B3
Slagnäs S 195 E9
Slaidburn GB 40 B1
Slane IRL 30 A2
Slangerup DK 61 D2
Slano HR 139 C3
Slantsy RUS 8 C6
Slany CZ 84 B2
Šlapanice CZ 97 B4
Slåstad N 48 B3
Slatina
BIH 139 B3
HR 125 B3
RO 17 C6
Slatiňany CZ 97 B3
Slatinice CZ 98 B1
Slättberg S 50 A1
Slattum N 48 C2
Slavičín CZ 98 B1
Slavkov CZ 98 C1
Slavkovica SRB . .127 C2
Slavkov u Brna CZ .97 B4
Slavonice CZ 97 C3

Slavonski Brod
HR 125 B4
Slavonski Kobas
HR 125 B3
Slavõsovce SK 99 C4
Slavskoye RUS 69 A5
Slavuta UA. 13 C7
Sława
Lubuskie PL. 85 A4
Zachodnio-Pomorskie
PL 67 A4
Slawharad BY 13 B9
Sławków PL 86 B3
Sławno
Wielkopolskie PL .76 B2
Zachodnio-Pomorskie
PL 68 A1
Sławoborze PL 67 C4
Sl'ažany SK 98 C2
Sleaford GB 40 C3
Sleðbrjótur IS 191 B11
Sledmere GB. 40 A3
Sleights GB 37 B6
Slemmestad N 54 A1
Ślesin PL 76 B3
Sliač SK 99 C3
Sliema M 175 C3
Sligo IRL 26 B2
Slite S 57 C4
Slitu N 54 A2
Sliven BG. 17 D7
Sljeme HR 123 B4
Slobozia RO 17 C7
Slochteren NL 71 A3
Slöinge S 60 C2
Słomniki PL. 87 B4
Slonim BY 13 B6
Słońsk PL 75 B3
Slootdorp NL. 70 B1
Slottsbron S 55 A4
Slövag N 46 B2
Slovenj Gradec
SLO 110 C2
Slovenska Bistrica
SLO 123 A4
Slovenská L'upča
SK 99 C3
Slovenská-Ves SK. .99 B4
Slovenské Darmoty
SK 112 A3
Slovenske Konjice
SLO 123 A4
Słubice PL 74 B3
Sluderno I 108 C1
Sluis NL 78 A3
Sluknov CZ 84 A2
Slunj HR 123 B4
Słupca PL 76 B2
Słupia PL 87 A3
Słupiec PL 85 B4
Słupsk PL 68 A2
Slutsk BY 13 B7
Smålandsstenar S .60 B3
Smalåsen N. 195 E4
Smardzewo PL 75 B4
Smarhon BY 13 A7
Šmarje SLO 123 B4
Šmarjeta SLO 123 B4
Šmartno SLO 123 A3
Smečno CZ 84 B2
Smedby S 63 B4
Smědec CZ 96 C2
Smederevo SRB . .127 C2
Smederevska Palanka
SRB 127 C2
Smedjebacken S . . .50 B2
Smęgorzów PL 87 B5
Smeland N 53 B4
Smidary CZ 84 B3
Śmigiel PL 75 B5
Smilde NL 71 B3
Smilčić HR 137 A4
Smithfield GB 36 B4
Šmitovo PL 75 A5
Smögen S 54 B2
Smogulec PL 76 A2
Smołdzino PL 68 A2
Smolenice SK 98 C1
Smolensk RUS 13 A10
Smolník SK 99 C4
Smolyan BG 183 B6
Smuka SLO 123 B3
Smygehamn S 66 A2
Smykow PL 87 A4
Snainton GB 40 A3
Snaith GB 40 B2
Snaptun DK 59 C3
Snarby N 192 C3
Snarum N 48 B1
Snåsa N 199 A9
Snedsted DK 58 B1
Sneek NL 70 A2
Sneem IRL 29 C2
Snejbjerg DK 59 B1
Snilldfjord N 198 B6
Snillfjord N 198 B6
Snina SK 12 D5
Šnjegotina BIH . . .125 C3
Snøde DK 65 A3
Snøfjord N 193 B8
Snogebæk DK 67 A4
Snyatyn UA. 13 D6
Soave I 121 B4
Sober E 140 B3
Sobernheim D 93 B3
Soběslav CZ 96 B2
Sobota
Dolnośląskie PL. .85 A3
Łódzkie PL. 77 B4
Sobótka SK 98 C1
Sobotka CZ 84 B3
Sobótka
Dolnośląskie PL. .85 B4
Wielkopolskie PL .86 A1
Sobra HR 139 C3
Sobrado
Coruña E 140 A2
Lugo E 141 B3
Sobral da Adica P .161 A2
Sobral de Monte
Agraço P 154 C1

Sobreira Formosa
P 154 B3
Søby DK. 64 B3
Soca SLO 122 A2
Sochaczew PL. 77 B5
Sochos GR 183 C5
Socodor RO. 113 C5
Socol RO 127 C3
Socovos E 164 A3
Socuéllamos E . . .158 B1
Sodankylä FIN. . . .197 B9
Soderåkra S. 63 B4
Söderala S 51 A3
Söderbärke S 50 B2
Söderby-Karl S. . . .51 C5
Söderfors S 51 B4
Söderhamn S 51 A4
Söderköping S 56 B2
Söderö S 56 B1
Södertälje S 57 A3
Södingberg A. 110 B2
Södra Finnö S 56 B2
Södra Ny S 55 A4
Södra Råda S 55 A5
Södra Sandby S . . .61 D3
Södra Vi S 62 A3
Sodražica SLO . . .123 B3
Sodupe E 143 A3
Soengas P 148 A1
Soest
D 81 A4
NL 70 B2
Sofades GR. 182 D4
Sofia = Sofiya BG .17 D5
Sofikon GR 184 B4
Sofiya = Sofia BG .17 D5
Şofronea RO 126 A3
Sögel D 71 B4
Sogliano al Rubicone
I 135 A5
Sogndalsfjøra N . . .46 A4
Søgne N 53 B3
Sögütköy TR 188 C3
Soham GB 45 A4
Sohland D 84 A2
Sohren D 93 B3
Soignies B 79 B4
Soissons F 90 B3
Söjtör H 111 C3
Sokal' UA 13 C6
Söke TR 188 B2
Sokna N 48 B1
Sokndal N 52 B2
Soknedal N 199 C7
Soko BIH 125 C4
Sokolac BIH. 139 B4
Sokółka PL. 13 B5
Sokolov CZ 83 B4
Sokołów Podlaski
PL. 12 B5
Sola N 52 B1
Solana de los Barros
E 155 C4
Solana del Pino E .157 B3
Solánas I 179 C3
Solares E 143 A3
Solarino I 177 B4
Solarussa I 179 C2
Solas GB 31 B1
Solberg S 200 C3
Solberga S 62 A2
Solber-gelva N 53 A6
Solčany SK 98 C2
Solčava SLO 123 A3
Solda I 108 C1
Solec Kujawski PL .76 A3
Soleils F. 132 B2
Solenzara F 180 B2
Solera E 163 A4
Solesmes F 79 B3
Soleto I 173 B4
Solgne F 92 C2
Solheim N 46 B2
Solheimsvik N 52 A2
Solignac F 115 C5
Solihull GB 44 A2
Solin HR. 138 B2
Solingen D 80 A3
Solivella E 147 C2
Solkan SLO 122 B2
Söll A 108 B3
Sollana E 159 B3
Sollebrunn S 54 B3
Sollefteå S 200 C3
Sollenau A 111 B3
Sollen-tuna S 57 A3
Søller E 166 B2
Sollerön S 50 B1
Søllested DK 65 B4
Solliès-Pont F 132 B2
Sollihøgda N 48 C2
Solnechnogorsk
RUS. 9 D10
Solnice CZ 85 B4
Solofra I 170 C2
Solomiac F 129 C3
Solopaca I 170 B2
Solórzano E. 143 A3
Solothurn CH 106 B2
Solre-le-Château F .79 B4
Solsona E 147 C2
Solsvik N 46 B1
Solt H 112 C3
Soltau D 72 B2
Soltsy RUS 9 C7
Soltszentimre H . . .112 C3
Soltvadkert H 112 C3
Solumsmoen N 48 C1
Solund N 46 A1
Solva GB 39 C1
Sölvesborg S 63 B2
Solymár H 112 B2
Soma TR 186 C2
Somberek H 125 A4
Sombernon F 104 B3

Sombor SRB 125 B5
Sombreffe B 79 B4
Someren NL. 80 A1
Somero FIN 8 B3
Somersham GB. 9 B7
Somerton GB. 43 A4
Somma Lombardo
I 120 B1
Sommariva del Bosco
I 119 C4
Sommarøy N 192 C2
Sommarset N 194 C6
Sommatino I 176 B2
Sommeilles F 91 C4
Sommen S 55 B5
Sommepy-Tahure
F 91 B4
Sömmerda D 82 A3
Sommerfeld D 74 B2
Sommersted DK . . .59 C2
Sommesous F 91 C4
Somme-Tourbe F . .91 B4
Sommières F 131 B3
Sommières-du-Clain
F 115 B4
Somo E 143 A3
Somogyfajsz H . . .111 C4
Somogyjád H 111 C4
Somogysámson
H 111 C4
Somogysárd H . . .125 A3
Somogyszíl H 112 C2
Somogyszob H . . .124 A3
Somogyvár H 111 C4
Somontín E 164 B2
Somosierra E 151 A4
Somoskõújfalu
H 113 A3
Sompolno PL 76 B3
Sompuis F 91 C4
Son N 54 A1
Son Bou E 167 B4
Sonceboz CH 106 B2
Soncillo E 143 B3
Soncino I 120 B2
Sóndalo I 120 A3
Søndeled N 53 B4
Sønder Bjert DK . . .59 C2
Sønderby DK 64 B2
Sønder Felding DK .59 C1
Sønderho DK 59 C1
Sønder Hygum DK .59 C1
Sønder Omme DK .59 C1
Sondershausen D. .82 A2
Søndersø DK 59 C3
Søndervig DK 59 B1
Søndre Enningdal
Kappel N 54 B2
Sóndrio I 120 A2
Soneja E 159 B3
Son en Breugel NL .80 A1
Sønsterud N 48 B2
Sonstorp S 56 B1
Sonta SRB 125 B5
Sontheim D 94 C2
Sonthofen D 107 B5
Sontra D. 82 A1
Sopelana E 143 A4
Sopje HR 125 B3
Soporňa SK 111 A4
Sopot
PL 69 A3
SRB 127 C2
Sopotnica MK 182 B3
Sopron H 111 B3
Šor SRB 127 C1
Sora I 169 B3
Soragna I 120 C3
Söråker S 200 D3
Sorano I 168 A1
Sorbara I 121 C4
Sorbas E 164 B2
Sórbolo I 121 C3
Sörbygden S 200 D2
Sordal N 52 B3
Sordale GB 32 C3
Sore F 128 B2
Sörenberg CH 106 C3
Soresina I 120 B2
Sorèze F 146 A3
Sörfjärden N 200 D3
Sörfors S 200 C5
Sorges F 115 C4
Sórgono I 179 B3
Sorgues F 131 A3
Sorgun TR 23 B8
Soria E 143 C4
Soriano Cálabro I .175 C2
Soriano nel Cimino
I 168 A2
Sorihuela del
Guadalimar E. . .164 A1
Sorisdale GB 34 B1
Sørkjosen N. 192 C4
Sørli N 199 A10
Sormás H 111 C3
Sörmjöle S 200 C6
Sørmo N. 194 B9
Sornac F 116 B2
Sörö DK 61 D1
Soroca MD 17 A8
Sørreisa N 194 A9
Sorrento I 170 C2
Sorsele S 195 E8
Sörsjön S 49 A5
Sorso I 178 B2

Sort E 146 B2
Sortavala RUS. 9 B7
Sortino I 177 B3
Sortland N 194 B6
Sørumsand N 48 C3
Sorunda S 57 A3
Sörup D 64 B2
Sørvågen N 194 C3
Sørværøy N 192 B6
Sorvik S 50 B2
Sørvika N 199 C8
Sos F 128 B3
Sösdala S 61 C3
Sos del Rey Católico
E 144 B2
Sošice HR 123 B4
Sośnica PL. 75 A5
Sośnicowice PL. . . .86 B2
Sośno PL 76 A2
Sosnovyy Bor RUS. . .9 C6
Sosnowiec PL 86 B3
Sospel F 133 B3
Šoštanj SLO 123 A4
Sotaseter N 198 D4
Sotillo de Adrada
E 150 B3
Sotillo de la Ribera
E 143 C3
Sotin HR 125 B5
Sotkamo FIN 3 D11
Sotobañado y Priorato
E 142 B2
Soto de la Marina
E 143 A3
Soto del Barco E . .141 A4
Soto de los Infantes
E 141 A4
Soto de Real E . . .151 B4
Soto de Ribera E. .141 A5
Sotoserrano E 149 B3
Soto y Amío E 141 B5
Sotresgudo E 142 B2
Sotrondio E 142 A1
Sotta F 180 B2
Sottomarina I 122 B1
Sottrum D 72 A2
Sottunga FIN 51 B7
Sotuelamos E 158 B1
Souain F 91 B4
Soual F 146 A3
Soucy F 104 A2
Souda GR 185 D5
Soudron F 91 C4
Souesmes F 103 B4
Soufflenheim F 93 C3
Soufli GR 186 A1
Souillac F 129 B4
Souilly F 91 B5
Soulac-sur-Mer F .114 C2
Soulaines-Dhuys F 91 C4
Soulatgé F 146 B3
Soultz-Haut-Rhin
F 106 B2
Soultz-sous-Forêts
F 93 C3
Soumagne F 80 B1
Soumoulou F 145 A3
Souppes-sur-Loing
F 103 A4
Sourdeval F. 88 B3
Soure P 154 A2
Sournia F 146 B3
Souro Pires P 149 B2
Sourpi GR 182 D4
Sours F 90 C1
Sousceyrac F 116 C2
Sousel P. 155 C3
Soustons F 128 C1
Söğüt
Bilecik TR. 187 B5
Burdur TR 189 B5
Souteulo de Montes
E 140 B2
Southam GB 44 A2
Southampton GB . .44 C2
Southborough GB. .45 B4
South Brent GB . . .42 B3
South Cave GB . . .40 B3
Southend GB 34 C2
Southend-on-Sea
GB 45 B4
South Hayling GB . .44 C3
South Molton GB. . .42 A3
South Ockendon
GB 45 B4
South Petherton
GB 43 B4
Southport GB 38 A3
South Shields GB . .37 B5
South Tawton GB . .42 B3
Southwell GB 40 B3
Southwold GB 45 A5
South Woodham
Ferrers GB. 45 B4
Söğütlü TR. 187 B5
Souto P 148 B2
Soutochao E 141 C3
Souto da Carpalhosa
P 154 B2
Souvigny F 104 C2
Souzay-Champigny
F 102 B1
Soverato I 175 C2
Soveria Mannelli I 175 B2
Sövestad S 66 A2
Sovetsk RUS 12 A4
Sovići BIH 138 B3
Sovicille I 135 B4
Søvik N 198 C3
Sowerby GB 37 B5
Soyaux F 115 C4
Sozopol BG 17 D7
Spa B 80 B1
Spadafora I 177 A4
Spaichingen D. . . .107 A3

Spakenburg NL 70 B2
Spalding GB 41 C3
Spálené Pořiči CZ . .96 B1
Spalt D 94 B2
Spangenberg D 82 A1
Spangereid N 52 B3
Spantekow D 74 A2
Sparanise I 170 B2
Sparbu N 199 B8
Sparkær DK 58 B2
Sparkford GB 43 A4
Sparreholm S 56 A2
Sparta = Sparti
GR 184 B3
Spartà I 177 A4
Sparti = Sparta
GR 184 B3
Spean Bridge GB . .34 B3
Speicher D 92 B2
Speichersdorf D . . .95 B3
Speke GB 38 A4
Spello I 136 C1
Spenge D 72 B1
Spennymoor GB . . .37 B5
Spentrup DK 58 B3
Sperenberg D 74 B2
Sperlinga I 177 B3
Sperlonga I 169 B3
Spetalen N 54 A1
Spetses GR 184 B4
Speyer D 93 B4
Spézet F 100 A2
Spezzano Albanese
I 174 B2
Spezzano della Sila
I 174 B2
Spiddle IRL 28 A2
Spiegelau D 96 C1
Spiekeroog D 71 A4
Spiez CH 106 C2
Spigno Monferrato
I 133 A4
Spijk NL 71 A3
Spijkenisse NL 79 A4
Spilamberto I 135 A4
Spili GR 185 D5
Spilimbergo I 122 A1
Spilsby GB 41 B4
Spinazzola I 172 B2
Spincourt F 92 B1
Spind N 52 B2
Spindleruv-Mlyn
CZ 84 B3
Spinoso I 174 A1
Špišić Bukovica
HR 124 B3
Spišská Belá SK . . .99 B4
Spišská Nová Ves
SK 99 C4
Spišská Stará Ves
SK 99 B4
Spišské-Hanušovce
SK 99 B4
Spišské Podhradie
SK 99 C4
Spišské Vlachy SK .99 C4
Spišský-Štvrtok
SK 99 C4
Spital A 110 B1
Spital am Semmering
A 110 B2
Spittal an der Drau
A 109 C4
Spittle of Glenshee
GB 35 B4
Spitz A 97 C3
Spjald DK 59 B1
Spjærøy N 54 A1
Spjelkavik N 198 C3
Spjutsbygd S 63 B3
Split HR 138 B2
Splügen CH 107 C4
Spodsbjerg DK 65 B3
Spofforth GB 40 B2
Spohle D 71 A5
Spoleto I 136 C1
Spoltore I 169 A4
Spondigna I 108 C1
Sponvika N 54 A2
Spornitz D 73 A4
Spotorno I 133 A4
Spraitbach D 94 C1
Sprakensehl D 72 B3
Sprecowo PL 69 B5
Spremberg D 84 A2
Spresiano I 122 B1
Sprimont B 80 B1
Springe D 72 B2
Sproatley GB 41 B3
Spydeberg N 54 A2
Spytkowice PL 99 B3
Squillace I 175 C2
Squinzano I 173 B4
Sračinec HR 124 A2
Srbac BIH 124 B3
Srbobran SRB 126 B1
Srebrenica BIH 127 C1
Srebrenik BIH 125 C4
Sredets BG 17 D7
Središče SLO 124 A2
Šrem PL 76 B2
Sremska Mitrovica
SRB 127 C1
Sremski Karlovci
SRB 126 B1
Srní CZ 96 B1
Srnice Gornje BIH 125 C4
Srock PL 86 A3
Środa Śląska PL . . .85 A4
Środa Wielkopolski
PL 76 B2
Srpska Crnja SRB 126 B2
Srpski Itebej SRB .126 B2
Srpski Miletić
SRB 125 B5
Staatz A 97 C4
Stabbursnes N 193 B8

Staberdorf D 65 B4
Stabroek B 79 A4
Stachy CZ 96 B1
Staðarfell IS 190 B3
Stade D 72 A2
Staden B 78 B3
Stadl an der Mur
A 109 B4
Stadskanaal NL 71 B3
Stadtallendorf D . . .81 B5
Stadthagen D 72 B2
Stadtilm D 82 B3
Stadtkyll D 80 B2
Stadtlauringen D . . .82 B2
Stadtlengsfeld D . . .82 B2
Stadtlohn D 71 C3
Stadtoldendorf D . .82 A1
Stadtroda D 83 B3
Stadtsteinach D 82 B3
Stäfa CH 107 B3
Staffanstorp S 61 D3
Staffelstein D 82 B2
Stafford GB 31 B2
Stafford GB 40 C1
Stainach A 110 B1
Stainville F 91 C5
Stainz A 110 C2
Staithes GB 37 B6
Staiti I 175 D2
Stäket S 57 A3
Stakroge DK 59 C1
Štalcerji SLO 123 B3
Stalden CH 119 A4
Stalham GB 41 C5
Stalheim N 46 B3
Stallarholmen S 56 A3
Ställberg S 50 C1
Ställdalen S 50 C1
Stallhofen A 110 B2
Stalon S 195 F6
Stalowa Wola PL . . .12 C5
Stamford GB 40 C3
Stamford Bridge
GB 40 B3
Stamnes N 46 B2
Stams A 108 B1
Stamsried D 95 B4
Stamsund N 194 B4
Stanford le Hope
GB 45 B4
Stånga S 57 C4
Stange N 48 B3
Stanghella I 121 B4
Stanhope GB 37 B4
Stanišić SRB 125 B5
Staňkov CZ 95 B5
Stankovci HR 137 B4
Stanley GB 37 B5
Stans CH 106 C3
Stansted Mountfitchet
GB 45 B4
Stanzach A 108 B1
Stapar SRB 125 B5
Staphorst NL 70 B3
Staplehurst GB 45 B4
Staporków PL 87 A4
Stara Baška HR . . .123 C3
Starachowice PL . . .87 A5
Stara Fužina SLO .122 A2
Stara Kamienica
PL 84 B3
Stara Kiszewa PL . .68 B3
Stará L'ubovňa SK .99 B4
Stara Moravica
SRB 126 B1
Stara Novalja HR . .137 A3
Stara Pazova SRB 127 C2
Stará Turá SK 98 C1
Staraya Russa RUS .9 D7
Stara Zagora BG . . .17 D6
Stärbsnäs S 51 C6
Starčevo SRB 127 C2
Stare Dłutowo PL . .77 A4
Staré Hamry CZ . . .98 B2
Stare Jablonki PL . .69 B5
Staré Město CZ 98 B1
Stare Pole PL 69 A4
Stare Sedlo CZ 96 B2
Stare Strącze PL . . .85 A4
Stargard Szczeciński
PL 75 A4
Stårheim N 198 D2
Stari Banovci
SRB 127 C2
Starigrad
Ličko-Senjska
HR 123 C3
Splitsko-Dalmatinska
HR 138 B2
Stari Gradac HR . .124 B3
Starigrad-Paklenica
HR 137 A4
Stari Jankovci HR 125 B4
Stari Majdan BIH . .124 C2
Stari-Mikanovci
HR 125 B4
Staritsa RUS 9 D9
Starkenbach A 108 B1
Starnberg D 108 B2
Starogard PL 75 A4
Starogard Gdański
PL 69 B3
Starokonstyantyniv
UA 13 D7
Staro Petrovo Selo
HR 124 B3
Staro Selo
HR 124 B1
SRB 127 C3
Stary Brzozów PL . .77 B5
Stary Dzierzgoń PL 69 B4
Starý Hrozenkov
CZ 98 C1
Stary Jaroslaw PL . .68 A1
Stary Plzenec CZ . .96 B1
Stary Sącz PL 99 B4

Starý Smokovec
SK 99 B4
Staryy Chartoriysk
UA 13 C6
Staškov SK 98 B2
Stassfurt D 82 A3
Staszów PL 87 B5
Stathelle N 53 A5
Staufen D 106 B2
Staunton GB 39 C4
Stavang N 46 A2
Stavanger N 52 B1
Stavåsnäs S 49 B4
Stavby S 51 B5
Staveley GB 40 B2
Stavelot B 80 B1
Stavenisse NL 79 A4
Stavern N 53 B6
Stavnäs S 55 A3
Stavoren NL 70 B2
Stavros
CY 181 A1
GR 183 C5
Stavroupoli GR . . .183 B6
Stavseng N 47 A6
Stavsiø N 48 B2
Stavsnäs S 57 A4
Stawiszyn PL 76 C3
Steane N 53 A4
Steblevë AL 182 B2
Stechelberg CH . . .106 C2
Stechovice CZ 96 B2
Stechow D 73 B5
Steckborn CH 107 B3
Stede Broek NL 70 B2
Steeg A 107 B5
Steenbergen NL 79 A4
Steenvoorde F 78 B2
Steenwijk NL 70 B3
Štefanje HR 124 B2
Steffisburg CH 106 C2
Stegaurach D 94 B2
Stege DK 65 B5
Stegelitz D 74 A2
Stegersbach A 111 B3
Stegna PL 69 A4
Steimbke D 72 B2
Stein GB 31 B2
Steinach
A 108 B2
Baden-Württemberg
D 106 A3
Bayern D 82 B2
Thüringen D 82 B3
Stein an Rhein CH 107 B3
Steinau
Bayern D 81 B5
Niedersachsen D . . .64 C1
Steinbeck D 74 B2
Steinberg am Rofan
A 108 B2
Steindorf A 109 C5
Steine N 46 B2
Steinen D 106 B2
Steinfeld
A 109 C4
D 71 B5
Steinfurt D 71 B4
Steingaden D 108 B1
Steinhagen D 72 B1
Steinheid D 82 B3
Steinheim
Bayern D 107 A5
Nordrhein-Westfalen
D 81 A5
Steinhöfel D 74 B3
Steinhorst D 72 B3
Steinigtwolmsdorf
D 84 A2
Steinkjer N 199 A8
Steinsholt N 53 A5
Stekene B 79 A4
Stelle D 72 A3
Stellendam NL 79 A4
Stenåsa S 63 B4
Stenay F 91 B5
Stenberga S 62 A3
Stendal D 73 B4
Stenhammar S 55 B4
Stenhamra S 57 A3
Stenhousemuir GB .35 B4
Stenlose DK 61 D2
Stensätra S 50 B3
Stensele S 195 E8
Stenstorp S 55 B4
Stenstrup DK 65 A3
Stenudden S 195 D8
Stenungsund S 54 B2
Štěpánov CZ 98 B1
Stephanskirchen
D 108 B3
Stepnica PL 74 A3
Stepojevac SRB . . .127 C2
Stepping DK 59 C2
Sterbfritz D 82 B1
Sternberg D 65 C4
Šternberk CZ 98 B1
Sterup D 64 B2
Stes Maries-de-la-Mer
F 131 B3
Stęszew PL 75 B5
Štěti CZ 84 B2
Stevenage GB 44 B3
Stewarton GB 36 A2
Steyerburg D 72 B2
Steyning GB 44 C3
Steyr A 110 A1
Stężyca PL 68 A2
Stezzano I 120 B2
Stia I 135 B4
Stibb Cross GB 42 B2
Sticciano Scalo I . .135 C4
Stidsvig S 61 C3
Stiens NL 70 A2
Stige DK 59 C3
Stigen S 54 B3
Stigliano I 174 A2
Stigtomta S 56 B2
Stilida GR 182 E4
Stilla N 192 C7

Stillington GB 40 A2
Stilo I 175 C2
Stintino I 178 B2
Stio I 172 B1
Štip MK 182 B4
Stira GR 185 A5
Stirling GB 35 B4
Štítnik SK 99 C4
Štity CZ 97 B4
Stjärnhov S 56 A3
Stjärnsund S 50 B3
Stjørdalshalsen N 199 B7
Stobnica PL 87 A3
Stobno PL 75 A5
Stobreč HR 138 B2
Stochov CZ 84 B1
Stockach D 107 B4
Stöckalp CH 106 C3
Stockaryd S 62 A2
Stockbridge GB 44 B2
Stockerau A 97 C4
Stockheim D 82 B3
Stockholm S 57 A4
Stocksbridge GB . . .40 B1
Stockton-on-Tees
GB 37 B5
Stod CZ 96 B1
Stöde S 200 D2
Stødi N 195 D6
Stöðvarfjörður
IS 191 C12
Stoer GB 32 C1
Stoholm DK 58 B2
Stoke Ferry GB 41 C4
Stoke Fleming GB . .43 B3
Stoke Mandeville
GB 44 B3
Stoke-on-Trent GB .40 B1
Stokesley GB 37 B5
Stokke N 54 A1
Stokkemarke DK . . .65 B4
Stokken N 53 B4
Stokksseyri IS 190 D4
Stokkvågen N 195 D4
Stokmarknes N 194 B6
Štoky CZ 97 B3
Stølaholmen N 46 A3
Stolberg D 80 B2
Stolin BY 13 C7
Stollberg D 83 B4
Stöllet S 49 B5
Stollhamm D 71 A5
Stolno PL 76 A3
Stolpen D 84 A2
Stolzenau D 72 B2
Stompetoren NL 70 B1
Ston HR 139 C3
Stonařov CZ 97 B3
Stone GB 40 C1
Stonehaven GB 33 E4
Stonehouse GB 36 A3
Stongfjorden N 46 A2
Stonndalen N 47 B4
Stony Stratford GB 44 A3
Stopnica PL 87 B4
Storå S 56 A1
Storås N 198 B6
Storby FIN 51 B6
Stordal
Møre og Romsdal
N 198 C4
Nord-Trøndelag
N 199 B8
Store GB 33 B4
Storebø N 46 B2
Storebro S 62 A3
Store Damme DK . . .65 B5
Store Heddinge DK .65 A5
Store Herrestad S . .66 A2
Store Levene S 55 B3
Storelv N 192 B6
Store Molvik N 193 B12
Støren N 199 B7
Store Skedvi S 50 B2
Store Vika S 57 B3
Storfjellseter N 199 D7
Storfjord N 192 C3
Storfjorden N 198 C3
Storfors S 55 A5
Storforshei N 195 D5
Storhøliseter N 47 A6
Storjord N 195 D6
Storkow
Brandenburg D 74 B2
Mecklenburg-
Vorpommern D 74 A3
Storli N 198 C6
Storlien S 199 B9
Stornara I 171 B3
Stornoway GB 31 A2
Storo I 121 B3
Storozhynets UA . . .17 A6
Storrington GB 44 C3
Storseleby S 200 B2
Storsjön S 50 A3
Storslett N 192 C5
Storsteinnes N 192 C3
Storsund S 196 D3
Storuman S 195 E8
Störvattnet S 199 C9
Storvik
N 195 D4
S 50 B3
Storvreta S 51 C4
Štos SK 99 C4
Stössen D 83 A3
Stotel D 72 A1
Stötten D 108 B1
Stotternheim D 82 A3
Stouby DK 59 C2
Stourbridge GB 40 C1
Stourport-on-Severn
GB 39 B4
Støvring DK 58 B2
Stow GB 35 C5
Stowbtsy BY 13 B7
Stowmarket GB 45 A5

Stow-on-the-Wold
GB 44 B2
Straach D 73 C5
Strabane GB 27 B3
Strachan GB 33 D4
Strachur GB 34 B2
Stracin MK 182 A4
Strackholt D 71 A4
Stradbally IRL 29 B1
Stradella I 120 B2
Straelen D 80 A2
Stragari SRB 127 C2
Strakonice CZ 96 B1
Strålsnäs S 55 B6
Stralsund D 66 B2
Strand N 48 A3
Stranda N 198 C3
Strandby DK 58 A3
Strandebarm N 46 B3
Strandhill IRL 26 B2
Strandlykkja N 48 B3
Strandvik N 46 B2
Strangford GB 27 B5
Strängnäs S 56 A3
Strångsjö S 56 B2
Stráni CZ 98 C1
Stranice SLO 123 A4
Stranorlar IRL 26 B3
Stranraer GB 36 B1
Strasatti I 176 B1
Strasbourg F 93 C3
Strasburg D 74 A2
Strašice CZ 96 B1
Stråssa S 56 A1
Strassburg A 110 C1
Strass im Steiermark
A 110 C2
Strasskirchen D 95 C4
Strasswalchen A . . .109 B4
Stratford-upon-Avon
GB 44 A2
Strathaven GB 36 A2
Strathdon GB 32 D3
Strathkanaird GB . .32 D1
Strathpeffer GB 32 D2
Strathy GB 32 C3
Strathyre GB 34 B3
Stratinska BIH 124 C2
Stratton GB 42 B2
Straubing D 95 C4
Straulas I 178 B3
Straume N 53 A5
Straumen
Nordland N 194 C6
Nord-Trøndelag
N 199 B8
Straumsjøen N 194 B5
Straumsnes N 194 C6
Straupitz D 74 C3
Strausberg D 74 B2
Straussfurt D 82 A3
Strawczyn PL 87 B4
Straža
SLO 123 B4
SRB 127 C3
Stražnad Nezárkou
CZ 96 B2
Strážnice CZ 98 C1
Strážný CZ 96 C1
Stráž Pod Ralskem
CZ 84 B2
Štrbské Pleso SK . .99 B4
Strečno SK 98 B2
Street GB 43 A4
Strehla D 83 A5
Strekov SK 112 B2
Strem A 111 B3
Stremska-Rača
SRB 127 C1
Strengberg A 110 A1
Strengelvåg N 194 B6
Stresa I 119 B5
Streufdorf D 82 B2
Strib DK 59 C2
Striberg S 55 A5
Štribro CZ 95 B4
Strichen GB 33 D4
Strigno I 121 A4
Strijen NL 79 A4
Strizivojna HR 125 B4
Strmica HR 138 A2
Strmilov CZ 97 B3
Ströhen D 72 B1
Strokestown IRL 28 A3
Stromberg
Nordrhein-Westfalen
D 81 A4
Rheinland-Pfalz D .93 B3
Stromeferry GB 31 B3
Strömnäs S 200 B2
Stromness GB 33 C3
Strömsberg S 51 B4
Strömsbruk S 200 E3
Strömsfors S 56 B2
Strömsnäsbruk S . .61 C3
Strömstad S 54 B2
Strömsund
Jämtland S 199 B12
Västerbotten S 195 E7
Stronachlachar GB 34 B3
Stróngoli I 174 B3
Stronie Śląskie PL .85 B4
Strontian GB 34 B2
Stroppiana I 119 B5
Stroud GB 43 A4
Stroumbi CY 181 B1
Stróża PL 99 B3
Strücklingen D 71 A4
Struer DK 58 B1
Struga MK 182 B2
Strugi Krasnyye
RUS 9 C6
Strumica MK 182 B4
Strumien PL 98 B2
Struy GB 32 D2
Stružec HR 124 B2
Stryków PL 77 C4
Stryn N 198 D3
Stryy UA 13 D5

Strzałkowo PL 76 B2
Strzegocin PL 77 B5
Strzegom PL 85 B4
Strzegowo PL 77 B5
Strzelce PL 77 B4
Strzelce Krajeńskie
PL 75 B4
Strzelce Kurowo
PL 75 B4
Strzelce Opolskie
PL 86 B2
Strzelin PL 85 B5
Strzelno PL 76 B3
Strzepcz PL 68 A3
Strzybnica PL 86 B2
Strzygi PL 77 A4
Stubbekøbing DK . .65 B5
Stuben A 107 B5
Stubenberg A 110 B2
Stubline SRB 127 C2
Studená CZ 97 B3
Studenci HR 138 B3
Studenka CZ 98 B2
Studenzen A 110 B2
Studienka SK 98 C1
Studland GB 43 B5
Studley GB 44 A2
Studzienice PL 68 A2
Stuer D 73 A5
Stugudal N 199 C8
Stugun S 200 C1
Stuhr D 72 A1
Stukenbrock D 81 A4
Stülpe D 74 B2
Stupava SK 111 A4
Stupnik HR 124 B1
Stupsk PL 77 A5
Sturkö S 63 B3
Sturminster Newton
GB 43 B4
Šturovo SK 112 B2
Sturton GB 40 B3
Stuttgart D 94 C1
Stvolny CZ 96 A1
Stykkishólmur IS . .190 B3
Styri N 48 B3
Stysö S 60 B1
Suances E 142 A2
Subbiano I 135 B4
Subiaco I 169 B3
Subotica SRB 126 A1
Subotište SRB 127 C1
Sučany SK 98 B2
Suceava RO 17 B7
Sucha-Beskidzka
PL 99 B3
Suchacz PL 69 A4
Suchań PL 75 A4
Suchdol nad Lužnice
CZ 96 C2
Suchedniów PL 87 A4
Suchorze PL 68 A2
Suchteln D 80 A2
Sucina E 165 B4
Sück CH 107 C5
Süčuraj HR 138 B3
Súčovci SRB 127 C1
Sudbury GB 45 A4
Suddesjaur S 195 E10
Suden D 64 B1
Süderbrarup D 64 B2
Süderlügum D 64 B1
Sudoméřice u Bechyně
CZ 96 B2
Sudovec HR 124 A2
Suðureyri IS 190 A2
Sueca E 159 B3
Suelli I 179 C3
Sugenheim D 94 B2
Sugères F 117 B3
Sugny B 91 B4
Suhl D 82 B2
Suhlendorf D 73 B3
Suhopolje HR 124 B3
Suho Polje BIH 125 C5
Şuhut TR 189 A5
Šuica BIH 138 B3
Suippes F 91 B4
Sukošan HR 137 A4
Sükösd H 125 A4
Suków PL 87 B4
Šul'a SK 99 C3
Suldalsosen N 52 A2
Suldrup DK 58 B2
Sulechów PL 75 B4
Sulęcin PL 75 B4
Sulęczyno PL 68 A2
Sulejów PL 87 A3
Süleymanlı TR 186 D2
Sulgen D 107 B4
Sulibórz PL 75 A4
Sulina RO 17 C8
Sulingen D 72 B1
Suliszewo PL 75 A4
Sulitjelma N 195 C7
Sulkowice PL 99 B3
Süller TR 189 A4
Sully-sur-Loire F . . .103 B4
Sulmierzyce
Łódzkie PL 86 A3
Wielkopolskie PL . .85 A5
Sulmona I 169 A3
Süloğlu TR 186 A1
Sułoszowa PL 87 B3
Sulów PL 85 A5
Sulsdorf D 65 B4
Sultandağı TR 189 A6
Sulviken S 199 B11
Sulzbach
Baden-Württemberg
D 94 B1
Baden-Württemberg
D 94 C1
Bayern D 93 B5
Saarland D 92 B3

Sulzbach-Rosenberg
D 95 B3
Sülze D 72 B3
Sulzfeld D 82 B2
Sumartin HR 138 B2
Sumburgh GB 33 B5
Sümeg H 111 C4
Šumiswald CH 106 B2
Sumná CZ 97 C3
Šumperk CZ 97 B4
Šumvald CZ 98 B1
Sunbilla E 144 A2
Sünching D 95 C4
Sund
FIN 51 B7
S 54 A2
Sundborn S 50 B2
Sundby DK 58 B1
Sunde N 46 C2
Sunde bru N 53 B5
Sunderland GB 37 B5
Sundern D 81 A4
Sundhultsbrunn S . .62 A2
Sundnäs S 195 D8
Sundom S 196 D5
Sunds DK 59 B2
Sundsfjord N 195 D5
Sundsvall S 200 D3
Sungurlu TR 23 A8
Suni I 178 B2
Sunja HR 124 B2
Sunnansjö S 50 B1
Sunnaryd S 60 B3
Sunndalsøra N 198 C5
Sunne S 49 C5
Sunnemo S 49 C5
Sunnersberg S 55 B4
Suolovuopmio N . .192 C7
Suomussalmi FIN . .3 D11
Suoyarvi RUS 9 A8
Super Sauze F 132 A2
Supetar HR 138 B2
Supetarska Draga
HR 123 C3
Supino I 169 B3
Šuplja Stijena
MNE 139 B5
Surahammar S 56 A2
Šurany SK 112 A2
Surazh BY 13 A9
Surbo I 173 B4
Surčin SRB 127 C2
Surgères F 114 B3
Surhuisterveen NL .70 A3
Súria E 147 C2
Surin F 115 B4
Surka N 48 B2
Surnadalsøra N . . .198 C5
Sursee CH 106 B3
Surte S 60 B2
Surwold D 71 B4
Sury-le-Comtal F . .117 B4
Susa I 119 B4
Šušara SRB 127 C3
Susch CH 107 C5
Susegana I 122 B1
Süsel D 65 B3
Sušice CZ 96 B1
Sušnjevica HR 123 B3
Sussen D 94 C1
Susurluk TR 186 C3
Susz PL 69 B4
Sütçüler TR 189 B5
Sutivan HR 138 B2
Sutjeska SRB 126 B2
Sutri I 168 A2
Sutton GB 44 B3
Sutton Coldfield
GB 40 C2
Sutton-in-Ashfield
GB 40 B2
Sutton-on-Sea GB . .41 B4
Sutton-on-Trent
GB 40 B3
Sutton Scotney GB .44 B2
Sutton Valence GB .45 B4
Suvaja BIH 124 C2
Suvereto I 135 B3
Suwałki PL 12 A5
Suze-la-Rousse F .131 A3
Suzzara I 121 C3
Svabensverk S 50 A2
Svalbarð IS 191 A10
Svalöv S 61 D3
Svanabyn S 200 B2
Svanberga S 51 C5
Svaneke DK 67 A4
Svanesund S 54 B2
Svängsta S 63 B2
Svannäs S 195 D9
Svanskog S 54 A3
Svanstein S 196 C6
Svappavaara S 196 B4
Svärdsjö S 50 B2
Svarstad N 53 A5
Svartå S 55 A5
Svärta S 56 B3
Svartå S 55 A4
Svartbyn S 196 C5
Svärtinge S 56 B2
Svartlå S 196 D4
Svartnäs S 50 B3
Svartnäs S 195 C5
Svarttjärn S 195 E7
Svatsum N 48 A1
Svätý Jur SK 111 A4
Svatý Peter SK 112 B2
Svedala S 61 D3
Sveg S 199 C11
Sveindal N 52 B3
Sveio N 52 A1
Svejbæk DK 59 B2
Svelgen N 198 D2
Svelvik N 54 A1
Svenljunga S 60 B3
Svennevad S 56 A1
Svenstavik S 199 C11
Svendborg DK 65 A3
Svene N 53 A5
Svenljunga S 60 B3
Svennevad S 56 A1
Svenstavik S 199 C11
Svenstrup DK 58 B2

Švermov CZ. . . .84 B2
Sveti Ivan Zabno HR. 124 B2
Sveti Ivan Zelina HR. 124 B2
Sveti Nikole MK. . .182 B3
Sveti Rok HR. . .137 A4
Světlá nad Sázavou CZ. 97 B3
Svetlyy RUS. . . .69 A5
Svetvinčenat HR. .122 B2
Švica HR 123 C4
Svidnik SK. . . .12 D4
Švihov CZ. 96 B1
Svilajnac SRB. . .127 C3
Svilengrad BG. . .183 B8
Svindal N. 54 A2
Svinhult S. 62 A3
Svinna SK 98 C2
Svinninge
DK. 61 D1
S. 57 A4
Sviritsa RUS 9 B8
Svishtov BG . . .17 D6
Svislach BY. . . .13 B6
Svit SK. 99 B4
Svitavy CZ. . . .97 B4
Svodin SK. . . .112 B2
Svolvær N. . . .194 B5
Svortemyr N . . .46 A2
Svortland N. . . .52 A1
Svratka CZ. . . .97 B4
Svrčinovec SK. . .98 B2
Svullrya N. 49 B4
Svyetlahorsk BY . .13 B8
Swadlincote GB. .40 C2
Swaffham GB . . .41 C4
Swanage GB. . . .43 B5
Swanley GB. . . .45 B4
Swanlinbar IRL . .26 B3
Swansea GB . . .39 C3
Swarzęd PL 76 B2
Swatragh GB. . . .27 B4
Świątki PL. 69 B5

Świdnica
Dolnośląskie PL. .85 B4
Lubuskie PL. . . .84 A3
Świdnik PL. . . .12 C5
Świdwin PL. . . .67 C4
Świebodzice PL. .85 B4
Świebodzin PL. . .75 B4
Świecie PL. 76 A3
Świedziebnia PL . .77 A4
Świeradów Zdrój
PL. 84 B3
Świerki PL. 85 B4
Świerzawa PL. . .85 A3
Świerzno PL. . . .67 C3
Święta PL. 74 A2
Świeta Anna PL. .86 B3
Świętno PL. 75 B5
Swifterbant NL. . .70 B2
Swindon GB 44 B2
Swineshead GB. . .41 C4
Swinford IRL . . .26 C2
Świnoujście PL. . .66 C3
Swinton GB. . . .35 C5
Swobnica PL. . . .74 A3
Swords IRL 30 A2
Swornegacie PL. . .68 B2
Sya S 56 B1
Syasstroy RUS . . .9 B8
Sycewice PL. . . .68 A1
Sychevka RUS . . .9 E9
Syców PL. 86 A1
Sycowice PL. . . .75 B4
Sydnes N. 52 A1
Syfteland N. . . .46 B2
Syke D 72 B1
Sykkylven N .198 C3
Sylling N 48 C2
Sylt N. 198 C4
Symbister GB. . . .33 A5
Symington GB. . .36 A3
Symonds Yat GB. .39 C4
Sypniewo
Kujawsko-Pomorskie PL. . . .76 A2
Wielkopolskie PL. .68 B1
Syserum S. 62 A4
Sysslebäck S. . . .49 B4
Syvälahti FIN .197 B8
Szabadbattyán H. .112 B2
Szabadegyháza H .112 B2
Szabadszállás H. .112 C3
Szadek PL. 86 A2
Szajol H 113 B4
Szakály H. 112 C2
Szakcs H. 112 C2
Szakmár H. 112 C3
Szalánta H 125 B4
Szałas PL. 87 A4
Szalkszentmárton H. 112 C3
Szalonna H. . . .99 C4
Szamocin PL. . . .76 A2
Szamotuly PL. . . .75 B5
Szany H 111 B4
Szarvas H. 113 C4
Szarvaskő H . . .113 B4
Szászvár H 125 A4
Százhalombatta H. 112 B2
Szczawa PL. . . .99 B4
Szczawnica PL. . .99 B4
Szczecin PL. . . .74 A3
Szczecinek PL. . .68 B1
Szczekociny PL. . .87 B3
Szczerców PL. . . .86 A3
Szczucin PL. . . .87 B5
Szczuczarz PL. . .75 A5
Szczuki PL. 77 B5
Szczurowa PL. . . .87 B4
Szczyrk PL. 99 B3
Szczytna PL. . . .85 B4
Szczyty PL. 77 A5
Szécsény H 112 A3
Szederkény H . . .125 B4
Szedres H 112 C2

Szeged H 126 A2
Szeghalom H. . . .113 B5
Szegvár H 113 C4
Székesfehérvár H. 112 B2
Székkutas H. . . .113 C4
Szekszárd H 125 A4
Szemplino Czarne PL. 77 A5
Szemud PL. 68 A3
Szendehely H . . .112 B3
Szendrő H 99 C4
Szentendre H. . . .112 B3
Szentes H 113 C4
Szentgotthárd H . .111 C3
Szentlászló H . . .125 A3
Szentlőrinc H . . .125 A3
Szentmártonkáta H. 113 B3
Szenyér H 111 C4
Szeremle H 125 A4
Szerencs H 113 A5
Szerep H 113 B5
Szigetszentmiklós H. 112 B3
Szigetvár H 125 A3
Szikáncs H. 126 A2
Szikszó H 113 A4
Szil H 111 B4
Szilvásvárad H . . .113 A4
Szklarska Poreba PL. 84 B3
Szlichtyngowa PL. .85 A4
Szob H. 112 B2
Szolnok H 113 B4
Szombathely H . .111 B3
Szorosad H 112 C2
Szpetal Graniczny PL. 77 B4
Szprotawa PL. . . .84 A3
Szreńsk PL. 77 A5
Sztum PL. 69 B4
Sztutowo PL. . . .69 A4
Szubin PL. 76 A2
Szulmierz PL. . . .77 B5
Szulok H 124 A3
Szumanie PL. . . .77 B4
Szumanów PL. . .75 A5
Szydłów
Łódzkie PL. . . .86 A3
Świętokrzyskie PL. .87 B5
Szydłowiec PL. . .87 A4
Szydlowo PL. . . .77 A5
Szydlowo PL. . . .75 A5
Szymanów PL. . .77 B5
Szynkielów PL. . .86 A2

T

Taastrup DK. . . .61 D2
Tab H 112 C2
Tabanera la Luenga E. 151 A3
Tabaqueros E. . .158 B2
Tábara E. 149 A4
Tabenera de Cerrato E. 142 B2
Taberg S. 62 A2
Tabernas E. . . .164 B2
Taboada E. 140 B3
Taboadela E. . . .140 B3
Tábor CZ. 96 B2
Táborfalva H . . .112 B3
Taborište HR . . .124 B2
Tábua P. 148 B1
Tabuaco P. 148 A2
Tabuenca E. . . .152 A2
Tabuyo del Monte E. 141 B4
Taby S 57 A4
Tác H. 112 B2
Tachov CZ. 95 B4
Tadcaster GB. . . .40 B2
Tadley GB 44 B2
Tafalla E. 144 B2
Tafjord N 198 C4
Tågarp S 61 D2
Taggia I 133 B3
Tagliacozzo I. . .169 A3
Táglio di Po I. . .121 B5
Tagnon F 91 B4
Tahal E. 164 B2
Tahitótfalu H . . .112 B3
Tahtaköprü TR. . .187 C4
Tailfingen D . . .107 A4
Taillis F. 101 A4
Tain-l'Hermitage F. 117 B4
Taipadas P. . . .154 C2
Taivalkoski FIN .197 D11
Takene S 55 A4
Takovo SRB. . . .127 C2
Taksony H 112 B3
Tal E. 140 B2
Talachyn BY. 13 A8
Talamello I. . . .135 B5
Talamone I. . . .168 A1
Talant F 105 B3
Talarrubias E. . .156 A2
Talaván E. 155 B4
Talavera de la Reina E. 150 C3
Talavera la Real E. 155 C4
Talayuela E. . . .150 C2
Talayuelas E. . . .159 B2
Talgarth GB 39 C3
Talgje N 52 A1
Talhadas P. . . .148 B1
Táliga E. 155 C3
Talizat F. 116 B3
Tálknafjörður IS . .190 B2
Talla I 135 B4
Talladale GB 31 B3
Tallard F. 132 A2

Tällberg S. 50 B1
Tallberg S. 196 C5
Tallinn EST 87 B5
Talloires F. 118 B3
Tallow IRL 29 B3
Tallsjö S. 200 B4
Tallvik S. 196 C5
Talmay F 105 B4
Talmont-St Hilaire F. 114 B2
Talmont-sur-Gironde F. 114 C3
Talne UA. 13 D9
Talsano I. 173 B3
Talsi LV. 8 D3
Talvik N. 192 B6
Talybont GB. . . .39 B3
Tal-Y-Llyn GB. . .38 B3
Tamajón E 151 B4
Tamames E. . . .149 B3
Tamarit de Mar E. 147 C3
Tamarite de Litera E. 145 C4
Tamariu E. 147 C4
Tamási H. 112 C2
Tambach-Dietharz D. 82 B2
Tameza E. 141 A4
Tammisaari FIN. . .8 B3
Tampere FIN 8 B3
Tamsweg A. . . .109 B4
Tamurejo E. . . .156 B3
Tamworth GB. . . .40 C2
Tana bru N 193 B12
Tañabueyes E. . .143 B3
Tanakajd H 111 B3
Tananger N 52 B1
Tanaunella I. . . .178 B3
Tancarville F . . .89 A4
Tandsjöborg S. . .199 D11
Tånga S 61 C2
Tangelic H 112 C2
Tangen N 48 B3
Tangerhütte D . . .73 B4
Tangermünde D. . .73 B4
Tanhua FIN .197 B10
Taninges F. 118 A3
Tankavaara FIN .197 A10
Tann D 82 B2
Tann D 83 B3
Tannadice GB . . .35 B5
Tännäker S. 60 C3
Tännäs S. 199 C9
Tannay
Ardennes F . . .91 B4
Nièvre F 104 B2
Tannenbergsthal D 83 B4
Tännesberg D . . .95 B4
Tannheim A 108 B1
Tannila FIN. . . .197 D8
Tanowo PL. 74 A3
Tanum S. 54 B2
Tanumshede S . . .54 B2
Tanus F 130 A1
Tanvald CZ. 84 B3
Taormina I 177 B4
Tapa EST 8 C4
Tapfheim D 94 C2
Tapia de Casariego E. 141 A4
Tapio F. 146 A2
Tapiobicske H. . .112 B3
Tápiógyörgye H .113 B3
Tápióság H 112 B3
Tápiószecsö H . .112 B3
Tápiószele H. . . .113 B3
Tápiószentmárton H. 113 B3
Tapolca H. 111 C4
Tapolcafő H 111 B4
Tar HR 122 B2
Tarabo S. 60 B2
Taradell E. 147 C3
Taraklı TR. 187 B5
Taramundi E . . .141 A3
Tarancón E 151 B4
Táranto I. 173 B3
Tarare F 117 B4
Tarascon F. 131 B3
Tarascon-sur-Ariège F. 146 B2
Tarashcha UA. . . .13 D9
Tarazona E. 144 C2
Tarazona de la Mancha E. 158 B2
Tarbena E. 159 C3
Tarbert
GB. 34 C2
IRL 29 B2
Tarbes F 145 A4
Tarbet GB. 34 B3
Tarbolton GB. . . .36 A2
Tarcento I. 122 A2
Tarčin BIH 139 B4
Tarczyn PL. 77 C5
Tardajos E 143 B3
Tardelcuende E. .151 A5
Tardets-Sorholus F. 144 A3
Tardienta E 145 C3
Tärendö S 196 B5
Targon F. 128 B2
Târgovişte RO. . .17 C6
Târgu-Jiu RO. . .17 C5
Târgu Mureş RO .17 B6
Târgu Ocna RO. .17 B7
Târgu Secuiesc RO. 17 C7
Tarifa E. 162 B2
Tariquejas E. . . .161 B2
Tarján H 112 B2
Tárkány H 112 B2
Tarland GB. 33 D4
Tarłów PL. 87 A5
Tarm DK. 59 C1
Tarmstedt D 72 A2
Tärnaby S 195 E6
Tarnalelesz H. . .113 A4
Tarnaörs H. 113 B4

Târnăveni RO. . .17 B6
Tårnet N 193 C14
Tarnobrzeg PL. . .87 B5
Tarnos F 128 C1
Tarnów
Lubuskie PL. . . .75 B3
Małopolskie PL. .87 B4
Tarnowo Podgórne PL. 75 B5
Tarnowskie Góry PL. 86 B2
Tärnsjö S. 51 B3
Tårnvik N. 194 C6
Tarouca P. 148 A2
Tarp D. 64 B2
Tarquínia I. 168 A1
Tarquinia Lido I. .168 A1
Tarragona E. . . .147 C2
Tàrrajaur S. 196 C2
Tàrrega E. 147 C2
Tarrenz A. 108 B1
Tårs
Nordjyllands DK. .58 A3
Storstrøms DK. . .65 B4
Tarsia I. 174 B2
Tarsus TR. 23 C8
Tartas F. 128 C2
Tartu EST. 8 C5
Tarves GB 33 D4
Tarvísio I. 109 C4
Taşağıl TR. 189 C6
Tasch CH. 119 A4
Taşköprü TR. . . .23 A8
Tasov CZ. 97 B4
Tasovčići BIH. . .139 B3
Taşucuo TR. . . .23 C7
Tát H. 112 B2
Tata H. 112 B2
Tatabánya H. . . .112 B2
Tataháza H. . . .126 A1
Tatarbunary UA. .17 C8
Tatárszentgyörgy H. 112 B3
Tatranská-Lomnica SK. 99 B4
Tau N 52 A1
Tauberbischofsheim D. 94 B1
Taucha D 83 A4
Taufkirchen D . .95 C4
Taufkirchen an der Pram A. 96 C1
Taulé F. 100 A2
Taulignan F. . . .131 A3
Taunton GB. . . .43 A3
Taunusstein D. . .81 B4
Tauragė LT. 12 A5
Tauriano I. 175 C2
Taurianova I. . . .175 C2
Taurisano I. . . .173 C4
Tauste E. 144 C2
Tauves F 116 B2
Tavankut SRB. . .126 A1
Tavannes CH. . . .106 B2
Tavarnelle val di Pesa I. 135 B4
Tavas TR 188 B4
Tavaux F. 105 B4
Tävelsås S. 62 B2
Taverna I. 175 B2
Taverne CH 120 A1
Tavernelle I. . . .135 B5
Tavernes de la Valldigna E . . .159 B3
Tavérnola Bergamasca I. 120 B3
Taverny F. 90 B2
Tavescan E 146 B2
Taviano I. 173 C4
Tavira P 160 B2
Tavistock GB. . . .42 B2
Tavşanlı TR. . . .187 C4
Tayinloan GB. . . .34 C2
Taynuilt GB. 34 B2
Tayport GB. 35 B5
Tázlár H 112 C3
Tazones E. 142 A1
Tczew PL. 69 A3
Tczów PL. 87 A5
Teangue GB. . . .31 B3
Teano I. 170 B2
Teba E. 162 B3
Tebay GB. 37 B4
Techendorf A. . .109 C4
Tecklenburg D. . .71 B4
Tecko-matorp S. .61 D3
Tecuci RO. 17 C7
Tefenni TR. 189 B4
Tegelsmora S . . .51 B4
Tegelen NL. 80 A2
Tegernsee D . . .108 B2
Teggiano I. 172 B1
Tegoleto I. 135 B4
Teichel D. 82 B3
Teignmouth GB. .43 B3
Teillay F. 101 B4
Teillet F. 130 B1
Teisendorf D . . .109 B3
Teistungen D. . . .82 A2
Teixeiro E. 140 A2
Tejada de Tiétar E 150 B2
Tejado E. 152 A1
Tejares E. 150 B2
Tejn DK. 67 A3
Teke TR. 187 A4
Tekirdağ TR 186 B2
Tekovské-Lužany SK. 112 A2
Telavåg N. 46 B1
Telč CZ. 97 B3
Telese Terme I. . .170 B2
Telford GB. 38 B4
Telfs A. 108 B2
Telgárt SK. 99 C4
Telgte D. 71 C4
Tellingstedt D. . . .64 B2
Telšiai LT. 8 E3
Telti I. 178 B3
Tembleque E. . . .157 A4
Temelín CZ. 96 B2

Temerin SRB . . .126 B1
Temiño E 143 B3
Témpio Pausánia I. 178 B3
Templederry IRL . .28 B3
Templemore IRL . .28 B4
Temple Sowerby GB. 37 B4
Templin D. 74 A2
Temse B 79 A4
Tenay F 118 B2
Ten Boer NL. . . .71 A3
Tenbury Wells GB .39 B4
Tenby GB. 39 C2
Tence F. 117 B4
Tende F. 133 A3
Tenhult S. 62 A2
Tenja HR 125 B4
Tenneville B. . . .92 A1
Tennevoll N 194 B8
Tensta S. 51 B4
Tenterden GB . . .45 B4
Teo E 140 B2
Teora I 172 B1
Tepasto FIN 196 B7
Tepelenë AL. . . .182 C2
Teplá CZ. 95 B4
Teplice CZ 84 B1
Teplička nad Váhom SK. 98 B2
Tepsa FIN 197 B8
Tera E 143 C4
Téramo I. 169 A3
Ter Apel NL 71 B4
Terborg NL. 71 C3
Terchová SK. . . .99 B3
Terebovlya UA. . .13 D6
Teremia Mare RO .126 B2
Terena P. 155 C3
Terento I. 108 C2
Teresa de Cofrentes E. 159 B2
Terešov CZ. 96 B1
Terezín CZ. 84 B2
Terezino Polje HR .124 B3
Tergnier F 90 B3
Teriberka RUS . . .3 B14
Terlizzi I. 171 B4
Termas de Monfortinho P. 155 A4
Terme di Súio I. .169 B3
Terme di Valdieri I .133 A3
Termens E. 145 C4
Termes F 116 C3
Términi Imerese I .176 B2
Terminillo I. . . .169 A2
Térmoli I. 170 B3
Termonfeckin IRL .27 C4
Ternberg A. 110 B1
Terndrup DK. . . .58 B3
Terneuzen NL . . .79 A3
Terni I. 168 A2
Ternitz A 111 B3
Ternopil UA 13 D6
Terpni GR. 183 C5
Terracina I. 169 B3
Terrak N 195 E3
Terralba I 179 C2
Terranova di Pollino I. 174 B2
Terranova di Sibari I. 174 B2
Terras do Bouro P. 148 A1
Terrasini I 176 A2
Terrassa E. 147 C3
Terrasson-la-Villedieu F. 129 A4
Terrazos E. 143 B3
Terriente E. 152 B2
Terrugem P 155 C3
Tertenía I. 179 C3
Tervola FIN 196 C7
Tervuren B. 79 B4
Terzaga E. 152 B2
Tešanj BIH 125 C3
Tešáske-Mlyňany SK. 98 C2
Teslić BIH. 125 C3
Tessin D 66 B1
Tessy-sur-Vire F. .88 B2
Têt H 111 B4
Tetbury GB. 43 A4
Teterchen F 92 B2
Teterow D 65 C5
Teteven BG 17 D6
Tetiyev UA. 13 D8
Tetovo MK 182 A2
Tettau D. 82 B3
Tettnang D 107 B4
Teublitz D. 95 B4
Teuchern D 83 A4
Teulada
E. 159 C4
I. 179 D2
Teupitz D. 74 B2
Teurajärvi S 196 C5
Teutschenthal D. .83 A3
Tevel H 112 C2
Teviothead GB. . .36 A4
Tewkesbury GB. .39 C4
Thale D. 82 A3
Thalfang D. 92 B2
Thalgau A. 109 B4
Thalkirch CH . . .107 C4
Thalmässing D . . .95 B3
Thalwil CH. 107 B3
Thame GB. 44 B3
Thann F. 106 B2
Thannhausen D . .94 C2
Thaon-les-Vosges F. 105 A5
Tharandt D. 83 B5
Tharsis E. 161 B2
Thasos GR. 183 C6
Thatcham GB . . .44 B2
Thaxted GB. 45 B4
Thaya A. 97 C3
Thayngen CH . . .107 B3
Theale GB. 44 B2
The Barony GB. . .33 B3
Temelín CZ. 96 B2

Thebes = Thiva GR. 185 A4
Theding-hausen D .72 B2
Theessen D 73 B5
The Hague = 's-Gravenhage NL. .70 B1
Themar D. 82 B2
Temse B 79 A4
Tenay F 118 B2

Thebes = Thiva GR. 185 A4
Theding-hausen D .72 B2
Theessen D 73 B5
The Hague = 's-Gravenhage NL. .70 B1
Themar D. 82 B2
The Mumbles GB. .39 C3
Thénezay F. . . .102 C1
Thenon F 129 A4
Therouanne F . . .78 B2
Thessaloniki = Salonica GR. 182 C4
Thetford GB. 45 A4
Theux B 80 B1
Thézar-les-Corbières F. 146 A3
Thèze F. 145 A3
Thiberville F 89 A4
Thibie F. 91 C4
Thiéblemont-Farémont F. 91 C4
Thiendorf D 84 A1
Thiene I. 121 B4
Thierrens CH . . .106 C1
Thiers F 117 B3
Thiesi I. 178 B2
Thiessow D 66 B2
Thiezac F. 116 B2
Þingeyri IS. . . .190 B2
Þingvellir IS. . . .190 C4
Thionville F 92 B2
Thira GR. 185 C6
Thiron-Gardais F . .89 B4
Thirsk GB. 37 B5
Thisted DK. 58 B1
Thiva = Thebes GR. 185 A4
Thivars F 90 C1
Thiviers F. 115 C4
Thizy F 117 A4
Tholen NL 79 A4
Tholey D 92 B3
Thomas Street IRL .28 A3
Thomastown IRL. .30 B1
Thônes F 118 B3
Thonnance-les-Joinville F . . .91 C5
Thonon-les-Bains F. 118 A3
Thorame-Basse F .132 A2
Thorame-Haute F .132 A2
Thorens-Glières F 118 A3
Thorigny-sur-Oreuse F. 91 C3
Thörl A 110 B2
Þorlákshöfn IS . .190 D4
Thornaby on Tees GB. 37 B5
Thornbury GB . . .43 A4
Thorne GB 40 B3
Thornhill
Dumfries & Galloway GB. 36 A3
Stirling GB . . .35 B3
Thornthwaite GB. .36 B3
Thornton-le-Dale GB. 40 A3
Þorshöfn IS. . . .191 A10
Thouarcé F 102 B1
Thouars F. 102 C1
Thrapston GB. . . .44 A3
Threlkeld GB. . . .36 B3
Thrumster GB. . . .32 C3
Thueyts F. 117 C4
Thuin B. 79 B4
Thuir F. 146 B3
Thumau D 95 A3
Thun CH. 106 C2
Thuret F 116 B3
Thurey F 105 C4
Thüringen A. . . .107 B4
Thurins F 117 B4
Thürkow D 65 C5
Thurles IRL 29 B4
Thurmaston GB. . .40 C2
Thurø By DK. . . .65 B3
Thursby GB. 36 B3
Thurso GB 32 C3
Thury-Harcourt F .89 B3
Thusis CH 107 C4
Thyborøn DK. . . .58 B1
Thyregod DK. . . .59 C2
Tibi E 159 C3
Tibro S. 55 B5
Tidaholm S 55 B4
Tidan S. 55 B5
Tidersrum S. 62 A3
Tiedra E. 150 A2
Tiefenbach D. . . .95 B4
Tiefencastel CH. .107 C4
Tiefenort D 82 B2
Tiefensee D 74 B2
Tiel NL. 79 A5
Tielmes E. 151 B4
Tielt B. 78 A3
Tienen B. 79 B4
Tiengen D 106 B3
Tiercé F 102 B1
Tierga E. 152 A2
Tiermas E. 144 B2
Tierp S. 51 B4
Tierrantona E. . .145 B4
Tighina MD 17 B8
Tighnabruaich GB. .34 C2
Tignes F. 119 B3
Tigy F 103 B4
Tihany H. 111 C4
Tijnje NL. 70 A2
Tijola E. 164 B2
Tikhvin RUS. 9 C8
Tilburg NL 79 A5
Til Châtel F 105 B4
Tilh F. 128 C2
Tillac F. 145 A4
Tillberga S. 56 A2
Tille F. 90 B2
Tillicoultry GB. . .35 B4
Tilloy Bellay F. . .91 B4

Tilly F. 115 B5
Tilly-sur-Seulles F. .88 A3
Tim DK. 59 B1
Timau I 109 C4
Timbaki GR 185 D5
Timi CY 181 B1
Timişoara RO . . .126 B3
Timmele S. 60 B3
Timmendorfer Strand D. 65 C3
Timmernabben S. .62 B4
Timmersdala S. . .55 B4
Timoleague IRL. . .29 C3
Timolin IRL 30 B2
Timrå S 200 D3
Timsfors S. 61 C3
Timsgearraidh GB. .31 A1
Tinajas E 152 B1
Tinalhas P. 155 B3
Tinchebray F. . . .88 B3
Tincques F 78 B2
Tineo E. 141 A4
Tinglev DK. 64 B2
Tingsryd S. 63 B2
Tingstäde S 57 C4
Tingvoll N. 198 C5
Tinlot B 79 B5
Tinnoset N. 53 A5
Tinos GR 185 B6
Tintagel GB 42 B2
Tinténiac F. 101 A4
Tintern GB 39 C4
Tintigny B 92 B1
Tione di Trento I .121 A3
Tipperary IRL. . . .29 B3
Tiptree GB 45 B4
Tirana = Tiranë AL. 182 B1
Tiranë= Tirana AL .182 B1
Tirano I. 120 A3
Tiraspol MD 17 B8
Tire TR 188 A2
Tires I. 108 C2
Tiriez E. 158 C1
Tirig E. 153 B4
Tiriolo I. 175 C2
Tirnavos GR . . .182 D4
Tírrenia I. 134 B3
Tirschenreuth D . .95 B4
Tirstrup DK. 59 B3
Tirteafuera E . . .157 B3
Tisno HR 137 B4
Tišnov CZ. 97 B4
Tisovec SK. 99 C3
Tisselskog S 54 B3
Tistedal N. 54 A2
Tistrup DK. 59 C1
Tisvildeleje DK. . .61 C2
Tiszaalpár H . . .113 C3
Tiszabö H 113 B4
Tiszacsege H. . .113 B5
Tiszadorogma H. .113 B4
Tiszaföldvár H. . .113 C4
Tiszafüred H . . .113 B4
Tiszajenő H 113 B4
Tiszakécske H . . .113 C4
Tiszakeszi H . . .113 B4
Tiszakürt H 113 C4
Tiszalök H 113 A5
Tiszalúc H 113 A5
Tiszanána H. . . .113 B4
Tiszaörs H. 113 B4
Tiszaroff H. 113 B4
Tiszasüly H. . . .113 B4
Tiszasziget H. . .126 A2
Tiszaszőlős H . . .113 B4
Tiszaújváros H. . .113 B5
Tiszavasvári H. . .113 B5
Titaguas E. 159 B2
Titel SRB. 126 B2
Titisee-Neustadt D. 106 B3
Tito I 172 B1
Titova Korenica HR. 123 C4
Titran N 198 B5
Tittling D. 96 C1
Tittmoning D . . .109 A3
Titz D. 80 A2
Tiurajärvi FIN . . .196 B7
Tived S. 55 B5
Tiverton GB. 43 B3
Tivisa E 153 A4
Tívoli I. 168 B2
Tizsadob H. . . .113 A5
Tjåmotis S 195 D9
Tjæreborg DK. . .59 C1
Tjautjas S. 196 B3
Tjøme N. 54 A1
Tjong N 195 D4
Tjonnefoss N. . . .53 B4
Tjörn IS 190 B5
Tjörnarp S 61 D3
Tjøtta N 195 E3
Tkon HR 137 B4
Tleň PL. 69 B3
Tlmače SK. 98 C2
Tłuchowo PL. . . .77 B4
Tlumačov CZ. . . .98 B1
Tóalmás H 112 B3
Toano I. 134 A3
Toba D 82 A2
Tobarra E. 158 C2
Tobermore GB . . .27 B4
Tobermory GB. . .34 B1
Toberonochy GB. .34 B2
Tobha Mor GB . . .31 B1
Tobo S 51 B4
Tocane-St Apre F .129 A3
Tocha P 148 B1
Tocina E. 162 A2
Töcksfors S. 54 A2
Tocón E. 163 A4
Todal N. 198 C5
Todi I 136 C1
Todmorden GB . . .40 B1

Todorici BIH. 138 A3
Todtmoos D. 106 B3
Todtnau D. 106 B2
Toén E. 140 B3
Tofta
  Gotland S. 57 C4
  Skaraborg S. 55 B4
Toftbyn S. 50 B2
Tofte N. 54 A1
Töftedal S. 54 B2
Tofterup DK. 59 C1
Toftlund DK. 59 C2
Tófü H. 125 A4
Tohmo FIN. 197 C10
Tokaj H. 113 A5
Tokarnia PL. 87 B4
Tokary PL. 76 C3
Tokod H. 112 B2
Tököl H. 112 B2
Tolastadh bho Thuath
  GB. 31 A2
Toledo E. 151 C3
Tolentino I. 136 B2
Tolfa I. 168 A1
Tolg S. 62 A2
Tolga N. 199 C8
Tolkmicko PL. 69 A4
Tollarp S. 61 D3
Tollered S. 60 B2
Tølløse DK. 61 D1
Tolmachevo RUS. 9 C6
Tolmezzo I. 122 A2
Tolmin SLO. 122 A2
Tolna H. 112 C2
Tolnanémedi H. 112 C2
Tolob GB. 33 B5
Tolosa
  E. 144 A1
  P. 155 B3
Tolox E. 162 B3
Tolpuddle GB. 43 B4
Tolva
  E. 145 B4
  FIN. 197 C11
Tolve I. 172 B2
Tomar P. 154 B2
Tomaševac SRB. 126 B2
Tomašica BIH. 124 C2
Tomášikovo SK. 111 A4
Tomašouka BY. 13 C5
Tomášovce SK. 99 C3
Tomaszów Mazowiecki
  PL. 87 A4
Tomatin GB. 32 D3
Tombeboeuf F. 129 B3
Tomdoun GB. 32 D1
Tomelilla S. 66 A2
Tomellosa E. 151 B5
Tomelloso E. 157 A4
Tomiño E. 140 C2
Tomintoul GB. 32 D3
Tomislavgrad BIH. 138 B3
Tomisław PL. 84 A3
Tomisławice PL. 76 B3
Tomnavoulin GB. 32 D3
Tompa H. 126 A1
Tompaládony H. 111 B3
Tomra N. 198 C3
Tomter N. 54 A1
Tona E. 147 C3
Tonara I. 179 B3
Tonbridge GB. 45 B4
Tondela P. 148 B1
Tønder DK. 64 B1
Tongeren B. 79 B5
Tongue GB. 32 C2
Tönisvorst D. 80 A2
Tønjum N. 47 A4
Tonkopuro FIN. 197 C11
Tonnay-Boutonne
  F. 114 C3
Tonnay-Charente
  F. 114 C3
Tonneins F. 129 B3
Tonnerre F. 104 B2
Tonnes N. 195 D4
Tönning D. 64 B1
Tonsåsen N. 47 B6
Tønsberg N. 54 A1
Tonstad N. 52 B2
Toomyvara IRL. 28 B3
Toormore IRL. 29 C2
Topares E. 164 B2
Topas E. 150 A2
Topliţa RO. 17 B6
Topola SRB. 127 C2
Topolčani MK. 182 B3
Topol'čany SK. 98 C2
Topol'čianky SK. 98 C2
Topolje HR. 124 B2
Topólka PL. 76 B3
Topol'niky SK. 111 B4
Topolovăţu Mare
  RO. 126 B3
Toponár H. 125 A3
Toporów PL. 75 B4
Topsham GB. 43 B3
Topusko HR. 124 B1
Toques E. 140 A3
Torà E. 147 C2
Toral de los Guzmanes
  E. 142 B1
Toral de los Vados
  E. 141 B4
Torbalı TR. 188 A2
Torbjörntorp S. 55 B4
Torbole I. 121 B3
Torchiarolo I. 173 B4
Torcross GB. 43 B3
Torcy-le-Petit F. 89 A5
Torda SRB. 126 B2
Tørdal N. 53 A4
Tordehumos E. 142 C1
Tordera E. 147 C3
Tordesillas E. 150 A2
Tordesilos E. 152 B2
Töre S. 196 D5

Töreboda S. 55 B5
Toreby DK. 65 B4
Torekov S. 61 C2
Torella dei Lombardi
  I. 170 C3
Torelló E. 147 B3
Toreno E. 141 B4
Torfou F. 114 A2
Torgau D. 83 A5
Torgelow D. 74 A3
Torgueda P. 148 A2
Torhamn S. 63 B3
Torhop N. 193 B11
Torhout B. 78 A3
Torigni-sur-Vire F. 88 A3
Torija E. 151 B4
Toril E. 152 B2
Torino = Turin I. 119 B4
Toritto I. 171 C4
Torkovichi RUS. 9 C7
Torla E. 145 B3
Tormac RO. 126 B3
Törmänen FIN. 193 D11
Tormestorp S. 61 C3
Tórmini I. 121 B3
Tornada P. 154 B1
Tornal'a SK. 99 C4
Tornavacas E. 150 B2
Tornby DK. 58 A2
Tornesch D. 72 A2
Torness GB. 32 D2
Torniella I. 135 B4
Torrita di Siena I. 135 B4
Torroal P. 154 C2
Tornimparte I. 169 A3
Torning DK. 59 B2
Tornio FIN. 196 D7
Tornjoš SRB. 126 B1
Tornos E. 152 B2
Toro E. 150 A2
Törökszentmiklós
  H. 113 B4
Toropets RUS. 9 D7
Torpa S. 61 C3
Torpè I. 178 B3
Torphins GB. 33 D4
Torpo N. 47 B5
Torpoint GB. 42 B2
Torquay GB. 43 B3
Torquemada E. 142 B2
Torralba de Burgo
  E. 151 A5
Torralba de Calatrava
  E. 157 A4
Torralba del Pinar
  E. 157 B4
Torre Annunziata
  I. 170 C2
Torreblacos E. 143 C4
Torreblanca E. 153 B4
Torreblascopedro
  E. 157 B4
Torrecaballeros E. 151 A3
Torrecampo E. 156 B3
Torre Canne I. 173 B3
Torre Cardela E. 163 A4
Torrecilla E. 152 B1
Torrecilla de la Jara
  E. 156 A3
Torrecilla de la Orden
  E. 150 A2
Torrecilla del Pinar
  E. 151 A3
Torrecilla en Cameros
  E. 143 B4
Torrecillas de la Tiesa
  E. 156 A2
Torre das Vargens
  P. 154 B3
Torre de Coelheiros
  P. 154 C3
Torre de Dom Chama
  P. 149 A2
Torre de Juan Abad
  E. 157 B4
Torre de la Higuera
  E. 161 B3
Torre del Bierzo E. 141 B4
Torre del Burgo E. 151 B4
Torre del Campo
  E. 163 A4
Torre del Greco I. 170 C2
Torre del Lago Puccini
  I. 134 B3
Torre dell'Orso I. 173 B4
Torre del Mar E. 163 B3
Torredembarra E. 147 C2
Torre de Miguel
  Sesmero E. 155 C4
Torre de Moncorvo
  P. 149 A2
Torre de Santa Maria
  E. 156 A1
Torredonjimeno E. 163 A4
Torre do Terranho
  P. 148 B2
Torre Faro I. 177 A4
Torregrosa E. 147 C1
Torreira P. 148 B1
Torrejoncillo E. 155 B4
Torrejón de Ardoz
  E. 151 B4
Torrejón de la Calzada
  E. 151 B4
Torrejón del Rey
  E. 151 B4
Torrejon el Rubio
  E. 156 A1
Torrelaguna E. 151 B4
Torrelapaja E. 152 A2
Torre la Ribera E. 145 B4
Torrelavega E. 142 A2
Torrelobatón E. 150 A2
Torrelodones E. 151 B4
Torre los Negros
  E. 152 B2
Torremaggiore I. 171 B3
Torremanzanas E. 159 C3
Torremayor E. 155 C4
Torremezzo di
  Falconara I. 174 B2
Torremocha E. 156 A1

Torremolinos E. 163 B3
Torrenieri I. 135 B4
Torrenostra E. 153 B4
Torrenova I. 168 B2
Torrent E. 159 B3
Torrente de Cinca
  E. 153 A4
Torrenueva
  Ciudad Real E. 157 B4
  Granada E. 163 B4
Torreorgaz E. 155 B4
Torre Orsáia I. 172 B1
Torre Péllice I. 119 C4
Torreperogil E. 157 B4
Torres E. 163 A4
Torres-Cabrera E. 163 A3
Torres de la Alameda
  E. 151 B4
Torres Novas P. 154 B2
Torres Vedras P. 154 B1
Torrevieja E. 165 B4
Torricella I. 173 B3
Torri del Benaco I. 121 B3
Torridon GB. 31 B3
Torriglia I. 134 A2
Torrijos E. 151 C3
Tørring DK. 59 C2
Torroella de Montgrì
  E. 147 B4
Torrox E. 163 B4
Torrskog S. 54 A3
Torsåker S. 50 B3
Torsang S. 50 B2
Torsås S. 63 B4
Torsby S. 49 B4
Torsetra N. 48 B2
Torshälla S. 56 A2
Tórshavn FO. 4 A3
Torslanda S. 60 B1
Torsminde DK. 59 B1
Torsnes N. 46 B3
Törtel H. 113 B4
Tórtoles E. 150 B2
Tórtoles de Esgueva
  E. 142 C2
Tortoli I. 179 C3
Tortona I. 120 C1
Tórtora I. 174 B1
Tortoreto Lido I. 136 C2
Tortorici I. 177 A3
Tortosa E. 153 B4
Tortosendo P. 148 B2
Tortuera E. 152 B2
Tortuero E. 151 B4
Toruń PL. 76 A3
Torup S. 60 C3
Tor Vaiánica I. 168 B2
Torver GB. 36 B3
Tørvikbygde N. 46 B3
Torviscón E. 163 B4
Torzhok RUS. 9 D9
Torzym PL. 75 B4
Tosbotn N. 195 E3
Toscolano-Maderno
  I. 121 B3
Tosno RUS. 9 C7
Tossa de Mar E. 147 C3
Tossåsen S. 199 C10
Tosse F. 128 C1
Tösse S. 54 B3
Tossicia I. 169 A3
Tostedt D. 72 A2
Tosya TR. 23 A8
Tószeg H. 113 B4
Toszek PL. 86 B2
Totana E. 165 B3
Totebo S. 62 A4
Tôtes F. 89 A5
Tótkomlós H. 113 C4
Totland N. 198 D2
Tøtlandsvik N. 52 A2
Totnes GB. 43 B3
Tótszerdahely H. 124 A2
Totton GB. 44 C2
Touça P. 149 A2
Toucy F. 104 B2
Toul F. 92 C1
Toulon F. 132 B1
Toulon-sur-Allier
  F. 104 C2
Toulon-sur-Arroux
  F. 104 C3
Toulouse F. 129 C4
Tourcoing F. 78 B3
Tour de la Parata
  F. 180 B1
Tourlaville F. 88 A2
Tournai B. 78 B3
Tournan-en-Brie F. 90 C2
Tournay F. 145 A4
Tournon-d'Agenais
  F. 129 B3
Tournon-St Martin
  F. 115 B4
Tournon-sur-Rhône
  F. 117 B4
Tournus F. 105 C3
Touro E. 140 B2
Tourouvre F. 89 B4
Tourriers F. 115 C4
Tours F. 102 B2
Tourteron F. 91 B4
Tourves F. 132 B1
Toury F. 103 A3
Touvedo P. 148 A1
Touvois F. 114 B2
Touzim CZ. 83 B4
Tovačov CZ. 98 B1
Tovariševo SRB. 126 B1
Tovarnik HR. 125 B5
Tovdal N. 53 B4

Towcester GB. 44 A3
Town Yetholm GB. 35 C5
Tråastølen N. 47 B4
Trabada E. 141 A3
Trabadelo E. 141 B4
Trabanca E. 149 A3
Trabazos E. 149 A3
Traben-Trarbach D. 92 B3
Trabia I. 176 B2
Tradate I. 120 B1
Trädet S. 60 B3
Trafaria P. 154 C1
Tragacete E. 152 B2
Tragwein A. 96 C2
Traiguera E. 153 B4
Trainel F. 91 C3
Traisen A. 110 A2
Traismauer A. 97 C3
Traitsching D. 95 B4
Trákhonas CY. 181 A2
Tralee IRL. 29 B2
Tramacastilla de Tena
  E. 145 B3
Tramagal P. 154 B2
Tramariglio I. 178 B2
Tramatza I. 179 B2
Tramelan CH. 106 B2
Tramonti di Sopra
  I. 122 A1
Tramore IRL. 30 B1
Trampot F. 92 C1
Trana I. 119 B4
Tranås S. 55 B5
Tranbjerg DK. 59 B3
Tranby N. 54 A1
Trancoso P. 148 B2
Tranebjerg DK. 59 C3
Tranekær DK. 65 B3
Tranemo S. 60 B3
Tranent GB. 35 C5
Tranevåg N. 52 B2
Trängslet S. 49 A5
Tranhult S. 60 B3
Trani I. 171 B4
Trans-en-Provence
  F. 132 B2
Transtrand S. 49 A5
Tranum DK. 58 A2
Tranvik S. 57 A4
Trápani I. 176 A1
Trappes F. 90 C2
Traryd S. 61 C3
Trasacco I. 169 B3
Trasierra E. 156 B1
Träslövsläge S. 60 B2
Trasmiras E. 140 B3
Traspinedo E. 150 A3
Trate SLO. 110 C2
Trauchgau D. 108 B1
Traun A. 110 A1
Traunstein D. 109 B3
Traunwalchen D. 109 B3
Trávad S. 55 B4
Travemünde D. 65 C3
Traversétolo I. 120 C3
Travnik
  BIH. 139 A3
  SLO. 123 B3
Travo
  F. 180 B2
  I. 120 C2
Trawsfynydd GB. 38 B3
Trbovlje SLO. 123 A4
Trbušani SRB. 127 D2
Treban F. 116 A3
Trebatsch D. 74 B3
Trebbin D. 74 B2
Třebechovice pod
  Orebem CZ. 85 B3
Trebel D. 73 B4
Třebenice CZ. 84 B1
Trébeurden F. 100 A2
Třebíč CZ. 97 B3
Trebinje BIH. 139 C4
Trebisacce I. 174 B2
Trebitz D. 83 A4
Trebnje SLO. 123 B4
Třeboň CZ. 96 B2
Třebovice CZ. 97 B4
Trebsen D. 83 A4
Trebujena E. 161 C3
Trecate I. 120 B1
Trecenta I. 121 B4
Tredegar GB. 39 C3
Tredózio I. 135 A4
Treffen A. 109 C4
Treffort F. 118 A2
Treffurt D. 82 A2
Trefnant GB. 38 A3
Tregaron GB. 39 B3
Trégastel-Plage F. 100 A2
Tregnago I. 121 B4
Tregony GB. 42 B2
Tréguier F. 100 A2
Trégunc F. 100 B2
Treharris GB. 39 C3
Trehörningsjö S. 200 C4
Tréia I. 136 B2
Treignac F. 116 B1
Treignat F. 116 A2
Treignes B. 91 A4
Treis-Karden D. 80 B3
Trekanten S. 63 B4
Trélazé F. 102 B1
Trelech GB. 39 C2
Trélissac F. 129 A3
Trelleborg S. 66 A2
Trélon F. 91 A4
Trélou-sur-Marne F. 91 B3
Tremblay-le-Vicomte
  F. 89 B5
Tremés P. 154 B2
Tremezzo I. 120 B2
Tremolo I. 120 B1
Tremp E. 145 B4
Trenčianska Stankovce
  SK. 98 C1

Trenčianska Turná
  SK. 98 C2
Trenčianske Teplá
  SK. 98 C2
Trenčianske Teplice
  SK. 98 C2
Trenčín SK. 98 C2
Trendelburg D. 81 A5
Trengereid N. 46 B2
Trensacq F. 128 B2
Trent D. 66 B2
Trento I. 121 A4
Treorchy GB. 39 C3
Trept F. 118 B2
Trepuzzi I. 173 B4
Trescore Balneário
  I. 120 B2
Tresenda I. 120 A3
Tresfjord N. 198 C4
Tresigallo I. 121 C4
Trešnjevica SRB. 127 D3
Tresnurághes I. 178 B2
Trespaderne E. 143 B3
Třešť CZ. 97 B3
Trestina I. 135 B5
Tretower GB. 39 C3
Trets F. 132 B1
Tretten N. 48 A2
Treuchtlingen D. 94 C2
Treuen D. 83 B4
Treuenbrietzen D. 74 B1
Treungen N. 53 A4
Trevelez E. 163 B4
Trevi I. 136 C1
Treviana E. 143 B3
Treviglio I. 120 B2
Trevignano Romano
  I. 168 A2
Trevi nel Lázio I. 169 B3
Treviso I. 122 B1
Trévoux F. 117 B4
Treysa D. 81 B5
Trézelles F. 117 A3
Trezzo sull'Adda I. 120 B2
Trhová Kamenice
  CZ. 97 B3
Trhové Sviny CZ. 96 C2
Triacastela E. 141 B3
Triaize F. 114 B2
Trianda GR. 188 C3
Triaucourt-en-Argonne
  F. 91 C5
Tribanj Kruščica
  HR. 137 A4
Triberg D. 106 A3
Tribsees D. 66 B1
Tribuče SLO. 123 B4
Tricárico I. 172 B2
Tricase I. 173 C4
Tricésimo I. 122 A2
Trieben A. 110 B1
Triebes D. 83 B4
Triepkendorf D. 74 A2
Trier D. 92 B2
Trieste I. 122 B2
Trie-sur-Baïse F. 145 A4
Triggiano I. 173 A2
Triglitz D. 73 A5
Trignac F. 101 B3
Trigueros E. 161 B3
Trigueros del Valle
  E. 142 C2
Trikala GR. 182 D3
Trikeri GR. 183 D5
Trikomo CY. 181 A2
Trilj HR. 138 B2
Trillo E. 152 B1
Trilport F. 90 C2
Trim IRL. 30 A2
Trimdon GB. 37 B5
Trindade
  Beja P. 160 B2
  Bragança P. 149 A2
Třinec CZ. 98 B2
Tring GB. 44 B3
Trinità d'Agultu I. 178 B2
Trinitápoli I. 171 B4
Trino I. 119 B5
Trinta P. 148 B2
Triora I. 133 B3
Tripoli GR. 184 B3
Triponzo I. 136 C1
Triptis D. 83 B3
Triste F. 144 B3
Trittau D. 72 A2
Trivento I. 170 B2
Trivero I. 119 B5
Trivigno I. 172 B1
Trn BIH. 124 C3
Trnava
  HR. 125 B4
  SK. 98 C1
Trnovec SK. 112 A1
Trnovo BIH. 139 B4
Trnovska vas
  SLO. 110 C2
Troarn F. 89 A3
Trochtelfingen D. 94 C1
Tródje S. 51 B4
Troense DK. 65 A3
Trofa P. 148 A1
Trofaiach A. 110 B2
Trofors N. 195 E4
Trøgstad N. 54 A2
Tróia I. 171 B3
Troia P. 154 C2
Troina I. 177 B3
Troisdorf D. 80 B3
Trois-Ponts B. 80 B1
Troisvierges L. 92 A2
Trojane SLO. 123 A3
Trolldhede DK. 59 C1
Trollhättan S. 54 B3
Trolog BIH. 138 B2
Tromello I. 120 B1
Tromøy N. 53 B4
Tromsø N. 192 C3
Trondheim N. 199 B7
Tronget F. 116 A3

Trönninge S. 61 C2
Trönningeby S. 60 B2
Trönö S. 51 A3
Tronzano-Vercellese
  I. 119 B5
Trôo F. 102 B2
Troon GB. 36 A2
Tropea I. 175 C1
Tropy Sztumskie
  PL. 69 B4
Trosa S. 57 B3
Trösken S. 50 B3
Trosly-Breuil F. 90 B3
Trossingen D. 107 A3
Trostberg D. 109 A3
Trouville-sur-Mer F. 89 A4
Trowbridge GB. 43 A4
Troyes F. 104 A3
Trpanj HR. 138 B3
Trpinja HR. 125 B4
Tršće HR. 123 B3
Tršice CZ. 98 B1
Trstená SK. 99 B3
Trstenci BIH. 125 B3
Trsteno HR. 139 C3
Trstice SK. 111 A4
Trstin SK. 98 C1
Trubia E. 141 A5
Trubjela MNE. 139 C4
Truchas E. 141 B4
Trujillanos E. 155 C4
Trujillo E. 156 A2
Trumieje PL. 69 B4
Trun
  CH. 107 C3
  F. 89 B4
Truro GB. 42 B1
Trusetal D. 82 B2
Truskavets' UA. 13 D5
Trustrup DK. 59 B3
Trutnov CZ. 85 B3
Truyes F. 102 B2
Trysil N. 49 A4
Tryszczyn PL. 76 A2
Trzcianka PL. 75 A5
Trzciel PL. 75 B4
Trzcińsko Zdrój PL. 74 B3
Trzebiatów PL. 67 B4
Trzebiel PL. 84 A2
Trzebielino PL. 68 A2
Trzebień PL. 84 A3
Trzebiez PL. 74 A3
Trzebinia PL. 86 B3
Trzebnica PL. 85 A5
Trzebnice PL. 85 A4
Trzeciewiec PL. 76 A3
Trzemeszno PL. 76 B2
Trzemeszno-Lubuskie
  PL. 75 B4
Trzetrzewina PL. 99 B4
Tržič SLO. 123 A3
Tsamandas GR. 182 D2
Tschagguns A. 107 B4
Tschernitz D. 84 A2
Tsebrykove UA. 17 B9
Tsyelyakhany BY. 13 B6
Tua P. 148 A2
Tuam IRL. 28 A3
Tubbercurry IRL. 26 B2
Tubbergen NL. 71 B3
Tubilla del Lago E. 143 C3
Tübingen D. 93 C5
Tubize B. 79 B4
Tučapy CZ. 96 B2
Tučepi HR. 138 B3
Tuchan F. 146 B3
Tüchen D. 73 A5
Tuchola PL. 76 A2
Tuchomie PL. 68 A2
Tuchów PL. 99 B5
Tuczno PL. 75 A5
Tuddal N. 53 A4
Tudela E. 144 B2
Tudela de Duero
  E. 150 A3
Tudweiliog GB. 38 B2
Tuejar E. 159 B2
Tuffé F. 102 A2
Tufsingdalen N. 199 C8
Tuhaň CZ. 84 B2
Tui E. 140 B2
Tukhkala RUS. 197 D13
Tukums LV. 8 D3
Tula I. 178 B2
Tul'chyn UA. 13 D8
Tulcea RO. 17 C8
Tulette F. 131 A3
Tuliszków PL. 76 B3
Tulla IRL. 28 B3
Tullamore IRL. 30 A1
Tulle F. 116 B1
Tullins F. 118 B2
Tulln A. 97 C4
Tullow IRL. 30 B2
Tułowice PL. 85 B5
Tulppio FIN. 197 B12
Tulsk IRL. 28 A3
Tumba S. 57 A3
Tummel Bridge GB. 35 B3
Tun S. 55 B3
Tuna
  Kalmar S. 62 A4
  Uppsala S. 51 B5
Tuna Hästberg S. 50 B2
Tunçbilek TR. 187 C4
Tunes P. 160 B1
Tungelsta S. 57 A4
Tunnerstad S. 55 B5
Tunnhovd N. 47 B5
Tunstall GB. 45 A5
Tuohikotti FIN. 8 B5
Tuoro sul Trasimeno
  I. 135 B5
Tupadły PL. 76 B3
Tupanari BIH. 139 A4
Tupik RUS. 9 E8
Tuplice PL. 84 A2
Tura H. 112 B3
Turanj HR. 137 B4
Turany SK. 99 B3

Turbe BIH. 139 A3
Turbenthal CH. 107 B3
Turcia E. 141 B5
Turčianske Teplice
  SK. 98 C2
Turcifal P. 154 B1
Turckheim F. 106 A2
Turda RO. 17 B5
Turégano E. 151 A4
Turek PL. 76 B3
Türgovishte BG. 17 D7
Turgutlu TR. 188 A2
Turi I. 173 B3
Turin = Torino I. 119 B4
Turis E. 159 B3
Türje H. 111 C4
Turka UA. 12 D5
Túrkeve H. 113 B4
Türkheim D. 108 A1
Türkmenli TR. 186 C1
Turku FIN. 8 B3
Turleque E. 157 A4
Turňa nad Bodvou
  SK. 99 C4
Turnberry GB. 36 A2
Turnhout B. 79 A4
Türnitz A. 110 B2
Turnov CZ. 84 B3
Turnu RO. 126 A3
Turnu Măgurele
  RO. 17 D6
Turón E. 164 C1
Turoszów PL. 84 B2
Turowo PL. 77 A5
Turquel P. 154 B1
Turri I. 179 C2
Turries F. 132 A2
Turriff GB. 33 D4
Tursi I. 174 A2
Turtmann CH. 119 A4
Turtola FIN. 196 C6
Turze PL. 86 A1
Turzovka SK. 98 B2
Tusa I. 177 B3
Tuscánia I. 168 A1
Tuse DK. 61 D1
Tušilovic HR. 123 B4
Tuszyn PL. 86 A3
Tutow D. 66 C2
Tutrakan BG. 17 C7
Tuttlingen D. 107 B3
Tutzing D. 108 B2
Tuzla
  BIH. 125 C4
  TR. 23 C8
Tuzlukçu TR. 189 A6
Tvååker S. 60 B2
Tvärålund S. 200 B5
Tvärskog S. 63 B4
Tvedestrand N. 53 B4
Tveit
  Hordaland N. 47 B4
  Rogaland N. 52 A2
Tver RUS. 9 D9
Tverrelvmo N. 192 D3
Tversted DK. 58 A3
Tving S. 63 B3
Tvrdošin SK. 99 B3
Tvrdošovce SK. 112 A2
Twardogóra PL. 85 A5
Twatt GB. 33 B3
Twello NL. 70 B3
Twimberg A. 110 C1
Twist D. 71 B4
Twistringen D. 72 B1
Tworóg PL. 86 B2
Twyford
  Hampshire GB. 44 B2
  Wokingham GB. 44 B3
Tyachiv UA. 17 A5
Tychówka PL. 67 C5
Tychowo PL. 67 C5
Tychy PL. 86 B2
Tydal N. 199 B8
Týec nad Labem
  CZ. 97 A3
Tyfors S. 49 B6
Tygelsjö S. 61 D2
Tylldal N. 199 C7
Tylstrup DK. 58 A2
Tymbark PL. 99 B4
Tymowa PL. 99 B4
Tyndrum GB. 34 B3
Týnec nad Sázavou
  CZ. 96 B2
Tynemouth GB. 37 A5
Tyngsjö S. 49 B5
Týniště nad Orlicí
  CZ. 85 B4
Týn nad Vltavou
  CZ. 96 B2
Tynset N. 199 C7
Tyresö S. 57 A4
Tyringe S. 61 C3
Tyristrand N. 48 B2
Tysnes N. 46 B2
Tysse N. 46 B2
Tyssebotn N. 46 B2
Tyssedal N. 46 B3
Tystberga S. 56 B3
Tysvær N. 52 A1
Tywyn GB. 39 B2
Tzermiado GR. 185 D6
Tzummarum NL. 70 A2

U

Ub SRB. 127 C2
Ubby DK. 61 D1
Úbeda E. 157 B4
Überlingen D. 107 B4
Ubidea E. 143 A4
Ubli HR. 138 C2
Ubrique E. 162 B2
Ucero E. 143 C3
Uchaud F. 131 B3
Uchte D. 72 B1

Uckerath D 80 B3
Uckfield GB 45 C4
Ucklum S 54 B2
Uclés E 151 C5
Ucria I 177 A3
Udbina HR 137 A4
Uddebo S 60 B3
Uddeholm S 49 B5
Uddevalla S 54 B2
Uddheden S 49 C4
Uden NL 80 A1
Uder D 82 A2
Udiča SK 98 B2
Údine I 122 A2
Udvar H 125 B4
Ueckermünde D 74 A3
Uelsen D 71 B3
Uelzen D 73 B3
Uetendorf CH 106 C2
Uetersen D 72 A2
Uetze D 72 B3
Uffculme GB 43 B3
Uffenheim D 94 B2
Ugarana E 143 A4
Ugento I 173 C4
Ugerldse DK 61 D1
Uggerby DK 58 A3
Uggerslev DK 59 C3
Uggiano la Chiesa
I 173 B4
Ugíjar E 164 C1
Ugine F 118 B3
Uglejevik BIH 125 C5
Uglenes N 46 B2
Uglich RUS 9 D11
Ugljane HR 138 B2
Ugod H 111 B4
Uherské Hradiště
CZ 98 B1
Uherský Brod CZ 98 B1
Uherský Ostroh
CZ 98 C1
Uhingen D 94 C1
Uhlířské-Janovice
CZ 96 B3
Uhříněves CZ 96 A2
Uhyst D 84 A2
Uig GB 31 B2
Uitgeest NL 70 B1
Uithoorn NL 70 B1
Uithuizen NL 71 A3
Uithuizermeeden
NL 71 A3
Uivar RO 126 B2
Ujazd
Łódzkie PL 87 A3
Opolskie PL 86 B2
Ujezd u Brna CZ 97 B4
Ujhartyán H 112 B3
Újkígyós H 113 C5
Ujpetre H 125 B4
Ujście PL 75 A5
Ujsolt H 112 C3
Újszász H 113 B4
Újszentmargita H 113 B5
Ujué E 144 B2
Ukanc SLO 122 A2
Ukmergė LT 13 A6
Ukna S 56 B2
Ula TR 188 B3
Ul'anka SK 99 C3
Ulaş TR 186 A2
Ulássai I 179 C3
Ulbjerg DK 58 B2
Ulbster GB 32 C3
Ulceby GB 40 B3
Ulcinj MNE 16 E3
Uldum DK 59 C2
Ulefoss N 53 A5
Uleila del Campo
E 164 B2
Ulëz AL 182 B1
Ulfborg DK 59 B1
Uljma SRB 127 B3
Ullånger S 200 C4
Ullapool GB 32 D1
Ullared S 60 B2
Ullatti S 196 B4
Ullatun N 52 A2
Ulldecona E 153 B4
Ulldemolins E 147 C1
Ullerslev DK 59 C3
Ullervad S 55 B4
Üllés H 126 A1
Üllö H 112 B3
Ulm D 94 C1
Ulme P 154 B2
Ulmen D 80 B2
Ulnes N 47 B6
Ulog BIH 139 B4
Ulricehamn S 60 B3
Ulrichstein D 81 B5
Ulrika S 56 B1
Ulriksfors S 200 C1
Ulrum NL 71 A3
Ulsberg N 198 C6
Ulsta GB 33 A5
Ulsted DK 58 A3
Ulsteinvik N 198 C2
Ulstrup
Vestsjællands Amt.
DK 59 C3
Viborg Amt. DK 59 B2
Ulsvåg N 194 B6
Ulubey TR 188 A4
Uluborlu TR 189 A5
Ulukışla TR 23 C8
Ulverston GB 36 B3
Ulvik N 46 B3
Umag HR 122 B2
Uman UA 13 D9
Umba RUS 3 C14
Umbértide I 135 B5
Umbriático I 174 B2
Umčari SRB 127 C2
Umeå S 200 C6
Umgransele S 200 B4
Umhausen A 108 B1
Umka SRB 127 C2
Umljanovic HR 138 B2
Umnäs S 195 E7
Umurbey TR 186 B1
Unaðsdalur IS 190 A3
Unapool GB 32 C1
Unari FIN 197 B8
Unbyn S 196 D4
Uncastillo E 144 B2
Undenäs S 55 B5
Undersaker S 199 B10
Undredal N 46 B4
Unešić HR 138 B2
Úněšov CZ 96 B1
Ungheni MD 17 B7
Unhais da Serra P 148 B2
Unhošt CZ 84 B2
Unichowo PL 68 A2
Uničov CZ 98 B1
Uniejów PL 76 C3
Unisław PL 76 A3
Unkel D 80 B3
Unken A 109 B3
Unna D 81 A3
Unnaryd S 60 C3
Unquera E 142 A2
Unterach A 109 B4
Unterägeri CH 107 B3
Unterammergau D 108 B2
Unterhaching D 108 A2
Unteriberg CH 107 B3
Unterkochen D 94 C2
Unter Langkampfen
A 108 B3
Unterlaussa A 110 B1
Unterlüss D 72 B3
Untermünkheim D 94 B1
Unterschächen
CH 107 C3
Unterschleissheim
D 95 C3
Unterschwaningen
D 94 B2
Untersiemau D 82 B2
Unter-steinbach D 94 B2
Unterweissenbach
A 96 C2
Unterzell D 95 B4
Upavon GB 44 B2
Úpice CZ 85 B4
Upiłka PL 68 B2
Upphärad S 54 B3
Uppingham GB 40 C3
Upplands-Väsby S 57 A3
Uppsala S 51 C4
Uppsjøhytta N 48 A1
Upton-upon-Severn
GB 39 B4
Ur F 146 B2
Uras I 179 C2
Uraz PL 85 A4
Urbánia I 136 B1
Urbino I 136 B1
Urçay F 103 C4
Urda E 157 A4
Urdax E 144 A2
Urdilde E 140 B2
Urdos F 145 B3
Urk NL 70 B2
Úrkút H 111 B4
Urla TR 188 A1
Urlingford IRL 30 B1
Urnäsch CH 107 B4
Urnes N 47 A4
Uroševac KOS 16 D4
Urracal E 164 B2
Urries E 144 B2
Urroz E 144 B2
Ursensollen D 95 B3
Urshult S 63 B2
Uršna Sela SLO 123 B4
Urszulewo PL 77 B4
Ury F 90 C2
Urziceni RO 17 C7
Urzulei I 178 B3
Usagre E 156 B1
Uşak TR 187 D4
Usedom D 66 C2
Useldange L 92 B1
Uséllus I 179 C2
Ushakovo RUS 69 A5
Usingen D 81 B4
Usini I 178 B2
Usk GB 39 C4
Uskedal N 46 C2
Üsküdar TR 186 A4
Uslar D 82 A1
Úsov CZ 97 B5
Usquert NL 71 A3
Ussássai I 179 C3
Ussé F 102 B2
Usséglio I 119 B4
Ussel
Cantal F 116 B2
Corrèze F 116 B2
Usson-du-Poitou
F 115 B4
Usson-en-Forez F 117 B3
Usson-les-Bains
F 146 B3
Ustaoset N 47 B5
Ustaritz F 144 A2
Uštěk CZ 84 B2
Uster CH 107 B3
Ústi CZ 98 B1
Ustikolina BIH 139 B4
Ústínad Labem CZ 84 B2
Ústínad Orlicí CZ 97 B4
Ustipračа BIH 139 B5
Ustka PL 68 A1
Ust Luga RUS 8 C6
Ustroń PL 98 B2
Ustronie Morskie
PL 67 B4
Ustyuzhna RUS 9 C10
Uszód H 112 C2
Utåker N 52 A1
Utansjö S 200 D3
Utebo E 152 A3
Utena LT 13 A6
Utery CZ 95 B5
Uthaug N 198 B6
Utiel E 159 B2
Utne N 46 B3
Utö S 57 B4
Utrecht NL 70 B2
Utrera E 162 A2
Utrillas E 153 B3
Utsjoki FIN 193 C11
Utstein kloster N 52 A1
Uttendorf A 109 B3
Uttenweiler D 107 A4
Utterslev DK 65 B4
Uttoxeter GB 40 C2
Utvälinge S 61 C2
Utvorda N 199 A7
Uusikaarlepyy FIN 3 E8
Uusikaupunki FIN 8 B2
Uvaly CZ 96 A2
Uvdal N 47 B5
Uza F 128 B1
Uzdin SRB 126 B2
Uzdowo PL 77 A5
Uzein F 145 A3
Uzel F 100 A3
Uzerche F 116 B1
Uzès F 131 A3
Uzhhorod UA 12 D5
Uzhok UA 12 D5
Užice SRB 127 D1
Uznach CH 107 B3
Üzümlü
Konya TR 189 B6
Muğla TR 188 C4
Uzunköprü TR 186 A1

V

Vaalajärvi FIN 197 B9
Vaas F 102 B2
Vaasa FIN 8 A2
Vaasen NL 70 B2
Vabre F 130 B1
Vác H 112 B3
Vacha D 82 B2
Váchartyán H 112 B3
Väckelsång S 63 B2
Vacqueyras F 131 A3
Vad S 50 B2
Vada I 134 B3
Väddö S 51 C5
Väderstad S 55 B5
Vadheim N 46 A2
Vadillo de la Sierra
E 150 B2
Vadillos E 152 B1
Vadla N 52 A2
Vado I 135 A4
Vado Lígure I 133 A4
Vadsø N 193 B13
Vadstena S 55 B5
Vadum DK 58 A2
Vaduz FL 107 B4
Vafos N 53 B5
Vág H 111 B4
Vågåmo N 198 D6
Væggerløse DK 65 B4
Vaggeryd S 62 A2
Vaghia GR 184 A4
Vaglia I 135 B4
Váglio Basilicata I 172 B1
Vagney F 106 A1
Vagnhärad S 57 B3
Vagnsunda S 57 A4
Vagos P 148 B1
Vai GR 185 D7
Vaiano I 135 B4
Vaiges F 102 A1
Vaihingen D 93 C4
Vaillant F 105 B4
Vailly-sur-Aisne F 91 B3
Vailly-sur Sauldre
F 103 B4
Vairano Scalo I 170 B2
Vaison-la-Romaine
F 131 A4
Vaite F 105 B4
Väjern S 54 B2
Vajszló H 125 B3
Vaksdal N 46 B2
Vál H 112 B2
Valaam RUS 9 B7
Valada P 154 B2
Vålådalen S 199 B10
Valadares P 148 A1
Valado P 154 B1
Valandovo MK 182 B4
Valaská SK 99 C3
Valaská Belá SK 98 C2
Valaská Dubová
SK 99 B3
Valašská Polanka
CZ 98 B1
Valašské Klobouky
CZ 98 B2
Valašské Meziříčí
CZ 98 B1
Valberg F 132 A2
Vålberg S 55 A4
Valbo S 51 B4
Valbom P 148 A1
Valbondione I 120 A3
Valbonnais F 118 C2
Valbuena de Duero
E 142 C2
Válcani RO 126 B2
Valdagno I 121 B4
Valdahon F 105 B5
Valdaracete E 151 B4
Valday RUS 9 D8
Valdealgorfa E 153 B3
Valdecaballeros E 156 A2
Valdecabras E 152 B1
Valdecarros E 150 B2
Valdeconcha E 151 B5
Valdeflores E 161 B3
Valdefresno E 142 B1
Valdeganga E 158 B2
Valdelacasa E 150 B2
Valdelacasa de Tajo
E 156 A2
Valdelarco E 161 B3
Valdelosa E 149 A4
Valdeltormo E 153 B4
Valdelugeros E 142 B1
Valdemanco de Esteras
E 156 B3
Valdemarsvik S 56 B2
Valdemorillo E 151 B3
Valdemoro E 151 B4
Valdemoro Sierra
E 152 B2
Valdenoceda E 143 B3
Valdeobispo E 149 B3
Valdeolivas E 152 B1
Valdepeñas E 157 B4
Valdepeñas de Jaén
E 163 A4
Valdepiélago E 142 B1
Valdepolo E 142 B1
Valderas E 142 B1
Valdérice I 176 A1
Valderrobres E 153 B4
Valderrueda E 142 B2
Val de San Lorenzo
E 141 B4
Val de Santo Domingo
E 150 B3
Val d'Esquières F 132 B2
Valdestillas E 150 A3
Valdetorres E 156 B1
Valdetorres de Jarama
E 151 B4
Valdeverdeja E 150 C2
Valdevimbre E 142 B1
Valdieri I 133 A3
Valdilecha E 151 B4
Val-d'Isère F 119 B3
Valdobbiádene I 121 B4
Valdocondes E 143 C3
Valdoviño E 140 A2
Valea lui Mihai RO 16 B5
Vale de Açor
Beja P 160 B2
Portalegre P 154 B3
Vale de Agua P 160 B1
Vale de Cambra P 148 B1
Vale de Lobo P 160 B1
Vale de Prazeres
P 148 B2
Vale de Reis P 154 C2
Vale de Rosa P 160 B2
Vale de Santarém
P 154 B2
Vale de Vargo P 160 B2
Vale do Peso P 155 B3
Valega P 148 B1
Valéggio sul Mincio
I 121 B3
Valeiro P 154 C2
Valença P 140 B2
Valençay F 103 B3
Valence
Charente F 115 C4
Drôme F 117 C4
Valence d'Agen F 129 B3
Valence d'Albigeois
F 130 A1
Valence-sur-Baise
F 129 C3
Valencia E 159 B3
Valencia de Alcántara
E 155 B3
Valencia de Don Juan
E 142 B1
Valencia de las Torres
E 156 B1
Valencia del Ventoso
E 161 A3
Valencia de Mombuey
E 161 A2
Valenciennes F 79 B3
Valensole F 132 B1
Valentano I 168 A1
Valentigney F 106 B1
Valentine F 145 A4
Valenza I 120 B1
Valenzuela E 163 A3
Valenzuela de
Calatrava E 157 B4
Våler
Hedmark N 48 B3
Østfold N 54 A1
Valera de Abajo E 158 B1
Valeria E 158 B1
Valestrand N 52 A1
Valestrandsfossen
N 46 B2
Valevåg N 52 A1
Valfabbrica I 136 B1
Valflaunes F 131 B2
Valga EST 8 D5
Valgorge F 131 A3
Valgrisenche I 119 B4
Valguarnera Caropepe
I 177 B3
Valhelhas P 148 B2
Valjevo SRB 127 C1
Valka LV 8 D4
Valkeakoski FIN 8 B4
Valkenburg NL 80 B1
Valkenswaard NL 79 A5
Valkó H 112 B3
Valla S 56 A2
Vallada E 159 C3
Vallado E 141 A4
Valladolid E 150 A3
Vallåkra S 61 D2
Vallata I 172 A1
Vallberga S 61 C3
Vall d'Alba E 153 B3
Valldemossa E 166 B2
Valle N 52 A3
Valle Castellana I 136 C2
Valle de Abdalajís
E 163 B3
Valle de Cabuérniga
E 142 A2
Valle de la Serena
E 156 B2
Valle de Matamoros
E 155 C4
Valle de Santa Ana
E 155 C4
Valledolmo I 176 B2
Valledoria I 178 B2
Vallelado E 150 A3
Vallelunga Pratameno
I 176 B2
Valle Mosso I 119 B5
Vallendar D 81 B3
Vallentuna S 57 A4
Vallerås S 49 B5
Valleraugue F 130 A2
Vallermosa I 179 C2
Vallet F 101 B4
Valletta M 175 C3
Valley GB 38 A2
Vallfogona de Riucorb
E 147 C2
Valli del Pasúbio I 121 B4
Vallo della Lucánia
I 172 B1
Valloire F 118 B3
Vallombrosa I 135 B4
Vallon-Pont-d'Arc
F 131 A3
Vallorbe CH 105 C5
Vallouise F 118 C3
Valls E 147 C2
Vallset N 48 B3
Vallsta S 50 A3
Vallstena S 57 C4
Valmadrid E 153 A3
Valmiera LV 8 D4
Valmojado E 151 B3
Valmont F 89 A4
Valmontone I 169 B2
Valö S 51 B5
Valognes F 88 A2
Valonga P 148 B1
Valongo P 148 A1
Válor E 164 C1
Valoria la Buena
E 142 C2
Valøy N 199 A7
Valozhyn BY 13 A7
Valpaços P 148 A2
Valpelline I 119 B4
Valpiana I 135 B3
Valpovo HR 125 B4
Valras-Plage F 130 B2
Valréas F 131 A3
Vals CH 107 C4
Valsavarenche I 119 B4
Vålse DK 65 B4
Valsequillo E 156 B2
Valsjöbyn S 199 A11
Vals-les-Bains F 117 C4
Valsonne F 117 B4
Valstagna I 121 B4
Val-Suzon F 105 B3
Valtablado del Rio
E 152 B1
Valþjofsstaður IS 191 B11
Val Thorens F 118 B3
Valtice CZ 97 C4
Valtiendas E 151 A4
Valtierra E 144 B2
Valtopina I 136 B1
Valtorta I 120 B2
Valtournenche I 119 B4
Valverde E 144 C2
Valverde de Burguillos
E 155 C4
Valverde de Júcar
E 158 B1
Valverde de la Vera
E 150 B2
Valverde de la Virgen
E 142 B1
Valverde del Camino
E 161 B3
Valverde del Fresno
E 149 B3
Valverde de Llerena
E 156 B2
Valverde de Mérida
E 156 B1
Valvträsk S 196 C4
Vamberk CZ 85 B4
Vamdrup DK 59 C2
Våmhus S 50 A1
Vamlingbo S 57 D4
Vammala FIN 8 B3
Vamos GR 185 D5
Vámosmikola H 112 B2
Vámosszabadi H 111 B4
Vanault-les-Dames
F 91 C4
Vandel DK 59 C2
Vandenesse F 104 C2
Vandenesse-en-Auxois
F 104 B3
Vandóies I 108 C2
Väne-Åsaka S 54 B3
Vänersborg S 54 B3
Vänersnäs S 54 B3
Vang N 47 A5
Vänge S 51 C4
Vangsnes N 46 A3
Vänjaurbäck S 200 B4
Vännacka S 54 A3
Vannareid N 192 B3
Vännäs S 200 C5
Vannes F 101 B3
Vannsätter S 51 A3
Vannvåg N 192 B3
Vansbro S 49 B6
Vanse N 52 B2
Vantaa FIN 8 B4
Vanttauskoski
FIN 197 C9
Vanviken N 199 B7
Vanyarc H 112 B3
Vaour F 129 B4
Vapnyarka UA 13 D8
Vaprio d'Adda I 120 B2
Vaqueiros P 160 B2
Vara S 55 B3
Varacieux F 118 B2
Varades F 101 B4
Varages F 132 B1
Varaldsøy N 46 B2
Varallo I 119 B5
Varangerbotn N 193 B12
Varano de'Melegari
I 120 C3
Varaždin HR 124 A2
Varaždinske Toplice
HR 124 A2
Varazze I 133 A4
Varberg S 60 B2
Vardal N 48 B2
Varde DK 59 C1
Vårdö FIN 51 B7
Vardø N 193 B15
Vardomb H 125 A4
Varejoki FIN 196 C7
Varel D 71 A5
Varėna LT 13 A6
Vårenes N 52 A1
Varengeville-sur-Mer
F 89 A4
Varenna I 120 A2
Varennes-en-Argonne
F 91 B5
Varennes-le-Grand
F 105 C3
Varennes-St Sauveur
F 105 C4
Varennes-sur-Allier
F 117 A3
Varennes-sur-Amance
F 105 B4
Vareš BIH 139 A4
Varese I 120 B1
Varese Ligure I 134 A2
Vârfurile RO 16 B5
Vårgårda S 60 A2
Vargas
E 143 A3
P 154 B2
Vargön S 54 B3
Varhaug N 52 B1
Variaş RO 126 A2
Variaşu Mic RO 126 A3
Varilhes F 146 A2
Varin SK 98 B2
Väring S 55 B4
Váriz P 149 A3
Varkaus FIN 8 A5
Varmahlíð IS 190 B6
Varmaland IS 190 C4
Värmlands Bro S 55 A4
Värmskog S 55 A3
Varna
BG 17 D7
SRB 127 C1
Värnamo S 60 B4
Varnhem S 55 B4
Varnsdorf CZ 84 B2
Värö S 60 B2
Varoška Rijeka
BIH 124 B2
Városlöd H 111 B4
Várpalota H 112 B2
Varreddes F 90 C2
Vars F 118 C3
Varsi I 120 C2
Varsseveld NL 71 C3
Vårsta S 57 A3
Vartdal N 198 C3
Vartofta S 55 B4
Vårvik S 54 A3
Várvölgy H 111 C4
Varzi I 120 C2
Varzjelas P 148 B1
Varzo I 119 A5
Varzy F 104 B2
Vasad H 112 B3
Väse S 55 A4
Vašica SRB 125 B5
Vasilevichi BY 13 B8
Väskinde S 57 C4
Vaskút H 125 A4
Vaslui RO 17 B7
Vassbotn N 53 B4
Vassenden N 47 A6
Vassieux-en-Vercors
F 118 C2
Vassmolösa S 63 B4
Vassy F 88 B3
Västansjö S 195 E6
Västanvik S 50 B1
Västerås S 56 A2
Västerby S 50 B2
Västerfärnebo S 50 C3
Västergarn S 57 C4
Västerhaninge S 57 A4
Västervik S 62 A4
Vasto I 170 A2
Västra Ämtervik S 55 A4
Västra-Bodarne S 60 B2
Västra Karup S 61 C2
Vasvár H 111 B3
Vasylkiv UA 13 C9
Vát H 111 B3
Vatan F 103 B3
Väte S 57 C4
Vathia GR 184 C3
Vatican City = Cittàdel
Vaticano I 168 B2
Vatili CY 181 A2
Vatin SRB 126 B3
Vatland N 52 B3
Vatnar N 53 A5
Vatnås N 48 C1
Vatne N 53 B3
Vatnestrøm N 53 B4
Vätö S 51 C5
Vatra-Dornei RO 17 B6
Vatry F 91 C4
Vattholma S 51 B4
Vättis CH 107 C4
Vauchamps F 91 C3
Vauchassis F 104 A2
Vaucouleurs F 92 C1
Vaudoy-en-Brie F 90 C3
Vaulen N 52 B1
Vaulruz CH 106 C1
Vaulx Vraucourt F 90 A2
Vaumas F 104 C2
Vausseroux F 115 B3
Vauvenargues F 132 B1
Vauvert F 131 B3
Vauvillers F 105 B5
Vaux-sur-Sure B 92 B1
Vawkavysk BY 13 B6
Vaxholm S 57 A4
Växjö S 62 B2
Våxtorp S 61 C3
Vayrac F 129 B4
Važec SK 99 B3
Veberöd S 61 D3
Vechelde D 72 B3
Vechta D 71 B5
Vecinos E 149 B4
Vecsés H 112 B3
Vedavågen N 52 A1
Veddige S 60 B2
Vedersø DK 59 B1
Vedeseta I 120 B2
Vedevåg S 56 A1
Vedra E 140 B2
Vedum S 55 B3
Veendam NL 71 A3
Veenendaal NL 70 B2
Vega
Asturias E 142 A1
Asturias E 142 A1
Vega de Espinareda
E 141 B4
Vega de Infanzones
E 142 B1
Vegadeo E 141 A3
Vega de Pas E 143 A3
Vega de Valcarce
E 141 B4
Vega de Valdetronco
E 150 A2
Vegårshei N 53 B4
Vegas de Coria E 149 B3
Vegas del Condado
E 142 B1
Vegby S 60 B3
Vegger DK 58 B2
Veggli N 47 B6
Veghel NL 80 A1
Veglast D 66 B1
Véglie I 173 B3
Veguillas E 151 B4
Vegusdal N 53 B4
Veidholmen N 198 B4
Veidnes N 193 B10
Veikåker N 48 B1
Veinge S 61 C3
Vejbystrand S 61 C2
Vejen DK 59 C2
Vejer de la Frontera
E 162 B2
Vejle DK 59 C2
Vejprty CZ 83 B5
Velada E 150 B3
Vela Luka HR 138 C2
Velayos E 150 B3
Velbert D 80 A3
Velburg D 95 B3
Velde N 199 A8
Velden
Bayern D 95 B3
Bayern D 95 C4
Velden am Worther See
A 109 C5
Velefique E 164 B2
Velen D 80 A2
Velenje SLO 123 A4
Veles MK 182 B3
Velesevec HR 124 B2
Velešín CZ 96 C2
Velestino GR 182 D4
Velez Blanco E 164 B2
Vélez de Benaudalla
E 163 B4
Vélez-Málaga E 163 B3
Vélez Rubio E 164 B2
Veliiki Radinci
SRB 127 B1
Velika HR 125 B3
Velika Gorica HR 124 B2
Velika Grdevac
HR 124 B3
Velika Greda SRB 126 B3
Velika Ilova BIH 125 C3
Velika Kladuša
BIH 124 B1
Velika Kopanica
HR 125 B4
Velika Krsna SRB 127 C2
Velika Obarska
BIH 125 C5
Velika Pisanica
HR 124 B3
Velika Plana SRB 127 C3
Velika Zdenci HR 124 B3
Velike Lašče SLO 123 B3
Velike Središte
SRB 126 B3
Veliki Gaj SRB 126 B3
Veliki Popović
SRB 127 C3
Velikiye Luki RUS 9 D7
Veliko Gradište
SRB 127 C3
Veliko Orašje
SRB 127 C3
Veliko Selo SRB 127 C3
Veliko Tŭrnovo BG 17 D6
Velilla del Río Carrió
E 142 B2
Velilla de San Antonio
E 151 B4
Veli Lošinj HR 137 A3
Velingrad BG 183 A5
Velizh RUS 9 E7
Veljun HR 123 B4
Velká Bíteš CZ 97 B4

Velka Hled'scbe CZ . 95 B4
Velká Lomnica SK. .99 B4
Velkánad Veličkou
CZ 98 C1
Velké Bystřice CZ. .98 B1
Velké Heraltice CZ. .98 B1
Velké Karlovice SK . .98 C1
Vel'ke'Kostol'any
SK 98 C1
Vel'ké Leváre SK . .97 C5
Velké Losiny CZ . . .98 A1
Velké Meziříčí CZ. .97 B4
Velké Pavlovice
CZ 97 C4
Vel'ké Rovné SK . . .98 B2
Vel'ké Uherce SK. .98 B1
Vel'ké Zálužie SK. .98 C1
Vel'ký Blahovo SK. .99 C4
Velky Bor CZ 96 B1
Vel'ký Cetin SK . . .112 A2
Vel'ký Krtiš SK . . .112 A3
Vel'ký Meder SK . .111 B4
Velky Ujezd CZ . . .98 B1
Vellahn D 73 A3
Vellberg D 94 B1
Velles F 103 C3
Velletri I 168 B2
Vellinge S. 66 A2
Vellisca E 151 B5
Velliza E 150 A3
Vellmar D 81 A5
Velp NL. 70 B2
Velten D 74 B2
Velvary CZ. 84 B2
Velvendos GR 182 C4
Vemb DK 59 B1
Vemdalen S 199 C10
Veme N. 48 B2
Véménd H 125 A4
Vemmedrup DK. . .61 D2
Vena S 62 A3
Venaco F 180 A2
Venafro I 169 B4
Venarey-les-Laumes
F 104 B3
Venaría I 119 B4
Venasca I 133 A3
Vençane SRB. 127 C2
Vence F 132 B3
Venda Nova
Coimbra P 154 A2
Leiria P 154 B2
Vendas Novas P . .154 C2
Vendays-Montalivet
F. 114 C2
Vendel S. 51 B4
Vendelso S 57 A4
Vendeuil F 91 B3
Vendeuvre-sur-Barse
F. 104 A3
Vendoeuvres F . . .115 B5
Vendôme F 103 B3
Venelles F 131 B4
Veness GB. 33 B4
Venézia = Venice
I. 122 B1
Venialbo E 150 A2
Venice = Venézia
I. 122 B1
Vénissieux F 117 B4
Venjan S. 49 B5
Venlo NL. 80 A2
Vennesla N 53 B3
Vennesund N 195 E3
Vennezey F 92 C2
Venn Green GB 42 B2
Venosa I 172 B1
Venray NL 80 A1
Vent A. 108 C1
Venta de Baños E .142 C2
Venta del Moro E. .158 B2
Venta de los Santos
E 157 B4
Venta las Ranas E .142 A1
Ventanueva E 141 A4
Ventas de Huelma
E 163 A4
Ventas de Zafarraya
E 163 B3
Ventavon F 132 A1
Ventimíglia I. 133 B3
Ventnor GB 44 C2
Ventosa de la Sierra
E 143 C4
Ventosilla E 143 C4
Ventspils LV. 8 D2
Venturina I 134 B3
Venzolasca F 180 A2
Venzone I 122 A2
Vép H 111 B3
Vera
E. 164 B3
N. 199 B9
Vera Cruz E 160 A2
Vera de Bidasoa
E 144 A2
Vera de Moncayo
E 144 C2
Verbánia I 119 B5
Verberie F 90 B2
Verbicaro I 174 B1
Verbier CH 119 A4
Vercelli I 119 B5
Vercel-Villedieu-le-
Camp F 105 B5
Verchen D 66 C1
Vercheny F 118 C2
Verclause F 131 A4
Verden D 72 B2
Verdens Ende N . . .54 A1
Verdikoussa GR . .182 D3
Verdille F 115 C3
Verdú E 147 C2
Verdun F 92 B1
Verdun-sur-Garonne
F. 129 C4

Verdun-sur-le-Doubs
F. 105 C4
Veresegyház H . . .112 B3
Verfeil F 129 C4
Vergato I 135 A4
Vergel E 159 C4
Vergeletto CH 120 A1
Verges E 147 B4
Vergiate I 120 B1
Vergt F. 129 A3
Veria GR. 182 C4
Verín E 141 C3
Veringenstadt D . .107 A4
Verl D 81 A4
Verma N. 198 C5
Vermand F 90 B3
Vermelha P 154 B1
Vermenton F 104 B2
Vernago I 108 C1
Vernante I 133 A3
Vernantes F 102 B2
Vernár SK 99 C4
Vernayaz CH 119 A4
Vernazza I 134 A2
Vern-d'Anjou F . . .102 B1
Verneřice CZ. 84 B2
Vernet F 146 A2
Vernet-les-Bains
F. 146 B3
Verneuil F 91 B3
Verneuil-sur-Avre
F. 89 B4
Vernier CH 118 A3
Vernio I 135 A4
Vérnole I 173 B4
Vernon F 90 B1
Vernoux-en-Vivarais
F. 117 C4
Veróce H 112 B3
Verolanuova I 120 B3
Véroli I 169 B3
Verona I 121 B4
Verpelét H 113 B4
Verrabotn N 199 B7
Verrès I. 119 B4
Verrey-sous-Salmaise
F. 104 B3
Verrières F 115 B4
Versailles F 90 C2
Versam CH. 107 C4
Verseg H 112 B3
Versmold D 71 B5
Versoix F 118 A3
Verteillac F 115 C4
Vértesacsa H 112 B2
Vertou F 101 B4
Vertus F 91 C3
Verviers B 80 B1
Vervins F 91 B3
Verwood GB 43 B5
Veryan GB 42 B2
Veržej SLO 111 C3
Verzuolo I 133 A3
Verzy F 91 B4
Vescovato F 180 A2
Vése H 124 A3
Veselínad Lužnicí
CZ 96 B2
Veselínad Moravou
CZ 98 C1
Veseliy BG 17 D7
Vésime I 119 C5
Veskoniemi FIN . .193 D11
Vesoul F 105 B5
Vespolate I 120 B1
Vessigebro S. 60 C2
Vestbygd N 52 B2
Vestenanova I 121 B4
Vester Husby S. . . .56 B2
Vester Nebel DK . .59 C2
Vesterøhavn DK . .58 A3
Vester Torup DK . .58 A2
Vester Vedsted DK .59 C1
Vestervig DK 58 B1
Vestfossen N 53 A5
Vestmannaeyjar
IS 190 D5
Vestmarka N 48 C3
Vestnes N 198 C4
Vestone I 120 B3
Vestre Gausdal N . .48 A2
Vestre Jakobselv
N 193 B13
Vestre Slidre N . . .47 A5
Vesyegonsk RUS . .9 C10
Veszprém H 112 B1
Veszprémvarsány
H 112 B1
Vésztö H 113 C5
Vetlanda S 62 A3
Vetovo HR 125 B3
Vetralla I. 168 A2
Větrný Jeníkov CZ .97 B3
Vétroz CH 119 A4
Vettasjärvi S 196 B4
Vetto I. 134 A3
Vetulónia I 135 C3
Veules-les-Roses F .89 A4
Veulettes-sur-Mer
F 89 A4
Veum N 53 A4
Veurne B 78 A2
Veverská Bítýška
CZ 97 B4
Vevey CH 106 C1
Vevi GR 182 C3
Vevring N 46 A2
Vex CH 119 A4
Veynes F 132 A1
Veyre-Monton F . .116 B3
Veyrier F 118 B3
Vézelay F 104 B2
Vézelise F 92 C2
Vézenobres F 131 A3
Vezins F 102 B1
Vézins-de-Lévézou
F. 130 A1
Vezirhan TR 187 B5

Vezirköprü TR 23 A8
Vezza di Óglio I . . .120 A3
Vezzani F 180 A2
Vezzano I 121 A4
Vezzano sul Cróstolo
I. 121 C3
Vi S. 200 D3
Viadana I 121 C3
Via Gloria P 160 B2
Viana E. 143 B4
Viana do Alentejo
P. 154 C2
Viana do Bolo E. . .141 B3
Viana do Castelo
P. 148 A1
Vianden L 92 B2
Viannos GR 185 D6
Viaréggio I 134 B3
Viator E. 164 C2
Vibble S 57 C4
Viborg DK 58 B2
Vibo Valéntia I . . .175 C2
Vibraye F 102 A2
Vic E 147 C3
Vicar E 164 C2
Vicarello I. 134 B3
Vicari I 176 B2
Vícchio I. 135 B4
Vicdesses F. 146 B2
Vic-en-Bigorre F . .145 A4
Vicenza I 121 B4
Vic-Fézensac F . . .129 C3
Vichy F. 117 A3
Vickan S. 60 B2
Vickerstown GB . . .36 B3
Vic-le-Comte F. . . .116 B3
Vico F. 180 A1
Vico del Gargano
I 171 B3
Vico Equense I . . .170 C2
Vicopisano I. 134 B3
Vicosoprano CH . .120 A2
Vicovaro I. 169 A2
Vic-sur-Aisne F. . . .90 B3
Vic-sur-Cère F 116 C2
Victoria = Rabat
M 175 C3
Vidago P 148 A2
Vidauban F 132 B2
Vide P. 148 B2
Videbæk DK. 59 B1
Videm SLO. 123 B3
Videseter N 198 D4
Vidigueira P 160 A2
Vidin BG. 16 D5
Vidlin GB 33 A5
Vidsel S 196 D3
Vidzy BY. 13 A7
Viechtach D 95 B4
Vieille-Brioude F . .117 B3
Vieira P. 154 B2
Vieira do Minho P .148 A1
Vieiros P 155 C3
Vielha E 145 B4
Vielle-Aure F 145 B4
Viellespesse F 116 B3
Viellevigne F 114 B2
Vielmur-sur-Agout
F. 130 B1
Vielsalm B 80 B1
Viels Maison F 91 C3
Vienenburg D 73 C3
Vienna = Wien A . .111 A3
Vienne F 117 B4
Vieritz D 73 B5
Viernheim D 93 B4
Vierraden D 74 A3
Viersen D. 80 A2
Vierville-sur-Mer F .88 A3
Vierzon F 103 B4
Vieselbach D 82 B3
Vieste I 171 B4
Vietas S 194 C9
Vieteren B 78 B2
Vietri di Potenza I .172 B1
Vietri sul Mare I . .170 C2
Vieux-Boucau-les-
Bains F 128 C1
Vif F 118 B2
Vig DK 61 D1
Vigásio I 121 B3
Vigaun A. 109 B4
Vigeland N 52 B3
Vigeois F 116 B1
Vigévano I 120 B1
Viggianello I 174 B2
Viggiano I. 174 A1
Vigliano I 169 A3
Vigmostad N 52 B3
Vignale I 119 B5
Vignanello I 168 A2
Vigneulles-lès-
Hattonchâtel F . .92 C1
Vignevieille F 146 B3
Vignola I. 135 A4
Vignory F 105 A4
Vignoux-sur Barangeon
F. 103 B4
Vigo E. 140 B2
Vigo di Fassa I . . .121 A4
Vigone I 119 C4
Vigrestad N 52 B1
Vihiers F 102 B1
Viitasaari FIN. 3 E9
Vik IS 190 D6
Vik
Nordland N 195 E3
Rogaland N 52 B1
Sogn og Fjordane
N 46 A3
S 63 C2
Vika S. 50 B2
Vikajärvi FIN 197 C9
Vikane N 54 A1
Vikarbyn S 50 B2
Vike N. 46 B3
Vikedal N 52 A1
Vikeland N 53 B3
Viken
Jämtland S. 199 A10

Viken continued
Skåne S. 61 C2
Viker N. 48 B2
Vikersund N. 48 C1
Vikeså N. 52 B2
Vikevåg N. 52 A1
Vikingstad S 56 B1
Vikmanshyttan S. . .50 B2
Vikna N. 199 A7
Vikøy N. 46 B3
Vikran
Troms N 192 C2
Troms N 194 B7
Viksjö S 200 D3
Viksøyri N 46 A3
Viksta S. 51 B4
Vila Boim P 155 C3
Vila Chã de Ourique
P 154 B2
Vila de Cruces E . .140 B2
Vila de Rei P 154 B2
Vila do Bispo P . . .160 B1
Vila do Conde P. . .148 A1
Viladrau E. 147 C3
Vila Flor P 149 A2
Vila Franca das Navas
P 149 B2
Vilafranca del Maestrat
E 153 B3
Vilafranca del Penedès
E 147 C2
Vila Franca de Xira
P. 154 C1
Vila Fresca P 154 C1
Vilagarcía de Arousa
E 140 B2
Vilamarín E 140 B3
Vilamartín de
Valdeorras E . . .141 B3
Vila Nogueira P . . .154 C1
Vila Nova da Baronia
P. 154 C2
Vila Nova de Cerveira
P. 140 C2
Vila Nova de Famalicão
P 148 A1
Vila Nova de Foz Côa
P. 149 A2
Vila Nova de Gaia
P. 148 A1
Vila Nova de Milfontes
P 160 B1
Vila Nova de Paiva
P. 148 B2
Vila Nova de São Bento
P 160 B2
Vilanova de Sau E .147 C3
Vilanova i la Geltrú
E 147 C2
Vilapedre E 140 A3
Vila Pouca de Aguiar
P 148 A2
Vila Praja de Ancora
P 148 A1
Vilar de Santos E. .140 B3
Vilardevós E. 141 C3
Vila Real P. 148 A2
Vila-real dos Infantes
E 159 B3
Vila Real de Santo
António P 160 B2
Vilar Formosa P . .149 B3
Vila-Rodona E 147 C2
Vila Ruiva P 160 A2
Vilasantar E 140 A2
Vilaseca E 147 C2
Vila Seca P. 148 B1
Vilassar de Mar E .147 C3
Vilasund S 195 D5
Vila Velha de Ródão
P. 155 B3
Vila Verde
Braga P 148 A1
Lisboa P. 154 B1
Vila Verde de Filcalho
P 161 B2
Vila Viçosa P 155 C3
Vilches E 157 B4
Vildbjerg DK 59 B1
Vilémov CZ 97 B3
Vileyka BY 13 A7
Vilhelmina S 200 B3
Vília GR 184 A4
Viljandi EST 8 C4
Villabáñez E. 150 A3
Villablanca E 161 B2
Villablino E 141 B4
Villabona E. 144 A1
Villabragima E 142 C1
Villabuena del Puente
E 150 A2
Villacadima E. 151 A4
Villacañas E. 157 A4
Villacarriedo E. . . .143 A3
Villacarrillo E. 164 A1
Villa Castelli I 173 B3
Villacastín E. 150 B3
Villach A 109 C4
Villacidro I 179 C2
Villaconejos E 151 B4
Villaconejos de
Trabaque P 152 B1
Villa Cova de Lixa
P 148 A1
Villada E 142 B2
Villadangos del
Páramo E 141 B5
Villadecanes E 141 B4
Villa del Prado E . .150 B3
Villa del Rio E 157 C3
Villadepera E. 149 A3
Villa de Peralonso
E 149 A3
Villa di Chiavenna
I. 120 A2

Villadiego E. 142 B2
Villadompardo E. . .163 A3
Villadóssola I. 119 A5
Villaeles de Valdavia
E 142 B2
Villaescusa de Haro
E 158 B1
Villafáfila E 142 C1
Villafeliche E. 152 A2
Villaflores E 150 A2
Villafrades de Campos
E 142 B2
Villafranca
Avila E 150 B2
Navarra E 144 B2
Villafranca de Córdoba
E 157 C3
Villafranca del Bierzo
E 141 B4
Villafranca de los
Barros E 155 C4
Villafranca de los
Caballeros E. . . .157 A4
Villafranca di Verona
I 121 B3
Villafranca in Lunigiana
I. 134 A2
Villafranca-Montes de
Oca E. 143 B3
Villafranca Tirrena
I. 177 A4
Villafranco del Campo
E 152 B2
Villafranco del
Guadalquivir E. .161 B3
Villafrati I 176 B2
Villafrechós E 142 C1
Villafruela E 143 C3
Villagarcia de las
Torres E. 156 B1
Villaggio Mancuso
I. 175 B2
Villagonzalo E 156 B1
Villagotón E 141 B4
Villagrains F 128 B2
Villaharta E 156 B3
Villahermosa E. . . .158 C1
Villaherreros E 142 B2
Villalhoz E. 142 B3
Villaines-la-Juhel F 89 B3
Villajoyosa E 159 C3
Villalago E 169 B3
Villalba
E 140 A3
I. 176 B2
Villalba de Calatrava
E 157 B4
Villalba de Guardo
E 142 B2
Villalba del Alcor
E 161 B3
Villalba de la Sierra
E 152 B1
Villalba de los Alcores
E 142 C2
Villalba de los Barros
E 155 C4
Villalba del Rey E .151 B5
Villalcampo E 149 A3
Villalcázar de Sirga
E 142 B2
Villalengua E 152 A2
Villalgordo del Júcar
E 158 B1
Villalgordo del
Marquesado E . .158 B1
Villalmóndar E 143 B3
Villalón de Campos
E 142 B1
Villalonga E 159 C3
Villalonso E 150 A2
Villalpando E 142 C1
Villaluenga E 151 B4
Villalumbroso E . . .142 B2
Villálvaro E 143 C3
Villamalea E 158 B2
Villamanán E. 142 B1
Villamanín E 142 B1
Villamanrique E . . .157 B5
Villamanrique de la
Condesa E 161 B3
Villamanta E 151 B3
Villamantilla E 151 B3
Villamar I 179 C2
Villamartín E 162 B2
Villamartín de Campos
E 142 B2
Villamartin de Don
Sancho E 142 B1
Villamassárgia I . . .179 C2
Villamayor E 142 A1
Villamayor de Calatrava
E 157 B3
Villamayor de Campos
E 142 C1
Villamayor de Santiago
E 157 A5
Villamblard F 129 A3
Villamejil E 141 B4
Villamesías E. 156 A2
Villaminaya E 157 A4
Villa Minozzo I . . .134 A3
Villamor de los
Escuderos E . . .150 A2
Villamoronta E 142 B2
Villamuelas E 151 C4
Villamuriel de Cerrato
E 142 B2
Villandraut F 128 B2
Villanova I 173 B3
Villanova d'Asti I . .119 C4
Villanova del Battista
I. 171 B3
Villanova Mondovì I
. . . . .133 A3
Villanova Monteleone
I 178 B2
Villante E 143 B3
Villantério I 120 B2
Villanubla E 142 C2

Villanueva de Alcardete
E 157 A4
Villanueva de Alcorón
E 152 B1
Villanueva de Algaidas
E 163 A3
Villanueva de Argaña
E 143 B3
Villanueva de Bogas
E 157 A4
Villanueva de Córdoba
E 156 B3
Villanueva de Gállego
E 144 C3
Villanueva del Aceral
E 150 A3
Villanueva del
Arzobispo E 164 A2
Villanueva de la Serena
E 156 B2
Villanueva de la Sierra
E 149 B3
Villanueva de las
Manzanas E 142 B1
Villanueva de las Peras
E 141 C5
Villanueva de la Vera
E 150 B2
Villanueva del Campo
E 142 C1
Villanueva del Duque
E 156 B3
Villanueva del Fresno
E 155 C3
Villanueva del Huerva
E 152 A2
Villanueva de los
Castillejos E 161 B2
Villanueva de los
Infantes E 157 B5
Villanueva del Rey
E 156 B2
Villanueva del Rio
E 162 A2
Villanueva del Río y
Minas E 162 A2
Villanueva del Rosario
E 163 B3
Villanueva del Trabuco
E 163 A3
Villanueva de Mesia
E 163 A4
Villanueva de Nía
E 142 B2
Villanueva de Oscos
E 141 A4
Villanueva de San
Carlos E 157 B4
Villanueva de San Juan
E 162 A2
Villanueva de Tapia
E 163 A3
Villanueva de
Valdegovia E . . .143 B3
Villány H. 125 B4
Villaputzu I. 179 C3
Villaquejida E 142 B1
Villaquilambre E . .142 B1
Villaquiran de los
Infantes E 142 B2
Villaralto E 156 B3
Villarcayo E 143 B3
Villard-de-Lans F . .118 B2
Villar de Barrio E . .140 B3
Villar de Cañas E . .158 B1
Villar de Chinchilla
E 158 C2
Villar de Ciervo E . .149 B3
Villardeciervos E . .141 C4
Villar de Domingo
Garcia E 152 B1
Villardefrades E . . .142 C1
Villar del Arzobispo
E 159 B3
Villar del Buey E . .149 A3
Villar del Cobo E . .152 B2
Villar del Humo E .158 B2
Villar de los Navarros
E 152 A2
Villar del Pedroso
E 156 A2
Villar del Rey E . . .155 B4
Villar del Rio E 143 B4
Villar del Saz de
Navalón E 152 B1
Villar de Rena E . . .156 A2
Villarejo E 151 A4
Villarejo de Fuentes
E 158 B1
Villarejo de Orbigo
E 141 B5
Villarejo de Salvanes
E 151 B4
Villarejo-Periesteban
E 158 B1
Villares del Saz E .158 B1
Villaretto I 119 C4
Villargordo del Cabriel
E 158 B2
Villarino E 149 A3
Villarino de Conso
E 141 B3
Villarluengo E 153 B3
Villarobe E 143 B3
Villarosa I 177 B3
Villar Perosa I 119 C4
Villarramiel E 142 B2
Villarrasa E 161 B3
Villarreal de San Carlos
E 150 C1

Villarrín de Campos
E 142 C1
Villarrobledo E 158 B1
Villarroya de la Sierra
E 152 A2
Villarroya de los
Pinares E 153 B3
Villarrubia de los Ojos
E 157 A4
Villarrubia de Santiago
E 151 C4
Villarrubio E 151 C5
Villars-les-Dombes
F 117 A5
Villarta E 158 B2
Villarta de los Montes
E 156 A3
Villarta de San Juan
E 157 A4
Villasana de Mena
E 143 A3
Villasandino E 142 B2
Villa San Giovanni
I 175 C1
Villa Santa Maria I 169 B4
Villasante E 143 A3
Villa Santina I 122 A1
Villasarracino E . . .142 B2
Villasayas E 151 A5
Villasdardo E 149 A3
Villaseca de Henares
E 151 B5
Villaseca de Laciana
E 141 B4
Villaseca de la Sagra
E 151 C4
Villaseco de los
Gamitos E 149 A3
Villaseco de los Reyes
E 149 A3
Villasequilla de Yepes
E 151 C4
Villasimíus I. 179 C3
Villasmundo I 177 B4
Villasor I. 179 C2
Villastar E 152 B2
Villastellone I 119 C4
Villatobas E 151 C4
Villatorp E 150 B2
Villatoya E 158 B2
Villavaliente E 158 B2
Villavelayo E 143 B4
Villavella E 141 B3
Villaver de de
Guadalimar E . . .158 C1
Villaverde del Rio
E 162 A2
Villaviciosa E 142 A1
Villaviciosa de
Córdoba E. 156 B3
Villaviciosa de Odón
E 151 B4
Villavieja de Yeltes
E 149 B3
Villayón E. 141 A4
Villé F. 93 C3
Villebois-Lavalette
F 115 C4
Villecerf F 90 C2
Villecomtal F 130 A1
Villedieu-les-Poêles
F 88 B2
Villedieu-sur-Indre
F 103 C3
Ville-di-Pietrabugno
F 180 A2
Villedômain F 103 B3
Villefagnan F 115 B4
Villefontaine F 118 B2
Villefort F 131 A2
Villefranche-
d'Albigeois F . . .130 B1
Villefranche-d'Allier
F 116 A2
Villefranche-de-
Lauragais F 146 A2
Villefranche-de-
Lonchat F 128 B3
Villefranche-de-Panat
F 130 A1
Villefranche-de-
Rouergue F 130 A1
Villefranche-du-
Périgord F 129 B4
Villefranche-sur-Cher
F 103 B3
Villefranche-sur-Mer
F 133 B3
Villefranche-sur-Saône
F 117 A4
Villegenon F 103 B4
Villel E 152 B2
Villemaur-sur-Vanne
F 104 A2
Villemontais F 117 B3
Villemur-sur-Tarn
F 129 C4
Villena E 159 C3
Villenauxe-la-Grande
F 91 C3
Villenave-d'Ornon
F 128 B2
Villeneuve
CH 119 A3
F 129 B5
Villeneuve-d'Ascq
F 78 B3
Villeneuve-de-Berg
F 131 A3
Villeneuve-de-Marsan
F 128 C2
Villeneuve-de-Rivière
F 145 A4
Villeneuve-la-Guyard
F 90 C3
Villeneuve-
l'Archevêque F . .104 A2
Villeneuve-le-Comte
F 90 C2